THE SCIENTIFIC STUDY OF GENERAL INTELLIGENCE:

TRIBUTE TO ARTHUR R. JENSEN

Journal Titles of Related Interest

DOUGLAS K. DETTERMAN
Intelligence

G. GUDJONSSON AND S. B. G. EYSENCK
Personality and Individual Differences

M. L. COOPER
Journal of Research in Personality

THE SCIENTIFIC STUDY OF GENERAL INTELLIGENCE:
TRIBUTE TO ARTHUR R. JENSEN

EDITED BY

HELMUTH NYBORG

University of Aarhus, Risskov, Denmark

2003

Pergamon
An Imprint of Elsevier Science

Amsterdam – Boston – Heidelberg – London – New York – Oxford
Paris – San Diego – San Francisco – Singapore – Sydney – Tokyo

ELSEVIER SCIENCE Ltd
The Boulevard, Langford Lane
Kidlington, Oxford OX5 1GB, UK

First edition 2003

Library of Congress Cataloging in Publication Data
A catalog record from the Library of Congress has been applied for.

British Library Cataloguing in Publication Data
A catalogue record from the British Library has been applied for.

ISBN: 0-08-043793-1

♾ The paper used in this publication meets the requirements of ANSI/NISO Z39.48-1992 (Permanence of Paper).
Printed in The Netherlands.

Contents

Contributors

Phillip L. Ackerman — School of Psychology
Georgia Institute of Technology
Atlanta, GA, USA

Britt Anderson — Department of Neurology (JT 1209)
University of Alabama at Birmingham
Birmingham, AL, USA

Rosalind Arden — 8 Hillfield Road
Redhill, Surrey RH1 4AP, U.K.

Gerald V. Barrett — Barrett & Associates, Inc.
Human Resource Consulting
500 West Exchange Street
Akron, OH, USA

Christopher R. Brand — Consultant to the Woodhill Foundation (USA)
71 South Clerk Street
Edinburgh, U.K.

Nathan Brody — Department of Psychology
Wesleyan University
Middletown, CT, USA

Thomas R. Carretta — Air Force Research Laboratory
Wright-Patterson AFB
OH, USA

John B. Carroll — University of North Carolina at Chapel Hill
Chapel Hill, NC, USA

Denis Constales — Department of Mathematical Analysis
University of Ghent
Ghent University, Ganglaan 2
Gent, Belgium

Ian J. Deary — Department of Psychology
University of Edinburgh
Edinburgh, Scotland, U.K.

Lee Ellis   Department of Sociology
                         Minot State University
                         Minot, ND, USA

Gilles Gignac   Assessment Unit
                         Swinburne Centre for Neuropsychopharmacology
                         Swinburne University of Technology
                         Hawthorn, Vic., Australia

Linda S. Gottfredson   School of Education
                         University of Delaware
                         Newark, USA

Mark T. Green   Center for Leadership Studies
                         Our Lady of the Lake University
                         San Antonio, TX, USA

Richard J. Haier   Department of Pediatrics
                         University of California at Irvine
                         Irvine, CA, USA

Harrison Kane   Exceptional Student Education
                         University of Nevada
                         Putnam County School District
                         FL, USA

Alissa J. Kramen   Barrett & Associates, Inc.
                         Human Resource Consulting
                         500 West Exchange Street
                         Akron, OH, USA

David F. Lohman   Psychological and Quantitative Foundations
                         College of Education
                         University of Iowa
                         Iowa City, IA, USA

Sarah B. Lueke   Barrett & Associates, Inc.
                         Human Resource Consulting
                         500 West Exchange Street
                         Akron, OH, USA

Richard Lynn   Department of Psychology
                         University of Ulster
                         Coleraine, N. Ireland

Ted Nettelbeck   Department of Psychology
                         University of Adelaide
                         Adelaide, Australia

Helmuth Nyborg   Department of Psychology
                         University of Aarhus
                         Risskov, Denmark

Robert Plomin   Social, Genetic and Developmental Psychiatry Research
Centre
Institute of Psychiatry
London, U.K.

Malcolm J. Ree   Center for Leadership Studies
Our Lady of the Lake University
San Antonio, TX, USA

J. Philippe Rushton Department of Psychology
University of Western Ontario
London, Ontario, Canada

Dean Keith Simonton Department of Psychology
University of California at Davis
Davis, CA, USA

Herman H. Spitz   389 Terhune Road
Princeton, NJ 08540–3637, USA

Robert J. Sternberg Department of Psychology
Yale University
New Haven, CT, USA

Philip A. Vernon   Department of Psychology
University of Western Ontario
London, Ontario, Canada

Anthony Walsh   Department of Criminal Justice Administration
Boise State University
Boise, ID, USA

John C. Wickett   Assessment Strategies Inc.
Ottawa, Ontario, Canada

General Introduction: Arthur Jensen — The Man, His Friends and This Book

Helmuth Nyborg

This book celebrates two triumphs in modern psychology: the successful development and application of a solid measure of general intelligence, and the personal courage and skills of the man who made this possible — Arthur R. Jensen from Berkeley University.

This photo is the property of Time Incorporated. Published with permission of LIFE Editorial Services, New York, USA.

The photo of Art Jensen is taken in his studio at home in 1969 — right at the time his famous Harvard Educational Review article came out. That article changed his life as well as the fields of education, psychometrics, differential psychology and behavior genetics forever.

The Man

Arthur Robert Jensen is a great scientist but he will probably never ". . . receive the kind of recognition others with even lesser accomplishments have been given. He will not receive the honors his work merits from organizations like the American Psychological Association, The National Academy of Science, or the National Association for the Advancement of Science, to name a few. The reasons for this lack of recognition are obvious. He has taken controversial and politically unpopular stands on issues that are important to the study of intelligence".

These thought-provoking words by editor Douglas K. Detterman open a special honorary issue — *A king among Men: Arthur Jensen* — appearing in the journal *Intelligence* (1998).

There is, of course, nothing new in clashes between eminent scientists and the Establishment. Pioneers are by definition ahead of their time and they often stray far beyond the prevailing Zeitgeist. However, in the case of Arthur Jensen the controversy soon turned into a remarkably vicious sequence of events, that started immediately after he made public, in the (in)famous article in 1969, that he now felt obliged to acknowledge, contra his previous view, that certain genetic restrictions affected development — after inspecting a mountain of largely neglected evidence, that he had stumbled upon almost by accident.

Jensen's change of mind elicited nothing less than an academic disaster, and marked a sharp turning point in his professional career. From being considered by most as a well recognized, honest, exclusively data-oriented scientist, perhaps a bit boring, but very clever educational psychologist who specialized in the not too emotionally arousing area of serial learning effects, Jensen suddenly found his work grossly distorted and misrepresented, and himself threatened and ridiculed. Colleagues low and high competed for stabbing him in the back, influential professional organizations published issue statements against him, and not few asked for his removal from office. Over a short time a massive opposition developed and began to form the sinister contours of a well-organized, widespread, self-reinforcing, collective fraud in modern academia. Later analyses suggest that the infection actually had begun to infect deep layers of academia and the public press since the early 1930s, but its full impact became particularly obvious in connection with the publication of Jensen's 1969 article. It spread and now threatens academic freedom in many modern universities in the United States and elsewhere.

The photo (opposite) is taken when controversy encircled Jensen, and shows one of the first graphical illustrations of the different IQ distributions for blacks and whites.

I know Art well enough to appreciate that he personally prefers to entirely side-step all emotionally and politically motivated controversy, and to get on with what really

This photo is the property of Time Incorporated. Published with permission of LIFE Editorial Services, New York, USA.

matters to him: work, solid work, much of it! In terms of controversy, Art contrasts his mentor and classmate in the *London School of Differential Psychology*, Hans Eysenck. Both are industrious beyond measure, but Hans simply loved a good fight (Gray 1997: xi), whereas Art thinks it is basically a waste to time.

The major bulk of the present volume is accordingly devoted to a scientific treatment of what interests Art most as a professional scientist — the origin, the models, the brain base, the methods and the validity (but curiously enough less the broad application) of general intelligence, *g*. However, considering its unique history-of-science interest, I could not resist the temptation to analyze the nature of the ghastly story of the controversy that surrounds Art ever since 1969, but out of respect for his general attitude I have relegated it to a remote Chapter 20 in this volume. I find the story must be told for at least two reasons. First, it reveals the remarkably fine personal qualities and the rare application of Gandhian principles of an eminent scientist that stood headstrong and almost alone in a true Ibsen's sense against a dreadfully strong head wind. Second, it illustrates how easily even a solid scientific case can be bogged down by a majority if not single scientists takes upon them the troublesome responsibility of defending academic freedom, even if being hounded personally and professionally, and threatened to his life and family by hoards of angry politically correct ideologues drawing their nourishment from the prevailing Zeitgeist.

His Friends

It has been said: If you have no enemies, you have no point of view. Art has many enemies, and I will describe some of the more prominent in Chapter 20 in this volume. Fortunately, he also has friends. What do they say about him?

Sandra Scarr (1998), herself certainly no stranger to controversy, understands quite well that Art Jensen was bound to run into trouble because he "relentlessly pursues a hard-edged, hypothetic-deductive science that treads on a more emotional, humanistic psychology. Art has no sympathy for mushy thinking. For him, impressions and feelings are not data and have no place in psychology . . ." (p. 227).

The friends (and fiends) know immediately that emotionality is no important part of Art. All who watch Art at close quarters recognize that he always looks opponents straight in the face, listens carefully and patiently, and then pours out counter data if there are any, or surprisingly readily admits to total agnosticism in the matter — or he begins to speculate aloud on the best way to find a solution. Data and analysis, not emotions, are what matters. Art spent three years working at the late Hans Eysenck's Psychology Department in the University of London's Institute of Psychiatry. Hans once remarked with a smile that he probably had "high emotional stimulus value", as judged by the violent reactions of many of his critics that often went berserk when they saw, heard, or read anything from or about him. I think this applies in spades to Art as well. While Art is always cool, he easily gets critics boiling over his sharpness.

The photo of Art (opposite) is taken when he visited Hans in London in 1971.

It was Hans who introduced Art to the details of Galton, Spearman, and Thurstone's works and thus provided ". . . a much needed antidote to the predominantly Freudian or psychoanalytic concepts that informed my clinical work" (Jensen 1998: 184). It was Hans who planted Art's view of psychology as a natural science branch of biology, and it was Hans who made Art believe that ". . . differential psychology, broadly conceived, was exactly the path for me."

Hans and Art were invited to present the Fink Memorial lectures at the University of Melbourne in Australia in September 1977, and that tour ended in a disaster. Art was to talk first, but his lecture was disrupted by bullies, and he had to run for his life, protected by at least 50 police officers. Hans was scheduled to talk the next day, but he was bullied too, and nobody could hear a word. The photo on page xviii was taken on that occasion by professor Brian Start, in his office.

If Art is loyal to data, he is entirely unfaithful to theory. I know this comes as a surprise to many of his opponents, who claim he is square, preconceived, and immovable. "In fact" writes Detterman (1998: 177) "I have never known anybody with fewer prejudices . . . Jensen has no loyalty whatsoever to any theory or hypotheses even if they come from his own ideas."

Allow me to give a recent example of this. Art has long been of the opinion that the sexes do not differ in *g*, and further that those who nevertheless find a difference are not

using proper methods (Jensen 1998: Chapter 13). It was therefore not entirely without trepidation I in December 2002 gave a lecture on the matter in front of him at the meeting of the *Third Annual Conference for the International Society for Intelligence Research* at Vanderbilt University in Nashville, TN. The main point of the lecture was that there is, in fact, a moderate male lead in *g*, but you will see it only if you use Art's own highly sophisticated factor-analytic methods, which, by the way, were the same methods that led Art to believe that there is no difference (see the details in Chapter 10

Photo taken in London in 1971 by Methuen Publishers.

in this volume). After the lecture Art came up to me and just said: This is the best lecture I have ever heard on sex difference." To another colleague he said: "It seems I have to rethink the matter." The point of the story: give Art a proper analysis and good data, and his mind will follow, entirely independently of his previous view. That is far more than one can say about most of his critics!

Jensen is courageous! Sandra Scarr admires Jensen's never failing personal courage in defending data as he sees them. Sandra's words have particular weight here, because she has herself often proved willing to step into the frying pan to defend controversial behavior genetics data. Sandra thus ". . . witnessed his steadfastness in the face of a screaming, unruly mob who disrupted his lecture on learning and intelligence and threatened his personal safety. I learned what it was like to be spat upon and to put my body on the line to get Art out of a University of Minnesota auditorium. It was shocking and frightening, as surely the radicals intended, but it was most of all infuriating, because no disciplinary actions were taken against those who assaulted us." What the audience missed that day was a treatment of test bias, which eventually came to totally redefine expert opinion in this important matter (Chapter 20 reports on many such unworthy attempts to repress unpopular scientific information).

Where does Art's courage come from? Well, it surely is partly a function of his particular personality organization, partly due to a principle, and partly due to a rational need for change. Art thus writes: ". . . rather than duck for cover, which I peculiarly felt would be disgracefully un-Gandhian, I resolved not to be whipsawed by the prevailing

Photo taken near American Embassy, New Delhi, October 1980.

orthodoxy in the social and behavioral science, but to do whatever I could to reform the social sciences" (Jensen 1998: 198).

Art has traveled and lectured extensively in India, and has adhered for much of his life to Gandhian principles. The photo (opposite) shows Art feeding holy cows near the American Embassy in New Delhi in October 1980, the year his famous citation classic *Bias in Mental Testing* came out.

Art is a calm person. This does not only show up when he faces an unruly mob, but also in the private sphere. My wife, Mette, and I spent some working days at his beautiful second house at a huge lake in 1999. Hardly had I fallen asleep before Mette woke me up and said there is a smell of smoke! Dressed for the night we went to the living room, and yes, there was smoke. I woke up Art and all three of us inspected the first floor rooms. No smoke, he declared, this is not a thing I would worry about, go back to sleep. The next morning it became all too obvious that the cellar was totally burned out, and only luck prevented the fire from spreading to the rest of the house. There is no doubt Art's extroversion score is low, but I bet his neuroticism score is even lower. In that respect he seems very much like Hans Eysenck — both are rather stable introverts.

Art is generous! Scarr observed, for example, that Art thinks he even understands the motives of harsh critics like the Marcus Feldmans, Steven Jay Goulds, and Leon Kamins of the intellectual world, even if she finds them ". . . despicable, because they have the knowledge and intellect to know that they deliberately corrupt science (again consult Chapter 20, if in doubt). Sandra readily admits that Art has contributed enormously to psychological science, but perhaps his most important contribution is ". . . intellectual honesty and integrity to a psychological science that is threatened with Politically Correct corruption" (1998: 232).

Art is meticulous (bordering on the pedantic, I dare say)! Alan S. Kaufman tells an instructive story about Art's insistence on data rather than emotion and opinion in scientific matters (1998: 249–250). Alan was preparing a rebuttal to 13 articles, commenting on the Kaufman Assessment Battery for Children, and felt rather well after reading the first dozen articles by several notabilities in psychology "... filled with test, opinion, and sometimes emotion". Then, when Kaufman "... got to Jensen's article ... [he] began to sweat ... Jensen buttressed his text with original data analyses that occupied four new tables and six new figures. He used these analyses to challenge and provoke, to some extent, but mostly to inquire, to seek the truth." I think not only Alan but anybody who has worked with Art, or had him review one's work, will recognize his extreme meticulousness, if perhaps not always at first with gratitude.

Art is obsessed with work, and it shows! The eminent twin researcher Thomas J. Bouchard, Jr. (1998) characterized Art's bibliography as "... breathtaking and his scientific work as intensive, detailed, exhaustive, fair-minded, temperate, and courageous." At the time Tom wrote this, Jensen's biography reflected, that: a) he is the first author on 357 of the 384 items, b) he is the sole author of 319 of the 384 items, c) he has four citation classics, d) he has published nearly 10 items a year (including books) since 1962, e) there is no indication that he is slowing down, and f) the quality is not only superb, it is getting better! One disconcerting feature of the bibliography is the paucity of items that have been reprinted", Tom adds (p. 283). The reader may consult the updated bibliography at the end of this volume and see that Art keeps up the stunning pace.

Art is gracious! Bouchard wonders why so few of Art's works have been reprinted, and provides the following answer: "He had dared to study and speak straight forwardly about important issues that most other social scientists only whisper about — race and class differences in IQ, lack of bias in intelligence testing, the biological basis of general intelligence, genetic influences on intelligence, and the fallacious research methods in developmental psychology." Like everybody who knows Art, Tom is duly impressed by Jensen's personality: "For someone who has been attacked so vituperatively, both in public and in the published literature, I continue to be astounded at the lack of anger and hostility in his replies and the astuteness with which he dissects the arguments of his critics" (p. 285).

When invited to say a few words at a commemorative event at the Institute of Psychiatry in London in connection with the all too early death of Hans Eysenck in 1997, I draw attention to the fact that if the audience went to any good library or well-assorted book store, they would inevitably find the collected works of Freud, Marx, Gould, and other popular writers, but would seek in vain for the collected works of Hans. I could have added: and the collected works of Art Jensen. We here see another manifestation of the ugly collective intellectual fraud (to be exposed in Chapter 20), of neglecting or avoiding politically incorrect literature.

In stark contrast, Art Jensen's critics are not only legion, but they are often also quite popular in professional circles and quite powerful there. The recently deceased Steven Jay Gould was one such person, and he certainly never missed any occasion to fire a broadside on Arthur Jensen or his work. In his *The Mismeasure of Man* (1981/1996) Gould thus wrote: "The chimerical nature of *g* is the rotten core of Jensen's edifice, and of the entire hereditarian school" (p. 320; see Chapter 20 for details). This book sold 125,000 copies, was translated into 10 languages, and became required reading for undergraduate and even graduate classes in anthropology, psychology and sociology (Rushton 1997). Gould eventually became president of the prestigious *American Academy for the Advancement of Science*. Another critic, Robert Sternberg, teases Arthur Jensen by calling him a *g*-ocentrist, or compares him to a naïve little boy, too afraid to leave his own little *g* house and visit other and more interesting (I suppose: Triarchic) houses, so he is still under the illusion that his little *g* house is the best of all houses (see Chapter 17 in this volume). Bob has received many awards and honors over the years, and has recently been elected the 2003 president of the *American Psychological Association*. One of Bob's priorities for the APA is to infuse more psychology in schools and ". . . propose a set of standards of accountability — a school children's bill of right", to counter the fact that "Schools are becoming factories for test-taking". (Daw 2002). For other rebuttals, see Dennett (1995), Gross (2002), and Jensen (1982).

Most of Art's enemies come from the academic left, or from the associated post-modernist quarter. These critics are well-known for their resistance to notions of individual and group differences in IQ and inheritance (see Chapter 20 in this volume). Art has no difficulty in competing with them for professional citations, but they completely overpower Art by several factors in media mentioning. Gould is thus number 9 among the 10 public intellectuals most cited in the States, the others being in rank order: Michel Foucault, Pierre Bourdieu, Jürgen Habermas, Jackques Derrida, Noam Chomsky, Max Weber, Gary Becker, Anthony Giddens and Richard Posner.

Art has a phenomenal memory. Once Art was asked to a meeting in order to prepare for an invited speech to the House of Lords in London. As I stayed for a couple of days in the apartment, his lovely wife Barbara and I were left alone for the evening, and we began to wonder what to eat for dinner. Then, just before Art left, Barbara asked him about the details of an Indian receipt. In a great hurry, Art leaned over the dinner table, hastily scribbled down all the 32 ingredients that went into that particular course and then, on the run to the door, gave several pieces of advice as how to prepare the meal, and off he went. Likewise, in professional conversation his association horizon is remarkably broad. Anybody, who has had the pleasure of hearing him talk about some of the many outstanding people he has met throughout his long career, are stunned by the richness of the details. Just ask him to say a few words about Wagner, Toscanini, Gandhi, Eysenck, William Shockley, or many others, and you will have enlightening entertainment for hours. When working, I have seen him sitting in deep concentration without a word for 10 or more minutes, carefully running over, and over again, a large number of raw data, tables, and figures, then suddenly raise his head and exclaim: Yes, now I have got it all. Now, I can write it up. It all clicks in my head! And then it all really is in there! Writing it up is the least part of it.

Art is a devoted music lover. He is on print for saying: ". . . my interest in music has never been second to my interest in psychology, though I have necessarily devoted more time to the latter, of course, since it has been my livelihood. When I wasn't on Columbia campus, chances are I was hanging out in Carnegie Hall, either at a concert or a rehearsal" (Jensen 1998: 183). When attending out-of-town conferences he usually inquires into the musical life of the various cities, and does not shy away from taking the most expensive seat in order to hear and see more of the concert. I was therefore more than touched when I went with Art and Barbara to a concert in London, and found that he had seated Barbara and me in excellent front seats, whereas he sat behind the orchestra, right up to the percussionist, and could probably not hear anything much else. After the concert I realized he hadn't been able to get three seats in a row, and became double thankful, because I "knew" what he must have gone through back there. In his youth Art played the second clarinet in the San Diego Symphony Orchestra. However, with his high goals for perfection, he soon realized that he probably would neither make it to the top as a musician nor as a maestro, and accordingly decided to put his full force behind an academic life.

Even then his interest in music is unabated. I recently assured him that I would follow his advice and give Wagner a second try. I never really understood the greatness of

Arthur Jensen, December 1993, Berkeley, USA.

Wagner's music, so I bought *Deutsche Grammonphon*'s 14 compact disc version of Karajan's *Der Ring Des Nibelungen* to get an idea of what was in store. Art was not too happy with my choice, though. "I wish", he said, "that you had begun our study of Wagner with *Die Meistersinger*, which is more easily accessible than the Ring. The Karajan version of *Meistersinger* is probably the best available, although the one by Varviso (recorded at a live performance at Beyreuth) is also excellent. Solti also does a fine job, but doesn't have quite the "gemütlichkeit" that Karajan brings and which is needed for this warm opera. The great pianist Paderewski considered *Meistersinger* the greatest work of art (of any kind) ever created. The score is certainly a work of incredible genius and for it, I think, Wagner can be forgiven all his personal faults! The *Ring* is a whole world of its own and takes a while to get used to. "*The Ring Resounding*" by Robert Culshaw is an excellent brief introduction to the whole thing. *Die Walküre* (especially Act I) is probably the most easily grasped part of the whole *Ring*. The finale of *Götterdämmerung* is marvelous. One wonders how a composer would end such a tremendous work as the Ring, and it's always a thrill to see how only a genius would have done it — as of course Wagner did. No lesser genius could have, or would have, done it as Wagner did. But I hope you get a chance to see the whole Ring to get the full impact. It's especially worth the trouble even to go considerably out of your way, to see a live performance of *Meistersinger*. Worth a trip to Copenhagen, at least." Thank you for all this, Art!

Eysenck once remarked with a smile that he probably had "high emotional stimulus value", as judged by the violent reactions of many of his critics that often went berserk when they saw, heard, or read anything from or about him. I think this applies in spades to Art as well, even if he looks quite peaceful in the photo (opposite). It is taken in Berkeley in 1993, the year before his formal — but certainly not practical — retirement.

Senior editor Frank Miele of *Skeptic Magazine* (2002) has written a wonderful book about his conversations with Art, and the reader is well advised to consult it. In dialog form, Art here answers all the hard questions pertaining to his view on general intelligence, race differences, cultural test bias, heredity, public policy and affirmative action, in a clear, non-technical language.

This Book

This book arose out of conversation with many colleagues, some of them differential psychologist, some educational psychologists, neuropsychologists, clinical psychologists, occupational psychologists, behavioral geneticists, brain imaging specialists, sociologists or general psychologists. A consensus to produce a tribute to Arthur R. Jensen was a prerequisite for these discussions, and it was soon envisioned that the book would reflect an attempt to cover all essential aspects of Jensen's work, even if this task seemed daunting.

We thus wanted the book to trace the historical roots of general intelligence *g* as well as the incredible controversy surrounding Jensen's work. We wanted the book to provide the most recent account of the hierarchical structure of cognitive abilities, and to document the transition from a hopelessly confused concept of *intelligence in general*, IQ, to the development of an objective measure of *general intelligence*, *g*. We wanted the book to scrutinize the best available evidence on individual and group differences in *g*. We wanted the book to illustrate the impressive power *g* has with respect to predicting educational achievement, getting an attractive job, or social stratification in general, and we wanted the book to document what we know today about the molecular basis of *g*. We even wanted to take intelligence testing into the courtroom and inspect how it fared.

Each single author's task was defined much along the line Irene Martin suggested for Nyborg's (1997) *The Scientific Study of Human Nature: Tribute to Hans J. Eysenck*. First describe Art's contribution to the field (including theory where relevant); then what research has developed from it, and what kinds of amendments/modifications/additions to his work (theory) are appropriate; and, finally, describe your thoughts about the future of the field. Not every author followed the scheme, but then, it is a free country.

I further asked Rosalin Arden to write a non-academic chapter on her changing impressions of Art, and Anthony Vernon to collect the memories of former students, who have had Art as a teacher or mentor.

I, in fact, also asked a number of outspoken opponents of *g*-theory to write a chapter, and reserved a full part of the book for them, with the explicit purpose of seeking a balanced presentation of *g* theory. Unfortunately, I did not have much success in reaching this goal. One opponent said he had over the years had so many occasions to criticize *g* that he would consider it inappropriate to once more present his critical points in a book of this kind. He nobly added that his respect for Arthur Jensen was so great that he would rather see the book appear as laudatory as could be. Other opponents were rather brisk: "I do not want to contribute to such a book". Still others, such as Howard Gardner and Daniel Goleman, could neither find the time nor the motive to write a chapter. From the balance point of view, this is regrettable because science progresses best by first presenting all the pros and cons and then making an informed decision. But then again, it is a free country. Perhaps Robert Sternberg from Yale University is not directly opposing *g* theory, but he has his reservations, so I asked him to write a chapter for this honorary volume for Arthur Jensen. Surely he did. He paid back by comparing Arthur Jensen to a naïve little boy living in his little house of *g*, too afraid to leave his narrow site and find out that the world outside has many more houses, that are much more interesting and, not to forget, also Sternberg's own tower! As an editor I welcomed the scientific aspects of Bob's chapter, but I must admit that it caused me personal grief to see the undeserving ad hominem remarks about Art's immaturity, in particular in a tribute such as the present. I decided, nevertheless, to include Bob's chapter, and will invite the reader to form his/her own judgment in the matter.

The book is divided into 6 parts. The introduction to each part provides an abstract, which allows the reader a quick overview of the full content of that part.

However, to point out the overall organization of the book — Part I presents the most recent higher-stratum analysis of cognitive abilities. Part II deals with biological aspects of *g*, such as research on brain imaging, glucose uptake, working memory, reaction time, inspection time, and other biological correlates, and concludes with the latest findings in *g*-related molecular genetics. Part III addresses demographic aspects of *g*, such as geographic-, race-, and sex differences, and introduces differential psychological aspects as well. Part IV concentrates on the *g* nexus, and relates such highly diverse topics as sociology, genius, retardation, training, education, jobs, and crime to *g*. Part V contains chapters critical of research on *g* and of its genetic relationship, and also presents a rejoinder. Part VI mediates a number of personal impressions of one of the greatest contemporary psychologists, Professor Emeritus Arthur R. Jensen as a public figure, teacher, and mentor.

The Gratefully Acknowledged

It takes two to tango. It takes many more for a book. Let me first thank two colleagues for their never failing and enthusiastic help in launching this book — Linda Gottfredson and Phil Rushton. Thanks also to the many distinguished contributors who so willingly took the time off to honor Art. Thanks to the very able people at Elsevier in Oxford — Fiona Barron, Diane Cogan, Charlotte Dewhearst, Dianna Jones, and Deborah Raven for their expert assistance and immense patience, and thanks to Sarah Medford, Ph.D. student, for her linguistic services. Thanks to my wife, Mette, for being so understanding when I despaired, and for her teaching Art the Tango. Thanks to Rosalind Arden for sharing her admiration for Art with us, and for being such a lovely person in general. Thanks to Tony Vernon for undertaking the not so easy task of locating and organizing contributions from Art's former students. Finally, thanks to my secretary through many years, Lone Hansen. Frankly, I do not know where this book would have landed without her unfailing personal and professional assistance. Du bist ein Schatz, Lone.

Thanks to Art for lending me the photos used in the introduction. I am grateful to Pergamon for allowing me to design the cover. Not really trusting the articulateness of my varying artistic talent, I perhaps ought to spell out the details. Spread out over the brain, and by and large in place, are the various main components of the hierarchical *g* model. The differently colored eyes refer to the moderate average sex difference in *g* (Chapter 10, if you are a non-believer). The nose roughly represents the proportional black and white IQ distributions, and the mouth spells out the formula for heritability, or that part of the population variance in a trait that can be ascribed to genes. The ears could have signaled, that the positive effect of compensatory education depends to a large extent on the level of *g*, but that would probably be to push the matter too far.

Let me conclude this introduction by admitting that it has been a privilege to edit this tribute to Arthur R. Jensen. We all wanted to pay back in each our small way the inspiration and headship you — Art — have provided over half a century for all of us in the fields of differential psychology, educational psychology, psychometrics, or behavioral genetics. We wanted to express our admiration for the guidance you have provided in terms of honest science, never failing supportiveness, courage, and personal integrity.

May your molecules be with you for many years to come, Art!

Helmuth Nyborg
University of Aarhus
Risskov, Denmark

References

Bouchard, T. J. (1998). Intensive, detailed, exhaustive. *Intelligence, 26* (3), 283–290.

Daw, J. (2002). Sternberg chosen as APA's new president. *Monitor on Psychology, 33* (1), January.

Dennett, D. C. (1995). *Darwin's dangerous idea: Evolution and the meaning of life*. New York: Simon & Schuster.

Detterman, D. K. (1998). Kings of Men: Introduction to a special issue. *Intelligence, 26* (3), 175–180.

Gould, S. J. (1981/1996). *The Mismeasure of Man*. New York: W. W. Norton.

Gross, P. R. (2002). The apotheosis of Stephen Jay Gould. *The New Criterion, 21* (2).

Gray, J. (1997). Foreword. In: H. Nyborg (Ed.), *The scientific study of human nature. Tribute to Hans J. Eysenck*. Oxford: Pergamon.

Jensen, A. R. (1982). The debunking of scientific fossils and straw persons. *Review of The Mismeasure of Man*. New York: W. W. Norton, 1981, by Stephen Jay Gould. *Contemporary Education Review, 1* (2), 121–135.

Jensen, A. R. (1998). Jensen on "Jensenism". *Intelligence, 26* (3), 181–208.

Kaufman, A. S. (1998). A new twist on Jensenism. *Intelligence, 26* (3), 249–253.

Miele, F. (2002). *Intelligence, race, and genetics: Conversations with Arthur R. Jensen*. Boulder, CO: Westview Press.

Nyborg, H. (Ed.) (1997). *The scientific study of human nature. Tribute to Hans J. Eysenck*. Oxford: Pergamon.

Rushton J. P. (1997). Race, Intelligence, and the Brain: The Errors and Omissions of the Revised Edition of S. J. Gould's *The Mismeasure of Man* (1996). *Personality and Individual Differences, 23*, 169–180.

Scarr, S. (1998). On Arthur Jensen's integrity. *Intelligence, 26* (3), 227–232.

Part I

The *g* Factor

Part I — Introduction

John Carroll is unquestionably a world authority on factor analysis and g modeling. I therefore asked him to specifically comment on higher-stratum structure models for cognitive abilities, to see whether the classical model of general intelligence would still stand strong in the light of current and new evidence.

Carroll begins chapter 1 by considering three somewhat different views about the higher-stratum structure of cognitive abilities: (a) The classical view of Spearman, Thurstone (in his later years), Jensen, Carroll, and many others. This view says that a general factor of intelligence g exists and can be confirmed, along with a series of about 10 broad second-stratum factors, including factors called G_f and G_c, defined by specifiable types of variables; (b) The view of Gustafsson, Undheim, and some others, that a general factor of intelligence exists and can be confirmed (along with various second-stratum factors), but that it is highly or even perfectly correlated with a second-stratum factor G_f as proposed by others; and (c) The view of Horn and some others, that there is "no such thing" as a general factor of intelligence, because it cannot be properly conceived or experimentally demonstrated. However, the factors G_f and G_c exist as second-stratum factors (along with about 8 others) and can be confirmed.

Carroll then analyzes datasets, assembled and studied by McGrew, Werder and Woodcock, by both exploratory and confirmatory factoring methods, in order to investigate the statistical hypotheses implied in the above mentioned three views. The re-analyses of these datasets suggests the following conclusions:

(a) Classical hypotheses, claiming a general factor g and, orthogonal to it and to each other, two or more second-stratum factors, can be confirmed even when the second-stratum factors include G_f. The existence of G_f as a second-stratum factor separate from g is no longer doubtful, but there may be problems in validly measuring it.

(b) The notion (favored by Gustafsson) that there exists a general factor of intelligence g in addition to broad second-stratum factors, including a factor G_f with which it is highly or perfectly correlated, can be accepted, with the provision that in some datasets, G_f can be clearly distinguished from g.

(c) The notion (favored by Horn) that factor g does not exist cannot be accepted. It ignores the fact that with the use of confirmatory analysis techniques in which a general intelligence factor is postulated, such a factor can easily be confirmed, even when G_f and G_c factors independent of g can be shown to be present. If suitable test variables are present in the test battery analyzed, factor *g* shows significant loadings on a great variety of mental tests (though not necessarily all such tests).

However, John cautiously stresses that it remains to verify these conclusions by analyses of further datasets.

Chapter 1

The Higher-stratum Structure of Cognitive Abilities: Current Evidence Supports *g* and About Ten Broad Factors

John B. Carroll

1. Introduction

As I proposed in my volume *Human Cognitive Abilities* (Carroll 1993), cognitive abilities may be assumed to exist at three principal levels or strata: a first, lower-order stratum comprising some 50 to 60 or more narrow abilities that are linearly independent of each other (that is, possibly inter-correlated but with clearly separated vectors in the factorial space); a second stratum comprising approximately 8 to 10 or more broad abilities, also linearly independent of each other; and a third still higher stratum containing only a single, general intellectual ability commonly termed *g*. (For consistency with the custom observed in the literature, I use only the lower case letter to refer to the supposed factor *g* occupying the highest level.) The present chapter is concerned with the structure of the two higher levels, that is, with questions about whether there actually exist two higher-order levels, and with what factors can be shown to occupy each of these levels.

The title of the present volume of essays written in tribute to Arthur Jensen, as well as the title of Jensen's most recent masterwork, *The G Factor* (Jensen 1998), would appear to guarantee definitively that there exists a unitary factor of cognitive ability (or "intelligence") that can be termed *g*. Indeed, ever since the publication of Charles Spearman's seminal writings on intelligence (1904, 1923, 1927) the almost universally accepted assumption among many psychologists, educators, and even popular writers has been that there does indeed exist a single general factor of intelligence, possibly along with other, more specialized dimensions of ability (Eysenck 1994). The assertion that a general factor of intelligence exists would be the principal statement to make about the higher-stratum structure of cognitive abilities.

At the time of writing *Human Cognitive Abilities*, I did not think it reasonable to question the existence of a general factor because I tended to accord with the

The Scientific Study of General Intelligence: Tribute to Arthur R. Jensen
Copyright © 2003 by Elsevier Science Ltd.
All rights of reproduction in any form reserved.
ISBN: 0-08-043793-1

widespread acceptance of such a factor in the psychometric research community. Nevertheless, even in the several decades after the publication of Spearman's writings about a general factor in 1904 and later, concern (reviewed by Burt 1949a, 1949b) about the genuine existence of such a factor began to appear, particularly in England. However, considerable evidence for a general factor was accumulated in the early years of the nineteenth century, and Holzinger (1936) and even Thurstone & Thurstone (1941), who had endorsed the existence of first-order "primary" factors, published evidence supporting a *g* factor. In his book on technical considerations in performing multiple factor analyses, Thurstone (1947: 421) included a chapter on the computation of second-order factors, one of which, he thought, might be a general factor similar to that espoused by Spearman.

In recent times the most pertinent developments concerning the higher-order structure of cognitive abilities have been based on technical advances in factor-analytic methodology, in particular the development of *confirmatory factor analysis* as opposed to the exploratory factor analysis techniques formulated earlier by Thurstone (1938, 1947) and many others. In confirmatory factor analysis (Jöreskog & Sörbom 1989), it has become possible readily to apply statistical significance tests to factorial results in order to confer on them a greater degree of scientific plausibility. Using structural equation models involved in confirmatory factor analysis, Gustafsson and others (Gustafsson 1984, 1989, 2001; Gustafsson & Balke 1993; Gustafsson & Undheim 1996) have consistently found what they interpret as a general factor *g*, but they also have found and confirmed two factors similar to those proposed by Cattell as early as 1941 (Cattell 1941) and later studied by Cattell (1971) and Cattell & Horn (1978; see also Horn 1965), namely, a G_f (fluid intelligence) factor and a G_c (crystallized intelligence) factor. Gustafsson and his colleagues report that their factor tends to be highly or even perfectly correlated with *g*, but Cattell and Horn have tended to reject the notion of a general factor at a third stratum in the hierarchy of abilities. Further, Gustafsson and colleagues found and confirmed what they call a cultural knowledge factor G_c as previously described by Cattell (1971) and Cattell & Horn (1978). Such findings at least raise questions about the interpretation and even the existence of a general factor.

In the early writings of Cattell and Horn, there was already an insistence that the type of *g* factor identified by Spearman and many others, including Thurstone, might be suspect and not confirmable. For example, Chapter 5 in Cattell's (1971) treatise on cognitive abilities was an extensive attempt to discredit the Spearman *g* factor, chiefly because, in Cattell's opinion, it could not be supported within the theory of rotated factors. Cattell and Horn's rejection of a Spearman-type *g* factor has been carried forward to recent articles by Horn (1991, 1998; Horn & Noll 1994, 1997), which summarize Horn's current views.

2. Three Somewhat Different Views

In the present chapter, then, we may consider three somewhat different views about the higher-order structure of cognitive abilities:

(1) The classic view of Spearman (1927, or particularly in a book published posthumously, Spearman & Wynn Jones 1950), Thurstone & Thurstone (1941), Jensen (1998), and many others, that one can accept the existence of a general factor and of a series of non-general "broad" factors that together contribute variance to a wide variety of mental performances, but not necessarily to all of them. This is the view adopted by the present author (Carroll 1993) in proposing that all human cognitive abilities can be classified as occupying one of three hierarchical strata, as mentioned previously. I call this the *"standard multifactorial view"* of cognitive abilities.

(2) The view of Gustafsson and others (Gustafsson 1984, 1989, 2001; Gustafsson & Balke 1993; Gustafsson & Undheim 1996) that a general factor exists but is essentially identical to, or highly correlated with, a second-order fluid intelligence factor G_f, but linearly independent of a second-order crystallized intelligence factor G_c and other possible second-order factors. For present purposes, I call this the *"limited structural analysis view"*.

(3) The view of Horn and some others (Cattell 1971: 87; Horn 1998; Horn & Noll 1994) that there is "no such thing" (as Horn likes to phrase it) as a general factor, but that non-zero inter-correlations among lower-stratum factors can be explained by accepting the existence of two or more second-stratum factors, mainly G_f and G_c. Because this view denies the existence of a third stratum, it may be termed the *"second-stratum multiplicity view"*.

In this relatively brief chapter, I assemble and analyze sample data and arguments favoring or disfavoring each of these alternative views, eventually to permit drawing conclusions as to which of them is most nearly correct in terms of logical reasonableness and closeness of fit to a wide range of empirical data. Some of these data and arguments appeared in previous publications (Carroll 1993, 1995, 1997a, 1997b), which may be consulted for more detailed information. It is, however, my present belief that although currently available evidence tends to favor the standard multi-factorial view, we still do not have enough objective evidence to permit making any final decision on which view merits acceptance over the others.

3. How Decide Among These Views?

Each of the three views cited above can be expressed as a series of statements that could be put to the test by statistical analyses of appropriate datasets either newly designed for the purpose or drawn from the literature on human cognitive abilities — datasets containing measurements of a large number of people on a suitable variety of tests or other measurements of these abilities. The people for whom measurements are obtained should be a respectable sample of some defined population — preferably one that could be regarded as representative of an important segment of the general population of, say, English-speaking inhabitants of the United States of America or of some other country, within some defined age range. Furthermore, the tests should be reliable and valid measurements of the main types of known cognitive abilities at the first stratum — that is, tests designed to measure narrow abilities as opposed to broader or more general abilities, which show up only in correlations among different types of narrow abilities. Any dataset chosen for analysis should contain a table of the actual or estimated population inter-correlations of all the tests used in the dataset. It is desirable that there be at least three somewhat different tests of each narrow ability that the dataset was designed to measure, in order to insure that the ability is adequately defined for logical and statistical analysis.

3.1. First Dataset

A dataset that would be truly adequate for studying the higher-stratum structure of cognitive abilities would probably be too large, in terms of its number of test variables, to include in this necessarily brief chapter to illustrate a possible solution to the problem posed. There is a real question whether any such dataset yet exists in the literature. In its place, it may be sufficient, for drawing conclusions about the higher-stratum structure of cognitive abilities, to portray the application of factorial methods to two relatively small datasets developed and analyzed by McGrew *et al.* (1991). It is a dataset that was designed to test factorial structure only at a second or higher stratum, as suggested by Carroll (1993: 579), in that it has sufficient test variables to define several second-stratum factors, as well as the single third-stratum factor, but not necessarily any first-stratum factors. Table 1.1 shows the inter-correlations among the 16 variables used in the first of these datasets, derived from data from the administration of the *Woodcock-Johnson Psycho-Educational Battery — Revised* (McGrew *et al.* 1991, Appendix I, Table I-1) to 2,261 persons of both sexes from kindergarten to adult educational levels. The developers of this battery had the specific objective of preparing a series of tests that would reliably and validly measure the more important general and special abilities that had been discovered in the past fifty or sixty years of research on cognitive abilities. I therefore consider the data shown in Table 1.1 to be appropriate for analysis in order to draw at least tentative conclusions about the structure of higher-stratum cognitive abilities by testing the statistical hypotheses implied by the different views of that structure that I have been considering.

My intention is to perform what I consider to be appropriate exploratory and/or confirmatory analyses of the correlations shown in Table 1.1 (and later, the correlations from a related dataset shown in Table 1.4). From the results, it should be possible to reach the desired conclusions.

All analyses presented here assume that the factors obtained can be represented as completely orthogonal to each other; this is true not only for analyses made by the exploratory Schmid & Leiman (1957) technique described below but also for analyses made by the confirmatory LISREL 7 factor analysis program (Jöreskog & Sörbom 1989), which can provide factor loadings on orthogonal factors by allowing the user to specify that the matrix of correlations among factors at the highest level of analysis is to be an identity matrix (a square matrix containing 1's in all diagonal entries, 0s elsewhere; or, in the language of the program, PH = ID). This method of representing factors is theoretically sound even though it is impossible to compute, from empirical data, error-free and uncorrelated estimates of factor scores on orthogonal factors. It has

Table 1.1: Pearsonian intercorrelation matrix, combined kindergarten to adult sample (decimals omitted). 16 variables from the Woodcock-Johnson psycho-educational battery — revised. $N = 2261$ (correlations corrected for age).

Variable:	1	2	3	4	5	6	7	8	9	10	11	12	13	14	15	16
1 Memory for Name	1000															
2 Memory for Sentences	310	1000														
3 Visual Matching	271	269	1000													
4 Incomplete Words	246	347	295	1000												
5 Visual Closure	239	160	310	291	1000											
6 Picture Vocabulary	396	413	331	381	378	1000										
7 Analysis-Synthesis	331	369	351	321	276	396	1000									
8 Visual-Auditory Learning	561	349	316	290	338	424	464	1000								
9 Memory for Words	235	562	244	298	126	258	286	297	1000							
10 Cross Out	248	271	671	293	354	365	364	336	221	1000						
11 Sound Blending	283	372	326	486	268	433	356	410	358	355	1000					
12 Picture Recognition	334	239	297	248	338	320	327	377	205	321	269	1000				
13 Oral Vocabulary	400	523	406	410	350	706	502	479	387	407	492	347	1000			
14 Concept Formation	367	417	354	324	289	404	541	445	283	370	356	330	516	1000		
15 Calculation	292	341	496	241	246	453	464	403	278	433	380	264	586	460	1000	
16 Applied Problems	353	433	456	300	264	548	502	447	342	424	432	304	672	537	702	1000

Note: Reprinted with permission: McGrew, K. S., Werder, J. K. & Woodcock, R. W. (1991). *WJ-R Technical Manual* (p. 345). Allen, TX: DLM.

the advantage that conceptualizing results does not require consideration of possible correlations among factors at different levels of analysis. Also, it is mathematically equivalent to other procedures of analysis in that all these procedures seek to predict the matrix of empirical correlations found for a dataset. That matrix can be predicted from either orthogonal or oblique factor matrices, but if orthogonal matrices are used, it is not necessary to take account of correlations among the factors.

For exploratory factor analysis, Schmid & Leiman (1957) developed a procedure whereby data on different orders (or strata) of factors could be represented in a single matrix showing the predicted loadings of tests on orthogonal factors at different strata. Typically, just one factor would be found at the highest stratum, and such a factor might be considered to be a "general factor" when the tests or variables which had substantial loadings on it were sufficiently diverse, and preferably, identical or similar to tests or variables having loadings on general factors in other datasets. I used the exploratory factor analysis Schmid/Leiman procedure, incorporated in a factor analysis program I developed (Carroll 1989), to produce Table 1.2, which shows factor loadings of the 16 tests on a third-stratum g factor and eight second-stratum factors. All tests have substantial loadings on factor 1, which can be regarded as a general factor because the 16 tests that have substantial loadings on it are quite diverse in terms of test content and required mental operations. The eight second-stratum factors generally have substantial loadings on only two tests each, indicating that they cover restricted types of content and mental operation. Other loadings on these factors approach zero except for a few values that are still strikingly different from zero, though not as high as the two values that mainly define a given factor. From this, it is clear that the results support the classical or standard multifactorial view that postulates a general factor g at the third stratum and a series of broad abilities at the second stratum.

It may help the reader unfamiliar with factor analysis to realize that "cross-multiplying" any two rows of the factor-loading table (ordinarily termed a "factor matrix") should yield a fairly good estimate of the correlation between the two variables involved. (Cross-multiplying means finding the sum, over the number of entries in each row, of the products of the two values in a given column. Cross-multiplying a row by itself yields the value of the "communality" (h^2) or amount of common factor variance associated with a given variable.) The last two rows of the table (labeled SMSQ and %CCV) provide information on the relative weight of the factors in determining the predicted correlations. The entries labeled SMSQ are the sums of squared values in a given column, indicating the amount of variance contributed by a given factor, and the entries labeled %CCV are percents of common factor variance for that factor. The SMSQ values are highest for the factor g, and the percentage of common covariance is 51.07 for that factor, in contrast to the relatively low values for each of the second-stratum factors. At the same time, sizable loadings of particular tests on second-stratum factors are seen. For example, note the loadings of the Analysis-Synthesis Test and the Concept Formation Test on the so-called *Gf*, Fluid Reasoning factor, 0.310 and 0.403, respectively. In factor analysis, it is often shown that tests have loadings on more than one factor, indicating that their scores are to be regarded as functions of two or more latent abilities. Thus, it is not at all surprising to find, in Table 1.2, tests with substantial loadings on two or more factors. The "substantial" loadings are printed in **bold**. In exploratory factor analysis, loadings are customarily computed for all entries in matrices of results; many of these, of course, are very close to zero, confirming the "simple structure" principle that is one of the bases of exploratory factor analysis. It is common to find that values close to zero are simply not shown in tables of factor-analytic results in the literature, but they are, of course, shown in Table 1.2.

Table 1.2: Orthogonal hierarchical exploratory factor matrix for 16 variables and 9 factors: Factor loadings (decimals omitted).

Stratum:	3	2	2	2	2	2	2	2	2	
Factor:	*g*	Glr	Gsm	Gs	Ga	Gv	Gc	Gf	Gq	h²
Factor No.:	1	2	3	4	5	6	7	8	9	
Var.										
1 MEMNAM	**511**	**585**	–012	–001	002	003	014	002	–014	604
2 MEMSEN	**544**	–014	**466**	027	–020	–174	**275**	166	016	649
3 VISMAT	**595**	016	004	**779**	–012	–000	002	001	–004	961
4 INCWDS	**481**	–061	109	087	**238**	022	193	132	–117	380
5 VISCLO	**434**	002	–015	–002	–013	**531**	020	001	–002	471
6 PICTVO	**597**	027	–001	003	007	011	**639**	001	**381**	912
7 ANLSYN	**632**	023	001	–016	016	058	–023	**310**	025	501
8 VISAUD	**625**	**434**	008	–092	076	193	–135	051	031	652
9 MEMWDS	**451**	016	**670**	–015	014	000	004	001	–010	653
10 CRSOUT	**564**	–025	–002	**410**	030	164	–001	055	019	518
11 SNDBND	**612**	004	001	003	**732**	–006	002	001	–003	910
12 PICREC	**460**	152	033	020	–005	**264**	–044	073	–049	316
13 ORALVO	**710**	–020	103	–013	008	–023	**490**	085	**407**	930
14 CNCPTF	**662**	–001	–012	003	–008	–016	025	**403**	–028	602
15 CALCUL	**626**	000	–019	029	–004	097	–002	003	**566**	723
16 APLPRB	**689**	–001	026	–016	–004	015	149	078	**524**	779
SMSQ	5394	561	692	794	600	460	806	328	926	10561
%CCV	51.07	5.31	6.55	7.51	5.68	4.35	7.63	3.10	8.76	100.00

Note: Based on the correlation matrix of Table 1.1, which see for full names of variables. Salient loadings of variables on common factors are shown in **bold**. Factor Names: *g*: General Intellectual Ability; Glr: Long-Term Retrieval; Gsm: Short-Term Memory; Gs: Processing Speed; Ga: Auditory Processing; Gv: Visual-Spatial Thinking; Gc: Comprehension-Knowledge; Gf: Fluid Reasoning; Gq: Mathematics; h²: Communality. SMSQ: Sums of Squares. %CCV: Percentages of Common Covariance.

Literally hundreds of tables of exploratory factor-analytic results based on the classical view of factor structure were published in the 20th century from about 1940 to about 1990. The present author (Carroll 1993) reported re-analyses of about 450 of the datasets that generated these tables. The main advantage of the author's re-analyses was that they were based on a largely uniform exploratory methodology that was believed to be the best available at the time these analyses were conducted (Carroll 1995). The chief disadvantage of this methodology was that it suffered from a lack of adequate procedures for establishing the statistical significance of findings. Nevertheless, it is probable that most of the many *g* factors found in Carroll's analyses would be found statistically significant if the corresponding data could be submitted to appropriate analyses.

When the correlation matrix shown in Table 1.1 was submitted to confirmatory analysis with the Jöreskog & Sörbom (1989) LISREL 7 program, the resulting maximum likelihood estimates of the factor loadings are shown in Table 1.3, the general pattern of which is comparable in many ways to that of Table 1.2. The confirmatory analysis procedure requires the researcher to specify the general form of the model to be tested (for example, the number of factors to be assumed and whether the factors are to be uncorrelated or correlated), and exactly which variables are hypothesized to measure each factor (either positively or negatively); the researcher is not required to specify a value or even a range of possible values for factor loadings. The actual determination of each specified value is accomplished by iterative computational procedures leading to an approximation of the empirically observed correlation matrix as predicted from the LISREL estimates. Occasionally the iterations cannot be completed after a programmed number of them have taken place, because of improperly selected hypotheses about the structure. For further understanding of the procedure used here, see useful articles by Keith (1997) and Gustafsson (2001).

In the present case, the model that was tested assumed (or hypothesized) that the correlations could be explained by loadings (weights) on a single third-stratum general factor *g* plus a series of eight second-stratum factors, each of which was to be defined by 2 or 3 tests that previous research with these tests suggested would load on a given factor. It was also specified that the factors were to be orthogonal to each other. In the hope of attaining a complete solution for all factors, an attempt was made to find values of loadings on at least 3 variables for each of the second-stratum factors, but it was found not easily possible to do this for all of these factors, most likely because the battery was in fact not designed to include tests such that there would be more than two significant loadings on each second-order factors. For each factor found not easily possible to define in this way, the loadings for each of the two variables known (from previous research) to define the factor were set equal to each other (as indicated by asterisks placed next to certain values in the table). The principal difference from Table 1.2 was that information on the statistical significance of the results was provided. All non-zero loadings presented in Table 1.3 (i.e. those not shown as "—") were statistically significant at $p \leq 0.001$, and the goodness of fit indices (noted at the end of Table 1.3) for the whole model were at levels deemed to indicate satisfactory fit.

As found with Table 1.2, all variables (tests) had very substantial loadings on the third-order *g* factor, leaving only so much room, as it were, for high loadings on second-

Table 1.3: LISREL estimates of orthogonal factor loadings for 16 variables on 9 factors (decimals omitted).

Stratum:	3	2	2	2	2	2	2	2	2	
Factor:	g	Glr	Gsm	Gs	Ga	Gv	Gc	Gf	Gq	h^2
Factor No.:	1	2	3	4	5	6	7	8	9	
1 MEMNAM	504	488*	—	—	—	—	—	—	—	492
2 MEMSEN	566	—	551*	—	—	—	136	—	—	642
3 VISMAT	551	—	—	496	—	—	—	—	—	550
4 INCWDS	485	—	—	—	445*	—	—	—	—	433
5 VISCLO	418	—	—	152	—	402	—	—	—	359
6 PICTVO	676	—	—	—	—	—	371	—	—	595
7 ANLSYN	646	—	—	—	—	—	—	336*	—	530
8 VISAUD	623	488*	—	—	—	172	—	—	—	656
9 MEMWDS	457	—	551*	—	—	—	—	—	—	512
10 CRSOUT	549	—	—	743	—	—	—	—	—	853
11 SNDBND	594	—	—	—	445*	—	—	—	—	551
12 PICREC	461	—	—	—	—	334	—	—	—	316
13 ORALVO	812	—	—	—	—	—	425	—	—	840
14 CNCPTF	663	—	—	—	—	—	—	336*	—	602
15 CALCUL	684	—	—	—	—	—	—	—	415*	640
16 APLPRB	774	—	—	—	—	—	—	—	415*	771
SMSQ	**5762**	476	607	821	396	303	337	226	344	9302
%CCV	**61.94**	5.11	6.52	8.82	4.25	3.25	3.62	2.42	3.69	100.00

Measures of goodness of fit for the whole model:
CHI-square with 90 degrees of freedom = 798.90 ($p = 0.000$)
Goodness of fit index = 0.959
Adjusted goodness of fit index = 0.938
Root mean square residual = 0.035

Note: Based on the correlation matrix of Table 1.1, which see for full names of variables, and Table 1.2 for full names of factors. h^2: Communality or Squared Multiple Correlation. SMSQ: Sums of Squares.%CCV: Percentages of Common Factor Covariance. "*": Loadings equated within factor.

order factors (because the sum of squares of the 2 loadings for a given variable could not exceed 1.000). Overall, however, the second-order loadings conformed to expectations, and the results suggested that the hypothesized model for the dataset was valid, confirming the classical view of higher-stratum factorial structure.

The results show that there is indeed a factor *Gf* (Fluid Reasoning) that is significantly separate and different from factor *g*, tending to disconfirm any view that *Gf* is identical to *g*. If provisions for factor loadings of *g* are removed from the hypothesized pattern of factor loadings (leaving only 8 orthogonal factors), the goodness of fit of the model deteriorates significantly. Specifically, in this case the value of chi-square increases to 7108.02 with 106 degrees of freedom, and the Goodness of Fit Index decreases to 0.601, casting doubt on the validity of any view that denies the existence of a factor *g*. Because the model without *g* is nested within the model that includes *g*, the statistical significance of this finding is captured in the change of 6309.12 in the chi-square value, associated with a change of 16 in the number of degrees of freedom, making it clearly significant at $p < 0.0005$. Alternatively, the model tested could be specified as PH = ST, meaning that the second-order factors could be estimated as being correlated. In this case, chi-square with 78 degrees of freedom becomes 479.02, with a Goodness of Fit Index of 0.974. The change in the chi-square value is 319.88 with 12 degrees of freedom, clearly significant with a virtually zero probability. With correlated factors, it would be possible to assume at least one third-order factor. But it has already been demonstrated, above, that the existence of a third-order general factor in the first-order correlations can be accepted; it is unnecessary to perform further calculations unless one is interested in further third-order factors.

There is still a problem with *Gf*, namely, that it appears to be a rather weak, poorly defined factor, at least in the dataset examined here. Note the relatively small factor loadings for the two tests indicated as measuring *Gf* in both Table 1.2 and Table 1.3, also the relatively low values of %CCV for *Gf* in these tables (3.1% and 2.42%, respectively). In view of the undoubtedly careful and persistent efforts that were made in constructing these tests at the time the battery was being developed, the low *Gf* factor loadings most likely indicate that factor *Gf* is inherently difficult to measure reliably independently of its dependence on *g* (as indicated by the high *g* loadings for these tests). This may account for the finding by Gustafsson (1989, 2001; see also Gustafsson & Balke 1993; Gustafsson & Undheim 1996) that it is often difficult to distinguish *Gf* from *g*. Thus, Gustafsson's views on factor structure may be affected more by characteristics of tests than by factor structure as such. I have been tempted to suggest, on the basis of these and similar findings in other studies, that the reality of a Fluid Reasoning factor independent of *g* is at least questionable, and that Horn's (1998) support for a *Gf* factor can possibly be conceived of as support for a *g* factor (when no other factor interpretable as *g* is present in a given dataset).

3.2. Another Dataset

To provide information illustrating the generality of the higher-stratum structure found with the analysis of the correlation matrix shown in Table 1.1, a correlation matrix from a related dataset is presented in Table 1.4 and its confirmatory factor analysis is shown in Table 1.5. The 29-variable correlation matrix and a confirmatory factor analysis of it were published by McGrew *et al.* (1991), in the Technical Manual pertaining to the 1989 version of the Woodcock-Johnson Psycho-Educational Battery — Revised. The

Table 1.4: Pearsonian intercorrelation matrix, combined kindergarten to adult sample (decimals omitted). 29 variables from the Woodcock-Johnson psycho-educational battery — revised, $N = 1425$ (correlations corrected for age).

Variable:	1	2	3	4	5	6	7	8	9	10	11	12	13	14	15	16	17	18	19	20	21	22	23	24	25	26	27	28	29
Memory for Names	1	1000																												
Memory for Sentences	2	279	1000																											
Visual Matching	3	213	254	1000																										
Incomplete Words	4	167	255	191	1000																									
Visual Closure	5	148	103	178	176	1000																								
Picture Vocabulary	6	404	403	202	267	229	1000																							
Analysis-Synthesis	7	275	324	280	205	161	323	1000																						
Visual-Auditory Learning	8	542	343	267	192	205	382	376	1000																					
Memory for Words	9	208	559	221	245	046	225	215	246	1000																				
Cross Out	10	170	241	621	168	241	242	291	265	203	1000																			
Sound Blending	11	245	323	245	367	133	323	265	332	335	246	1000																		
Picture Recognition	12	293	216	212	123	234	256	233	299	155	335	212	1000																	
Oral Vocabulary	13	388	534	310	319	234	632	419	405	364	315	389	304	1000																
Concept Formation	14	306	382	306	236	206	325	484	376	227	305	275	269	458	1000															
Memory for Names (Delayed Recall)	15	721	236	155	168	129	383	269	460	173	123	242	236	359	284	1000														
Visual-Auditory Learning (Delayed Recall)	16	345	164	162	120	192	255	269	460	110	168	192	275	271	323	446	1000													
Numbers Reversed	17	259	384	227	129	129	255	368	321	401	309	316	206	396	354	225	182	1000												
Sound Patterns	18	233	257	204	221	109	269	271	259	243	229	294	168	331	299	222	214	282	1000											
Spatial Relations	19	280	266	278	158	265	317	389	369	189	343	225	288	388	404	240	289	311	294	1000										
Listening Comprehension	20	331	469	266	334	204	576	349	344	279	263	351	256	642	375	294	221	308	274	320	1000									
Verbal Analogies	21	379	454	334	228	242	522	455	445	310	344	355	322	639	496	377	330	403	304	465	526	1000								
Calculation	22	256	331	435	142	132	299	423	347	252	358	293	208	471	401	249	242	413	257	376	374	483	1000							
Applied Problems	23	337	416	419	206	175	439	470	388	312	388	360	273	603	489	313	268	438	315	486	524	631	655	1000						
Science	24	380	437	260	285	233	633	368	364	246	280	323	246	658	389	362	270	336	260	385	619	544	440	570	1000					
Social Studies	25	371	477	298	262	200	626	386	374	270	278	323	255	693	411	348	245	332	256	344	619	595	508	617	702	1000				
Humanities	26	390	447	308	281	252	622	343	414	297	284	355	283	665	359	368	283	326	282	340	572	598	427	536	633	672	1000			
Word Attack	27	281	370	356	263	119	316	303	366	322	255	484	202	468	329	269	228	398	316	312	326	415	422	450	346	354	398	1000		
Quantitative Concepts	28	342	427	408	205	162	497	437	416	309	361	320	244	615	413	337	280	433	299	440	513	624	656	728	602	637	576	471	1000	
Writing Fluency	29	225	350	494	193	123	260	309	347	266	410	358	196	398	335	197	194	365	229	276	285	394	420	426	293	336	409	488	434	1000

Note: Reprinted with permission: McGrew, K. S., Werder, J. K. & Woodcock, R. W. (1991). *WJ-R Technical Manual* (p. 345). Allen, TX: DLM.

Table 1.5: LISREL estimates of orthogonal factor loadings for 29 variables on 10 factors (decimals omitted).

Stratum:	3	2	2	2	2	2	2	2	2	2	
Factor:	*g*	Glr	Gsm	Gs	Ga	Gv	Gc	Gf	Gq	Lang	h²
Factor No.:	1	2	3	4	5	6	7	8	9	10	
01 MEMNAM	478	695	—	—	—	—	—	—	—	—	712
02 MEMSEN	587	—	396	—	—	—	—	—	—	—	501
03 VISMAT	499	—	—	709	—	—	—	—	—	—	752
04 INCWDS	340	—	—	—	308	—	—	—	—	—	210
05 VISCLO	279	—	—	—	—	472	—	—	—	—	301
06 PICVOC	566	—	—	—	—	—	531	—	—	—	602
07 ANLSYN	591	—	—	—	—	—	—	213	—	—	395
08 VISAUD	579	343	—	—	—	—	—	—	—	—	453
09 MEMWDS	424	—	782	—	—	—	—	—	—	—	791
10 CRSOUT	478	—	—	539	—	—	—	—	—	—	519
11 SNDBND	490	—	—	—	642	—	—	—	—	—	652
12 PICREC	398	—	—	—	—	260	—	—	—	—	226
13 ORALVO	749	—	—	—	—	—	377	—	—	—	703
14 CNCPTF	623	—	—	—	—	—	—	543	—	—	683
15 MMNADR	439	729	—	—	—	—	—	—	—	—	724
16 VSAUDR	404	320	—	—	—	—	—	—	—	—	266
17 NMRVRS	571	—	203	—	—	—	—	—	—	—	367
18 SNDPAT	436	—	—	—	144	—	—	—	—	—	211
19 SPAREL	580	—	—	—	—	219	—	—	—	—	384
20 LISCMP	619	—	—	—	—	—	424	—	—	—	563
21 VBLANL	761	—	—	—	—	—	162	052	—	—	608
22 CALCUL	652	—	—	—	—	—	—	—	432	—	612
23 APLPRB	783	—	—	—	—	—	—	—	335	—	725
24 SCIENC	651	—	—	—	—	—	491	—	—	—	665
25 SOCSTU	686	—	—	—	—	—	488	—	—	—	709
26 HUMANI	661	—	—	—	—	—	448	—	—	107	649
27 WDATCK	587	—	—	—	273	—	—	—	—	197	458
28 QUANCN	743	—	—	—	—	—	177	—	400	—	743
29 WRIFLU	549	—	—	286	—	—	—	—	—	685	852
SMSQ	9515	1235	810	875	602	338	1341	343	459	519	16037
%CCV	59.33	7.70	5.05	5.45	3.75	2.10	8.36	2.13	2.23	3.23	100.00

Measures of goodness of fit for the whole model:
CHI-square with 343 degrees of freedom = 1488.60 ($p = 0.000$)
Goodness of fit index = 0.931; Adjusted goodness of fit index = 0.912
Root mean square residual = 0.039

Note: Analysis of the correlation matrix of Table 1.4, which see for full names of variables. Factor Names (as given by McGrew *et al.*, 1991): *g*: General Intellectual Ability; Glr: Long-Term Retrieval; Gsm: Short-Term Memory; Gs: Processing Speed; Ga: Auditory Processing; Gv: Visual-Spatial Thinking; Gc: Comprehension-Knowledge; Gf: Fluid Reasoning: Gq: Mathematics; Lang: Language. h²: Communality or Squared Multiple Correlation; SMSQ: Sums of Squares; %CCV: Percentages of Common Factor Covariance.

confirmatory factor analysis presented here was run by the present author from the original correlations (Table 1.4) with a slightly different model from that employed by McGrew *et al.*, with computations to parallel the analysis presented in Table 1.2; specifically, there was provision for determining the factor loadings of all 29 variables on a general factor *g* and for computing data on the relative importance of the factors.

The results in Table 1.5 confirm the classical, standard multifactorial model of the higher-stratum structure even more clearly than the results in Table 1.2. That is, the presence and generality of a *g* factor for all 29 tests is supported, and the existence, separate from *g*, of nine second-stratum factors (including G_f and G_c) is shown, each with from 3 to 8 significant loadings on a specific group of tests, which help to define the nature of the factor. One of these factors, labeled "Lang" (Language), was not present in the previous dataset; its presence here invites further research on the nature of this factor.

At the same time, the results in Table 1.5 tend to disconfirm other views on the higher-stratum structure of cognitive abilities. They deny the view that a factor *g* does not exist, and some doubt is cast on the view that emphasizes the importance of a G_f factor, in view of the relatively low factor loadings of some tests (numbered 07 and 21) on this factor. Thus, these data tend to discredit the *limited structural analysis view* and the *second-stratum multiplicity view*.

4. Discussion

There is need for consideration of certain important features of recent publications — tests, test manuals, and writings concerned with the higher-stratum structure of cognitive abilities.

In some of the literature that has been cited, one finds a consistent bias against full acknowledgment of the existence of a general factor and its role in commonly used tests of cognitive ability. Consider, for example, the technical manual of the 1991 version of the Woodcock-Johnson cognitive test battery — the WJ-R (McGrew *et al.* 1991), from which the correlational data of Tables 1.1 and 1.4 were taken and further analyzed in the present chapter. Over many of its pages, this manual reveals a studious neglect of the role of any kind of general factor in the WJ-R. Confirmatory factor analyses of correlational data either are based on orthogonal structures (e.g. Table 6-27, p. 166) or assume oblique structure, with correlations between factors presented (e.g. Table 6-28, p. 167), but there is no mention of a possible general factor, despite the fact that appropriate analysis would have revealed an important role of what I would call a third-order general factor (as shown in Table 1.3 of the present chapter). On page 170 is found Figure 6-5, a path diagram which on page 169 is described as providing "a highly restricted and parsimonious representation of the factor structure of the WJ-R", but Figure 6-5 contains no representation of a general factor. Only on page 171 could one find a statement about the possibility that a hierarchical *g* factor might influence what were (erroneously) called first-order factors, but with a comparison of fit statistics said to be obtained with a hierarchical *g* model versus a "G_f-G_c model" (that did not include) the reader would be left with the impression that the G_f-G_c model was in every way superior to a "hierarchical *g* model". This impression would have been reinforced by Horn's (1991) essay, constituting Chapter 7 of the manual, that reviewed theory on the measurement of intellectual capabilities and emphasized the presumed superiority of the G_f-G_c theory. Thus for some ten years before a further revision of the WJ-R became available, users of the WJ-R were left largely uninformed of the fact that scores on the subtests in the battery were likely to be heavily influenced by a general factor of ability.

Fortunately, this situation changed in 2001 when a new version of the test, its scoring, and its technical manual became available (McGrew & Woodcock 2001), introducing a so-called CHC (Cattell-Horn-Carroll) theory of cognitive abilities that supplemented Horn's G_f-G_c theory with essentially a three-stratum theory similar to that proposed by the present writer (Carroll 1993).

Even though I was to some extent involved in this change (as an occasional consultant to the authors and publisher), I am still not quite sure what caused or motivated it. For a number of years, Horn had espoused the so-called G_f-G_c theory, and had written a number of papers that included criticisms of a hierarchical *g* theory (Horn & Noll 1994, 1997). For example, as he reported:

> "Carroll (1993) identified a general factor at the third stratum in 33 separate analyses in his reanalysis of the data of 461 studies. These factors are general in the sense that they are defined at the highest order in higher-order analyses, and each is defined by non-chance correlations with many different cognitive tests. The problem for theory of general intelligence is that the factors are not the same from one study to another. For example, in one case (an analysis labeled ARNO01) the factor is defined by lexical knowledge, spatial relations, memory span, general interest, and an unidentified first-order factor, whereas in another case (analysis DENT01) the factor is defined by reasoning, number, word fluency, short-term memory, and perceptual speed. The different general factors do not meet the requirements for the weakest form of invariance (Horn & McArdle 1992) or satisfy the conditions of the Spearman model. The general factors represent different mixture measures, not one general intelligence" (Horn & Noll 1997: 68).

In response, I will not speak of technical problems relating to invariance or the conditions of the Spearman model. I merely point out that it is not the case that the *g* factor in the ARNO01 analysis was "defined by lexical knowledge, spatial relations . . ." as Horn claimed; it was defined by whatever was common to a series of tests or factors at a lower stratum. Nor was the *g* factor in the DENT01 study "defined by reasoning, number, . . ."; it was defined by whatever was common to a series of factors (or tests) at a lower stratum, namely, loadings on a *g* factor. All the *g* factors that I studied and characterized as general factors can be considered to be the same if they indeed measure a single factor, which they do, according to the Schmid & Leiman (1957) procedure by which, generally, they were computed. Perhaps this conclusion can be better understood if one looks at either Table 1.2 or Table 1.3 in the present chapter. In either case, one notes that all the tests are shown as measuring a single factor *g*, along with a variety of second-order factors. We can doubtless agree that this factor g is the same for all 16 tests. Now, if we conduct two new analyses (either exploratory or confirmatory) of these data, one of them using tests 1–4 and 8–11 (i.e. using tests with high loadings on factors Glr, Gsm, Gs and Ga) and the other using tests 5–7 and 12–16 (i.e. tests with high loadings on factors Gv, Gc, Gf and Gq), both analyses would yield a factor g — the "same" g in each case. It would be difficult to argue that the g factors yielded by the two analyses are different, even though they involve different second-order factors. Horn's comment suggests that he conveniently forgets a fundamental principle on which factor analysis is based (a principle of which he is undoubtedly aware) — that the nature of a single factor discovered to account for a table of inter-correlations does not necessarily relate to special characteristics of the variables involved in the correlation matrix; it relates only to characteristics or underlying measurements (latent variables) that are common to those variables. I cannot regard Horn's comment as a sound basis for denying the existence of a factor g, yet he succeeded in persuading himself and many others to do exactly this for an extended period of years.

I believe I have covered the more important theoretical problems in describing the higher-stratum structure of cognitive abilities. Researchers who are concerned with this structure in one way or another, like Burns & Nettelbeck (in press), Case, Demetriou, Platsidou & Kazi (2001), Deary (2000), Garlick (in press), Jensen (1998), and Plomin (1999) can be assured that a general factor g exists, along with a series of second-order factors that measure broad special abilities. Special facts that should be considered, however, are that more and better tests of factor G_f are needed to establish this factor as linearly independent of factor g, if indeed this is possible, and that factor G_c, as a factor in certain kinds of tests of general knowledge, is also a factor that can strongly influence certain tests intended to measure factor g; it is suggested that this influence needs to be statistically controlled. Indeed, it may be recommended that estimates of scores on factor g should be based on multiple regression formulas for determining factor scores (Gorsuch 1983) rather than simple weighted sums of scores like those recommended in the WJ-III Technical Manual (McGrew & Woodcock 2001). Further research is needed on the best tests and procedures to use in estimating scores on all higher-stratum factors of cognitive ability, and continued psychological and even philosophical examination of the nature of factor g is a *must*.

References

Burns, N. R., & Nettelbeck, T. (in press). Inspection time in the structure of cognitive abilities: Where does IT fit? *Intelligence*.

Burt, C. (1949a). The two-factor theory. *British Journal of Psychology, Statistical Section, 2*, 151–178.

Burt, C. (1949b). The structure of the mind: A review of the results of factor analysis. *British Journal of Educational Psychology, 19*, 100–111, 176–199.

Carroll, J. B. (1989). *Exploratory factor analysis programs for the IBM PC (and compatibles)*. Chapel Hill, NC: The L. L. Thurstone Psychometric Laboratory, University of North Carolina at Chapel Hill, May 1989.

Carroll. J. B. (1993). *Human cognitive abilities: A survey of factor-analytic studies.* New York: Cambridge University Press.

Carroll, J. B. (1995). On methodology in the study of cognitive abilities. *Multivariate Behavioral Research, 30,* 429–452.

Carroll, J. B. (1997a). Theoretical and technical issues in identifying a factor of general intelligence. In: B. Devlin, S. E. Fienberg, D. P. Resnick, & K. Roeder (Eds), *Intelligence, genes, and success: Scientists respond to The Bell Curve* (pp. 125–156). New York: Springer-Verlag.

Carroll, J. B. (1997b). The three-stratum theory of cognitive abilities. In: D. P. Flanagan, J. L. Genshaft, & P. L. Harrison (Eds), *Contemporary intellectual assessment: Theories, tests, and issues* (pp. 122–130). New York: Guilford.

Case, R., Demetriou, A., Platsidou, M., & Kazi, S. (2001). Integrating concepts and tests of intelligence from the differential and developmental traditions. *Intelligence, 29,* 307–336.

Cattell, R. B. (1941). Some theoretical issues in adult intelligence testing. *Psychological Bulletin, 38,* 592.

Cattell, R. B. (1971). *Abilities: Their structure, growth, and action.* Boston: Houghton Mifflin. [Revised edition: Amsterdam: North-Holland, 1987.]

Cattell, R. B., & Horn, J. L. (1978). A check on the theory of fluid and crystallized intelligence with description of new subtest designs. *Journal of Educational Measurement, 15,* 139–164.

Deary, I. J. (2000). *Looking down on human intelligence: From psychometrics to the brain.* Oxford, England: Oxford University Press.

Eysenck, H. J. (1994). A biological theory of intelligence. In: D. K. Detterman (Ed.), *Current topics in human intelligence* (Vol. 4), *Theories of intelligence* (pp. 117–149). Norwood, NJ: Ablex.

Garlick, D. (in press). Understanding the nature of the general factor of intelligence: The role of individual differences in neural plasticity as an explanatory mechanism. *Psychological Review.*

Gorsuch, R. L. (1983). *Factor analysis* (2nd ed.). Hillsdale, NJ: Erlbaum.

Gustafsson, J-E. (1984). A unifying model for the structure of intellectual abilities. *Intelligence, 8,* 179–203.

Gustafsson, J-E. (1989). Broad and narrow abilities in research on learning and instruction. In: R. Kanfer, P. L. Ackerman, & R. Cudeck (Eds), *Abilities, motivation, and methodology: The Minnesota Symposium on Learning and Individual Differences* (pp. 203–237). Hillsdale, NJ: Erlbaum.

Gustafsson, J-E. (2001). On the hierarchical structure of ability and personality. In: J. M. Collis & S. Messick (Eds), *Intelligence and personality: Bridging the gap in theory and measurement* (pp. 25–42). Mahwah, NJ: Erlbaum.

Gustafsson, J-E., & Balke, G. (1993). General and specific abilities as predictors of school achievement. *Multivariate Behavioral Research, 28,* 407–434.

Gustafsson, J-E., & Undheim, J. O. (1996). Individual differences in cognitive functions. In: D. C. Berliner & R. C. Calfee (Eds), *Handbook of educational psychology* (pp. 186–242). New York: Macmillan Library Reference USA.

Holzinger, K. J. (1936). Recent research on unitary traits. *Character and Personality, 4,* 335–343.

Horn, J. L. (1965). Fluid and crystallized intelligence: A factor analytic study of the structure among primary mental abilities. Unpublished doctoral dissertation, University of Illinois. (University Microfilms 65–7113).

Horn, J. L. (1991). Measurement of intellectual capabilities: A review of theory. In: K. S. McGrew, J. K. Werder, & R. W. Woodcock (Eds), *Woodcock-Johnson technical manual: A reference on theory and current research* (pp. 197–246). Allen, TX: DLM Teaching Resources.

Horn, J. L. (1998). A basis for research on age differences in cognitive capabilities. In: J. J. McArdle, & R. Woodcock (Eds), *Human cognitive abilities in theory and practice* (pp. 57–91). Mahwah, NJ: Erlbaum.

Horn, J. L., & McArdle, J. J. (1992). A practical and theoretical guide to measurement invariance in aging research. *Experimental Aging Research, 18*, 117–144.

Horn, J. L., & Noll, J. (1994). A system for understanding cognitive capabilities: A theory and the evidence on which it is based. In: D. K. Detterman (Ed.), *Current topics in human intelligence* (Vol. 4), *Theories of intelligence* (pp. 151–203). Norwood, NJ: Ablex.

Horn, J. L., & Noll, J. (1997). Human cognitive capabilities: Gf-Gc theory. In: D. P. Flanagan, J. L. Genshaft, & P. L. Harrison (Eds). *Contemporary intellectual assessment: Theories, tests, and issues* (pp. 53–81). New York: Guilford.

Jensen, A. R. (1998). *The G factor: The science of mental ability.* Westport, CT: Praeger.

Jöreskog, K. G., & Sörbom, D. (1989). *LISREL 7 user's reference guide.* Scientific Software, Inc.

Keith, T. Z. (1997). Using confirmatory factor analysis to aid in understanding the constructs measured by intelligence tests. In: D. P. Flanagan, J. L. Genshaft, & P. L. Harrison (Eds), *Contemporary intellectual assessment: Theories, tests, and issues* (pp. 373–402). New York: Guilford.

McGrew, K. S., Werder, J. K., & Woodcock, R. W. (1991). *WJ-R technical manual.* Allen, TX: DLM Teaching Resources.

McGrew, K. S. & Woodcock, R. W. (2001). *Woodcock-Johnson III Technical Manual.* Itasca, IL: Riverside Publishing Co.

Plomin, R. (1999). Genetics and general cognitive ability. *Nature, 402* (Supp. 2, December), C25–C29.

Schmid, J., & Leiman, J. M. (1957). The development of hierarchical factor solutions. *Psychometrika, 22*, 53–61.

Spearman, C. (1904). "General intelligence", objectively determined and measured. *American Journal of Psychology, 15*, 201–293.

Spearman, C. (1923). *The nature of 'intelligence' and the principles of cognition.* London, England: Macmillan.

Spearman, C. (1927). *The abilities of man: Their nature and measurement.* New York: Macmillan.

Spearman, C., & Wynn Jones, L. (1950). *Human ability: A continuation of "The abilities of man".* London, England: Macmillan.

Thurstone, L. L. (1938). Primary mental abilities. *Psychometric Monographs,* (No. 1).

Thurstone, L. L. (1947). *Multiple factor analysis: A development and expansion of The Vectors of Mind.* Chicago: University of Chicago Press.

Thurstone, L. L., & Thurstone, T. G. (1941). Factorial studies of intelligence. *Psychometric Monographs,* (No. 2).

Part II

The Biology of *g*

Part II — Introduction

This part addresses the fact that *g* has many biological correlates, and thereby confirms a long-held view by Jensen and others that *g* is more than just a superficial product of factor analytic abstractions. The 6 chapters deal with such various aspects of *g* as research on brain imaging, glucose uptake, reaction time, working memory, inspection time and other biological correlates, and the part concludes with the latest findings in *g*-related molecular genetics.

In Chapter 2, Britt Anderson takes a closer look at the brain size–*g* relationship. He first discusses the low and variable relationships found in earlier studies using such rough measures as external head circumference, and then presents the outcome of studies using more exacting *in vivo* neuro-imaging techniques. The overall conclusion is that anatomical and metabolic imaging techniques using magnetic resonance technology suggest a correlation in the order of 0.35 between brain size and IQ, a finding that is consistent across multiple experimental groups. Another important conclusion is that the majority of individual variation in intelligence is not explained by variation in brain volume. A third conclusion is, that we still do not know whether specific brain regions or compartments are the principal basis for the size–IQ correlation, and this sets the stage for further experiments exploiting the many new capabilities of magnetic resonance imaging and other brain image techniques.

Chapter 3 treats *g* in the light of positron emission tomography. Richard Haier, a pioneer in the area, tells the story of the first presentation of results from a study using this technique to measure on line glucose uptake while subjects solve problems in a Raven test. The first study addressed a preliminary question — where in the brain is intelligence? — and produced informative PET images of which parts of the brain were active in terms of glucose metabolism, taken as a proxy for neural firing. The result was a surprise: the *harder* a brain area works, the *lower* the glucose metabolism! Haier *et al.* then tested whether training lowers brain activity, and found that subjects learn which brain areas not to use, resulting in lower glucose uptake. They also found that the brightest subjects became the most brain efficient with learning. Further investigations involved the use of Jensen's correlated vector method and sophisticated research designs. A PET study of mental retardation examined whether retardation relates to higher than normal glucose uptake. It does! The chapter then presents a fascinating catalogue of future studies, some of them focusing on individual differences, some on consciousness, and concludes with a discussion of the important transition of intelligence research from its psychometric origins to the next level of neuroscience exploration and explanation.

Ian Deary reviews Jensen's contributions to what is now known about the association between reaction times and psychometric intelligence in Chapter 4, and recounts the major evaluations and critiques of that research. He finds that several aspects of reaction time have significant correlations of small effect size with intelligence test scores, but also that little is known about the causes of these correlations. He suggests that the Hick task and its slope have had unnecessary attention, but Jensen may be credited for firmly establishing this area of research and bringing it sufficient attention to ensure its persistence.

Chapter 5 by Ted Nettelbeck reviews the evidence for a moderately strong correlation between a measure termed "inspection time" (IT) and scores on psychometric ability tests. He also addresses the theoretically important issue about what this might mean in terms of developing an improved understanding of human intelligence. Arthur Jensen's contribution to this work has been considerable. In a series of articles, published with John Kranzler during the late 1980s and early 1990s, he has helped to establish the size of this correlation at around –0.5; and applied IT together with other chronometric measures based on reaction times (RTs) to the task of shifting the description of intelligence from the psychometric to a psychological level. The realization of the potential of this exploratory approach must await an established account of what IT measures. IT appears to measure individual differences in a capacity to detect change in a very briefly presented stimulus array, and this may be psychologically distinct from whatever RTs measure. However, this capacity captured by IT is also probably influenced by more than one psychological function. Moreover, the extent to which each of these functions is involved may depend on whether participants are children, or young, or elderly adults, or persons with an intellectual disability. Nonetheless, Kranzler and Jensen's research has demonstrated that unitary psychometric general cognitive ability is almost certainly a consequence of the contribution of several psychological functions.

Gilles Gignac, Tony Vernon and John Wickett outline in Chapter 6 the factors that influence the relationship between brain size and intelligence. They begin by stressing the importance of determining whether a correlation between a physical variable and IQ is mediated by environmental or biological causes. If a correlation exists only between-families, it probably is due to sociological factors, such as cross-assortative mating — like the height-IQ correlation. Brain volume correlates about 0.40 with IQ, and the correlation does not appear to be limited to adults. Then follows a discussion of the role of white versus grey matter as a substrate to the biological basis of IQ, a question leading to mixed results. The authors conclude this part of the chapter by saying that although speed of information processing correlates with IQ, larger or more abundant neuronal constituents may not necessarily explain the correlation. Perhaps individual differences in neurochemistry provide alternative or complementary explanations. They then go on to report on correlations between the rank of a group of subtests' factor loadings on *g* with the same group of subtests' ranked correlations with head size, and find a positive so-called Jensen effect of 0.64, suggesting that the extent to which a given test is correlated with head size is related positively and strongly to its correlation with *g*. Gignac *et al.* then report on studies suggesting that between 80–90% of brain volume is heritable, and that the genetic correlation between brain volume and IQ is 0.48.

However, as there are mixed evidence with respect to whether the brain size–IQ relationship is a within-family or between-family phenomenon, they conclude that it would be prudent to await the results of additional studies before any conclusion about the causal basis for the correlation is drawn.

The final chapter in Part II, Chapter 7, deals with the molecular genetics and *g*, and is written by a world authority in the area — Robert Plomin. He emphasizes, that during the decade following Jensen's 1969 *Harvard Educational Review* monograph, more research on the genetics of *g* was conducted than in the previous 50 years combined, in large part because of his monograph and the controversy and criticism it aroused. These bigger and better twin and adoption studies confirmed the conclusions that Jensen reached in his monograph, and also extended the field in new directions such as multivariate genetic analysis of specific cognitive abilities, developmental genetic research on change and continuity, and genetic research at the interface between nature and nurture. The goal of Chapter 7 is to provide an overview of another new direction in genetic research on *g*: harnessing the power of molecular genetics to begin to identify some of the genes responsible for the substantial heritability of *g*.

Chapter 2

Brain Imaging and *g*

Britt Anderson

1. Introduction

The "super-intelligent" alien with an enlarged head is a cliché of science fiction movies. This popular character is accepted because lay people believe a larger brain is a better brain. At the turn of the last century this was also the scientifically accepted view (for an example see Spitzka's (1907) 133-page monograph on the brains of famous men). However, popular opinion is not a particularly reliable guide to scientific truth, and among scientists the issue has remained controversial and the debate heated. In large measure, this was because the investigational methods were severely limited; they consisted either of correlating the wet weight of post-mortem brains to idiosyncratic estimates of intellectual eminence (Passingham 1979) or correlating IQ with surrogate measures of brain size such as height, weight, or head size (Jensen 1994). Jensen & Sinha (1993) reviewed these data, and concluded that there was a probable correlation in the neighborhood of 0.35 between brain size and intelligence. Their review also provides a thoughtful critique of the methodological limitations of using surrogate variables for brain size and the implications for observing relationships between somatic and intellectual variables. Ultimately, and despite thoughtful analyses such as Jensen and Sinha's, the low and variable relationship between external head measures and brain size left the ability-size question unresolved; until the advent of magnetic resonance imaging (MRI).

The last twenty-five years have seen a huge leap in the technology of neuro-imaging and it has become possible using MRI and magnetic resonance spectroscopy (MRS) to provide excellent *in vivo* estimates of brain size and brain metabolites. This review will show that these new data provide definitive evidence that there is a positive correlation between brain size and IQ. More importantly these studies demonstrate that most of the interindividual variance in IQ cannot be explained in this way, and thus they encourage additional investigations, many of which could profitably use MRI and MRS, to refine our understanding of the biological bases of normal variation in human intelligence.

The first major advance in *in vivo* neuro-imaging was Computed Tomography (CAT) scanning. After reviewing the seminal study using this technology, the data on

The Scientific Study of General Intelligence: Tribute to Arthur R. Jensen
© 2003 Published by Elsevier Science Ltd.
ISBN: 0-08-043793-1

anatomical MR imaging will be presented. A summary of some of the recent studies using MRS will conclude the discussion.

2. Prelude — Computed Tomography

CAT scanning uses x-rays. The "A" in CAT scan stands for "axial". Even though scans can be made in other planes, the use of the term CAT scan for a computed tomographic image, regardless of the anatomical plane of reconstruction, is common parlance. In the current generation of scanners it is common for an x-ray source to rotate through a circle of x-ray detectors with the subject's head at the center of this circle. The intensity of the x-ray beam detected at each position is then used to compute and reconstruct the physical image.

Since its dissemination to clinical centers in the mid-1970s, CAT scanning has been reported for a variety of clinical populations in which intelligence is abnormally low. As one example, Schofield *et al.* (1995) reported that intracranial size calculated from two CAT scan slices, and used as a proxy estimate of pre-morbid brain size, correlated with the age of onset of Alzheimer's disease.

Studies such as these are not necessarily helpful in understanding the relationship between IQ and brain size in *normal* subjects. Just because a small brain size is associated with a pathologically low intelligence or increased susceptibility to a disease that affects cognitive function, it does not necessarily follow that in a normal population variation in intelligence depends on a variation in brain size; there could be a threshold effect. Therefore, this review will focus on data from "normal" populations.

The quotations around normal in the above sentence reflect the fact that some of the populations used have had clinical complaints not felt to be associated with an important change in neurological functioning. For example, Yeo *et al.* (1987) reported a comparison, in 41 subjects, between WAIS IQ scores and volumetric estimates of brain and ventricle volumes calculated from CAT scans. While the CT scans were normal to clinician review, the scans were obtained as part of the clinical evaluations of individuals presenting for neurological symptoms such as headaches and dizziness. This study found no relationship between brain size and intelligence, although an asymmetry measure of hemisphere size correlated $r = 0.57$ ($p < 0.001$) with an asymmetry measure of IQ (verbal IQ–performance IQ). As pointed out by one of the authors, this early study had significant limitations (Bigler 1995). Foremost, the CT imaging and post-imaging processing software technology available at the time was limited. For example, the CAT scans in this study had a slice thickness of 1 cm. It is not uncommon for MRI studies today to use a slice thickness of 3 mm. While this study had a limited empirical impact it did point the way for similar anatomic-ability comparisons using the technically superior technology of MRI.

3. Anatomical MR Imaging

MRI can yield either anatomical images or metabolite profiles. In this section I focus on the results for anatomical images.

Anatomical MRI imaging relates primarily to the density of hydrogen protons contained in water within a volume of tissue and the protons "relaxation" constants which are affected by the chemical matrix in which the water molecules are embedded. Hydrogen ions "spin" and this rotation of an electrical object produces a magnetic field which, when a person is placed in a magnetic field, there is an alignment of protons with the magnetic field. For the actual imaging, a radio-frequency (RF) pulse is applied to tip the protons out of alignment. A separate "coil" is used to measure the RF emissions as the protons return to equilibrium. How long it takes for the protons to relax back into alignment and to return to random precession, results in the recorded RF information that is used for image reconstruction.

The first reported comparison of intelligence and brain volume using MRI was by Willerman *et al.* (1991). Forty college students were selected to represent a high and low SAT test group. Each subject underwent MRI with 5 mm thick sections separated by 2.5 mm. Automated and manual techniques were used to delete the bone, meninges, and other non-brain structures. This was done blind to subject IQ and sex. From this processed data, the authors took the total number of pixels per slice as a measure of brain size. With the sexes pooled, the IQ-brain size correlation was $r = 0.51$ ($p < 0.01$); applying a statistical correction for the fact that this correlation was based on the selection of extreme groups, the authors reported a corrected correlation of $r = 0.35$. This figure has held to be remarkably consistent in subsequent studies and is essentially identical to that computed by Jensen & Sinha (1993) from their comprehensive review of the pre-CAT/MRI literature.

Willerman *et al.* (1992) performed further analyses on this cohort (excluding one woman) evaluating hemispheric effects. Using a similar MRI analysis they divided the brain into left and right hemisphere volumes, and compared the asymmetry of hemisphere size with the VIQ–PIQ difference and the Vocabulary–Block design subtests from the WAIS for each sex. For men these correlations were positive and neared significance, but for women the relationships were opposite in sign. The authors interpreted this finding to mean that non-verbal skills were more likely to be served by both hemispheres in women. As will be seen below, subsequent studies have failed to find consistent hemisphere effects or different patterns for the two sexes.

The next group to publish on the brain size–IQ association was from the University of Iowa. In their first report, Andreasen *et al.* (1993) imaged 67 (37 male) normal subjects recruited through newspaper advertisements. Their scanner was a 1.5T unit and analyses drew from two data sets, one with 5 mm thick sections and a 2.5 mm gap, and a second set concentrating on central brain regions with 3 mm slices and 1.5 mm gaps. Brain volumes were determined through a combination of automated edge detection and manual tracing. For another set of measures, statistical techniques were used to segment the brain, based on training classes, into gray matter, white matter, and cerebrospinal fluid components.

The major finding from this study was a positive correlation between brain size and IQ (WAIS-R), even when the data were evaluated at the level of individual brain structures. The overall correlation for Full scale IQ and total brain volume was $r = 0.38$ ($p < 0.01$). Positive correlations were found for left and right hemispheres, temporal lobe, hippocampal, and cerebellar structures. No significant correlations were found for caudate or intraventricular cerebrospinal fluid volumes.

One theory advanced for the positive relationship between brain structure and IQ has been differences in the volume of myelinated structures or the characteristics of myelin (Miller 1994). In Andreasen's study, the significant positive correlation between brain volume and IQ held only for the gray matter ($r = 0.35$, $p < 0.01$, Pearson partial correlation with height partialed out) and not the white matter ($r = 0.14$, $p > 0.01$).

The Andreasen group has continued to work on this issue with their most recent data analysis being in 1997. For this report (Flashman *et al.* 1997) there were 90 normal subjects (48 male). After pre-processing, to remove the skull and other non-brain structures, the volume rendered brains were transformed into Talairach Atlas space. This atlas is a commonly used referent for brain imaging studies.

There were no important differences in the correlations between men and women, so most analyses were pooled. As the population was skewed to an above average IQ group, a correction for restriction of range was employed. The researchers also partialed height out of their analyses. After all these steps, a statistically significant correlation was found for brain size and IQ ($r = 0.25$). Both performance and verbal IQs (WAIS-R) were positively correlated, but only performance IQ was statistically significant. In the regional analyses, the strongest correlations were between performance IQ and the size of the frontal and temporal regions. However, when the investigators looked to see whether correlation coefficients for VIQ and PIQ with the same brain region were statistically different from each other, the results were negative. No regionally specific pattern underlying either PIQ or VIQ was determined.

Another early report was by Raz *et al.* (1993). This group used a permanent magnet system (0.3T) to measure brain volume (however, the frontal and occipital poles were excluded from their coronal imaging sequence) in 29 subjects. Intelligence tests were Cattell's Culture Fair (for fluid intelligence) and the Extended Vocabulary test (for crystallized intelligence). The cross sectional area of the dorso-lateral prefrontal cortex and the cerebral hemisphere volumes correlated ($r = 0.43$) with the fluid intelligence measure, but not with the crystallized intelligence measure.

The issue of correlations between IQ and specific brain regions was considered by two groups of researchers that looked at the corpus callosum area. The corpus callosum is the major white matter tract connecting the two cerebral hemispheres and is principally composed of axons and their myelin sheaths. In a group of 47 epileptics, Strauss *et al.* (1994) found a significant correlation between the posterior portion of the corpus callosum (the splenium) and IQ (WAIS-R or WISC) of $r = 0.347$ ($p < 0.05$). This basic result was confirmed in a group of 23 children (6–12 years of age) by Rowe *et al.* (1997). They demonstrated significant correlations between the splenium of the corpus callosum and the Information ($r = 0.49$), Similarities ($r = 0.61$), and Comprehension ($r = 0.49$) sub-tests of the WISC. As they found no significant correlations with performance subtests they argued that the callosum was preferentially involved in verbal ability. Despite these two callosal studies, when one looks at this literature in general, specific relationships for particular brain regions and specific intellectual measures have not been found consistently.

Harvey *et al.* (1994) published an article on brain volumes in subjects with psychiatric conditions which included a control group of 32 healthy volunteers solicited from hospital staff, a Salvation Army training college, and an employment agency. IQ was estimated with the New Adult Reading Test. This test uses the subjects' pronunciation of words of varying frequency to estimate an IQ. MRI scanning was conducted on a 0.5T unit. A single short inversion time ('STIR') sequence was used for estimating volumes. Slice thickness was 5 mm, and the slices were interleaved. Their imaging in the coronal plane, and the limitation to 20 slices, included all of the temporal lobes (the region of interest for their schizophrenia study), but did not include the entire brain. Brain size measurement was done by a single rater. For the controls, the correlation (Spearman) between total intracranial volume and IQ was $r = 0.69$ ($p = 0.001$).

At about the same time, Wickett *et al.* (1994) reported positive results for a study of 40 normal women. The subjects were recruited through newspaper advertisements and screened for neurological and medical diseases. Subjects were selected only if they were right handed. The Multi-dimensional Aptitude Battery (MAB) was used as the IQ test. For the MR imaging, 6 mm slices with 1 mm gaps were used and selection of the brain area for measurement was manual. The correlation between Full Scale IQ and total brain volume was $r = 0.395$ ($p < 0.05$). The highest correlations were found for the verbal components of the battery. An important incidental result from this study was that the authors also measured external cranial size with a tape measure and found that head circumference correlated only $r = 0.228$ with brain volume. While a subsequent study found a higher correlation, this study emphasizes the modest relationship between head size and brain size.

Subsequently, Wickett *et al.* (in press) pursued their analyses in 68 right-handed men. The MAB was again used as the main intelligence test, but the Kit of Factor Referenced Tests, *Der Zahlen-Verbindungs*-Test, two Reaction Time tests, Vandenberg mental rotation test, and forward and backward digit span were also administered to broaden the range of cognitive domains sampled. Brain imaging used a 0.5T MRI unit with 4 mm thick slices and a 0 mm gap. Image tracing was manual and the brain volumes were computed from pixel counts. The correlation between Full Scale IQ and total brain volume was the familiar $r = 0.35$. With a correction for restriction for range this rose to 0.51. There were no significant results when comparing VIQ and PIQ asymmetries to structural asymmetries between the hemispheres. The two hemispheres were themselves highly correlated ($r = 0.99$) in size. Verbal scores again seemed to be slightly more correlated with brain volume measures than did performance measures. Each of the two RT measures was significantly and negatively correlated with brain volume.

To evaluate more directly the relationship between *g* and brain volume, these investigators subjected their behavioral data to a principal components analysis. The extracted factors that correlated positively and significantly with brain volume were in addition to the general factor, fluid ability ($r = 0.23$), crystallized ability ($r = 0.31$) and memory ($r = 0.38$). When using Jensen's method of vector correlations the investigators found that the more highly *g* loaded on a test, the more highly it correlated with brain volume, a so-called Jensen effect.

Reiss *et al.* (1996) evaluated brain development in 85 children and adolescents (21 male) by MRI. For 69 subjects, IQ data were known. The correlation of IQ to total *cerebral* (not brain) volume was 0.45 ($p = 0.0005$). Fitting a curve to their data, they found the best fit was a second order polynomial and they concluded that there might be an optimal brain size for the normal population with larger brains actually showing a decline in IQ. After removing the effects of age, Reiss *et al.* examined by regression techniques the predictive value for IQ of gray matter, white matter, and CSF volumes. Again, it was the gray matter volume that was significantly correlated to IQ (more gray: higher IQ).

On a subset of subjects, Reiss *et al.* divided the total gray matter into cortical and subcortical components. Both compartments contributed to predicting the variance in IQ. When the gray matter was divided regionally and analyzed by a stepwise regression, the prefrontal gray matter was the only tissue region retained in the regression equation.

The only published study of normal subjects that has failed to find a statistically significant correlation between MR measured brain volume and IQ is that by Tramo *et al.* (1998). Their population was smaller (20 subjects) and composed of 10 identical twin pairs. The authors found significant genotype effects on brain volume and large intercorrelations between the anatomical measures (forebrain volume, cortical surface area, midsaggital callosal area, and head circumference). The correlations between these variables and Full Scale IQ (WAIS-R) ranged from –0.05 to 0.06). Addressing the discrepancy between their work and the others, Tramo & Gazzaniga (1999) point out that some of the other studies did not measure the entire brain, but only selected regions. Tramo and Gazzaniga noted that for the callosal studies, only specific regions of the callosum and not total callosal areas (such as they measured) were reported to correlate with IQ measures. They also critiqued the other studies for using intellectual measures which frequently were not "IQ" tests. These authors conceded the possibility of a small positive correlation undetected by them secondary to sample size, but emphasized that they felt questions of quality rather than quantity explained differences in general cognitive ability.

Two more recent studies use current state of the art image analysis methods. Gur *et al.* (1999) reported a study of sex differences in brain compartmental volumes that also included subject performance measures. Subjects were 40 men and 40 women screened to exclude cognitive, psychiatric and medical problems. Neuropsychological measures included the WAIS-R. MRI measures came from 5 mm slices with 0 mm gaps in which the skull was automatically "stripped" and bone marrow and eyeball components were manually removed. The tissue of the brain was automatically segmented into white and gray matter compartments using an adaptive Bayesian algorithm. While the focus of their article was on differences due to sex (e.g. that women have a greater proportion of gray matter) they also found correlations between total intracranial volume and global performance ($r = 0.39$ men and $r = 0.40$ women). In contrast to the two earlier studies that analyzed segmented white and gray matter, this group found a larger effect for white matter volumes. Additionally, and discrepant from some earlier studies, Gur *et al.* also found larger correlations for the spatial tests than the verbal tests. Despite these differences, the overall correlation between ability and size was remarkably consistent with earlier studies. An important negative finding was the failure, again, to show important relationships between structural asymmetries and patterns of cognitive performance. The authors conclude, "It seems that sheer tissue volume, rather than proportion, is associated with better performance."

Pennington *et al.* (2000) reported a larger twin study. They had neuropsychological data on 9 pairs of monozygotic (MZ) and 9 pairs of dizygotic (DZ) twins which were the control group in a larger study of reading disability (an additional 48 twin pairs were in the reading disability group). Analyzing the control sample alone, there was a correlation of $r = 0.31$ between Full Scale IQ and total cerebral volume ($p = 0.07$, two tailed). Although the authors report a two tailed result, a one tailed test of significance might be more appropriate given the preponderance of evidence pointing to a specific direction for the ability-size effect.

Dividing brain volume into a cortical and subcortical factor (based on a factor analysis of their anatomical data), the authors found greater correlations for the subcortical factor. While the relationship between cerebral volume and IQ in twins reported from this study is at odds with that of Tramo *et al.*, the finding of significant genetic effects on brain size and structure were confirmed.

The large number of MR studies replicated multiple times by independent groups has unequivocally confirmed a relationship between brain volume and higher IQ scores for normal men and women. The value of this correlation hovers near $r = 0.35$. While the studies are consistent for their global findings, they are less consistent for their details. Most of the studies, especially the more recent studies with larger numbers of subjects and more sophisticated imaging protocols, fail to find any important contributions of left-right size asymmetries. The evidence for a differential effect of gray matter and white matter volumes favors gray matter volume being more important, but the issue cannot be considered fully resolved. No specific pattern of regional differences correlates with a specific pattern of cognitive skills in normal subjects, but it is important to note that the sizes of individual brain structure are themselves highly intercorrelated. There seem to be general factors for brain size as well as intelligence.

While the consistent finding of a correlation between intelligence and total brain size is important and reassuring, perhaps more important is the relatively small size of the correlation. Far less of the normal variation in human intelligence is explained by brain size than is explained because of it. This observation suggests that additional investigations are necessary to determine the biological bases of individual differences in intelligence and leads directly to the additional ways in which MRI can be employed.

4. Spectroscopic MR Imaging

The technique that is used for anatomical MRI grew from the nuclear magnetic resonance technology used in chemistry for identifying the atomic spectra of specific compounds. This same approach can be used in MRI for determining a spectrogram within an anatomically defined volume (voxel) of tissue. This allows measurement of neurotransmitters, chemical constituents, and pH in the brains of normal subjects who have known IQ's. The application of MRS to individual difference research has not progressed to the state that anatomical MRI has, but its potential is greater.

One of the first applications of this technique was that of Rae *et al.* (1996), who reported on a cohort of 42 boys. These children were a control group for a study on the brain metabolic changes associated with Duchenne's muscular dystrophy. Using the established relationship between phophocreatinine and inorganic phosphorous as a function of pH, these investigators calculated from the phosphorous NMR spectra the brain intracellular pH. When compared to WISC IQ's there was a highly significant correlation of $r = 0.523$ (Spearman's ranked).

Anderson *et al.* (1998) were unable to replicate this result in a cohort of 33 epileptic subjects who had undergone phosphorous NMR imaging and also had Wechsler IQ scores. A further result of the Anderson *et al.* study was a poor correlation between the pH of the left and right temporal areas, suggesting that this physiological measure may be quite variable and not as amenable for correlational studies as the relatively stable measure, brain volume. There were additional differences between the two studies: mixed gender versus all boys, adults versus children, and region of the brain used for pH measurement. Perhaps the pH:IQ correlation is developmentally transient.

Another application of MRS is seen in two papers by Jung *et al.* (1999a, b) They measured n-acetlyaspartate (NAA). This compound is a chemical constituent of neuronal membranes. When measured from gray matter areas, it has been taken as an index of neuronal number, although studies showing a direct correlation between NAA levels and neuronal number in normal populations, either animal or human, are lacking. In the Jung *et al.* studies, their voxel of interest was primarily white matter. They therefore interpreted their measurements as indexing the number or size of myelinated axonal processes. In their more recent report (Jung *et al.* 1999b), they recorded the results from 46 subjects (24 women). The voxel of interest was in the left occipital-parietal white matter. Neuropsychological measures included the Paced serial addition test, California Verbal Learning test, and Stroop interference test. This full battery of tests was composed of both timed and untimed components. Lower correlations were found between the untimed tasks and NAA levels. However, when a total z score was developed for the timed tasks it correlated $r = 0.65$ with NAA levels.

MRS is also capable of determining the level of specific neurotransmitters. In unpublished data, Anderson, Martin, and Kuzniecky measured levels of the inhibitory neurotransmitter gamma-aminobutyric acid (GABA) in 17 young healthy adults who were control subjects in a study of the effects of anti-convulsants on brain GABA levels. In addition to their baseline scans, the subjects were also tested, prior to medication administration, on choice reaction time tests, visual serial addition test, symbol digits modalities test, selective reminding test, and semantic and phonemic fluency tests. Brain GABA levels showed no consistent relationship to these behavioral variables. The confidence intervals that were computed from these correlations put a severe constraint on any possible GABA-behavioral relationship in the normal brain. It is unlikely (< 0.05) that variation in brain GABA can account for more than 10% of normal variation in *g*, and it is possible it has no relation at all. This is despite the fact that in pathological states or as a result of medications that perturbations of brain GABA levels are associated with alterations of mental performance (Kuzniecky *et al.* 1998;

Martin *et al.* 1999). These data emphasize the need to be cautious when inferring the basis for normal variation in cognitive function from studies on clinical populations.

5. Conclusions

Anatomical and metabolic imaging techniques using magnetic resonance technology have provided a clear answer to the question of whether brain size is correlated to intelligence. The correlation is positive and in the order of $r = 0.35$. This result has been so consistent across multiple experimental groups that its veracity should not be in dispute. Still open are questions as to whether there are specific brain regions or compartments (e.g. gray matter versus white matter) that are the principal basis for this relationship.

While providing a clear answer to the gross size-ability question, these studies have also pointed out that the majority of individual variation in intelligence is not explained by variation in brain volume. This sets the stage for further experiments using additional capabilities of MRI and other technologies to assess the physiological function of the brain. So far, the most dramatic result has been the correlation between white matter NAA levels and performance on timed cognitive tasks. However, both reports of this relationship have come from a single research group and await independent confirmation. Other applications of MRS, such as measuring brain neurotransmitter levels and intracellular pH, have only really been demonstrations of technical feasibility. While these new techniques have not resolved open question about normal variation in brain-behavior relations they light the way to a bright future for understanding the biological bases of interindividual variation in general cognitive ability, a research aspiration that one can trace from Spearman through Jensen to many of the authors of the present volume, this one included.

References

Anderson, B., Elgavish, G. A., Chu, W-J., Simor, T., Martin, R. C., Hugg, J. W., & Kuzniecky, R. I. (1998). Temporal lobe pHi and IQ: no consistent correlation. *Intelligence, 26,* 75–79.

Andreasen, N. C., Flaum, M., Swayze II, V., O'Leary, D. S., Alliger, R., Cohen, G., Ehrhardt, J., & Yuh, W. T. C. (1993). Intelligence and brain structure in normal individuals. *American Journal of Psychiatry, 150,* 130–134.

Bigler, E. D. (1995). Brain morphology and intelligence. *Developmental Neuropsychology, 11,* 377–403.

Flashman, L. A., Andreasen, N. C., Flaum, M., & Swayze II, V. W. (1997). Intelligence and regional brain volumes in normal controls. *Intelligence, 25,* 149–160.

Gur, R. C., Turetsky, B. I., Matsui, M., Yan, M., Bilker, W., Hughett, P., & Gur, R. E. (1999). Sex differences in brain gray and white matter in healthy young adults: correlations with cognitive performance. *Journal of Neuroscience, 19,* 4065–4072.

Harvey, I., Persaud, R., Ron, M. A., Baker, G., & Murray, R. M. (1994). Volumetric MRI measurements in bipolars compared with schizophrenics and healthy controls. *Psychological Medicine, 24,* 689–699.

Jensen, A. R. (1994). Psychometric *g* related to differences in head size. *Personality and Individual Differences, 17*, 597–606.

Jensen, A. R., & Sinha, S. N. (1993). Physical correlates of human intelligence. In: P. A. Vernon (Ed.), *Biological approaches to the study of human intelligence* (pp. 139–242). Norwood: Ablex.

Jung, R. E., Brooks, W. M., Yeo, R. A., Chiulli, S. J., Weers, D. C., & Sibbitt, W. L. Jr (1999a). Biochemical markers of intelligence: a proton MR spectroscopy study of normal human brain. *Proceedings of the Royal Society of London, B series, 266*, 1375–1379.

Jung, R. E., Yea, R. A., Chiulli, S. J., Sibbitt, W. L. Jr, Weers, D. C., Hart, B. L., & Brooks, W. M. (1999b). Biochemical markers of cognition: a proton MR spectroscopy study of normal human brain. *NeuroReport, 10*, 1–5.

Kuzniecky, R., Hetherington, H., Ho, S., Pan, J., Martin, R., Gilliam, F., Hugg, J., & Faught, E. (1998). Topirimate increases cerebral GABA in healthy humans. *Neurology, 51*, 627–629.

Martin, R., Kuzniecky, R., Ho, S., Hetherington, J., Pan, J., Sinclair, K., Gilliam, F., & Faught, E. (1999). Cognitive effects of topiramate, gabapentin, and lamotrigine in healthy young adults. *Neurology, 52*, 321–327.

Miller, E. M. (1994). Intelligence and brain myelination: a hypothesis. *Personality and Individual Differences, 17*, 803–832.

Passingham, R. E. (1979). Brain size and intelligence in man. *Brain, Behavior, and Evolution, 16*, 253–270.

Pennington, B. F., Filipek, P. A., Lefly, D., Chabildas, N., Kennedy, D. N., Simon, J. F., Filley, C. M., Galaburda, A., & DeFries, J. C. (2000). A twin MRI study of size variations in the human brain. *Journal of Cognitive Neuroscience, 12*, 223–232.

Rae, C., Scott, R. B., Thompson, C. H., Kemp, G. J., Dumughn, I., Styles, P., Tracey, I., & Radda, G. K. (1996). Is pH a biochemical marker of IQ? *Proceedings of the Royal Society of London, B series, 263*, 1061–1064.

Raz, N., Torres, I. J., Spencer, W. D., Millman, D., Baertschi, J. C., & Sarpel, G. (1993). Neuroanatomical correlates of age-sensitive and age invariant cognitive abilities: an *in vivo* MRI investigation. *Intelligence, 17*, 407–422.

Reiss, A. L., Abrams, M. T., Singer, H. S., Ross, J. L., & Denckla, M. B. (1996). Brain development, gender and IQ in children. A volumetric imaging study. *Brain, 119*, 1763–1774.

Rowe, L. A., Kranzler, J., & Leonard, C. M. (1997). Corpus callosum morphology and cognitive functioning in normal children. *Society of Neuroscience Abstracts, 23*, 212.

Schofield, P. W., Mosesson, R. E., Stern, Y., & Mayeux, R. (1995). The age at onset of Alzheimer's disease and an intracranial measurement. A relationship. *Archives of Neurology, 52*, 95–98.

Spitzka, E. A. (1907). A study of the brains of six eminent scientists and scholars belonging to the American Anthropometric Society, together with a description of the skull of Professor E. D. Cope. *Transactions of the American Philosophical Society, 21*, 175–308.

Strauss, E., Wada, J., & Hunter, M. (1994). Callosal morphology and performance on intelligence tests. *Journal of Clinical and Experimental Neuropsychology, 16*, 79–83.

Tramo, M. J., & Gazzaniga, M. S. (1999). Brain size, head size, and intelligence quotient in monozygotic twins (reply to Letter to the Editor). *Neurology, 53*, 243–244.

Tramo, M. J., Loftus, W. C., Stukel, T. A., Green, R. L., Weaver, J. B., & Gazzaniga, M. S. (1998). Brain size, head size, and intelligence quotient in monozygotic twins. *Neurology, 50*, 1246–1252.

Wickett, J. C., Vernon, P. A., & Lee, D. H. (1994). *In vivo* brain size, head perimeter, and intelligence in a sample of healthy adult females. *Personality and Individual Differences, 16*, 831–838.

Wickett, J. C., Vernon, P. A., & Lee, D. H. (in press). Relationships between factors of intelligence and brain volume. *Personality and Individual Differences*.

Willerman, L., Schultz, R., Rutledge, J. N., & Bigler, E. D. (1991). *In vivo* brain size and intelligence. *Intelligence*, *15*, 223–228.

Willerman, L., Schultz, R., Rutledge, J. N., & Bigler, E. D. (1992). Hemisphere size asymmetry predicts relative verbal and nonverbal intelligence differently in the sexes: an MRI study of structure-function relations. *Intelligence*, *16*, 315–328.

Yeo, R. A., Turkheimer, E., Raz, N., & Bigler, E. D. (1987). Volumetric asymmetries of the human brain: intellectual correlates. *Intelligence*, *6*, 15–23.

Chapter 3

Positron Emission Tomography Studies of Intelligence: From Psychometrics to Neurobiology*

Richard J. Haier

1. Genes or Environment?

Well into the 1960s, a furious debate considered whether schizophrenia had a genetic component or not. Evidence from twin studies was strongly suggestive but always confounded with shared environment. Then researchers funded by the American NIMH (National Institute of Mental Health) reported the first data from the Denmark Adoption studies (Kety *et al.* 1971). They found that adopted-away offspring of biological parents with schizophrenia were more likely to have a diagnosis of schizophrenia spectrum disorders in adulthood than adopted-away controls of normal biological parents. A researcher opposing the genetic hypothesis literally had a heart attack at the scientific meeting when this was presented. Although far from perfect, the Denmark studies helped shift the debate decisively to those favoring a genetic component with the important insight that if there were a genetic component to schizophrenia, there must be a biological basis to the disease because genes act through biology. One impact of this reasoning was a fundamental shift in research orientation. More federal funds were directed at neurobiological studies of schizophrenia than ever before. In fact, at the NIMH, the premiere center for mental illnesses research in the United States, the Intramural Research Program's Adult Psychiatry Branch was renamed the "Biological Psychiatry Branch". Now, more than 30 years later, the nature of the genetic component to schizophrenia and the neurobiological pathways involved remain a mystery despite an enormous worldwide research effort. Most researchers in the field, nonetheless, value this approach as the most likely to some day solve the puzzle of schizophrenia as measured ultimately by profound advances in treatment, cure and prevention.

* Parts of this paper were presented at the APA-sponsored conference on Models of Intelligence for the Next Millennium, Yale University, June, 2000.

The debate over the role of genetics in intelligence has a longer history and even more data than the early debate over the genetic role in schizophrenia. The Public debate about the role of genes in explaining individual differences in intellectual abilities and general intelligence continues, at times with considerable fury. Most researchers now interpret the findings of studies of identical twins reared apart and much other data as showing that there is a genetic component involved in general intelligence, although some fury is not unknown among researchers on this point. The importance of establishing that there is a genetic component, usually estimated at about 50% of the variance, is that there is a neurobiological basis of intelligence to be discovered. Unlike schizophrenia research, however, no major redirection of research funds toward this end has happened. In fact, among many researchers and policy-makers, the topic is an unwelcome one. Arthur Jensen, partially and unintentionally, may be to blame.

2. The Problem with Intelligence

In the late 1960s Arthur Jensen reviewed attempts to raise IQ with early environmental interventions like the federally funded Head Start pre-school program (Jensen 1969). In so doing, he detailed the psychometric difference between blacks and whites on measures of IQ (about one standard deviation). He argued that the failure of compensatory education programs to close this gap suggested the gap might have a genetic (and therefore biological) basis. Public and scientific reaction was swift, brutal, and incessant. The turmoil continues to this day (recently reinvigorated by publication of Herrnstein and Murray's, *The Bell Curve*, 1994) and one major result is that funding to explore the neurobiological basis of intelligence has not been forthcoming. Even the 1990s "Decade of the Brain", based on rapid scientific advances in the neurosciences and driven largely by the illnesses of schizophrenia, depression, and Alzheimer's Disease, never included any focus on intelligence. Although it could be argued that intelligence and IQ are controversial, hard to measure concepts and therefore unworthy of major research funding, the same could be said of schizophrenia. In fact, in the 1960s some argued that schizophrenia was not an illness at all but a convenient social myth to label unorthodox behavior. Seymour Kety, one of the NIMH authors of the Denmark Adoption studies, remarked that if schizophrenia was a myth, it was a myth with a genetic component. The same might be said for intelligence. Twin and adoption data support a genetic component to intelligence and the search for a neurobiological basis to intelligence is certainly warranted. Such a search may have profound relevance for treating or preventing disorders of low IQ like some forms of mental retardation, and for developing cognitive enhancing drugs to treat Alzheimer's Disease and other dementias. Whether drugs can be developed to treat mental retardation or to raise IQ in general, is an open question.

3. *g* and Glucose Metabolic Rate

Not surprisingly, Arthur Jensen has advocated research directed at discovering the neurobiological basis of intelligence, especially "*g*", the general factor first proposed by

Spearman and later defined by psychometric studies of intelligence tests. We first met in June of 1987 at the Toronto meeting of the Society for the Study of Individual Differences (ISSID). It was the first presentation of the results of a study using Positron Emission Tomography (PET) aimed (naively) at the question, "where in the brain is intelligence?" The study intended to identify areas of the brain activated while subjects performed the Raven's Advanced Progressive Matrices (RAPM), a test of non-verbal, abstract reasoning highly loaded on *g*. PET was a new and powerful technique to image regional brain functioning. The entire brain, including deep subcortical areas, could be imaged based on the uptake of glucose labeled with a radioactive tracer (i.e. flurodeoxyglucose or FDG). The harder a brain region works while performing a mental task like the RAPM, the more glucose is used in that area since neuronal firing is dependent on energy derived from glucose in the blood. Both glucose metabolic rate and blood flow increase in the brain as the brain works harder. The pattern of increases and decreases is shown by color coding so PET images look different in even the same person depending on the mental task used during the uptake period. For glucose PET studies, this period is about 32 minutes, so this kind of scanning has a time resolution of 32 minutes, meaning that the images show the accumulated brain activity over this period. By contrast, the newer technique of functional Magnetic Resonance Imaging (fMRI) has a time resolution of about 2 seconds (see Haier 1998 for a review of brain imaging techniques). However, in 1987, PET was the most important new tool available to psychologists (although there were few available and it cost at least $2500 per subject; fMRI now is available widely for about $400 per subject).

The PET/RAPM data presented at the 1987 ISSID meeting (and again in February 1988 at the AAAS meeting in Boston) were somewhat provocative (Haier *et al.* 1988). We had expected to see glucose increases denoting activation of more neurons in the areas of the brain used to solve the RAPM problems during the 32 minute uptake period when compared to controls performing a simple attention test with no *g* loading. Some brain areas were uniquely activated during the RAPM condition. Were these the "IQ" areas of the brain? Because the 8 subjects were recruited from a list of normal volunteers unselected for IQ, the range of RAPM scores attained during the uptake was 11 to 33 out of a total possible score of 36. We correlated these scores with glucose metabolic rate (GMR) in each region of the cortex. By today's standards, the anatomical localization of cortical areas was rudimentary. Nonetheless, the results were striking. There were statistically significant correlations between several cortical areas bilaterally and RAPM scores but all the correlations were negative.

The higher the RAPM score, the *lower the GMR*. Thus, it would appear that the harder the brain was working, the less well a subject solved the non-verbal, *g*-loaded problems of the RAPM. We interpreted this as evidence for a brain efficiency model of intelligence.

It was one of those findings that no one anticipated but that make sense *post-hoc*. Some subjects mentally struggled, scored poorly but their brains seemed working very hard whereas other subjects solved the problems accurately and apparently without greater brain activity. A host of questions are implied — are poor performers more anxious and does anxiety increase cerebral GMR? Is the test just easier for some who expend less effort and therefore have lower cerebral GMR? Is the cerebral GMR at rest (i.e. when no mental performance is required) lower in high *g* people? The inverse correlations reported in this study were one of the first and most powerful demonstrations of how individual differences in performance of a mental task was key to interpreting functional imaging data. When these data were presented at the Toronto ISSID meeting, Arthur Jensen was particularly intrigued with the possibilities for new research on *g* opened by the PET technology.

4. Brain Efficiency Concepts

Brain efficiency concepts have a long history in intelligence research. Early EEG studies, for example, suggested that evoked potential waveforms generated by bright people had shorter latencies (faster mind?) and smaller amplitudes (fewer neurons firing?). Even some psychometric research pointed to an efficiency explanation for why loadings on a general factor in good readers were smaller than for poor readers (Maxwell *et al.* 1974; see also Detterman & Daniel 1989). Based on an earlier model by Thompson (1939), the theory was that a general cognitive factor would reflect a large number of neurons sampled from many brain areas, whereas, factors of more specific abilities would reflect smaller subgroups of neurons. Assuming factor loadings estimate the proportions of neurons involved in general and specific factors, the lower loadings on the general factor in good readers was interpreted as showing fewer neurons involved, consistent with a concept of brain efficiency (see Haier 1993 for a review of these efficiency ideas). Other subsequent PET studies also reported inverse correlations between regional GMR and performance on *g*-related tasks (Parks *et al.* 1988; Boivin *et al.* 1992).

We decided our next PET study would test the concept of brain efficiency further. We wondered whether the brain would show less activity after learning, consistent with the idea that learning causes the brain to become more efficient. We studied 8 new normal male volunteers with FDG PET while they performed the computer game Tetris, a visual spatial task. None of the subjects had ever played this game before. Each received instruction, a brief practice session, and then were injected with FDG while they played for the 32 minute uptake period. Each subject then practiced 4–8 weeks and, on average, improved performance 7-fold. A second post-practice PET session was completed. GMR decreases in several brain areas were related to improvement in Tetris performance, consistent with a brain efficiency concept.

We concluded that with practice and improved performance, subjects learn what areas of the brain not to use and this results in GMR decreases (Haier *et al.* 1992a).

5. The Conservation of *g*

Remarkably, in the same subjects, we found inverse correlations between degree of GMR decreases after practice and scores on the RAPM, suggesting that the brightest subjects become the most brain efficient with learning (Haier *et al.* 1992b). Scores on

WAIS-R subtests in these subjects were also correlated with whole brain GMR. Arthur Jensen analyzed these data using the correlated vector approach (Jensen 1998: 157–158). He reported the vector of WAIS subtest/GMR correlations was correlated –0.79 with the corresponding vector of the subtests' *g*-loadings. Thus, the largest GMR decreases with practice were found on subtests with the highest *g* loadings. Jensen noted this finding was consistent with what he termed the conservation of *g*. Namely, with practice and training, tasks become more automatized and require less *g*. Subsequent PET studies of learning also show functional brain decreases along with increases in some circumstances but virtually all of these subsequent studies are designed to study brief learning over a period of minutes rather than training over weeks (see Haier 2001 for a review).

6. More Sophisticated Designs

We undertook two additional PET studies of intelligence, each with a more sophisticated research design to explore brain efficiency further. The first, funded by the Office of Naval Research, addressed the role of mental effort. We screened a large number of normal volunteer males on the RAPM and selected 14 with average scores and 14 with high scores (Larson *et al.* 1996). Each subject then completed two PET sessions performing a digit-span backward task. During one session, the digit span task was easy because the length of the digit string to remember was kept short for a 90% accuracy rate; during the other session (random, counterbalanced order), the string was longer with a 75% accuracy rate. The starting number of digits to attain these rates was predetermined for each subject. Thus, we selected high and average ability subjects based on a *g*-loaded test and each was then scanned while performing an easy (low effort) and a hard (high effort) version of the same task. The comparison of GMR among the groups and conditions showed a significant interaction between ability and effort. The high ability subjects had higher GMR during the hard task than the average ability subjects. Both groups had similar GMR consumption during the easy task. In discussing this study, Arthur Jensen wrote, "This increase in GMR by the high-IQ subjects suggests that more neural units are involved in their level of performance on a difficult task that is beyond the ability of the average-IQ subjects" (Jensen 1998: 159). Certainly, more experimental data are needed, but this is a good demonstration of the importance of using a research design that incorporates subject ability and task effort during a functional imaging study. Without these design elements, interpretations of brain activity and its relation to *g* will be difficult to interpret (see for example Ducan *et al.* 2000).

About the same time, we completed another PET study aimed at investigating brain efficiency in volunteers selected for high or average mathematical reasoning ability (Haier & Benbow 1995). This study's design also included a comparison between men and women. Subjects were recruited from a university population based on admission SAT-Math scores. High ability groups were defined by SAT-M scores between 700 and 800 ($n = 11$ men and 11 women). SAT-M scores in the 410–540 range defined average ability groups ($n = 11$ men and 11 women). All subjects ($N = 44$) completed one PET session during which they solved a set of SAT mathematical reasoning problems. High ability subjects were hypothesized to show lower GMR. All four groups showed similar GMR patterns.

There were no significant main effects or interactions (ANOVA, group X sex X hemisphere X lobe X segment). In the total sample of men ($N = 22$), there were significant correlations between SAT-M score attained during the FDG uptake period and GMR in the temporal lobes (bilaterally). In the women ($N = 22$), this comparison showed a near zero correlation. Furthermore, in the women none of the correlations between SAT-M score and regional GMR were significant. It would appear that high math ability men use more neurons in the temporal lobes to solve math-reasoning problems but women solve the problems (just as well) in some other way. Additional experiments cry out for completion.

7. Brain Inefficiency in Mental Retardation

The final project completed in this series of PET studies of intelligence was a one-year pilot funded by the National Institute of Child Health and Development (NICHD) to study mental retardation. We hypothesized the counter-intuitive idea that people with mild mental retardation of unknown etiology might have higher than normal GMR. Based in part on the findings of high RAPM score correlated with lower GMR, we had speculated (Haier 1993) that the neural pruning that takes place developmentally during childhood and adolescence may fail for some reason and this could result in more neurons and less efficient neuro-circuitry. People with this abnormality may be poor problem solvers, score low on IQ tests, and have higher than normal cerebral GMR during a cognitive task. We tested this in a group of 10 people with mild mental retardation (MR) defined by WAIS-R scores between 52 and 78; seven other people with Down Syndrome (DS) were age, sex, and IQ matched to the MR group as were 10 normal controls (Haier *et al.* 1995). Each subject completed an FDG PET session while performing a version of the Continuous Performance Test (CPT) of attention. Structural MRIs were also obtained. Both the MR and the DS groups showed higher whole brain GMR than the normals, with the largest difference in the posterior temporal lobe (bilaterally).

Both the MR and the DS groups showed 20% smaller brain sizes compared to normals based on MRI measurements, whereas, overall, these groups showed about a 30% increase in GMR compared to normals. Combining all subjects into one group, the correlation between brain size and IQ was 0.65 ($p < 0.005$ one tailed) which became 0.36 after correction for extreme groups. IQ and GMR were correlated -0.58 ($p < 0.005$ one tailed) and the correlation between brain size and GMR was -0.69 ($p < 0.005$ one tailed). Moreover, in the normals there was a pattern of correlations among GMR in several brain areas that differed from the pattern in DS, suggesting specific functional neuro-circuitry abnormalities in the frontal lobe (Haier *et al.* 1998). These intriguing results were discussed as consistent with brain inefficiency in mental retardation. Nonetheless, a renewal grant application for replication and extension in larger samples with other cognitive tasks was approved but not funded (after numerous "very responsive" revisions), bringing a temporary end to this series of functional imaging projects aimed at helping to understand the neurobiology of intelligence.

8. New Directions

The inclusion of the DS comparison group, however, led us in a new direction. We are funded currently by NICHD for a five-year longitudinal study using PET and MRI to chart the progression and sequence of brain changes as dementia develops in middle-aged people with DS and in comparison groups of people with early Alzheimer's Disease and in normal controls. Since part of the data collection includes the WAIS-R, we may generate data of interest concerning intelligence as well as dementia.

In the meantime, we have published another series of PET studies using a focus of individual differences in combination with drug probes. These studies investigate alcohol's effect on divided attention (Haier *et al.* 1999), and the mechanism of anesthetic drugs and their relation to the neurobiology of consciousness (Alkire *et al.* 1995, 1996, 1997, 1999, 2000; Alkire & Haier 2001). Individual differences also were critical to the understanding of PET results in studies of emotional memory (Alkire *et al.* 1998; Cahill *et al.* 1996, 2001). These studies did not include a focus on intelligence but pilot data suggest that the IQ of the subjects in these studies may interact with main effects of drug or cognitive condition. We are now pursuing this possibility. For example, we are designing functional imaging studies to address questions such as, are intelligent people more conscious than others and does the neuro-circuitry of consciousness, as revealed by studies of anesthetic drugs, overlap with the neuro-circuitry of intelligence? We can address these questions with new image analysis software, PET hardware, MRI co-registration (for anatomical localization), and fMRI techniques that were not available for our first series of studies. These new studies can be more hypothesis driven than the earlier studies. For example, we have reviewed rat lesion studies to compare brain areas implicated in specific and in general task ability to results of human PET studies (Haier *et al.* 1993). We have also reviewed brain studies of autism, Down syndrome, and mental retardation to generate a short list of six brain factors with abnormalities in all these conditions where intelligence is often abnormal (Lawrence *et al.*, in press). Such comparisons suggest more focus for better hypothesis testing in new studies.

9. Individual Differences

Individual differences as a mainstream discipline within psychology may be about to reassert itself after near banishment in the wake of the controversies of the last 30 years. This has already happened in cognitive psychology where new fMRI studies abound. Correlating cognitive task performance with functional brain data has yielded some spectacular results (e.g. Haier *et al.* 1988, 1992a, b; Cahill *et al.* 1996; Nyberg *et al.* 1996). Such correlations are fast becoming the norm in a branch of psychology where effects of individual differences were typically regarded as noise and error variance. Even more dramatic is the growing attention to the profound individual differences in drug response. Psychopharmacology may well be the most amenable field for a new appreciation of individual differences. Virtually every psychoactive drug produces a wide range of clinical response. Some people respond to a drug in one way and others respond differently or not at all. Understanding the neuro-biology of these differences is a major problem for neuroscience in the 21st century. Moreover, whereas the causes of schizophrenia and Alzheimer's Disease (AD) were among the major clinical problems driving neuroscience in the last few decades, the next wave may well derive from the problems of understanding diseases of low intelligence. The first advances may come from research based on learning and memory studies linked to Alzheimer's Disease. Pharmaceutical companies are close to having drugs to treat AD which work to improve learning and memory by boosting neurotransmitter effectiveness or even by stimulating new neuron growth. What will be the effect of such cognitive-enhancing drugs on normal children or adults? If the drugs increase learning and memory, will IQ be raised? Will treatments for some forms of mental retardation follow? Why will some people respond to these drugs more than other people?

10. Neurophysiology and Individual Differences in *g*

At the start of the 1990s Decade of the Brain, we noted (Haier 1990) that 50 core questions were enumerated by neuroscience advocates. The word "intelligence" never appeared but four of the fifty questions were relevant:

(1) What are the neural substrates of higher cognitive properties of the human cerebral cortex?
(2) What essential properties of the brain give rise to conscious awareness?
(3) Why is thinking so easy for normal people and so aberrant in schizophrenics?
(4) Given the degree of homology between the human brain and those of other species, what makes us unique?

It may be time to revisit these questions and recast them in terms familiar to intelligence researchers. Arthur Jensen is leading the way. His most recent book (Jensen 1998) summarizes all data and arguments concerning the *g* factor and ends with a discussion of future research on the neurophysiological basis of *g*. He proposes the following working hypothesis: "Individual differences in behavioral capacities do not result from intraspecies differences in the brain's structural operating mechanisms per se, but result entirely from other aspects of cerebral physiology that modify the sensitivity, efficiency, and effectiveness of the basic information processes that mediate the individual's response to certain aspects of the environment" (p. 579). He further notes that there are two basic questions here — the first dealing with brain processes that allow intelligent behavior and the second dealing with what produces individual differences. "The highest priority in *g* research, therefore, is to discover how certain anatomical structures and physiological processes of the brain cause individual differences in *g*" (p. 579).

Imagine that a Foundation announced a competition for a single $25,000,000 award to one intelligence researcher. The application was one question: "After spending our money, what important problem about intelligence will you have solved?" Arthur's general hypothesis is a good starting place. I would focus on experiments using functional brain imaging in combination with drug probes to identify neuro-circuitry used in high level problem solving. I also have a keen interest in whether mitochondria, the energy producing parts of cells, differ in number or efficiency within the neurons of bright and average people. The fact that we can now consider such questions demonstrates the transition of intelligence research from its psychometric origins (and confines) to the next level of neuroscience exploration and explanation.

11. The Nature-Nurture Question Revisited

Moreover, this transition is forcing another dramatic and ironic shift in perspective. In the later 20th Century, a prevalent assumption underlying the (artificial) nature versus nurture debate was that something caused mostly by environment could be changed relatively easily, whereas, something caused mostly by genes was essentially immutable. As we enter the 21st Century, just the opposite may be true. We are becoming quite expert at changing biology and genes; we still don't improve environments with much precision of positive outcome. To the extent that low intelligence is genetic/biological, the prospects are increasing that neuroscience-based manipulations over the next decades may promise improvement where environmental-based manipulations have so far proved mostly unsuccessful.

12. The Bright Future of the Neurobiology of Intelligence and Individual Differences

Over the last 13 years we have produced a body of work using PET to begin to explore the neurobiological basis of intelligence. The data are intriguing and a number of specific questions are now raised that can be addressed experimentally. We are focusing on the neuro-circuitry of consciousness and intelligence and whether any overlap may help understand why some people learn certain subjects better than other people do. PET access has been so limited that little replication or extension of earlier work has been possible, especially with the large samples normally required to address questions of individual differences. The wide availability of fMRI may result in a surge of studies addressing neurobiological questions about *g*, brain efficiency, mental effort, sex differences and individual differences. The near future for psychology is going to be quite exciting as this frontier expands. Additional funding for this worldwide effort is inevitable. Arthur Jensen's vibrant intellectual influence continues to encourage researchers in this field as knowledge about the neurobiology of intelligence and individual differences begins to unfold.

References

Alkire, M. T., & Haier, R. J. (2001). The *in vivo* regional cerebral metabolic effects of the anesthetic propofol and not isoflurane correlate with human benzodiazepine receptor density. *British Journal of Anesthesia, 86* (5), 618–626.

Alkire, M. T., Haier, R. J., Barker, S., Shah, K., & Kao, J. (1995). Cerebral metabolism during propofol anesthesia in human volunteers studied with positron emission tomography. *Anesthesiology, 82,* 393–403.

Alkire, M. T., Haier, R. J., & Fallon, J. H. (2000). Toward a unified theory of narcosis: brain imaging evidence for a thalamocortical switch as the neurophysiologic basis of anesthetic-induced unconsciousness. *Consciousness and Cognition, 9* (3), 370–386.

Alkire, M. T., Haier, R. J., Fallon, J., & Barker, S. J. (1996). PET imaging of conscious and unconscious memory. *Journal of Consciousness Studies, 3* (5–6), 448–462.

Alkire, M. T., Haier, R. J., Fallon, J. H., & Cahill, L. (1998). Hippocampal, but not amygdala, activity at encoding correlates with long-term, free recall of non-emotional information. *Proceedings of the National Academy of Sciences, 95,* 14506–14510.

Alkire, M. T., Haier, R. J., Shah, N. K., & Anderson, C. T. (1997). A positron emission tomography study of regional cerebral metabolism in humans during Isoflurane anesthesia. *Anesthesiology, 86* (3), 549–557.

Alkire, M. T., Pomfrett, C., Haier, R. J., Gianzero, M. V., Chan, C., Jacobsen, B., & Fallon, J. H. (1999). Functional brain imaging during anesthesia in humans: effects of halothane on global and regional cerebral glucose metabolism. *Anesthesiology, 90* (3), 701–709.

Boivin, M. J., Giordani, B., Berent, S., Amato, D. A., Koeppe, R. A., Buchtel, H. A., Foster, N. L., & Kuhl, D. E. (1992). Verbal fluency and positron emission tomographic mapping of regional cerebral glucose metabolism. *Cortex, 28,* 231–239.

Cahill, L., Haier, R. J., Fallon, J., Alkire, M., Tang, C., Keator, D., Wu, J., & McGaugh, J. (1996). Amygdala activity at encoding correlated with long-term, free recall of emotional information. *Proceedings of the National Academy of Sciences, 93,* 8016–8321.

Cahill, L., Haier R. J., White, N. S., Fallon, J., Kilpatrick, L., Lawrence, C., Potkin, S., & Alkire, M. T. (2001). Sex-related difference in amygdala activity during emotionally influenced memory storage. *Neurobiology of Learning & Memory, 75* (1), 1–9.

Detterman, D. K., & Daniel, M. H. (1989). Correlations of mental tests with each other and with cognitive variables are highest for low IQ groups. *Intelligence, 13,* 349–359.

Ducan, J., Seitz, R. J., Kolodny, J., Bor, D., Herzog, H., Ahmed, A., Newell, F. N., & Emslie, H. (2000). A Neural Basis for General Intelligence. *Science, 289,* 457–460.

Haier, R. J. (1990). The end of intelligence research. *Intelligence, 14,* 371–374.

Haier, R. J. (1993). Cerebral glucose metabolism and intelligence. In: P. A. Vernon (Ed.), *Biological approaches to the study of human intelligence.* New Jersey: Ablex Publishing.

Haier, R. J. (1998). Brain scanning and neuroimaging. In: H. S. Friedman (Ed.), *Encyclopedia of mental health.* New York: Academic Press.

Haier, R. J. (2001). PET studies of learning and individual differences. In: J. L. McClelland, & R. S. Siegler (Eds), *Mechanisms of cognitive development: behavioral and neural perspectives. Carnegie Mellon symposium on cognition* (pp. 123–145). Mahwah, NJ.: Lawrence Erlbaum Associates.

Haier, R. J., & Benbow, C. (1995). Gender differences and lateralization in temporal lobe glucose metabolism during mathematical reasoning. *Developmental Neuropsychology, 11,* 405–414.

Haier, R. J., Chueh, D., Touchette, P., Lott, I., MacMillan, D., Sandman, C., Lacasse, L., & Sosa, E. (1995). Brain size and glucose metabolic rate in mental retardation and Down Syndrome. *Intelligence, 20,* 191–210.

Haier, R. J., Hazen, K., Fallon, J., Alkire, M. T., Schell, M., & Lott, I. (1998). Brain imaging and classification of mental retardation. In: S. Soraci, & W. McIlvane (Eds), *Perspectives on Fundamental Processes in Intellectual Functioning*. New Jersey: Ablex Press.

Haier, R. J., Schandler, S. L., MacLachlan, A., Soderling, E., Buchsbaum, M. S., & Cohen, M. (1999). Alcohol induced changes in regional cerebral glucose metabolic rate during divided attention. *Personality & Individual Differences, 26,* 425–439.

Haier, R. J., Seigel, B., Crinnella, F., & Buchsbaum, M. S. (1993). Biological and psychometric intelligence: Testing an animal model in humans. In: D. Detterman (Ed.), *New trends in intelligence research*. New Jersey: Ablex Publishing.

Haier, R. J., Siegel, B. V., MacLachlan, A., Soderling, E., Lottenberg, S., & Buchsbaum, M. S. (1992a). Regional glucose metabolic changes after learning a complex visuospatial/motor task: A PET study. *Brain Research, 570,* 134–143.

Haier, R. J., Siegel, B. V., Tang, C., Abel, L., & Buchsbaum, M. S. (1992b). Intelligence and changes in regional cerebral glucose metabolic rate following learning. *Intelligence, 16,* 415–426.

Haier, R. J., Siegel, B. V., Nuechterlein, K. H., Hazlett, E., Wu, J., Paek, J., Browning, H., & Buchsbaum, M. S. (1988). Cortical glucose metabolic rate correlates of abstract reasoning and attention studied with positron emission tomography. *Intelligence, 12,* 199–217.

Herrnstein, R. J., & Murray, C. (1994). *The bell curve: intelligence and class structure in American life*. New York: Free Press.

Jensen, A. R. (1969). How much can we boost IQ and scholastic achievement? *Harvard Educational Review, 39* (1), 1–123.

Jensen, A. R. (1998). *The "g" factor: The science of mental ability*. Westport, CT: Praeger.

Kety, S., Rosenthal, D., Wender, P. H., & Schulsinger, F. (1971). Mental illness in the biological and adoptive families of adopted schizophrenics. *American Journal of Psychiatry, 128* (3), 302–306.

Larson, G., Haier, R. J., Lacasse, L., & Hazen, K. (1996). Evaluation of a "Mental Effort" hypothesis for correlations between cortical metabolism and intelligence. *Intelligence, 21,* 267–278.

Lawrence, C., Lott, I., & Haier, R. J. (in press). Brain studies of autism, mental retardation and down syndrome: What can we learn about intelligence? In: C. Stough (Ed.), *Neurobiology of exceptionality*. New York: Plenum Press.

Maxwell, A. E., Fenwisk, P. B., Fenton, G. W., & Doillimore, J. (1974). Reading ability and brain function: A simple statistical model. *Psychological Medicine, 4,* 274–280.

Nyberg, L., McIntosh, A. R., Houle, S., Nilsson, L. G., & Tulving, E. (1996). Activation of medial temporal structures during episodic memory retrieval. *Nature, 380* (6576), 715–717.

Parks, R. W., Loewenstein, D. A., Dodril, K. L., Barker, W. W., Toshii, F., Chang, J. Y., Emran, A., Apicella, A., Sheramata, W., & Duara, R. (1988). Cerebral metabolic effects of a verbal fluency test: A PET scan study. *Journal of Clinical & Experimental Neuropsychology, 10,* 565–575.

Thomson, G. H. (1939). *The factorial analysis of human ability*. London: University of London Press.

Chapter 4

Reaction Time and Psychometric Intelligence: Jensen's Contributions

Ian J. Deary

1. Introduction

When a scientist has made a significant contribution to a field of research there occurs the problem of writing a chapter such as the present one. It is not just that Jensen has written so extensively on reaction time, it is that he has in addition written so much of the field's literature himself. The article that began the modern era of reaction time and intelligence studies was written by Jensen (Jensen & Munro 1979), the historical precedents, first gatherings of new data and theory came next (Jensen 1982), after that there were detailed and thoughtful contributions on methodology and statistical issues to do with reaction times and the study of intelligence (Jensen 1985), followed by the first sizeable meta-analysis and rebuttings of 'top-down' explainings-away of the correlation between reaction time and intelligence test scores (Jensen 1987a), comments on the possible reasons for the correlations (Jensen 1993), and more recently a review of the field in the context of information processing (Jensen 1998a). Add to this the influence on his one-time Ph.D. student P. A. Vernon (e.g. Vernon 1983, 1987) and one has covered a substantial percentage of the pioneering modern work on reaction times and intelligence. Without Jensen's contribution, then, one would be in a much less confident position in stating that reaction times correlate significantly with psychometric intelligence. And, with respect to evaluations of Jensen's work, there are recent non-quantitative reviews that summarise the field and do not require repeating here (Neubauer 1997; Mackintosh 1998, Chapter 7; Nettelbeck 1998; Deary 2000, Chapter 6).

   With so much relevant material easily available in this quite-small field, the present chapter should properly be an 'appreciation,' which is defined both as 'grateful recognition' or 'estimation or judgement.' Given that this same word comfortably holds these two meanings, the present contribution will attempt to do the same; highlighting Jensen's contributions, it shall document the main findings of the research, evaluate the

The Scientific Study of General Intelligence: Tribute to Arthur R. Jensen
Copyright © 2003 by Elsevier Science Ltd.
All rights of reproduction in any form reserved.
ISBN: 0-08-043793-1

progress in understanding of intelligence to which it has led, and pick out some newer developments in the area.

2. The First Study

Jensen's reviving of reaction time as a part of intelligence research began with a five-and-a-half page paper in *Intelligence* in 1979 (Jensen & Munro 1979). The rationale for the study is contained in two paragraphs which make the following points: (i) differential psychologists prematurely abandoned the use of reaction time measures at the turn of the 20th century; (ii) reaction time attracted new interest because of an information theory interpretation of the lawful association between the number of stimulus alternatives and overall reaction times (Hick 1952; Hyman 1953); and (iii) that individual differences in the slope function — when the log of the number of stimulus alternatives was plotted against the reaction time — were, according to Roth (1964), correlated significantly with psychometric intelligence, whereas simple reaction time was not. The one additional idea raised in the introduction was to separate movement time (MT) from reaction time (RT). However, because RT often refers to the time taken for the entire response, the latter measurement will be referred to hereinafter as decision time (DT) except in direct quotations from Jensen.

Jensen & Munro (1979) tested 39 14–15 years old schoolgirls on the 'Jensen box' version of the Hick device (Jensen 1987a: 108). This console has a home button and a semicircular array of target buttons. In this original study the stimulus lights were situated half an inch above the target pushbuttons. In later versions the stimulus lights and the pushbuttons were one and the same (Jensen 1998a: 212). By covering up different numbers of potential targets on the console, the size of the stimulus set was varied to include 1, 2, 4, 6, and 8 potential targets. The order of events was as follows. The subject placed their index finger on the home button. A warning tone sounded. After a variable delay of between 1 and 4 seconds one of the target lights was lit. The subject's task was to press the switch below the corresponding target light as fast as possible. The device had two timers. The first began at the onset of the target light, and ended when the person lifted their finger from the home button. This measures decision time (DT; what Jensen consistently called reaction time, RT). The second timer began with the person lifting their finger from the home button and ended when the target stimulus light was switched off. This measured the movement time (MT). Thirty trials were given at each of the five stimulus set sizes. It is not stated in the article but, from what was stated later, it appears that the order of stimulus sets was always from lesser to greater, i.e. from simple RT progressively up to the eight-choice condition. The psychometric test was Raven's Standard Progressive Matrices with a one hour time limit, which was long enough for all subjects to attempt all items.

Most subjects' data fitted Hick's law, with a mean Pearson correlation coefficient of 0.97 between decision time and 'bits' (log to the base 2 of the number of lights in the stimulus set). The corresponding correlation with movement time was 0.54. Split-half reliabilities for reaction and movement times were 0.90 and 0.89, respectively. Reaction

Table 4.1: Correlations between psychometric intelligence scores and indices from the Hick-type reaction time procedure (data from Jensen & Munro 1979).

	Jensen & Munro (1979)
	Uncorrected *r*
DT Mean	−0.39
DT Slope	−0.30
DT Intraindividual variability	−0.31
MT Mean	−0.43
MT Intraindividual variability	0.07

and movement times correlated only 0.37. Correlation within the five reaction times to the different set sizes was 0.85, and among the five movement times was 0.77.

The key results were those between reaction time indices and Raven's Matrices scores, as shown in Table 4.1. The overall mean of the decision times for the five stimulus set sizes and the overall standard deviation of the decision time showed modest correlations with Raven scores. Surprisingly, so did the overall mean of the movement times, though its standard deviation did not. People with higher psychometric intelligence had, on average, faster and less variable decision times and faster movement times. The slope of the increase in reaction time from zero to three bits of information correlated −0.30 with Raven scores (−0.36 after correcting for unreliability of the slope and the Raven scores); higher Raven scorers had flatter slopes. Jensen & Munro (1979) commented:

> Our expectation, from the study of Roth (1964) suggesting that the slope of RT with increasing information is the best measure of information processing capacity, and from consideration of the linear relationship of RT to *bits* of information found in other studies (Hick 1952; Hyman 1953), was that the slope of regression of RT on *bits* would have the highest correlation with Raven scores. Along the same lines, we expected RT to show higher correlations than MT with Raven scores. The fact that these specific expectations were not borne out seems somewhat puzzling; at present we can offer no explanation (p. 125).

> These correlations seem most interesting when one considers that the RT and MT measures are not based on past learning or on any intellectual content whatsoever (p. 126).

3. Developing the Field

From that small study to Jensen's (1982) overview and review only three years later there was enormous development. He considered that reaction time-intelligence research was important for two reasons. First, the correlation between the two was evidence that intelligence was not just related to knowledge and skills. Second, it offered a theoretical avenue for understanding differences in intelligence. This second aspect saw Jensen strongly commenting that factor analysis was unable to help our understanding intelligence differences and that more tractable measures like RT might be more help in this. Jensen then reviewed the chronology of RT research as it related to intelligence (see Table 4.2). He then described the RT apparatus that he used in the Jensen & Munro (1979) study and in so many other studies, and summarised the findings on, by then, about 900 subjects. Non-retarded groups and most individuals fitted Hick's law for DT. MT was much shorter than DT. MT showed very little increase or correlation with increases in stimulus uncertainty. For a number of reasons — including the zero correlation between DT and MT within individuals (paired over trials) and the modest correlation between decision and movement times between individuals — Jensen concluded that decision and movement times contained common and unique sources of variance and should be kept separate, as was done by his device. Jensen foregrounded intraindividual variability in DT, which he found to increase linearly with the number of stimulus alternatives. He also reported details of trial-to-trial and day-to-day variation, and the effects of age.

Jensen (1982) did not leap in with 'the' correlation between g and reaction time. He noted that people with higher psychometric test scores typically had faster and less variable reaction times, lower intercepts, and flatter slopes in cases where there were two or more levels of RT complexity. He pointed out that there were hardly any correlations in the wrong direction. And he pointed vaguely to an effect size of approximately 0.35. However, it was not possible accurately to come up with an effect size because of the day-to-day instability of RT parameters and the non-representative-ness of almost all extant samples, which were either highly restricted (often because they were students) or artificially wide (because they might be drawn from two different sub-samples such as people with mental retardation and healthy people). In any case, it is better to leave the matter of the effect size until a consideration of Jensen's (1987a) later review, which is more complete. In this article Jensen (1982) pointed out that, at that time, no-one had examined the correlations between the S. Sternberg and Posner RT procedures and intelligence test scores (for a review of these associations see Neubauer 1997). He also suggested the better prediction of intelligence test score variance that would come with combinations of RT procedures.

In the third important part of his article, Jensen (1982) turned to the development of a theory of RT differences as related to intelligence test scores. Refreshingly, Jensen's first contribution was to banish armchair formulations — 'the bright mind is the quick mind,' for example — and the lazy but easy assumption that brighter people have faster speed of work throughout the mental domain:

> If we invariably settle for an explanation of every new phenomenon in terms of a few simple and familiar psychological concepts, then the discovery and further investigation of new phenomena have no possibility of increasing our theoretical understanding of the nature of these phenomena, which virtually everyone agrees is inadequate. I also believe

Table 4.2: Landmarks in the history of the research on reaction time (RT) and psychometric intelligence (summarised from Jensen 1982).

Who?	When?	What?
Bessell	1823	Discovers the 'personal equation'. Individual differences in RT noted.
Von Helmholtz	1850	Measures of the speed of nerve conduction in frogs and humans.
Galton	1862	Suggests reaction times as a measure of mental ability differences.
Donders	1868	Choice RT is longer than simple RT. Devises the 'subtraction method'.
Exner	1873	Coins term 'reaction time' and studies effect of preparatory interval.
Merkel	1885	Discovers systematic increase in RT with increasing number of choice alternatives in stimulus and response arrangement.
Gilbert	1894	Finds relationship between RT and intelligence in groups of children.
Wissler	1901	Finds correlation of -0.02 between reaction times and course grades in male students at Columbia College.
Peak & Boring	1926	Find correlation of -0.9 between RT and intelligence test scores in 5 graduate students.
Lemmon	1927	Finds correlations between RT and intelligence test scores in 100 students: -0.25 for choice RT, and -0.08 for simple RT.
Hick	1952	Describes linear increase in RT as a function of the log to the base 2 of the number of stimulus alternatives; suggests that the slope indexes people's 'rate of gain of information'.
Roth	1964	Finds correlation of -0.39 between Hick slope and intelligence test scores.
Jensen & Munro	1979	Find correlations between various simple and choice RT indices and Raven's Matrices scores in 15-year-old girls.

that adequate theoretical formulations will have to involve concepts at a molecular, neurophysiological level, rather than at just the conceptual level of psychological factors or cognitive processes (p. 121).

But in advance of the biological information Jensen (1982) found a few serviceable ideas to work with. Speed of mental processing might be useful in the situation of a limited channel processor where memory traces were subject to rapid decay. He reviewed ideas about RT that he considered to be important for examining the reaction time-intelligence correlation.

- Individual differences in reaction times are common across a number of procedures in different modalities, suggesting shared central processes;
- Most reaction times were much longer than the 'irreducible minimum' of about 100–150 ms needed for peripheral and central processing, and the individual differences were probably more marked in these additions to the minimum;
- The facts that more intense RT stimuli resulted in faster and less variable reaction times led Jensen to suggest that the bases of RT differences might be the number of 'neural elements' activated by a stimulus and 'rate of oscillation of the excitatory-refractory phases of the activated elements.' He called this his hypothesis of individual differences in "hologramic neural redundancy";
- Among groups of people taking Hick RT tasks, the intercepts, slopes and RT variabilities were highly correlated;
- Choice-based reaction times were longer as the to-be-discriminated stimuli became more similar;
- Reaction times are related to the length of the preparatory interval;
- RT and its variability from childhood to the teens showed a typical growth curve, leading Jensen to speculate that, "*some constant proportion of a limited number of undeveloped or dormant neural elements gradually becomes functional during each year of the developmental period*".

Jensen then sketched a hypothetical model of oscillating neural nodes arranged in binary decision trees and produced evidence in accord and discord with such a model. That such a model made relatively little contact with neuroscience is not that important. The notable feature of this effort was that it nicely rounds off an astonishingly detailed book chapter, which has been cited over 100 times. The historical resume, the data and the theoretical development were all considerable, firmly founding the new study of reaction time and intelligence.

4. Addressing Methodology

Over the next few years the methodological and empirical aspects of RT and intelligence were developed in two more gargantuan book chapters. Jensen (1985) offered a methodological compendium that, at the time, was one of the most substantial and genuine attempts really to bring together cognitive-experimental psychology and individual differences. Jensen again went over the history of RT procedures but, as the material came up to date, showed great awareness of RT as an experimental tool (for divining the modal nature of cognitive processing) *and* a differential tool (for parameterising individual differences in cognitive processes). There's a passage in that chapter that this author quoted elsewhere (Deary 2000) and needs repeating here. It showed Jensen's modesty with respect to the achievements and potential for the psychometric approach to intelligence, and it demonstrated how genuine was his interest in combining with experimental psychology. Has a cognitive psychologist ever welcomed so humbly the differential psychology community?

> For some time there has been a growing consensus among differential psychologists that the traditional methodology of studying mental ability in terms of classical psychometrics, factor analysis, and external validation, over the last 75 years or so, has accumulated an impressive amount of solid empirical facts on the range, correlational structure, and practical consequences of IDs [individual differences] in ability, but has not contributed to the further development of theoretical explanations of the main abilities identified by factor analysis of psychometric tests. In the traditional framework, explanations of IDs have not advanced beyond statements that, to put it in the simplest form, individuals A and B differ in performance on task X, because X is highly saturated (or loaded) with ability factor Y, and A and B differ in ability factor Y. But ability Y is a hypothetical or mathematical construct that is not invariant to the method of factor analysis used to identify it. There is unfortunately nothing in the raw psychometric data that can compel the factor theorist to explain A's and B's difference in performance on task X in terms of their differing on factor Y. Factor rotation could displace the IDs variance on factor Y and divide it between two other factors P and Q, so that the difference between A and B would be attributed to their differing in factors P and Q. And factors P and Q would be different from factor Y, according to the usual method of psychologically describing factors in terms of the characteristics of those content-homogeneous tests that show the highest loadings on the factor. This, in essence, is the theoretical blind alley that differential psychologists find themselves in if they confine their methodology to traditional psychometric tests and factor analysis. The measurements and methods of psychometry reveal only the end products of mental activity, and, by themselves, cannot expose the processes between problem presentation and a subject's response (pp. 59–60).

For the researcher wishing to get into the field of RT procedures and wishing to be aware of the methodological and statistical pitfalls, Jensen's (1985) chapter is still worth reading. Its job was not to produce new data, but firmly to weld experimental and differential psychology. Jensen knew that the field was still young, but he had high hopes:

It is a seemingly remarkable and almost counterintuitive fact that chronometric variables derived from elementary cognitive tasks that include virtually no intellectual *content* that would be a source of IDs [individual differences] nevertheless show significant, even substantial, correlations with scores on complex psychometric tests of general intelligence and of scholastic achievement, the item contents of which comprise a great variety of acquired knowledge and skills ... Thus, IDs in mental test performance must also reflect IDs in fundamental cognitive and even neural processes that lie below the level of information content and scholastic skills *per se*. Galton's original intuition would seem to be vindicated. But much research remains to be done. The prospect of measuring IDs in human intelligence in terms of IDs in such basic and content-irrelevant processes is still a major challenge for researchers in differential psychology and mental chronometry. Research toward this goal is still exploratory. The techniques are too undeveloped and too lacking in sufficiently substantiated theoretical underpinnings and construct validity for chronometric techniques to be recommended as replacements for standard psychometric tests of intelligence (pp. 113–114).

Is this comment somewhat off the mark? Isn't the point of employing chronometric tests actually to explain some of the variance in psychometric intelligence rather than to act as replacement tests (Deary *et al.* 2000)? Perhaps some think that one achievement follows the other? This seems unlikely, given the complexity of administering chronometric tasks compared with standard psychometric tests. Nevertheless, Matarazzo (1992) had the same opinion of the future of testing, seeing chronometric tests, among other biological measures, as coming in as adjuncts to psychometric tests. Jensen (1985) envisaged progress on this front within a decade, and Matarazzo reset the prediction to sometime in the 21st century. Progress between 1985 and the decade up to 1995 was certainly much slower than Jensen envisaged. But before examining the reasons for that, the next major contribution by Jensen is the review of the Hick paradigm in 1987.

5. The Comprehensive Review

Jensen's (1987a) next comprehensive review appeared as a book chapter in Vernon's (1987) edited volume and is the touchstone for research on the Hick task as applied to intelligence research. Almost 80 pages long, it is the largest document on the research to that date. Some history and basic methodology concerning the Hick task were covered, but the empirical substance of the article is a combined analysis of 33 study samples of the Hick task and psychometric intelligence. The total N of the samples was 2,317 (individual N's ranged from 10 to 182). Of the 33 samples, 24 were tested in Jensen's own lab ($N = 1,584$). A substantial proportion of the subjects were university students or otherwise gifted, and another sizeable proportion were mentally handicapped. Conformity to Hick's law was high at the group level, except for severely retarded people. Individual conformity to Hick's law was high, with exceptions showing unreliable non-conformity. By comparison with DT, MT showed very little increase with increasing stimulus uncertainty. Thus, the equations were:

$$\text{Decision time (in ms)} = 336 + 34*\text{bits}$$

$$\text{Movement time (in ms)} = 246 + 3*\text{bits}.$$

A concern about the Hick apparatus as used by Jensen — which separated overall RT into decision and movement times — was that people might move off the home button before they had fully determined which stimulus light they were heading for (e.g. see Smith & Carew 1987; Neubauer 1991). If this were the case, Jensen argued, it was reasonable to suggest that, within individuals and across trials, there should be increasingly negative correlations between decision and movement times as the number of bits increased. He found no such consistent trend. Jensen's separation of RT into decision and movement time would later become a contentious issue with regard to the optimal way forward in measuring reaction times in intelligence research (e.g. see Neubauer 1991; Deary *et al.* 2001). Another, even more contentious issue would be the effect of practice across Hick RT set sizes (Longstreth 1984; Widaman & Carlson 1989). The Hick slope was a prime reason for studying this RT procedure. People with higher psychometric intelligence, it was reckoned, had flatter slopes than people with lower intelligence as they proceeded from fewer to more choices in the RT task. But Jensen's studies always confounded practice with stimulus complexity; people started at the single light and went through 2, 4 and 8 lights in sequence. Therefore, it might be the case that higher ability people simply learned faster on the task and thereby achieved a flatter slope, this phenomenon being nothing to do with 'rate of gain of information.' Jensen's own findings suggested that it was not a problematic issue:

> Practice effects are nil with the present apparatus and procedure, at least within the number of trials used in the studies of the relation of RT parameters to IQ. Since practice effects across trials within each set size are nil, it is so highly improbable that practice effects would transfer across set sizes that, so far, we have not performed a direct experimental test for such an effect by varying the order of administering the different set sizes (pp. 132–133).

Table 4.3 shows a 'pocket' version of Jensen's (1987a) review of the associations among parameters in the Hick procedure. First, note the redundancy among measures, even though these associations are conservative. Second, note that the negative correlation between the slope and the intercept is artefactual. These two measures are typically derived from the same data and share correlated error variance that assures that, as the slope increases the intercept goes down and vice versa. Ideally, these two parameters should be calculated from independent data, something that Jensen explained and performed elegantly in an undervalued paper in the same year and again later (Jensen 1987b, 1998b). Table 4.3 also shows the reliabilities of the principal Hick RT measures that are correlated with intelligence test scores (Jensen 1987a, Table 19). The split-half

Table 4.3: *N*-weighted mean correlations and corrected correlations* (Ns) among parameters extracted from the Hick task (from Jensen 1987a, Tables 18, 19 and 25).

	Median DT	DT intercept	Hick slope	$DT_{\sigma i}$	MT	$MT_{\sigma i}$
Decision time intercept (DT intercept)	0.90 1.0* (125)	—				
Hick slope	0.32 0.41* (553)	–0.06 –0.23* (537)	—			
Decision time intraindividual variability ($DT_{\sigma i}$)	0.62 0.71* (606)	0.40 0.49* (375)	0.39 0.48* (698)	—		
Movement time (MT)	0.51 0.59* (787)	0.41 0.49* (375)	0.09 0.24* (965)	0.35 0.44* (797)	—	
Split-half reliability	0.94	0.95	0.81	0.66	0.87	0.79
Test-retest reliability	0.84	0.72	0.39	0.40	0.86	0.54
N-weighted mean correlation (*N*) with intelligence measures	–0.20 (1195)	–0.12 (774)	–0.12 (1558)	–0.21 (1397)	–0.19 (1302)	–0.01 (1154)
Corrected correlation with intelligence measures (Jensen 1987a: 157)	–0.32	–0.25	–0.28	–0.48	–0.30	–0.02

reliabilities are generally high, but the test-retest reliabilities of the slope and intraindividual variability of the DT measures are very modest (see Jensen 1998b, for a rescue package for the Hick slope). Note, too, that this lack of test-retest reliability appears alongside quite different correlations with intelligence test scores: intra-individual variability of decision times correlate higher than slope.

The most recounted data from Jensen's (1987a) review were the correlations between Hick measures and measures of intelligence based upon 26 independent samples. These have been included in Table 4.3 here. The correlations with individual measures have small effect sizes, with only the mean median DT and the intraindividual variability of DT reaching 0.2. The theoretically interesting slope measure correlates only 0.12 with intelligence. Table 4.3 also shows, predictably, that the DT intraindividual variability and slope measures benefit most from correction for unreliability, with (still conservative) estimates of their effect sizes rising to –0.48 and –0.28, respectively. Jensen estimated the multiple correlation between Hick parameters and intelligence test scores between 0.35 and 0.50. Jensen also reported the *N*-weighted mean correlations (based on 15 independent samples with a total *N* of 1129) between intelligence measures and reaction times as the number of stimulus alternatives increased, as follows: 1 stimulus (simple RT) = –0.18; 2 stimuli = –0.19; 4 stimuli = –0.22; and 8 stimuli = –0.23. Though the correlations increase, the increments are tiny. Across the studies that contributed to these means, the rank order correlation between set size of RT stimuli and correlation with intelligence was only 0.39. The fact that DT intraindividual variability did not show increasing correlations with intelligence measures as the stimulus set size increased was seen as a refutation of one of the suggestions of Jensen's (1982) oscillatory model of the neural basis of RT differences. However, because this model is based on speculation rather than known cognitive or biological constructs, it seems that it is better to concentrate here on data.

The last contribution in Jensen's (1987a) masterwork on RT was to address explanations for the association between RT and intelligence. The importance of this task cannot be overstated. Demonstrating correlations between intelligence and parameters from experimental procedures is important, and any replicable associations promise an understanding of intelligence differences that is more profound than the psychometric-level analysis can deliver. But finding and replicating correlations is a job less than half done, because correlations do not bring with them explanations. Two things remain undone. First, there is the problem of the causes of the correlation. Is the experimental parameter somehow a cause of intelligence differences or is the true account vice versa. Or are both variables caused by some other, unmeasured factor? And, further, even where there is reasonable confidence in the direction of the association — that it goes from experimental measure to intelligence differences — there can only be as much insight into the nature of intelligence as the experimental measure affords (Mackintosh 1998). If the nature of differences in reaction times is obscure — if there is no mechanistic account of the measure and its differences — then all that has occurred is the loose tying (a very modest association in most cases) of one unknown to another. Jensen's (1987a) summing up was admirable in its common sense. He made the following points: there was no adequate theory to explain the intelligence-Hick parameter correlations; many of the Hick parameters have similar correlations with intelligence test scores; the same situation occurs in other RT procedures (Jensen 1987b); and the Hick intercept and MT parameters were supposedly uninteresting with respect to human information processing differences, yet they correlate with intelligence test scores just as well, if not better than, the Hick slope, the supposedly central theoretical parameter. He summed up as follows:

> Although it is not yet unarguable, the evidence on the Hick parameters seems to indicate that *g* is more highly correlated with a general factor common to all of the Hick RT and MT variables than with any particular cognitive processing components that can be inferred from certain parameters of the Hick paradigm.

In fact, much of the theoretical work in reaction time-intelligence research has been 'defence' rather than attack in so far as it involved refuting 'explainings-away' of the correlations rather than explanatory accounts proper (see, especially, the exchange between Longstreth 1984 and Jensen & Vernon 1986). The correlations are not the result of a general speed factor in test taking, as RT parameters correlate just as highly with unspeeded intelligence tests (Vernon 1985; Vernon & Kantor 1986). They are not the result of speed-accuracy trade-offs. Nor are they the result of greater general motivation or arousal on the part of the higher ability subjects, argued Jensen (1987a, 1998a; see also Neubauer 1997 and Deary 2000, Chapter 6, for reviews of these disputes).

6. Causal Accounts

Jensen (1993) addressed possible explanations of reaction time-*g* correlations at the neural level. The use of '*g*' in this context follows Jensen's (1998a: 236) demonstration that a psychometric test's *g*-loading correlates highly with the task's correlation with RT. This is demonstrated by what Jensen called the 'method of correlated vectors.' As a basis of the reaction time-*g* correlation Jensen (1993) suggested speed of nervous system transmission, perhaps at its most basic in peripheral and central nerve conduction velocity. It seems unlikely, though, that nerve conduction velocity (especially peripheral nerve conduction velocity) can fulfil this role. When differences in conduction velocity are partialled out of the reaction time-intelligence test score correlations, they hardly alter (Vernon & Mori 1992). The second suggestion made by Jensen (1993) was that noise (or error rates) in neural transmission might underpin the association between intelligence test scores and RT variability. Eysenck (1987) considered this to be the aspect of reaction time-intelligence association of prime interest. These two giants converging on this explanation cannot, though, be seen as convincing. Jensen's ideas were speculative constructions on the data themselves, and Eysenck's ideas were based upon the highly speculative ideas of Hendrickson (1982). In short, Jensen's reductionist ideas about nervous 'speed' and 'oscillation' don't proceed much further than the data themselves.

   Jensen's (1998a) later summary of the research on reaction times and psychometric intelligence embraced a number of so-called 'elementary cognitive tasks' (ECTs) in addition to the Hick procedure. Jensen only briefly reviewed evidence, but did touch on a number of explanatory issues. He suggested that reaction time-intelligence correlations: were not to do with speed of test taking; were not to do with conscious awareness of reacting in the ECTs; intraindividual variability in RT correlates better with intelligence than mean RT and the two do not fully overlap; and composites of ECTs have higher correlations with intelligence than one ECT alone. There were other substantive issues. The last of this list was Jensen's demonstration, using a number of data sets, that the correlations between reaction times and psychometric tests tended to be with the *g* factor rather than a group factor of intelligence. There then followed Jensen's rebutting again various 'blind alley' explanations of the correlations between ECTs and intelligence, and a stab at a biological account which drew little on data (there are few that are relevant to date). One of the constructs addressed was working memory. Polczyk & Necka (1997) tested and confirmed a hypothesis that the correlation between intelligence and RT should be less in people with a relatively capacious and retentive working memory, lending some support to Jensen's (1998a) ideas.

7. Evaluations of Jensen's Reaction Time Research

7.1. *Longstreth (1984)*

Longstreth's (1984) critique of Jensen's reaction time-intelligence research raised procedural and theoretical issues that have been prominent in the research ever since. He raised the issues of order effects (people in Jensen's experiments tended to take the experimental conditions in ascending order), visual attention effects (as the set sizes became smaller the light got closer to the centre of the display), response bias (responses to different set sizes involved different physical responses) and other factors such as the speed-accuracy trade-off. This critique combined with Jensen & Vernon's (1986) reply set out much of the research agenda for the following years. Most of Longstreth's comments were geared toward finding explanations for the intelligence-reaction time association that were other than a straightforward 'basic processes' account.

7.2. *Eysenck (1987)*

Eysenck's evaluation of the Jensen RT research was set in the context of the Galton versus Binet approach to intelligence, with Jensen's work being construed in the Galton lineage of the search for the latent aspects of intelligence. Eysenck rehearsed Jensen's views of the limited channel information processor and the speediness of information decay. Eysenck viewed the following findings as established: reaction times, even simple reaction times, are correlated with psychometric measures of intelligence; the correlation between reaction times and intelligence increases, up to a point, as the number of choices in the reaction time condition increases (it is doubtful whether this holds; see Deary 2000); the slope of the Hick procedure relates to intelligence; the variability of RT relates to intelligence, and Eysenck saw this as the major finding; including short and long term memory in the reaction time procedure (in the shape of the S. Sternberg and Posner procedures) does not increase the correlations between reaction times and intelligence. Eysenck concluded by stating that:

> Work on reaction times demonstrates, as does even more powerfully the recent work on the relationship between evoked potentials and IQ . . . that there is a central core to IQ tests which is quite independent of reasoning, judgement, problem-solving, learning, comprehension, memory, etc. (p. 293).

Eysenck spent some time discussing neural theories on the reaction time-intelligence association, which might be seen as too speculative to recount now, but his main theme was that the then-current theories of intelligence would not predict such an association.

7.3. *Carroll (1987)*

Carroll's review of Jensen's work that accompanied the Eysenck review had a different tone:

> I have come to be somewhat astonished and disturbed by the imprecise, oblique, and unrevealing manner in which Jensen has presented his data and findings (p. 297).

One concern of Carroll's was that Jensen had reported many key data in reviews rather than empirical reports. As others did, Carroll pointed out the relatively weak evidence for the correlation between measured intelligence and Hick slope and the increased correlation between intelligence and increasingly complex RT conditions. Carroll also rehearsed some of Longstreth's objections, though he alluded to some situations in which Jensen's or others' data rebutted some of those. He concluded:

> The findings examined here indicate a high probability that there are some true relations between one or more dimensions of cognitive ability and measures derived from Jensen's RT-MT task. The exact nature of these relations ... the conditions under which they arise or vary, their stability over time, and their interpretation are matters in need of much further investigation and clarification. The relations are small, seldom greater than what is indicated by correlation coefficients of 0.30 to 0.40 in absolute magnitude.
>
> My hunch is that many of the RT-MT findings can be explained by supposing that lower IQ individuals are less capable of meeting the attentional requirements of the RT-MT task (p. 306).

This latter comment finds agreement in Mackintosh (1998). Carroll concluded that the reaction time-intelligence correlations were interesting but that theories of the relations were premature. Carroll preferred a strategy that analysed cognitive test items themselves.

Most interestingly, here was a section of Eysenck's (1987) reply to Carroll's (1987) critical assessment:

> Specifically, I would suggest that Jensen has succeeded in establishing that a relationship exists between choice reaction time, variability in reaction time and possibly other parameters of the RT experiment on the one hand, and intelligence on the other. I believe that he is probably wrong in thinking that the slope of the Hick line is closely related to intelligence, or that within the choice reaction time paradigm differences in the number of alternatives are important (p. 309).

These comments are all the more important because it was Eysenck (1967) who first brought the possibility of the Hick slope-intelligence correlation to the English-speaking world.

Carroll's (1987) final word in response to Eysenck was to suggest that perhaps too much credit was being offered to Jensen in establishing reaction times as a tool for examining intelligence. He suggested that R. Sternberg and Hunt had been active in that field also, but perhaps Jensen had been central in examining the relatively non-cognitive choice reaction time task.

7.4. Neubauer (1997)

Neubauer's (1997) review of 'mental speed' approaches to intelligence covered matters including and beyond reaction times. Within his review he examined evidence for the three premier RT procedures used in intelligence research: the Hick, S. Sternberg and Posner tasks. In each of these he found significant associations with psychometric intelligence. But, crucially, the most consistent and largest correlations were not with the cognitive components extracted using the subtractive or pure insertion methods. Rather, the correlations tended to be with the more prosaic overall reaction times and their variabilities. One of Neubauer's main concerns was to examine 'top-down' versus 'bottom-up' accounts of the reaction time-intelligence association. He decided in favour of the latter:

> On the basis of the present state of knowledge, I would, therefore, conclude that a unitary process seems to be responsible for the relationship between psychometric intelligence and SIP [speed of information processing] (p. 168).

7.5. Nettelbeck (1998)

Nettelbeck (1998) highlighted the sheer amount of Jensen's research and his persistence with a consistent procedural set-up for the study of RT and intelligence. He pointed to the fact that theoretical expectations were sometimes found wanting: the Hick slope was a less good correlate of intelligence than other measures and the MT aspect of the Hick task appeared just as good a predictor of intelligence as supposedly more cognitive aspects. Nevertheless, Nettelbeck credited Jensen with providing enough output to convince the field, especially the sceptics, that RT indices were significantly correlated with psychometric intelligence, at a level greater than many expected. Nettelbeck addressed the explanation of the reaction time-intelligence correlation. He suggested that RT procedures were 'psychological' rather than 'biological' and that the epithet 'elementary cognitive tasks' often applied to RT procedures was a misnomer. Nettelbeck predicted that reaction times would be affected by higher-order cognitive processes; he simply did not accept RT indices as being as basic as Jensen suggested (contra Neubauer 1997). In conclusion, and in agreement with Eysenck's review over 10 years before, Nettelbeck saw Jensen's main contribution as the clear demonstration of a correlation, but without having explained the association.

7.6. Mackintosh (1998)

Mackintosh (1998) would rank among the sceptics rather than advocates of the so-called 'mental speed' approach to intelligence. Nevertheless, he accepted that there was a secure correlation between RT and intelligence, perhaps between –0.2 and –0.3. With regard to explaining the reaction time-intelligence correlation Mackintosh's opinion was similar to Nettelbeck's (1998), namely that RT was not the 'simple' variable that many differential psychologists had assumed and that higher order factors might cause the correlation rather than simple mental speed or speed of nervous transmission. Apart from pointing out that reaction times were not understood in mechanistic terms — a prerequisite for their being informative about intelligence — Mackintosh also was concerned that there was insufficient research on exactly the aspect of the intelligence hierarchy to which reaction times correlated most strongly (though Jensen (1998a: 234–238) insists it is the *g* factor). This last point finds agreement with Roberts & Stankov (1999) who have attempted to use multiple speed of processing tests alongside multiple psychometric measures better to understand the associations between intelligence and RT procedures.

7.7. Deary (2000)

Deary's (2000) critical appraisal of reaction time-intelligence research will be briefly summarised here. First, the accumulated evidence confirms a significant association between reaction times and their variabilities and psychometric intelligence. However, the main anomalies dwelt upon were that the 'entry point' for the Hick task's introduction to intelligence was the importance of the slope. Despite that, the slope appeared to have no especial (sometimes just no) correlation with psychometric intelligence, and even supposedly non-cognitive aspects of RT such as MT did correlate with intelligence test scores (Barrett *et al.* 1986; Deary *et al.* 1992; Beauducel & Brocke 1993).

Deary (2000) rehearsed Longstreth's (1984) original suggestions that might explain-away the reaction time-intelligence test score correlations, and reviewed research which had countered many of these. Jensen (1998a: 238–248) also attempted to deal with these matters, what he called "blind alley explanations of the RT-*g* relationship." Of Longstreth's suggestions, the one that gained some support was that which pointed out that flatter Hick slopes might arise owing to practice rather than higher IQ, and that Jensen's confounding of order of conditions and practice might be a serious methodological problem. Widaman & Carlson (1989) provided evidence that practice was the crucial factor causing the reaction time-intelligence correlation, but see Kranzler *et al.* (1988) and Widaman (1989) for an exchange on this matter. Deary (2000), though, reckoned that this lively interchange and the subsequent studies that addressed the slope-versus-practice issue and other Hick slope concerns were to a large extent irrelevant. Many of Longstreth's (1984) key comments (not all of them) were about the Hick slope, and others related to the separation of MT and DT in the Jensen apparatus. But the Hick slope has a less strong correlation with intelligence than do other aspects of the Hick task, the Hick slope does not actually figure in Jensen's own theoretical account of the reaction time-intelligence correlation, and the correlation still appears when RT and MT are not separated. Perhaps, then, the specific Hick-related concerns may be removed from 'problems' with the reaction time-intelligence association. Perhaps, also, the separation of movement and decision times was unnecessary, despite the ingenuity that went into examining possible counters to the strategies that might counter peoples' moving from the home button too early (Smith &

Carew 1987; Neubauer 1991; Stough *et al.* 1995; Bates & Stough 1998). That largely leaves the more general, high-level factors as putative partial explanations, such as those favoured by Nettelbeck (1998) and Mackintosh (1998) but partly refuted by Neubauer (1997) and Jensen (1998a).

The conclusion?: that the reappearance of reaction times into intelligence research after a long absence (see Beck 1933) in the guise of the Hick procedure might have been a distraction. Perhaps attention should be refocused on the basics of simple and choice reaction times (see Deary *et al.*, 2001). These have the merits of apparent simplicity. Another acceptable move would be to put more effort into procedures with better-established theoretical tractability than the Hick task. Lohman (1999) suggested that the Hick slope and other 'difference' or slope measures have inherent problems and cannot be used informatively to derive measures of individual differences, though Jensen (1987b, 1998b) suggested some means for salvaging the Hick slope from unreliability and Bates & Stough (1998), in a small study, reported an IQ-Hick slope correlation over –0.5.

With regard to understanding the reaction time-intelligence association, Deary (2000) was critical of those extensions of RT-intelligence research that appear to complicate RT even more, either by bundling together indices from multiple RT procedures (Vernon 1983) or by adding extra complications to the RT task itself as, say, found in the 'odd man out' procedure (Frearson & Eysenck 1986). These procedures do, though, improve the prediction of intelligence using RT procedures. But it must be understanding intelligence test variance rather than grabbing it in any old fashion that drives this research (Deary *et al.* 2000). More research was urged which examined: the psychopharmacological bases of reaction times and intelligence (e.g. Bates *et al.* 1994), the evoked potential correlates of reaction times and intelligence (e.g. Houlihan *et al.* 1994), and the shared heritability of RT and intelligence (e.g. Neubauer *et al.* 2000).

8. The Future of Reaction Time and Intelligence

Though some have suggested that the Hick slope has not been given a fair chance to correlate with intelligence test scores (Jensen 1998b), it seems best to advise retrenchment in the study of reaction times as applied to intelligence differences. Since there does appear to be a significant correlation between even simple and four choice RT and their variabilities and intelligence test scores it seems advisable to study these relatively simple procedures if we are to understand the associations. Accounting for IQ-score variance is another matter, and certainly multiple and more complex measures do better there. There follow three short accounts of recent studies that might suggest some ways forward.

8.1. Back to Ordinary RT?

One of the statistics that has been called for but not forthcoming is the effect size of the relation between psychometric intelligence and RT in the general population. In 1982 Jensen commented that:

Although there are now quite extensive data linking RT and intelligence, I find it virtually impossible at present to draw any firm conclusion about the true magnitude of the relationship as it would be expressed in terms of a coefficient of correlation. The reason for this uncertainty is mainly two fold: (a) little, if any, RT research has been based on large representative samples of the general population . . . (p. 94).

The other reason was to do with the stability of RT. But a study of a representative sample has been two decades in arriving. Deary *et al.* (2001) examined a sample of nine hundred 55-year-old Scots. They had a narrow age range, almost equal numbers of men and women, and were closely related to the nation as a whole in terms of social characteristics. They were tested on the Alice Heim 4 test, Part 1. The RT device tested simple and four-choice RT. The four-choice task was of the fingers-on-buttons type (cf. Hick 1952) in which 'decision' and 'movement' times were not separated. Psychometric intelligence scores correlated −0.31 with simple RT, −0.49 with choice RT and −0.26 with intraindividual variability in both simple and choice reaction times. The correlation between Alice Heim scores and the difference between choice and simple reaction times was −0.15. Separating the sample into subgroups by sex, educational level, social class grouping and numbers of errors made on the RT task had no significant effect on the correlations. The study might be a benchmark for the reaction time-mental ability test score correlation at that specific age. It suggests a larger effect size than those reported in extant studies that are often dominated by student samples with restricted ranges of mental ability.

8.2. Psychopharmacology

An experimental rather than correlational test of the hypothesis that nerve conduction velocity might underlie the association between RT and intelligence was carried out by Strachan *et al.* (2001). They examined 16 healthy subjects in counterbalanced hypoglycaemia (low blood glucose) and euglycaemia (normal blood glucose) conditions. It is well known that controlled moderate hypoglycaemia of the degree employed by Strachan *et al.* temporarily and reversibly deranges cognitive functions in a widespread manner (Deary 1998). Indeed, hypoglycaemia affected, in Strachan *et al.*'s study, digit symbol from the Wechsler test battery, trail-making from the Halstead Reitan battery, and speed of information processing from the British Ability Scales. These are all psychometric, paper-and-pencil tests. In addition, decision times and movement times from a 'Jensen box'-type RT device and inspection time were significantly slowed during hypoglycaemia. Therefore, there was continuity of derangement at the psychometric, experimental and psychophysical levels. On the other hand, peripheral motor nerve conduction velocities in the arms and the legs were unaffected. Though such a study is not definitive, it is hard to sustain the argument that nerve conduction velocity might be the basis of the reaction time-intelligence association in the face of these data.

8.3. Animal Hick Reaction Times

The Hick phenomenon has been explored in other species, namely pigeons. In a series of experiments, Vickrey & Neuringer (2000) found that Hick's law of increasing reaction times as a function of the log of the number of bits does apply. They found evidence that practice on the Hick task reduced the intercept, though the evidence for the slope was less clear. Perhaps contrary to a simple assumption that pigeons are less intelligent than humans, they had flatter Hick slopes and no more variable reaction times. Slopes and intercepts on the pigeon Hick task were affected by what the authors called 'response topography.' They concluded:

> Taken together, our results do not support complex RT as an index of heritable general intelligence. Parameters are affected by training, thus arguing against heritability; and functions for pigeons indicate an intelligence that is higher than that of humans, thus arguing against a generally valid measure (p. 291).

It is hard fully to go along with their view that a flatter Hick slope, or whatever, would make another species more or less intelligent in humans. Even if the phenomenon is related to intelligence within a species, when it comes to between species comparisons the information processing parameters being measured are parts of different systems. If a calculator could do some isolated function better or faster than a large computer it would be an odd conclusion to state that the calculator, given this one isolated advantage, was overall more powerful than the computer. The more important lesson from this study is that RT parameters can be obtained in animals. Together with the tentative finding that there might be a psychometric structure to animal abilities that includes *g* (in mice, at least; Locurto & Scanlon 1998) we should look forward to experiments in non-human animals that predicts their cognitive differences in terms of information processing parameters.

Perhaps these recommendations are obvious. Employing the simplest-seeming — those that appear theoretically most tractable — information processing tasks that deliver the associations. More population-level studies, in order to gain trustworthy effect sizes. More studies of the biological links — psychopharmacology, evoked potentials, functional brain scanning — between intelligence at the psychometric level and information processing parameters (though a possibility here is that intelligence researchers might proceed to biology, bypassing cognitive tasks based on information processing models; Duncan *et al.* 2000). And parallel studies in non-human animals. It must be stated clearly, though, that the principal barrier to our progress in understanding human intelligence differences is the lack of any task of human information processing that both correlates with intelligence differences and has a validated model of performance based on brain processes.

9. Conclusions

A short summing up of Jensen's contribution is attempted (for others see Carroll 1987; Eysenck 1987; Nettelbeck 1998). Jensen made contributions to reaction time-intelligence research in the following fields: recalling the almost-forgotten history of the topic, the methodology for RT measurement, the 'theory' of the reaction time-intelligence association, the data sets, and the refutation of 'confounding' accounts. He contributed a great deal more experimental work than people now cite (see, especially, Jensen 1985, 1987a, 1987b). A great deal of methodological thought went into his writings. What is needed now is more big-scale research that chases down the many ideas generated by the reaction time-intelligence linkage; at present there are orders of magnitude too few studies. Jensen's speculative ideas about the intelligence-reaction time association are still too little connected with modern cognitive or neuroscience, though the idea of neural oscillators attracts new attention (Poppel 1994; Plenz & Kital 1999). Jensen put the topic of RT and intelligence on the research agenda, and it won't go away now, the way it did before. There are solid findings of correlations, but we still do not know the population effect sizes and we still do not know what they mean.

Detterman (1987) commented on RT research and intelligence:

> What is required, then, is a research program which uses multiple basic tasks, employs extremely sophisticated measurement techniques to collect data for each task, begins from a precise model of performance on each task, makes predictions supported by simulation, and uses ample sample sizes in the experimental confirmation of predictions. When such a research program is launched, we will be well on our way to understanding the important relationship between choice reaction time measures and intelligence (p. 198).

The fuel for that launch is the 'precise model of performance on each task.' When cognitive science delivers any such model perhaps the program will take off properly.

References

Barrett, P., Eysenck, H. J., & Lucking, S. (1986). Reaction time and intelligence: A replicated study. *Intelligence, 10*, 9–40.

Bates, T., Pellett, O., Stough, C., & Mangan, G. L. (1994). The effects of smoking on simple and choice reaction time. *Psychopharmacology, 114*, 365–378.

Bates, T., & Stough, C. (1998). Improved reaction time method, information processing speed, and intelligence. *Intelligence, 26*, 53–62.

Beauducel, A., & Brocke, B. (1993). Intelligence and speed of information processing: further results and questions on Hick's paradigm and beyond. *Personality and Individual Differences, 15*, 627–636.

Beck, L. F. (1933). The role of speed in intelligence. *Psychological Bulletin, 30*, 169–178.

Carroll, J. B. (1987). Jensen's mental chronometry: some comments and questions. In: S. Modgil, & C. Modgil (Eds), *Arthur Jensen: Consensus and controversy* (pp. 297–307 & 310–311). New York: Falmer.

Deary, I. J. (1998). The effects of diabetes on cognitive function. *Diabetes Annual, 11*, 97–118.

Deary, I. J. (2000). *Looking down on human intelligence: From psychometrics to the brain.* Oxford, England: Oxford University Press.

Deary, I. J., Austin, E. J., & Caryl, P. G. (2000). Testing versus understanding human intelligence. *Psychology, Public Policy and Law, 6*, 180–190.

Deary, I. J., Der, G., & Ford, G. (2001). Reaction times and intelligence differences: A population-based cohort study. *Intelligence, 29,* 389–399.

Deary, I. J., Langan, S. J., Graham, K. S., Hepburn, D., & Frier, B. M. (1992). Recurrent severe hypoglycaemia, intelligence, and speed of information processing. *Intelligence, 16,* 337–359.

Detterman, D. K. (1987). What does reaction time tell us about intelligence? In: P. A. Vernon (Ed.), *Speed of information processing and intelligence* (pp. 177–200). Norwood, NJ: Ablex.

Duncan, J., Seitz, R. J., Kolodny, J., Bor, D., Herzog, H., Ahmed, A., Newell, F. N., & Emslie, H. (2000). A neural basis for general intelligence. *Science, 289,* 457–460.

Eysenck, H. J. (1967). Intelligence assessment: A theoretical and experimental approach. *British Journal of Educational Psychology, 37,* 81–97.

Eysenck, H. J. (1987). Intelligence and reaction time: The contribution of Arthur Jensen. In: S. Modgil, & C. Modgil (Eds), *Arthur Jensen: Consensus and controversy* (pp. 285–295 & 308–309). New York: Falmer.

Frearson, W., & Eysenck, H. J. (1986). Intelligence, reaction time (RT) and a new 'odd-man-out' RT paradigm. *Personality and Individual Differences, 7,* 807–817.

Hendrickson, A. E. (1982). The biological basis of intelligence. Part 1: Theory. In: H. J. Eysenck (Ed.), *A Model for Intelligence.* Berlin: Springer-Verlag.

Hick, W. E. (1952). On the rate of gain of information. *Quarterly Journal of Experimental Psychology, 4,* 11–26.

Houlihan, M., Campbell, K., & Stelmack, R. M. (1994). Reaction time and movement time as measures of stimulus evaluation and response processes. *Intelligence, 18,* 289–307.

Hyman, R. (1953). Stimulus information as a determinant of reaction time. *Journal of Experimental Psychology, 45,* 188–196.

Jensen, A. R. (1982). Reaction time and psychometric *g.* In: H. J. Eysenck (Ed.), *A Model for Intelligence.* Berlin: Springer-Verlag.

Jensen, A. R. (1985). Methodological and statistical techniques for the chronometric study of mental abilities. In: C. R. Reynolds & V. L. Willson (Eds), *Methodological and statistical advances in the study of individual differences* (pp. 51–116). New York: Plenum.

Jensen, A. R. (1987a). Individual differences in the Hick paradigm. In: P. A. Vernon (Ed.), *Speed of information processing and intelligence* (pp. 101–175). Norwood, NJ: Ablex.

Jensen, A. R. (1987b). Process differences and individual differences in some cognitive tasks. *Intelligence, 11,* 153–179.

Jensen, A. R. (1993). Why is reaction time correlated with psychometric *g? Current Directions in Psychological Science, 2,* 53–56.

Jensen, A. R. (1998a). *The g factor: The science of mental ability.* New York: Praeger.

Jensen, A. R. (1998b). The suppressed relationship between IQ and the reaction time slope parameter of the Hick function. *Intelligence, 26,* 43–52.

Jensen, A. R., & Munro, E. (1979). Reaction time, movement time, and intelligence. *Intelligence, 3,* 121–126.

Jensen, A. R., & Vernon, P. A. (1986). Jensen's reaction-time studies: A reply to Longstreth. *Intelligence, 10,* 153–179.

Kranzler, J. H., Whang, P. A., & Jensen, A. R. (1988). Jensen's use of the Hick paradigm: visual attention and order effects. *Intelligence, 12,* 379–392.

Locurto, C., & Scanlon, C. (1998). Individual differences and a spatial learning factor in two strains of mice (*Mus musculus*). *Journal of Comparative Psychology, 112,* 344–352.

Lohman, D. F. (1999). Minding our p's and q's: on finding relationships between learning and intelligence. In: P. L. Ackerman, P. C. Kyllonen, & R. D. Roberts (Eds), *Learning and individual differences: Process, trait, and content determinants* (pp. 55–76). Washington, D.C.: American Psychological Association.

Longstreth, L. E. (1984). Jensen's reaction time investigations of intelligence: A critique. *Intelligence, 8,* 139–160.

Mackintosh, N. J. (1998). *IQ and human intelligence.* Oxford, England: Oxford University Press.

Matarazzo, J. D. (1992). Psychological testing and assessment in the 21st century. *American Psychologist, 47,* 1007–1018.

Nettelbeck, T. (1998). Jensen's chronometric research: neither simple nor sufficient but a good place to start. *Intelligence, 26,* 233–241.

Neubauer, A. C. (1991). Intelligence and RT: a modified Hick paradigm and a new RT paradigm. *Intelligence, 15,* 175–193.

Neubauer, A. C. (1997). The mental speed approach to the assessment of intelligence. In: J. Kingma, & W. Tomic (Eds), *Advances in cognition and education: Reflections on the concept of intelligence.* Greenwich, CT: JAI Press.

Neubauer, A. C., Spinath, F. M., Riemann, R., Borkenau, P., & Angleitner, A. (2000). Genetic and environmental influences on two measures of speed of information processing and their relation to psychometric intelligence: evidence from the German Observational Study of Adult Twins. *Intelligence, 28,* 267–289.

Plenz, D., & Kital, S. T. (1999). A basal ganglia pacemaker formed by the subthalamic nucleus and external globus pallidus. *Nature, 400,* 677–682.

Polczyk, R., & Necka, E. (1997). Capacity and retention capability of working memory to modify the strength of the RT/IQ correlation: a short note. *Personality and Individual Differences, 23,* 1089–1091.

Poppel, E. (1994). Temporal mechanisms in perception. *International Review of Neurobiology, 37,* 185–202.

Roberts, R., & Stankov, L. (1999). Individual differences in speed of mental processing and human cognitive abilities: Toward a taxonomic model. *Learning and Individual Differences, 11,* 1–120.

Roth, E. (1964). Die Geschwindigkeit der Verabeitung von Information und ihr Zusammenhang mit Intelligenz. *Zeitschrift fur Experimentelle und Angewandte Psychologie, 11,* 616–622.

Smith, G. A., & Carew, M. (1987). Decision time unmasked: individuals adopt different strategies. *Australian Journal of Psychology, 39,* 339–351.

Stough, C., Nettelbeck, T., Cooper, C., & Bates, T. (1995). Strategy use in Jensen's RT paradigm: relationships to intelligence? *Australian Journal of Psychology, 47,* 61–65.

Strachan, M. W. J., Deary, I. J., Ewing, F. M. E., Ferguson, S. S. C., Young, M. J., & Frier, B. M. (2001). Acute hypoglycaemia impairs functions of the central but not the peripheral nervous system. *Physiology and Behavior, 72* (1–2), 83–92.

Vernon, P. A. (1983). Speed of information processing and general intelligence. *Intelligence, 7,* 53–70.

Vernon, P. A. (1985). Reaction times and speed of processing: their relationship to timed and untimed measures of intelligence. *Intelligence, 9,* 357–374.

Vernon, P. A. (Ed.) (1987). *Speed of information processing and intelligence.* Norwood, NJ: Ablex.

Vernon, P. A., & Kantor, L. (1986). Reaction time correlations with intelligence test scores obtained under either timed or untimed conditions. *Intelligence, 10,* 315–330.

Vernon, P. A., & Mori, M. (1992). Intelligence, reaction times, and peripheral nerve conduction velocity. *Intelligence, 16,* 273–288.

Vickrey, C., & Neuringer, A. (2000). Pigeon reaction time, Hick's law, and intelligence. *Psychonomic Bulletin and Review, 7,* 284–291.

Widaman, K. F. (1989). When failure to replicate is not failure to replicate: a comment on Kranzler, Whang and Jensen (1988). *Intelligence*, *13*, 87–91.

Widaman, K. F., & Carlson, J. S. (1989). Procedural effects on performance on the Hick paradigm. *Intelligence*, *13*, 63–86.

Chapter 5

Inspection Time and *g*

Ted Nettelbeck

1. Introduction

This chapter examines what is known about correlation between inspection time (IT) and IQ, and what is known about the nature of IT. The main consideration is whether IT has revealed anything about the nature of human intelligence; and the main conclusions are that it has; and that it may yet help to uncover more.

Arthur Jensen's contributions to these issues have been very important. He became interested in IT research during the late 1970s, soon after its inception and, although his preferred tool for investigating a role for speed of information processing in explaining human intelligence has been choice reaction time (RT), he has frequently promoted IT as an important chronometric procedure (e.g. Jensen 1982, 1998, ch. 8). His article with Kranzler on the nature of psychomotor *g* (Kranzler & Jensen 1991a) is an important analysis of this key question. Besides such published accounts, to my certain knowledge he has, as a self-identified referee to several pre-publication drafts, made many insightful suggestions that have significantly improved the final products. Also, he has been actively involved in comprehensive meta-analyses of available data. Because of the formal rigor that these analyses have provided and because of Jensen's standing as a foremost scholar in the field of intelligence, these analyses have with considerable authority set the size of the IT-IQ correlation at around –0.5, a moderately strong outcome (Kranzler & Jensen 1989). Moreover, Jensen has consistently kept his eye on the main prize — a testable theory about the contribution of fundamental psychological and biological processes to human intelligence (e.g. Jensen 1998, ch. 8). This has been a major accomplishment. Twenty years ago most cognitive psychologists would have resoundingly dismissed a suggestion that speed of thought could play more than a relatively trivial part in accounting for individual differences in intelligence. Despite an age-old intuition embedded in our language in terms like "quick wit", main stream psychology was convinced that the pursuit of an explanation for intelligence in terms of speed of processing was not likely to yield much of significance (e.g. Das *et al.* 1978: 18). Yet, Jensen's RT research has persuaded many psychologists otherwise (Nettelbeck 1998). Reliable correlations between chronometric tasks with low performance requirements and conventional psychometric ability tests have confirmed that these are relationships that beg a theoretical explanation.

From the outset it will be useful to distinguish between the *measure* IT and the psychological *construct* purportedly estimated by the procedures involved. Douglas Vickers (Adelaide University) developed both the initial theoretical account and the first procedure for estimating IT around 1970. The first published report of IT research by Vickers *et al.* (1972) maintained the theoretical-procedural distinction by symbolizing their particular measure as λ. This practice was discontinued beyond the late 1980s, however, largely because of the diverse criteria used by different researchers to define high accuracy of performance in the IT task, as well as by debate generated by psychophysical theory about the most efficient criterion to apply (Levy 1992). Nonetheless, as will become clear from what follows, it is an important distinction to observe.

2. Measuring Inspection Time (IT)

The measurement of visual IT is described here because, thus far, this has been the most widely applied version. Measures of auditory and tactile IT have also been developed and there have been several studies involving the former but very few for the latter (refer to Deary 2000, ch. 7 and Nettelbeck 1987, respectively). Unless otherwise stated, in what follows "IT" refers to visual IT.

Measuring IT requires discrimination between alternatives (typically just two vertical lines of markedly different lengths, joined horizontally across the top to form what has commonly been described as a "pi" figure; see Figure 5.1). Without restriction to

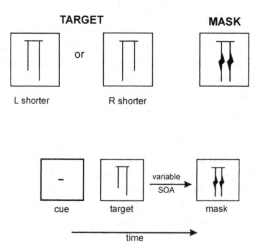

Figure 5.1: Examples of the target and pattern backward masking figures and the sequence in which these occur when measuring inspection time. Greg Evans developed this mask (Evans & Nettelbeck 1993).

viewing time, a decision about whether the shorter (or longer) line in the target figure is located to left or right is so easy that no-one makes any errors, irrespective of age or IQ level — at least within the limits tested; children as young as 5 years, adults up to 86 years and IQs in the 40s. However, having first displayed the target, a similar figure but with vertical lines of equal length is used to overlay the target. The second figure is termed a "backward pattern mask". In other words, it follows the target ("backward"), it has similar contours ("pattern"); and phenomenologically the target disappears, becoming integrated with the "mask". A tachistoscope was initially used to present these figures but as computer monitors with increasingly faster refresh rates have become available this method of display has become most common. The duration for which the target is exposed, from target onset to mask onset, is termed the "stimulus-onset-asynchrony" (SOA), typically measured in milliseconds (ms). Very brief exposures of the target render the task excessively difficult.

An individual's IT is defined as a critical SOA, specifically the SOA required to achieve a predetermined high level of discriminative accuracy (e.g. exactly 75% correct on all trials at that SOA).[1] For some participants this critical SOA (i.e. IT) will be considerably shorter than 100 ms but there are marked and reliable individual differences in the measure, even within relatively homogeneous age or IQ samples. Even within an IQ distribution that specifically excludes intellectual disability some ITs will exceed 200 ms. So defined, IT can typically be estimated with high reliability (test-retest r's from 0.7 to 0.8, with generally only marginally changed absolute outcomes) within a session lasting about 10 minutes, from approximately 100–150 trials. Although critical SOA can be estimated by a number of different procedures, the most common method has used an adaptive staircase procedure to control and modify SOA in accordance with ongoing performance characteristics. Detailed accounts of these and similar procedures are available from several reviews (e.g. Deary 2000, ch. 7; Deary & Stough 1996; Nettelbeck 1987).

It is important to note that a participant's responses when making the required discriminations are not time constrained, so that IT is not a direct measure of performance speed. Instead, IT is effectively a threshold measure, reflecting some limitation to accuracy of performance. Thus "speed of information processing" is inferred, with shorter IT consistent with faster processing. As a measure of processing speed, IT has advantages over more widely applied RT procedures because it excludes the influence of both motor delays and conceptual factors reflecting a participant's motivation and confidence that confound the speed and accuracy of RTs. To summarize, the measure IT is well prescribed, highly reliable and very convenient to make. However, this preliminary description of the IT measure has scarcely addressed IT as a *theoretical construct*, other than as some putative basic limitation to processing efficiency. Suffice to acknowledge here, there has been wide debate concerning the nature of IT and this is an issue that will be explored further in the sections to follow on the nature of inspection time and its relationship with psychometric abilities.

---

[1] Adelaide research generally followed Vickers, Nettelbeck & Willson's (1972) accuracy criterion of 97.5% correct until Levy (1992) persuaded us to revise this practice.

3. A Correlation between IT and IQ

Nettelbeck & Lally (1976) were the first to report a correlation between IT and IQ. The aim of their study was to test an idea, previously advanced by several authors but picked up from Savage (1970: 37), that low IQs associated with mental retardation may reflect slow "mental speed". A small sample ($N = 10$) was necessary because of the clumsy and time consuming procedures followed at that time and to maximize any IT-IQ relationship the sample was deliberately selected to provide a very wide range of IQ; it spanned 72 points. Although this method obviously inflated any correlation existing between IT and IQ in a normally distributed population, the outcomes in excess of $r = -0.9$ between IT and Performance IQ (PIQ) from the Wechsler Adult Intelligence Scale (WAIS) startled many, including the authors.

Along with Christopher Brand at Edinburgh University, Arthur Jensen at the University of California, Berkeley was quick to appreciate the potential of this initial report. His interest having been triggered by Eysenck's (1967) theoretical account of the importance of mental speed to intelligence, Jensen had already established a chronometric laboratory in his department based substantially on the Hick procedure that tests RT as a function of stimulus-response choice (Jensen & Munro 1974). In the late 1970s Jensen included IT as an adjunct procedure. Jensen (1982: 120) reported a correlation of –0.31 between IT and Raven's matrices, obtained by Tony Vernon (now at the University of Western Ontario) with a sample of 25 university students. However, this promising outcome was not replicated by Vernon (1983), for whose sample of 50 university students the IT-WAIS Full Scale IQ correlation was near zero.

Brand & Deary (1982) were early convinced that IT was capable of accounting for 60% and higher variance in IQ, providing that highly reliable measuring procedures could be developed and a fully representative, normal distribution for IQ was available. Deary has long since revised his opinion about this effect size (e.g. "somewhere between [negative] 0.3 and 0.5", Deary 2000: 188) but Brand has continued to support a substantially higher value ("around –0.75", Brand 1996: 86). Sitting plumb in the middle of this range, Nettelbeck (1987) concluded on the basis of his review of 29 studies (the majority at Adelaide or Edinburgh) that 16 of these addressed the IT-IQ correlation without including participants with mental retardation who tended to inflate outcome, and that the best estimate for an effect size corrected for restricted range in IQ was –0.5 (without correction –0.35).

Kranzler & Jensen (1989) subsequently carried out a series of meta-analyses of 31 studies that provided a database of more than 1,100 participants without mental retardation. Four studies involved auditory or tactile versions of IT but numbers for these were too small to warrant separate analyses. Kranzler and Jensen's results essentially supported Nettelbeck's (1987) conclusions. The overall uncorrected average correlation between IT and "general" IQ was –0.29. After correcting for sampling and measurement error and for restricted range of IQ, Kranzler and Jensen's best estimates for the effect size were –0.49 overall, –0.54 for adults and –0.47 for children. Meta-analyses of a subset of 25 studies that excluded those identified by Nettelbeck (1987) as having serious methodological deficiencies returned marginally larger corrected effect sizes of –0.56 and –0.59 for adults and children, respectively.

Most recently, Grudnik & Kranzler (2001) have replicated these estimates on an extended and updated sample of about 4,200 participants in 92 studies; 62 with adults and 30 with children. Across all studies, including some for auditory IT, the uncorrected mean effect size was –0.30. Corrected values were –0.51 overall, –0.51 with adults and –0.44 with children. The outcomes for visual and auditory IT separately were –0.49 and –0.58, respectively. A word of caution about these average correlations is warranted because, prior to correction for artifactual effects, the 95% confidence intervals for most meta-analyses contained zero correlation. Nonetheless, the size of this sample, built up across several laboratories using somewhat different procedures, is considerable. A reasonable conclusion, after some 25 years of investigation into this association, is that there is a moderately strong correlation between IT and IQ. As Jensen (1998, ch. 8) has noted, these effect sizes with IT are higher than any achieved by the application of choice RT. What this might mean, however, is another matter.

4. The Nature of Inspection Time

According to the original conception, IT was thought of as a discrete, constant duration in time that determined the rate at which proximal stimulation could be sampled, thereby setting a limit on speed of information processing early within the visual system (Vickers *et al.* 1972). Brand (1996) has consistently supported this view. Based on his assumption that differences in speed of early apprehension of input are the major cause of differences in intelligence, he predicted that correlations between IT and *g* would be stronger among persons with lower IQ, for whom there is less differentiation in specific abilities (Brand 1996). However, apart from those studies that provided the basis for his discussion of this matter (Brand 1996: 81–82), his prediction finds no support from other quarters. Kranzler & Jensen (1989) found virtually the same correlations between IT and PIQ from the Wechsler scales among both mentally retarded and non-retarded adults. Similarly, Nettelbeck & Kirby (1983) found about the same IT-IQ correlations (–0.3) among samples with IQs above and below IQ 80, where the IQ range for 185 adults was from 40 to 130.

In any case, the position of Vickers *et al.* (1972) has been challenged on grounds that on a number of counts IT is psychologically complex and the particular measuring procedures involved do not have special status (Levy 1992; White 1996). In particular, White (1996) argued that, as with other backward masking tasks, the psychophysical function describing typical performance accuracy as a function of increasing SOA would be found to include two discernible stages. Burns *et al.* (1998) subsequently tested this prediction, finding strong support. Chance levels of performance accuracy did not improve until SOAs were beyond about 10 ms and longer. Beyond this initial "lag", performance improved rapidly as SOAs were lengthened. Thus, instead of a single outcome measure (i.e. IT), there were two; the lag to improving performance at very brief SOAs might reflect focused attention or vigilance, for example, whereas the rate of accrual parameter could reflect a different psychological function, like capacity to detect change in a briefly exposed visual array — in other words, speed of perception, or "stimulus apprehension" as Jensen (1998: 251) has termed this capacity. One recent investigation of latent characteristics underpinning IT measurement is consistent with the perceptual speed interpretation. Deary *et al.* (1997) examined the differences between performances on IT, on two tasks designed to measure detection of change in a visual array under time constraints, and on a measure of contrast sensitivity without any time restriction. Whereas the latter task, which would require the same levels of compliance with instructions, motivation and so on as the others, did not correlate with IQ, the other three tasks that required processing of very briefly available information all correlated about −0.5 with IQ; and moderately to strongly with each other.

These findings are not inconsistent with Jensen's speculations about what IT measures. Although he has long been committed to the theory that it is the efficiency of some general property of neural transmission that causes or at least is substantially responsible for individual differences in general cognitive ability (Jensen 1982), his account of this has remained sufficiently flexible to accommodate the possibility that different chronometric procedures may tap different psychological constructs (Jensen 1998). Thus, he has speculated that IT may principally measure speed of apprehension, whereas choice RT may make more demands on discrimination and encoding; and, with even more complex chronometric procedures, working memory may become increasingly involved (Jensen 1998: 252). Moreover, consistent with Gf-Gc theory, he has emphasized the important difference between speed in intellectually undemanding circumstances (Gs) and speed that he equates with mental power (e.g. Correct Decision Speed, Horn & Noll 1997).

Jensen's cognitive model of information processing components (see Jensen 1998: 251) includes the critical importance of focused attention to cognitive efficiency. Consistent with this, Nettelbeck (2001) has speculated that IT may be sensitive to low-level strategic capacities that, although intrinsic in the sense that they are not driven by conscious intent, set limits on executive capabilities. This idea was intended to accord with the efficiency of some basic attentional mechanism and to be fundamentally different therefore from suggestions that better IT performance is simply the outcome of higher intelligence, which provides access to more effective cognitive strategies in all manner of tasks (Mackintosh 1981), or of some other mediating variable, like task motivation (Howe 1990). In fact, although it is very difficult to disprove such influences absolutely, a number of versions of these ideas have been explored, without finding any support for them (Egan 1994; Simpson & Deary 1997; Stough *et al.* 1996). Moreover, although it is undoubtedly the case that some participants in IT studies have been able to utilize cues of apparent movement when the backward pattern mask overwrites the target figure, there is no evidence that this capacity is related to IQ (e.g. Mackenzie & Bingham 1985). Nonetheless, there is still little empirical evidence to support Nettelbeck's suggestion. As Levy (1992) emphasized, the possible contribution of various attentional factors to IT performance had not been thoroughly explored at that time and that is still so. In fact, as Deary (2000) has stressed, there has as yet been very little progress in identifying and understanding the psychological or biological processes that support IT.

It is even possible that processes reflected in IT are either different in different populations or produce differential effects for different groups. For example, Nettelbeck & Kirby (1983) found that when their participants were subdivided into two groups, above and below IQ 80, the IT estimates from low IQ participants were disproportionately slower than those from higher IQ participants. In other words, although IT-IQ regression slopes were about the same in both groups, the regression intercept was markedly higher for the low IQ group; an additive effect. A possible explanation is that IT is more sensitive to distractibility among lower IQ participants. In principle, of course, any distraction, either immediately prior to the appearance of the target figure or following the appearance of the masking figure, has potential to increase errors on this kind of task and one can readily appreciate why some mentally retarded persons — or even very young children or very elderly persons — might do less well on an IT task because of less focused attention. For example, as found by Lally & Nettelbeck (1980) for mentally retarded participants, more demanding response selection requirements can result in higher error rates and therefore longer estimates for IT. However, besides such an obvious influence, IT is probably sensitive to a number of different psychological functions.

It also seems probable that whatever role speed of processing plays for determining individual differences in intelligence is more important during old age and during childhood development than during young and middle-aged adulthood. Thus, like Jensen (e.g. 1982), Salthouse (1985) has afforded speed of information processing a primary causal influence on the quality of general ability. However, Salthouse has been concerned exclusively with a theory of cognitive ageing. His critical propositions have been, first, that slower processing speed is a generally inevitable consequence of normal old age. Secondly, slower speed of processing directly impairs general cognitive ability. Thirdly, the decline to general cognitive ability causes more specific abilities (other than well learned crystallized capabilities) to decline also. Thus, if Salthouse's theory is correct, then processing speed as tapped by IT may occupy an important causal role — but not necessarily sufficient (Wilson *et al.* 1992) — for explaining the nature of intelligence. Of course, it is possible that IT taps different aspects of information processing among elderly persons than among younger adults; and in any case the situation may also be quite different among children. Hints that this could be so are found in different patterns of correlations between IT and different combinations of Wechsler subscales for different age groups. Thus Kranzler & Jensen's meta-analyses (1989) found that, unlike the results from adult samples where IT-PIQ correlation typically exceeds IT-Verbal IQ (VIQ) correlation, IT correlations with PIQ and VIQ among children were about the same size; although there were appreciably fewer studies with children than with adults, from which to draw conclusions. Similarly, Nettelbeck & Rabbitt (1992; $N = 104$ adults aged 55 to 85 years) reported correlations between IT and WAIS PIQ subtests that were appreciably stronger (uncorrected average $r = -0.61$) than has typically been found with younger adults (c.f. Kranzler & Jensen 1989, -0.45 for "adults").

These are issues that require further research. Nonetheless, Salthouse (1996) has found strong evidence for his theory that old age directly affects general cognitive ability, which in turn influences group factors or specific abilities, rather than age influencing these directly. And there is one dataset that implicates IT as an index for speed of processing and supports the possibility that processing speed fulfills a causal role in shaping individual differences in general cognitive ability. Nettelbeck & Rabbitt

(1992) set out to test Salthouse's prediction that all age-related cognitive decline is mediated by speed of processing. Although Nettelbeck and Rabbitt's results provided strong support on the whole for Salthouse's prediction, their interpretation focused on an exception, whereby an aspect of long term memory performance was not mediated by speed. However, Deary (2000: 244–246) has re-analyzed Nettelbeck and Rabbitt's data using structural equation modeling. His finding was that processing speed (defined in part by IT) acted as a mediator variable between age and a general factor. Although intriguing, however, this was not the only plausible interpretation from this re-analysis. The general factor was derived from just three WAIS PIQ subtests and all shared substantial age-related variance to about the same extent and there was a very high relationship between the speed of processing latent trait and the general factor. Thus, rather than being mediated through general cognitive ability, age may have simply affected everything to about the same extent. Again, this is an issue for future research. Nonetheless, Deary's re-analysis has demonstrated one way in which speed of processing might cause individual differences in multiple abilities, by directly influencing general cognitive ability. A test of this idea involving a large sample of elderly participants and large psychometric and chronometric batteries to define all relevant constructs adequately is not difficult to envisage.

If one assumes that old age is accompanied by some reduction to brain efficiency that slows rate of information processing to about the same extent for everyone, irrespective of prior adulthood capacities, then performance in old age should be predicted by younger age performance but with the former a constant multiple of the latter. This is what Cerella (1985) and others have found for RT comparisons and this outcome is consistent with Salthouse's (1996) theory. Jensen (1998) has speculated about how loss of myelin within the central nervous system (CNS) might contribute to slower rate of information processing in old age. Noting also Kail's (1991) report that children's RTs are well predicted by adult levels to which a constant is added, Jensen has pointed out that this is what would be predicted by increasing CNS myelination during childhood development. This theory is plausible in light of what is currently known about changes in myelination during the life span and how myelination contributes to speed of nerve conduction, although at the present time there is no direct evidence linking physiological status to speed on chronometric tasks like IT or RT. However, whatever aspects of neural activities are eventually found to be responsible for these universal changes to intellectual capacities, the bases of individual differences within any age cohort may be independent from such changes and require separate explanation. This is the point emphasized by Anderson (1992), whose theory is based on the proposition that individual differences within age cohorts (IQ) and improving capacities across childhood (Mental Age) are driven by separate mechanisms. Anderson's attempt to implicate IT as a measure of an inborn, stable, basic processing capacity has raised important theoretical issues that have scarcely yet been addressed. Anderson's (1992) monograph did not extend beyond a theory of childhood development to include questions about old age but it is obviously possible that mechanisms responsible for intellectual decline during old age could be different from those involved in childhood developmental improvement. Again, these are important issues for future research.

5. Inspection Time and Psychometric Abilities

As outlined above, Jensen's view (1982, 1998) is that IT taps fundamental processes that underpin general cognitive ability. This may well be so, although on present evidence the IT-IQ relationship, at least for normal young adults, may reflect the speed of processes used in relatively undemanding circumstances, rather than speed involved with abstract problem solving and other intellectually demanding circumstances, as has previously been supposed by several researchers (Deary & Stough 1996; Jensen 1998; Nettelbeck 1987). Currently, the most comprehensive definition of psychometric intelligence against which to test the role of IT is that provided by Carroll (1993a). His comprehensive analyses of 461 large psychometric datasets, each screened to meet stringent inclusion criteria, have returned a hierarchical "three stratum" model. This has a large number of specific abilities at the first level but, because these were only relatively independent from one another, they combined to define some nine factors at the second level. These are effectively the same broad factors promoted by Gf-Gc theory (Horn & Noll 1997). However, Carroll's analysis found some common variance at this level also, thereby supporting a general cognitive factor at the third level, which accounted for substantial variance in all of the tests involved. A question, still unresolved although there are some leads, is where within this hierarchy should IT be located?

Kranzler & Jensen's (1989) meta-analyses confirmed an early observation by Nettelbeck & Lally (1976), noting that, among those studies using Wechsler Adult Intelligence Scales (WAIS: WAIS-R), stronger correlations have generally been found between IT and PIQ than with VIQ. Kranzler and Jensen's best estimates for effect sizes were −0.44 and −0.32 for IT with PIQ and VIQ, respectively. Deary (1993; $N = 87$ adults) has since supported this outcome, reporting a reliably higher IT-PIQ correlation (−0.42), compared with IT-VIQ (−0.19).

Consistent with earlier widely accepted interpretations of WAIS structure, this outcome has been taken to support a suggestion that IT reflects fluid abilities (Nettelbeck 1987), although Kranzler & Jensen (1989) early suggested that IT appeared to measure perceptual organization, as well as a general factor. Crawford *et al.* (1998; $N = 184$ adults) also found that IT loaded strongly on a perceptual organization factor (−0.39), which was defined principally by the Block Design and Object Assembly WAIS-R subtests; and less so on a general factor (−0.19).

McGrew's (1997) recent analysis of WAIS and WAIS-R in terms of Gf-Gc theory offers a different approach to investigating the association between IT and psychometric structures. McGrew concluded that the Wechsler PIQ scale measures the psychometric constructs processing speed (Gs; measured in intellectually undemanding tasks) and visual processing (Gv; a similar construct to perceptual organization); but not fluid reasoning (Gf). Following this suggestion, Burns *et al.* (1999; $N = 64$ adults) attempted to locate IT in terms of Gf-Gc theory. They found that IT correlated significantly with a marker test for Gs (−0.43) but not with a marker for Gf (−0.18). Most recently, Nettelbeck & Burns (2000, April; $N = 90$ adults) have confirmed this result. They found that IT loaded strongly on a well-defined Gs factor but not on Gf. However, IT also shared about 20% variance with a strong general cognitive factor. Taken together with research that has investigated decline in cognitive capabilities among elderly people, this result suggests one way in which speed of information processing may impact on human intelligence.

A further consideration at this point is how the measure IT can be applied to exploring whether general cognitive ability defined by psychometric tests is necessarily also unitary at a psychological level of explanation. There is no reason why this should be so and several theories have been based on the idea that a general psychometric factor may reflect the extent to which all cognitive activities either sample from a range of elementary processes or draw on the same basic functions, but to different degrees, depending upon specific circumstances (Detterman 1982; Humphreys 1979; Snow 1986; Thomson 1939). When describing Vernon's early correlational study ($N = 25$ university students) of IT and Raven's matrices, Jensen (1982: 120) noted that the prediction of the Raven score by chronometric means was significantly increased by adding a choice RT variable to the regression of IT on Raven. In other words, the different speed measures each made a unique contribution to the predicted outcome, suggesting that RT and IT were each measuring different relevant psychological processes to some extent.

Kranzler & Jensen (1991a) subsequently followed up this lead, by examining the performance of 101 university students on a test battery that included IT and various RT measures, as well as Raven's Advanced Progressive Matrices and the full Multi-dimensional Aptitude Battery (MAB), a group test designed to assess the same abilities as WAIS-R (Jackson 1984). With the exception of IT, the other chronometric procedures permitted separation of a decision time from a movement time component. Different RT tasks were designed to operationalize rate and efficiency of processing in relatively straight forward choice situations, the speed of visual search and of short-term and long-term memory retrieval, and speed of spatial discrimination (the "odd-man-out" procedure devised by Frearson & Eysenck 1986).

Kranzler and Jensen concluded that their psychometrically defined general cognitive ability factor was psychologically complex. It was made up of four relatively independent components that corresponded with their chronometric measures for choice RT, short and long-term memory retrieval and IT. Each component contributed significantly to variance in general cognitive ability. However, commenting on their analysis, Carroll (1991a, 1991b, 1993b) disagreed with Kranzler and Jensen's interpretation (see also Kranzler & Jensen 1991b, 1993 for an exchange of opinions about interpretation). Instead, Carroll presented a unitary factor solution based on a single factor analysis of all variables, which identified a strong second order general factor defined by all the MAB subtests and the decision components of the various RT tasks, together with IT. There was also a second general factor loaded by the movement times from those chronometric tasks that included separate decision and movement times. Carroll acknowledged, however, that because the mainly decision components of the chronometric measures loaded together with the psychometric tests on the general cognitive factor, this tended to highlight the importance to general cognitive ability of the speed and consistency of information processes. Nonetheless, he also emphasized that the general factor defined by this data set differed from the factor that more commonly emerged from batteries of exclusively psychometric tests, instead reflecting the large number of chronometric tasks in this battery. As Jensen (1998) has pointed out, however, argument about the extent to which any derived *g* factor is more or less "pure" (i.e. not contaminated by including non-*g* tests in the battery) cannot serve much empirical purpose while it remains ultimately impossible to define with complete confidence those tests that should or should not be included in a battery.

The study by Nettelbeck & Burns (2000, April) referred to above included the odd-man-out RT procedure, as well as two versions of IT and another backward masking task. Whereas both IT versions and the backward masking task loaded on Gs, the contribution of the decision component from the odd-man-out task was different; it loaded strongly on Gf. This outcome was therefore consistent with Jensen's (1982: 120) account of Vernon's early study that found separate contributions from IT and RT to the Raven score, commonly accepted as a good test of cognitive ability (Jensen 1998). It was also consistent with Kranzler and Jensen's (1991a) finding that IT and other chronometric tasks made separate contributions to general cognitive ability.

One more study is relevant to this discussion of the contribution that speed of processing might make to intelligence. A recent large-scale investigation ($N = 179$ university students) by Roberts & Stankov (1999) included a large psychometric test battery of 25 tests to define six broad factors within Gf-Gc theory. Twelve of these tests were timed and there were also 11 additional chronometric measures. In addition to recovering the expected broad psychometric factors defining Gf-Gc theory, and a higher-order general cognitive ability factor, as predicted by Carroll (1993b), Roberts and Stankov's analyses identified nine different speed factors that combined at a higher level to form three broad factors. They labeled these Correct Decision Speed (i.e. speed on intellectually challenging tasks), Psychometric Speed (i.e. Gs) and Response Speed (i.e. motor). These results therefore confirmed that various kinds of speed contribute to an understanding of intelligence. However, by this account speed was not unitary; and the different types of speed could not be combined to provide a sufficient account for general cognitive ability.

6. Conclusions

Although the links are not yet understood, some 25 years of research with IT have confirmed that this measure taps low-level aspects of psychological processes that contribute to general cognitive ability. Essentially, IT appears to capture individual differences in capacity to detect change in a very briefly exposed visual array. However, whether this capacity is properly described as speed of apprehension, in the sense of some fundamental perceptual capacity, is by no means clear. In fact, on current evidence there must now be considerable doubt about whether the measure IT reflects a single mechanism, as was initially proposed, or whether a number of different functions are involved. For example, IT is probably sensitive to focused attention and can be shown also under some circumstances to reflect decision processes that must continue beyond the onset of the masking figure that defines the termination of an IT trial. Thus far, these are issues that seem most important when estimating IT among persons with an intellectual disability. Nonetheless, it is also possible that for measures made outside of this group, IT is psychologically complex.

There are also signs that different chronometric tasks may reflect other psychological processes than those indexed by IT, and that these too may be equally important to the psychological description of psychometric intelligence. Nonetheless there are many inconsistencies across the studies reviewed in the foregoing account. In part, some of these differences may turn out to be allied with whether participants are children, younger adults or elderly adults. RT studies have raised the possibility that RT taps different psychological processes in different age groups during childhood and old age. The same possibility exists for IT. Irrespective of what is found with young adults, it is possible that the psychological bases for an IT-IQ correlation among elderly persons or for children or adolescents will turn out to be different. At least among normal young adults, the correlation of IT with general cognitive ability may be mediated by speed processes involved in performance that is less intellectually demanding, rather than by speed required under more demanding circumstances. However, this is an issue that requires further research to confirm or disconfirm it.

Also most researchers have continued to rely heavily on university students as participants, thereby severely restricting the range of abilities involved. However, as Deary (2000) has emphasized the major issue that drives all of these considerations remains the psychological and biological bases to IT and other chronometric tasks. Researchers have as yet scarcely begun to address the problem of adequately addressing the construct validity of the various chronometric tasks that they devise to measure putative underlying psychological processes. It remains the case that, as yet for any specified population, no one can confidently identify exactly what IT is measuring.

Although Jensen's investigations of RTs and their correlations with psychometric abilities have more widely been recognized, he has made substantial contributions to IT research, particularly regards the size of the IT-IQ correlation. Thus, his analyses with Kranzler determined that the correlation between IT and general cognitive ability is around −0.5, an effect size larger than has been found for any single parameter of RT. Again with Kranzler he was also at the forefront of attempts to apply IT, along with other chronometric measures, to exploring the psychological bases to psychometric general cognitive ability. This work has been influential in advancing the proposition that although general cognitive ability is unitary at the psychometric level of explanation, it is not unitary at the psychological level.

References

Anderson, M. (1992). *Intelligence and development: A cognitive theory.* Oxford, U.K.: Blackwell.

Brand, C. R. (1996). *The g factor.* Chichester, U.K.: Wiley.

Brand, C., & Deary, I. J. (1982). Intelligence and "inspection time". In: H. J. Eysenck (Ed.), *A model for intelligence* (pp. 133–148). Berlin: Springer-Verlag.

Burns, N. R., Nettelbeck, T., & Cooper, C. J. (1999). Inspection time correlates with general speed of processing but not with fluid ability. *Intelligence, 27,* 37–44.

Burns, N. R., Nettelbeck, T., & White, M. (1998). Testing the interpretation of inspection time as a measure of sensory processing. *Personality and Individual Differences, 24,* 25–39.

Carroll, J. B. (1991a). No demonstration that *g* is not unitary, but there's more to the story: Comment on Kranzler and Jensen. *Intelligence, 15*, 423–436.

Carroll, J. B. (1991b). Still no demonstration that *g* is not unitary: Further comment on Kranzler and Jensen. *Intelligence, 15*, 449–453.

Carroll, J. B. (1993a). *Human cognitive abilities: A survey of factor analytic studies*. Cambridge, U.K.: Cambridge University Press.

Carroll, J. B. (1993b). The unitary *g* problem once more: On Kranzler and Jensen. *Intelligence, 17*, 15–16.

Cerella, J. (1985). Information processing rates in the elderly. *Psychological Bulletin, 98*, 67–83.

Crawford, J. R., Deary, I. J., Allan, K. M., & Gustafsson, J-E. (1998). Evaluating competing models of the relationship between inspection time and psychometric intelligence. *Intelligence, 26*, 27–42.

Das, J. P., Kirby, J. R., & Jarman, R. F. (1978). *Simultaneous and successive cognitive processes*. New York: Academic Press.

Deary, I. J. (1993). Inspection time and WAIS-R IQ subtypes: A confirmatory factor analysis study. *Intelligence, 17*, 223–236.

Deary, I. J. (2000). *Looking down on human intelligence: From psychophysics to the brain*. Oxford, U.K.: Oxford University Press.

Deary, I. J., McCrimmon, R. J., & Bradshaw, J. (1997). Visual information processing and intelligence. *Intelligence, 24*, 461–479.

Deary, I. J., & Stough, C. (1996). Intelligence and inspection time: Achievements, prospects and problems. *American Psychologist, 51*, 599–608.

Detterman, D. K. (1982). Does *g* exist? *Intelligence, 6*, 99–108.

Egan, V. (1994). Intelligence, inspection time and cognitive strategies. *British Journal of Psychology, 85*, 305–316.

Evans, G., & Nettelbeck, T. (1993). Inspection time: A flash mask to reduce apparent movement effects. *Personality and Individual Differences, 15*, 91–94.

Eysenck, H. J. (1967). Intelligence assessment: A theoretical and experimental approach. *British Journal of Educational Psychology, 37*, 81–98.

Frearson, W., & Eysenck, H. J. (1986). Intelligence, reaction time (RT) and a new 'odd-man-out' RT paradigm. *Personality and Individual Differences, 7*, 807–817.

Grudnik, J. L., & Kranzler, J. H. (2001). Meta-analysis of the relationship between intelligence and inspection time. *Intelligence, 29*, 525–537.

Horn, J. L., & Noll, J. (1997). Human cognitive abilities: Gf-Gc theory. In: D. P. Flanagan, J. L. Genshaft, & P. T. Harris (Eds), *Contemporary intellectual assessment: Theories, tests, and issues* (pp. 53–91). New York: Guilford Press.

Howe, M. J. A. (1990). Does intelligence exist? *The Psychologist, 3*, 490–493.

Humphreys, L. G. (1979). The construct of general intelligence. *Intelligence, 3*, 105–120.

Jackson, D. N. (1984). *Multidimensional aptitude test battery manual*. Port Huron, MI: Research Psychologists Press.

Jensen, A. R. (1982). Reaction time and psychometric *g*. In: H. J. Eysenck (Ed.), *A model for intelligence* (pp. 93–132). Berlin: Springer-Verlag.

Jensen, A. R. (1998). *The g factor: The science of mental ability*. New York: Praeger.

Jensen, A. R., & Munro, E. (1974). Reaction time, movement time and intelligence. *Intelligence, 3*, 121–126.

Kail, R. (1991). Development of processing speed in childhood and adolescence. In: H. W. Reese (Ed.), *Advances in child development and behavior* (Vol. 23, pp. 151–185). New York: Academic Press.

Kranzler, J. H., & Jensen, A. R. (1989). Inspection time and intelligence: A meta-analysis. *Intelligence, 13,* 329–347.

Kranzler, J. H., & Jensen, A. R. (1991a). The nature of psychometric *g*: Unitary process or a number of independent processes. *Intelligence, 15,* 397–422.

Kranzler, J. H., & Jensen, A. R. (1991b). Unitary *g*: Unquestioned postulate or empirical fact? *Intelligence, 15,* 437–448.

Kranzler, J. H., & Jensen, A. R. (1993). Psychometric *g* is still not unitary after eliminating supposed "impurities": Further comments on Carroll. *Intelligence, 17,* 11–14.

Lally, M., & Nettelbeck, T. (1980). Intelligence, inspection time, and response strategy. *American Journal of Mental Deficiency, 84,* 553–560.

Levy, P. (1992). Inspection time and its relation to intelligence: Issues of measurement and meaning. *Personality and Individual Differences, 13,* 987–1002.

MacKenzie, B., & Bingham, E. (1985). IQ, inspection time and response strategies in a university sample. *Australian Journal of Psychology, 37,* 257–268.

Mackintosh, N. J. (1981). A new measure of intelligence? *Nature, 289,* 529–530.

McGrew, K. S. (1997). Analysis of the major intelligence batteries according to a proposed comprehensive Gf-Gc framework. In: D. P. Flanagan, J. L. Genshaft, & P. T. Harris (Eds), *Contemporary intellectual assessment: Theories, tests, and issues* (pp. 151–179). New York: Guilford Press.

Nettelbeck, T. (1987). Inspection time and intelligence: In: P. A. Vernon (Ed.), *Speed of information processing and intelligence* (pp. 295–346). Norwood, NJ: Ablex.

Nettelbeck, T. (1998). Jensen's chronometric research: Neither simple nor sufficient but a good place to start. *Intelligence, 26,* 233–241.

Nettelbeck, T. (2001). Correlation between inspection time and psychometric abilities: A personal interpretation. *Intelligence, 29,* 459–474.

Nettelbeck, T., & Burns, N. R. (2000, April). Reductionism and "intelligence": The case of inspection time. Paper presented at the Australasian Experimental Psychology Conference, Noosa, Queensland, Australia.

Nettelbeck, T., & Kirby, N. H. (1983). Retarded-nonretarded differences in speed of processing. *Australian Journal of Psychology, 35,* 445–453.

Nettelbeck, T., & Lally, M. (1976). Inspection time and measured intelligence. *British Journal of Psychology, 67,* 17–22.

Nettelbeck, T., & Rabbitt, P. M. A. (1992). Age, intelligence, and speed. *Intelligence, 16,* 189–205.

Roberts, R. D., & Stankov, L. (1999). Individual differences in speed of mental processing and human cognitive abilities: Towards a taxonomic model. *Learning and Individual Differences, 11,* 1–120.

Salthouse, T. A. (1985). *A theory of cognitive aging.* Amsterdam: North Holland.

Salthouse, T. A. (1996). The processing speed theory of adult age differences in cognition. *Psychological Review, 103,* 403–428.

Savage, R. D. (1970). Intellectual assessment. In: P. Mittler (Ed.), *The psychological assessment of mental and physical handicaps* (pp. 29–81). London: Methuen.

Simpson, C. R., & Deary, I. J. (1997). Strategy use and feedback in inspection time. *Personality and Individual Differences, 23,* 787–797.

Snow, R. E. (1986). On intelligence. In: R. J. Sternberg, & D. K. Detterman (Eds), *What is intelligence? Contemporary viewpoints on its nature and definition* (pp. 133–139). Norwood, NJ: Ablex.

Stough, C., Brebner, J., Nettelbeck, T., Cooper, C. J., Bates, T., & Mangan, G. L. (1996). The relationship between intelligence, personality and inspection time. *British Journal of Psychology, 81*, 255–268.

Thomson, G. H. (1939). *The factorial analysis of human ability.* London: University of London Press.

Vernon, P. A. (1983). Speed of information processing and general intelligence. *Intelligence, 7*, 53–70.

Vickers, D., Nettelbeck, T., & Willson, R. J. (1972). Perceptual indices of performance: the measurement of "inspection time" and "noise" in the visual system. *Perception, 1*, 263–295.

White, M. (1996). Interpreting inspection time as a measure of the speed of sensory processing. *Personality and Individual Differences, 20*, 351–363.

Wilson, C., Nettelbeck, T., Turnbull, C., & Young, R. (1992). IT, IQ and age: a comparison of developmental function. *British Journal of Developmental Psychology, 10*, 179–188.

Chapter 6

Factors Influencing the Relationship Between Brain Size and Intelligence

Gilles Gignac, Philip A. Vernon and John C. Wickett

1. Introduction

With the publication of Jensen & Sinha's (1993) book chapter, "Physical Correlates of Human Intelligence," the psychological community was given the most extensive review of the topic. In Eysenck's (1994) review of the chapter, he writes, "... the coverage, discussion and theoretical sophistication are impressive; nothing like it has appeared in print before" (p. 657). In fact, it is now almost 10 years later and, although there have been smaller, more up-to-date reviews published, none have likely made as large an impact.

The review has a substantial emphasis on genetics. It is considered important, for theoretical reasons, argue Jensen & Sinha (1993), to determine whether the correlation between a physiological variable and intelligence is mediated simply by environmental causes. This can be determined by estimating the within-family as well as the between-family correlation between two variables. If a correlation can be found only between-families, then the correlation has likely arisen due to sociological factors, such as cross-assortive mating. A good example is the correlation between height and intelligence (Jensen & Sinha 1993).

The N-weighted mean correlation between height and IQ is reported by Jensen & Sinha (1993) to be 0.23. The within-family correlation, however, is estimated to be essentially zero. Jensen & Sinha (1993) also note that the trend appears to be that more recent studies (i.e. 1951–1979) have found larger between-family correlations than those reported in an early review by Paterson (1930). Jensen & Sinha (1993) interpret this finding as consistent with an increase in assortive mating for height and intelligence. Thus, even though it is a significant physical correlate of intelligence, height cannot be expected to reveal anything about the essential nature of mental abilities.

The largest section of the Jensen & Sinha (1993) chapter is devoted to the head/brain size and IQ literature. They conclude that the correlation between brain size and IQ is not less than 0.2 and may be considerably higher, but this could not then be determined,

The Scientific Study of General Intelligence: Tribute to Arthur R. Jensen
Copyright © 2003 by Elsevier Science Ltd.
All rights of reproduction in any form reserved.
ISBN: 0-08-043793-1

because the correlation between brain size and external cranial capacity, controlling for body height, had yet to be established firmly (Jensen & Sinha 1993). This question is no longer an issue. At the time of writing their chapter, only one magnetic resonance imaging (MRI) and IQ study had been conducted. Since that time, the area of brain size and IQ has been revolutionized by the very consistent results that this new technology has afforded. The most important issue now appears to be whether the correlation can be found within-families. If it cannot, the significance of the correlation will have to be re-evaluated.

By reviewing approximately the last decade's research in the area of brain volume and IQ, it will become apparent that there can be little question that brain volume is correlated positively with intelligence. Future directions for the area will be suggested. Also, the notion that white matter volume is a more substantial mediator of intelligence than grey matter volume will be discussed. It will be argued, from the existing data, that this argument is untenable, but that there may be particular qualities of white matter, other than volume, that may be contributors to intelligence. The method of correlated vectors will also be reviewed in the context of brain volume and intelligence. Finally, the possibility that there may be a causal relationship between brain volume and IQ will be assessed.

2. Brain Volume and Intelligence

The history of head size and IQ studies should be regarded as superseded greatly by the studies that have used magnetic resonance imaging (MRI) to quantify brain volume. In fact, head size as a proxy for brain size is far from perfect, with validity coefficients reported to be in the area of 0.7, when using calipers (Tan *et al.* 1999; Wickett *et al.* 2000), and as low as 0.23, when using a tape measure (Wickett 1992). The number of brain volume and IQ studies that have used neurologically normal subjects and an established measure of cognitive ability is now up to 14 and consists of a combined total sample size of 858 subjects. There now seems little doubt that brain volume correlates with IQ at approximately 0.40. Of the 14 studies, all but one has obtained a positive correlation close to 0.4 (see Table 6.1).

The only study that did not find the expected positive correlation is that of Tramo *et al.* (1998). Their subject sample consisted of 10 pairs of MZ twins. Assuming that the true correlation between brain volume and IQ is in the area of 0.4, it is clear that a study of this size should be considered inadequate in terms of power.

In a sample of 48 healthy adults, Egan *et al.* (1994) found a correlation of 0.32 between brain volume and IQ (WAIS-R). The correlation rose to 0.48, once corrected for restriction in IQ range (Egan *et al.* 1995). It was also found that white matter volume correlated more substantially (0.27) with full-scale IQ (FSIQ) than grey matter volume (0.08, ns). Thus, based on this study, it appears that white matter volume may be carrying the majority of the effect between brain volume and IQ. This differential effect is possible, because grey matter volume and white matter volume were themselves found to correlate only moderately (0.52). This issue will be discussed more fully below.

Table 6.1: Brain volume and IQ literature using neurologically normal subjects and established psychometric tests.

Study	*N*	Age characteristics	IQ test	*r*[a]
Willerman *et al.* (1991)	40	mean = 18.9 (SD = 0.6)	WAIS-R	0.35
Andreason *et al.* (1993)	67	mean = 38 (SD = 16)	WAIS-R	0.38
Raz *et al.* (1993)	29	mean = 43.8 (SD = 21.5)	CFIT	0.43
Egan *et al.* (1994)	48	mean = 22.5 (SD = 5)	WAIS-R	0.32 (0.48)
Wickett *et al.* (1994)	40	range = 20 to 30	MAB	0.40 (0.54)
Reiss *et al.* (1996)	69	range = 5 to 17	WISC-R[b]	0.40
Flashman *et al.* (1998)	90	mean = 27 (SD = 10)	WAIS-R	0.25 (0.31)[c]
Tramo *et al.* (1998)	20	median = 34 (24 to 43)	WAIS-R	–0.05
Gur *et al.* (1999)	80	mean = 26 (SD = 5.5)	various	0.41
Tan *et al.* (1999)	103	range = 18 to 26	CFIT	0.40
Wickett *et al.* (2000)	68	range = 20 to 35	MAB	0.35 (0.51)
Pennington *et al.* (2000)	36	mean = 19 (SD = 3.7)	WISC-R/ WAIS-R	0.31 (0.46)
Pennington *et al.* (2000)	96	mean = 17 (SD = 4.1)	WISC-R/ WAIS-R	0.42 (0.57)
Schoenemann *et al.* (2000)	72	mean = 23 (SD = 5.1)	'*g*'	0.45

N = 858
Unweighted mean *r* = 0.35 (0.41)
N-weighted mean *r* = 0.37 (0.43)

[a] Correlations in parentheses are corrected for restriction in IQ score range.
[b] Reiss (2000), personal communication.
[c] Corrected for restriction in IQ score range by the first author using Guilford & Fruchter (1978).

Of particular note is that a serendipitous correlation of 0.60 was found between cerebral spinal fluid (CSF) and FSIQ (Egan *et al.* 1994). Because CSF and total brain volume were found to correlate only at 0.30, CSF should be regarded as a unique predictor of FSIQ. A possible explanation of the CSF/IQ correlation is that CSF volume is a proxy for cortical surface area (Egan *et al.* 1995). That is, the human brain is extensively convoluted and CSF fills the subarachnoid space which envelopes the brain. Consequently, the more convoluted a particular brain is, the more CSF that brain likely has enveloping the cortical surface area.

The hypothesis follows that a brain with above average cortical surface area likely also has an above average number of neurons, which would allow for greater cognitive capacity. In fact, Haug (1987) estimated the within human species correlation between brain volume and number of neurons to be only moderate (0.48). This moderate correlation allows cortical surface area to be a potentially much better estimator of neuron number, because brain volume and cortical surface area were found to correlate at only 0.59 (Haug 1987). Unfortunately, Haug (1987) did not correlate cortical surface area with total amount of neurons. In another study (Pakkenberg & Gundersen 1997), however, a correlation of 0.73 was found between brain weight and pial surface area, which is synonymous with cortical surface area (Pakkenberg, personal communication 2000). There was also a correlation of 0.73 between pial surface area and total number of neurons. As would be expected, the correlation of 0.73 was much higher than the correlation between brain weight and total number of neurons (0.56), a difference of 22% in terms of percentage of variance accounted for. Thus, if brain volume is correlated with intelligence because it is a proxy for neuron number, then the correlation between cortical surface and IQ should be larger than 0.4.

With the publication of Haier *et al.*'s (1995) study (see Chapter 3 in this volume), that combined both brain volume and glucose metabolic rate (GMR), it has become possible to hypothesise that brain volume may be mediating a substantial proportion of the effects reported in the glucose uptake and IQ literature. Haier *et al.* (1995) found a correlation of –0.58 between GMR and IQ, suggesting that more intelligent individuals have more efficient brains. A correlation of 0.65 was also found between brain volume and IQ, as would be predicted from previous studies (corrected for extreme groups, the correlation fell to 0.36). Of particular interest is that a correlation of –0.69 was found between brain volume and GMR, i.e. larger brains tend to be more efficient. This finding replicated a previous study that found a similar correlation of –0.75 between brain volume and GMR (Hatawa *et al.* 1987). Based on these data, the correlation between GMR and IQ, controlling for brain volume, can be estimated to be reduced to –0.24. Evidence from electrophysiology suggests that the relationship between brain volume and GMR is not an artefact of PET (e.g. pixel count). Blumberg (1989) found a correlation of –0.92 between brain volume and theta frequency (known to be associated with energy use) in a between-species analysis: humans had the lowest theta frequency and mice the highest. It is difficult to determine the significance (or direction of influence) of the correlation between brain volume and GMR, because of the non-experimental nature of the data. However, it appears doubtful that both brain volume and GMR (at rest) are independent correlates of intelligence.

The correlation between brain volume and IQ does not appear limited to adults. In Reiss *et al.*'s study (1996), children aged 5 to 17 had their brain volumes and IQs estimated: a correlation of 0.4 between brain volume and IQ, controlling for gender and age, was reported. Age did not have an appreciable effect on the correlation, because there was no correlation between age and brain size. This should come as no surprise, because 92% of adult brain weight is achieved by age 6 (Ho *et al.* 1980). The fact that children possess brain volumes of almost the same magnitude as adults is important to note, because it stresses the fact that the relationship between brain volume and IQ is not simple: six-year-old children, for example, do not have the intellectual capacity of normal 25-year-old adults.

Reiss *et al.* (1996) also found a negative correlation of –0.44 between age and grey matter volume. Consequently, one must consider the fact that adults manifest greater cognitive capacity with less grey matter and possibly fewer neurons. The reason there is no developmental loss in total brain volume is because white matter volume is correlated positively with age (0.40), during the developmental period from 5 to 17 years of age. After the age of 30, however, brain volume begins to decrease (Ho *et al.* 1980) at a rate of approximately 2 grams per year until the age of 80, after which the loss increases to 5 grams per year. The weight loss appears to be due both to neuronal loss and to a reduction in white matter volume. For instance, Pakkenberg & Gundersen (1997) found that, from the age of 20 to 90, a 12.3% reduction in neocortical volume could be expected. Similarly, a 28% reduction in white matter volume was observed in the same age group. The loss in neocortical volume appears to be due to the loss of neurons (as opposed to shrinking), because a reduction of 9.5% in neuron number was established. Further support for a concomitant decrease in both grey matter and white matter during adulthood has been provided by Raz *et al.* (1993), who found a negative correlation of –0.43 between dorsolateral prefrontal cortex volume and age, as well as a negative correlation of –0.36 between prefrontal white matter and age. This is important to note, because IQ (or fluid intelligence) is known to begin its decrease in adults at around the age of 30, precisely the time at which brain volume (grey and white) begins to decrease.

3. White Matter Versus Grey Matter

Miller (1994) has proposed that the substrate to the biological basis of intelligence is mediated by white matter and not grey matter. Essentially, his thesis is that there should be a positive correlation between the amount of myelin sheaths, which are wrapped around neuronal axons, and intelligence, because more myelin should allow for faster information processing. A recent factor analytic study (Pennington *et al.* 2000) provides some support for Miller's (1994) thesis.

Pennington *et al.* (2000) estimated brain volume in two groups: (1) a reading disordered (RD) group, comprised of 25 pairs of MZ twins and 23 pairs of DZ twins; and (2) a control sample comprised of 9 pairs of normal MZ twins and 9 pairs of normal DZ twins. As would be expected from previous research, a correlation of 0.42 was found between brain volume and IQ in the RD sample (0.57 corrected for restriction in IQ range) and 0.31 (0.46 corrected) in the control group. Unlike any other brain volume and IQ study, the authors estimated the size of various structures of the brain and then performed a factor analysis on the data. Two factors were extracted: a cortical factor and a subcortical factor. Both factors combined accounted for 64% of the variance. What is particularly intriguing is that white matter had a factor loading of essentially zero (–0.002) on the cortical factor and a loading near unity (0.911) on the subcortical factor. Consequently, the amount of white matter in a particular brain appears to be independent of the amount of cortical grey matter. Thus, whereas there is a positive correlation between all cognitive ability tests, there is not an analogous positive manifold in brain anatomy. Of perhaps even greater significance is that the two factors correlated with IQ differentially. The cortical factor correlated with IQ at 0.16 in the RD sample, while the subcortical factor correlated 0.41. In the control group, the same effect proved apparent, with the cortical factor correlating with IQ at 0.13 and the subcortical factor correlating at 0.34. These results suggest that white matter is carrying the weight of the relationship between brain volume and IQ.

Table 6.2: White matter volume and grey matter volume correlations with IQ.

Study	White Matter Volume	Grey Matter Volume
Andreason *et al.* (1993)	0.14	0.35
Raz *et al.* (1993)	0.32	0.51
Egan *et al.* (1994)	0.27	0.08
Gur *et al.* (1999)	0.36	0.34
Pennington *et al.* (2000)	0.34	0.13
Pennington *et al.* (2000)	0.41	0.16
Schoenemann *et al.* (2000)	0.31	0.31
Unweighted mean *r* =	0.31	0.27

However, the results of a more comprehensive survey of the brain volume and intelligence studies that obtained estimates of grey and white matter separately do not substantiate Miller's (1994) claim. For instance, Andreason *et al.* (1993) found white matter to correlate with FSIQ at 0.14. In contrast, grey matter correlated with FSIQ at 0.35. Schoenemann *et al.* (2000) found grey and white matter to correlate with g at approximately the same magnitude, 0.23 and 28, respectively. Gur *et al.* (1999) also found grey and white matter to correlate at virtually the same magnitude: 0.34 and 0.36, respectively. Listed in Table 6.2 are the brain volume and IQ studies that estimated both white and grey matter and reported separate correlations between each of these and IQ. Two studies found that grey matter tended to correlate with IQ to a greater extent than did white matter, two studies found grey matter and white matter to correlate at approximately the same magnitude, and three studies found that white matter correlated more highly with IQ than did grey matter. Across all seven samples, the average correlation between white matter and IQ is 0.31. The average correlation between grey matter volume and IQ is so similar in magnitude at 0.27 that one cannot consider Miller's hypothesis tenable.

The hypothesis that white matter plays a potentially larger role in mediating intelligence does receive support from studies that have examined particular qualities of myelin other than volume. For instance, Willerman *et al.* (1991) measured the degree of contrast between a particular brain's grey and white matter. That is, there exist individual differences in the intensity with which white and grey matter are depicted in an MRI image, with white and grey matter appearing darker when there is more water bound to membrane surfaces. For white matter, an increase in water bound to membranes is interpreted by Willerman *et al.* (1991) as an increase in myelin sheaths wrapped around axons. A correlation of 0.54 between white/grey matter contrast and FSIQ was found. This is a study that Miller (1994) cites in support of his "white matter hypothesis". However, Willerman *et al.* (1991) acknowledge that other variables (e.g. biochemical) can also affect the degree of white/grey matter contrast. Magnetic Resonance Spectroscopy (MRS) is a procedure that can measure some of these biochemicals more accurately.

The principles of operation underlying MRS are the same as those underlying MRI (Orrison *et al.* 1995). Effectively, the difference is that the signal derived and analysed by MRS produces a frequency spectrum that allows researchers to quantify *in vivo* concentrations of particular neurometabolites in a particular area of the brain.

The first study to use MRS in intelligence research with neurologically normal subjects (Rae *et al.* 1996), estimated occipitalparietal white matter intracellular pH levels in a sample of 42 boys (mean age = 10). pH was estimated by "using the difference in chemical shift between phosphocreatine resonance and inorganic phosphate" (Rae *et al.* 1996: 1061). The WISC-III was administered to determine the subjects' IQs. A correlation of 0.52 was found between pH level and FSIQ, indicating that a higher pH level was associated with greater intelligence. The effect of pH levels on the nervous system is far ranging. For instance, experimental *in vitro* research on rats (Elis 1969) has shown a very close correspondence between pH level and nerve action potential amplitude (0.92) and conduction time (–0.86). Consequently, Rae *et al.* (1996) interpreted their result in the context of the neural efficiency theory, implicating higher intelligence as associated with faster conductivity and transmission.

In another MRS study (Jung *et al.* 1999), levels of *N*-acetylaspartate (NAA) and choline (Cho) were measured in 26 male and female college students. The authors chose NAA because it has been shown to be positively related to neuronal injury and death. Further, the authors report, levels of Cho appear to be related positively to demyelination (that may or may not appear on MRI brain images), because increased levels have been observed in patients with stroke and multiple sclerosis. Intelligence was assessed with the WAIS-III. NAA and Cho correlated with FSIQ at 0.52 and –0.32, respectively. A multiple *R* of 0.67 was obtained with a multiple regression using NAA and Cho as predictors of IQ.

Thus, although speed of information processing is a well-replicated correlate of IQ (Vernon 1987), it does not appear to necessarily hinge upon an exclusive theory of larger or more abundant neuronal constituents, such as myelin sheaths. Rather, individual differences in neurochemistry provide an alternative or complementary perspective to the area.

4. Method of Correlated Vectors

Because an individual's factor score based on a factor analysis of cognitive ability tests is an *estimate* of a person's level of *g* (and not a person's true level of *g*), there is the likelihood that a group of subjects' factor scores will be contaminated by processes other than *g* (e.g. Performance IQ, Verbal IQ, test specificity). To accommodate this problem, Jensen (1998) proposed the method of correlated vectors. This procedure consists of correlating the rank of a group of subtests' factor loadings on *g* with that same group of subtests' ranked correlations with a particular physiological or chronometric variable. Thus, if *g* is really mediating the correlation between a cognitive and a non-cognitive variable (a so-called Jensen effect — see Chapter 9 in this volume), the correlation between the subtests' correlation with the *g* factor (i.e. its factor loading) and the respective subtests' correlation with the physiological or chronometric variable should be larger than the simple correlation between the variable of interest and *g*.

The first study to apply the method of correlated vectors to a head size study is that of Jensen (1994). The data were obtained from Osborne (1980) and came from 286 subjects. A *g* factor was extracted from an extensive battery of 17 well-known cognitive ability tests (e.g. PMA reasoning, Cattell Culture Fair). The correlation between head circumference and *g* was estimated at 0.19. The method of correlated vectors revealed a vector correlation of 0.64. Thus, the extent to which a given test is correlated with head size is related positively and strongly to its correlation with *g*.

Thus far, there have been only two brain volume and IQ studies to apply the method of correlated vectors. This is unfortunate, because most studies have administered a large enough battery of cognitive ability tests to extract a *g* factor, which would have permitted the requisite calculations. In Wickett *et al.* (2000), brain volume via MRI was estimated in 68 adult subjects. A *g* factor was extracted from an extensive cognitive ability battery that was comprised also of the subjects' mean and standard deviation reaction times. Reaction time (RT) mean and RT sd loaded at 0.79 and 0.74 on *g*, respectively. Total brain volume correlated with *g* at 0.38. The method of correlated vectors estimated a correlation of 0.59 between a subtest's *g* loading and its correlation with brain volume. A very similar study, that also included reaction time tasks in the *g* factor, is that of Schoenemann *et al.* (2000). They obtained a correlation of 0.45 between brain volume and *g*. Jensen (1998) calculated the vector correlation to be 0.51, which is remarkably similar to the vector correlation of 0.59 found by Wickett *et al.* (2000).

5. The Heritability of Brain Volume and the Possible Causal Relationship between Brain Volume and Intelligence

In Pennington *et al.*'s (2000) MZ/DZ study, the heritability of total brain volume was estimated to be 97% in the reading disordered (RD) sample. No variance was found to be accounted for by shared environment, while 3% was accounted for by unique environment and/or error. In the control sample, heritability of total brain volume was estimated to be somewhat lower at 80%. Shared environment in this sample was estimated to account for 18% of the variance and unique environment and/or error was estimated at 2%. In another MZ/DZ study (Bartley *et al.* 1997), it was estimated that 94% of the variance in total brain volume could be accounted for by additive genetic effects. Similarly to the RD sample above, shared environmental influences could not be found to account for any of the variability in brain volume. Consequently, it is reasonable to contend that at the very least 80% and likely closer to 90% of brain volume is heritable. The bivariate heritability between brain volume and IQ was estimated to be 0.32. Using a formula provided by Falconer & Mackay (1996), Pennington *et al.* (2000) estimated that the genetic correlation between brain volume and IQ is 0.48. The authors also estimated that about 80% of the phenotypic brain volume and IQ correlation is mediated by common genetic effects.

As has been argued previously (Jensen 1998), it is important to establish a correlation between a physiological variable and a cognitive variable within- as well as between-families. An effect found only between families (e.g. height and IQ) suggests that there is no pleitropic (i.e. two or more phenotypically unique traits mediated by the same gene) or causal effect between the two variables. In one within-family study (Schoenemann *et al.* 2000), a battery of cognitive and RT tasks were administered to female sibling pairs. The scores on all of these tasks were subjected to a principal components analysis, from which a '*g*' factor was extracted. To circumvent violating the assumption of within-group independence, the authors averaged each sibling pairs' factor score ('*g*') and brain volume and correlated these means. A correlation of 0.45 was found between sibling-average brain volume and sibling-average *g*, further replicating previous work.

In contrast to Pennington *et al.* (2000), a suggestive causal relation between brain volume and IQ was not found. The within-family correlation between brain volume and *g* was found to be virtually zero (–0.05). If the relationship between brain volume and IQ does not exist within families then one would hypothesise, the authors reasoned, that perhaps a between-family variable such as socioeconomic status (SES) may mediate some of the variation in brain volume. The Schoenemann *et al.* (2000) study in fact had SES data on their subjects, which permitted the testing of this hypothesis: the hypothesis was not supported — SES did not correlate (0.05, ns) with brain volume. The fact that no correlation was found supports the previously cited twin studies that found that shared environment did not have an influence on brain volume.

In our own research (Wickett *et al.* 2000), a battery of intelligence, paper-and-pencil tests of mental ability, and computerized RT tests were administered to a sample of 34 right-handed, adult male siblings. These measures yielded a FSIQ score and, through factor analysis, factor scores on a *g* factor, fluid and crystallized intelligence factors, a spatial factor, and a memory factor. The subjects' head perimeter was measured with a tape measure, and their head length, width and height were measured with callipers. Right- and left-hemisphere as well as total brain volume were measured in 32 pairs of these siblings using MRI. Tables 6.3 and 6.4 show the between- and within-family correlations between brain volume (Table 6.3), head size (Table 6.4), and the several measures and factors of intelligence, both before and (in italics) after correction for attenuation. These particular results have not been previously published.

Inspection of Table 6.3 reveals that the phenotypic correlations between brain volume and mental ability reported by Wickett *et al.* (2000) have both a between- and a within-family component. The between-family correlations are somewhat larger than the corresponding within-family correlations but, in combination, they indicate that both between- and within-family factors are important in the relation between brain volume and intelligence. Thus, families with larger brains overall tend also to have higher IQs and, within a family, the siblings with the larger brains tend to be the more intelligent. This is particularly the case for the *g*, the fluid intelligence, and the memory factors.

Overall, the ratio of within- to between-family correlations is 0.63, indicating that a substantial portion of the correlation between brain volume and mental abilities occurs within a family, and so must be functional in nature. This further suggests that such between-family factors as nutrition, SES, and cross-assortative mating are not the main causes of the brain volume/IQ correlation, although they may contribute. Rather, the results suggest that brain volume is causally related to IQ, with pleiotropy being the

Table 6.3: Within- and between-family correlations between brain volume and IQ and factor scores.

		Brain volume					
		right		left		total	
FSIQ	r_B	0.302	*0.307*	0.320	*0.325*	0.311	*0.316*
	r_W	0.145	*0.155*	0.145	*0.155*	0.146	*0.156*
G	r_B	**0.356**	*0.360*	**0.376**	*0.380*	**0.366**	*0.370*
	r_W	0.230	*0.240*	0.226	*0.235*	0.229	*0.238*
Fluid Ability	r_B	0.335	*0.341*	0.344	*0.351*	0.340	*0.347*
	r_W	0.248	*0.259*	0.248	*0.259*	0.249	*0.260*
Crystallized Ability	r_B	0.198	*0.202*	0.200	*0.203*	0.199	*0.203*
	r_W	0.082	*0.087*	0.110	*0.117*	0.097	*0.102*
Spatial Imaging	r_B	−0.115	*−0.119*	−0.105	*−0.108*	−0.110	*−0.114*
	r_W	−0.207	*−0.223*	−0.282	*−0.303*	−0.246	*−0.264*
Memory	r_B	0.246	*0.253*	0.273	*0.282*	0.260	*0.268*
	r_W	0.197	*0.212*	0.218	*0.236*	0.208	*0.225*

Note: $P < 0.05$ for r_B and r_W greater than 0.345 (in bold). $N = 32$ (number of sibships). Disattenuated correlations (in italics) do not have significance levels associated with them.

likely agent considering the high heritabilities of both IQ and brain volume. Although some aspect of a within-family correlation may be environmental, it is unlikely that environmental factors exert much influence on the relations observed in this study. Within-family environmental effects have to be unique or non-shared and what makes it unlikely that non-shared environmental factors are operating here is that the same factor(s) would have to lead both to a change in brain volume and to a change in the same direction in intelligence. Nutrition could have such an effect, but is unlikely because siblings in the same family typically receive similar levels of nutrition. Illness is another possibility, leading to a developmental delay in both brain growth and intelligence, but the subjects in Wickett *et al.* (2000) were carefully screened to exclude any with pathologies of the type that could affect either cognitive ability or brain development. Again, then, it appears much more likely that genetic factors contribute to the relation between brain size and intelligence.

Table 6.4 shows a similar pattern of results for the head size measures. The correlations here are typically small but a within-family component is evident more often than not. With FSIQ and with *g* there is a significant within-family correlation with head width (0.398 and 0.371, respectively); width also shows smaller (and non-significant) within-family correlations with the fluid and crystallized factors, and to a

Table 6.4: Within- and between-family correlations between head size and IQ and factor scores.

		Head size							
		perimeter		height		length		width	
FSIQ	r_B	*0.026*	0.026	*-0.148*	-0.146	*-0.029*	-0.029	*0.098*	0.097
	r_W	*0.101*	0.095	*-0.182*	-0.170	*-0.088*	-0.082	*0.426*	**0.398**
g	r_B	*0.058*	0.057	*-0.128*	-0.127	*-0.004*	-0.004	*0.161*	0.159
	r_W	*0.123*	0.118	*-0.129*	-0.124	*-0.018*	-0.017	*0.386*	**0.371**
Fluid Ability	r_B	*0.162*	0.159	*-0.192*	-0.188	*0.050*	0.049	*0.318*	0.312
	r_W	*0.172*	0.164	*-0.003*	-0.003	*0.180*	0.173	*0.224*	0.215
Crystallized Ability	r_B	*-0.024*	-0.024	*-0.125*	-0.123	*-0.092*	-0.090	*0.099*	0.097
	r_W	*0.138*	0.130	*0.001*	0.001	*-0.039*	-0.037	*0.309*	0.291
Spatial Imaging	r_B	*-0.256*	-0.249	*-0.032*	-0.031	*-0.212*	-0.207	*-0.276*	-0.268
	r_W	*-0.225*	-0.209	*-0.222*	-0.206	*-0.233*	-0.217	*-0.087*	-0.081
Memory	r_B	*0.176*	0.171	*0.179*	0.174	*0.246*	0.239	*0.040*	0.039
	r_W	*0.009*	0.008	*-0.102*	-0.095	*-0.094*	-0.087	*0.187*	0.173

Note: $P < 0.05$ for r_B and r_W greater than 0.335 (in bold). $N = 34$ (number of sibships). Disattenuated correlations (in italics) do not have significance levels associated with them.

lesser extent with memory. The other head size variables typically do not show correlations large enough to be taken as meaningful.

6. Conclusion

In conclusion, as Jensen & Sinha (1993) predicted, there is now no question that brain volume and IQ are significantly and positively correlated, with the best estimate being a correlation of approximately 0.40. In addition to this phenotypic correlation, there is also evidence that brain volume and IQ have a genetic correlation (Pennington *et al.* 2000). Jensen & Sinha (1993) also emphasised the importance of establishing whether the correlation between brain volume and intelligence occurred both within- as well as between-families. The sibling data from Wickett *et al.* (2000) strongly suggest that a within-family relationship does exist but, given the contrary results of Schoenemann *et al.* (2000), it would be prudent to await the results of additional studies. A large-scale twin study would be ideal because this would also allow Pennington *et al.*'s (2000) results regarding the genetic correlation between brain volume and IQ to be replicated.

References

Andreason, N. C., Flaum, M., Swayze, V., O'Leary, D. S., Alliger, R., Cohen, G., Ehrhardt, J., & Yuh, W. T. C. (1993). Intelligence and brain structure in normal individuals. *American Journal of Psychiatry, 150* (1), 130–134.

Bartley, A. L., Jones, D. W., & Weinberger, D. R. (1997). Genetic variability of human brain size and cortical gyral patterns. *Brain, 120,* 257–269.

Blumberg, M. S. (1989). An allometric analysis of the frequency of hippocampal theta: The significance of Brain Metabolic Rate. *Brain Behavior and Evolution, 34,* 351–356.

Egan, V., Chiswick, A., Santosh, C., Naidu, K., Rimmington, J. E., & Best, J. J. K. (1994). Size isn't everything: a study of brain volume, intelligence and auditory evoked potentials. *Personality and Individual Differences, 17* (3), 357–367.

Egan, V., Wickett, J. C., & Vernon, P. A. (1995). Brain size and intelligence: erratum, addendum, and correction. *Personality and Individual Differences, 19* (1), 113–115.

Elis, F. R. (1969). Some effects of Pco2 and pH on nerve tissue. *British Journal of Pharmacology, 35,* 197–201.

Eysenck, H. J. (1994). Special review. *Personality and Individual Differences, 16* (4), 657.

Falconer, D. S., & Mackay, T. F. C. (1996). *Introduction to quantitative genetics* (4th ed.). London: Longman Group.

Flashman, L. A., Andreasen, N. C., Flaum, M., & Swayze, V. W. (1998). Intelligence and regional brain volumes in normal controls. *Intelligence, 25* (3), 149–160.

Guilford, J. P., & Fruchter, B. (1978). *Fundamental statistics in psychology and education.* New York: McGraw-Hill.

Gur, R. C., Turetsky, B. I., Matsui, M., Yan, M., Bilker, W., Hughett, P., & Gur, R. E. (1999). Sex differences in brain grey and white matter in healthy young adults: Correlations with cognitive performance. *The Journal of Neuroscience, 19* (10), 4065–4072.

Haug, H. (1987). Brain sizes, surfaces, and neuronal sizes of the cortex cerebri: a stereological investigation of man and his variability and a comparison with some mammals (primates, whales, marsupials, insectivores, and one elephant). *The American Journal of Anatomy, 180*, 126–142.

Haier, R. J., Chueh, D., Touchette, P., Lott, I., Buchsbaum, M., Macmillan, D., Sandman, C., Lacasse, L., & Sosa, E. (1995). Brain size and cerebral glucose metabolic rate in nonspecific mental retardation and Down Syndrome. *Intelligence, 20*, 191–210.

Hatawa, J., Brooks, R. A., Di Chiro, G., & Bacharach, S. L. (1987). Glucose utilization rate versus brain size in humans. *Neurology, 37*, 583–588.

Ho, K-C., Roessmann, U., Straumfjord, J. V., & Monroe, G. (1980). Analysis of brain weight. I. Adult brain weight in relation to sex, race, and age. *Archives of Pathology and Laboratory Medicine, 104*, 635–645.

Jensen, A. R. (1994). Psychometric *g* related to differences in head size. *Personality and Individual Differences, 17*, 597–606.

Jensen, A. R. (1998). *The g Factor. The science of mental ability.* WestPort, CT: Praeger.

Jensen, A. R., & Sinha, S. N. (1993). Physical correlates of human intelligence. In: P. A. Vernon (Ed.), *Biological approaches to the study of human intelligence* (pp. 139–242). Norwood, NJ: Ablex.

Jung, R. E., Brooks, W. M., Yeo, R. A., Chiulli, S. J., Weers, D. C., & Sibbit, W. L. (1999). Biochemical markers of intelligence: A proton MR spectroscopy study of normal human brain. *Proceedings of the Royal Society of London: B, 266*, 1375–1379.

Miller, E. M. (1994). Intelligence and brain myelination: A hypothesis. *Personality and Individual Differences, 17*, 803–832.

Orrison, W. W., Lewine, J. D., Sanders, J. A., & Hartshorne, M. F. (1995). *Functional brain imaging.* St. Louis: Mosby.

Osborne, R. T. (1980). *Twins: Black and white.* Athens, GA: Foundation for Human Understanding.

Pakkenberg, B., & Gundersen, H. J. G. (1997). Neocortical neuron number in humans: Effect of sex and age. *The Journal of Comparative Neurology, 384*, 312–320.

Paterson, D. G. (1930). *Physique and intellect.* Westport, CT: Greenwood Press.

Pennington, B. F., Filipek, P. A., Lefly, D., Chabildas, N., Kennedy, D. N., Simon, J. H., Filley, C. M., Galaburda, A., DeFries, J. C. (2000). A twin MRI study of size variations in the human brain. *Journal of Cognitive Neuroscience, 12* (1), 223–232.

Rae, C., Scott, R. B., Thompson, C. H., Kemp, G. J., Dumughn, I., Styles, P., Tracey, I., & Radda, G. K. (1996). Is pH a biochemical marker of IQ? *Proceedings of the Royal Society of London: B, 263*, 1061–1064.

Raz, N., Torres, I. J., Spencer, W. D., Millman, D., Baertschi, J. C., & Sarpel, G. (1993). Neuroanatomical correlates of age-sensitive and age-invariant cognitive abilities: an *in vivo* MRI investigation. *Intelligence, 17*, 407–422.

Reiss, A. L., Abrams, M. T., Singer, H. S., Ross, J. L., & Denckla, M. B. (1996). Brain development, gender and IQ in children. *Brain, 119*, 1763–1774.

Schoenemann, P. T., Budinger, T. F., Sarich, V. M., & Wang, W. (2000). Brain size does not predict general cognitive ability within families. *Proceedings of the National Academy of Science, 97*(9), 4932–4937.

Tan, U., Tan, M., Polat, P., Ceylan, Y., Suma, S., & Okur, A. (1999). Magnetic resonance imaging brain size/IQ relations in Turkish university students. *Intelligence, 27* (1), 83–92.

Tramo, M. J., Loftus, W. C., Stukel, T. A., Green, R. L., Weaver, J. B., & Gazzaniga. M. S. (1998). Brain size, head size, and intelligence quotient in monozygotic twins. *Neurology, 50*, 1246–1252.

Vernon, P. A. (1987). *Speed of information-processing and intelligence.* Norwwod, NJ: Ablex.

Wickett, J. C. (1992). *Unpublished master's dissertation.* London, Ontario: Canada.

Wickett, J. C., Vernon, P. A., & Lee, D. H. (1994). *In vivo* brain size, head perimeter, and intelligence in a sample of healthy adult females. *Personality and Individual Differences, 16* (6), 831–838.

Wickett, J. C., Vernon, P. A., & Lee, D. H. (2000). Relationships between factors of intelligence and brain volume. *Personality and Individual Differences, 29* (6), 1095–1122.

Willerman, L., Schultz, R., Rutledge, J. N., & Bigler, E. D. (1991). *In vivo* brain size and intelligence. *Intelligence, 15*, 223–228.

Chapter 7

Molecular Genetics and *g*

Robert Plomin

1. Introduction

Although a review of behavioral genetic research on *g* was published in *Science* in 1963 (Erlenmeyer-Kimling & Jarvik 1963), it was Arthur Jensen's *Harvard Educational Review* monograph (Jensen 1969) that made it no longer possible to avoid the issue in the social and behavioral sciences. He clearly and carefully described quantitative genetic theory with a minimum of jargon, reviewed the data, and concluded that individual differences in IQ scores are substantially due to genetic differences. The section of the monograph entitled 'The Inheritance of Intelligence' (pp. 28–59) is still one of the best introductions to the genetics of *g*. I especially like his section 'Common Misconceptions about Heritability' (pp. 42–46). What is most impressive to me is that this monograph was written only one year after his first article on behavioral genetics appeared (Jensen 1967). In his 1981 book *Straight Talk About Mental Tests*, Jensen admirably explains research on the genetics of *g* for readers with no technical background.

An autobiographical statement (Jensen 1972) reminds us of the extent to which genetic influences on *g* were ignored just three decades ago and also provides interesting insights into his reasons for writing about genetic influences on *g*:

> What struck me as most peculiar as I worked my way through the vast bulk of literature on the disadvantaged was the almost complete lack of any mention of the possible role of genetic factors in individual differences in intelligence and scholastic performance. In the few instances where genetics was mentioned, it was usually to dismiss the issue as outmoded, irrelevant, or unimportant, or to denigrate the genetic study of human differences and to proclaim the all-importance of the social and cultural environment as the only source of individual and group differences in the mental abilities relevant to scholastic perform-ance. So strongly expressed was this bias in some cases, and so inadequately buttressed by any evidence, that I began to surmise that the

topic of genetics was ignored more because of the particular author's social philosophy than because the importance of genetic factors in human differences had been scientifically disproved. It seemed obvious to me that a book dealing with the culturally disadvantaged would have to include a chapter that honestly comes to grips scientifically with the influence of genetic factors on differences in mental ability (Jensen 1972: 7–8).

The case for substantial genetic influence on g is stronger than for any other (Mackintosh 1998) human characteristic. As Jensen says in his overview of genetic research in *The g Factor*, "the following concatenation of several overwhelmingly well-established facts in behavioral genetics is impossible to explain or understand without invoking a substantial degree of broad heritability of IQ" (Jensen 1998: 177). Correlations for first-degree relatives living together average 0.43 for more than 8000 parent-offspring pairs and 0.49 for more than 27,000 pairs of siblings. However, g might run in families for reasons of nurture or of nature. In studies involving more than 10,000 pairs of twins, the average g correlations are 0.86 for identical twins and 0.60 for same-sex fraternal twins. These twin data suggest a genetic effect size (heritability) that explains about half of the total variance in g scores. Adoption studies also yield estimates of substantial heritability. For example, in two recent studies, identical twins reared apart are almost as similar for g as are identical twins reared together, with an average correlation of 0.78 for 93 such pairs (Bouchard *et al*. 1990; Pedersen *et al*. 1992). Adoption studies of other first-degree relatives also indicate substantial heritability, as illustrated by recent results from the longitudinal 25-year Colorado Adoption Project (Plomin *et al*. 1997). All the data converge on the conclusion that the heritability of 'g' is about 50%, that is, genes account for about half of the variance in 'g' scores (Bouchard, Jr & McGue 1981; Plomin *et al*. 1997). Even an attempt to explain as much of the variance of 'g' as possible in terms of prenatal effects nonetheless yielded a heritability estimate of 48% (Devlin *et al*. 1997; McGue 1997). Although heritability could differ in different cultures, moderate heritability of g has been found, not only in twin studies in North American and western European countries, but also in Moscow, former East Germany, rural India, urban India, and Japan.

During the decade following Jensen's 1969 monograph, more research on the genetics of g was conducted than in the previous 50 years combined in large part because of the monograph and the controversy and criticism it aroused. These bigger and better twin and adoption studies confirmed the conclusions that Jensen reached in his monograph and also extended the field in new directions such as multivariate genetic analysis of specific cognitive abilities, developmental genetic research on change and continuity, and genetic research at the interface between nature and nurture (Plomin 1999a).

Jensen has made other important contributions to genetic theory and methodology such as genotype-environment correlation (Jensen 1976), assortative mating (Jensen 1978), and inbreeding (Jensen 1983). The chapter on the heritability of g in Jensen's definitive tome *The g Factor* (Jensen 1998) extends his thinking on each of these topics. Rather than repackaging some of his previous reviews on the topic, Jensen begins by using his important distinction of between-family and within-family variance to ask whether the same *g* factor emerges between and within families. For first-degree relatives whose genetic relatedness is 50%, genetic factors operate equally to create differences between and within families. In contrast, different environmental factors operate between and within families. For example, socioeconomic status affects differences between families but is largely the same for two children growing up in the same family. Thus, if the factor structure of *g* is the same between and within families, this suggests that between-family factors such as socioeconomic factors cannot be responsible for the factor structure of *g*. Using data from his large sibling study, Jensen shows that the *g* factor structures derived from sibling sums (an index of between-family factors) and sibling differences (within-family factors) are virtually identical with congruence coefficients in excess of 0.98 (Jensen 1980), a finding replicated in another sibling study (Nagoshi & Johnson 1987). Multivariate genetic research, mentioned later, pins down the implication from these findings that the factor structure of *g* is almost entirely due to genetic factors.

In his chapter on heritability in *The g Factor*, Jensen also notes one of the most surprising findings from behavioral genetics research: the heritability of *g* increases throughout development and the importance of shared environmental factors that make family members similar decreases. His hypothesis to explain this fascinating finding involves genotype-environment correlation:

> "From early childhood to late adolescence the predominant component of the GE covariance gradually shifts from *passive* to *reactive* to *active*, which makes for increasing phenotypic expression of individuals' genotypically conditioned characteristics. In other words, as people approach maturity they seek out and even create their own experiential environment. With respect to mental abilities, a 'good' environment, in general, is one that affords the greatest freedom and the widest variety of opportunities for reactive and active GE covariance, thereby allowing genotypic propensities their fullest phenotypic expression" (Jensen 1998: 181).

What are the non-shared environmental factors that are responsible for environmental influence on *g* after adolescence? Jensen summarizes his important view of this perplexing problem in *The g Factor*:

> "The causes of the nonshared environmental variance are still somewhat obscure. I have presented analyses of MZ twin data elsewhere which suggest that the nonshared environmental variance is mainly the result of a great many small random effects that are largely of a biological nature (Jensen 1974). Such effects as childhood diseases, traumas, and the like, as well as prenatal effects such as mother-fetus incompatibility of blood antigens, maternal health, and perinatal effects of anoxia and other complications in the birth process, could each have a small adverse effect on mental development. Such environmental effects could differ randomly among twins or ordinary siblings. Some individuals would

have the good luck of being 'hit' by very few such adverse random effects, compared to the average, and others would have the bad luck of being 'hit' by many more than the average" (Jensen 1998: 181).

Concerning assortative mating, Jensen (1978) noted that the correlation between spouses for *g* is above 0.40, which is much higher than for other traits. In *The g Factor*, he uses his important 'method of correlated vectors' to show that assortative mating is largely a matter of *g*. That is, the degree to which cognitive tests show assortative mating is highly correlated with the tests' loadings on the *g* factor. Similar results for the method of correlated vectors are found for kinship correlations and for heritabilities — tests with greater *g* loadings show greater heritability. All of these findings suggest that the *g* is the central plot in the story of cognitive abilities.

Jensen also describes the results of multivariate genetic analysis that suggest that what the genetics of cognitive abilities is about is *g*. Although it is surprising that *g* accounts for about 40% of the phenotypic variance of diverse cognitive tests, it is truly amazing that about 80% of the genetic variance of such tests is explained by *g*. That is, multivariate genetic analyses have consistently found that genetic correlations among cognitive abilities exceed 0.80. In other words, if a gene associated with a particular cognitive ability were identified, the same gene would be expected to be associated with other cognitive abilities as well. This finding suggests that, despite its complexity, *g* is the best target for molecular genetic research aimed at identifying specific genes for cognitive abilities. The finding is also important for cognitive neuroscience, a field in which *g* has hardly entered the lexicon. The genetic nexus responsible for *g* provides clues for understanding how the brain works from an individual differences perspective. It suggests that there must be genetically-driven mechanisms that affect performance across diverse cognitive tasks. Although genetic *g* does not imply that *g* is due to genes that affect a single process, the multivariate genetic results indicate that the same genes affect different cognitive processes. The genetic links among cognitive processes may have been forged by evolution to coordinate effective problem solving across the modules of mind.

The goal of this chapter is to provide an overview of another new direction in genetic research: harnessing the power of molecular genetics to begin to identify some of the genes responsible for the substantial heritability of *g*. This is one of the few topics related to *g* that Jensen has not written about, in part because the techniques to identify genes for complex traits are new and solid findings in the area have not yet been established. Nonetheless, the importance that Jensen would assign to molecular genetics can be seen in the last words of *The g Factor* which he gives to Charles Spearman: the final understanding of *g* "must needs come from the most profound and detailed direct study of the human brain in its purely physical and chemical aspects" (Spearman 1927: 403). Finding some of the genes associated with *g* will provide discrete windows through which we can view the brain mechanisms that mediate genetic effects on *g*.

The following discussion of molecular genetics begins with a brief description of some of the breathtaking advances from the Human Genome Project which have far-reaching implications for identifying genes associated with *g*. After discussing a few fundamental issues such as the likelihood that many genes of small effect size are responsible for the heritability of *g*, a molecular genetic study is described whose goal is to identify genes associated with *g*. Details about DNA and methods such as linkage and allelic association used to identify genes are beyond the scope of this paper, but these methods are described elsewhere (e.g. Plomin *et al.* 2001; Plomin & Crabbe 2000).

2. The Human Genome Project

The 20th century began with the re-discovery of Mendel's laws of heredity. The word *genetics* was only invented in 1903. Fifty years later it was understood that DNA was the mechanism of heredity. The genetic code was cracked in 1966 — the 4-letter alphabet (G, A, T, C) of DNA is read as 3-letter words that code for the 20 amino acids that are the building blocks of proteins. The crowning glory of the century and a tremendous start to the new century is the Human Genome Project, which has provided a working draft of the sequence of the 3 billion letters of DNA in the human genome.

The most exciting development for behavioral genetics is the identification of the DNA sequences that make us different from each other. There is no human genome sequence — we each have a unique genome. Indeed, about one in every thousand DNA letters differs, about 3 million variations in total. Half of these DNA differences have already been identified. The Human Genome Project has spawned new technologies that will make it possible to investigate simultaneously thousands of DNA variants as they relate to behavioral traits. These DNA differences are responsible for the widespread heritability of psychological disorders and dimensions. That is, when we say that a trait is heritable, we mean that variations in DNA exist that cause differences in behavior.

DNA variation has a unique causal status in explaining behavior. When behavior is correlated with anything else, the old adage applies that correlation does not imply causation. For example, as alluded to earlier in relation to genotype-environment correlation, when parenting is shown to be correlated with children's behavioral outcomes, this does not imply that the parenting caused the outcome environmentally. Parental behavior to some extent reflects genetic effects on children's behavior. When it comes to interpreting correlations between biology and behavior, such correlations are often mistakenly interpreted as if biology causes behavior. For example, correlations between neurotransmitter physiology and behavior or between neuroimaging indices of brain activation and behavior are often interpreted as if brain differences cause behavioral differences. However, these correlations do not necessarily imply causation. Behavioral differences can cause brain differences. In contrast, in the case of correlations between DNA variants and behavior, the behavior of individuals does not change their genome. Expression of genes can be altered but the DNA sequence itself does not change. For this reason, correlations between DNA differences and behavioral differences can be interpreted causally: DNA differences cause the behavioral differences and not the other way around.

When the working draft of the human genome sequence was published in February 2001, much publicity was given to the finding that there are fewer than half as many genes (30,000) in the human genome as expected — about the same number of genes as mice and worms. A bizarre spin in the media was that having only 30,000 genes implies that nurture must be more important than we thought. The idea that fewer genes means more free will is silly. Do flies have more free will than us because they have fewer genes? However, the finding that the human species does not have more genes than other species is important in suggesting that the number of genes is not responsible for the greater complexity of the human species. In part, the greater complexity of the human species occurs because during the process of decoding genes into proteins, human genes more than the genes of other species are spliced in alternative ways to create a greater variety of proteins. The greater complexity of the human species may be due to quality rather than quantity: other subtle variations in genes rather than the number of genes may be responsible for differences between mice and men. If subtle DNA differences are responsible for the differences between mice and men, even more subtle differences are likely to be responsible for individual differences within the species.

Another interesting finding from the Human Genome Project is that only 5% of the 3 billion letters in our DNA code involves genes in the traditional sense, that is, genes that code for amino acid sequences. This 5% figure is similar in other mammals. Mutations are quickly weeded out from these bits of DNA which are so crucial for development. When mutations are not weeded out, they can cause one of the thousands of severe but rare single-gene disorders. However, it seems increasingly unlikely that the other 95% of DNA is just along for the ride. For example, variations in this other 95% of the DNA are known to regulate the activity of the classical genes. For this reason, the other 95% of DNA might be the place to look for genes associated with quantitative rather than qualitative effects on behavioral traits.

3. Quantitative Trait Loci (QTLs)

The heritability of complex traits such as *g* is likely to be due to multiple genes of varying but small effect size rather than one gene or a few genes of major effect. Genes in such multiple-gene systems are inherited in the same way as any other gene but they have been given a different name — quantitative trait loci (QTLs) — in order to highlight some important distinctions. Unlike single-gene effects that are necessary and sufficient for the development of a disorder, QTLs contribute interchangeably and additively, analogous to probabilistic risk factors. If there are multiple genes that affect a trait, it is likely that the trait is distributed quantitatively as a dimension rather than qualitatively as a disorder; this was the essence of Fisher's classic 1918 paper on quantitative genetics (Fisher 1918).

From a QTL perspective, common disorders are just the extremes of quantitative traits caused by the same genetic and environmental factors responsible for variation throughout the dimension. In other words, the QTL perspective predicts that genes found to be associated with complex disorders will also be associated with normal variation on the same dimension and vice versa (Plomin *et al.* 1994; Deater-Deckard *et al.* 1997). Although the QTL perspective has some specific implications for the design and analysis of molecular genetic studies, the general importance of a QTL perspective is conceptual. At the most general conceptual level, a common mistake is to think that we are all basically the same genetically except for a few rogue mutations that lead to disorders. In contrast, the QTL perspective suggests that genetic variation is normal. Many genes affect most complex traits and, together with environmental variation, these QTLs are responsible for normal variation as well as for the abnormal extremes of these quantitative traits. This QTL perspective has some implications for thinking about mental illness because it blurs the etiological boundaries between the normal and the abnormal. That is, we all have many alleles that contribute to mental illness but some of us are unluckier in the hand that we draw at conception from our parents' genetic decks of cards. A more subtle conceptual advantage of a QTL perspective is that it frees us to think about both ends of the normal distribution — the positive end as well as the problem end, abilities as well as disabilities, and resilience as well as vulnerability. It has been proposed that we move away from an exclusive focus on pathology towards considering positive traits that improve the quality of life and perhaps prevent pathology (Seligman & Csikszentmihalyi 2000).

The QTL perspective is the molecular genetic version of the quantitative genetic perspective which assumes that genetic variance on complex traits such as *g* is due to many genes of varying effect size. The QTL goal is not to find the gene for *g*, but rather some of the many genes that make contributions of varying effect sizes to the variance of *g*. Perhaps one gene will be found that accounts for 5% of the variance, 5 other genes might each account for 2% of the variance, and 10 other genes might each account for 1% of the variance. If the effects of these QTLs are independent, together these QTLs would account for 25% of the variance, or half of the heritable variance of *g*. If the genes interact, they would in sum account for less of the heritable variance. All of the genes that contribute to the heritability of *g* are unlikely to be identified because some of their effects may be too small or too complicated to detect. The problem is that we do not know the distribution of effect sizes of QTLs for any complex trait in plant, animal or human species. Not long ago, a 10% effect size was thought to be small, at least from the single-gene perspective in which the effect size was essentially 100%. However, for behavioral disorders and dimensions, a 1% effect size may turn out to be a large effect. If effect sizes are so small, this would explain the slow progress to date in identifying genes associated with behavior.

4. Slow Progress So Far

Although the tremendous advances during the past few years from the Human Genome Project warrant optimism for the future, progress in identifying genes associated with behavioral traits has been slower than expected. For example, although there are several promising leads (Baron 2001), no clear-cut associations with schizophrenia and bipolar affective disorder have been identified despite a huge effort during the past decade. Part of the reason for this slow progress may be that because these were the first areas in which molecular genetic approaches were applied, they happened at a time in the 1980s when large pedigree linkage designs were in vogue. It is now generally accepted that such designs are only able to detect genes of major effect size. Recent research has been more successful for finding QTLs for complex traits because they have employed different designs that can detect genes of much smaller effect size. QTL linkage designs use many small families (usually siblings) rather than a few large families and they are able to detect genes that account for about 10% of the variance. Association studies such as case-control comparisons make it possible to detect genes that account for much smaller amounts of variance (Plomin *et al.* 1994; Risch 2000; Risch & Merikangas 1996) A daunting target for molecular genetic research on complex traits such as behavior is to design research powerful enough to detect QTLs that account for 1% of the variance while providing protection against false positive results in genome scans using thousands of markers. In order to break the 1% QTL barrier (which no study has yet done), samples of many thousands of individuals are needed for research on disorders (comparing cases and controls) and on dimensions (assessing individual differences in a representative sample). The main reason why progress in identifying QTLs for complex traits has been slower than expected is likely to be that studies have been underpowered to detect and replicate QTLs of small effect size (Cardon & Bell 2001).

5. The IQ QTL Project

The quantitative genetic findings mentioned earlier suggest that *g*, despite its complex nature, is a reasonable target for QTL research. More than 100 rare genetic syndromes include mental retardation as a symptom (Wahlström 1990). One study, called the IQ QTL Project, has begun a systematic search for QTLs associated with normal variation in *g*. The project uses an association design that compares the frequency of alleles in cases of high *g* individuals to control individuals. It is the first QTL study to investigate high functioning. The goal is not to find genes for genius but to use very high-functioning individuals to identify QTLs that operate throughout the entire distribution, including the low (mental retardation) end of the ability distribution. This goal is based on the simple hypothesis that, although any one of many genes can disrupt normal development, very high functioning requires most of the positive alleles and few of the negative alleles. This is just an hypothesis, but one that can be tested when QTLs are found because it predicts that QTLs found for high ability will have a similar effect throughout the rest of the distribution, including the low end of the distribution.

Why does the IQ QTL Project use an association design rather than linkage? The major strength of linkage designs is that they are systematic in the sense that a few hundred DNA markers can be used to scan the genome. However, as indicated above, QTL linkage designs can only detect QTLs that account for at least 10% of the variance. In contrast, association designs can detect QTLs of much smaller effect size limited only by the size of the samples of cases and controls. If as seems likely many genes affect a trait as complex as *g*, any one gene will have a very small effect which can only be detected by an association design. Association designs can use an unselected sample and simply correlate the presence of a particular allele with *g* scores. Another strategy to boost power that is used by the IQ QTL Project is to sample from the extremes where most of the information in the normal distribution lies. There is a tremendous gain in power to detect QTLs of small effect size as well as in cost-effectiveness in genotyping by selecting from the extremes of a very large sample, as explained below.

The problem with an association design is that association with a quantitative trait can only be detected if a DNA marker is itself the QTL or is very close to it. Thousands of DNA markers are thus needed in order to scan the genome. For this reason, allelic association has been used primarily to investigate associations with candidate genes. In early work on the IQ QTL Project, 100 DNA markers in or near genes involved in brain functioning, primarily neurotransmitters, were genotyped, but no replicated associations with *g* were found (Petrill *et al.* 1998; Plomin *et al.* 1995). A problem with such a candidate gene approach is that any of the thousands of genes expressed in the brain could be considered as candidate genes for *g*. If just about any gene can be considered as a candidate then this approach does not help much to narrow the field.

Rather than examining a few candidate genes, allelic association can be made more systematic by using a dense map of thousands of markers throughout the genome. The IQ QTL Project took a first step in this direction by genotyping 47 short-sequence repeat (SSR) markers on the long arm of chromosome 6 (Chorney *et al.* 1998). A replicated association was found for a marker that happened to be in the gene for insulin-like growth factor-2 receptor (*IGF2R*), a gene that has been subsequently shown to be especially active in brain regions most involved in learning and memory (Wickelgren 1998). We replicated this result using larger samples and a different polymorphism in *IGF2R* (Hill *et al.* 1999), but this finding needs to be replicated in other samples and other laboratories before we can place much confidence in it.

The problem with using a dense map of markers for a genome scan for QTLs of small effect is the amount of genotyping required. Current estimates suggest that at least 100,000 markers are needed for a complete genome scan using allelic association. These markers would need to be genotyped on many individuals in order to achieve the power needed to detect QTLs of small effect size. Despite the daunting amount of genotyping for such a systematic genome scan, there has recently been a sharp swing in favor of genome scans using association approaches that have the power to detect genes of small effect size operating throughout the distribution, as suggested by the QTL perspective. This change in attitude has been fueled by advances in high-throughput genotyping that can quickly genotype thousands of DNA markers, although it is still very expensive to use these techniques to genotype thousands of individuals.

In order to address these issues, the IQ QTL Project developed a technique called DNA pooling (Daniels *et al.* 1998). DNA pooling greatly reduces the need for genotyping by pooling DNA from all individuals in a group and genotyping the pooled groups. For example, with a group of 100 high *g* individuals and 100 control individuals, one marker would require 200 genotypings. However, when DNA is pooled for the high *g* group and for the control group, only 2 genotypings are required. DNA pooling cannot be used with unselected samples because pooling requires groups whose DNA can be pooled. Because most of the power of an unselected sample comes from its extremes, it is reasonable to select the extremes for purposes of pooling. The logic of the QTL perspective is that greater power can be achieved by selecting more extreme individuals as well as by selecting larger samples. The IQ QTL Project focuses specifically on high *g* rather than low *g* because quantitative genetic results suggest that genetic influences on high *g* individuals are the same as genetic influences throughout the distribution (Saudino *et al.* 1998; Saudino *et al.* 1994), whereas very low *g* functioning is often due to chromosomal abnormalities and rare single-gene disorders (Plomin 1999b).

The IQ QTL Project selected a high *g* group of 101 individuals with scores more than two standard deviations above the mean (an IQ score greater than 130), which represents the 98th percentile of an unselected sample of 5,000 individuals. Because greater power is needed to replicate results, a replication high *g* group of 100 individuals was selected from some of the brightest adolescents in the U.S. with estimated IQs greater than 160 which would represent the top 0.00003 of an unselected sample of three million. Although all subjects were Caucasian, it is nonetheless possible that QTL associations could be due to ethnic stratification. For this reason and to provide further confirmation of results, replication was sought in a third sample consisting of 197 parent-child trios in which the offspring had estimated IQs greater than 160 which provides a within-family test called the transmission disequilibrium test (TDT) that protects against population stratification as a possible source of QTL associations. Preliminary proof-of-principle papers were published for systematic searches of chromosome 4 (Fisher *et al.* 1999) and chromosome 22 (Hill *et al.* 1999) using just the two case-control studies and with samples only half the size of the present study.

The IQ QTL Project currently employs a five-stage design in order to provide a balance between false positives and false negatives rather than using a stringent p value in a single study, which protects against false positives but also greatly increases false negatives for QTLs of small effect size. The five-stage design uses a more lenient significance criterion in the first stage (which reduces false negatives for QTLs of small effect size) and then removes false positives in later stages. The five stages include: (1) case-control DNA pooling; (2) case-control DNA pooling; (3) individual genotyping of Stage 1 sample; (4) individual genotyping of Stage 2 sample; (5) individual genotyping of parent-offspring trios. Using DNA pooling, markers that yielded nominally significant ($p < 0.05$) results in the first case-control sample (Stage 1) were replicated using the second case-control sample (Stage 2). Markers that survived Stage 2 were individually genotyped for the first sample (Stage 3) and markers surviving Stage 3 were individually genotyped for the second sample (Stage 4). Markers surviving stage 4 were individually genotyped for the parent-child trios for TDT analysis (Stage 5). The approach was made even more conservative by requiring that, at each stage, a single allele show a significant allelic frequency difference as compared to all other alleles and that the same allele had to be replicated in the same direction in the replication case-control and TDT samples. Data simulation and analytic power analyses indicate that the use of extreme selected sampling provides power to detect QTLs of small effect (Plomin *et al.* 2001). The overall Type I (false positive) error rate for the three samples is 0.000005 which protects against false positive results.

The IQ QTL Project has recently reported results from a preliminary genome scan of 1,847 markers (Plomin *et al.* 2001). As mentioned above, the rationale for the multiple-stage design is to increase power to detect QTLs of small effect by using nominal significance levels that screen out Type I (false positive) errors sequentially. Using an alpha of 0.05 implies that the number of false positive findings expected for 1,847 markers are 92 for the first case-control sample, 5 for the second case-control sample, and 0 for the third sample of parent-offspring trios. Fewer false positives are actually expected because markers must pass additional hurdles such as yielding a significant result for a specific allele in the same direction at each stage and the results of individual genotyping must confirm the results from DNA pooling.

In summary, the numbers of markers surviving each stage using a conservative allele-specific directional test were 108, 6, 4, 2, and 0, respectively, for the five stages. Two markers (*D4S2460* and *D14S65*) met the multiple criteria in the two independent case-control samples. However, these two markers did not replicate in the TDT sample. It should be noted that the criteria for replication used in the IQ QTL Project were conservative if not extreme. No other study has required replication in three samples using two different designs (case-control and parent-offspring trios). However, a conservative approach seems warranted given the problems in the literature with replicating QTL associations (Cardon & Bell 2001).

Concerning *D4S2460* and *D14S65*, it is possible that these markers were significant in the two case-control samples but not the TDT sample because ethnic stratification, which is controlled in the within-family TDT analysis, artificially created the association in the case-control samples. However, this explanation seems unlikely because all subjects were Caucasian and ethnic stratification is unlikely to account for case-control differences unless the cases and controls differ substantially in ethnicity. Furthermore, another test of ethnic stratification called genomic control yielded no evidence of ethnic stratification (Plomin *et al.* 2001).

What is responsible for the failure to find replicable QTLs? One part of the answer is that many more markers are needed for a genome scan for allelic association. Compared to the 300 markers needed for a genome scan for linkage, 1,847 markers seem like a lot of markers; however, at least 100,000 markers are needed to exclude QTL association. The problem for allelic association analysis is that power drops off precipitously when a marker is not very close to the QTL. When the marker is very close to the QTL, in the IQ QTL Project the power to detect a QTL with 5%, 2.5% and 1% heritability is, respectively, 100%, 93% and 56% for the original case-control sample; 100%, 100% and 98% for the replication case-control sample; and 100%, 100% and 99% for the TDT sample (Plomin *et al.* 2001). When a marker is about 100,000 DNA base pairs away from the QTL (that is, linkage disequilibrium between the marker and QTL is 0.50 rather than 1.0), the power estimates decline to 73%, 42% and 19% for the original case-control sample; 100%, 92% and 54% for the replication case-control sample; and 100%, 96% and 64% for the TDT sample.

Given these considerations of genome coverage and power, the IQ QTL Project would have been lucky to detect one QTL associated with *g* using 1,847 markers. Although the design attempts to balance false positives and false negatives in the quest for QTLs of small effect size, it does a much better job of protecting against false positives than false negatives. This balance seems appropriate given the many unreplicable QTL associations that have been reported previously for other complex traits (Cardon & Bell 2001). The balance is especially appropriate for a trait as controversial as *g*.

Although it will soon be possible to conduct a genome scan using 100,000 evenly spaced DNA markers, a more appropriate strategy at the present time may be to go back to using potentially functional polymorphisms. However, rather than focusing on a few candidate genes or gene systems we can look forward to a systematic search using all functional polymorphisms in coding sequences and in regulatory regions. The IQ QTL Project is now using such markers with our five-stage design in order to identify QTL associations that meet our strict criteria for significance.

A gloomier prospect is that QTLs for *g* account for less than 1% of the variance. Although the distribution of effect sizes for *g* or any other complex trait is not known, if QTL heritabilities are less than 1% or if QTLs interact epistatically, it will be difficult to detect them reliably. Nonetheless, the convergence of evidence for the strong heritability of *g* from family, twin and adoption studies implies that *g*-relevant DNA polymorphisms exist. The solution of course is that the power of our designs will need to be increased in order to detect the QTLs responsible for the heritability of *g*, even if the QTL heritabilities are less than 1%. DNA pooling will be useful in this context because it costs no more to genotype 1,000 individuals than 100 individuals.

6. Using Genes Rather Than Finding Genes

Despite the slow progress to date in finding genes associated with *g*, the substantial heritability of *g* means that there are DNA polymorphisms that affect *g*. I am confident that we will find some of them. Although attention is now focused on finding specific genes associated with complex traits, the greatest impact for behavioral science will come after genes have been identified. Few behavioral scientists are likely to join the hunt for genes because it is difficult and expensive, but once genes are found, it is relatively easy and inexpensive to use them (Plomin & Rutter 1998). DNA can be obtained painlessly and inexpensively from cheek swabs — blood is not necessary. Cheek swabs yield enough DNA to genotype thousands of genes, and the cost of genotyping can be surprisingly inexpensive. Although some psychology departments already have DNA laboratories, it is likely that most psychological research with DNA will be accomplished through collaborations with molecular geneticists or through commercial arrangements.

It is critical for the future of the behavioral sciences that we be prepared to use DNA in our research and eventually in our clinics. What has happened in the area of dementia in the elderly will be played out in many areas of the behavioral sciences. As mentioned earlier, the only known risk factor for late-onset Alzheimer's dementia (LOAD) is a gene, apolipoprotein E, involved in cholesterol transport. A form of the gene called allele 4 quadruples the risk for LOAD but is neither necessary nor sufficient to produce the disorder; hence, it is a QTL. Although the association between allele 4 and LOAD was reported less than a decade ago (Corder *et al.* 1993), it has already become de rigueur to conduct research on dementia without genotyping subjects for apolipoprotein E in order to ascertain whether the results differ for individuals with and without this genetic risk factor. Genotyping apolipoprotein E will become clinically routine if a genetic risk factor is found to predict differential response to interventions or treatments.

In terms of clinical work, DNA may eventually lead to gene-based diagnoses and treatment programs. The most exciting potential for DNA research is to be able predict genetic risk for an individual and intervening to prevent problems before full-blown disorders emerge and create cascades of complications that are difficult to counteract. Interventions for behavioral disorders, and even for single-gene disorders, are likely to involve environmental rather than genetic engineering. For example, as mentioned earlier, phenylketonuria (PKU), a metabolic disorder that can cause severe mental retardation, is caused by a single gene on chromosome 12. A particular form of the gene, found in 1 per 10,000 babies, damages the developing brain postnatally. This form of mental retardation has been largely prevented, not by high-tech solutions such as correcting the mutant DNA or by eugenic programs or by drugs, but rather by a change in diet that prevents the mutant DNA from having its damaging effects. For this reason, newborns have been screened for decades for PKU, in order to identify those with the disorder so their diet can be changed. The example of PKU serves as an antidote to the mistaken notion that genetics implies therapeutic nihilism, even for a single-gene disorder. This point is even more important in relation to complex disorders that are influenced by many genes and by many environmental factors as well.

The search for genes involved in behavior has led to a number of ethical concerns (Plomin 1999a). For example, there are fears that the results will be used to justify social inequality, to select individuals for education or employment, or to enable parents to pick and choose among their fetuses. These concerns are largely based on misunderstandings about how genes affect complex traits (Rutter & Plomin 1997), but it is important that behavioral scientists knowledgeable about DNA continue to be involved in this debate. Students in the behavioral sciences must be taught about genetics in order to prepare them for this future.

As the recent advances from the Human Genome Project begin to be absorbed in behavioral genetic research, optimism is warranted about finding more QTLs associated with behavioral dimensions and disorders. The future of genetic research will involve moving from finding genes (genomics) to finding out how genes work (functional genomics). Functional genomics is usually considered in terms of bottom-up molecular biology at the cellular level of analysis. However, a top-down behavioral level of analysis may be even more valuable in understanding how genes work at the level of the intact organism, in understanding interactions and correlations between genes and environment, and in leading to new treatments and interventions. The phrase 'behavioral genomics' has been suggested to emphasise the importance of top-down levels of analysis in understanding how genes work (Plomin & Crabbe 2000). Bottom-up and top-down levels of analysis of gene-behavior pathways will eventually meet in the brain. The grandest implication for science is that DNA will serve as an integrating force across diverse disciplines.

References

Baron, M. (2001). Genetics of schizophrenia and the new millennium: Progress and pitfalls. *American Journal of Human Genetics*, 68, 299–312.

Bouchard, T. J., Jr, Lykken, D. T., McGue, M., Segal, N. L., & Tellegen, A. (1990). Sources of human psychological differences: The Minnesota Study of Twins Reared Apart. *Science, 250,* 223–228.

Bouchard, T. J., Jr, & McGue, M. (1981). Familial studies of intelligence: A review. *Science, 212,* 1055–1059.

Cardon, L. R., & Bell, J. (2001). Association study designs for complex diseases. *Nature Genetics, Feb* (2), 91–99.

Chorney, M. J., Chorney, K., Seese, N., Owen, M. J., Daniels, J., McGuffin, P., Thompson, L. A., Detterman, D. K., Benbow, C. P., Lubinski, D., Eley, T. C., & Plomin, R. (1998). A quantitative trait locus (QTL) associated with cognitive ability in children. *Psychological Science, 9,* 1–8.

Corder, E. H., Saunders, A. M., Strittmatter, W. J., Schmechel, D. E., Gaskell, P. C., Small, G. W., Roses, A. D., Haines, J. L., & Pericak Vance, M. A. (1993). Gene dose of apolipoprotein E type 4 allele and the risk of Alzheimer's disease in late onset families. *Science, 261,* 921–923.

Daniels, J., Holmans, P., Plomin, R., McGuffin, P., & Owen, M. J. (1998). A simple method for analyzing microsatellite allele image patterns generated from DNA pools and its application to allelic association studies. *American Journal of Human Genetics, 62,* 1189–1197.

Deater-Deckard, K., Reiss, D., Hetherington, E. M., & Plomin, R. (1997). Dimensions and disorders of adolescent adjustment: A quantitative genetic analysis of unselected samples and selected extremes. *Journal of Child Psychology and Psychiatry, 38,* 515–525.

Devlin, B., Daniels, M., & Roeder, K. (1997). The heritability of IQ. *Nature, 388,* 468–471.

Erlenmeyer-Kimling, L., & Jarvik, L. F. (1963). Genetics and intelligence: A review. *Science, 142,* 1477–1479.

Fisher, P. J., Turic, D., McGuffin, P., Asherson, P. J., Ball, D. M., Craig, I. W., Eley, T. C., Hill, L., Chorney, K., Chorney, M. J., Benbow, C. P., Lubinski, D., Plomin, R., & Owen, M. J. (1999). DNA pooling identifies QTLs for general cognitive ability in children on chromosome 4. *Human Molecular Genetics, 8,* 915–922.

Fisher, R. A. (1918). The correlation between relatives on the supposition of Mendelian inheritance. *Transactions of the Royal Society of Edinburgh, 52,* 399–433.

Hill, L., Chorney, M. J., Chorney, K., Craig, I. W., Fisher, P., Owen, M. J., McGuffin, P., & Plomin, R. (1999). IGF2R and cognitive ability. *Molecular Psychiatry, 4,* S108.

Hill, L., Craig, I. W., Ball, D. M., Eley, T. C., Ninomiya, T., Fisher, P. J., McGuffin, P., Owen, M. J., Chorney, K., Chorney, M. J., Benbow, C. P., Lubinski, D., Thompson, L. A., & Plomin, R. (1999). DNA pooling and dense marker maps: A systematic search for genes for cognitive ability. *NeuroReport, 10,* 843–848.

Jensen, A. R. (1967). Estimation of the limits of heritability by comparison of monozygotic and dizygotic twins. *Proceedings of the National Academy of Sciences, 58,* 149–156.

Jensen, A. R. (1969). How much can we boost IQ and scholastic achievement? *Harvard Educational Review, 39,* 1–123.

Jensen, A. R. (1972). *Genetics and education.* New York: Harper & Row.

Jensen, A. R. (1974). The problem of genotype-environment correlation in the estimation of heritability from monozygotic and dizygotic twins. *Acta Geneticae Medicae et Gemellologicae, 25,* 86–99.

Jensen, A. R. (1976). The problem of genotype-environment correlation in the estimation of heritability from monozygotic and dizygotic twins. *Acta Geneticae Medicae et Gemellologiae, 25,* 86–99.

Jensen, A. R. (1978). Genetic and behavioural effects of nonrandom mating. In: R. T. Osbourne, C. E. Noble, & N. Weyl (Eds), *Human variation: The biopsychology of age, race, and sex* (pp. 51–105). New York: Academic Press.

Jensen, A. R. (1980). Uses of sibling data in educational and psychological research. *American Educational Research Journal, 17*, 153–170.

Jensen, A. R. (1983). Effects of inbreeding on mental-ability factors. *Personality and Individual Differences, 4*, 71–87.

Jensen, A. R. (1998). *The g factor: The science of mental ability*. Wesport: Praeger.

Mackintosh, N. J. (1998). *IQ and human intelligence*. Oxford: Oxford University Press.

McGue, M. (1997). The democracy of the genes. *Nature, 388*, 417–418.

Nagoshi, C. T., & Johnson, R. C. (1987). Between-versus within-family factor analyses of cognitive abilities. *Intelligence, 11*, 305–316.

Pedersen, N. L., Plomin, R., Nesselroade, J. R., & McClearn, G. E. (1992). A quantitative genetic analysis of cognitive abilities during the second half of the life span. *Psychological Science, 3*, 346–353.

Petrill, S. A., Ball, D. M., Eley, T. C., Hill, L., & Plomin, R. (1998). Failure to replicate a QTL association between a DNA marker identified by EST00083 and IQ. *Intelligence, 25*, 179–184.

Plomin, R. (1999a). Genetics and general cognitive ability. *Nature, 402*, C25-C29.

Plomin, R. (1999b). Genetic research on general cognitive ability as a model for mild mental retardation. *International Review of Psychiatry, 11*, 34–36.

Plomin, R., & Crabbe, J. C. (2000). DNA. *Psychological Bulletin, 126*, 806–828.

Plomin, R., DeFries, J. C., McClearn, G. E., & McGuffin, P. (2001). *Behavioral genetics* (4th ed.). New York: Worth Publishers.

Plomin, R., DeFries, J. C., McClearn, G. E., & Rutter, M. (1997). *Behavioral genetics*. New York: W. H. Freeman.

Plomin, R., Fulker, D. W., Corley, R., & DeFries, J. C. (1997). Nature, nurture and cognitive development from 1 to 16 years: A parent-offspring adoption study. *Psychological Science, 8*, 442–447.

Plomin, R., Hill, L., Craig, I., McGuffin, P., Purcell, S., Sham, P., Lubinski, D., Thompson, L., Fisher, P. J., Turic, D., & Owen, M. J. (2001). A genome-wide scan of 1847 DNA markers for allelic associations with general cognitive ability: A five-stage design using DNA pooling. (submitted).

Plomin, R., McClearn, G. E., Smith, D. L., Skuder, P., Vignetti, S., Chorney, M. J., Chorney, K., Kasarda, S., Thompson, L. A., Detterman, D. K., Petrill, S. A., Daniels, J., Owen, M. J., & McGuffin, P. (1995). Allelic associations between 100 DNA markers and high versus low IQ. *Intelligence, 21*, 31–48.

Plomin, R., Owen, M. J., & McGuffin, P. (1994). The genetic basis of complex human behaviors. *Science, 264*, 1733–1739.

Plomin, R., & Rutter, M. (1998). Child development, molecular genetics, and what to do with genes once they are found. *Child Development, 69*, 1223–1242.

Risch, N. J. (2000). Searching for genetic determinants in the new millennium. *Nature, 405*, 847–856.

Risch, N., & Merikangas, K. R. (1996). The future of genetic studies of complex human diseases. *Science, 273*, 1516–1517.

Rutter, M., & Plomin, R. (1997). Opportunities for psychiatry from genetic findings. *British Journal of Psychiatry, 171*, 209–219.

Saudino, K. J., Dale, P. S., Oliver, B., Petrill, S. A., Richardson, V., Rutter, M., Simonoff, E., Stevenson, J., & Plomin, R. (1998). The validity of parent-based assessment of the cognitive abilities of two-year-olds. *British Journal of Developmental Psychology, 16*, 349–363.

Saudino, K. J., Plomin, R., Pedersen, N. L., & McClearn, G. E. (1994). The etiology of high and low cognitive ability during the second half of the life span. *Intelligence, 19*, 353–371.

Seligman, M. E. P., & Csikszentmihalyi, M. (2000). Positive psychology: An introduction. *American Psychologist, 55,* 5–14.

Spearman, C. (1927). *The abilities of man: Their nature and measurement.* New York: Macmillan.

Wahlström, J. (1990). Gene map of mental retardation. *Journal of Mental Deficiency Research, 34,* 11–27.

Wickelgren, I. (1998). Tracking insulin to the mind. *Science, 280,* 517–519.

Part III

The Demography of *g*

Part III — Introduction

Part III examines selected demographic aspects, such as geographic, race, and sex differences in *g*.

Richard Lynn begins chapter 8 — The geography of intelligence — by discussing the interesting observation that the intelligence levels of peoples throughout the world vary consistently with their geographical location and race, even if there certainly are considerable overlaps. Lynn uses a common classification to distinguish eight major geographical-racial groups, and then presents an updated version of data on their average IQ scores, originally collected in the late 1980s using progressive matrices, WAIS, or Cattell's Culture Fair Tests. The IQs are expressed in relation to a British average of IQ = 100, and adjusted for the Lynn-Flynn effect of increasing IQ scores over time.

IQs in north and west Europe (with Ireland excluded) range between 98–103; lower values are observed in southeast and east Europe. European Caucasoids living outside Europe tend toward slightly lower IQs, but are still located within the full European range of 93–102. East Asian Mongoloids have increased IQs (range: 98–110), but South East Asian and Pacific Islanders earn lower IQs (range: 82–91). Still lower IQs are found in the rest of the world.

Lynn makes it clear, that the tests used load high on *g*, and that the *g* differences among populations arise from a mix of genetic and environmental factors. However, race is still found to be the most important determinant of the IQs of the populations. Lynn points to the fact that the average IQ of American blacks is around 85, which is roughly 15 IQ points above the African black average, and suggests living in a white society has considerably raised the IQs of American blacks. Lynn concludes chapter 8 with a discussion of how proximate IQs can be deduced from populations of racial admixtures, and of whether evolution may explain the genetics behind racial differences in IQ.

Phil Rushton continues the thread from chapter 9, by commenting on race differences in *g* and the "Jensen Effect". His review of the literature confirms that black-white IQ differences are more pronounced on highly *g*-loaded tests than on low *g*-loaded tests, *g* being the general factor of intelligence. Black-white differences on the *g*-factor occur regardless of whether testing is performed in the United States, in South Africa, or in the Netherlands. Rushton then finds that the Lynn-Flynn effect may not be a "Jensen Effect", and goes on to review, in considerable detail, the evidence for what Jensen calls the "default hypothesis" — that genetic and cultural factors carry the same weight in causing black-white IQ differences, as they do in causing individual differences within each race. Rushton's general conclusion is that the robustness of the Spearman-Jensen hypothesis — that the more g-loaded a test, the larger the race difference — implies, that a scientific understanding of the individual, group, or developmental differences depends on understanding the nature of g. The reader may find it enlightening to compare Rushton's arguments and data to those provided by Nathan Brody in chapter 18 in this volume.

Helmuth Nyborg pursues a further controversial demographic thread in chapter 10, by discussing whether males and females differ in general intelligence g. Most experts agree that there are important sex differences in group factors, like verbal and spatial ability, but they visibly disagree about a sex difference in general intelligence. Part of the problem seems to be that many proponents for a sex difference in general intelligence, such as Richard Lynn, rely on a total summed IQ score and find a difference, whereas sceptics, such as Arthur Jensen, use correlational factor analytic approaches and find no consistent sex difference. Nyborg begins the analysis by arguing, that both total summed IQ scores of intelligence in general and the Principal Component or Principal Factor analytic g scores of general intelligence g might, under certain methodological circumstances, represent a slightly contaminated proxy for the latent variable g. Were that the case, methodological shortcomings would overshadow a potentially small sex difference in g. A six-point scale for evaluating sex difference studies in term of adequacy of methodology was therefore developed and applied to a number of selected studies — some of them reporting a sex difference, some not. Studies earning less than 5 points run, according to the chosen scale cut-off point an unacceptable high risk of committing either a type I or type II error. The literature review indicates that only two contemporary studies earn five or more points, and thus satisfy the quality demand. Both studies used the Schmid-Leiman hierarchical factor analytic approach, both factored in the relevant point-biserial correlations, and both studies found a significant male lead in general intelligence g. Nyborg finally demonstrates that a simple tape measure of head circumference (a proxy for brain size) correlates significantly with g (0.34), and that brain size under-predicts the sex difference in g by about 1.1 IQ point. Suggestions for future research on sex differences conclude the chapter.

Chapter 8

The Geography of Intelligence

Richard Lynn

1. Introduction

In this chapter it is shown that the intelligence levels of peoples throughout the world varies consistently with their geographical location and with their race. There is a considerable overlap between geography and race. The most recent and thorough classification of the world's peoples by geography and race has been produced by Cavalli-Sforza *et al.* (1994). From an analysis of genetic differences between populations they distinguish eight major geographical-racial groups. Although they prefer to avoid the classical descriptive terms of Caucasoids, Mongoloids and so forth, their categories are so similar to these that it is convenient to use them. In terms of the classical taxonomy, their geographical-racial groups are European Caucasoids, South Asian and North African Caucasoids, Northeast Asian Mongoloids, Southeast Asians extending from Thailand to Indonesia and the Philippines, Pacific Islanders, Australian Aborigines, Negroids and American Indians. This is the classification adopted in this chapter. The data presented here are an updated version of the evidence collected in the late 1980s (Lynn 1991). The IQs have been calculated from the Progressive Matrices or from other tests of general intelligence such as the Wechsler tests and the Cattell Culture Fair. IQs are expressed in relation to a British IQ of 100 and take into account Flynn effects of 2 IQ points per decade for the Progressive Matrices and similar tests and 3 IQ points per decade for Wechsler and similar tests. This is responsible for a number of minor differences between the present calculations and those presented previously, which were not adjusted for Flynn effects. A number of studies presented previously have been omitted here because of defects of various kinds and because they have been superseded by better studies. For example, Vernon (1969) reported data for 50 children in Uganda showing that their IQ was about 80. The sample was drawn from a selective academic secondary school so this must have been an overestimate of the IQ in Uganda. The study reported here was based on a representative sample of 2,019 children tested with the Progressive Matrices and is so much more satisfactory in terms of representativeness and sample size that the Vernon results have been discarded.

2. IQ Distribution of the World

2.1. European Caucasoids — Europe

Mean IQs derived from 26 data sets for the populations of 21 European nations are shown in Table 8.1. This table omits Buj's (1981) IQ data for 21 European cities on the grounds that his sample sizes are in many cases rather small (e.g. 75 for Ireland and 100 for Norway) and in 13 of the countries his standard deviations are greater than 20, suggesting sampling defects. For most countries his results have been superseded by more recent data based on greater sample sizes and these have been entered in the table. The European IQs fall in the range between 92 for Ireland and 103 for Germany (the average of the two results). The median of the 26 data sets is 98, which can be taken as the best estimate of the IQ of the European peoples.

The lowest IQ of 92 for Ireland is probably explicable in terms of the backward economy until quite recently and the long history of selective emigration of the more intelligent, which is documented in Lynn (1979). With this exception, IQs in north and west Europe are generally higher than elsewhere, lying in the range of 98–103, while IQs in southeast and east Europe lie in the range of 88–96, and the IQ of 98 in the two central European countries of the Czech and Slovak Republics is intermediate. The relatively low IQs in east and southeast Europe are probably due in part to the lower living standards in these counties, brought about by half a century of impoverishment caused by communist economies. Particular interest is attached to the IQ of 96 for Russia which has recently been obtained from a study in the city of Briansk, which lies about two hundred miles south west of Moscow. Work on intelligence was prohibited throughout the Soviet Union in the 1930s as contrary to Marxist-Leninism and it was not until 1997 that normative data on intelligence were collected from which the IQ of 96 has been calculated.

2.2. European Caucasoids — Outwith Europe

During the last four centuries European Caucasoids have colonised and occupied a number of parts of the world, notably North and South America, Australia, New Zealand and South Africa. IQs from 15 studies for eight of these populations are shown in Table 8.2. The IQs fall between 93 and 102 and are thus in the same range as IQs in Europe. The studies for Argentina and Uruguay are derived from norms for the total population. In Argentina this is 85% white and 15% Mestizo and Native American, and in Uruguay it is 88% white, 8% Mestizo and 4% black (Ramsay 2000). A notable feature of these results is the consistency of the IQs over a period of many decades in the cases of Argentina, Australia, New Zealand and the United States. These results show that wherever European populations are located their IQs fall in the European range of between 92 and 103.

2.3. South Asian and North African Caucasoids

IQs for 15 samples from ten South Asian and North African countries are shown in Table 8.3. Apart from Israel, all the IQs lie between 78 and 90 and the median IQ is 83.

Table 8.1: IQs of European caucasoids.

Country	IQ	Reference	Country	IQ	Reference
Belgium	99	Goosens 1952a	Ireland	92	Raven 1981
Belgium	103	Goosens 1952b	Italy	103	Tesi & Young 1962
Britain	100	Raven 1981	Netherlands	99	Raven et al. 1995
Bulgaria	91	Lynn et al. 1998	Netherlands	101	Raven et al. 1996
Croatia	90	Sorokin 1954	Poland	92	Jarorowska & Szustrowa 1991
Czech Rep.	98	Raven et al. 1996	Portugal	91	Simoes 1989
Denmark	97	Vejleskov 1968	Romania	94	Zahirnic et al. 1974
Finland	98	Kyostio 1972	Russia	96	Raven 1998
France	102	Dague et al. 1964	Slovak Rep.	98	Raven et al. 1995
France	97	Bourdier 1964	Spain	96	Raven et al. 1995
Germany	105	Raven 1981	Sweden	100	Scandinavia Test 1970
Germany	101	Raven et al. 1995	Switzerland	101	Raven et al. 1995
Greece	88	Fatouros 1972	Switzerland	102	Raven et al. 1995

Table 8.2: IQs of other European caucasoids.

Country	IQ	Reference	Country	IQ	Reference
Argentina	93	Rimoldi 1948	N. Zealand	101	Reid & Gilmore 1989
Argentina	98	Raven *et al.* 1998	South Africa	96	Owen 1992
Australia	95	McIntyre 1938	Uruguay	96	Risso 1961
Australia	98	Raven *et al.* 1995	United States	100	Scottish Council 1933
Australia	99	Raven *et al.* 1996	United States	99	Scottish Council 1949
Canada	97	Raven *et al.* 1996	United States	100	Hodgkiss 1978
N. Zealand	100	Redmond & Davies 1940	United States	100	Raven *et al.* 1996

Table 8.3: IQs of South Asian and North African caucasoids.

Country	IQ	Reference	Country	IQ	Reference
Egypt	83	Dennis 1957	Israel	97	Miron 1977
Egypt	83	Ahmed 1989	Israel	90	Lynn 1994
India	81	Sinha 1968	Lebanon	86	Dennis 1957
India	82	Rao & Reddy 1968	Morocco	84	Te Nijenhuis & van der Flier 1997
India	82	Raven et al. 1996	Nepal	78	Sunberg & Ballinger 1968
Iran	84	Valentine 1959	Qatar	78	Bart et al. 1987
Iraq	87	Abul-Hubb 1972	Turkey	90	Sahin & Duzen 1994
Iraq	85	Abul-Hubb 1972			

We note that in these populations the IQ is highest in Turkey (90), reflecting their close genetic similarity with Greeks (shown by Cavalli-Sforza *et al.* 1994), who have the same IQ. The IQs in the remaining nine countries fall in the range of 78 to 86. Thus, there is not a sharp break at the Dardanelles between the European and the Asian Caucasoids but rather a continuous gradient reflecting the genetic admixture of peoples with their neighbors all the way from North-West to South-East Europe through to Turkey and on to South-East Asia and North Africa.

The IQ in Israel requires separate consideration. If the two results of 90 and 97 are averaged to 94, the IQ is evidently higher than among any of the other South Asian and North African Caucasoids. Israel is an ethnically diverse nation with about equal numbers of Western (European) and Eastern (Asian) Jews. Western Jews have an IQ 12 points higher than Eastern Jews (Lieblich *et al.* 1972; Zeidner 1987). It can be inferred that the IQ of Eastern Jews in Israel is about 88 and falls into place in the intelligence gradient running from Turkey east and south. The IQ of Western Jews in Israel is about 100, and about the same as that of other North-Western European populations. Most Western Jews migrated to Israel during the second half of the twentieth century and have raised the intelligence level above that of other south Asian populations.

2.4. IQs of East Asian Mongoloids

IQs for 24 samples of East Asian Mongoloids from six countries are shown in Table 8.4. The results of the 24 studies lie between 98 and 110. The median of the studies is an IQ of 104. Of the three studies from China, the IQ of 98 is obtained from children and adults in which the IQ for children is higher than that for adults, reflecting a substantial increase in intelligence in China during the last half century. The IQ of 108 is derived from a standardisation of the WISC-R in Shanghai and is likely to be too high because the IQ in Shanghai is probably higher than in China as a whole. The ten results for Japan all lie between 103 and 110 with the exception of the IQ of 100 derived from the Japanese standardisation of the McCarthy test. The explanation for this is probably that this test is for 2 to 8-year-old children and Oriental children mature more slowly than European (Rushton 2000).

An explanation is required for the IQs of 104 for Japan and for Taiwan entered for the study by Stevenson *et al.* (1985). This study compared the IQs of 240 6-year-olds and 240 10-year-olds in the American city of Minneapolis, the Japanese city of Sendai and the Taiwanese city of Taipei. The investigators constructed their own tests of various abilities. These did not include a test of non-verbal reasoning but did include a vocabulary and a spatial test. The results were that there were no overall differences in the scores obtained by the children in the three cities, which led the investigators to conclude that the Japanese and Chinese have the same IQ as Europeans. A defect of this study is that Minneapolis is not representative for intelligence of American cities. A series of studies have shown that intelligence in the state of Minnesota, in which Minneapolis is situated, is higher than in the United States as a whole. In the military draft in World War I, the whites from Minnesota obtained the highest score on the Army Beta Test of all American States (Ashley Montagu 1945). In the draft for the Vietnam

Table 8.4: IQs of North East Asian mongoloids.

Country	IQ	Reference	Country	IQ	Reference
China	98	Raven et al. 1996	Japan	103	Li et al. 1996
China	108	Li et al. 1990	Hong Kong	103	Lynn et al. 1988
China	103	Li et al. 1996	Hong Kong	110	Lynn et al. 1988
Japan	103	Lynn 1977a	Hong Kong	109	Chan & Lynn 1989
Japan	107	Lynn & Dziobon 1980	Hong Kong	107	Lynn et al. 1988
Japan	110	Misawa et al. 1984	Singapore	106	Lynn 1977b
Japan	105	Stevenson et al. 1985	South Korea	105	Moon 1988
Japan	100	Lynn & Hampson 1986a	South Korea	106	Lynn & Song 1994
Japan	103	Lynn & Hampson 1986b	Taiwan	102	Rodd 1959
Japan	107	Kaufman et al. 1989	Taiwan	103	Hsu 1976
Japan	110	Shigehisa & Lynn 1991	Taiwan	104	Stevenson et al. 1985
Japan	104	Takeuchi & Scott 1992	Taiwan	105	Lynn 1997

war, the percentage of draftees (blacks and whites) who failed the pre-induction mental assessments was the second lowest in Minnesota among the American states (Office of the Surgeon General 1968: 45). On the basis of these data, Flynn (1980) has calculated that the average IQ in Minnesota is 105. Hence, as the Japanese and Taiwanese IQs are the same as those in Minnesota, they must be 105 in relation to that of the United States. It is another defect of this study that the authors do not say whether the sample was all white or, if not, what percentage was black. Since Minnesota is very largely white, it is assumed that the sample was white and therefore that it had an IQ 5 points higher than that of American whites.

The four results from Hong Kong are reasonably consistent, all lying in the range of 103–110. The two results from South Korea yielding IQs of 105 and 106 are highly consistent. The four results from Taiwan are highly consistent, all lying in the range of 102–105. The explanation for entering an IQ of 105 for the Stevenson *et al.* (1985) study has been given above. A curious feature of the Stevenson *et al.* study is that Hsu, the member of Stevenson's team who conducted the study in Taiwan, had already published a study of the performance of all 6 and 7-year-old children numbering 43,825 in Taipei on the Coloured Progressive Matrices. The result, as shown in Table 8.4, is that the Chinese children had an IQ of 103 in relation to the British mean of 100. This result from this huge sample should have alerted the investigators to the inconsistency with their own result. Furthermore, since Hsu's result from this huge sample for one of the best tests of *g* was already available, it is difficult to understand the point of Stevenson and his group carrying out a further study of 480 children using tests of unknown properties.

2.5. South East Asia and Pacific Islanders

IQs for 13 samples from nine countries are given in Table 8.5. The IQs lie in the range between 82–91 and the median is 89. The IQs in these populations are discernibly lower than those of the North-East Asian Mongoloids (median = 104) and higher than those of the South Asian and North African Caucasoids (median = 82). The explanation for this is that the South-East Asians are a hybrid population consisting of South Asians from the Indian sub-Continent who migrated east into South-East Asia and then into the Pacific islands, interbred with Mongoloids who migrated southwards.

2.6. IQs of Australian Aborigines

The IQs of six samples of Australian Aborigines are given in Table 8.6. They fall in the range of 65–79 and the median is 71. There is no overlap between the IQs of these samples and those of the South-East Asians and Pacific Islanders, whose lowest recorded IQ is 82. The explanation for this is that the Australian Aborigines are genetically distant from the South East Asians and Pacific Islanders. Their ancestors migrated from South East Asia around 50,000 years ago and were not followed by other South-East Asian migrants, so they remained genetically isolated from other populations throughout South-East Asia and the Pacific Islands.

Table 8.5: IQs of South East Asians and Pacific islanders.

Country	IQ	Reference	Country	IQ	Reference
Fiji	82	Chandra 1975	NZ Maoris	95	St. George 1983
Indonesia	89	Thomas & Sjah 1961	NZ Maoris	90	St. George & Chapman 1983
Malaysia	89	Chaim 1994	Philippines	86	Flores & Evans 1972
Marshall Is.	84	Jordheim & Olsen 1963	Singapore	90	Lynn 1977b
NZ Maoris	90	Walters 1958	Thailand	91	Pollitt *et al.* 1989
NZ Maoris	84	Du Chateau 1967	Tonga	86	Beck & St.George 1983
NZ Maoris	9	Harker 1978			

Table 8.7: IQs of sub-saharan African negroids.

Country	IQ	Reference	Country	IQ	Reference
Congo	73	Ombredane et al. 1952	South Africa	67	Owen 1992
Congo	72	Nkaya et al. 1994	South Africa	63	Lynn & Holmshaw 1990
Ethiopia	67	Lynn 1994	Sudan	72	Ahmed 1989
Ghana	62	Glewwe & Jacoby 1992	Tanzania	78	Klingelhofer 1967
Guinea	70	Faverge & Falmagne 1962	Tanzania	69	Boissiere et al. 1985
Kenya	69	Boissiere et al. 1985	Uganda	73	Heyneman & Jamison 1980
Kenya	75	Costenbader & Ngari 2000	Zaire	68	Laroche 1959
Nigeria	69	Wober 1969	Zaire	62	Boivin & Giordani 1993
Nigeria	69	Fahrmeier 1975	Zaire	68	Boivin et al. 1995
Sierra Leone	67	Berry 1966	Zambia	65	Giordani et al. 1996
South Africa	65	Fick 1929	Zambia	75	MacArthur et al. 1964
South Africa	75	Notcutt 1950	Zimbabwe	61	Zindi 1994
South Africa	71	Notcutt 1950	Zimbabwe	70	Zindi 1994

Table 8.8: IQs of native American indians.

Country	IQ	Reference	Country	IQ	Reference
Canada	85	MacArthur 1965	United States	81	Haught 1934
Mexico	87	Modiano 1962	United States	85	Reschly & Jipson 1976
Peru	87	Raven *et al.* 1995	United States	94	Raven & Court 1989
United States	88	Telford 1932			
United States	83	Beiser & Gotoweic 2000			

With regard to the intelligence difference between blacks and whites in the United States, the consistency of the black-white differences worldwide corroborates the thesis that genetic factors are largely responsible for the difference in the United States. We have seen that whites from North West Europe, which is where the ancestors of most American whites came from, almost invariably have IQs close to 100, whether they are in Europe, Canada, Australia, New Zealand or South Africa, while blacks in sub-Saharan Africa invariably obtain IQs in the range of 62–78. The IQ of blacks in the United States is around 85 and hence substantially higher than the IQs of blacks in sub-Saharan Africa. There are two explanations for this. The first is that American blacks are a hybrid population with about 25% of white ancestry (Reed 1969; Chakraborty *et al.* 1992). According to genetic theory this would raise their IQs above the level of blacks in Africa. The second is that American blacks live in a society run by whites and enjoy much higher standards of living, nutrition, education and health care than they have in societies run by blacks. This enriched environment can be expected to have some advantageous impact on their IQ. When we look at the IQs of blacks in Africa we have to conclude that living in a white society has raised rather than lowered the IQs of American blacks.

This conclusion is the opposite to that of a number of environmentalists who contend that the low IQ of American blacks is due to "white racism". For instance, Mackintosh writes: "it is precisely the experience of being black in a society permeated by white racism that is responsible for lowering black children's IQ scores" (1998: 152). The IQs of blacks in Africa is compelling evidence against this theory. African countries gained independence from white rule in the 1960s and African children born from 1970 onwards no longer experienced white racism. The theory that white racism has been responsible for the low IQ of American blacks leads to the prediction that recent generations of young African blacks would show significant IQ gains. Studies carried out in the 1990s show that this has not happened. African blacks have continued to obtain the same low IQs of 62 (Ghana), 75 (Kenya), 62–68 (Zaire) and 61–70 (Zimbabwee) as they have obtained from the 1920s onwards. The theory that white racism has been responsible for the low IQ of American blacks was never plausible because its proponents have not identified the mechanism by which racism could lower intelligence and because racism has had no adverse impact on the intelligence of Asians and Jews. The evidence from Africa finally discredits it.

This association between intelligence and race is sufficiently close for it to be possible to predict the approximate IQs of nations and of sub-populations within nations from their racial identity. For instance, the population of Jamaica is 90% black, 7% mixed and 3% Indian (Ramsay 2000). It would be predicted that the population's IQ should be a little above the median IQ of 68 of blacks in sub-Saharan Africa. The mean IQ is 72 (Manley 1963). In neighboring Cuba the population is 37% white, 11% black and 51% Afro-European. Assigning IQs of 98 for whites, 69 for blacks and 83 for Afro-Europeans, the IQ of the population should be 87. The actual IQ derived from the standardisation of the Progressive Matrices by Alonso (1974) is 84. Numerous other predictions can be made and tested from the genetic theory of race differences in intelligence. The theory has crossed the threshold from descriptive to predictive science.

The causes of genetically based racial differences in intelligence should be sought in their evolutionary history. Differences in IQ must have developed together with differences in skin color, morphology and resistance to diseases as adaptations to the environments in which the races evolved. We can reconstruct the broad outline of how this occurred. Modern humans evolved in Central East Africa about a quarter of a million years ago. Their brain size was the same as that of living blacks and it can be assumed that their intelligence was the same, represented by an IQ of 69. About 100,000 years ago some of these migrated into South West Asia. Here they encountered cold winters and a lack of plant foods during winter and spring. These conditions exerted selection pressure for an increase of intelligence to enable them to make clothing and shelters to protect themselves from the cold winters and to hunt large animals to obtain meat when plant foods were not available. By around 50,000 years ago these selection pressures raised the IQ of these peoples to about 75, represented by the present day Australian Aborigines, who migrated to Australia at about this time and whose IQ stabilized at around this figure.

During the next 25,000 years some of the peoples of South Asia migrated into North East Asia and others migrated into Europe. Some of those who migrated into North East Asia evolved into the Mongoloids. Others crossed into America and evolved into the Native Americans. Those who migrated into Europe evolved into the European Caucasoids. About 25,000 years ago the climate in the northern hemisphere began to grow colder with the onset of the last ice age. Winter temperatures fell by around 10 degrees centigrade. This made survival more difficult and exerted further selection pressure for enhanced intelligence. This selection pressure was weakest on the peoples of South Asia but it was sufficient to raise their IQs to the present day level of about 83; it was about the same on the Native Americans because these had migrated into America before the onset of the ice age and their IQs were raised to about the same level as that of South Asians. Climatic conditions were more severe in Europe and North East Asia, where the environment resembled that of present day Alaska and Siberia. This increased the selection pressure for enhanced intelligence and drove the IQs of the European Caucasoids up to its present day figure of around 98. In North East Asia the climate was even more severe than in Europe and drove the IQs of the Mongoloids up to the present day figure of around 104. The morphological basis of the increase in intelligence in the Caucasoids and Mongoloids was an enlargement of brain size the evidence for which is set out by Rushton (2000).

The ice age came to an end about 10,000 years ago. In the more benign climate that followed the South Asian Caucasoids and the Mongoloids were able to use their enhanced intelligence to develop the early civilisations along the river valleys of the Tigris, Euphrates, Indus, Nile and Yangtze, where the flood plains and the favourable climate made it possible to produce the agricultural surpluses required to feed urban populations and sustain an intellectual class. The Native Americans had also evolved sufficiently high intelligence to develop the quasi-civilizations of the Aztecs, Mayas and Incas. Europe, Northern China and Japan did not have the flood plains or the favorable climate necessary for the development of these early civilizations but in the last two millennia these peoples have used their high IQs to overcome these problems and produce the advanced civilisations of today.

References

Abul-Hubb, D. (1972). Application of Progressive Matrices in Iraq. In: L. J. Cronbach, & P. J. Drenth (Eds), *Mental tests and cultural adaptation*. The Hague: Mouton.

Ahmed, R. A. (1989). The development of number, space, quantity and reasoning concepts in Sudanese schoolchildren. In: L. L. Adler (Ed.), *Cross cultural research in human development*. Westport, CT: Praeger.

Alonso, O. S. (1974). Raven, *g* factor, age and school level. *Havana Hospital Psiquiatrico Revista, 14*, 60–77.

Ashley Montagu, F. M. (1945). Intelligence of northern Negroes and southern whites in the First World War. *American Journal of Psychology, 58*, 161–188.

Bart, W., Kamal, A., & Lane, J. F. (1987). The development of proportional reasoning in Qatar. *Journal of Genetic Psychology, 148*, 95–103.

Beck, L. R., & St. George, R. (1983). The alleged cultural bias of PAT: reading comprehension and reading vocabulary tests. *New Zealand Journal of Educational Studies, 18*, 32–47.

Beiser, M., & Gotoweic, A. (2000). Accounting for native/non-native differences in IQ scores. *Psychology in the Schools, 37*, 237–253.

Berry, J. W. (1966). Temne and Eskimo perceptual skills. *International Journal of Psychology, 1*, 207–229.

Boissiere, M., Knight, J. B., & Sabot, R. H. (1985). Earnings, schooling, ability and cognitive skills. *American Economic Review, 75*, 1016–1030.

Boivin, M. J., & Giordani, B. (1993). Improvements in cognitive performance for school children in Zaire following an iron supplement and treatment for intestinal parasites. *Journal of Pediatric Psychology, 18*, 249–264.

Boivin, M. J., Giordani, B., & Bornfeld, B. (1995). Use of the tactual performance test for cognitive ability testing with African children. *Neuropsychology, 9*, 409–417.

Bourdier, G. (1964). Utilisation et nouvel etalonnage du P. M. 47. *Bulletin de Psychologie, 235*, 39–41.

Bruce, D. W., Hengeveld, M., & Radford, W. C. (1971). *Some cognitive skills in aboriginal children in Victorian primary schools*. Hawthorn, Victoria: ACER.

Buj, V. (1981). Average IQ values in various European countries. *Personality and Individual Differences, 2*, 168–169.

Cavalli-Sforza, L. L., Menozzi, P., & Piazza, A. (1994). *The history and geography of human genes*. Princeton, NJ: Princeton University Press.

Chaim, H. H. (1994). Is the Raven Progressive Matrices valid for Malaysians? Unpublished.

Chakraborty, R., Kamboh, M. I., Nwankwo, M., & Ferrell, R. E. (1992). Caucasian genes in American blacks. *American Journal of Human Genetics, 50*, 145–155.

Chan, J., & Lynn, R. (1989). The intelligence of six year olds in Hong Kong. *Journal of Biosocial Science, 21*, 461–464.

Chandra, S. (1975). Some patterns of response on the Queensland Test. *Australian Psychologist, 10*, 185–191.

Costenbader, V., & Ngari, S. M. (2000). A Kenya standardisation of the coloured progressive matrices. *Personality and Individual Differences*.

Dague, P., Garelli, M., & Lebettre, A. (1964). Recherches sur l'echelle de maturite mentale de Columbia. *Revue de Psychologie Applique, 14*, 71–96.

Dennis, W. (1957). Performance of near eastern children on the draw-a-man test. *Child Development, 28*, 427–430.

Du Chateau, P. (1967). Ten point gap in Maori aptitudes. *National Education, 49*, 157–158.

Edwards, L. D., & Craddock, L. J. (1973). Malnutrition and intellectual development. *Medical Journal of Australia*, (5 May), 880–884.

Fahrmeier, E. D. (1975). The effect of school attendance on intellectual development in Northern Nigeria. *Child Development, 46*, 281–285.

Fatouros, M. (1972). The influence of maturation and education on the development of abilities. In: L. J. Cronbach, & P. J. Drenth (Eds), *Mental tests and cultural adaptation*. The Hague: Mouton.

Faverge, J. M., & Falmagne, J. C. (1962). On the interpretation of data in intercultural psychology. *Psychologia Africana, 9*, 22–96.

Fick, M. L. (1929). Intelligence test results of poor white, native (Zulu), coloured and Indian school children and the social and educational implications. *South African Journal of Science, 26*, 904–920.

Flores, M. B., & Evans, G. T. (1972). Some differences in cognitive abilities between selected Canadian and Filipino students. *Multivariate Behavioral Research, 7*, 175–191.

Flynn, J. R. (1980). *Race, IQ and Jensen*. London: Routledge & Kegan Paul.

Giordani, B., Boivin, M. J., Opel, B., Nseyila, D. N., & Lauer, R. E. (1996) Use of the K-ABC with children in Zaire. *International Journal of Disability, Development and Education, 43*, 5–24.

Glewwe, P., & Jacoby, H. (1992). *Estimating the determinants of cognitive achievement in low income countries*. Washington, D.C.: World Bank.

Goosens, G. (1952a). Etalonnage du matrix 1947 de J. C. Raven. *Revue Belge de Psychologie et de Pedagogie, 14*, 74–80.

Goosens, G. (1952b). Une application du test d'intelligence de R. B. Cattell. *Revue Belge de Psychologie et de Pedagogie, 14*, 115–127.

Harker, R. K. (1978). Achievement and ethnicity: environmental deprivation or cultural difference. *New Zealand Journal of Educational Studies, 13*, 107–124.

Haught, B. F. (1934). Mental growth of the southwest Indian. *Journal of Applied Psychology, 18*, 137–142.

Heyneman, S. P., & Jamison, D. T. (1980). Student learning in Uganda. *Comparative Education Review, 24*, 207–220.

Hotgkiss, J. (1978). Differential Aptitude Test: British manual. Windsor: NFER.

Hsu, C. (1976). The learning potential of first graders in Taipei city as measured by Raven's Coloured Progressive Matrices. *Acta Pediatrica Sinica, 17*, 262–274.

Jarorowska, A., & Szustrowa, T. (1991). *Podrecznik do testu matryc ravena*. Warsaw: Pracownia Testow Psychologicznych.

Jensen, A. R. (1998). *The g Factor*. Westport, CT: Praeger.

Jordheim, G. D., & Olsen, I. A. (1963). The use of a non-verbal test of intelligence in the trust territory of the Pacific. *American Anthropologist, 65*, 1122–1125.

Kaufman, A. S., McLean, J. E., Ishikuma, T., & Moon, S. B. (1989) Integration of the literature on the intelligence of Japanese children and analysis of the data from a sequential-simultaneous perspective. *School Psychology International, 10*, 173–183.

Klingelhofer, E. L. (1967). Performance of Tanzanian secondary school pupils on the Raven Standard Progressive Matrices test. *Journal of Social Psychology, 72*, 205–215.

Kyostio, O. K. (1972). Divergence among school beginners caused by different cultural influences. In: L. J. Cronbach, & P. J. Drenth (Eds), *Mental tests and cultural adaptation*. The Hague: Mouton.

Laroche, J. L. (1959). Effets de repetition du matrix 38 sur les resultats d'enfants Katangais. *Bulletin du Centre d'Etudes et Recherches Pychotechniques, 1*, 85–99.

Li, D., Jin, Y., Vandenberg, S. G., Zhu, Y., & Tang, C. (1990). Report on Shanghai norms for the Chinese translation of the Wechsler intelligence scale for Children – revised. *Psychological Reports, 67*, 531–541.

Li, X., Sano, H., & Merwin, J. C. (1996). Perception and reasoning abilities among American, Japanese and Chinese adolescents. *Journal of Adolescent Research, 11*, 173–193.

Lieblich, A., Ninio, A., & Kugelmas, S. (1972). Effects of ethnic origin and parental SES on WPPSI performance of pre-school children in Israel. *Journal of Cross Cultural Psychology, 3*, 159–168.

Lynn, R. (1977a). The intelligence of the Japanese. *Bulletin of the British Psychological Society, 30*, 69–72.

Lynn, R. (1977b). The intelligence of the Chinese and Malays in Singapore. *Mankind Quarterly, 18*, 125–128.

Lynn, R. (1979). The social ecology of intelligence in the British Isles. *British Journal of Social and Clinical Psychology, 18*, 1–12.

Lynn, R. (1991). Race differences in intelligence: a global perspective. *Mankind Quarterly, 31*, 255–296.

Lynn, R. (1994). The intelligence of Ethiopian immigrant and Israeli adolescents. *International Journal of Psychology, 29*, 55–56.

Lynn, R. (1997). Intelligence in Taiwan. *Personality and Individual Differnces, 22*, 585–586.

Lynn, R., & Dziobon, J. (1980). On the intelligence of the Japanese and other Mongoloid peoples. *Personality and Individual Differences, 1*, 95–96.

Lynn, R., & Hampson, S. (1986a). The structure of Japanese abilities: an analysis in terms of the hierarchical model of intelligence. *Current Pyschological Research and Reviews, 4*, 309–322.

Lynn, R., & Hampson, S. (1986b). Intellectual abilities of Japanese children: an assessment of 2–8 year olds derived from the McCarthy Scales of Children's Abilities. *Intelligence, 10*, 41–58.

Lynn, R., & Holmshaw, M. (1990). Black-white differences in reaction times and intelligence. *Social Behavior and Personality, 18*, 299–308.

Lynn, R., Pagliari, C., & Chan, J. (1988). Intelligence in Hong Kong measured for Spearman's *g* and the visuospatial and verbal primaries. *Intelligence, 12*, 423–433.

Lynn, R., Plaspalanova, E., Stetinsky, D., & Tzenova, B. (1998). Intelligence in Bulgaria. *Psychological Reports, 82*, 912–914.

Lynn, R., & Song, M. J. (1994). General intelligence, visuospatial and verbal abilities of Korean children. *Personality and Individual Differences, 16*, 363–364.

MacArthur, R. S. (1965). *Mackenzie district norming project*. Ottawa: Dept. of Northern Affairs.

MacArthur, R. S., Irvine, S. H., & Brimble, A. R. (1964). *The Northern Rhodesia mental ability survey*. Lusaka: Rhodes Livingstone Institute.

Mackintosh, N. J. (1998). *IQ and human intelligence*. Oxford: University Press.

Manley, D. R. (1963). Mental ability in Jamaica. *Social and Economic Studies, 12*, 51–77.

McElwain, D. W., & Kearney, G. E. (1973). Intellectual development. In: G. E. Kearney, P. R. de Lacey, & G. R. Davidson (Eds), *The psychology of aboriginal Australians*. New York: Wiley.

McIntyre, G. A. (1938). *The standardisation of intelligence tests in Australia*. Melbourne: University Press.

Miron, M. (1977). A validation study of a transferred group intelligence test. *International Journal of Psychology, 12*, 193–205.

Misawa, G., Motegi, M., Fujita, K., & Hattori, K. (1984). A comparative study of intellectual abilities of Japanese and American children on the Columbia Mental Maturity Scale. *Personality and Individual Differences, 5*, 173–181.

Modiano, N. (1962). *Mental testing among Tzeltas and Tzotzil children* (unpublished).

Moon, S. B. (1988). *A cross cultural study of the Kaufman assessment battery for children with Korean children*. Ph.D thesis, University of Alabama.

Nkaya, H. N., Huteau, M., & Bennet, J-P. (1994). Retest effect on cognitive performance on the Raven matrices in France and in the Congo. *Perceptual and Motor Skills, 78*, 503–510.

Notcutt, B. (1950). The measurement of Zulu intelligence. *Journal of Social Research, 1*, 195–206.

Nurcombe, B., & Moffitt, P. (1963). Cultural deprivation and language deficit. In: G. E. Kearny, P. R. de Lacey, & D. R. Davidson (Eds), *The psychology of Australian aborigines*. Sydney: John Wiley.

Office of the Surgeon General (1968). *Supplement to health of the Army*. Washington, D.C.: Dept of the Army.

Ombredane, A., Robaye, F., & Robaye, E. (1952). Analyse des resultats d'une application experimentale du matrix 38 a 485 noirs Baluba. *Bulletin Centre d'Etudes et Researches Psychotechniques, 7*, 235–255.

Owen, K. (1992). The suitability of Raven's Progressive Matrices for various groups in South Africa. *Personality and Individual Differences, 13*, 149–159.

Piddington, M. (1932). Report of field work in northwestern Australia. *Oceania, 2*, 342–358.

Pollitt, E., Hathirat, P., Kotchabhakdi, N., Missell, L., & Valyasevi, A. (1989). Iron deficiency and educational achievement in Thailand. *American Journal of Clinical Nutrition, 50*, 687–697.

Porteus, S. D. (1965). *Porteus maze test*. Palo Alto: Pacific Books.

Ramsay, F. J. (2000). *Global studies: Africa*. Guilford, CT: Dushkin/McGraw-Hill.

Rao, S. N., & Reddy, I. K. (1968). Development of norms for Raven's Coloured Progressive Matrices on elementary school children. *Psychological Studies, 13*, 105–107.

Raven, J. (1981). *Irish and British standardisations*. Oxford: Oxford Psychologists Press.

Raven, J. (1998). *Manual for Raven's progressive matrices*. Oxford: Oxford Psychologists Press.

Raven, J., & Court, J. H. (1989). *Manual for Raven's progressive matrices and vocabulary scales*. London: Lewis.

Raven, J., Court, J. C., & Court, J. H. (1998). *Coloured progressive matrices*. Oxford: Oxford Psychologists Press.

Raven, J. C., Court, J. H., & Raven, J. (1995). *Coloured progressive matrices*. Oxford: Oxford Psychologists Press.

Raven, J. C., Court, J. H., & Raven, J. (1996). *Standard progressive matrices*. Oxford: Oxford Psychologists Press.

Redmond, M., & Davies, F. R. (1940). *The standardisation of two intelligence tests*. Wellington: New Zealand Council for Educational Research.

Reed, T. E. (1969). Caucasian genes in American Negroes. *Science, 165*, 762–768.

Reid, N., & Gilmore, A. (1989). The Raven's standard progressive matrices in New Zealand. *Psychological Test Bulletin, 2*, 25–35.

Reschly, D. J., & Jipson, F. J. (1976). Ethnicity, geographical locale, age, sex and urban-rural residence as variables in the prevalence of mild mental retardation. *American Journal of Mental Deficiency, 81*, 154–161.

Rimoldi, H. J. (1948). A note on Raven's progressive matrices. *Educational and Psychological Measurement, 8*, 347–352.

Risso, W. L. (1961). *El test de matrice progressivas y el test domino*. Proceedings of the 1961 Conference of the Psychological Society of Uruguay.

Rodd, W. G. (1959). A cross cultural study of Taiwan's schools. *Journal of Social Psychology, 50*, 30–36.

Rushton, J. P. (2000). *Race, evolution and behavior*. Port Huron, MI: Charles Darwin Research Institute.

Sahin, N., & Duzen, E. (1994). *Turkish standardisation of Raven's SPM*. Proceedings of the 23rd International Congress of Applied Psychology, Madrid.

Scottish Council for Research in Education (1933). *The Intelligence of Scottish children*. London: University of London Press.

Scottish Council for Research in Education (1949). *The trend of Scottish intelligence*. London: University of London Press.

Shigehisa, T., & Lynn, R. (1991). Reaction times and intelligence in Japanese children. *International Journal of Psychology, 26*, 195–202.

Simoes, M. M. R. (1989). Un estudo exploratorio com o teste des matrizes progressivas de Raven para criancas. Proceedings of the Congress of Psychology, Lisbon, Portugal.

Sinha, U. (1968). The use of Raven's Progressive Matrices in India. *Indian Educational Review, 3*, 75–88.

Skandinaviska Testforlaget (1970). *Manual of the Swedish WISC*. Stockholm: Skandinaviska Testforlaget.

Smith, K. K. (1966). *A validation study of the Queensland test*. B.A. Thesis, University of Queensland.

Sorokin, B. (1954). *Standardisation of the progressive matrices test*. Unpublished Report.

St. George, R. (1983). Some psychometric properties of the Queensland test of cognitive abilities with New Zealand European and Maori children. *New Zealand Journal of Psychology, 12*, 57–68.

St. George, R., & Chapman, J. W. (1983). TOSCA results from a New Zealand sample. *New Zealand Journal of Educational Studies, 18*, 178–183.

Stevenson, H. W., Stigler, J. W., Lee, S., Lucker, G. W., Kitanawa, S., & Hsu, C. (1985). Cognitive performance and academic achievement of Japanese, Chinese and American children. *Child Development, 56*, 718–734.

Sundberg, N., & Ballinger, T. (1968). Nepalese children's cognitive development as revealed by drawings of man, woman and self. *Child Development, 39*, 969–985.

Takeuchi, M., & Scott, R. (1992). Cognitive profiles of Japanese and Canadian kindergarten and first grade children. *Journal of Social Psychology, 132*, 505–512.

Te Nijenhuis, J., & van der Flier, H. (1997) Comparability of GATB scores for immigrant and majority group members: Some Dutch findings. *Journal of Applied Psychology, 82*, 675–685.

Telford, C. W. (1932). Test performance of full and mixed-blood North Dakota Indians. *Journal of Comparative Psychology, 14*, 123–145.

Tesi, G., & Young,B. H. (1962). A standardisation of Raven's Progressive Matrices. *Archive de Psicologia Neurologia e Pscichologia, 5*, 455–464.

Thomas, R. M., & Skah, A. (1961). The draw-a-Man test in Indonesia. *Journal of Educational Psychology, 32*, 232–235.

Valentine, M. (1959). Psychometric testing in Iran. *Journal of Mental Science, 105*, 93–107.

Vejleskov, H. (1968). An analysis of Raven matrix responses in fifth grade children. *Scandinavian Journal of Psychology, 9*, 177–186.

Vernon, P. E. (1969). *Intelligence and cultural environment*. London: Methuen.

Walters, R. H. (1958). The intelligence test performance of Maori children: A cross-cultural study. *Journal of Abnormal and Social Psychology, 58*, 107–114.

Wober, M. (1969). The meaning and stability of Raven's matrices test among Africans. *International Journal of Psychology, 4*, 229–235.

Zahirnic, C., Girboveanu, M., Onofrai, A., Turcu, A., Voicu, C., & Visan, O. M. (1994). Etolonarea matricelor progressive colorate Raven. *Revista de Psihologie, 20*, 313–321.

Zeidner, M. (1987). Test of the cultural bias hypothesis: some Israeli findings. *Journal of Applied Psychology, 72*, 38–48.

Zindi, F. (1994). Differences in psychometric performance. *The Psychologist, 7*, 549–552.

Chapter 9

Race Differences in *g* and the "Jensen Effect"

J. Philippe Rushton

1. The Spearman-Jensen Hypothesis

Jensen (1980: 535) formally designated the view that Black-White differences were largely a matter of *g* as "Spearman's hypothesis", because Spearman (1927: 379) was the first to suggest it. Subsequently, Osborne (1980a) dubbed it the "Spearman-Jensen hypothesis" because it was Jensen who brought Spearman's hypothesis to widespread attention, and it was Jensen who did all the empirical work confirming it. More recently, to honor one of the great psychologists of our time, Rushton (1998) proposed that the term "Jensen Effect" be used whenever a significant correlation occurs between *g*-factor loadings and any variable, X; otherwise there is no name for it, only a long explanation of how the effect was calculated. Jensen Effects are not omnipresent and their absence can be as informative as their presence. For example, the "Flynn Effect" (the secular rise in IQ) is probably not a Jensen Effect because it does not appear to be on *g*.

The Black-White difference on the *g*-factor is the best known of all the Jensen Effects. The reason Jensen pursued Spearman's (1927) hypothesis was because it so exquisitely solved a problem that had long perplexed him. The average 15 to 18 IQ point difference between Blacks and Whites in the U.S. had not changed since IQ testing began almost 100 years ago. But Jensen (1969a) noted that the race differences were markedly smaller on tests of rote learning and short-term memory than they were on tests of abstract reasoning and transforming information. Moreover, culture-fair tests tended to give Blacks slightly *lower* scores than did conventional tests, as typically did non-verbal tests compared with verbal tests. Furthermore, contrary to purely cultural explanations, race differences could be observed as early as three years of age, and controlling for socioeconomic level only reduced the race differences by 4 IQ points.

Jensen (1968) initially formalized these observations in his so-called Level I-Level II theory. Level I tasks were those that required little or no mental manipulation of the input in order to arrive at the correct response whereas Level II tasks required mental manipulation. A classic example of Level I ability is Forward Digit Span in which people recall a series of digits in the same order as that in which they are presented. A clear example of a Level II task is Backward Digit Span in which people recall a series of digits in the *reverse* order to that in which they were presented. Jensen found that Black-White differences were twice as large for Backward as for Forward Digit Span.

After Jensen (1980) re-read Spearman, he realized that the Black-White differences (and his Level I-Level II formulation) were specific examples of the more general hypothesis proposed by Spearman (1927: 379), namely that the Black-White difference "was most marked in just those [tests] which are known to be saturated with *g*". It was Spearman (1904, 1927), of course, who had generated the seminal concept of *g* in the first place. The *g* factor, derived from factor analysis of the correlations among a number of tests of mental abilities, is typically the largest factor.

To test Spearman's hypothesis, Jensen developed the *method of correlated vectors*. Essentially, this method correlates the standardized Black-White mean differences on a set of cognitive tests (a vector of scores, i.e. possessing both direction and quantity), with the tests' *g* loadings (a second vector of scores). A positive and substantial correlation provides support for Spearman's hypothesis. The rationale is straightforward: if *g* is the main source of between- *and* within-group differences, then there should be a positive relationship between a test's *g*-loading and the Black-White difference on the test; the more *g*-loaded the test, the greater the Black-White difference on that test. A methodological corollary is the prediction that when the point-biserial correlations of race (Black-White) with a number of diverse cognitive tests are entered into the total matrix of correlations among all the tests, the race variable will have its largest loading on the general factor of the correlation matrix.

According to Jensen (1998: 372–373), an ideal test of Spearman's hypothesis using the method of correlated vectors, must meet several methodological requirements. These are: (1) the samples being compared must be representative of their respective populations; (2) the samples being compared must be large enough to overcome the sampling error of the correlations among tests; (3) the samples being compared must not be selected on the basis of any *g*-loaded criterion; (4) the *g* factor should be extracted from enough tests to be reliable, as would be indicated by high coefficients of congruence in independent samples from the same population; (5) any test showing psychometric test bias for the groups being compared must be excluded; (6) the tests must be sufficiently diverse to allow significant differences between their *g* loadings; (7) the scores must be corrected for reliability; (8) the *g* values must be computed separately in the different groups; (9) the scores must measure the same latent traits in the different groups (i.e. the vector of *g* loadings extracted separately from each group must show a high congruence coefficient); and (10) the hypothesis must be tested for statistical significance by both Pearson's *r* and Spearman's rank-order correlation, rho.

As also noted by Jensen, tests of Spearman's hypothesis are necessarily stringent because the degrees of freedom used for statistical rejection of the null hypothesis are based on the number of pairs of variables in the correlated vectors (e.g. 13 sub-tests from the Wechsler Scales) and not on the subject sample size. It is also worth emphasizing that Spearman's hypothesis concerns the *relative* magnitude of the group difference across various tests that differ in their *g* loadings and not the *absolute* magnitude of group differences. It is therefore conceptually independent of any secular trend in absolute test scores, viz., the Flynn Effect (discussed below).

Jensen summarized his early tests of Spearman's hypothesis and responded to the open-peer commentary in *Behavioral and Brain Sciences* (Jensen 1985, 1987). Chapter 11 of *The g Factor* (1998) describes his subsequent analysis of 17 independent data sets of nearly 45,000 Blacks and 245,000 Whites derived from 171 psychometric tests (see Figure 9.1). The *g* loadings consistently predicted the relative magnitude of the Black-White differences ($r = 0.63$; Spearman rho $= 0.71$, $P < 0.05$) on the various tests. Spearman's hypothesis was borne out even among 3-year-olds administered eight sub-tests of the Stanford-Binet, where the rank correlation between *g* loadings and the Black-White differences was 0.71 ($P < 0.05$; Peoples *et al.* 1995).

These *g* related race differences are not due to factors such as the reliability of the test, social class differences, or the inevitable result of factor analysis. Indeed, the Spearman-Jensen hypothesis applies even to the *g* factor extracted from reaction time (RT) performance on elementary cognitive tasks. For example, in the "odd-man-out" task (Frearson & Eysenck 1986), 9- to 12-year-olds are asked to decide which of several lights is illuminated and then move their hand to press a button to turn that light off. All children can perform this and other tasks in less than 1 second, but children with higher IQ scores perform faster than do those with lower scores, and White children, on average, perform faster than do Black children (Vernon & Jensen 1984; Jensen 1993). The correlations between the *g* loadings of these types of RT tasks and the Black-White differences range from 0.70 to 0.81.

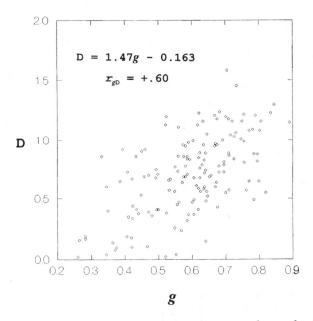

Figure 9.1: Scatter diagram of the correlation between the *g* loadings and the standardized mean White-Black differences (*D*) on 149 psychometric tests. With the tests' reliability coefficients partialled out, the correlation is 0.63 ($P < 0.001$). (After Jensen 1998: 378).

When Jensen examined East Asian-White comparisons using these same reaction time measures, the direction of the correlation was *opposite* to that in the Black-White studies, with East Asians scoring higher in g than Whites (Jensen & Whang 1993, 1994). Dozens of other studies indicate an East Asian advantage on conventional IQ tests (Lynn 1991, 1997; Lynn & Vanhanen 2002; see also Chapter 8 in this volume). So far, however, only one study seems to have looked at East Asian-White differences on conventional psychometric tests as a direct function of their g loadings. Nagoshi *et al.* (1984) administered 15 cognitive tests to two generations of Americans of Japanese, Chinese and European ancestry. Of the four reported correlations between g loadings and ethnic group differences, only one was significant, albeit in the predicted direction. It is interesting to note, in light of the above, that in an early reply to a charge of "white supremacy", Jensen wrote (1969b: 240) "[I]f I were asked to hypothesize about race differences in what we call g or abstract reasoning ability, I should be inclined to rate Caucasians on the whole somewhat below Orientals, at least those in the United States."

2. Studies of Race Differences

2.1. U.S. Black-White Differences in g Since 1998

Following publication of *The g Factor* (Jensen 1998), Nyborg & Jensen (2000) provided further evidence for the generality of the Spearman-Jensen hypothesis. They analyzed a unique battery of 19 highly diverse cognitive tests made available by the Centers for Disease Control (CDC: 1988) from an archival data set of 4,462 males who had served in the U.S. Armed Forces. Since approximately half had served in the Vietnam War, the CDC made the data available for researchers to examine the effects of exposure to toxic substances such as Agent Orange used during that war. The sample was fairly representative of the U.S. population in terms of race, education, income and occupation, though the lower tail of the ability distribution was truncated because those who scored below the 10th percentile on a pre-induction general aptitude test were excluded from military service.

Five of the tests were administered at the time of induction into the armed forces while the others were given approximately 17 years later. The battery included the Grooved Pegboard Test, the Paced Auditory Serial Addition Test, the Rey-Osterrieth Complex Figure Drawing Test, the Wisconsin Card Sorting Test, the Wide Range Achievement Test, the California Verbal Learning Test, the General Information Test, and various sub-tests from the Wechsler Adult Intelligence Scale-Revised, and the Army Classification Battery. The g factor was extracted using different methods. Spearman's hypothesis was confirmed regardless of procedure, with an average correlation between the race differences on a test and its g loading across the extraction procedures of 0.81. This value is higher than the average correlation of 0.62 for all previous studies. Nyborg & Jensen (2000) concluded that Spearman's original conjecture about the Black-White difference on the g factor "should no longer be regarded as just an hypothesis but as an empirically established fact" (p. 599).

Subsequently, Roth *et al.* (2001) carried out a meta-analytic review that extended the range of the 1.1 standard deviation effect size of Black-White IQ differences to college and university application tests such as the Scholastic Aptitude Test (SAT; $N = 2.4$ million) and the Graduate Record Examination (GRE; $N = 2.3$ million), as well as to tests for job applicants in corporate settings ($N = 0.5$ million), and in the military ($N = 0.4$ million). Their review also noted that in any particular work settings where the Black-White difference was less than 1.1 standard deviations, it resulted from selection factors and restriction of range (as in studies of complex versus simple jobs, within- versus across-jobs, and of job incumbents versus applicants). Roth *et al.* (2001) report that the tests with the greatest *g* loadings showed the largest Black-White differences, again confirming Spearman's hypothesis. Since IQ scores are the best predictor of economic success in Western society (Schmidt & Hunter 1998), group differences in IQ scores help to explain the differences in societal outcomes (Gottfredson 1997).

Jensen's (in press) most recent study of Black-White differences compared 8- to 13-year-old pupils (877 White, 855 Black) on up to 17 tests. As usual, race differences at all ages were mainly on the *g* factor. Age differences also showed a Jensen Effect, that is, older children had higher levels of *g*, rather than just more acquired knowledge. The race effect (which was equal to about two years of chronological age) differed from the age effect by being greater on tests with higher *g* loadings (such as verbal and figural reasoning) whereas the age effect was greater on tests with lower *g* loadings (such as digit span memory). This age x race interaction suggests that for both racial groups, cognitive development during childhood involves mental growth factors other than *g*, while the Black-White difference at any given age is almost exclusively a matter of *g*.

2.2. Studies of g in South Africa

Since the studies so far described were all carried out in the U.S., it might be argued that the results are solely due to local conditions. However, the race differences on the *g* factor have been confirmed in several independent studies carried out in sub-Saharan Africa (this section) and in the Netherlands (next section). It is surprising that only recently has research on the *g* factor been carried out in Africa because the low mean test scores obtained there are of considerable interest. They came to widespread attention in the U.S. with Richard Herrnstein and Charles Murray's best-selling 1994 book *The Bell Curve* (and my own 1995 *Race, Evolution, and Behavior*). *The Bell Curve* considered the hypothesis that: "The African black population has not been subjected to the historical legacy of American black slavery and discrimination and might therefore have higher scores". However, after examination of the literature, the IQ for Black Africans turned out to be, on average, substantially below African Americans, who are of mixed Black and White ancestry.

Both *The Bell Curve* and *Race, Evolution, and Behavior* cited a 1991 review by Richard Lynn of 11 studies from West, East, Central, and Southern Africa which reported an average IQ of 70 (median = 75), 15 points (1 standard deviation (SD)) lower than the mean of 85 typically found for Black Americans and 30 points (2 SDs) lower than the mean of 100 typically found for Whites. Subsequent reviews by Lynn (1997;

see also his Chapter 8 in this volume) that examined additional published studies have confirmed a mean African IQ of 70. In their recent book *IQ and the Wealth of Nations*, Lynn & Vanhanen (2002) reviewed over two-dozen studies from the African sub-continent finding the lowest recorded IQ scores in the world.

University students in South Africa also achieve low mean test scores. Sixty-three undergraduates at the all-Black universities of Fort Hare, Zululand, the North, and the Medical University of South Africa were given the Wechsler Adult Intelligence Scale-Revised (WAIS-R) and found to have a full scale IQ of 77 (Avenant 1988; cited by Nell 2000: 26–28). A study at the University of Venda in South Africa's Northern Province by Grieve & Viljoen (2000) found 30 students in 4th-year law and commerce averaged a score of 37 out of 60 on the Standard Progressive Matrices. This is equivalent to an IQ of 78 on the 1993 U.S. norms (Raven *et al.* 1990: 98; 1998: 77). A study at South Africa's University of the North by Zaaiman, van der Flier & Thijs (2001) found the highest scoring African sample to that date — 147 first-year mathematics and science students who scored 52 out of 60 on the Standard Progressive Matrices, with an IQ equivalent of 100. Their relatively high mean score may have been because they were mathematics and science students, and also because they had been specially selected for admission to the university from a pool of 700 applicants on the basis of a mathematics and science selection test.

Lynn & Owen (1994) were the first to explicitly test Spearman's hypothesis in sub-Saharan Africa. They administered the Junior Aptitude Test, a paper-and-pencil test, consisting of ten sub-tests (four verbal, six nonverbal), to 1,056 White, 1,063 Indian, and 1,093 Black 16-year-old high school students in South Africa. They found a 2 SDs difference between the Africans and Whites (yielding an average African IQ of about 70) and a 1 SD difference between the Whites and Indians (yielding an average Indian IQ of 85). Lynn and Owen tested Spearman's hypothesis and found the African-White differences correlated 0.62 ($P<0.05$) with the *g*-factor extracted from the African sample (although only 0.23 with *g* extracted from the White sample). However, unlike the African-White differences, the White-Indian differences they found were *not* on the *g* factor.

Six studies by Rushton, Skuy, and other colleagues in Southern Africa also support Spearman's hypothesis, including of university students. In the first study, Rushton & Skuy (2000) gave 309 17- to 23-year-old first-year psychology students at the University of the Witwatersrand in Johannesburg the untimed Standard Progressive Matrices. The 173 African students solved an average of 44 of the 60 problems, while the 136 White students solved an average of 54 of the 60 problems. These scores placed the African students at the 14th percentile and the White students at the 61st percentile, which yielded IQ equivalents of 84 and 104, respectively. Because the total score on the Standard Progressive Matrices is an excellent measure of *g*, Rushton and Skuy used the item-total correlations as an estimate of each item's *g* loading and found that item *g* loadings showed a significant positive correlation with the standardized differences in the percentage of Africans and Whites passing the same items. These Jensen Effects were found using both the African item-total correlations, $r=0.39$ ($P<0.01$, $N=58$, with rho $=0.43$, $P<0.01$), and the White item-total correlations, $r=0.34$ ($P<0.01$, $N=46$, rho $=0.41$, $P<0.01$).

The second study (Rushton 2001) analyzed ten sub-tests of the Weschler Intelligence Scale for Children-Revised (WISC-R) from data published by Skuy *et al.* (2001) on 154 Black South African high school students from Johannesburg. Table 9.1 presents the African means and SDs for the various WISC-R sub-tests. The table shows the African mean scores are 1 to 2 SDs below American norms. The mean score for Whites was set at the U.S. standardization sample mean of 10 (which included African Americans). The mean African-White differences were then calculated and also expressed in SD units, using the African SDs. When the g loadings from the WISC-R national standardization data were extracted they correlated $r = 0.77$ ($P < 0.05$) with the standardized African-White differences, thereby showing the Jensen Effect. For many of the African students, English was not their first language. However, the Jensen Effect remained even after the Vocabulary sub-test was excluded from the data (in Table 9.1), and the mean of the 11 other sub-tests substituted in its place ($r = 0.66$, $P < 0.05$). Nor did the Jensen Effect disappear if g was extracted from the African rather than from the White standardization sample ($r = 0.60$, $P < 0.05$), or if Spearman's rho was used instead of Pearson's r to measure the magnitude of the correlation (rhos $= 0.74$, 0.74, respectively, $Ps < 0.005$).

The third study (Rushton 2002) re-analyzed published data from Owen (1992) who had given the Standard Progressive Matrices in South Africa without time limits to 1,056 White, 1,063 Indian, 778 Colored, and 1,093 Black 14-year-olds. Out of a total of 60 items, Owen (1992) found the Whites averaged 45 correct, East Indians, 42, Coloreds, 37, and Blacks 28, placing them at the 57th, 42nd, 19th, and 5th percentiles, yielding IQ equivalents of 103, 97, 87 and 75 on the 1993 U.S. norms. Importantly, Owen found that the item-total test score correlations predicted the pass rate differences between the ethnic groups on these same items and concluded that this indicated an absence of test bias. Rushton proposed a stronger inference, that all the group differences (viz., White-African, White-Colored, White-Indian, Indian-African, Indian-Colored, Colored-African) were primarily on g. To test this possibility, he carried out a purely non-parametric re-analysis of Owen's data and found that, indeed, the more highly correlated an item was with g (the item-total correlation), the more it predicted the differences among the (now ranked) item pass rates for Whites, Indians, Coloreds, and Africans, (Spearman's rhos from 0.35 to 0.85; all $Ps < 0.01$). The effects remained regardless of the ethnic group from which the item g-loadings were taken.

In the fourth study, I teamed up with Arthur Jensen himself (Rushton & Jensen 2003) to analyze a set of data published by Zindi (1994), an African Zimbabwean educational psychologist. Zindi had reported data on 10 sub-tests of the WISC-R for 204 Black Zimbabwean children with a total IQ score of 70, a difference of nearly 2 SDs below White norms. Because the sub-test correlations were not available, Rushton and Jensen compared the Zimbabwean means and SDs against those for 1,868 White Americans from the U.S. standardization sample. A principal factor analysis of the correlation matrix was carried out for the White standardization sample, along with the point-biserial correlation of the African-White standardized differences on each sub-test, a measure of the racial "effect size". Table 9.2 shows the loadings of the African-White variable and of the 10 WISC-R sub-tests on the g factor, and on the next three largest unrotated principal factors (regardless of sign and whether the eigenvalues were less than 1). The g loading is considerably larger than the largest non-g factor, and the ratio

Table 9.1: Means and standard deviations (*SDs*) of African secondary school students aged 13 to 15 years on sub-tests of the WISC-R and U.S.-African differences (After Skuy *et al.* 2001; Rushton 2001).

WISC-R Scale	African mean	African SD	U.S.-African difference	z-score difference	g for U.S.	g for Africa	Reliability
Information	4.66	2.33	5.34	2.29	0.67	0.65	0.85
Picture Completion	7.06	2.28	2.94	1.29	0.51	0.57	0.77
Similarities	4.89	2.32	5.11	2.20	0.67	0.62	0.81
Picture Arrangement	6.42	2.68	3.58	1.34	0.49	0.49	0.73
Arithmetic	6.01	2.20	3.99	1.81	0.57	0.60	0.77
Blocks	6.58	2.49	3.42	1.37	0.65	0.61	0.85
Vocabulary	2.85	1.64	7.15	4.36	0.72	0.71	0.86
Object Assembly	6.29	2.81	3.71	1.32	0.50	0.53	0.70
Comprehension	4.79	2.46	5.21	2.12	0.60	0.61	0.77
Coding	6.18	2.25	3.82	1.70	0.37	0.36	0.72
Digits	6.93	2.64	3.07	1.16	0.44	0.59	0.78
Mazes	7.60	2.90	2.40	0.83	0.37	0.45	0.72

U.S. standardization sample mean = 10, *SD* = 3.

Table 9.2: Principal factor analysis of correlation matrix for 1,868 whites plus the African-White standardized effect size. (After Rushton & Jensen in press).

WISC-R Sub-tests	g	Non-g factors		
		1 >	2 >	3 >
Information	0.724	-0.274	0.106	-0.164
Similarities	0.711	-0.217	0.144	0.002
Arithmetic	0.592	-0.138	-0.077	-0.195
Vocabulary	0.772	-0.313	0.032	0.002
Comprehension	0.705	-0.247	-0.084	0.319
Picture completion	0.556	0.158	0.194	0.066
Picture arrangement	0.517	0.078	0.157	-0.023
Block design	0.697	0.311	0.154	-0.112
Object assembly	0.582	0.426	0.188	0.062
Coding	0.429	0.107	-0.365	-0.204
Race	0.882	0.236	-0.389	0.124
Percent Total Variance Explained	44.073	6.164	4.131	2.228

of g variance to all non-g variance is 3.5 to 1. The race variable has a larger g loading than do any of the sub-test variables. It appears to reflect almost pure g. Fully 77% of the between-group race variance can be attributed to a single source, namely g.

The fifth study (Rushton *et al.* 2002) gave the Standard Progressive Matrices to an academically select population of 342 17- to 23-year-old first-year engineering students (198 Africans, 58 Indians, 86 Whites) in the Faculties of Engineering and the Built Environment at the University of the Witwatersrand. Out of the 60 problems, the African students solved an average of 50, the Indian students, 53, and the White students, 56, placing the Africans at the 41st percentile, the Indians at the 50th, and the Whites at the 75th, with IQ equivalents of 97, 105, and 110, respectively. Several analyses showed that even for this very select group, the standardized African-Indian-White differences were most pronounced on those items with the highest item-total correlations, indicating a difference in g. Indeed, the g-loadings showed cross-cultural generality; for example, item-total correlations calculated on the Indian students predicted the magnitude of the African-White differences. When the 60 items were aggregated into 10 "sub-tests" of six items each, the magnitude of the Jensen Effect was similar to that from studies based on whole sub-tests (median rho = 0.53).

In a sixth study, Rushton *et al.* (2003) gave the Advanced version of the Progressive Matrices to 294 of the same engineering students (187 Africans, 40 Indians, 67 Whites) as in the previous study. Out of the 36 problems, the African students solved an average of 22, the Indian students, 24, and the White students, 29, placing the Africans at the 57th percentile, the Indians at the 64th, and the Whites at the 86th, with IQ equivalents of 103, 106, and 117, respectively, making this the now highest scoring African sample on record. External validities were established, with both the African and the non-African students' scores on the Advanced Progressive Matrices predicting their scores on the Standard Progressive Matrices taken three months earlier (mean $r = 0.60$; mean $Ps < 0.01$) and their final examination marks taken three months later (mean $rs = 0.30$; mean $Ps < 0.01$). Once again, the standardized African-Indian-White differences were Jensen Effects, being most pronounced on those items with the highest item-total correlations. Moreover, the g-loadings again showed cross-cultural generality, with those calculated on the Indian students predicting the magnitude of the African-White differences.

2.3. Ethnic Differences in g from The Netherlands

Several studies of g-factor differences among various populations have been carried out in The Netherlands by Jan te Nijenhuis and his colleagues who compared the majority Dutch population with immigrants from the Third World who now comprise 6% of the Dutch population. About 40% of these immigrants came from the West Indies — the Netherland Antilles and Surinam. The Antilleans are predominantly of mixed African descent and the Surinamese are a diverse population of Creoles (mixed African, White, and Native American), East Indians, and individuals of Indonesian and Chinese descent. They speak Dutch as their first language. About 60% of the immigrants came from Turkey and Morocco. These are Caucasian, and do not have Dutch as their first language. The IQ scores of all immigrants averaged over 1 SD lower than did those of the Dutch majority, with the North Africans and Turks scoring lower than the Surinamese and Antilleans, especially on tests with a verbal component. Immigrant children tended to perform poorly in school and the adult unemployment rate was 20% for immigrants versus 7% for the total population (te Nijenhuis & van der Flier 2001).

In one study, te Nijenhuis & van der Flier (1997) compared the test results of all first generation immigrant job applicants to the Dutch Railways between 1988 and 1992 with those of a random representative sample of all the majority group applicants over the same time period. The Dutch version of the General Aptitude Test Battery (GATB), consisting of eight speeded sub-tests, showed similar alpha coefficients and covariance matrices in all groups and, apart from a Dutch language proficiency factor, there was no evidence of test bias. The Dutch-Immigrant differences correlated highly with the g factor extracted separately for each of the five groups, before and after correcting for unreliability in the measures. (The after-correction correlations were: Dutch-Surinamese, $r = 0.76$; Dutch-Antilleans, $r = 0.78$; Dutch-North Africans, $r = 0.82$; and Dutch-Turks, $r = 0.64$.)

The Spearman-Jensen hypothesis was also tested on this sample using safety aptitude measures (ability to concentrate and sensori-motor coordination ability) that are important predictors for accident-related criteria for this sample of engine drivers, guards, train traffic controllers, bus drivers, shunters, and railway station assistants (te Nijenhuis 1997). The safety aptitude scores were consistently lower for all the immigrant groups than for the Dutch majority group. Group differences on the safety aptitude tests correlated $r = 0.81$ with their g loadings from the GATB, indicating that the group differences in safety aptitude were largely a function of g, i.e. they were Jensen Effects.

Subsequently, te Nijenhuis *et al.* (2000) gave the Dutch adaptation of the Differential Aptitude Test to 318 Dutch and 111 immigrant secondary school students (no details being available about the ethnic origin of the immigrant students). School grades and scholastic achievement test scores were used as criteria. On the g factor scores extracted from nine sub-tests, the mean of the immigrants was 1.14 SDs below that of the Dutch, with the pattern of g loadings similar for both. The immigrant group was also lower on the criteria measures, which were predicted equally well for both groups. Group differences in both test scores and educational achievement were predicted quite well by the g loadings of the various measures, making g the predominant factor accounting for the group differences.

In still another study, te Nijenhuis *et al.* (in press) examined the Revised Amsterdam Intelligence Test for Children (RAKIT), which consisted of 12 sub-tests. The study compared 604 Dutch children who constituted the nationally representative normative sample against 559 immigrant children who had been carefully selected to be generally representative of all immigrant children in the Netherlands. Little test bias was found; some differential prediction occurred, but its effects were small. The estimate of g as computed from the test showed strong predictive validity for most school subjects and standardized achievement tests. Moreover, the study confirmed Spearman's hypothesis that g is the predominant factor determining the size of the difference between the two groups.

In summarizing all the Dutch studies on the assessment of immigrants, te Nijenhuis & van der Flier (2001) stated that the lower scores of the immigrants could be generalized to the whole population of immigrants, yielding IQs under 100 for 84% of immigrants. However, second-generation immigrants were doing roughly one-third of an SD better than were first-generation immigrants, and the third generation may continue to improve their group's relative position. As many other West European countries also have immigrants from Third World countries, including former colonies, the Dutch findings may be generalizable.

2.4. The Flynn Effect May Not Be a Jensen Effect

Jensen Effects are not omnipresent and their absence can be as informative as their presence. For example, it is not universally true that all groups that differ, on average, in their overall score on a test battery will necessarily conform to the Spearman-Jensen hypothesis. A study in Spain by Colom *et al.* (2002), using the Spanish standardization sample of the Wechsler Adult Intelligence Scale (WAIS III), found that while 2 SDs divided the lowest IQ group (IQ = 84) from the highest IQ group (IQ = 112), Jensen Effects were not found on the 14 sub-tests: the people were apparently not less intelligent, merely less educated.

In a study by Lynn & Owen (1994) in South Africa, although there was a nearly 1 SD difference between Whites and East Indians, there was no correlation between g loadings and standardized mean differences on 10 sub-tests. Thus, it was not a Jensen Effect. (Several subsequent studies, however, found the Indian-White and Indian-African differences *were* on the g factor; Rushton 2002; Rushton *et al.* 2002). It is an interesting question which of the national differences documented in Lynn & Vanhanen's (2002) *IQ and the Wealth of Nations* are on the g factor.

Another apparent absence of the Jensen Effect is that shown for the secular increase in test scores. The Flynn Effect (sometimes also known as the Lynn-Flynn Effect) refers to the repeated demonstration by Flynn (1984, 1987, 1999; but see also Lynn 1982) that the average IQ in several countries has increased by about 3 points a decade over the last 50 years. The Flynn Effect seems to imply the 1 SD difference in the mean IQ between Blacks and Whites in the U.S. will simply disappear over time (Flynn 1999). However, analysis shows that the Flynn Effect is not on the g factor.

Table 9.3 (based on Rushton 1999) shows the results of a principal components analysis of the secular gains in IQ from the U.S., Germany, Austria and Scotland, along with Black-White IQ difference scores from the U.S., inbreeding depression scores from cousin marriages in Japan, and g-loadings from the standardization samples of the Wechsler Intelligence Scale for Children (WISC-R and WISC-III). The important findings are: (1) the IQ gains on the WISC-R and WISC-III form a cluster, showing that the secular trend is a reliable phenomenon; but (2) this cluster is *independent* of a second cluster formed by Black-White differences, inbreeding depression scores (a purely genetic effect), and g-factor loadings (a largely genetic effect). This analysis shows that the secular increase in IQ behaves in a different way than the mean Black-White IQ difference. The secular increase is unrelated to g and other heritable measures,

Table 9.3: Principal components analysis and varimax rotation for Pearson correlations of inbreeding depression scores, black-white differences, g loadings, and gains over time on the Wechsler intelligence scales for children with reliability partialled out. (After Rushton 1999).

Variables	Principal Components			
	Unrotated Loadings		Varimax Rotated Loadings	
	I	II	1	2
Inbreeding depression scores from Japan (WISC-R)	0.31	0.61	0.26	**0.63**
Black-White differences from the U.S. (WISC-R)	0.29	0.70	0.23	**0.72**
WISC-R g loadings from the U.S.	−0.33	0.90	−0.40	**0.87**
WISC-III g loadings from the U.S.	−0.61	0.64	−0.66	**0.59**
U.S. gains 1 (WISC to WISC-R)	0.73	−0.20	**0.75**	−0.13
U.S. gains 2 (WISC-R to WISC-III)	0.81	0.40	**0.77**	0.47
German gains (WISC to WISC-R)	0.91	0.03	**0.91**	0.11
Austria gains (WISC to WISC-R)	0.87	0.00	**0.86**	0.07
Scotland gains (WISC to WISC-R)	0.97	0.08	**0.96**	0.17
% of total variance explained	48.6	25.49	48.44	25.65

while the magnitude of the Black-White difference is related to heritable g and inbreeding depression.

Flynn's hypothesis that the "massive IQ gains over time" imply an environmental origin of race differences is not supported. Although the Flynn Effect does suggest that improving the environment, especially at the low end of the IQ distribution, can improve test scores, the cluster analysis show that effect is unrelated to the g-factor. Instead, g is associated with inbreeding depression, for which there is no non-genetic explanation, which implies strongly that g is less amenable to environmental manipulation.

Two Estonian studies confirm the finding that the Flynn Effect is not on the *g* factor (Must *et al.* in press (a), in press (b)). In the largest of these, Must *et al.* (in press (b)) analyzed ten sub-tests of the Estonian translation of the (U.S.) National Intelligence Test from comparable samples of 12- to 14-year-old children taken over a 60-year period (1936 to 1998). The loadings on the 1st Principal Component (which represents *g*) had a congruence coefficient across the 60-year time span of 0.996, but *negative* correlations of –0.24 to –0.54 with the 60-year Flynn Effect of sub-test gains (depending on how the sample was divided or how + *g* was extracted).

In Spain, however, Colom *et al.* (2001), have reported a positive correlation ($r = 0.78$; $P < 0.05$) between *g* and the amount of generational change in two successive standardizations of the Spanish Differential Aptitude Test across 16-years. There were 10 samples of males and females for each of five sub-tests (Verbal Reasoning, Space Relations, Numerical Ability, Mechanical Reasoning, and Abstract Reasoning). But 5 of the 10 samples showed a generational *decrement* (their Table 1), so ambiguities in the study raise questions about its generality. Moreover, the magnitude of the Jensen Effect on the secular rise in IQ that Colom *et al.* found is relatively small compared to the Jensen Effect for race (about 0.50 SD compared to >1.00 SD for Black-White differences).

In summary, no one has yet found a Flynn Effect that approaches the magnitude of the Jensen Effect. All but the Colom *et al.* (2001) study (i.e. Rushton 1999; Must *et al.* in press (a), in press (b)) showed no Jensen Effect at all (or even negative correlations between secular gains and *g* loadings). The complete explanation for the secular rise in IQ remains one of the unsolved psychometric mysteries.

2.5. Pushing Out the Envelope Even Further

From the beginning, "Jensenism" did not stop within the U.S. or with IQ. For example, Jensen (1969a: 86) cited studies showing the early development of motor behavior in Black infants, with some Black samples at six months of age scoring nearly 1 SD above White norms. Paralleling the behavioral precocity, Jensen (1969a: 87) reported evidence of faster bone development in Black infants (established using X-rays) and earlier maturation of brain wave patterns (measured using EEGs). Soon after, Jensen (1973: 289–290) suggested that race differences in the production of two-egg twins, being most common among Blacks and least common among East Asians, with Caucasians intermediate, "may be a reflection of evolutionary age". In a long footnote, he wrote: "[T]he three racial groups lie on a developmental continuum on which the Caucasian group is more or less intermediate. A related fact is that there is an inverse relationship throughout the phylogenetic hierarchy between the tendency for multiple births and the prolongation of immaturity."

Many researchers were inspired by "Jensenism". Richard Lynn (1977, 1978, 1982) and Philip E. Vernon (1982) not only pushed the envelope, but extended the "outside of the envelope" and made the race-IQ debate international in scope with their findings that East Asians average higher on tests of mental ability than do Whites, whereas Caribbeans (and especially Africans) average lower. As Lynn's (1997, 2003; Lynn &

Vanhanen 2002) most recent reviews show, East Asians, measured in North America and in Pacific Rim countries, typically average IQs in the range of 101 to 111; Whites in North America, Europe, and Australasia average IQs of 85 to 115, with an overall mean of 100; and Blacks, living south of the Sahara, in North America, in the Caribbean, and in Britain average IQs of 70 to 90.

As a budding sociobiologist, I too was inspired by Jensenism. It seemed to me that by its impact on diverse areas of behavioral science, Jensenism might help complete the Darwinian revolution. I began to review the international literature, studying not only IQ, but other behavioral traits like speed of physical maturation and longevity, personality and temperament, family structure and crime, and sexual behavior and fertility, and later brain size too (Rushton 1984a, 1984b, 1988). These studies culminated in a book *Race, Evolution, and Behavior* (Rushton 1995, 2000). East Asians are slower maturing, less fertile, less sexually active, with larger brains and higher IQ scores than Blacks, who tend towards the opposite in each of these areas. Whites fall between the other two groups (see Table 9.4). As Jensen (1984) elaborated in a commentary on my first (1984a) review, a network of such related evidence provides more opportunity for finding and testing alternative theories than does any single dimension drawn from the set.

Subsequently, I carried out experiments finding, for example, that the amount of inbreeding depression on 11 sub-tests of the WISC-R in Japan predicted the magnitude of the Black-White differences on the same sub-tests in the U.S. (Rushton 1989). Inbreeding depression, a purely genetic effect, was a sufficiently robust predictor to overcome generalization from the Japanese in Japan to Blacks and Whites in the U.S. There really is no explanation, other than a genetic one, for the correlation between inbreeding depression and Black-White differences.

I also examined the relation between intelligence and brain size, finding correlations of $r = 0.20$ between IQ scores and simple head size measures and of $r = 0.44$ with measures based on Magnetic Resonance Imaging (MRI) (Rushton & Ankney 1996). In one study, Rushton (1997) analyzed data from the enormous Collaborative Perinatal Project which recorded head circumference measurements and IQ scores from 50,000 children followed from birth to age seven (Broman *et al.* 1987). At birth, four months, one year, and seven years, the Asian American children averaged larger cranial volumes than did the White children, who averaged larger cranial volumes than did the Black children (Figure 9.2). Within each race, the children with the larger head sizes had the higher IQ scores. By age seven, the Asian American children averaged an IQ of 110, White children an IQ of 102, and Black children an IQ of 90. Since the Asian American children were the shortest in stature and the lightest in weight and the Black children were the tallest in stature and the heaviest in weight, these race differences in brain-size/IQ relations were not due to body size.

With adults, I used external head size measurements (length, width, height) to calculate cranial capacities from five large archival data sets. In the first of these studies, Rushton (1991) examined head size measures in 24 international military samples collated by the U.S. National Aeronautics and Space Administration. After adjusting for the effects of body height, weight, and surface area, it found the mean cranial capacity for East Asians was 1,460 and for Europeans 1,446 cm^3. The second (Rushton 1992)

Table 9.4: Relative ranking of races on diverse variables.

Variable	East Asians	Whites	Blacks
Brain size			
Autopsy data (cm^3 equivalents)	1,351	1,356	1,223
Endocranial volume (cm^3)	1,415	1,362	1,268
External head measures (cm^3)	1,356	1,329	1,294
Cortical neurons (billions)	13.767	13.665	13.185
Intelligence			
IQ test scores	106	100	85
Decision times	Faster	Intermediate	Slower
Cultural achievements	Higher	Higher	Lower
Maturation rate			
Gestation time	?	Intermediate	Earlier
Skeletal development	Later	Intermediate	Earlier
Motor development	Later	Intermediate	Earlier
Dental development	Later	Intermediate	Earlier
Age of first intercourse	Later	Intermediate	Earlier
Age of first pregnancy	Later	Intermediate	Earlier
Life-span	Longer	Intermediate	Shorter
Personality			
Activity	Lower	Intermediate	Higher
Aggressiveness	Lower	Intermediate	Higher
Cautiousness	Higher	Intermediate	Lower
Dominance	Lower	Intermediate	Higher
Impulsivity	Lower	Intermediate	Higher
Self-concept	Lower	Intermediate	Higher
Sociability	Lower	Intermediate	Higher
Social organization			
Marital stability	Higher	Intermediate	Lower
Law abidingness	Higher	Intermediate	Lower
Mental health	Higher	Intermediate	Lower
Administrative capacity	Higher	Higher	Lower
Reproductive effort			
Two-egg twinning (per 1000 births)	4	8	16
Hormone levels	Lower	Intermediate	Higher
Secondary sex characteristics	Smaller	Intermediate	Larger
Intercourse frequencies	Lower	Intermediate	Higher
Permissive attitudes	Lower	Intermediate	Higher
Sexually transmitted diseases	Lower	Intermediate	Higher

Note: From: Rushton, J. P. (1995). *Race, evolution, and behavior* (p. 5).

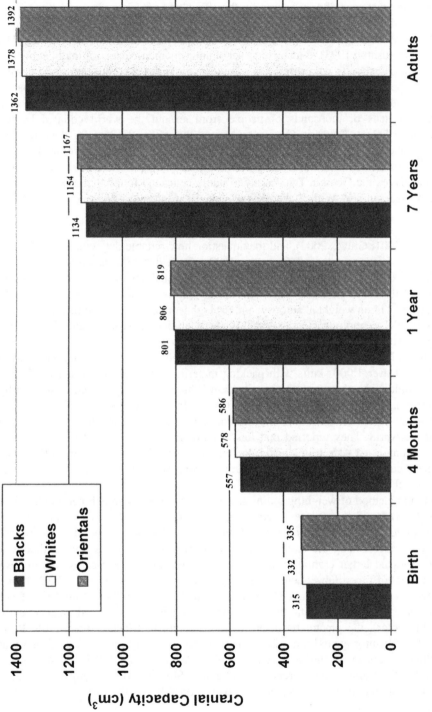

Figure 9.2: Average cranial capacity (cm³) from birth to adulthood for Blacks, Whites, and Orientals in the U.S. Birth through age 7 from U.S. Collaborative Perinatal Project; adults from U.S. Army. (After Rushton 1997: 15).

demonstrated that even after adjusting for the effects of body size, sex and military rank in a stratified random sample of over 6,000 U.S. Army personnel, East Asians, Whites and Blacks averaged cranial capacities of 1,416, 1,380 and 1,359 cm³, respectively. The third study (Rushton 1993) re-analyzed a set of anthropometric data originally published by Melville Herskovits who offered it as evidence against race differences in cranial capacity. The new analyses revealed that in fact Caucasoids averaged a cranial capacity of 1,421 and Negroids, 1,295 cm³. The fourth study (Rushton 1994) analyzed data obtained on tens of thousands of people from around the world collated by the International Labour Office in Geneva and found that after adjusting for the effects of body size and sex, samples from the Pacific Rim, Europe, and Africa averaged cranial capacities, of 1,308, 1,297, and 1,241 cm³, respectively. Finally, Rushton & Osborne (1995) analyzed the Georgia Twin Study of adolescents and found that after correcting for body size and sex, Whites averaged a cranial capacity of 1,269 and Blacks 1,251 cm³.

Many are surprised to learn that the races differ in brain size (Kamin & Omari 1998; Lieberman 2001; Graves 2002), and they question how reliable the evidence is. In fact, dozens of studies from the 1840s to the 1990s, using different methods on different samples, reveal the same strong pattern. Three other methods of measuring brain size also reveal the same pattern of race differences: (1) endocranial volume from empty skulls; (2) wet brain weight at autopsy; and (3) high tech MRI. For example, using state-of-the-art MRI technology, Harvey *et al.* (1994) found that 41 Africans and West Indians averaged a smaller brain volume than did 67 Caucasians.

Using endocranial volume, the American anthropologist Samuel George Morton (1849) filled over 1,000 skulls with packing material and found that Blacks averaged about 5 cubic inches less cranial capacity than Whites. His results were confirmed by Todd (1923), Gordon (1934) and Simmons (1942). In 1984, Beals *et al.* carried out the largest study of race differences in endocranial volume to date, using 20,000 skulls from around the world. They reported that East Asians, Europeans, and Africans averaged cranial volumes of 1,415, 1,362, and 1,268 cm³, respectively. The skulls from East Asia averaged 3 cubic inches larger than those from Europe, which in turn was 5 cubic inches larger than the African average.

Using the method of weighing brains at autopsy, the famous French neurologist Paul Broca (1873) found that Whites averaged heavier brains than did Blacks and showed more complex convolutions and larger frontal lobes. Broca corroborated the Black-White differences using the endocranial volume method as well as finding that East Asians averaged larger cranial capacities than did Europeans. These results too have stood the test of time. Subsequent autopsy studies have found an average Black-White brain weight difference of about 100 grams (Bean 1906; Mall 1909; Vint 1934; Pearl 1934). Some studies have found that the more White admixture (judged independently from skin color), the greater the average brain weight in Blacks (Bean 1906; Pearl 1934). A 1980 autopsy study of 1,261 American adults by Ho *et al.* (1980) found that 811 White Americans in this sample averaged 1,323 grams and 450 Black Americans averaged 1,223 grams — a difference of 100 grams. Since the Blacks and Whites in the study were similar in body size, it was not responsible for the differences in brain weight.

Rushton (1995) summarized the world database using the three methods on which there are a sufficient number of studies (autopsies, endocranial volume, head measurements) as well as head measurements corrected for body size (see pp. 126–132, Table 6.6). The results in cm^3 or equivalents were: East Asians = 1,351, 1,415, 1,335, 1,356 (mean = 1,364); Whites = 1,356, 1,362, 1,341, 1,329 (mean = 1,347); and Blacks = 1,223, 1,268, 1,284, and 1,294 (mean = 1,267). The overall mean for Asians is 17 cm^3 more than that for Europeans and 97 cm^3 more than that for Africans. Within-race differences, due to method of estimation, averaged 31 cm^3. Since one cubic inch of brain matter contains millions of brain cells and hundreds of millions of synapses or neural connections, these brain size differences help to explain why the races differ in average IQ.

As a committed Jensenist, I pursued these and many other hypotheses with vigor. To account for the trade-off between racial differences in brain size and egg-production and all the other traits shown in Table 9.4, Rushton (1988, 1995, 2000) proposed a gene-based "life-history theory" based on evolutionary biology's $r - K$ scale of reproductive strategies. This scale is generally used to compare the life histories of widely disparate species, but Rushton used it to describe the smaller but real differences between the human races. East Asians are more K and so tend to devote resources to producing small numbers of children and invest heavily in them and provide them with a high level of parental care; Africans are more r and devote resources to producing greater numbers of children, invest less heavily in them and give them less parental care; Whites are intermediate, though closer to East Asians. The r/K scale predicted a wide spectrum of characteristics including fertility, infant mortality, rate of physical maturation, intelligence, brain size, dizygotic twinning, crime, sexual potency, sexual precocity, number of sexual partners, and hormone levels. Highly K-selected women produce fewer eggs (and have bigger brains) than r-selected women. Highly K-selected men invest time and energy in their children rather than the pursuit of sexual thrills. They are "dads" rather than "cads".

Rushton (1988, 1995, 2000) also mapped the $r - K$ theory of racial differences onto the "Out of Africa" theory of human origins. Only when *Homo sapiens* left Africa, about 100,000 years ago, did they begin to develop the racial traits we see today, by adapting to the new regions and climates. The first major split was between the Africans and the non-Africans. Then about 40,000 years ago there was another major split, between the ancestors of today's Whites and East Asians. The African/non-African split occurred more than twice as early as the East Asian-White split. This explains why Whites average between East Asians and Africans on so many life history traits.

The climate differences influenced mental abilities. In Africa, food and warmth were available all year round. As *Homo sapiens* moved out of Africa they faced an entirely new problem — cold winters. Gathering and storing food, providing shelter, making clothes, and raising children during these long winters were more mentally demanding tasks than those that humans had faced previously. These tasks called for larger brains and slower rates of growth. They resulted in lower levels of sex hormones leading to fewer twins, less sexual behavior and aggression, and more family stability. Both parents had to provide more care to help their young survive in the harsher climates. Thus came about the pattern of traits in Table 9.4.

3. Genes? Environment? Or Both?

All the issues concerning Black-White differences in IQ that Jensen (1969a) raised in his famous *Harvard Educational Review* article are still with us today. Indeed, much of the opposition to IQ testing and heritability would probably disappear if it were not for the stubborn and unwelcome fact that, despite extensive well-funded programs of intervention, the Black-White difference refuses to go quietly into the night.

Jensen's long intellectual march on this topic led triumphantly to his latest book, *The g Factor* (1998). Jensen's tome does not draw back from Jensenist conclusions — that the average difference in IQ found between Blacks and Whites has a substantial hereditary component, that this difference is related mainly to the *g*-factor, and that it has important societal consequences. Jensen (1998: 418) proposed the "default hypothesis" for Black-White IQ differences, viz., that they are due to the same weight of genetic and environmental factors as are the causes of individual differences within each race. There is no need for any ad hoc hypothesis, or to postulate some Factor X, that is unique to either Blacks or Whites.

Chapter 12 of *The g Factor* presents Jensen's technical arguments for why he believes that Black-White IQ differences are about 50% genetic in origin. These include that: (1) the Black-White IQ differences are most pronounced on the more *g*-loaded components of IQ tests; (2) the Black-White IQ differences are most pronounced on the more heritable components of IQ tests; (3) IQ differences are associated with brain size within each race and there are significant Black-White (and East Asian) differences in average brain size; (4) Black-White (and East Asian) differences show up in myopia which has been linked to brain size; (5) the Black-White (and East Asian) IQ differences remain following transracial adoption; (6) the Black-White IQ differences are reflected in studies of racial admixture; (7) the Black-White IQ differences are predicted by "regression to the mean"; (8) Black-White-East Asian differences in neonate behavior, rate of maturation, and a suite of life-history traits parallel the IQ differences; (9) the Black-White-East Asian IQ differences cannot be explained by any culture-only theory; and (10) the Black-White-East Asian IQ differences dovetail with what is known about human evolution. What follows is a summary of some of the evidence from Jensen's (1998) The *g* Factor and Rushton's (1995, 2000) *Race, Evolution, and Behavior*.

4. Evidence for the Default Hypothesis for Black-White IQ Differences

4.1. Black-White IQ Differences are Most Pronounced on the More g-Loaded Components of IQ Tests

As reviewed early in this chapter, Black-White differences are Jensen Effects, being most pronounced on the more *g*-loaded subtests. Spearman's hypothesis thus constitutes a special case of the Jensen Effect. It applies even to the *g* factor extracted from reaction time measures taken from 9- to 12-year-old Black and White children. Jensen (1998) has shown that a test's *g* loading is the best predictor not just of that test's correlation with scholastic and work-place performance, but of heritability coefficients determined from twin studies, inbreeding depression scores calculated in children born from cousin-marriages, and many other variables including brain evoked potentials, brain pH levels, brain glucose metabolism, as well as nerve conduction velocity, reaction time and other physiological factors. These correlations establish the heritable and biological, as opposed to the mere statistical, reality of *g*. The general factor *g* is a product of human evolution. Indeed, massive evidence indicates that *g* is related to the size and functioning of the brain (Duncan *et al.* 2000; Rushton & Ankney 1996; see also Chapters 6 and 10 in this volume). As reviewed above, race differences in brain size occur at birth and continue through life.

4.2. Black-White IQ Differences are Most Pronounced on the More Heritable Components of IQ Tests

Individual differences are heritable *within* races, indeed within all species and sub-species so far studied. Dozens of twin, adoption, and family studies have confirmed the high heritabilities for intellectual and social variables within human races (as reviewed by Bouchard 1996; Bouchard & Loehlin 2001 and Chapter 7 of *The g Factor*). By simple generalization, therefore, we would expect that race differences are heritable too. If, however, environmental deprivation is stronger for Blacks than for Whites, the heritabilities for Blacks should be reduced. If so, greater environmental *damage* and not genes would be the cause of the race difference.

Loehlin *et al.* (1975: 114–116) reviewed the literature to date and found that while there was some evidence suggesting a lower heritability of intelligence for Blacks than for Whites (e.g. by Scarr-Salapatek 1971), a larger body of evidence suggested equal heritabilities in the two groups. Subsequently, Osborne's (1980b) Georgia Twin Study compared 123 Black and 304 White pairs of 12- to 18-year-old twins drawn from schools in Georgia, Kentucky, and Indiana, given the Basic Test Battery, along with smaller sub-sets of twins given the Primary Mental Abilities test and the Cattell Culture Fair Intelligence test. He found heritabilities of about 50% for both Blacks and Whites, all significantly different from zero but not from each other. (The heritabilities of the Basic, Primary, and Cattell tests respectively were, for Whites: 0.61, 0.37, and 0.71; and for Blacks: 0.75, 0.42, and 0.19; Osborne 1980b, pp. 68–69, 89, 98). Moreover, the heritabilities increased with age in Blacks, just as they did in Whites, indicating no evidence for the cumulative environmental deficits predicted by culture-only theory (Osborne 1980b, ch. XI).

Jensen (1998: 465) re-analyzed the Georgia Twin Study using structural equation modeling. This decomposes a phenotypic mean difference into its genetic and environmental components. Essentially, this methodology is a multiple regression technique that tests the "goodness-of-fit" of different alternative models that explain whether a difference between groups is due to the same genetic and environmental factors that cause individual differences within the groups, *or* whether some additional, minority-specific, cultural factor (an unknown Factor X) causes differences *between* groups but not differences *within* groups. Jensen (1998) tested three alternative models — *only* genetic factors, *only* environmental factors, or *neither* genes *nor* environment — against the default model (genes and environment). He found that the observed Black-White differences were best explained by both genetic and environmental factors, while either genetic or environmental explanations alone were inadequate.

Others too have used structural equation models to examine the genetic and cultural contributions to race differences. In a series of studies, Rowe (1994; Rowe *et al.* 1994, 1995) analyzed diverse but representative data sets. In one study of six data sources, Rowe *et al.* (1994) compared cross-sectional correlation matrices (about 10×10) for a total of 8,528 Whites, 3,392 Blacks, 1,766 Hispanics and 906 Asians. These matrices contained both independent variables (e.g. home environment, peer characteristics) and developmental outcomes (e.g. achievement, delinquency). When the matrices were compared by a LISREL goodness-of-fit test, each ethnic group's covariance matrix was equal to the matrix of the other groups. Not only were these matrices nearly identical but also they were no less alike than covariance matrices computed from random halves within one ethnic or racial group. There were no distortions in the matrices that required any minority-specific developmental Factor X to explain the correlations between the background variables and the outcome measures.

In another study, Rowe *et al.* (1995) extended this cross-sectional line of research by examining longitudinal data on academic achievement. Once again, the existence of any minority-specific cultural processes affecting achievement should produce different covariance structures among ethnic and racial groups. Correlation matrices were computed on academic achievement and family environment measures in 565 full-sibling pairs from the National Longitudinal Survey of Youth, each tested at ages 6.6 and 9.0 years (White $N = 296$ pairs; Black $N = 149$ pairs; Hispanic $N = 120$ pairs). Each population group was treated separately, yielding three 8×8 correlation matrices. When compared employing a LISREL method, the matrices were equal across the three groups. As a single structural equation model fitted all groups, the hypothesis of special minority-specific developmental processes affecting academic achievement was not supported.

Subsequently, Rowe & Cleveland (1996) extended the structural equation modeling studies to estimate explicitly the within-race heritabilities from Black and White full- and half-siblings, again with data from the National Longitudinal Survey of Youth (106 pairs of Black half-sibs, 53 pairs of White half-sibs; 161 pairs of Black full-sibs, 314 pairs of White full-sibs). Three Peabody Individual Achievement Tests were used (Mathematics, Reading Comprehension and Reading Recognition). The data fit the default hereditarian model that the sources of individual differences and of differences between racial means were the same — about 50% genetic and 50% environmental — extremely well.

Large-scale studies of military samples have also reported a nearly identical statistical structure on intellectual variables across races. Ree & Carretta (1995) examined a nationally representative sample of young Black, White and Hispanic men and women who took the Armed Services Vocational Aptitude Battery (ASVAB; $N = 9,173$). The ASVAB, which is used to select applicants for all military enlistments and assign them to first jobs, consists of 10 separately scored sub-tests (General Science, Arithmetic Reasoning, Word Knowledge, Paragraph Comprehension, Numerical Operations, Coding Speed, Auto and Shop Information, Mathematics Knowledge, Mechanical Comprehension, Electronics Information). Ree and Carretta found the hierarchical factor structure of ASVAB sub-test scores was virtually identical across the three groups. Similarly, Carretta & Ree (1995) examined the more specialized and diverse Air Force Officer Qualifying Test (AFOQT), a multiple-aptitude battery that had been given to 269,968 applicants (212,238 Whites, 32,798 Blacks, 12,647 Hispanics, 9,460 Asian Americans and 2,551 Native Americans). Hierarchical *g* accounted for the greatest amount of variance in all groups and its loadings differed little by ethnicity. Thus, the factor structure of cognitive ability is nearly identical for Blacks and for Whites. These findings are consistent with the default hereditarian hypothesis.

Heritability data are especially informative when genetic theory and culture-only theories of race differences make diametrically opposite predictions. For example, genetic theory predicts that race differences will be greater on those sub-tests that are more heritable within races, while culture-only theory predicts that race differences will be greater on those sub-tests that are culturally malleable (i.e. those with lower heritability) and on which races can grow apart as a result of dissimilar experiences. Analyses of independent data sets support the genetic hypothesis.

Jensen (1973, ch. 4) was one of the first to apply differential heritabilities to the study of race differences. He calculated the *environmentality* of tests in both Black and White children defined as the degree to which sibling correlations departed from the pure genetic expectation of 0.50. Environmentality was inversely related to the magnitude of the Black-White difference ($r = -0.70$), leading to the conclusion that the more environmentally influenced a test, the less pronounced its Black-White difference. Jensen (1973) also cited an unpublished study by Nichols (1972) that estimated the heritability of 13 tests from 543 pairs of 7-year-old siblings, including an equal number of Blacks and Whites. Jensen found a 0.67 correlation between the heritability of a test and the magnitude of the Black-White difference on that test.

Prompted by Jensen's approach, Rushton (1989) estimated genetic weights by using the amount of inbreeding depression found on the 11 tests of the Wechsler Intelligence Scale for Children (WISC). Inbreeding depression occurs in the offspring of closely related parents when harmful recessive genes combine. The fact that inbreeding depression lowers the IQ in offspring in itself provides evidence for the heritability of IQ. Rushton found a positive correlation between inbreeding depression scores calculated from 1,854 cousin marriages in Japan and the magnitude of the Black-White difference in the U.S. on the same 11 Wechsler tests ($r = 0.48$; Figure 9.3). This contradicts culture-only theory, which predicts that differences between Blacks and Whites should be greater on those sub-tests most affected by the environment (i.e. those showing lowest amount of inbreeding depression). There really is no non-genetic explanation for the relation between inbreeding depression scores from Japan and Black-White differences in the U.S. Figure 9.3 also shows the regression of Black-White differences on the *g* factor (reviewed earlier). As either the *g* loadings or the inbreeding depression scores increase, the differences between Blacks and Whites also increase.

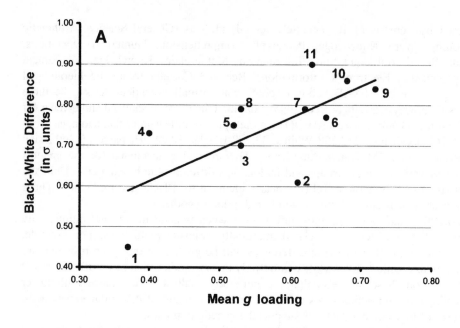

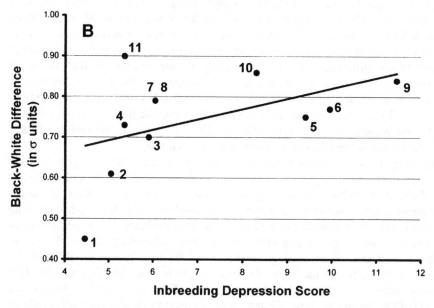

Figure 9.3: Regression of Black-White differences on *g* loadings (panel A) and on inbreeding depression scores (panel B). *Note:* The numbers indicate sub-tests from the Wechsler Intelligence Scale for Children—Revised: 1 Coding; 2 Arithmetic; 3 Picture completion; 4 Mazes; 5 Picture arrangement; 6 Similarities; 7 Comprehension; 8 Object assembly; 9 Vocabulary; 10 Information; 11 Block design. (After Rushton 1995: 188).

4.3. Black-White (and East Asian) IQ Differences Occur in Average Brain Size Which is Linked to IQ scores Within Races

The g Factor discusses Jensen's own studies on the relation between brain size and intelligence and to racial differences in brain size, as well as those reviewed earlier in this chapter. Jensen & Johnson (1994) showed that for Blacks, as for Whites, the head size $\times$ IQ correlation exists within-families as well as between-families, indicating the intrinsic or functional relationship mentioned earlier. Equally important is the fact that within each sex, Blacks and Whites fit the same regression line of head size on IQ. When Blacks and Whites are perfectly matched for true-score IQ (i.e. IQ corrected for measurement error), at either the Black mean or the White mean, the overall average White-Black difference in head circumference is virtually nil. (Matching Blacks and Whites for IQ eliminates the average difference in head size, but matching the groups on head size does not equalize their IQs. This is what one would expect if brain size is only one of a number of brain factors involved in IQ.)

In another analysis of the Georgia Twin Study, Jensen (1994) showed that the Black-White difference in head/brain size is also related to the magnitude of the Black-White difference in g. The correlation coefficient of each test with the head measurements was correlated with the magnitude of the Black-White difference on that test, thus forming two vectors. The column vector of test $\times$ head-size correlations correlated 0.51 ($P < 0.05$) with the vector of standardized White-Black differences on each of the tests.

The final piece of evidence that the race difference in brain size mediates the race difference in IQ comes from an "ecological correlation" (widely used in epidemiological research) of 0.998 between mean brain size measures and mean IQ scores across the three races (Jensen 1998: 443). Figure 9.4, which plots the regression of median IQ on mean cranial capacity is almost perfectly linear, with a Pearson $r = 0.998$. Mean cranial capacity for each of the three races accurately predicts their mean IQs.

4.4. Black-White (and East Asian) IQ Differences Show up in Myopia Which has been Linked to Brain Size

Myopia (near-sightedness) is positively correlated with IQ. The relationship appears to be pleiotropic, that is, a gene affecting one of the traits also has some effect on the other (Cohn *et al.* 1988). Further, there are significant racial and ethnic differences in the frequency of myopia, with the highest rates found in East Asians, the lowest rates among Africans and Europeans intermediate (Post 1982). Among Europeans, Jews have the highest rate of myopia, about twice that of gentiles and about on a par with that of Asians. Miller (1994) suggested that myopia is caused by extra myelinization in the eye and is similarly linked to brain size.

4.5. Black-White (and East Asian) IQ Differences Remain Following Transracial Adoptions

The g Factor also cites the evidence of transracial adoption studies. Three studies have been carried out on Korean and Vietnamese children adopted into White American and

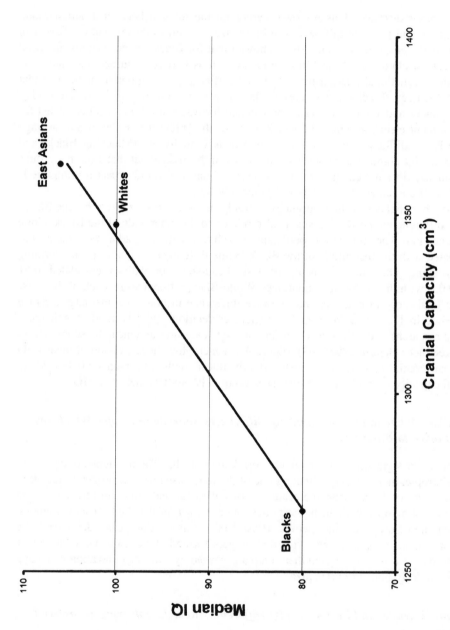

Figure 9.4: Median IQ of three populations (Mongoloid, Caucasoid, and Negroid) plotted as a function of the mean cranial capacity in each population. (Regression: IQ = 0.262 × cranial capacity − 252.6; r = 0.998.) (After Jensen 1998: 443).

White Belgian homes (e.g. Frydman & Lynn 1989). Though many had been hospitalized for malnutrition prior to adoption, they went on to develop IQs ten or more points higher than their adoptive national norms. By contrast, Black and Mixed-Race (Black/White) children adopted into White middle-class families typically perform at a lower level than similarly adopted White children. The largest and best known such study, the Minnesota Transracial Adoption Study, was designed specifically by Sandra Scarr and Richard Weinberg to separate genetic factors from rearing conditions as causal influences on the poor cognitive performance of Black children (Scarr & Weinberg 1976; Weinberg *et al.* 1992). It is also the only transracial adoption study that includes a longitudinal follow-up, with testing at ages 7 and 17 years.

Scarr and her colleagues compared the IQ and academic achievement scores of Black, White, and mixed-race Black/White children adopted into privileged White families in Minnesota by adopting parents whose mean IQ was more than 1 SD above the population mean of 100 (see Table 9.5). The biological children of these parents were also tested. The first testing of 265 children was carried out in 1975 when they were 7 years old and the second in 1986 when the 196 remaining in the study were 17 years old. The 7-year-old White biological (non-adopted) children had an average IQ of 117 (Table 9.5, 2nd column), similar to that found for other children of upper-middle-class parents. The adopted children with two White biological parents had a mean IQ of 112. The adopted children with one Black and one White biological parent averaged 109. The adopted children with two Black biological parents had an average IQ of 97. (A mixed group of 21 Asian, North American Indian, and Latin American Indian adopted children averaged an IQ of 100 but were not included in the main statistical analyses.)

Scarr & Weinberg (1976) interpreted the results of their testing at age 7 as strong support for the culture-only interpretation of racial differences in intelligence. They drew special attention to the fact that the mean IQ of 107 for all "socially classified" Black children (i.e. those with either one or two Black parents) was significantly above the U.S. White mean. The poorer performance of children with two Black biological parents was attributed to their more difficult and later placement. Scarr and Weinberg also pointed out that this latter group had both natural and adoptive parents with somewhat lower educational levels and abilities (two points lower in adoptive parents IQ). They found no evidence for "the expectancy effects" hypothesis that adoptive parent' beliefs about the child's racial background influence the child's intellectual development. The mean score for 12 children wrongly believed by their adoptive parents to have two Black biological parents was virtually the same as for 56 children correctly classified by their adoptive parents as having one Black and one White biological parent.

Table 9.5 also presents the results for the 196 children retested at 17 years old (Weinberg *et al.* 1992). There were four independent assessments of the children's cognitive performance at this later age: (1) an individually administered IQ test; (2) an overall grade point average; (3) a class rank based on school performance; and (4) four special aptitude tests in school subjects administered by the educational authority, which Rushton (1995) averaged. The results are strikingly concordant with the earlier testing. The non-adopted White children had a mean IQ of 109, a grade point average of 3.0, a class rank at the 64th percentile, and an aptitude score at the 69th percentile. The

Table 9.5: Comparison of white biological and white, mixed-race, and black adopted children at age 7 and 17 raised in middle-class white families.

Children's background	Age 7	Age 17	Age 17 Grade Point Average	Age 17 Class Rank (percentile)	Age 17 School Aptitude based on National Norms (weighted mean of 4 percentiles)
Biological Parents					
Non-adopted, with 2 White biological parents (N at 7 = 143; N at 17 = 104)	120 116	115 109	3.0	64	69
Adopted, With 2 White biological parents (N at 7 = 25; N at 17 = 16)	112	106	2.8	54	59
Adopted, with 1 White, 1 Black biological parent (N at 7 = 68; N at 17 = 55)	109	99	2.2	40	53
Adopted, with 2 Black biological parents (N at 7 = 29; N at 17 = 21)	97	89	2.1	36	42

Adapted from *Race, Evolution, and Behavior* (Rushton 1995). Based on data from Weinberg *et al.* (1992).

adopted children with two White biological parents had a mean IQ of 106, a grade point average of 2.8, a class rank at the 54th percentile, and an aptitude score at the 59th percentile. The adopted children with one Black and one White biological parent had a mean IQ of 99, a grade point average of 2.2, a class rank at the 40th percentile, and an aptitude score at the 53rd percentile. The adopted children with two Black biological parents had a mean IQ of 89, a grade point average of 2.1, a class rank at the 36th percentile, and an aptitude score at the 42nd percentile. (The 12 remaining mixed group of Amerindian and Asian children had an IQ of 96 with no data provided on school achievement.)

Because different tests based on different standardization groups were used in the first testing than were used in the follow-up, the overall average difference of about eight IQ points (evident for all groups, including the non-adopted group) between the two test periods is of no theoretical importance for the hypothesis of interest. The relevant comparisons are those between the adopted groups *within* each age level. The mean of 89 for adopted children with two Black parents was slightly above the national Black mean of 85 but not above the Black mean for Minnesota.

4.6. Black-White IQ Differences are Reflected in Studies of Racial Admixture

In the Minnesota Transracial Adoption Study, the Mixed-Race (Black/White) adoptees had a mean IQ between those of the "non-mixed" White and "non-mixed" Black adoptees, as predicted from a genetic hypothesis (see Table 9.5). Although Jensen (1998: 478–483) himself is equivocal on this topic, in fact many other studies report similar results. For example, with respect to IQ scores, Shuey (1966) found that in 16 of 18 studies, Blacks with lighter skin color averaged higher IQ scores than did those with darker skin. Shockley (1973) estimated that for low IQ Black populations there is a one-point increase in average "genetic" IQ for each 1% of Caucasian ancestry, with diminishing returns as an IQ of 100 is reached. The genetic hypothesis is also consistent with the African American mean IQ of 85 being 15 points above the African average of 70 (reviewed earlier), given the approximately 20% White admixture in this group (Chakraborty *et al.* 1992; Parra *et al.* 1998). Corroborating data come from the mixed-race "Colored" population of South Africa showing they too have an average IQ of 85, intermediate to the "pure" Africans and "pure" Whites (Owen 1992). What brain weight data are available also fit with the genetic hypothesis. Both Bean (1906) and Pearl (1934) found that the greater the amount of White admixture (judged independently from skin color), the higher the average brain weight at autopsy in Blacks.

Most recently, Lynn (2002) and Rowe (2002) have analyzed data from large, publicly available, archival data sets, which show that groups of mixed-race individuals have mean scores intermediate to unmixed groups of Blacks and of Whites. Lynn examined the 1982 National Opinion Research Center's survey of a representative sample of the adult population, excluding non-English speakers. The 442 Blacks in the sample were asked whether they would describe themselves as "very dark", "dark brown", "medium brown", "light brown", or "very light". The correlation between these self-ratings and a 10-word vocabulary test score was $r = 0.17$ ($p < 0.01$). Rowe examined the 1994

National Longitudinal Study of Adolescent Health's survey of a representative sample of youths, with intentional over-sampling of Black children of highly educated parents. The mean age for the entire sample (9,830 Whites, 4,017 Blacks, and 119 mixed-race individuals) was 16. The Black adolescents averaged a lower birth weight, a lower verbal IQ, and a higher number of sexual partners than did the White adolescents. For each characteristic, the mixed-race mean fell between the means of the other two groups. Rowe found the social class explanation of the group differences "unconvincing", because of the three variables, only verbal IQ showed a moderate correlation with social class and statistically adjusting for it left the main findings unchanged. He also rejected the "discrimination based on skin tone" hypothesis since it was eliminated by deliberately selecting only those mixed-race adolescents who were judged by their interviewers to be Black based on their physical appearance.

4.7. Blacks and Whites Regress Toward their Predicted Racial Means

Regression toward the mean provides still another way to test if race differences are genetic. Regression toward the mean is seen, on average, when high IQ people mate and their children are less intelligent than their parents. This is because the parents pass on some, but not all, of their exceptional genes to their offspring. The converse happens for very low IQ parents; they have children with higher IQs. Although parents pass on a random half of their genes to their offspring, they cannot pass on the particular combinations of genes that cause their own exceptionality. It's like rolling a pair of dice and having them come up two sixes or two ones. The odds are that on the next roll, you'll get some value that is not quite as high (or as low). Physical and psychological traits involving dominant and recessive genes show some regression effect. Genetic theory predicts the magnitude of the regression effect to be lesser the closer the degree of kinship (e.g. identical twin > full-sibling > half-sibling). Culture-only theory makes no systematic or quantitative predictions based on genetic kinship *per se.*

For any trait, regression predicts that scores will move towards the average for that race. So in the United States, genetic theory predicts that the children of Black parents of IQ 115 will regress toward the Black IQ average of 85, while children of White parents of IQ 115 will regress toward the White IQ average of 100. There are similar predictions for the low end of the scale. Children of Black parents of IQ 70 should move up toward the Black IQ average of 85, while children of White parents of IQ 70 should move up toward the White IQ average of 100. Regression to the mean has been tested and the predictions proved to be true many times over. But more importantly, both the White and Black groups show the same degree of regression throughout the entire range of IQs between ± 3 SDs from the group mean. The Law of Regression also explains why Black children born to high IQ, wealthy Black parents have test scores two to four points lower than do White children born to low IQ poor White parents (Jensen 1998: 358). The high IQ Black parents were unable to pass on their advantage to their children, even though they gave them a good upbringing and good schools. (The same phenomenon, of course, is also found for high IQ White parents.) Again, no culture-only theory *predicts* these results. To do so it would have to invoke the ad hoc hypothesis that cultural factors perfectly imitate the effect theoretically predicted by genetic theory and confirmed repeatedly in studies of physical traits and in animals.

Jensen (1973, Chapter 4) tested the regression predictions with data from siblings. These provide an even better test than parent-offspring comparisons because siblings share very similar environments. Black and White children matched for IQ had siblings who had regressed approximately halfway to their respective population means rather than to the mean of the combined population. For example, when Black and White children are matched with IQs of 120, the siblings of Black children average close to 100, while the siblings of White children average close to 110. A reverse effect is found with children matched at the lower end of the IQ scale. When Black and White children are matched for IQs of 70, the siblings of Black children average about 78, while the siblings of White children average about 85. The regression line showed no significant departure from linearity throughout the range of IQ from 50 to 150.

4.8. Black-White-East Asian Differences in Neonate Behavior, Rate of Maturation and a Suite of Life-History Traits Parallel the IQ Differences

On average, Black babies are born a week earlier than White babies, yet they are more mature as measured by bone development. In America, 51% of Black children have been born by week 39 of pregnancy compared with 33% of White children. In Europe, Black African babies, even those born to mothers in the professional classes, are born earlier than White babies. These Black babies are not born premature. They are born sooner, but biologically they are more mature. The length of pregnancy depends on the genes.

After birth, Black babies continue to mature faster than White babies, while East Asian babies mature more slowly. X-rays show that the bones grow faster in Black children than in White children and faster in Whites than in East Asians. Black babies also have greater muscular strength and can reach for objects better. Their neck muscles are often so developed that they can lift their heads up when they are only nine hours old. In a matter of days they can turn themselves over. Black children sit, crawl, walk, and put on their own clothes earlier than Whites or East Asians. East Asian children, on the other hand, mature more slowly than do White children. East Asian children often do not walk until 13 months while White children average walking at 12 months and Black children average walking at 11 months.

Blacks have faster dental development than do Whites, who mature faster than do East Asians. For example, Black children begin the first stage of permanent tooth growth at about 5.8 years while Whites and East Asians don't begin until 6.1 years. Blacks also reach sexual maturity sooner than do Whites, who in turn reach sexual maturity sooner than do East Asians. This is true for things like age of first menstruation, age of first sexual experience, and age of first pregnancy (Rushton 1995). It is unlikely that social factors could produce these differences. Across species a slower rate of development tends to go with greater brain size.

As reviewed earlier (Table 9.4), data from around the world on over 60 different variables including speed of maturation and longevity, personality and temperament, family stability and crime, sexual behavior and fertility, as well as intelligence and brain size, show East Asians and Africans consistently average at opposite ends of a continuum, with Europeans intermediate. Studies of personality show that Blacks are on average more extraverted, outgoing and uninhibited than Whites, who are in turn more extraverted, outgoing and uninhibited than Asians. These differences in personality may be reflected in international differences in rate of violent crime, as reported in the INTERPOL Yearbooks. Analyzes of these data throughout the 1980s and 1990s showed that African and Caribbean countries had double the rate of violent crime than that of European countries and three times that of countries in the Pacific Rim. For example, Rushton & Whitney (2002) averaged the rate of three of these violent crimes (murder, rape, and serious assault) per 100,000 population for the years 1984, 1990, and 1996 and found rates of 142, 74, and 43 for Blacks, Whites, and East Asians, respectively. Similarly, the matrifocal family pattern found disproportionately among African Americans, and often related to the crime statistics, is to be found in Britain, Canada, the Caribbean, and in South-of-Saharan Africa (Draper 1989).

Parallel race differences exist in average testosterone level. Studies show 3% to 19% more testosterone in Black college students and military veterans than in their White counterparts (Ellis & Nyborg 1992) and a lower amount of testosterone among the Japanese than among White Americans (Polednak 1989). Because testosterone is a sex hormone that travels everywhere throughout the body and affects many behavioral systems, it may be a "master switch" that sets the individual and the racial average position on an overall suite of characteristics. Testosterone level affects temperament, self-concept, aggression, altruism, crime and sexuality, in women as well as in men. Testosterone is also involved in secondary sexual characteristics such as muscularity and deepening of the voice.

Also associated with differences in sex hormones is the rate of double ovulation. For example, around the world, the rate of dizygotic twinning is less than 4 per 1,000 births among East Asians, 8 among Europeans, and 16 or greater among Africans (Table 9.4). Multiple birthing rates have been shown to be heritable. It is based on the race of the mother, regardless of the race of the father, as found in East Asian-European crosses in Hawaii and European-African crosses in Brazil (Bulmer 1970). Worldwide surveys also report higher average levels of sexual activity in Africans than in Europeans and especially in East Asians (Table 4). International fertility rates show the racial pattern. So do sexually transmitted disease rates within and between countries.

4.9. Black-White-East Asian Differences Cannot be Explained by Culture-Only Theory

When deciding whether genes are involved in the Black-White average IQ difference, or whether culture-only theory is correct, the following results should be considered. First, the mean difference in IQ scores has scarcely changed over the past 100 years (despite repeated claims that the gap is narrowing) and it can be observed as early as three years of age (Peoples *et al.* 1995). Controlling for overall socioeconomic level only reduces the mean difference by 4 IQ points. Culture-fair tests tend to give Blacks slightly *lower* scores, on the average, than do more conventional tests, as do non-verbal tests compared with verbal tests, and abstract reasoning tests compared with tests of acquired knowledge. Also, the Black-White differences show up on the *g*-factor extracted from culture-fair reaction time tests. The pattern of race differences shown in Table 9.4 is consistent across time and nation. Environmental explanations must account for *all* these differences — in IQ, brain size, myopia, speed of dental development, age of sexual maturity, testosterone level and number of multiple births. Genetic theory provides a single parsimonious explanation for all of them.

4.10. Black-White-East Asian Differences Map Onto Genetic Distance Measures and Dovetail with what is Known About Human Evolution

Finally, race differences can be examined from an evolutionary perspective to explain the worldwide clustering of traits. Jensen accepts the "Out-of-Africa" theory, that *Homo sapiens* arose in Africa about 200,000 years ago, expanded northwards beyond Africa about 140,000 years ago, with a European/East Asian split about 41,000 years ago (Stringer & McKie 1996). Evolutionary selection pressures were different in the hot savanna where Africans evolved than in the cold northern regions where Europeans evolved, or in the even colder Arctic regions where East Asians evolved. These ecological differences had not only morphologic but also behavioral consequences. Rushton (1995) proposed that the farther north the populations migrated out of Africa, the more they encountered the cognitively demanding problems of gathering and storing food, gaining shelter, making clothes and raising children during prolonged winters. As these populations evolved into present-day Europeans and East Asians, they underwent selective pressure for larger brains.

It is in this evolutionary context that Jensen (1998: 420–437) takes on the "race is a myth" brigade. As *Homo sapiens* migrated further away from Africa the random genetic mutations that occur at a constant rate in all living species accumulated, along with the adaptive changes. The resulting differences in allele frequencies are sufficient to warrant the designation of subspecies. Virtually every living species on earth has two or more subspecies. The human species is no exception, but then the subspecies are called races. Numerous and extensive genetic investigations yield essentially the same picture and identify the same major racial groupings as did the morphological markers of classical anthropology. The genetic evidence shows that, by far, the greatest divergence within the human species is between Africans (who have had the most time for random mutations to accumulate) and non-Africans (Cavalli-Sforza *et al.* 1994; Nei & Roychoudhury 1993). In a long footnote, Jensen (1998: 517–520) carried out a principal components analysis of data on genetic markers from Nei and Roychoudhury (1993) and found the familiar clustering of races: (1) Mongoloids; (2) Caucasoids; (3) South Asians and Pacific Islanders; (4) Negroids; (5) North and South Amerindians and Eskimos; and (6) Aboriginal Australians and Papuan New Guineans. Anyone wanting to argue, "race is only skin deep" has to confront the consistency of such results.

5. Conclusion

Most pieces of the scientific puzzle for why Blacks average lower IQ scores than do Whites are now falling into place. For example, the conclusion that intelligence is related to brain size and that there are racial differences in brain size, is becoming accepted. Ulric Neisser, Chair of the recent American Psychological Association's Task Force Report on *The Bell Curve* (Neisser *et al.* 1996), acknowledged that, with respect to "racial differences in the mean measured sizes of skulls and brains (with East Asians having the largest, followed by Whites and then Blacks) . . . there is indeed a small overall trend" (Neisser 1997: 80). Moreover, the average Black-White differences are now established using independent data sets and different test instruments around the world, in southern Africa and in the Netherlands, as in the United States. All are Jensen Effects. As Spearman (1927) predicted, those sub-tests that show the most pronounced Black-White differences are typically the ones with the highest g-loadings.

It is important to know that the Spearman-Jensen hypothesis is robust and that g is the same in southern Africa and the Netherlands as it is in the U.S. This tells us that the largest single source of Black-White differences around the world is essentially the same as the source of differences between individuals *within* each racial group — namely, g. This implies that a scientific understanding of Black-White, indeed of many individual, group and developmental differences, depends on understanding the nature of g. Race differences are not due to idiosyncratic cultural peculiarities in this or that test but to a general factor that all the ability tests measure in common.

Jensen's default hypothesis views mean population differences in g simply as aggregated individual differences and they are explainable by the same principles, thereby not violating Occam's razor by invoking unnecessary ad hoc hypotheses. Jensen's hypothesis is consistent with a preponderance of psychometric, behavior-genetic and evolutionary lines of evidence. And like true scientific hypotheses generally, it continually invites empirical refutation.

Jensen's methodological and theoretical analyses have distilled the deep essence of intelligence. Jensen has gone beyond proving the statistical reality and predictive validity of the general factor. He has shown Spearman's g to be a keystone of the behavioral sciences. If future psychometricians "see further", it will only be by standing on the shoulders of these two giants: Spearman and Jensen.

References

Avenant, T. J. (1988). *The establishment of an individual intelligence scale for adult South Africans. Report on an exploratory study conducted with WAIS-R on a sample of Blacks (Report No. P-91)*. Pretoria, South Africa: Human Sciences Research Council.

Beals, K. L., Smith, C. L., & Dodd, S. M. (1984). Brain size, cranial morphology, climate, and time machines. *Current Anthropology, 25*, 301–330.

Bean, R. B. (1906). Some racial peculiarities of the Negro brain. *American Journal of Anatomy, 5*, 353–432.

Bouchard, T. J. Jr (1996). Behaviour genetic studies of intelligence, yesterday and today: The long journey from plausibility to proof. *Journal of Biosocial Science, 28*, 527–555.

Bouchard, T. J. Jr, & Loehlin, J. C. (2001). Genes, evolution, and personality. *Behavior Genetics,* *31,* 243–273.

Broca, P. (1873). Sur les crânes de la caverne de l'Homme Mort (Loere). *Revue d'Anthropologie,* *2,* 1–53.

Broman, S. H., Nichols, P. L., Shaughnessy, P., & Kennedy, W. (1987). *Retardation in young children.* Hillsdale, NJ: Erlbaum.

Bulmer, M. G. (1970). *The biology of twinning in man.* Oxford: Clarendon.

Carretta, T. R., & Ree, M. J. (1995). Near identity of cognitive structure in sex and ethnic groups. *Personality and Individual Differences, 19,* 149–155.

Cavalli-Sforza, L. L., Menozzi, P., & Piazza, A. (1994). *The history and geography of human genes.* Princeton, NJ: Princeton University Press.

Centers for Disease Control (1988). Health status of Vietnam veterans. *Journal of the American Medical Association, 259,* 2701–2719.

Chakraborty, R., Kamboh, M. I., Nwankwo, M., & Ferrell, R. E. (1992). Caucasian genes in American Blacks. *American Journal of Human Genetics, 50,* 145–155.

Cohn, S. J., Cohn, C. M. G., & Jensen, A. R. (1988). Myopia and intelligence: A pleiotropic relationship? *Human Genetics, 80,* 53–58.

Colom, R., Abad, F. J., Garcia, L. F., & Juan-Espinosa, M. (2002). Education, Wechsler's full-scale IQ, and *g. Intelligence, 30,* 449–462.

Colom, R., Juan-Espinosa, M., & Garcia, L. F. (2001). The secular increase in test scores is a "Jensen effect". *Personality and Individual Differences, 30,* 553–559.

Draper, P. (1989). African marriage systems: Perspectives from evolutionary ecology. *Ethology and Sociobiology, 10,* 145–169.

Duncan, J., Seitz, R. J., Kolodny, J., Bor, D., Herzog, H., Ahmed, A., Newell, F. N., & Emslie, H. (2000). A neural basis for general intelligence. *Science, 289,* 457–460.

Ellis, L., & Nyborg, H. (1992). Racial/ethnic variations in male testosterone levels: A probable contributor to group differences in health. *Steroids, 57,* 72–75.

Flynn, J. R. (1984). The mean IQ of Americans: Massive gains 1932 to 1978. *Psychological Bulletin, 95,* 29–51.

Flynn, J. R. (1987). Massive IQ gains in 14 nations: What IQ tests really measure. *Psychological Bulletin, 101,* 171–191.

Flynn, J. R. (1999). Searching for justice: The discovery of IQ gains over time. *American Psychologist, 54,* 5–20.

Frearson, W., & Eysenck, H. J. (1986). Intelligence, reaction time (RT) and a new "odd-man-out" RT paradigm. *Personality and Individual Differences, 7,* 807–817.

Frydman, M., & Lynn, R. (1989). The intelligence of Korean children adopted in Belgium. *Personality and Individual Differences, 10,* 1323–1326.

Gordon, H. L. (1934). Amentia in the East African. *Eugenics Review, 25,* 223–235.

Gottfredson, L. S. (Ed.) (1997). Intelligence and social policy [Special Issue]. *Intelligence, 24,* 1–320.

Graves, J. L. Jr (2002). The misuse of life-history theory: J. P. Rushton and the pseudoscience of racial hierarchy. In: J. L. Fish (Ed.), *Race and intelligence: Separating science from myth* (pp. 57–94). Mahwah, NJ: Erlbaum.

Grieve, K. W., & Viljoen, S. (2000). An exploratory study of the use of the Austin Maze in South Africa. *South African Journal of Psychology, 30,* 14–18.

Harvey, I., Persaud, R., Ron, M. A., Baker, G., & Murray, R. M. (1994). Volumetric MRI measurements in bipolars compared with schizophrenics and healthy controls. *Psychological Medicine, 24,* 689–699.

Herrnstein, R. J., & Murray, C. (1994). *The bell curve.* New York: Free Press.

Ho, K. C., Roessmann, U., Straumfjord, J. V., & Monroe, G. (1980). Analysis of brain weight: I & II. *Archives of Pathology and Laboratory Medicine, 104,* 635–645.

Jensen, A. R. (1968). Patterns of mental ability and socioeconomic status. *Proceedings of the National Academy of Sciences, 60,* 1330–1337.

Jensen, A. R. (1969a). How much can we boost IQ and scholastic achievement? *Harvard Educational Review, 39,* 1–123.

Jensen, A. R. (1969b). Reducing the heredity-environment uncertainty. *Harvard Educational Review, 39,* 449–483.

Jensen, A. R. (1973). *Educability and group differences.* London: Methuen.

Jensen, A. R. (1980). *Bias in mental testing.* New York: Free Press.

Jensen, A. R. (1984). Sociobiology and differential psychology: The arduous climb from plausibility to proof. In: L. J. R. Royce, & L. P. Mos (Eds), *Annals of theoretical psychology* (Vol. 2, pp. 49–58). New York: Plenum.

Jensen, A. R. (1985). The nature of the black-white difference on various psychometric tests: Spearman's hypothesis. *Behavioral and Brain Sciences, 8,* 193–263.

Jensen, A. R. (1987). Further evidence for Spearman's hypothesis concerning the black-white differences on psychometric tests. *Behavioral and Brain Sciences, 10,* 512–519.

Jensen, A. R. (1993). Spearman's hypothesis tested with chronometric information-processing tasks. *Intelligence, 17,* 47–77.

Jensen, A. R. (1994). Psychometric g related to differences in head size. *Personality and Individual Differences, 17,* 597–606.

Jensen, A. R. (1998). *The g factor.* Westport, CT: Praeger.

Jensen, A. R. (in press). Do age-group differences on mental tests imitate racial differences? *Intelligence.*

Jensen, A. R., & Johnson, F. W. (1994). Race and sex differences in head size and IQ. *Intelligence, 18,* 309–333.

Jensen, A. R., & Whang, P. A. (1993). Reaction times and intelligence: A comparison of Chinese-American and Anglo-American children. *Journal of Biosocial Science, 25,* 397–410.

Jensen, A. R., & Whang, P. A. (1994). Speed of accessing arithmetic facts in long-term memory: A comparison of Chinese-American and Anglo-American children. *Contemporary Educational Psychology, 19,* 1–12.

Kamin, L., & Omari, S. (1998). Race, head size, and intelligence. *South African Journal of Psychology, 28,* 119–128.

Lieberman, L. (2001). How 'Caucasoids' got such big crania and why they shrank: From Morton to Rushton. *Current Anthropology, 42,* 69–95.

Loehlin, J. C., Lindzey, G., & Spuhler, J. N. (1975). *Race differences in intelligence.* San Francisco, CA: Freeman.

Lynn, R. (1977). The intelligence of the Japanese. *Bulletin of the British Psychological Society, 30,* 69–72.

Lynn, R. (1978). Ethnic and racial differences in intelligence: International comparisons. In: R. T. Osborne, C. E. Noble, & N. Weyl (Eds), *Human variation: The biopsychology of age, race, and sex* (pp. 261–286). New York, Academic.

Lynn, R. (1982). IQ in Japan and the United States shows a growing disparity. *Nature, 297,* 222–223.

Lynn, R. (1991). Race differences in intelligence: A global perspective. *Mankind Quarterly, 31,* 255–296.

Lynn, R. (1997). Geographical variation in intelligence. In: H. Nyborg (Ed.), *The scientific study of human nature: Tribute to Hans J. Eysenck at eighty.* London: Elsevier.

Lynn, R. (2002). Skin color and intelligence in African Americans. *Population and Environment, 23,* 365–375.

Lynn, R. (2003). The geography of *g*. In: H. Nyborg (Ed.), *The scientific study of general intelligence: Tribute to Arthur R. Jensen*. London: Elsevier.

Lynn, R., & Owen, K. (1994). Spearman's hypothesis and test score differences between Whites, Indians, and Blacks in South Africa. *Journal of General Psychology, 121*, 27–36.

Lynn, R., & Vanhanen, T. (2002). *IQ and the wealth of nations*. Westport, CT: Praeger.

Mall, F. P. (1909). On several anatomical characters of the human brain, said to vary according to race and sex, with special reference to the weight of the frontal lobe. *American Journal of Anatomy, 9*, 1–32.

Miller, E. M. (1994). Intelligence and brain myelination: A hypothesis. *Personality and Individual Differences, 17*, 803–832.

Morton, S. G. (1849). Observations on the size of the brain in various races and families of man. *Proceedings of the Academy of Natural Sciences Philadelphia, 4*, 221–224.

Must, O., Must, A., & Raudik, V. (in press (a)). The Flynn Effect for gains in literacy found in Estonia is not a Jensen Effect. *Personality and Individual Differences*.

Must, O., Must, A., & Raudik, V. (in press (b)). The secular rise in IQs: In Estonia the Flynn Effect is not a Jensen Effect. *Intelligence*.

Nagoshi, C. T., Johnson, R. C., DeFries, J. C., Wilson, J. R., & Vandenberg, S. G. (1984). Group differences and first principal-component loadings in the Hawaii Family Study of Cognition: A test of the generality of "Spearman's hypothesis". *Personality and Individual Differences, 5*, 751–753.

Nei, M., & Roychoudhury, A. K. (1993). Evolutionary relationships of human populations on a global scale. *Molecular Biology and Evolution, 10*, 927–943.

Neisser, U. (1997). Never a dull moment. *American Psychologist, 52*, 79–81.

Neisser, U., Boodoo, G., Bouchard, T. J. Jr, Boykin, A. W., Brody, N., Ceci, S. J., Halpern, D., Loehlin, J. C., Perloff, R., Sternberg, R. J., & Urbina, S. (1996). Intelligence: Knowns and unknowns. *American Psychologist, 15*, 77–101.

Nell, V. (2000). *Cross-cultural neuropsychological assessment: Theory and practice*. Mahwah, NJ: Erlbaum.

Nichols, P. L. (1972). *The effects of heredity and environment on intelligence test performance in 4- and 7-year-old white and Negro sibling pairs*. Unpublished doctoral dissertation, University of Minnesota.

Nyborg, H., & Jensen, A. R. (2000). Black-White differences on various psychometric tests: Spearman's hypothesis tested on American armed services veterans. *Personality and Individual Differences, 28*, 593–599.

Osborne, R. T. (1980a). The Spearman-Jensen hypothesis. *Behavioral and Brain Sciences, 3*, 351.

Osborne, R. T. (1980b). *Twins: black and white*. Athens, GA: Foundation for Human Understanding.

Owen, K. (1992). The suitability of Raven's Standard Progressive Matrices for various groups in South Africa. *Personality and Individual Differences, 13*, 149–159.

Parra, E. J., Marcini, A., Akey, J., Martinson, J., Batzer, M. A., Cooper, R., Forrester, T., Allison, D. B., Deka, R., Ferrell, R. E., & Shriver, M. D. (1998). Estimating African American admixture proportions by use of population specific alleles. *American Journal of Human Genetics, 63*, 1839–1851.

Pearl, R. (1934). The weight of the Negro brain. *Science, 80*, 431–434.

Peoples, C. E., Fagan, J. F. III, & Drotar, D. (1995). The influence of race on 3-year-old children's performance on the Stanford-Binet (4th ed.). *Intelligence, 21*, 69–82.

Polednak, A. P. (1989). *Racial and ethnic differences in disease*. Oxford: Oxford University.

Post, R. H. (1982). Population differences in visual acuity: A review, with speculative notes on selection relaxation. *Social Biology, 29,* 319–343.

Raven, J., Summers, B., Birchfield, M., Brosier, G., Burciaga, L., Byrkit, B., *et al.* (1990). *Manual for Raven's progressive matrices and vocabulary scales. Research supplement No. 3: American and international norms* (2nd ed.). Oxford: Oxford Psychologists Press.

Raven, J. C., Court, J. H., & Raven, J. (1998). *Manual for Raven's standard progressive matrices.* Oxford, U.K.: Oxford Psychologists Press.

Ree, M. J., & Carretta, T. R. (1995). Group differences in aptitude factor structure on the ASVAB. *Educational and Psychological Measurement, 55,* 268–277.

Roth, P. L., Bevier, C. A., Bobko, P., Switzer III, F. S., & Tyler, P. (2001). Ethnic group differences in cognitive ability in employment and educational settings: A meta-analysis. *Personnel Psychology, 54,* 297–330.

Rowe, D. C. (1994). No more than skin deep. *American Psychologist, 49,* 215–216.

Rowe, D. C. (2002). IQ, birth weight, and number of sexual partners in White, African American, and mixed race adolescents. *Population and Environment, 23,* 513–524.

Rowe, D. C., & Cleveland, H. H. (1996). Academic achievement in Blacks and Whites: Are the developmental processes similar? *Intelligence, 23,* 205–228.

Rowe, D. C., Vazsonyi, A. T., & Flannery, D. J. (1994). No more than skin deep: Ethnic and racial similarity in developmental process. *Psychological Review, 101,* 396–413.

Rowe, D. C., Vazsonyi, A. T., & Flannery, D. J. (1995). Ethnic and racial similarity in developmental process: A study of academic achievement. *Psychological Science, 6,* 33–38.

Rushton, J. P. (1984a). Sociobiology: Toward a theory of individual and group differences in personality and social behavior. In: J. R. Royce, & L. P. Mos (Eds), *Annals of theoretical psychology* (Vol. 2, pp. 1–48). New York: Plenum.

Rushton, J. P. (1984b). Group differences, genetic similarity theory, and the importance of personality traits: Reply to commentators. In: J. R. Royce, & L. P. Mos (Eds), *Annals of theoretical psychology* (Vol. 2, pp. 73–81). New York: Plenum Press.

Rushton, J. P. (1988). Race differences in behaviour: A review and evolutionary analysis. *Personality and Individual Differences, 9,* 1009–1024.

Rushton, J. P. (1989). Japanese inbreeding depression scores: Predictors of cognitive differences between blacks and whites. *Intelligence, 13,* 43–51.

Rushton, J. P. (1991). Mongoloid-Caucasoid differences in brain size from military samples. *Intelligence, 15,* 351–359.

Rushton, J. P. (1992). Cranial capacity related to sex, rank, and race in a stratified random sample of 6,325 U.S. military personnel. *Intelligence, 16,* 401–413.

Rushton, J. P. (1993). Corrections to a paper on race and sex differences in brain size and intelligence. *Personality and Individual Differences, 15,* 229–231.

Rushton, J. P. (1994). Sex and race differences in cranial capacity from International Labour Office data. *Intelligence, 19,* 281–294.

Rushton, J. P. (1995). *Race, evolution, and behavior: A life history perspective.* New Brunswick, NJ: Transaction.

Rushton, J. P. (1997). Cranial size and IQ in Asian Americans from birth to age seven. *Intelligence, 25,* 7–20.

Rushton, J. P. (1998). The "Jensen Effect" and the "Spearman-Jensen Hypothesis" of Black-White IQ differences. *Intelligence, 26,* 217–225.

Rushton, J. P. (1999). Secular gains in IQ not related to the *g* factor and inbreeding depression — unlike Black-White differences: A reply to Flynn. *Personality and Individual Differences, 26,* 381–389.

Rushton, J. P. (2000). *Race, evolution, and behavior: A life history perspective* (3rd ed.). Port Huron, MI: Charles Darwin Research Institute.

Rushton, J. P. (2001). Black-White differences on the *g* factor in South Africa: A "Jensen Effect" on the Wechsler Intelligence Scale for Children-Revised. *Personality and Individual Differences, 31*, 1227–1232.

Rushton, J. P. (2002). Jensen Effects and African/Colored/Indian/White differences on Raven's Standard Progressive Matrices in South Africa. *Personality and Individual Differences, 33*, 65–70.

Rushton, J. P., & Ankney, C. D. (1996). Brain size and cognitive ability: Correlations with age, sex, social class and race. *Psychonomic Bulletin and Review, 3*, 21–36.

Rushton, J. P., & Jensen, A. R. (in press). African-White IQ differences from Zimbabwe on the Wechsler Intelligence Scale for Children-Revised are mainly on the *g* factor. *Personality and Individual Differences.*

Rushton, J. P., & Osborne, R. T. (1995). Genetic and environmental contributions to cranial capacity in black and white adolescents. *Intelligence, 20*, 1–13.

Rushton, J. P., & Skuy, M. (2000). Performance on Raven's Matrices by African and White university students in South Africa. *Intelligence, 28*, 251–265.

Rushton, J. P., Skuy, M., & Fridjohn, P. (2002). Jensen effects among African, Indian, and White engineering students in South Africa on Raven's standard progressive matrices. *Intelligence, 30*, 409–423.

Rushton, J. P., Skuy, M., & Fridjohn, P. (2003). Performance on Raven's advanced progressive Matrices by African, East Indian, and White engineering students in South Africa. *Intelligence, 31*, 123–139.

Rushton, J. P., & Whitney, G. (2002). Geographic and populational variation in violent crime rates (from INTERPOL, 1993–1996). *Population and Environment, 23*, 501–511.

Scarr-Salapatek, S. (1971). Race, social class and IQ. *Science, 174*, 1285–1295.

Scarr, S., & Weinberg, R. A. (1976). IQ test performance of black children adopted by white families. *American Psychologist, 31*, 726–739.

Schmidt, F. L., & Hunter, J. E. (1998). The validity and utility of selection methods in personnel psychology: Practical and theoretical implications of 85 years of research findings. *Psychological Bulletin, 124*, 262–274.

Shockley, W. (1973). Variance of Caucasian admixture in Negro populations, pigmentation variability, and IQ. *Proceedings of the National Academy of Sciences, USA, 70*, 2180a.

Shuey, A. M. (1966). *The testing of Negro intelligence.* New York: Social Science Press.

Simmons, K. (1942). Cranial capacities by both plastic and water techniques with cranial linear measurements of the Reserve Collection: white and Negro. *Human Biology, 14*, 473–498.

Skuy, M., Schutte, E., Fridjhon, P., & O'Carroll, S. (2001). Suitability of published neuropsychological test norms for urban African secondary school students in South Africa. *Personality and Individual Differences, 30*, 1413–1425.

Spearman, C. (1904). General intelligence, objectively determined and measured. *American Journal of Psychology, 15*, 201–293.

Spearman, C. (1927). *The abilities of man: Their nature and measurement.* New York: Macmillan.

Stringer, C., & McKie, R. (1996). *African exodus.* London: Cape.

te Nijenhuis, J. (1997). *Comparability of test scores for immigrants and majority group members in the Netherlands.* Unpublished doctoral dissertation, Vrije Universiteit, Amsterdam, The Netherlands.

te Nijenhuis, J., Evers, A., & Mur, J. P. (2000). Validity of the Differential Aptitude Test for the assessment of immigrant children. *Educational Psychology, 20*, 99–115.

te Nijenhuis, J., & van der Flier, H. (1997). Comparability of GATB scores for immigrants and majority group members: Some Dutch findings. *Journal of Applied Psychology, 82*, 675–687.

te Nijenhuis, J., & van der Flier, H. (2001). Group differences in mean intelligence for the Dutch and Third World immigrants. *Journal of Biosocial Science, 33*, 469–475.

te Nijenhuis, J., Tolboom, E., Resing, W., & Bleichrodt, N. (in press). Does cultural background influence the intellectual performance of children from immigrant groups? Validity of the RAKIT intelligence test for immigrant children. *European Journal of Psychological Assessment.*

Todd, T. W. (1923). Cranial capacity and linear dimensions, in white and Negro. *American Journal of Physical Anthropology, 6*, 97–194.

Vernon, P. A., & Jensen, A. R. (1984). Individual and group differences in intelligence and speed of information processing. *Personality and Individual Differences, 10*, 573–576.

Vernon, P. E. (1982). *The abilities and achievements of Orientals in North America.* New York: Academic.

Vint, F. W. (1934). The brain of the Kenya native. *Journal of Anatomy, 48*, 216–223.

Weinberg, R. A., Scarr, S., & Waldman, I. D. (1992). The Minnesota Transracial Adoption Study: A follow-up of IQ test performance at adolescence. *Intelligence, 16*, 117–135.

Zaaiman, H., van der Flier, H., & Thijs, G. D. (2001). Dynamic testing in selection for an educational programme: Assessing South African performance on the Raven Progressive Matrices. *International Journal of Selection and Assessment, 9*, 258–269.

Zindi, F. (1994). Differences in performance. *The Psychologist, 7*, 549–552.

Chapter 10

Sex differences in *g*

Helmuth Nyborg

1. Introduction

Even a quick review of the research literature reveals a fundamental disagreement about the existence of a sex difference in general intelligence. It is imperative in this connection to clearly distinguish between *general intelligence* and *intelligence in general*. The use of these terms will become much clearer later in the chapter. For now it suffices to say that general intelligence can be estimated by the higher-order *g* factor score, that can be obtained by factor analyzing the pattern of correlations among test items. In clear distinction, *intelligence in general* — or total IQ score — can be obtained by summing the standardized item scores.

Empirical evidence abounds both for and against a difference in general intelligence. This chapter tests the hypothesis that there is actually a small male average superiority in general intelligence but it can be seen only if the most sophisticated contemporary methodology is brought into action. It is an interesting twist to this test that Arthur Jensen promotes the advanced tools needed to identify the difference, but at the same time comes to the conclusion that there is no consistent sex difference.

The chapter first lines up the positions, evaluates the methodological and analytic qualities of selected studies, and then comes to the conclusion that there is in fact a small difference in favor of males. It is shown how even such a small average sex difference can take on practical importance at the high end of the general intelligence distribution scale. Finally, some speculations are presented on the likely future of sex difference research.

1.1. The Positions

1.1.1. There is no sex difference in general intelligence! The possibility of sex differences in intelligence has fascinated researchers, philosophers and lay people for millennia, and they have aired their interest in such different places as in a religious ancient Sanskrit paper informing us that: "Ten shares of talk were handed down to earth; the nine went to the women", in literally hundreds of contemporary books and thousands of scientific articles, in Ladies' magazines, and in myriads of radio and TV shows.

Often, the conclusion reached is that there indeed are real sex differences in first order group factors like verbal or spatial abilities, but these are not terribly important. These lower order factors usually have only moderate to low validity in predicting sex differences in achievement in school, jobs or life, when compared to the considerable predictive validity of higher order general intelligence. The important point is, they say, that most studies find no real sex difference in a general intelligence (e.g. Brody 1992; Halpern & LaMay 2000; Neisser *et al.* 1996).

The theoretical implications of this widespread view cannot easily be overestimated. No other constructs in psychology come even close in predicting one's final level of education, occupational status and income, one's likely belongingness to the administrative or political elite or, conversely, to predict the risk of finding oneself caught in a wide range of unfavourably economic, social and criminal life circumstances (e.g. Herrnstein & Murray 1994). Researchers of various stripes usually have no difficulties in admitting the male over-representation at most societal top positions. However, given that there are no sex differences in general intelligence, they must explain this male superiority by "old boys network", unsavoury tradition, unfair differences in female opportunity, a lack of female role models, learned helplessness, male oppression, or socially induced differences in motivation or personality. The possibility that genes, hormones, neurobiology or evolutionary history may provide part of the explanation of a sex difference in general intelligence accordingly needs little consideration, or may even call for active resistance from the academic left (Gould 1996, see Chapter 20 in this volume for further details). The subject index for the authoritative *Handbook of Intelligence: Theories, measurements and applications* (Wolman 1985), does not even have an entry to sex differences.

1.1.2. There is a sex difference in general intelligence!   Defenders of this opposite view hold that it is, in fact, directly counterintuitive to assume that there is no sex difference in general intelligence. They point to good practical and theoretical reasons to back up their point.

On the practical side, they refer to the vast male over-representation in top positions in education, occupations, and in the social power structures. These areas no doubt call for capacity to deal with high degrees of complexity. Moreover, capacity to deal with complexity is just another way to define general intelligence. It would therefore, according to their view, be downright counterintuitive to assume intellectual equality among the sexes. The male over-representation in most elites will naturally raise the suspicion of a higher general intelligence, everything else equal.

Theoretically speaking we should also expect a male superiority in general intelligence. This idea is based on a paradox, the underlying logic of which cannot easily be dismissed. Thus, most experts agree that general intelligence correlates positively with head size, ranging in size from $r = 0.1$ to 0.45. Aside from measurement error, the differences in correlations depend essentially on whether the measure is based on simply taping head circumference or on the more exactly measured brain volume by modern imaging techniques. The rule seems to be: the more exact the measurement, the higher the IQ-brain size correlation (see Chapter 6 in this volume for details). Given this fact and given the common if debatable assumption, that males and females do not differ in overall intelligence, one would obviously expect to see on average equal head size or brain volume in males and females. This is not what we see, however. Males have larger heads with more brain tissue, on average of course, than females, quite as expected from a higher general intelligence (Ankney 1992, 1995; Lynn 1994, 1999; Rushton 1992).

This so-called anomaly has elicited contrasting interpretations. Lynn (1994, 1999) argues, for example, that there really is no problem here. Having averaged the IQs of a number of studies, he found that the male lead in general intelligence amounts to 3.8 IQ points. This value corresponds to a male SD advantage of 0.3 in intelligence. Lynn then demonstrated that the well-documented sex difference in brain size actually predicts the observed male average IQ lead closely enough to solve the apparent paradox. The details of Lynn's prediction are presented in Table 10.2. Jensen (1998: 541–543) disagrees with Lynn's interpretation, and suggests that perhaps there is a greater neural "packing density" in the female brain. This interpretation is, in turn, contradicted by an observation by Pakkenberg & Gundersen (1997). Applying a new neuronal counting technique they found equal packing density throughout male and female brains. Moreover, the average female brain contains 15% fewer neurons than the male brain. Lynn takes this to support for his particular interpretation, given the reasonable premise that more neurones are needed for a more efficient brain (even though one should always keep in mind that more is not always better!)

1.2. Diagnosing the Main Problem

As leading scientists disagreed about the existence of a genuine sex difference in general intelligence and also used different methods I began to suspect that the disagreement could be explained by the use of less than optimal methods for studying the sex difference.

On the one side, there was the longstanding tradition of summing standardized scores, an approach that loses important information on its way. Most clinicians and researchers sum standardized subtest scores to reach an overall intelligence score, as for example in the widely used WAIS or WISC IQ tests for adults and children, developed by David Wechsler in the mid-twentieth century. Two subscale scores — Performance and Verbal IQ — can be combined to form a Full Scale IQ score (FSIQ). Wechsler explicitly dismissed test items greatly favouring one sex when constructing the test, and then balanced out the remaining items so as to avoid male or female superiority in overall IQ. Males often lead in Performance IQ and females tend toward superiority in at least some verbal abilities. Considering Wechsler's manipulation with items in the construction, it is in fact a bit surprising to find that the average of recent studies points to a male superiority of 3.8 points in total FSIQ (Lynn 1997). The fabrication of the test and the use of summed scores leave us entirely in the dark about the origin of the observed sex difference in the WISC and WAIS. Is it due to bias in item selection or is it due to a true sex difference in general intelligence. The only way to find out is to apply analytic techniques that go well beyond summing scores.

On the other side, there was the quite sophisticated factor analytic approach.

Perhaps both types of approach may produce contaminated measures of general intelligence. Perhaps the main problem is that the key measure of general intelligence falls victim to fatal contamination. Perhaps we are looking for a petite sex difference, that will reveal itself only if we methodologically step up from simple summed scores, over the application of analytically speaking quite sophisticated psychometrics, to ultimately reach a position where we attain an uncontaminated and trustworthy higher order factor of general intelligence. Phrased differently, perhaps the fragile sex difference will appear reliably only after successful derivation of an uncontaminated measure of general intelligence.

The grand master of psychometrics, Jensen wrote in 1998 (p. 532) that the study of sex differences in general intelligence is "technically the most difficult to answer . . . the least investigated, the least written about, and, indeed, even the least often asked". Perhaps methodological uncertainty would explain why the field has for so long been beleaguered by confusion, occasional glimpses of clarification, wildly differing interpretations, and the hasty formation of conclusions not rarely based more on what "what ought to be" than on "what is" sexist attitudes.

Given the present discrepancy in opinions and the worries over the methodology, it became mandatory to ask how the methodology can be improved to decide the difficult question of the existence of a sex difference in general intelligence. A step on the way was to develop a simple questionnaire for ranking studies of sex differences in accordance with their analytic capability to avoid making type 1 or type 2 errors. This may enable us to grade studies in accordance with their potential for safely identifying even a subtle sex difference.

However, even having accomplished that, there are further methodological problems that researchers may run into when entering the minefield of sex differences. As they hold the potential to degrade the quality of the studies, I first name and use them to establish criteria for the proper scientific approach to sex difference research on general intelligence. Several studies are then measured up against the criteria, and ranked in accordance with how well they conform to them. This evaluation becomes the basis for deciding how much confidence we can ascribe to their conclusions about the sex difference.

1.3. Further Problems

1.3.1. Ideology gone awry   It is a sad fact that scientists finding a sex difference in intelligence too often become woven into an odd struggle, characterized by direct personal attacks or having to deal with tongue-tied politically correct terminological anomalies. The latter involves accusations of believing/postulating/wrongly assuming that he/she has found a gender/sex difference in intelligence/aptitude/achievement/ educational challenges rather than sticking to the numbers. The apparently unavoidable and pervasive influences of strong ideological and emotional loadings on the matter may force herself/himself into the process of academic and/or personal survival. The nature of this matter is discussed more fully in Lynn (2001), Segerstråle (2000), and summarized in Chapter 20 in this volume. Suffice it to say that the study of sex differences in general ability has long been hampered by ideology run amok, by academic or personal intimidation of researchers finding a difference, and by the near absence of research specifically capable of solving the problems.

1.3.2. Ambiguous definitions   A number of critiques point to the fact that there is little agreement about how to define intelligence. Therefore, they argue, even if a sex difference is found, it cannot be trusted. We would not know what it was all about. It is food for thought to realize that one of the truly great pioneers in psychometrics, Spearman, addressed this problem as far back in time as around 1900 (e.g. Spearman 1904, 1923, 1927; Spearman & Jones 1950). Unfortunately, even if he came of great age, he did not live long enough to see his important points getting generally accepted in the scientific community. This is all too bad because, without a full understanding of his particular reasoning on the matter, it is virtually impossible to see how easy and essential it is to substitute vague concepts of intelligence in general with proper operational definitions, and thereby realize how futile the whole discussion was all the time. Spearman's frustration clearly shines through in his report on reading a paper from a symposium: "Intelligence and Its Measurement" (The Editors 1921). The paper made it obvious that fourteen leading researchers featured fourteen different definitions of intelligence. Spearman reacted with despair: "Chaos itself can go no farther ... 'intelligence' has become a mere vocal sound, a word with so many meanings that finally it has none" (1927: 14). Sixty-five years later Sternberg & Detterman (1986) convened a symposium with the aim to answer the very same question: "What is Intelligence?" Now it was Jensen's turn to pass judgment on the report of the meeting. His conclusion was as depressing as the one Spearman had reached: "The overall picture remains almost as chaotic as it was in 1921" (1998: 48).

1.3.3. Competing "intelligences"   New definitions of intelligence continue to see the day of light. This is without doubt a sign of impatience with prevailing definitions. Unfortunately, Spearman's early ground work and Jensen's (1998) later development of a proper theory for the objective measurement of general intelligence (see below) seem either ignored by the inventers of the new intelligences or are met with persistent attempts to deny their methodological and practical validity (see Brody (in press) and Gottfredson (in press)). Several recent varieties of competing theories feed in part on the disagreement about how to define, measure or explain intelligence. One of these is Howard Gardner's (1983, 1993) model for *Multiple Intelligence*. Another is *Emotional Intelligence* by David Goleman (1995). A third is *Triarchic Mind* by Robert Sternberg (1988). Without going into details, three considerations about the alternatives are relevant here: a sex specific, a general theoretical, and an operational aspect.

With respect to sex, none of these new intelligences tells us anything useful about the question of sex differences in general ability. For that reason alone they can safely be sidestepped in the present chapter. A more general theoretical concern is that many contemporary uses of the term intelligence are so vague as to be of little use in a scientific study, a point Jensen (1998) discussed at some length in his Chapter 3 entitled: 'The Trouble with "Intelligence"' (but see also Jensen 1987, 1993, 1994a). Most importantly, a precise linguistic definition is not at all needed for a proper operational approach to the question of whether there is a sex difference in general intelligence, as will be illustrated shortly.

1.4. Summary

Previous research on sex differences in intelligence is characterized by exorbitant confusion due to a number of factors. One factor is that widely different sex-based ideologies weigh down the field. Other important points are the disagreement about how to define and measure general intelligence, and the undeniable existence of contrasting and paradoxical findings. It is in such situations a troubled field finds itself in desperate need for a knight in shining armour with the brainpower and vision needed to see what has to be done. Arthur Jensen is just that kind of person. He has the intellectual power and also musters the rugged personality and professional integrity, without which no battle can ever be won when sailing through the troubled waters of sex differences in general intelligence. He not only cut through the emotional parts, but also refined the methods and perspectives, and thereby changed the field radically. We shall discuss in detail how he accomplished this. This chapter focuses in particular on the use of the tools he recommended.

2. Clever But Disengaged

2.1. Jensen as a Slow Starter

Given that Jensen clarified vital aspects of the study of sex differences in intelligence, it is quite surprising to realize in hindsight that he actually entered the area rather late in his professional career. His first publication went to print in 1955 and was on an entirely different matter, followed by a series of works on aggression in fantasy, projective techniques, and learning. Full sixteen years went by before he in 1971 gradually began to close in on the area. It was then in terms of a possible "race X sex X ability" interaction, a finding he later dismissed. Apparently as a side effect, Jensen then wrote theoretical notes on sex linkage and race differences in spatial ability (1975, 1978). His classical book *Bias in mental testing* (Jensen 1980, ch. 13) naturally deals more with sex bias than with sex differences. Jensen states that, like racial and social-class differences, the question of a sex difference in selection rates ". . . has two main aspects: true differences in ability versus artifactual differences due to bias in the tests . . .". Summarizing the outcome of studies between 1966 and the late seventies, he concluded that ". . . a *majority* of the studies find no sex differences large enough to be significant beyond the 0.05 level", and ". . . when significant sex differences *are* found, they never consistently favor males or females for any given ability . . .". He notes that

Maccoby (1966) reached a similar conclusion from her review of pre-1966 studies. Pondering over the reality of sex differences in the ability realm, Jensen (1980: 622) found that they ". . . are a relatively small-magnitude phenomenon as compared with racial and social-class differences . . .". The inconsistencies among studies suggest that they ". . . are complexly determined and are conditional on a number of other factors, such as age of the subject, educational level, regional differences, and secular trends". The first report in which Jensen directly addressed the question of a sex difference on the WISC-R came as late as in 1983, and was followed by a commentary on arithmetic computation and reasoning in pre-pubertal boys and girls (Jensen 1988). Again seemingly in passing, Jensen later commented on the previously mentioned sex differences in head size and related differences in intelligence (Jensen 1994b; Jensen & Johnson 1994).

It may very well be that Jensen's interest in the study of sex differences in intelligence was tempered by the many inconsistencies in the results. This may explain why it took him so long to tackle the topic and pass a devastating judgment. Even then, it was not at all a spin-off of own interests. To the contrary, he was explicitly asked to add a chapter on sex differences to a manuscript, long time previously submitted to a major publisher for evaluation. Ironically, that publisher eventually declined to publish what later became probably the best book ever written on intelligence — *The g factor: The science of mental ability.* Praeger Press published the book in 1998. Luckily, the relatively short chapter on sex differences survived the transfer. On just 13 pages Jensen demonstrates his characteristic perfectionism, his preference for ruthless empiricism, and his blessed lack of taste for easy compromises.

2.2. The Rude Awakening

Jensen's characterization of previous research in the area of sex differences was devastating. He concluded:

> Past studies of a sex difference in general ability have often been confounded by improper definitions and measurement of "general ability" based on simple summation of subtest scores from a variety of batteries that differ in their group factors, by the use of unrepresentative groups selected from limited segments of the normal distribution of abilities, and by the interaction of sex differences with age-group differences in subtest performance. These conditions often yield a mean sex difference in the total score, but such results, in principle, are actually arbitrary, of limited generality, and are therefore of little scientific interest. The observed differences are typically small, inconsistent in direction, across different batteries, and, in above-average samples, usually favor males" (1998: 531).

This is simply another way of saying that most previous studies of sex differences in intelligence fail to obey strict scientific criteria, and that progress in the field depends on better definitions and methods. The rest of this chapter is devoted to a discussion of what this means.

2.3. Proper Criteria

Jensen's incisive characterization of previous studies, developed on top of Spearman's original insights, suggests that future studies of sex differences in general ability must conform to the following objective principles:

- Make sure samples are truly representative;
- Present a proper operational definition of intelligence;
- Incorporate a multitude of tests that differ widely in content;
- Go analytically well beyond simple summed scores; and
- Control for potential confounders (e.g. contamination by group factors or sex-age interaction).

3. The Proper Study of Sex Differences in Abilities

This section first expands on the above criteria, and then scrutinizes how closely a number of methodologically quite different studies come to conforming to the criteria. The overall purpose of this maneuver is first, to illustrate that studies can in fact be ranked by quality, so that we can grade the trustworthiness of their conclusions with respect to the existence of a sex difference in general ability, and second, to see whether the claim of a sex difference survives closer scrutiny.

3.1. Criteria

3.1.1. Subject sampling   It has been argued that the typical greater male variability in general ability poses a special problem that makes proper subject sampling critically important. A sample restriction towards the high end of the bell-shaped (Gaussian) curve would for example favor male superiority, whereas sample restriction towards the left side would favor female supremacy. In both cases this would misrepresent a true sex difference in the general population. More generally, a failure to recognize the typically greater male variance in test scores ". . . may cause both the direction and magnitude of the mean sex differences in test scores to vary across different segments of the total distribution for the general populations. The observed sex difference will therefore often vary across groups selected from different segments of the population distribution" (Jensen 1998: 536). With respect to educational bias this implies, for example, that samples should preferably be drawn from populations of elementary school children, because increasingly harsh sample restrictions apply the further we go up the ladder from elementary levels to junior high and beyond. A further consideration here is whether the male/female variance ratio on various subtests relates in balanced samples to the subtests' *g* loadings.

Allik *et al.* (1999: 1140–1941) dispute the importance of sample restriction based on higher male variability. Their main argument is based essentially on Feingold's (1992) extensive review of variability on the national norms of several standardized test batteries. They stress the fact that the theory of greater male variability is by no means conclusively established. Then again, it is worth noting that Feingold's own conclusion was that males were consistently more variable than females in quantitative reasoning, spatial visualization, spelling and general knowledge, mostly abilities that are heavily *g*-loaded. Anyway, we may concur with Allik *et al.*'s recommendation that further evidence is needed before we draw firm conclusions, as well as with Feingold's notion that ". . . sex differences in variability and sex differences in central tendency have to be considered together to form correct conclusions about the magnitude of cognitive gender differences" (p. 61).

3.1.2. Test item variation   The proper study will include a minimum of nine tests that all differ widely in content area. The more varied the tests, the more likely it is that bias in one direction cancels out bias in another direction, according to classical test theory. As mentioned previously, verbal and spatial tests typically benefit females and males differently; and their simultaneous presence in a test battery would tend to balance out the sex biasing effects.

3.1.3. Lexical definitions   With respect to the importance of definition for measurement, Jensen (1998) suggests, for reasons detailed in *The g Factor*, that we better give up all talk about "intelligence" or "intelligence in general". These terms are used by too many in too many different contexts to be of any scientific use. It is important to realize that there are basic differences between, on the one side:

> ". . . the simple sum or mean of various subtest scores [which] is a datum without scientific interest or generality." or "ability in general" . . . "an arbitrary variable that fails to qualify conceptually as a scientific construct", and,

> on the other side:

> "general ability, defined as g, [which] rests on the correlations among test scores" (Jensen's 1998: 537 emphasis).

In other words, summed or averaged subtest scores are no scientifically acceptable alternatives to measures of general ability based on inter-test correlations. Of course, in practice we might use IQ scores as a reasonable proxy to general intelligence *g,* because most standardized IQ tests load fairly high on *g*. However, in the process of establishing whether there is a sex difference, no IQ test results will suffice as a sole basis for deciding whether an observed difference in general ability *g* is real, or rather a mirror of biased test item composition.

None of the newly defined "intelligences" will solve this problem. Sternberg's (1988) Triarchic, Practical or Successful intelligences have not yet demonstrated proper construct and predictive validity (see Chapter 19 in this volume), and the various sub-components of the theory have also been criticized (Kline 1991; Messick 1992). Four of Gardner's Multiple "intelligences" (Gardner 1983, 1993) correlate closely enough to suggest considerable redundancy, and they seem to mainly tap general ability *g* (linguistic, logical-mathematical, spatial and musical), whereas the remaining "intelligences" (intra-personal, inter-personal and bodily-kinesthetic) neither inter-correlate well nor do they correlate noticeably with the first four "intelligences". There is also the problem that the latter "intelligences" do not reflect g well, and that their predictive validity has not yet been documented. Goleman's (1995) Emotional "intelligence" seems based more on psychobiographical anecdotes than on solid data obtained through nationally representative samples. No doubt, psycho-biographic evidence can be an interesting starting point, but it is a long shot from a serious empirical mission to establish an ability test. Left to itself, it surely does not suffice as a basis for sweeping generalizations, and it in no way substitutes for the predictive validity of this "intelligence". Finally, none of the new intelligences seem to satisfy obligatory criteria for legal or moral use (see Chapter 19 in this volume).

It is therefore a relief to realize from Jensen's many contributions over the years, culminating in *The g Factor* book (1998) that a precise lexical definition of intelligence is really not needed. It is no more a must than is the exact lexical definitions of time, space and gravity. What all these constructs really need is an operational definition, which will give us an idea of what kind of reality lies behind the constructs.

3.1.4. Operational definitions   The problem of how to properly estimate g is actually by and large solved by now. A chapter on sex differences is not the right place to discuss in details what a "good" g is, and the reader is referred to Jensen (1998), Jensen & Weng (1994), or to Carroll (1993, or Chapter 1 in this volume) for detailed expositions. It suffices to say here that all the different factor analytic solutions that allow for the existence of a g factor will identify g. Thurstone's simple structure rotation method is the exception to the rule, because it expressly forbids the appearance of a g. Even if all the g variance remains in the factor structure all the time, the mathematical solution does not allow it to appear as a separate higher order factor. The considerable predictive validity of psychometric g, and the fact that the heritability estimate for the various g's *increases* over the life span (i.e. it becomes larger with time rather than smaller, as previously expected), when derived as a second or third order factor, also speaks well for its usability, as does its multiple correlations with a variety of biological traits.

However, and this is vitally important in the present context: I have found that most factor analytic solutions are perhaps less than optimal in the search of a sex difference in g. The average sex difference may be rather small, and this means that it has to be protected by all means from the masking effect of confounding by other ability dimensions, or it will not be possible to identify at all. A brief comparison of the various factor analytic approaches demonstrates this analytic point, and the forthcoming grading of studies illustrates the important empirical implications.

3.1.5. Principal component (PC) and principal factor (PF) analyses   A drawback of PC and PF analyses is that they are somewhat sensitive to test bias. If the test battery contains a predominance of, say, visuo-spatial tests, second or third order PC1 and PF1 g run the risk of being contaminated by this over-representation, perhaps even as much as to side with general intelligence g in the case of a grossly biased test battery. In that case we would get a definitely false impression of a male superiority in general ability g. Contrariwise, a surplus of verbal fluency tests in the battery would easily induce the illusion of a female superiority in g. The mathematical reason for this outcome is straightforward: The PC1 and PF1 *g* factors derive directly from inter-test correlations. As such, they reflect to some extent the kind of abilities the test items cover.

3.1.6. Hierarchical factor analysis (HFA)   Hierarchical factor analysis is much less sensitive to this error of over-sampling same- or similar-ability type tests. One thus begins the analytic process by first identifying the primary or group factors using PF (or in some special cases PC) analysis, and forcing an oblique rotation of factor axes to determine their correlations. Another step is to derive the second-order (or third order in the case of a large and varied test battery) *g* from correlations among the group factors at the primary level. The bottom of the hierarchy of factors is, in other words, the least general: the factors there arise on the basis of correlations between only a few of the tests (say, a number of interrelated verbal tests or some interrelated visuo-spatial tests). The factors at the next higher level are a function of the correlations among a few group factors (say, verbal abilities or visuo-spatial abilities.) The highest second or third level is inhabited by the general ability factor *g*, which is a function of what is common to all the lower order group factors and test. In other words, because the sources of variances due to test specificity and possible group factor biases are sorted out already at lower levels, the higher order *g* factor emanates as a largely uncontaminated function of general ability, reflecting mostly the variance that is common to all factors below.

3.1.7. Orthogonal Schmid-Leiman rotation   The HFA analytic solution can be optimized by including a Schmid-Leiman (SL) transformation (Schmid & Leiman 1957). This procedure orthogonalizes all factors between and within all levels in the hierarchy, making them totally uncorrelated. One advantage is that the structure is easier to interpret. Another advantage is, that it prohibits the appearance of a general ability factor where none is present in a correlation matrix. This could happen in the case of the PC and PF approaches.

3.1.8. Test for differences   There are basically three ways to test for the significance of an observed sex difference in *g,* here presented in increasing order of scientific interest.

The least informative method is to factor *g* by any of the relevant factor analytic methods, and then simply use a *t*-test to see if the male-female difference is significant.

The next step, which is proposed by Arthur Jensen (and explained in details in Appendix B in Jensen 1998: 589–591), is to determine whether the vector of disattenuated *d* values correlates significantly with the vector of disattenuated *g* loadings. The sex difference on each subtest may, for example, be expressed in terms of effect size *d* (calculated according to the formula: $d = (X_M - X_F)/\text{sigma}$, where X_M is the male mean, X_F is the female mean, and sigma is the pooled SD). The *d* effects are now arranged according to size in a vector matrix, preferable after correction for attenuation or reliability. The next step is to determine whether the vector matrix of attenuated *d* values correlate significantly with the vector matrix of likewise attenuated test *g* loadings. Both Pearson product-moment correlation and Spearman's rank-order correlation coefficients are calculated, as a divergence between the two coefficients may reveal a hidden non-linearity. In case the magnitude of the sex differences are related to the tests' g loadings, we can with Rushton (see Chapter 9 in this volume) talk about the demonstration of a "Jensen Effect", a shorthand phrase that saves the many words needed to describe the monotonous calculation of relating g to test differences.

Unfortunately, there is an important caveat to the use of the correlated vector method in the search for a sex difference in g. Thus, the number of tests — and not the number of subjects — determines the degrees of freedom in the correlated matrix analysis. This means that the likelihood of committing a type 2 error is rather high with this method. After some testing I have therefore come to the conclusion that the use of the correlated vector approach, while perfectly suited for many other purposes, is counterproductive in the pursuit of a small sex difference in g.

The last mean for testing for a sex difference is also the best. Here sex differences are first expressed in terms of point-biserial correlations (r_{pbs}) between sex and scores on each of the various subtests. Jensen states (1998: 538–542) that: "The point-biserial correlation ... is simply a Pearson product-moment correlation that expresses the relationship between a metric variable (e.g. test scores) and a dichotomous variable (in this case sex, quantitized as male = 1, female = 0 ...".) The formula for I_{pbs} allows for corrections for inequalities in sample sizes and SDs. The I_{pbs} is then fitted into the correlation matrix along with the various subtests inter-correlations and subjected to factor analysis. A PC, PF, or a HFA SL orthogonal analysis will then reveal how heavily each factor dimension loads on sex, including the g dimension.

3.1.9. Confounding factors   The last requirement for a proper study of a sex difference in g is the analytic capability to identify and control for further confounders, such as sex-age interaction. It is common knowledge that the developmental tempo of boys and girls differ considerably. To conclude that there is an absolute sex difference in g among, say, 12-year boys and girls without taking the developmental advantage of girls into account would be risky at best. Age is usually taken to mean actual or chronological age in studies of school children, but it would actually be more correct to compare the sexes on basis of their biological rather than chronological age in developmental studies of children.

3.2. Summary of Analytic Considerations and Outline for the Optimal Study

We are now able to condense the analytic considerations and outline the optimal approach in a search for a sex difference in g. A study can be trusted only if it is based on representative samples of males and females, if it incorporates a large number of tests (i.e. ≥ 9), if there is no over-sampling of a particular type of ability in the test battery, and if data are subjected to a HFA analysis. The inclusion of the Schmid-Leiman (1957) orthogonal transformation is obligatory, because a small sex difference in g would otherwise too easily drown in contamination, either from first order group factors, some of which clearly favor females and others favor males, or from test specificity. The correlated vector analysis admittedly indicates the g-load of a sex difference, a so-called Jensen Effect, but the degrees of freedom are restricted to the number of tests, which makes it a too conservative estimate of a sex difference in *g*. The best solution is, as stated by Jensen (1998) to include the point-biserial correlations in the factor matrix along with the inter-test correlations, to inspect the loading of sex on *g*, and to test the factored correlations coefficient for significance.

4. Selective Review of Sex Differences Research

4.1. The Development of a Quality Questionnaire

The question of whether a sex difference in general ability *g* exists after proper methodological control is, as previously mentioned, technically quite demanding. In an attempt to keep matters as simple as possible, this section reviews only a few studies. Rather than aiming for an exhaustive overview, the examination is meant to illustrate a number of specific methodological points, and therefore includes studies that vary sufficiently in quality to illustrate just that. The simple point scale described in table 10.1 is then used to grade the studies in accordance with how well they conform to the criteria for a scientifically sound study of sex differences in general ability *g*.

Use of the quality questionnaire is straightforward. One point is given to a study if the sample is fairly representative, rather than restricted to, say, university students. As previously mentioned, correct sampling is particularly important in sex differences research, because differences in male and female distributions can greatly influence the size and direction of the sex difference, depending on the set point of the ability scale. This point deserves repetition because too many studies use biased samples and no controls.

The derivation of a good *g* depends on a sufficient number of tests. The minimum number of tests for a sound hierarchical factor solution is 9 (Jensen (1998: 85). Studies including nine or more tests are awarded one point.

A study is granted one point for diversity if it includes a wide variety of tests mapping obviously different abilities. A way to check diversity is to see if the factor analytic solution allows for the derivation of at least three different first order factors.

The application of a HFA analysis is awarded one point, because it allows for close to virtual independence among factor dimensions. Studies deriving *g* by non-hierarchical PC or PF analysis earn no point, because this *g* is too easily contaminated by influences from the other factor dimensions when a sex difference is suspected.

Studies adding a Schmid-Leiman (1958) orthogonal rotation to the hierarchical solution are awarded a further point, as this transformation secures correlational independence among all factors, in addition to allowing for easier interpretation of the factor structure.

Studies just summing subtest scores are not given points, as they reflect unspecific "intelligence in general" rather than general intelligence. Structural equation modeling studies are not awarded points either, because the *g* thus derived may be contaminated by non-*g* factors (Bollen 1989). In this connection is it interesting to note that Gustavsson (1992) was unable to support the widely accepted Spearman hypothesis that the white-black difference in g increases the more g-loaded a test one uses (e.g. Nyborg & Jensen 2001). Gustavsson analyzed the same WISC-R data used in the Jensen & Reynolds (1983) study, but he used a LISREL program to factor analyze it. The explanation for the divergence in results may be that LISREL and other structural equation solutions may produce a contaminated g that gives unexpected results.

One point is given if point-biserial correlations are calculated, included in the inter-test correlation matrix before factor analysis and, finally, tested for significance after factoring.

The use of a t-test or other straightforward statistical procedure to test for significance of sex differences in g earns no point. Neither does a correlated vector analysis. It will be remembered that the purpose of a correlated vector calculation is to inspect whether observed sex differences in various tests, often expressed in terms of d effects, correlate with the g-loading of the various tests, routinely after control for attenuation (a Jensen Effect). The problem is that a correlated vector calculation is a severe test that provides a highly conservative estimate of d–g relationships, because the degrees of freedom are restricted to the number of tests. This means that the relationship does not attain significance unless the sex difference is large, which seems unlikely (see later). In other words, the risk of committing a type 2 error of not correctly identifying a real sex difference, is unacceptably large, using this test. Obviously, proper use of the correlated vector method further presumes the availability of an uncontaminated g measure.

The scale thus allows for a total of 5 points in the case of a hierarchical analysis, and six points when the Schmid-Leiman transformation is added. Conversely, any study given less than five points provides an unacceptable shaky basis for conclusions about the existence of a sex difference in general intelligence.

4.2. Ranking of Studies

4.2.1. The Colom and García-López (2002) study.

This study — "Sex differences in fluid intelligence among high-school graduates" — was specifically designed to take a stand in the controversy over whether there is a sex difference in general intelligence. Where Lynn (1994, 1999) argued that there is a difference, Colom and *García-López* explicitly intended to demonstrate that this is not true. They did so by subjecting 301 females and 303 males to two tests: Cattell's Culture-Fair (CF) Intelligence test (scale 3) and Raven's Advanced Progressive Matrices (APM). They further subjected 1,471 females and 1,997 males to the PMA Inductive Reasoning (IR) Test from the Primary Mental Abilities Battery. The idea behind using these tests was that they basically tap reasoning g ability (G_f), precisely the general intelligence proxy Lynn claims males are better at than females.

Colom and García-López made three observations: No sex differences on the CF; a significant female advantage on the IR ($p = 0.000$); and a male advantage on the APM ($p = 0.000$). Their verdict: "Given that there is no systematic difference favoring any sex in the measures of G_f, and that there is no sex difference in the best available measure of G_f (the Culture-Fair Test), it is concluded that the sex difference in fluid intelligence is non-existent". They also concluded, that "The data reported in this study disconfirm the case set out by Lynn (1994, 1999) . . .", and further that they are ". . . contrary to the [results] reported by Allik *et al.* (1999). The main conclusion is that Lynn's notion of a sex difference in general intelligence is falsified.

How much confidence may we ascribe to the strong conclusions from this critical study? Not much according to the quality criteria in Table 10.1. First, subject sampling is biased (for details, see the comments to the Colom *et al.* (2000) and the Allik *et al.* (1999) studies). Second, the number of tests is too small to satisfy the minimum criteria. Third, the test battery does not satisfy the minimum diversity criteria. Fourth, intra-test scores are simply summed. Fifth, the more or less undetermined sex differences are averaged across tests. Colom and García-López thus mention that their measures of "Fluid intelligence (G_f) is usually seen as the core of intelligence behavior . . ." and they refer in this matter to Carroll (1993). However, Carroll (see Chapter 1 in this volume) has arrived at the conclusion that G_f largely dissolves when *g* is controlled for. Given

Table 10.1: Rough and ready grading scale for *g*-sex studies. Studies granted 5 points or less run an unacceptable high risk of committing either a type 1 or a type 2 error, that is, they permit no firm conclusion about the existence of a sex difference in general intelligence. Maximum is 6 points.

Qualifiers	**No = 0**	**Yes = 1**
Sample:		
Representative populations.		
Tests:		
Large number of tests (≥ 9).		
Diversity of tests		
Analytic Method:		
Hierarchical factor analysis (HFA).		
Orthogonal Schmid-Leiman transformation.		
(No points for:		
(1) Simple summing over standardized scores (reflecting "intelligence in general".)		
(2) Structural equation modeling (as it may give a *g* contaminated by non-*g* factors (Bollen, 1989)).		
Test:		
Inserting point-biserial correlations into the inter-test correlation matrix, co-factoring it, and then testing whether sex loads significantly on *g*.		
(No points for:		
Correlated vector analysis because it is too easy to make a type 2 error (i.e. not seeing a true difference)).		

this is correct, there is little reason to discuss G_f separately as a measure of general intelligence. Finally, by averaging summed scores over tests that probably differ in their g-loading, Colom and García-López end up with a less than optimal g-measure. In fact, the study earns no point.

4.2.2. Raven matrices.   Court (1983) reviewed the entire literature (117 studies from five continents) on sex differences on Raven's Standard Progressive Matrices test for adults and the Colored Progressive Matrices test for children — "Sex differences in performance on Raven's Progressive Matrices: A review". The Raven tests may be interesting in the present context to the extent they are good proxies for pure g, and their g-loading indeed amounts to about 0.80 (Jensen 1998: 38). Court concluded that there is no consistent evidence for a sex difference in the Raven tests, and that these studies represent all degrees of representativeness.

According to the quality scale, the analysis is tentatively awarded one point for sample representativity, even though it is difficult to know for sure if some bias sneaked into this huge compilation of rather different studies, rather than just cancelled out. The Raven study neither qualified for points by representing many and very different tests, nor did it earn points for the total score based on summing.

The single point earned leads to the conclusion that the many studies using the Raven tests do not permit any sober conclusions about the existence of a sex difference in general intelligence.

4.2.3. The Colum *et al.* (2000) (1) study.   This study — "Negligible sex differences in general intelligence" — subjected two samples, totaling no less than 10,475 adult subjects (6,219 males and 4,256 females, average age 23.12 years), to two cognitive test batteries, one with five and the other with six different tests. Raw data were factor analyzed and several tests for differences were applied in order to see whether the sexes differed in general ability, after having secured that the male and female factor structures were identical, as reflected in sufficiently high factor congruence coefficients. The main conclusion of the study was that there are only negligible sex differences in g.

Sampling bias is a problem in this study, as it is in most other studies. It is true that the majority of adult applicants for a private university may not actually pass the score level required for admission to a state university, but there are good reasons to believe that even these applicants do not represent an unselected population sample. Any bias toward the right side of the ability distribution will in general deflate the g loadings obtained, relative to samples better representing the general population, in addition to enhancing the probability of finding a male advantage to the extent their distribution is wider than that of the females. The possibility of ". . . some statistical sampling error . . ." is appropriately discussed by Colom *et al.* (p. 60), and related to the fact that there was close to 30% more males than females in the sample and to the possibility of some female self-selection. Thus, no point is given for proper sampling.

The two studies offered data from five or six different tests for analysis, respectively. This obviously reduces the likelihood of tapping into a large variety of abilities and in this way counter a possible ability bias. The study gets no points for using the first unrotated PF approach. A hierarchical analysis would have been a better choice, but this would require access to data from a minimum of nine tests from which at least three primary factors can be derived. As the study stands, the PF1 *g* measure most likely was contaminated to some undetermined degree by influences from the other factor dimensions (see below).

With respect to testing, it is interesting to note that when the sex differences in *g* are measured by Pearson's rs, *Rhos*, and *Taus*, they all turned out to be highly significant ($p < 0.000$) in both the first and second study. Colom *et al.* (p. 65) dismissed the significance of this finding as they "... could be explained by the non-g variance included in the *g* factor scores. It should be remembered that the *g* factor scores are not a pure measure of *g*". While the latter certainly is true, the size and consistency of the observed sex difference in *g* were considerable. The study earns no point for applying the method of correlated vectors, which by the way, did not come out statistically significant (Spearman $r = 0.000$; $p = 0.999$, after proper disattenuation). It is worth bearing in mind that it is highly unlikely that a correlated vector calculation based on only five or six tests (or even on the pooled 11 tests) will come out significant in sex difference research. The study earns one point for factoring in the point-biserial correlations. Curiously enough, the resulting loading of sex on *g* of 0.216 (found in Colom *et al.* 2002: 34) was never tested for significance. Given $N = 10,475$, I find the correlation to be highly significant ($p = 0.000$, Fisher $z = 0.219457$.) Had they done this testing, the authors obviously would have been forced to conclude that they had found a very real sex difference in *g* in male favor. On the other side, it should be realized that the derivation of *g* was based on the PF approach, which means that they probably operated with a contaminated *g*. That by itself renders any conclusion suspect.

The Colum *et al.* (2000) study of sex differences in *g* earns, in other words, a total of one point on the quality scale. This disqualifies it as a sound basis for deciding in the matter of a sex difference in general intelligence *g*. The methodological shortcomings, the divergence of data, and the observation of a significant sex load on *g*, should perhaps have tempered their main conclusion, of "... no sex difference in general intelligence" (p. 66).

4.2.4. The Jensen and Reynolds (1983) study. Jensen and Reynolds found a small but significant sex difference (M–F) of $d = 0.161$ ($p < 0.01$) in *g* factor scores in a study — "Sex differences on the WISC-R".

The study earns one point for drawing upon the national standardization sample of 6- to 16-year-old boys and girls, making it representative, at least for that age range. The study earns another point as data emanated from a fairly large number of subtests. However, as mentioned earlier, Wechsler purposely removed all test items during the construction of the test reflecting a large sex difference, carefully balanced out the remaining items so that what females would gain on verbal score side, males would gain on performance score, in order to present a neutral IQ test with no offensive overall sex difference. A test deliberately twisted that way cannot be trusted as an objective measure of sex differences. It may not represent a realistic distribution of abilities out there. No point could be given for the use of PF analysis. The study thus earned a total of 2 points on the quality scale.

Jensen (1998: 538) later carefully de-emphasized the value of the study, and the reasons he gave are illustrative. Basically, he argued, the precise size of the sex difference could not be estimated, because PF *g* factor scores might have been ". . . somewhat contaminated by small bits of the other factors and test specificity measured by the various subtests. This might either have increased or decreased the mean difference". I agree that the methodological flaws make it unlikely that this study can form a solid basis for the conclusion that there is no genuine sex difference in general ability *g*.

4.2.5. The Lynn *et al.* (2002) study. This study — "Sex differences in general knowledge" — applied a newly developed general information test (Irwing *et al.* 2001), covering 19 domains of general knowledge. The sample consisted of 469 female and 167 males. A second-order general factor was extracted that arguably reflects *g*, in addition to six first-order factors. Significant male superiority was found on the general factor and on four first-order factors, whereas females came out superior on one first-order factor. There were no sex differences in the remaining first-order factors.

Judging the methodological merits of this study, sampling cannot be claimed to be unbiased; the study drew on an unequal number of male and female undergraduates from three different academic areas. It gets one point for applying a large number of tests, but no points for diversity as general knowledge or information is but one, though heavily *g*-loaded, component of a broad-spectrum test battery. The study obtains one point for applying a hierarchical factor solution, but none for involving rather sophisticated MIMIC (multiple indicators and multiple causes models (Jöreskog & Sörbom 1993). Here, sex appears as the single predictor, the second-order general knowledge factor as a latent variable, and the first-order factors and domain levels of general knowledge as multiple indicators. Various models were tested using LISREL maximum likelihood estimation. A model with six effects on general knowledge domains was finally accepted. The coefficient for an effect of sex on overall general knowledge factor amounted to –0.42 (or 0.51*d*), but females performed better on factors reflecting Family and Fashion. The problem with structural equation modeling is, as mentioned previously that it may produce a contaminated *g* (Bollen 1989). The study concluded that males have more general knowledge than females. However, the earned total of two points on the quality scale makes it likely that we cannot learn much about sex differences in *g* from this study.

4.2.6. The Allik *et al.* (1999) study. This study — "Sex differences in general intelligence in high school students: Some results from Estonia" — found a substantial sex difference in *g* when testing 1,201 applicants for entry to the University of Tartu, Estonia. Raw data from four tests — verbal, reasoning, spatial abilities and scholastic knowledge — were factored, and a *g* was derived by the PC1 method. A large male effect size lead on *g* of *d* = 0.65, equal to 9.75 IQ points was found.

The sample consisted of applicants striving to enter a Social Science Faculty at the university. Obviously, this means that the sample was no more representative than the ones used in the Colum *et al.* (2000) and the Colom & García-López (2002) studies.

Potential university students are in general located well to the right of the mean in the normal ability distribution. Moreover, there were more than double as many female as male applicants (838 vs. 363, respectively). The battery consisted of four tests. The study thus misses the optimum requirements for numbers and diversity, even if each of the available tests loads heavily on *g*. The study gets no points for applying the PC approach, as the PC1 *g* measure is unacceptably vulnerable to biasing influence from tests with a clear male advantage, such as reasoning and spatial ability. The study checked for a sex difference in *g* by using a simple test for significance.

In other words, this study is compromised by sample bias, by the incorporation of a few and not widely varied tests, by the likely contamination of the PC1 *g* measure from other factors, and by the use of a simple statistical test for sex differences. It accordingly did not earn any points on the quality scale, and the finding of a rather large sex difference in general ability *g* cannot be trusted.

4.2.7. The Jensen (1998) analysis. Jensen analyzed five test batteries for which data were available for large and representative samples that encompass the full range of abilities in the general population, and presented the results in Jensen (1998: 538–541). Sex differences on each subtest were represented by point-biserial correlations that were inserted into the matrix of subtest inter-correlations. The loadings on sex on each of the factors, including *g*, were then determined after factor analysis. I leave out many of the interesting details of the analysis, and go directly to Jensen's two main conclusions:

- The sex difference in psychometric *g* is either totally nonexistent or is of uncertain direction and of inconsequential magnitude;
- The generally observed sex difference in variability of test scores is attributable to factors other than *g*.

However, there are methodological problems with this study. One of these relates to a critique voiced by Mackintosh (1996: 567). Mackintosh argued, ". . . research on sex differences suggests that different batteries yield significantly different general factors". He accordingly concluded that for the analysis of sex differences in *g* ". . . little will be gained by further pursuit of the precise nature of general intelligence defined in this way". Lynn (1999) follows up with further detailed critique of the analysis, some of which resonates with Mackintosh's. Lynn thus also finds that ". . . The nature of *g* depends on the kind of tests in the battery from which it is extracted", and further that the nature of the test batteries favored females and males to unequal extents, respectively. Lynn concluded that it is incorrect to average such greatly disparate estimates of *g* and then concludes that there is no sex difference in general ability. For reasons stated before and below I agree with Mackintosh's and Lynn's conclusion that the *g* measure was probably flawed. However, I disagree with Lynn's argument that a "global IQ obtained by summing the subtests . . ." will suffice. This measure is flawed, too. By the way, it should be remembered that this critique of the use of more or less contaminated *g* measures applies in particular to sex difference research. In most other cases, a *g* derived by different factor analytic solutions will usually also behave as a good *g* (Jensen & Weng 1994).

Lynn states incorrectly (1999: 8–9) that Jensen applied the PC method in the analysis. The analysis was actually based on the PF approach. Not that this matters much in the present context, because PC and PF analyses suffer equally with respect to the nagging problem of factor contamination. As in a PC analysis, one encounters the obligatory problem that ". . . contamination is especially significant when one extracts g as the first factor (PF1) in a principal factor analysis" (Jensen 1998: 86). Closer examination of data from the General Aptitude Test Battery, one of the five tests subjected to analysis, illustrates the nature of this problem rather well. Females performed significantly better than males in this test. However, the g factor was clearly compromised by a psychometric sampling excess of psychomotor tests that typically favor females. Jensen is, of course, too experienced to not note the danger. When he removed the female biased tests and performed a follow-up factor analysis, the remaining cognitive variables then showed only negligible sex loadings on PF1.

The analysis earns quite a number of points on the quality scale. One point is given for unbiased sampling, one for the large number of tests involved, and one for great test variety. It gets no points for the PF approach, but one for inserting point-biserial correlations in the factor analysis. However, the study earns a total of four points. This disqualifies it, according to the quality scale, as a trustworthy basis for conclusions about sex differences in g.

4.2.8. The Aluja-Fabregat *et al.* (2000) study. The title of this study is: "Sex differences in general intelligence defined as g among young adolescents". The investigation involved two independent samples of 678 primary school children in the first, and 887 children in the second. The average age was about 13 in both groups of volunteers, and there were an almost equal number of girls and boys.

With respect to the analytic approach, the authors state: "It seldom makes a difference whether g is represented by the highest order factor in a HFA analysis or by the first unrotated principal factor in a principal factor analysis. These typically have a congruence coefficient of $+0.99$ or more (Jensen & Weng 1994). We have used the first unrotated principal factor solution to extract g" (p. 815). This would be acceptable in cases where g research is tracing large group differences, such as among races or between social levels, but not in the search for a sex difference in g. Here test and sample bias may become THE basic problems to be dealt with effectively in order not to draw conclusions on the basis of the contaminated g. The Aluja-Fabregat *et al.* study thus earns no point for the PF approach. The point-biserial correlations were actually entered into the inter-test correlation matrix. The sex loading on g was –0.194 and –0.150 in the first and second study, respectively.

The authors offer an interesting interpretation of this: ". . . the percentage of g variance due to sex differences is 0.817 (first sample) and 0.420 (second sample) . . ." and this suggests, "A negligible sex difference in general intelligence defined as g in young adolescents" (pp. 818–819). This surely is not the optimal basis for deciding in the matter. The correct way is to check whether the two coefficients are statistically significant, and then a rather surprising result surfaces. Given a total N of 678 in the first sample, I find that the loading of sex on g of –0.194 is highly significant in the first sample ($p = 0.000$, Fisher $z = 0.196490$). In the second sample with $N = 887$, the sex loading on g of –0.150 also is highly significant ($p = 0.000$, Fisher $z = 0.151140$). The inescapable conclusion seems to be, that there are now two independent confirmations of a very convincing sex difference in g in **female** favor!

It will be remembered that the study was explicitly designed to disprove Lynn's (1994, 1999) developmental hypothesis. It says that boys have in fact higher g than girls, but this will be camouflaged by the girl's earlier maturation, so young girls ought to score similarly or even higher than same age boys. The statistical outcome of the Aluja-Fabregat study actually supports the hypothesis it was designed to falsify. We, nevertheless, cannot trust this conclusion. The two PF1 g measures were probably contaminated to an undetermined degree by a test bias, pointing in a female direction in both independent samples. One piece of evidence for this is that the girls in both samples outperformed the boys in all but an attention test. Another rather puzzling observation is that the girls in both samples outperformed the boys not only on the Math but also on the Natural Science test. Boys in practically all other studies surpass girls in these areas. This raises the suspicion that either the tests were not of sufficient complexity, or the female samples were biased in an upward direction.

The Aluja-Fabregat *et al*. (2000) study is tentatively awarded a total of three points: One for sampling, and two for using many and varied tests. This falls short of the five points needed for a solid g-sex study with reduced risk of committing type 1 or type 2 errors.

4.2.9. The Colom *et al*. (2002) study. This study — "Null sex differences in general intelligence: Evidence from the WAIS-III" — examined 703 females and 666 males, aged 15–94, from the Spanish standardization of the WAIS-III test. A male advantage of 3.6 IQ points was found in "ability in general", which is not far away from the 3.8 male average IQ lead observed by Lynn (1994).

Colom and colleagues, nevertheless, came to a very different conclusion, resting upon two other main findings. First, the non-significant outcome of the ". . . method of correlated vectors contradicts the conclusion that could be derived from the simple summation of the standardized mean group difference (d). Because of the greater scientific adequacy of the method of correlated vectors to test the null hypothesis concerning sex differences in general intelligence defined as g, we can conclude that there is no sex difference in general intelligence" (p. 34). Second, the factor loading of sex on g ". . . suggests a null sex difference". From this they deduced that the Ankney-Rushton paradox (a larger male brain predicts a male IQ lead) is irrelevant ". . . because there is no sex difference in general intelligence" (p. 34).

One of the eminent features of the study is, that Colum *et al*. first calculated point-biserial correlations among subtests' scores and the sex variable and included them within the matrix of subtest inter-correlations. They then performed a hierarchical Schmid-Leiman type factor analysis of the full matrix, which presently is the most adequate way to check for a sex difference in g. What they found was that sex loads 0.159 on g. Unfortunately, they lost this vital information again by combining the load value with all other available sex loadings on g coming from different studies. A meager average sex load of 0.02 came out of this averaging of sex loadings on g — clearly not an impressive figure!

The best approach is to directly test the observed sex load of 0.159 for significance. I did this, and found that the male lead in g is highly significant ($N = 1,369$; $p < 0.000$; Fisher $z = 0.160361$). This is all the more remarkable as the Colom *et al.* study operates with an excellent and probably entirely uncontaminated Schmid-Leiman transformed g identified in a representative sample.

Thus, rather than showing null sex differences, the overall conclusion of this methodologically sober study is that males significantly excel females in general intelligence g. The study gets one point for a representative sample, two points for using many and varied tests, one for a hierarchical factor analysis, and one for the Schmid-Leiman transformation. The earned total of five points indicates that the outcome of this study requires serious attention. I will take the last point for significance testing!

4.2.10. The Nyborg (2003) study. A final study — "Sex related differences in general intelligence, g, and group factors: A representative hierarchical orthogonal Schmid-Leiman type factor analysis" — found no sex difference in g before age 14, but identified a significant sex difference in the adult group of 52 males and females (as reported in Nyborg, 2001).

This is arguably the most carefully sampled study of those reviewed so far (Nyborg, unpublished data). The selection procedure began with a computer search in the late 1970s in the Danish Folkeregister for every twentieth child that was either 8, 10, 12, 14 or 16 years old, either a boy or a girl, and attending a school either in the countryside, in a suburb or in a larger city. Information about the socio-economic status of the parents, defined by father's occupational status, was also collected and categorized at five levels. If the twentieth child, or the parents, refused participation in the scheduled 20 years cohort-sequential study, the twenty-first (or in two cases the twenty-third) child on the computer list was invited. No particular pattern of reasons to refuse participation could be spotted in retrospect. Five preliminary age categories were established on basis of the results from this preliminary search protocol. The groups consisted of 8, 10, 12, 14 and 16+ year olds, respectively. When about 50% of the children were tested and filed, the distribution of all socio-economic and personal characteristics of the children were inspected for each group. The categories were then filled up with additional children, so that each age category finally mustered a total of 15 boys and 15 girls. During the fill-up process, great care was taken to ensure that each and all categories ended up being representative with respect to the general Danish socio-economic population distribution while also conforming to the nationwide proportional representation of rural, suburban and city residency. Data on children participating in the cross-sectional parts of the study were included in the present analysis, as were data on children participating in the longitudinal part of the study, but who had been examined only once. The particular selection procedure resulted in a total of 376 children and adults, with an identical number of girls and boys in each category.

All subjects were exposed to a large and varied battery of 20 or 21 ability tests (20 for the pooled 8 to 14 year-old-group, and 21 for the 16+ year-old group, with one subtest, Coding, making up the difference). The substantial number of highly varied tests permitted application of a hierarchical oblique factor analysis, which was supplemented with the Schmid-Leiman transformation. The factor structure coefficients for boys and girls were close to unity. A second order factor g and seven first-order factors were derived. Point-biserial correlations were computed, fitted into the inter-test correlation matrices, and factored in order to inspect the loading of sex on g, and tested for significance. The study also included a correlated vector analysis for Jensen effect, in addition to a traditional d effect analysis.

Point of departure for the analysis was a test of Lynn's prediction of a moderate but significant sex difference in g. The prediction could not be supported for the pooled 8 to 14-year-old children's sample, but the results of the adult sample actually confirmed the hypothesis. Thus, the point-biserial loading of sex on g was thus only 0.009 in children (ns), but reached 0.272 in the adult hierarchical orthogonal g factor analysis, which is significant (one-tailed $p = 0.026$) despite the very low $N = 52$. A correlated vector calculation reached significance neither for the children nor for the adult group, also as expected. Children's average sex difference d effect size was 0.18 or 2.62 IQ points, and the corresponding adult values were 0.26 or 3.94 IQ points, with positive signs indicating a male advantage in intelligence in general. The adult raw sex difference in g was 0.37 SD or 5.55 IQ points.

The study earns one point for being representative, and two for operating with a large battery of highly varied tests that allows for an adequate operational definition of g. It earns three points for factoring in the point-biserial correlations, for taking the hierarchical factor approach, for optimal orthogonalization through the Schmid-Leiman transformation, and for testing the loadings for significance. In other words, all likely precautions were taken against the likelihood of g-contamination in this study, due to the carefully chosen sample, the particular analytic approach, and the presence of a rich, varied and highly g-loaded test battery. The maximum of six points earned means that we can ascribe at least the same degree of confidence to the conclusions of this study as we did to the Colom *et al.* (2002) study.

This concludes the selective review of studies. Studies earning less than five points on the quality scale may either find a female advantage, a male advantage, or no sex difference in g, but none of these can be trusted due to the risk of contamination. Only two recent studies obtain five or six points, and both studies identify a significant adult advantage in g.

5. Discussion

This chapter specifically addressed the problem why sex difference research on g has been plagued for so long by analytic inconsistency and incompatible findings, and thus has provided little guidance for a scientifically based opinion whether there is in fact a sex difference in general intelligence which could explain, at least in part, the obvious sex-differentiated achievement in education, jobs, and societal power structures, as well as the repeated observation of an average male advantage in brain sizes.

The strategy chosen was to take point of departure in the analytic and empirical disagreement among two of the most prominent combatants in the field. On the one side, there is Lynn (1994, 1999) who uses the sum standardized scores, and finds an average significant male superiority in general intelligence, and uses the on average larger male brain to explain this difference. Jensen (1998) is, on the other side, moved neither by Lynn's finding of a sex difference in summed scores nor by the interpretation of its basis. Using the more advanced factor analytic inter-test correlation approaches, Jensen documents considerable inconsistency in the data: sometimes females obtain a higher score, sometimes males are in front, and sometimes there is no sex difference at all in *g*. In short, there is no reliable sex difference in *g*.

The way the present chapter addressed this analytic and empirical dilemma was, basically, to systematize Jensen's analytic critique in terms of the development of a brief catalogue of criteria for a proper study of sex differences in *g*. Then a number of typical studies were judged against these criteria, with the hope that this strategy promised a double advantage: to examine in detail whether Lynn's claimed male *g* advantage is a fact, and whether it would survive even at the highest levels of a Jensenist hierarchy of increasingly more demanding methodological environments.

5.1. Three Major Conclusions

The grading of *g*-studies allowed for three major conclusions.

First, studies granted less than five points on the quality scale routinely produce unreliable or inconsistent results, which means that their conclusions about the existence of a sex difference in *g* cannot be trusted. Most of these studies do not sample properly. Many studies remain satisfied with the summing of standardized scores, which makes them particularly vulnerable to the possibility of arriving at a contaminated IQ or "intelligence in general". To make things worse for sex differences research, the PC or PF analytic approaches cannot be trusted either, because the "general intelligence" or *g* thus derived may take on color to an undetermined degree from the non-*g* factors in the matrix. Jensen (1998: 539–540) elegantly demonstrated this danger in the previously discussed analysis of the GATB test battery. This test contains an unusual number of psychomotor tests for vocational aptitudes that favor females. It will be remembered that the observed female advantage in *g* disappeared after proper control for this test bias. The obvious implication is, that studies based on PC or PF analysis can neither be taken to confirm nor reject the possibility of a sex difference in *g*. We have to apply methodologically more stringent studies that take stronger precautions against test bias and the associated contamination of *g* by group or test specific factors, before they deserve our confidence in conclusions about a sex difference in *g*.

The second conclusion is that, provided the requirements set forth in the quality questionnaire in Table 10.1 are met, a significant adult sex difference in *g* appears. The Colom *et al.* (2002) and the Nyborg (2001, 2003) studies are the only ones that offer a hierarchical Schmid-Leiman transformation solution, in addition to conforming to other stated quality criteria. In both those cases, a moderate male lead in *g* is identified, as the factored point-biserial *g*-loading of sex on *g* came out unexpectedly significant at the two-tailed $p < 0.000$ level in the Colom case and, despite a critically low N of 52 in the Nyborg case, at a predicted one-tailed $p = 0.026$ level. The loading of sex on *g* did not reach significance in the 8 to 14-year-old child sample in the latter case.

The third conclusion is that the moderate male *g* advantage of 0.37 SD probably goes a long way in explaining why it was so difficult to pin it down in a multitude of inconsistent studies. A difference of that size easily drowns in studies not following the most stringent methodological rules, and where all sorts of influences from group factors and test specificity may contaminate the *g*. The cure against this danger seems to be to sample carefully, to use many and highly varied tests, and to exploit the mathematical approach behind the Schmid-Leiman orthogonalized transformation of the hierarchically organized factor dimensions. Such strict requirements for measuring *g* probably do not reach the same importance in studies of the well-documented much larger race or social level differences in *g*.

Obviously, the final establishment of an adult sex difference in *g* needs more than two replications!

5.2. Theoretical Implications

There are at least two theoretical lines of interests in knowing whether the sexes differ in *g*.

First, Jensen (1998: 541) states that no difference in *g* means that there is no sex difference in the "... general conditions of the brain's information-processing capacity that cause positive correlations among all of the modular functions on which there is normal variation and which account for the existence of *g*". It furthermore means that, "... the true sex differences reside in the modular aspects of brain functioning." In other words, the finding of a real sex difference in *g* would force us to acknowledge that whatever causes the positive manifold among abilities, observed by Spearman (1904), would be subjected to an effect of a general and not just specific nature.

Given that there is a small but real sex difference in *g*, and further given that the difference does not seem to appear before puberty (as suggested by the Nyborg 2001, 2003), one might speculate that some sex-related brain differentiation is taking place among boys and girls around that time. This could involve the general conditions of the brain's information-processing capacity, or it could provoke modular differentiation, or both. In either case, it is likely that individual and group differences in gonadal or adrenal hormones at puberty might be involved, because such hormones are known to significantly affect brain development (Nyborg 1994a). A study by Nyborg & Jensen (2000) suggested that only extremely high or low plasma testosterone concentrations significantly affect adult *g*, and then in a downward direction. However, it is worth keeping in mind that this sample consisted of middle-aged men with fully mature brains. The study might not adequately reflect the complex *g*-hormone concentration connections in much more sensitive younger people. In any case, the question whether sex hormones affect general or only modular aspects of the brain's information-processing capacity in a sex-related way can be fully answered only in carefully designed longitudinal studies. No such study is presently available, but one has been on its way since 1976 (Nyborg, unpublished data). The Nyborg (2001, 2003) analysis, referred to previously, took its data from this much more comprehensive study.

The second theoretical implication of a male advantage in g has to do with the Ankney-Lynn-Rushton brain size-IQ paradox mentioned previously. It will be remembered that Lynn (1994) was able to predict rather accurately a male lead in IQ from knowledge of a male lead in brain size. His calculations are presented in Table 10.2.

Given a male lead in brain size of SD = 0.78, and provided that the mean correlation between brain image size and IQ is 0.35 (Rushton & Ankney 1996), all we have to do is to multiply the male lead in brain size with the brain size-IQ correlation. We then get an SD of 0.27. When multiplied by 15 this 0.27 SD value translates into a male IQ lead of about 4 points. This theoretical prediction of intelligence from brain size matches the observed male average IQ lead of 3.8 quite well, but is for obvious reasons restricted to "intelligence in general". The Nyborg (2001, 2003) study allows us to re-test the prediction, but this time using an uncontaminated measure of g or "general intelligence". Like in the Lynn case, the arithmetics is straightforward. The observed sex difference in head circumference, a proxy for brain size, was SD = 0.87. This gives, when multiplied by the observed head circumference — g correlation of 0.34, an SD = 0.30, which, when multiplied by 15 turns into a predicted male IQ advantage of 4.437. The observed male lead in g was 0.37 which, when multiplied by 15, corresponds to a male IQ advantage of 5.55 points. In other words, Lynn underestimated the sex difference in g by 0.44 IQ point when using the questionable "intelligence in general" IQ measure.

5.3. The Very High End Male g Hypothesis

Obviously, the importance of the observed sex difference in g is not to be found in the group mean. No sensible prediction can be made for any individual male or female by referring to a mean average difference of just 0.37 SD. However, a brief consultation of the characteristics of Gaussian distribution theory teaches us that even a moderate mean advantage in g will have a considerable effect on the male/female ratio of individuals with high or very high g. In fact, the higher scoring group will be exponentially over-represented above a given high cut-off point on the scale. The growing disparity is graphically illustrated in Figure 10.1.

Equally obviously, a larger male variability would enhance this pattern, whereas the larger number of surviving females in each age category throughout life would to some small extent counter it. This means that the idealized curves must be inspected with caution, and this applies in particular at the extremes, as it is not given that they follow the normal distribution here. Finally, the sex difference in g variability in the Nyborg (2001, 2003) studies is larger than what is typically seen in most studies of IQ. It remains to be seen whether a sex difference of that size in g variability materializes in future g studies, or is just an artifact of the present study.

With these provisos in mind, we can begin to speculate about the practical predictive validity in the real world, outside the test room, of the male mean g advantage at the right side of the distribution. But first we have to realize that real life situations constitute a much, much broader test basis than the sex difference reported in this

Table 10.2: Predictions of **IQ** (intelligence in general) and *g* (general intelligence) from a sex difference in brain volume or head circumference, a proxy for brain size (from Nyborg (2002)).

Study	A: Observed sex differences in brain size	B: Correlations between volume[a] or circumference[b] and IQ[1] or g^2	C: A × B	D: Predicted male lead in IQ[3] or g^4 C × **15**	E: Observed male lead in IQ[5] or g^6
	d effects	*r*	**SD units**		
Lynn (1999): IQ data averaged over several studies	0.78	0.35^{a1}	0.27	4.05^3	3.85^5
Nyborg: Observed data in a specific study of *g*	0.87	0.34^{b2}	0.30	0.30^4 (IQ 4.44)	0.37^6 (IQ 5.55)

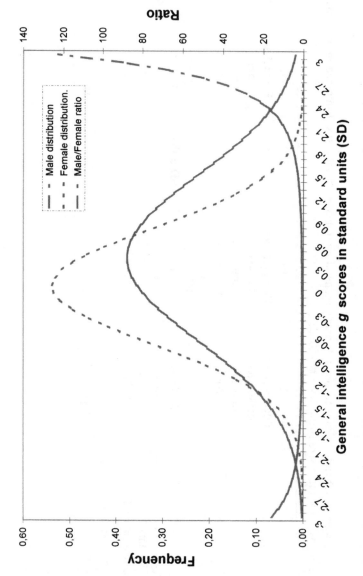

Figure 10.1: Male and female distributions and ratio as a function of male *g* = 0.36 (SD 1.06) and female *g* = –0.01 (SD 0.74). The theoretical ratio of males to females with *g* = 3 (IQ = 145) is about 120 : 1. 2.15% of the population obtains a *g* score ≥2 SDs, and only 0.13% a *g* score ≥3 SDs (from Nyborg 2002).

chapter, even if they emanated on the basis of relatively wide-ranging batteries of standardized tests in the two confirmatory studies. It has thus been argued that, in the largest possible scale, individuals coping with recurrent complex life problems can be viewed as participating in a gigantic longitudinal intelligence test (Gordon 1997; Gottfredson 1997, and Chapter 15 in this volume). In this all-encompassing perspective, all people can be seen as examinees in a gigantic and extremely varied set of tests, and many of these everyday tests undoubtedly are highly *g*-loaded. Given the male average lead in *g*, we can expect that more males will come out with a higher everyday success score, and more so the heavier the *g*-load of the every-day tests. For simplicity I will call this the "Very high end male *g* hypothesis". There actually is a growing body of evidence to support this hypothesis. Males typically outperform females in most top level educational, vocational, and political power areas — with a disproportionately higher proportion of males found as complexity and demands increase. This tendency is seen most clearly in complex problem-solving mathematics (Benbow 1992), engineering and physics (Lubinski *et al.* 2000), and in other areas calling for high spatial ability (Shea *et al.* (in press)). The "very high end male *g* hypothesis" might also provide part of the explanation for the massive male preponderance in high-level chess competition, musical composition, theoretical physics, economy and in the numerous other areas of demonstrated high-level male dominance.

This said, it is vitally important to realize that there is no question that a multitude of factors besides the sex difference in *g* will also have to be fitted into a realistic equation for predicting unequal participation in challenging areas of life (e.g. Nyborg, in press; Nyborg & Jensen 2001).

5.4. The Future of Sex Differences Research on g

Mainly thanks to Arthur Jensen we can now safely assume that both the definition and measurement of general intelligence are on safe ground and need little further attention. What needs closer attention, though, is the definition and measurement of sex. The division of mankind into male and female categories is awfully crude. More sophisticated approaches are possible but, unfortunately, vicious politically correct attempts to gloss over decisive biological differences among male and female are sure to surface whenever the attention is turned toward biologically based modeling of sex. Proofs of this are the widespread preference for terms like gender (supposed to have an environmental basis) over sex (supposed to have a biological basis), or the more wide-angled claim (with little hard evidence) that sex is just a social construct, or the aggressive claim that those who cannot see this must house a hidden hostile political agenda against females. This is empirically irresponsible and promotes more heat than light.

A realistic biological approach to sex differences research involves two things: deep knowledge of the operational definitions of sex, and the development of fine-grained, multi-spectered and continuous ways to classify males and females.

With respect to operational definitions, sex can be analyzed at many levels: the level of chromosomal sex (XX or XY, or multiple combinations thereof), sex hormonal sex (simplified here as estrogen or androgen in various ratios), internal sex organ sex, external sex organ sex, sexual inclination, gender identity, or sexually differentiated phenotypes. Usually, the sexual development at all these levels tends to co-vary, but any or all of the levels may co-vary differently in a given individual (Nyborg 1994a, 1994b). All causal modeling of sex will have to incorporate the interaction patterns among these levels, and only lazy social researchers may think they can get away with anything less.

It is an interesting hypothesis that, the causal factors that guide the coordinated sex-related development of the body and brain functions may also explain both the moderate sex-related difference in *g* and the much larger sex-related differences in group factors like verbal and spatial abilities. Sex hormones seem a good first choice here. Obviously, without sex hormones there will be no phenotypic sex-related differences at all. By implication, there will be no sex differences in body, brain, behavior and in *g*. A fetus, whether it is chromosomally male or female, will inevitably develop into a female in the absence of prenatal testosterone, *t*. *t* is a potent androgenic so-called male hormone — so-called because *t* can be aromatized into the so-called female hormone estradiol which, when present in sufficiently high concentrations, may exert masculinizing effects. Contrariwise, irrespective of male or female chromosomal complement, if the fetus is exposed to sufficiently high concentrations of *t*, it inevitably develops into a male with all the related bodily, brain and behavioral characteristics. One exception to this rule is, that if it is unable to induce *t* receptor molecules, the fetus will — despite it's male *t* level and even it's male XY karyotype — develop a female phenotype.

All this means that hormonally guided body and brain development is better considered a continuous than as a categorical phenomenon. It further means that, depending on the time-table for hormone exposure and transient individual differences in local body or brain receptor sensitivity, a given hormone exposure may during development provide an otherwise predominantly female individual with a couple of typical male traits, or an otherwise predominantly male individual with a couple of outstanding feminine traits, even if chromosomal and hormonal sex usually coincide in a species-specific evolutionary economic way (Nyborg 1994a).

With respect to the development of more fine-grained, multi-faceted and continuous ways to classify males and females, we can now begin to profit from an improved understanding of how sex hormones are capable of making multiple continuous mixings of male and female traits possible, on top of an individual's chromosomal sex. The causal basis is that hormones may alter the transcription of familial genes, whenever they are present in sufficient concentrations and specific receptor molecules can be induced in the target tissues. This mechanism allows us to classify males and females into more fine-grained categories, such as hormotypes (Nyborg 1984, 1994a, 1994b, 1997a, 1997b): I have tentatively established five different androtypes for XY males (low *t* A1s to high *t* A5s), and five estrotypes (low estradiol E1s to high estradiol E5s) for XX females (plus two A0 or A6, and two E0 or E6 categories for abnormally low or high hormone values — 1 or 99 percentiles, respectively).

The general Trait Co-variance — Androgen/Estrogen (GTC–A/E) model then generates a large number of empirically testable predictions about covariant body, brain, and behavioral development (see Nyborg 1994a, 1994b, 1997a, 1997b, for details).

With respect to estrotypes, young E1 individuals with relatively low early plasma estrogen and relatively high testosterone levels are thus expected to slowly develop high *g*, in addition to forming a slightly masculinized personality, and to expose few social interests. Such E1 females are expected to do well in male occupations like engineering, but they also encounter little reproductive success. They are thus expected to give birth to few and late children. A test in the U.S. of the GTC–A/E model confirmed that they have, in fact an unexpected high rate of unprovoked abortion (Hausman 1999). Clinical evidence suggests that E1 females, who for various medical or environmental reasons have been exposed prenatally to non-physiological amount of androgens, tend to score higher on academic achievement measures than normal females (Hoyenga & Hoyenga 1979, 1993). Another line of clinical evidence suggests that sex hormone treatment may affect the development of intelligence in young girls with Turner's syndrome (Turner 1938; Nyborg 1990; Nyborg & Nielsen 1981). These girls lack some X chromosome material and most remain psychosexually infantile, unless given proper hormone treatment. A pseudo-experimental study suggested that *t* treatment enhances *g*, whereas estradiol treatment elevates spatial abilities and depresses verbal abilities, and growth hormones do not affect intelligence (Nyborg *et al.* 2001; under revision).

With respect to males, we know that *g* is linearly and positively related to job status and income (Nyborg & Jensen 2001; see also Chapter 15 in this volume). Further analyses of a large sample of 4,000 + males suggest that plasma *t* is inversely related to these outcome variables, and that physical dominance and violence in interpersonal situations is related to high plasma *t*, whereas formal dominance, educational level and IQ is related to low *t* in A1 males (Nyborg, in press).

Obviously, this chapter is not the place for a more detailed elaboration of the host of modifying variables that come into play in the tangled webs of basically unexplored hormonally, genetically and environmentally based molecular, anatomical and functional interactions. The interested readers may consult Nyborg (1994a, 1994b, 1997a, 1997b) for suggestions on how to test the models for these complex relationships. Moreover, quite sophisticated analytical tools have recently been developed, so as to make it possible to not only directly take effects of hormones on intelligence and personality into account, but also to incorporate and test the power of the many indirect effects in such highly complex nexus (Netter *et al.* 2000; Reuter *et al.*, submitted.)

In conclusion we can — essentially thanks to Arthur R. Jensen — now remain satisfied with already available solid operational definitions and practical measures of general intelligence *g*. The next move in the study of sex-related differences in *g* is, accordingly, to enlighten its biological side. We already have some promising lines of evidence and models, telling us how to proceed in the future. The ultimate task is to unravel the material basis of physical *g* ". . . whereby physiology will achieve the greatest of all its triumphs" (Spearman 1927). Undoubtedly, an important part of this accomplishment consists of carefully modeling interaction effects of genes, hormones and environmental factors, with brain and body differentiation, and to inspect how all this affects specific and general life achievement measures in a coherent, consistent and causally satisfying way, including the possibility of experimental control.

With all this out in the open, the contemporary crude and dichotomous sex categorization analyses would surely abate to multi-faceted gene-hormone-body-brain-behavior-environment covariant interaction analyses (Nyborg 1997a, 1997b). This would hopefully assist in illuminating the causes for why low *t* A1 males and high *t* E1 females tend to converge developmentally towards high *g*, an androgynous body type with minimal sexual differentiation, and similarities in personality, and why high *t* A5 males and high estradiol E5 females tend toward developing low *g*, early and pronounced sexual development by maximal differentiation between their male or female body characteristics.

I feel quite confident that the two grand old masters of general intelligence — Charles Spearman and Arthur Robert Jensen — would not be too unhappy with the current situation. We may now begin to combine the almost unlimited possibilities in modern biological and molecular sciences with behavioral genetics' increased precision in identifying environmental effects. By probing deep down into the physical foundation of human nature, it might be possible to finally understand the basically physical and chemical nature of *g*, and the mechanisms for how hormones may affect *g* in a sex-related way by modulating the expression of familiarly transmitted genes. The "very high end male *g*" hypothesis may help us to understand why a modest average sex difference in *g* may have such large implications at the highest steps of the educational, occupational and political power hierarchies. There may, in fact, be no scientifically acceptable alternative approaches.

References

Allik, J., Must, O., & Lynn, R. (1999). Sex differences in general intelligence in high school students: Some results from Estonia. *Personality and Individual Differences, 26,* 1137–1141.

Aluja-Fabregat, A., Colom, R., Abad, F., & Juan-Espinosa, M. (2000). Sex differences in general intelligence defined as g among young adolescents. *Personality and Individual Differences, 28* (4), 813–820.

Ankney, C. (1992). Sex differences in relative brain size: The mismeasure of woman, too? *Intelligence, 16,* 329–336.

Ankney, C. (1995). Sex differences in brain size and mental abilities: Comments on R. Lynn and D. Kimura. *Personality and Individual Differences, 18,* 423–424.

Benbow, C. P. (1992). Academic achievement in mathematics and science of students between ages 13 and 23: Are there differences among students in the top one% of mathematical ability? *Journal of Educational Psychology, 84,* 51–61.

Bollen, K. A. (1989). *Structural equation with latent variables.* New York: Wiley.

Brody, N. (1992). *Intelligence* (2nd ed.). San Diego, CA: Academic Press.

Brody, N. (in press). Construct validation of the Sternberg Triarchic Abilities Test (STAT): Comment and reanalysis. *Intelligence, 30.*

Carroll, J. B. (1993). *Human cognitive abilities: A survey of factor-analytic studies.* Cambridge, U.K.: Cambridge University Press.

Colom, R., García, L. F., Juan-Espinosa, M., & Abad, F. (2002). Null sex differences in general intelligence: Evidence from the WAIS-III. *Spanish Journal of Psychology, 5* (1), 29–35.

Colom, R., & García-López, O. (2002). Sex difference in fluid intelligence among high school graduates. *Personality and Individual Differences, 32,* 445–451.

Colum, R., Juan-Espinosa, M., Abad, F., & García, L. (2000). Negligible sex differences in general intelligence. *Intelligence, 28* (1), 57–68.

Court, J. H. (1983). Sex differences in performance on Raven's Progressive Matrices: A review. *Alberta Journal of Educational Research, 29,* 54–74.

Feingold, A. (1992). Sex differences in variability in intellectual abilities: A new look at an old controversy. *Review of Educational Research, 62,* 61–84.

Gardner, H. (1983). *Frames of mind.* New York: Basic Books.

Gardner, H. (1993). *Creating minds.* New York: Basic Books.

Goleman, D. (1995). *Emotional intelligence.* New York: Bantam.

Gordon, R. A. (1997). Everyday life as an intelligence test: Effects of intelligence and intelligence context. *Intelligence, 24,* 203–320.

Gottfredson, L. (1997). Why *g* matters: The complexity of everyday life. *Intelligence, 24,* 79–132.

Gottfredson, L. Dissecting practical intelligence theory: Its claims and evidence. *Intelligence, 30* (in press).

Gould, S. J. (1996). *The mismeasure of man.* New York: Norton & Company.

Gustavsson, J-E. (1992). The "Spearman hypothesis" is false. *Multivariate Behavioral Research, 27,* 265–267.

Halpern, D. F., & LaMay, M. L. (2000). The smarter sex: A critical review of sex differences in intelligence. *Educational Psychology Review, 12* (2), 229–246.

Hausman, P. (1999). On the rarity of mathematically and mechanically gifted females: A life history analysis. *Dissertation Abstracts International: Section B: The Sciences & Engineering, 60* (6-B), 3006.

Herrnstein, R. J., & Murray, C. (1994). *The bell curve: Intelligence and class structure in American life.* New York: The Free Press.

Hoyenga, K. B., & Hoyenga, K. T. (1979). *The question of sex differences. Psychological, cultural, and biological issues.* Boston, MA: Little, Brown and Company.

Hoyenga, K. B., & Hoyenga, K. T. (1993). *Gender-related differences.* Boston, MA: Allyn and Bacon.

Irwing, P., Cammock, T., & Lynn, R. (2001). Some evidence for the existence of a general factor of semantic memory and its components. *Personality and Individual Differences, 30,* 857–871.

Jensen, A. R. (1975). A theoretical note on sex-linkage and race differences in spatial ability. *Behavior Genetics, 5,* 151–164.

Jensen, A. R. (1978). Sex linkage and race differences in spatial ability: A reply. *Behavioral Genetics, 8,* 213–217.

Jensen, A. R. (1980). *Bias in mental testing.* New York: Free Press.

Jensen, A. R. (1987). Psychometric *g* as a focus of concerted research effort. *Intelligence, 11,* 193–198.

Jensen, A. R. (1988). Sex differences in arithmetic computation and reasoning in prepubertal boys and girls. *Behavioral and Brain Sciences, 11,* 198–199.

Jensen, A. R. (1993). Psychometric *g* and achievement. In: B. R. Gifford (Ed.), *Policy perspectives on educational testing* (pp. 117–227). Boston: Kluwer Academic Publishers.

Jensen, A. R. (1994a). Phlogiston, animal magnetism, and intelligence. In: D. K. Detterman (Ed.), *Current topics in human intelligence* (Vol. 4), *Theories of intelligence* (pp. 257–284). Norwood, NJ: Ablex.

Jensen, A. R. (1994b). Psychometric g related to differences in head size. *Personality and Individual Differences, 17,* 597–606.

Jensen, A. R. (1998). *The g factor: The science of mental ability.* Westport, CT: Praeger.

Jensen, A. R., & Johnson, F. W. (1994). Race and sex differences in head size and IQ. *Intelligence, 18,* 309–333.

Jensen, A. R., & Reinolds, C. R. (1983). Sex differences on the WISC-R. *Personality and Individual Differences, 4*, 223–226.

Jensen, A. R., & Weng, L-J. (1994). What is a good *g*? *Intelligence, 18*, 231–258.

Jöreskog, K. G., & Sörbom, D. (1993). *LISREL 8: User's reference guide.* Chicago, IL: Scientific Software International.

Kline, P. (1991). Sternberg's components: Non-contingent concepts. *Personality and Individual Differences, 12*, 873–876.

Lubinski, D., Benbow, C. P., & Morelock. M. J. (2000). Gender differences in engineering and the physical sciences among the gifted: An inorganic-organic distinction. In: K. A. Heller, F. J. Monks, R. J. Sternberg, & R. F. Subotnik (Eds), *International handbook for research on giftedness and talent* (2nd ed., pp. 627–641). Oxford, U.K.: Pergamon Press.

Lynn, R. (1994). Sex differences in intelligence and brain size: A paradox resolved. *Personality and Individual Differences, 17*, 257–271.

Lynn, R. (1997). Sex differences in intelligence: Data from a Scottish standardization of the WAIS-R. *Personality and Individual Differences, 24* (2), 289–290.

Lynn, R. (1999). Sex difference in intelligence and brain size: A developmental theory. *Intelligence, 27* (1), 1–12.

Lynn, R. (2001). *The science of human diversity: A history of the Pioneer Fund.* New York: University Press of America.

Lynn, R., Irwing, P., & Cammock, T. (2002). Sex differences in general knowledge. *Intelligence, 30* (1), 27–39.

Maccoby, E. E. (1966). Sex differences in intellectual functioning. In: E. E. Maccoby (Ed.), *The development of sex differences.* Stanford, CA: Stanford University Press.

Mackintosh. N. J. (1996). Sex differences and IQ. *Journal of Biosocial Science, 28*, 559–572.

Messick, S. (1992). Multiple intelligences or multilevel intelligence? Selective emphasis on distinctive properties of hierarchy: On Gardner's Frames of Mind and Sternberg's Beyond IQ in the context of theory and research on the structure of human abilities. *Psychological Inquiry, 3*, 365–384.

Neisser, U., Boodoo, G., Bouchard, T., Boykin, A., Brody, N., Ceci, S., Halpern, D., Loehlin, J., Perloff, R., Sternberg, R., & Urbina, S. (1996). Intelligence: Knowns and unknowns. *American Psychologist, 51*, 77–101.

Netter, P., Toll, C., Rohrmann, S., Hennig, J., & Nyborg, H. (2000). Configural frequency analysis of factors associated with testosterone levels in Vietnam veterans. *Psychologische Beiträge,* (Band 42), 504–514.

Nyborg, H. (1984). Performance and intelligence in hormonally-different groups. In: G. Vries, J. Bruin, H. Uylings, & M. Corner (Eds), *Sex differences in the brain. Progress in Brain Research* (pp. 491–508). Amsterdam: Elsevier Biomedical Press.

Nyborg, H. (1990). Sex hormones, brain development, and spatio-perceptual strategies in Turner's syndrome. In: D. Berch, & B. Bender (Eds), *Sex chromosome abnormalities and human behavior: Psychological studies.* Boulder, CO: Westview Press.

Nyborg, H. (1994a). *Hormones, sex, and society: The science of physiology.* Westport, CT: Praeger.

Nyborg, H. (1994b). The neuropsychology of sex-related differences in brain and specific abilities: Hormones, developmental dynamics, and new paradigm. In: P. A. Vernon (Ed.), *The neuropsychology of individual differences* (pp. 59–113). San Diego: Academic Press.

Nyborg, H. (1997a). Molecular man in a molecular world: Applied physiology. *Psyche & Logos, 18* (2), 457–474.

Nyborg, H. (1997b). Personality, psychology, and the molecular wave: Covariation of genes with hormones, experience, and traits. In: J. Bermudez, B. De Raad, A. M. Perez, A. Sanchez-Elvira,

& G. L. van Heck (Eds), *Volume of Personality Psychology in Europe* (Chapter 16, pp. 159–173). Tilburg, The Netherlands: Tilburg University Press.

Nyborg, H. (2001). Early sex differences in general and specific intelligence: Pitting biological against chronological age. Paper presented at the Second Annual Conference for Intelligence Research (ISIR). Cleveland, OH, December 6–8th.

Nyborg, H. (2002). IQ and *g*: The art of uncovering the sex difference in general intelligence. Paper presented at the Third Annual Conference for Intelligence Research (ISIR). Vanderbilt University, Nashville, TN, December 5–7th (p. 37)

Nyborg, H. (2003). Sex-related differences in general intelligence, g, and group factors: A representative hierarchical orthogonal Schmid-Leiman rotation type factor analytic study (submitted).

Nyborg, H. (in press). Multivariate modeling of testosterone-dominance associations. *Behavior and Brain Sciences*.

Nyborg, H. *The Jutland School Project: A 25 year cohort-sequential study* (unpublished data)

Nyborg, H., & Jensen, A. R. (2000). Black-white differences on various psychometric tests: Spearman's hypothesis tested on American armed services veterans. *Personality and Individual Differences, 28*, 593–599.

Nyborg, H., & Jensen, A. R. (2001). Occupation and income related to psychometric *g*. *Intelligence, 29* (1), 45–55.

Nyborg, H., & Nielsen, J. (1981). Sex hormone treatment and spatial ability in women with Turner's syndrome. In: W. Schmid, & J. Nielsen (Eds), *Human behavior and genetics* (pp. 167–182). Amsterdam: Elsevier/North-Holland Biomedical Press.

Nyborg, H., Nielsen, J., Naeraa, R., & Kastrup, K. (2001). *Estrogen and androgen treatment affect the development of general and specific intelligence differently in young girls with Turner's syndrome*. Paper presented at the ISIR meeting, Cleveland, Ohio, December 4–7th.

Nyborg, H., Nielsen, J., Naeraa, R., & Kastrup, K. (under revision). Estrogen and androgen, but not growth hormone, treatment affect the development of general and specific intelligence differently in young girls with Turner's syndrome.

Pakkenberg, B., & Gundersen, H. J. (1997). Neocortical neurone number in humans: Effects of age and sex. *Journal of Comparative Neurology, 384*, 312–320.

Reuter, M., Netter, P., Hennig, J., Mohiyeddini, C., & Nyborg, H. (2003). Test of Nyborg's General Trait Covariance (GTC) model for hormonally guided development by means of structural equation modeling. *European Journal of Personality* (in press).

Rushton, J. P. (1992). Cranial capacity related to sex, rank and race in a stratified sample of 6,325 military personnel. *Intelligence, 16*, 401–413.

Rushton, J. P., & Ankney C. D. (1996). Brain size and cognitive ability: Correlations with age, sex, social class, and race. *Psychonomic Bulletin and Review, 3*, 21–36.

Schmid, J., & Leiman, J. M. (1957). The development of hierarchical factor solutions. *Psychometrika, 22*, 53–61.

Segerstråle, U. (2000). *Defenders of the truth: The battle for science in the sociobiology debate and beyond*. Oxford: Oxford University Press.

Shea, D. L., Lubinski, D., & Benbow, C. P. (in press). Importance of assessing spatial ability in intellectually talented young adolescents: A 20-year longitudinal study. *Journal of Educational Psychology*.

Spearman, C. (1904). General intelligence, objectively determined and measured. *American Journal of Psychology, 15*, 201–293.

Spearman, C. (1923). *The nature of "intelligence" and the principles of cognition*. London: Macmillan.

Spearman, C. (1927). *The abilities of man: Their nature and measurement*. New York: Macmillan.

Spearman, C., & Jones, L. W. (1950). *Human ability: A continuation of The abilities of man*. London: Macmillan.

Sternberg, R. J. (1988). *The triarchic mind: A new theory of intelligence*. New York. Viking Press.

Sternberg, R. J., & Detterman, D. K. (1986). *What is intelligence? Contemporary viewpoints on its nature and definition*. Norwood, NH: Ablex.

The Editors (1921). Intelligence and its measurement: A symposium. *Journal of Educational Psychology, 12*, 123–147, 195–216, 271–275.

Turner, H. (1938). A syndrome of infantilism, congenital webbed neck, and cubitus valgus. *Endocrinology, 23*, 566–574.

Wolman, B. B. (Ed.) (1985). *Handbook of intelligence: Theories, measurements, and applications*. New York: Wiley.

Part IV

The *g* Nexus

Part IV

Part IV — Introduction

Arthur Jensen wrote in 1998 in his major opus — The g factor: "The g factor derives its broad significance from the fact that it is causally related to many real-life conditions, both personal and social. These relationships form a complex correlational network, or nexus, in which g is a major node. The totality of real-world variables composing the g nexus is not yet known, but a number of educationally, socially, and economically critical elements in the nexus have already been identified and are the subject of ongoing research". He further wrote that it seems likely that "... g acts only as a threshold variable that specifies the essential minimum level required for different kinds of achievement. Other, non-g special abilities and talents, along with certain personality factors, such as zeal, conscientiousness and persistence of effort, are also critical determinants of educational and vocational success" ... "Future g research will extend our knowledge in two directions. In the horizontal direction, it will identify new nodes in the g nexus, by studying the implications for future demographic trends, employment demands and strategies for aiding economically developing countries. Research in the vertical direction will seek to discover the origins of g in terms of evolutionary biology and the causes of individual differences in terms of the neurophysiology of the brain (pp. 544–545).

Research in the vertical direction was presented in Part II. Part IV proceeds in the horizontal direction by addressing some of the critical elements, such as genius and exceptional achievement, mental retardation, the role of g in training, education, real life as a test for g in the sociological work realm, and crime and delinquency.

Dean Keith Simonton thus notes in Chapter 11 that the concept of genius is intimately related with concepts of intelligence, but also that genius relates to other unusual gifts that sets the bearer well apart from the average person. In fact, Simonton says, Jensen himself sees genius as far more rich and complex than the concept of general intelligence might imply. He accordingly takes Jensen's view as point of departure, even if this in certain places leads to definite disagreements. For example, Simonton finds Jensen's list of components in his tri-dimensional theory controversial and too short. In addition to discussing the multidimensionality of genius, Simonton also comments critically on genius as multiplicative and on aspects related to productivity. In section five he defends in some detail his own "chance-configuration theory" against Jensen's critique, and finds that it depends on a semantic misunderstanding. Simonton then regrets that Jensen could not possibly have read his *Origins of Genius* book that came years after Jensen's critique of his theory, and further that even his own 1999c work needs modification in terms of Huber's 1998a analysis. Things are moving fast in this area. Simonton then goes on to suggest that Jensen and he may nevertheless meet in considering genius as a result of multidimensional and multiplicative processes in terms of David Lykken's (1982) concept of emergenesis. It may be more doubtful whether agreement can be obtained between Simonton and Jensen with respect to the applicability of Gardner's psychometrically rather poorly defined multiple intelligences, instead of Spearman's operationally defined general intelligence measure and differentiation theory. Simonton concludes Chapter 11 by stating that he has mostly qualified and elaborated Jensen's position, but has also pointed to a few places where he profoundly disagrees with Jensen. Both agree, however, that exceptional g is not the same as genius.

In Chapter 12 Herman Spitz deals with the relationship between mental retardation and g. The evidence thus suggests that g is weak in low IQ groups, compared with the strength of g in groups of higher IQ. Low IQ groups also have fewer specific strengths; that is, they must depend on what g they have to deal with a variety of tasks, not just tasks that are, for the general population, highly g-loaded. Spitz suggests that many more tasks are g-loaded for the low IQ groups, whereas the higher IQ groups have not only a more potent g but, in addition, many more specific abilities that are not dependent on g.

Chapter 13 by Malcolm Ree, Thomas Carretta and Mark Green presents the wide-ranging literature examining relations between general cognitive ability, g, and an early part of occupational performance, training. The authors begin with an explication of a common problem in the examination of human characteristics — confusing constructs and methods. They then review theories about the configuration (structure) of ability and evidence regarding the near identity of factor structure for sex and ethnic groups. Next, the concepts of specific abilities, non-cognitive characteristics and knowledge, and their theoretical relations to training performance are introduced. Then the predictive validity of g for training is examined, as is the incremental validity of specific cognitive abilities, job knowledge, and personality. Next, path models are reviewed that document studies examining causal relations among g, job knowledge and training performance. They then briefly present findings on differential validity and predictive bias. The chapter concludes with an examination of the value of g as a predictor of organizational effectiveness.

Rather than providing a complete review of the relations between education and general intelligence g, Philip Ackerman and David Lohman attempt in Chapter 14 to highlight some of the central conceptual issues associated with evaluating the relationship between education and intelligence. They report on broad areas of research findings in the field, and attempt to integrate the literature to identify what is known and what fundamental questions remain for future study.

Linda Gottfredson points out in Chapter 15 that Jensen has drawn attention to the fact that tests and tasks differ systematically in g loading, that is, in the degree to which they call forth general intelligence g. This suggests a way to better understand the impact of differences in g in daily life: examine everyday tasks and broad life outcomes for their psychometric properties, including their g loadedness. That is, in what ways does life mimic or depart from a standardized intelligence test? The value of six specific questions is illustrated by applying them to the literature on job performance and occupational attainment: (1) What is the distribution, by *g* loading, of the many "subtests" we take in life's extensive mental test battery?; (2) To what extent do we take common vs. different "subtests" in life?; (3) To what extent do our differences in *g* determine which subtests we take?; (4) To what extent are life's tests standardized?; (5) Do many weakly *g*-loaded activities cumulate to produce highly *g*-loaded life outcomes?; and (6), How do a society's members (its "test takers") create and reshape the mental test battery that society "administers" to current and new generations? Applying the life-as-a-mental-test-battery analogy to the world of work yields predictions about where and why higher *g* will be an advantage elsewhere in life. The analogy also explains why even big effects can be hard to discern in the psychometrically messy real world.

Chapter 16 by Lee Ellis and Tony Walsh provides a review of the worldwide literature on crime, delinquency, and its relation to intelligence. They begin with the historically troubled story of an inverse relationship between intelligence and delinquent and criminal behavior, and argue that even today criminologists tend to downplay the role of intelligence. They then present, in the form of two tables, an updated review of intelligence-criminality relationships, one for intelligence in general, the other for intellectual imbalances among linguistic and non-linguistic components. As expected, the inverse IQ-crime and the intellectually imbalanced-crime relationships could be confirmed, usually with the linguistic component being the weaker. A number of social explanations for the IQ-criminality relationships are then rejected, and it is regretted that many textbooks on criminology leave students with the impression that intelligence has little or no importance in the matter. The authors then draw attention to moral maturation theory, hemispheric functioning theory, and the role of evolutionary forces in explaining the observations, supplemented by the genetic influence hypothesis.

Chapter 11

Genius and *g*: Intelligence and Exceptional Achievement

Dean Keith Simonton

1. Introduction

The concept of genius is intimately connected with the concept of intelligence. This connection is immediately evident in the most common definitions of genius found in the dictionary. In the *American Heritage Electronic Dictionary* (1992), for example, genius is defined as "extraordinary intellectual and creative power", "a person of extraordinary intellect and talent", "a person who has an exceptionally high intelligence quotient, typically above 140". These definitions give the primary meanings, and only later do we encounter indications that genius has meanings not explicitly associated with general intelligence. These include "a strong natural talent, aptitude, or inclination", "the prevailing spirit or distinctive character, as of a place, a person, or an era", "a tutelary deity or guardian spirit of a person or place" (in Roman mythology), "a person who has great influence over another", and "a jinni in Moslem mythology". The last few definitions, however remote from popular usage today, are much closer to the word's etymology (Murray 1989). In Roman mythology, each individual was born with a guardian spirit who watched out for the person's fate and distinctive individuality. With time, the term was taken to indicate the person's special talents or aptitudes. Although in the beginning everybody could be said to "have a genius", at least in the sense of possessing a unique capacity, the term eventually began to be confined to those whose gifts set them well apart from the average. These unusual gifts took the form of concrete achievements, such as noteworthy acts of creativity and leadership. Only much later did the concept of genius become so strongly associated with intelligence that the original definitions of genius moved into secondary and tertiary positions in the dictionary.

In this chapter I am expected to discuss the relation between genius and general intelligence, or what is often referred to as "Spearman's *g*" (Spearman 1927). However, because this chapter is also part of a tribute to Arthur Jensen, I must broaden the scope of the discussion. That necessity ensues from the fact that Jensen himself held a

The Scientific Study of General Intelligence: Tribute to Arthur R. Jensen
Copyright © 2003 by Elsevier Science Ltd.
All rights of reproduction in any form reserved.
ISBN: 0-08-043793-1

conception of genius that was far more rich and complex than the concept of general intelligence might imply. This is evident in his 1996 essay on "Giftedness and Genius: Crucial Differences" that he contributed to the volume on *Intellectual Talent: Psychometric and Social Issues* that was edited by Camilla Benbow & David Lubinski (1996). Therefore, I would like to use this essay as the basis for discussing Jensen's views. Even though I agree with him on most major issues, in certain places definite disagreements emerge.[1]

2. Genius as Multidimensional

Jensen (1996) at once declares that genius entails much more than just general intelligence. Instead, genius constitutes a multidimensional characteristic that included behavioral, motivational and dispositional attributes along with those more intellectual. Jensen's view can be considered a major departure from the position taken by Lewis Terman (1917, 1925), who tended to equate the two. Indeed, Terman can be considered the person underlying the dictionary's specification of IQ 140 as the "cutoff" for an individual attaining genius status. Jensen's position also stands in stark opposition to the many groups of self-proclaimed geniuses who use performance on tests of general intelligence as criteria for membership. The best known of these organizations is Mensa (Serebriakoff 1985).[2]

Despite these contrary viewpoints, many other researchers share Jensen's belief in the multidimensionality of genius, as he would be the first to admit. In fact, Jensen's essay was strongly influenced by Hans Eysenck's (1995) book *Genius: The Natural History of Creativity*, which he said leaves "little of potential scientific value that can be added to the subject at present, pending new empirical evidence" (p. 393). Actually, the notion of genius as multidimensional can be said to be well more than a century old. In particular, this idea goes back to Francis Galton, a pioneer totally ignored in Jensen's essay. Galton's (1869) *Hereditary Genius* defined genius in terms of exceptional "natural ability", but he made it very clear that this was not just intelligence: "by natural ability, I mean those qualities of intellect and disposition, which urge and qualify a man

---

[1] In line with Jensen's (1996) essay, this chapter confines itself to the discussion of genius domains that require creativity. Yet genius can manifest itself in other domains of achievement, most notably in great leaders. However, the connection between *g* and genius is probably far more complex in leadership than it is for creativity (Simonton 1995). For example, excessive general intelligence can undermine the effectiveness of a leader in a manner that has no counterpart in creative genius (Simonton 1985a). I must also note that Jensen's (1998) book devotes only a small amount of space to genius, and therefore Jensen's (1996) chapter still represents his most comprehensive treatment of this subject.

[2] My rejection of the IQ definition of genius cannot be dismissed as the "sour grapes" gesture of someone who has not done well on psychometric measures of general intelligence. In fact, my own IQ lies almost exactly midway between the requirement for Mensa membership (two standard deviations above the population average) and the stipulation for membership in the Four Sigma Society (self explanatory). Furthermore, as Jensen (1996) mentioned in his essay, I found that attending a Mensa meeting was seldom an inspiring experience. Some years ago there was a Dilbert cartoon in which the engineer protagonist, having just joined the group, learns that the president of the local chapter is the same guy who picks up his trash off the curb each week.

to perform acts that lead to reputation. I do not mean capacity without zeal, nor zeal without capacity, nor even a combination of both of them, without an adequate power of doing a great deal of very laborious work" (Galton 1892/1972: 77). Galton later refers to this as "the concrete triple event, of ability combined with zeal and with capacity for hard labour" (Galton 1892/1972: 78). Hence, Galton can be said to have advocated a tridimensional theory of genius.

Interestingly, Jensen (1996) also put forward a tridimensional theory. That is, genius consists of the following three components:

(1) *High Ability* — This component is general intelligence which Jensen conceived in terms of individual differences in the "efficiency of information processing" (also see Jensen 1998). Hence, in his view, *g* constitutes one essential ingredient of genius.

(2) *High Productivity* — By this misleading term Jensen (1996) meant "endogenous cortical stimulation", or "mental energy" (but not in Spearman's usage of this term). This component can be said to combine Galton's (1869) requisites of "zeal" and "capacity for hard labour".

(3) *High Creativity* — Following closely Eysenck's (1995) theory of creative genius, this component is called "trait psychoticism" in Jensen's (1996) scheme. The construct would be thus assessed by the psychoticism scale of Eysenck's Personality Questionnaire or some functional equivalent (see, e.g. Rushton 1990).

This list might be criticized on various grounds. One obvious criticism is that the terms are somewhat confusing. A second, and more critical complaint, is that the list is not long enough. Personality researchers have built up a large inventory of traits that appear correlated with creative genius (Simonton 1999a). Jensen (1996) was aware of this fact, but suggested that these diverse traits may be subordinate or auxiliary to the three core components, especially the last two. Furthermore, some psychologists might question the specific components selected for inclusion. To be sure, the second component looks pretty secure. If the research on genius agrees on anything, it is certainly the fact that geniuses display exceptional drive, persistence and effort (e.g. Cox 1926; Roe 1953). Yet the first and third components are more controversial.

In the case of the third component, many humanistic psychologists attempted to link creativity with mental health (e.g. Maslow 1959; May 1975; Rogers 1954), an association that has continuing echoes in the recent Positive Psychology movement (Simonton 2000). In defense of Jensen's (1996) position, however, it is easy to cite ample empirical and theoretical support (e.g. Barron 1963; Eysenck 1995; Ludwig 1995). It is not a matter that geniuses are truly "mad", unlike what Lombroso (1891) claimed, but rather it is the case that certain cognitive and dispositional traits associated with psychopathology tend to support the creative thought process (Eysenck 1995; Simonton 1999b).

Hence, the most problematic component may actually be the first — the dependence of genius on *g* or general intelligence. Howard Gardner (1983), for instance, identified what he considered to be seven distinct types of intelligence, each of which he later linked with a specific type of genius (Gardner 1993). More recently, Gardner (1998) has even expanded the list to encompass 10 intelligences. To resolve this controversy, we need a scientific concept of what exactly is encompassed by "general intelligence".

I will return to this question later in this chapter. But another issue needs more urgent attention.

3. Genius as Multiplicative

Let us assume that Jensen's (1996) tridimensional model is correct. The next question is how the three components are combined to create genius. On this point Jensen was quite emphatic: "My primary thesis is that the emergence of genius is best described using a multiplicative model" (p. 393). This view he expressed by the formula

$$\text{Genius} = \text{High Ability} \times \text{High Productivity} \times \text{High Creativity}$$

The argument on behalf of this formulation is that the distribution of genius appears to be highly skewed, whereas the components that make up genius may be normally distributed. That is, the distributions of general intelligence, mental energy and psychoticism are described by the bell curve, whereas the distribution of creative genius, like exceptional performance generally, is lognormal (Walberg et al. 1984).

This multiplicative model, like the multidimensionality concept, also has a long history. Although Jensen's (1996) essay does not contain Cyril Burt's name, Burt (1943) did propose a multiplicative model to explain the relation between ability and income. Even though ability is normally distributed (Burt 1963), income exhibits an extremely skewed "Pareto distribution" (Price 1963). Therefore, Burt assumed that the talent for making money was the joint function of two or more factors, the joint effect being multiplicative rather than additive. To illustrate, he provided a simple model consisting of just two components. These components were assumed to be measured on the same five-point ratio scale, including the zero point (i.e. 0, 1, 2, 3, 4). In addition, the scores on the two components were assumed to be distributed according to the binomial law, that is, the frequencies were set to be proportional to 1, 4, 6, 4, 1. In percentages, these proportions become 6.25, 25.0, 37.5, 25.0, and 6.25. This distribution is the discrete approximation to the continuous normal distribution. Burt then showed that the distribution of the product will not be symmetric even though the components are symmetrically distributed. In particular, rescaling the multiplicative score to the same five categories of the components, the percentages become 49.6, 36.0, 10.9, 3.1, and 0.4. Note that almost half of the cases receive the lowest possible multiplicative score, whereas fewer than 1% receive the highest possible score.

Several other investigators besides Burt (1943) and Jensen (1998) have also suggested that creative genius is a phenomenon involving the multiplicative combination of several distinct components (e.g. Lykken 1998; Shockley 1957; Walberg et al. 1984). Under such a model, general intelligence (g) has a somewhat ambivalent relation with genius. On the one hand, one cannot expect to display genius without a certain threshold level of intelligence (Simonton 1999d). The threshold that is often bandied about in the literature is a capacity comparable to an IQ of about 120 (e.g. Barron & Harrington 1981). Moreover, holding everything else constant, higher intellectual ability will be positively associated with higher levels of genius. Yet exceptional general intelligence will not automatically translate into genius when the various components are allowed to vary freely. According to Jensen's (1996) model, if an individual lacks High Productivity (mental energy) or High Creativity (psychoticism), then the product of the three components will be zero no matter how the person rates on High Ability (general intelligence). Hence, above-average *g* constitutes a necessary but not sufficient condition for genius. It may even be possible for someone with relatively mediocre general intelligence to exhibit more genius than someone else who is extremely brilliant, but is somewhat deficient in the other two components. For example, Catharine Cox (1926) observed with respect to her 301 geniuses that "high but not the highest intelligence, combined with the greatest degree of persistence, will achieve greater eminence than the highest degree of intelligence with somewhat less persistence" (p. 187).

4. Genius and Productivity

Earlier I noted that whatever it is that represents genius is not normally distributed in the population. On what basis can this statement be made? Once genius is divorced from intelligence, then the IQ test can no longer be used as even the most approximate indicator of genius. And, besides, the cross-sectional distributions are wrong. One solution is to adopt the definition favored by Galton (1869). He defined genius in terms of reputation, as gauged by "the opinion of contemporaries, revised by posterity . . . the reputation of a leader of opinion, of an originator, of a man to whom the world deliberately acknowledges itself largely indebted" (Galton 1892/1972: 77). James McKeen Cattell (1903) was the first to translate this concept into a workable operational definition. In fact, it was his measure that Cox (1926) used to establish a positive correlation between IQ and eminence (cf. Simonton 1976). Moreover, this type of assessment has excellent psychometric properties, including high reliability and stability (Simonton 1984b, 1998a, 1998b). In fact, it has been demonstrated that multiple indicators of genius by this criterion all load on a single general factor — what has been styled "Galton's G" (Simonton 1991c). Even more to the point, the distribution of reputation is extremely skewed, with a long upper tail (e.g. Martindale 1995; Zusne 1985).

Yet there are other ways of conceiving genius besides Galton's G (Albert 1992). The strongest single correlate of eminence is total lifetime output of contributions (Albert 1975; Dennis 1954a, 1954b; Simonton 1977b, 1991a, 1991b). It is on the basis of this alternative that Jensen (1996) spoke of the skewed distribution. To establish this latter fact, Jensen cited the Price Law (Price 1963). By this law, if *k* gives the total number of creators working in a given domain, then the square root of *k* gives the subset of creators who are responsible for *half* of all the creative products produced. This requires that the distribution be skewed right, with an extremely long upper tail. Total output has one conspicuous advantage over the reputational measure, namely that it is a purely behavioral measure. In that sense, it can be considered an objective rather than subjective indicator of genius.

Although Jensen (1996) got the skewed cross-sectional distribution right, he was led astray on one crucial matter: the relation between quantity and quality of output. He speculated that "high productivity and triviality are more frequently associated than low productivity and high importance", yielding a "scatter-diagram of the 'twisted pear' variety" (p. 402). If quantity is defined as total lifetime output regardless of impact and quality is defined as lifetime contributions that satisfy some standard — e.g. frequency of citation, performance, reprinting or showing — then the association is neatly described by the *equal-odds rule* (Simonton 1997). On the average, the more total output a creator produces, the more "hits" he or she can claim, but also the more "misses", the former growing in proportion to the latter. Hence, ratio of hits to total attempts does not systematically change as a function of total quantity of output (see, e.g. Davis 1987; Platz & Blakelock 1960; Simonton 1985b). This is precisely what would be expected if the functional relation between quantity and quality were roughly linear. That is, if total hits $H = cT$, where c is a positive constant indicating the "hit rate" and T is the total lifetime output, then $c = H/T$.[3] Of course, a stochastic error term should be added, because the association is not perfect. Typically, only about half of the variance is shared. This leaves considerable latitude for the emergence of so-called "perfectionists" and "mass producers", the former having more hits than their small output would predict, the latter having fewer hits than expected given their large output would predict. Yet there is no reason to believe that these departures represent taxonomically meaningful outliers.

What is more remarkable, this equal-odds rule applies not just across careers, but also within careers (Simonton 1988a, 1997). In other words, if a creator's career is divided into consecutive age periods, such as 5-year intervals, and the ratio of hits to total attempts calculated, that ratio fluctuates randomly across the career course (e.g. Simonton 1977a, 1985b, 1997). The hit rate neither increases nor decreases nor displays a curvilinear form. Hence, the number of hits generated in a particular career period is proportional to the total number of attempts during the same period. Put differently, age is irrelevant as a predictor of quality once adjustment is made for quantity (Over 1988, 1989). It is worth noting that this conspicuous longitudinal relation between quantity and quality was first demonstrated by Quételet (1835/1968), the statistician who first established the descriptive utility of the normal curve. Quételet's demonstration can be considered the first scientific study of creative genius published anywhere in the world.

I said that Jensen (1996) was misled because the equal-odds rule has powerful implications about how creativity operates in the genius.

5. Genius and Creativity

Jensen (1996) placed my 1988 book on *Scientific Genius* alongside Eysenck's (1995) *Genius* as the two "most promising efforts" toward a scientific treatment of genius as a

---

[3] If the hit rate decreases with lifetime output, then quality will be a negative quadratic function of quantity, whereas if the hit rate increases with lifetime output, then quality will be a positive quadratic function of quantity.

psychological phenomenon. Even so, the pleasure I received from this compliment was a bit diminished when I read his critique of the "chance-configuration theory" that I had presented in that book. Actually, Jensen's criticisms closely followed Eysenck's (1995) own, which were first expressed in a target article that appeared in a 1993 issue of *Psychological Inquiry*. As one of the commentators, I responded to Eysenck's (1993) complaints, showing that they largely stemmed from a misunderstanding of my theoretical claims (Simonton 1993). Jensen was evidently unaware of my 1993 comment when he wrote his 1996 article. In my defense, I would like to just say two things.

First, it seems to me that Jensen's (1996) objections to the "chance-configuration" theory represent nothing more than a semantic misunderstanding (Simonton 1999c). Although he argued that human beings cannot generate strictly random behavior (but see Miller 1997, for contrary view), the chance-configuration theory does not require that capacity to exist in the first place. Instead, the word "chance" closely follows the word's standard dictionary definition. According to the *American Heritage Electronic Dictionary* (1992), the noun "chance" can be "the unknown and unpredictable element in happenings that seems to have no assignable cause", "a force assumed to cause events that cannot be foreseen or controlled", "an accidental or unpredictable event", and "a risk or hazard; a gamble". As an adjective, chance can signify "caused by or ascribable to chance; unexpected, random, or casual". Among the idioms is the notion to "chance on" which means "to find or meet accidentally; happen upon", and "by chance" which means "without plan; accidentally". Its synonyms are random, causal, haphazard and desultory. Its etymology, interestingly enough, comes from the Latin word for "to fall", as in the English expression "let the chips fall where they may". Coin tosses and the casting of dices both entail the deliberate quest of a chance event by letting an object freely fall. A concept closely related to chance and luck is "random". By the same reference source, this means "having no specific pattern, purpose, or objective", "of or relating to the same or equal chances or probability of occurrence", and "without governing design, method, or purpose; unsystematically". These definitions are much more inclusive than the precise mathematical definitions that seem to have led Jensen (1996) and Eysenck (1995) astray.

Second, and most important, when Jensen wrote his 1996 essay he could not possibly have read my most recent book *Origins of Genius: Darwinian Perspectives on Creativity* (Simonton 1999c). This book basically continues where Simonton (1988b) and Eysenck (1995) left off, developing the "chance-configuration theory" into a comprehensive Darwinian theory of creative genius (also see Simonton 1999b). Chapter 1 begins by defining creativity and genius, and then discusses the nature of Darwinism, presenting its two major forms: Primary and secondary. Primary Darwinism is what emerged directly from Darwin's *Origin of Species*, and deals specifically with the evolution of biological forms through the differential reproduction of adaptive variants (whether through natural or sexual selection). Secondary Darwinism, in contrast, concerns those processes that operate in a fashion very much like those seen in primary Darwinism. Examples include, Darwinian theories of immunity, neurological development, operant conditioning, and, most notably, human creativity (Cziko 1995, 1998; Dennett 1995; Simonton 1999c). One critical issue addressed throughout the book is the interrelation between primary and secondary Darwinism. In particular, how can biological evolution support the emergence of a secondary Darwinian process like creative genius?

In great detail, Chapter 2 then treats the creative process in terms of a general Darwinian mechanism. The departure point is Donald T. Campbell's (1960) "blind-variation and selective-retention" model of creativity. Campbell's model is updated by linking it with: (a) introspective reports of creative geniuses (e.g. Hadamard 1945; Poincaré 1921); (b) laboratory experiments on problem solving (e.g. Finke *et al.* 1992; Rothenberg 1986); and (c) computer simulations of discovery and creativity (e.g. Boden 1991; Langley *et al.* 1987). In the latter category are the remarkable advances in computer science that are known as genetic algorithms and genetic programming (Goldberg 1989; Holland 1992; Koza 1992, 1994). These programs solve real problems through an explicitly Darwinian process. The chapter then closes with a discussion of the many objections that have been raised against this view of creative genius, including those voiced by Jensen (1996).

The remaining chapters extend the explanatory power of the Darwinian theory to encompass other aspects of creativity. In Chapter 3, the theory is extended to cover the creative personality, including individual differences in intelligence, cognitive style, motivation and psychopathology (e.g. Cox 1926; Guilford 1967; Ludwig 1995; Mednick 1962). Of course, strong links are forged between the theory and Eysenck's (1995) association of genius with psychoticism. Chapter 4 then directs the model's explanatory power toward creative development, including family background, educational experiences and career background (e.g. Galton 1874; Simonton 1984a; Sulloway 1996). Naturally, in this chapter I had to grapple with the nature-nurture issue, and proposed an integrated model from the Darwinian perspective. In Chapter 5 I scrutinized the creative product, devoting special attention to the characteristics of creative careers (e.g. Simonton 1988a, 1997), changes in aesthetic styles (Martindale 1990), and the phenomenon of multiple discovery and invention (e.g. Simonton 1979). The Darwinian implications of the equal-odds rule are here made explicit. Chapter 6 then contains a detailed treatment of creative genius in socially-defined groups, namely race, culture and gender. Here explanations based on primary Darwinism are replaced by explanations based on secondary Darwinism — especially sociocultural evolutionary theories. Chapter 7 then concludes the extensive documentation by arguing that secondary Darwinian theory holds the most promise for a comprehensive theory of creative genius.

Curiously, although *Origins of Genius* rendered obsolete Jensen's (1996) criticisms of the "chance-configuration theory", *Origins* is itself somewhat outdated. I say that because I was not able to incorporate the most recent research by John Huber (1998a, in press). This indicates that creativity operates as a random, Poisson process. In particular, the distribution of creative products across and within careers implies an underlying process where the chance of a "hit" is so minuscule that it can only be overcome by numerous trials. Furthermore, the parameter of the Poisson distribution ($\mu \approx 1$) is almost identical to the size I found in my earlier stochastic models of multiple discovery and invention (e.g. Simonton 1978, 1979, 1986). Translated into terms of the binomial distribution (which the Poisson approximates for low-likelihood events), this parameter suggests that the probability of a success may be, say, only 1 out of 100, and so it takes 100 trials for there to be any appreciable odds of success. As Alexander Bain (1855/1977) put it long ago, "the greatest practical inventions being so much dependent upon chance, the only hope of success is to multiply the chances by multiplying the experiments" (p. 597). The creativity may not be a random process, yet it certainly *acts* as if it were. This fact helps us appreciate why the only computer programs that successfully simulate human creativity — in the sense of producing something truly new and effective — always incorporate some kind of stochastic process, often in the form of the standard random number generator (Boden 1991).

6. Genius and Genes

I spent some time outlining the contents of my book for two reasons. First, and most obviously, I wish to defend my Darwinian theory of creativity against Jensen's (1996) criticisms. Second, and more subtly, the theory presented in that book presents a challenge to a premise that provides the *raison d'être* of Jensen's essay. Jensen proposed a multiplicative model because it explicates the highly skewed cross-sectional distribution of genius. The most notable geniuses stand way out at the extreme right-hand side of a very elongated upper tail. Yet according to the theory proposed in *Origins of Genius* (Simonton 1999a; see also Simonton 1997), the same skewed distribution can be obtained more simply, with only a single component process. If ideational variations are generated by a combinatorial process, then the number of available combinations does not increase linearly with the number of ideas undergoing permutation. On the contrary, as both Eysenck (1995) and Jensen (1996) observed, the supply of potential combinations grows "explosively". As a rough approximation, the inventory increases exponentially (Barsalou & Prinz 1997). That means that if the size of the initial stock of ideas is normally distributed in the population of creators operating within a given domain, then the supply of potential ideational variants will display a lognormal distribution (Simonton 1988a). This, too, is a highly skewed distribution with a long upper tail. Because the desired distribution can be obtained from a basic process intimately connected with the creativity, the supposition of a multidimensional and multiplicative process becomes superfluous. The latter is ruled out of court by the law of parsimony. Unless Jensen can come up with another reason for requiring that creative genius be multidimensional and multiplicative, there is no reason to go beyond the confines of the Darwinian model.

Fortunately for Jensen's thesis, such a justification exists. But it arrives from an unexpected quarter — behavioral genetics. I was somewhat surprised to see how little attention Jensen (1996) devoted to this subject, especially given how much time Eysenck (1995) spent on the genetics of genius. This surprise was all the more pronounced because modern behavioral genetics has produced a concept that suggests that creative genius may result from a multidimensional and multiplicative process. The concept is that of *emergenesis*, first suggested by David Lykken in 1982 and later developed in collaboration with his colleagues at the University of Minnesota (Lykken *et al.* 1992). Not only has Lykken (1998) specifically treated creative genius as an emergenic phenomenon, but also I have greatly elaborated the concept in terms of a formal developmental model, a model that applies to all forms of exceptional achievement (Simonton 1999d). The central feature of this model is the following multidimensional, multiplicative and epigenetic equation:

$$P_i(t) = \prod_{j=1}^{k} C_{ij}(t)^{w_j} \tag{1}$$

Here the amount of potential talent at chronological age $P(t)$ is expressed as a multiplicative function of the several components (the Cs, weighted by their corresponding ws), which are themselves functions of age (each with their own developmental growth trajectory).

Besides explaining the distinctive cross-sectional distribution of creativity, leadership, and performance (athletic and musical), this model can account for such epigenetic quirks as talent "burnout" and "late bloomers". One distinctive feature of emergenesis is that it predicts that genius, unlike giftedness, should not exhibit conspicuous familial inheritance — contrary to what Galton (1869) thought he had demonstrated. Because the genetics of genius is multiplicative rather than additive, only monozygotic twins can display family resemblance in creativity and other complex talents. A multiplicative model requires that all of the required genetic traits be inherited as a complete batch rather than piecemeal. I have reviewed evidence showing that this is indeed the case (Simonton 1999d; see, e.g. Waller *et al.* 1993).

Needless to say, among the components entering the multiplicative composite of inherited traits would probably be those listed in Jensen's (1996) multiplicative formula. Indeed, all of the components he included have substantial heritability coefficients, general intelligence featuring the highest heritability of them all (Jensen 1998).

7. Genius and Giftedness

But what is this general intelligence that is inherited? This question was raised at the beginning of this chapter, and it is now necessary that it be answered. As already noted, Jensen (1996) conceived g in terms of information-processing efficiency (also see Jensen 1992, 1998). I tend to view general intelligence in much the same way, though I am prone to conceive the construct in more explicitly Darwinian terms. That is, I assume that people vary in their latent capacity to adapt to their environment. This latent capacity is founded on the neural plasticity so prominent in *Homo sapiens*, and manifests itself in the speed with which an individual can master the knowledge and skills necessary for success in the local environment (e.g. home, school, the workplace, the subculture and society at large). There is absolutely nothing novel about this conception, for it harks back to Francis Galton (1869) and the Functionalist School of psychology.

More specifically, this notion of general intelligence formed the basis of Lewis Terman's (1925) concept of the intelligence quotient, or IQ. Those persons with a higher than normal innate intelligence would acquire mastery of their environment sooner than those with lower than normal innate capacity. In terms of Binet's original tests, the inherited ability would be reflected in how mental age compares with chronological age. Insofar as the Stanford-Binet tests assess adaptation to the school environment, it made perfectly good sense to use performance on these tests as criteria of "giftedness", even "genius". At least the IQ would identify those children who managed to learn the knowledge and skills necessary for success in school. However, the school environment does not represent all possible environments to which a child may have to adapt. Accordingly, Terman's (1925) manner of identifying intellectually gifted children could not help but produce many false negatives — children who were born with exceptional adaptive capacity but who applied that capacity to domains not strongly emphasized in school. For this reason, most of the so-called "Termites" attained their adulthood successes in areas most strongly associated with academic performance, such as science, engineering, medicine, law and teaching. For much the same cause, members of ethnic minorities were underrepresented in Terman's sample.

Happily, this limitation did not apply to the 301 geniuses who made up the Cox (1926) sample. It is often overlooked that many of those with superlative "IQs" would probably have done extremely poorly on the Stanford-Binet Intelligence Test. That discrepancy results from the fact that the IQ was largely defined in terms of how fast the subjects mastered the essential materials of their chosen domain of achievement. For instance, Mozart obtained his stellar IQ because he exhibited phenomenal precocity as a musician and composer — skills and knowledge that have no representation on any standard IQ test. To be sure, someone like J. S. Mill would probably have scored very high on the Stanford Binet. After all, his impressive IQ estimate was based on his precocious mastery of the kinds of things most strongly related to the content of intelligence tests. Nevertheless, what he mastered so quickly was also closely related to the expertise he would need for his adulthood career as thinker and writer.

It is often claimed that the development of creative genius must comply with the "10-year rule" (Ericsson 1996; Hayes 1989). This rule holds that no one can attain world-class status as a creator without first devoting a decade to the acquisition of the domain-relevant skills and knowledge. During this period, the future creator must devote a considerable amount of time and effort to what is termed *deliberate practice* (Ericsson *et al.* 1993). Unfortunately, this 10-year rule is almost invariably applied without due regard for individual differences (Simonton 1999d). If individuals vary in their intellectual capacity to adapt to their environments, they should certainly exhibit variation in the acquisition of domain-relevant expertise. This variation has been empirically demonstrated (e.g. Simonton 1991b, 1992, in press). Although expertise acquisition is always a time-consuming process, some do it in much less than 10 years, whereas others take longer than 10 years.

These individual differences in time to domain mastery have important implications regarding the relationship between intellectual giftedness and genius. The running head for Jensen (1996) basically summarizes a theme running throughout his chapter, namely "Giftedness & Genius". Jensen maintained that high general intelligence was a necessary but not sufficient basis for genius. Yet this point requires elaboration with respect to expertise acquisition. It is conceivable that the greater the magnitude of genius a creator displays, the higher should be his or her innate adaptive capacity. However, this greater innate adaptive power will not necessarily be manifested as extraordinary performance on IQ tests. Instead, it will be demonstrated in how fast the person obtains domain mastery.

This association has also been empirically established. Cox (1926) herself showed that the higher the magnitude of eminence attained by her geniuses, the higher was their estimated IQ (also see Simonton 1976; Walberg *et al.* 1978). Yet as already noted, the latter is best interpreted as a gauge of the youth's precocity in acquiring the tools and information needed for creativity. The same point was demonstrated in a different way in a study of 120 classical composers (Simonton 1991b). For each composer was assessed on the time interval between the age that they first began music lessons and the age that they first began composition. The shorter that "apprenticeship" period, the greater the degree of genius displayed, where the latter was measured in three distinct ways: maximum output rate, total lifetime output, and degree of eminence as a composer. Comparable results have been found in other domains of creativity, such as the sciences (e.g. Raskin 1936; Simonton 1991a, 1992).

In one crucial respect, this interpretation of genetically endowed general intelligence comes closer to Gardner's (1983, 1993) ideas about multiple intelligences than Jensen's (1996) ideas about Spearman's *g*. As creative talent develops over time, increasingly more of the general capacity of intellectual growth becomes channeled into domain-specific environments. This is especially true for creative domains in which specialization often comes relatively early, as happens in music and the visual arts. As a consequence, relatively little of the intellect will be allotted to acquiring the kind of knowledge and skills assessed by tests that purport to assess truly general intelligence. Instead, the creator's intelligence will become more specialized around the acquisition of a particular expertise. The kind of *g* measured by the generic tests will have correspondingly attenuated validity. There will be more than one kind of "intelligence", and some intelligences will have minimal overlap with *g*.

The foregoing argument raises the additional question about why a child or adolescent selects one particular developmental path in intellectual development. Why become an artist rather than a scientist, or a choreographer rather than an architect? Part of the answer may stem from innate talents, which can be conceived as the inborn capacity to master certain domains at an accelerated pace. In other words, expertise acquisition may "come easily" in some areas, but much less so in others (Simonton 1999d; Winner 1996). Another factor may be environmental influences, such as the encouragement of parents and teachers (Bloom 1985; Howe 1999). Among these influences might be a host of truly serendipitous events that deflect intellectual development in one arbitrary direction rather than another (Bandura 1982; Simonton 1999c). As Samuel Johnson (1781) said, "the true Genius is a mind of large general powers, accidentally determined to some particular direction" (p. 5).

8. Genius and *g*

This chapter was devoted to evaluating the ideas that Jensen (1996) presented in a chapter on the relation between genius and giftedness, where the latter was conceived largely in terms of *g*. I began by discussing Jensen's tridimensional multiplicative model of genius. Although this model is oversimplified, I believe it is basically correct postulating that genius is a product of many essential components, including factors that are more dispositional than intellectual. I then turned to his discussion of creative productivity, and pointed out that the relation between quantity and quality did not operate the way he suggested. In fact, the connection between quantity and quality is governed by the equal-odds rule, a rule that applies both across and within creative careers. This rule then leads to a discussion of creative genius. Although Jensen (1996) had criticized my earlier "chance-configuration theory", I point out that this theory has been developed into a far more comprehensive Darwinian theory of creativity. One repercussion of the combinatorial model is that it provides an alternative explanation for the highly skewed distribution of creativity. As a result, the multiplicative model needs another foundation besides the fact that it can account for the cross-sectional distribution. I accordingly show that this argument can be built from the genetic process of emergenesis. This requires the simultaneous inheritance of several essential components. Because one of those components must certainly be general intelligence, I conclude by treating *g* as the organism's innate capacity for successful adaptation to a local environment. This Darwinian conception is used to explain individual differences in both psychometric IQ and expertise acquisition. In particular, it is shown that greater genius implies superior intellectual giftedness.

All in all, I have mostly qualified and elaborated Jensen's (1996) position. In only a few places do we profoundly disagree. Moreover, on the really critical question there is no disagreement at all: exceptional *g* is not the same as genius. Hence, those who insist in defining genius in terms of exceptional scores on tests of general intelligence are distorting the meaning of the term. Someone who has a stratospheric IQ is certainly intellectually gifted, but genuine genius requires much, much more.

References

Albert, R. S. (1975). Toward a behavioral definition of genius. *American Psychologist, 30*, 140–151.

Albert, R. S. (Ed.) (1992). *Genius and eminence* (2nd ed.). Oxford: Pergamon Press.

American Heritage Electronic Dictionary (3rd ed.) (1992). Boston: Houghton Mifflin.

Bain, A. (1977). *The senses and the intellect* (D. N. Robinson (Ed.)). Washington, D.C.: University Publications of America. (Original work published 1855).

Bandura, A. (1982). The psychology of chance encounters in life paths. *American Psychologist, 37*, 747–755.

Barron, F. X. (1963). *Creativity and psychological health: Origins of personal vitality and creative freedom*. Princeton, NJ: Van Nostrand.

Barron, F. X., & Harrington, D. M. (1981). Creativity, intelligence, and personality. *Annual Review of Psychology, 32*, 439–476.

Barsalou, L. W., & Prinz, J. J. (1997). Mundane creativity in perceptual symbol systems. In: T. B. Ward, S. M. Smith, & J. Vaid (Eds), *Creative thought: An investigation of conceptual structures and processes* (pp. 267–309). Washington, D.C.: American Psychological Association.

Benbow, C. P., & Lubinski, D. J. (Eds). (1996). *Intellectual talent: Psychometric and social issues.* Baltimore: Johns Hopkins University Press.

Bloom, B. S. (Ed.) (1985). *Developing talent in young people.* New York: Ballantine Books.

Boden, M. A. (1991). *The creative mind: Myths & mechanisms.* New York: Basic Books.

Burt, C. (1943). Ability and income. *British Journal of Educational Psychology, 12,* 83–98.

Burt, C. (1963). Is intelligence distributed normally? *British Journal of Statistical Psychology, 16,* 175–190.

Campbell, D. T. (1960). Blind variation and selective retention in creative thought as in other knowledge processes. *Psychological Review, 67,* 380–400.

Cattell, J. M. (1903). A statistical study of eminent men. *Popular Science Monthly, 62,* 359–377.

Cox, C. (1926). *The early mental traits of three hundred geniuses.* Stanford, CA: Stanford University Press.

Cziko, G. (1995). *Without miracles: Universal selection theory and the second Darwinian revolution.* Cambridge, MA: MIT Press.

Cziko, G. A. (1998). From blind to creative: In defense of Donald Campbell's selectionist theory of human creativity. *Journal of Creative Behavior, 32,* 192–208.

Davis, R. A. (1987). Creativity in neurological publications. *Neurosurgery, 20,* 652–663.

Dennis, W. (1954a, September). Bibliographies of eminent scientists. *Scientific Monthly, 79,* 180–183.

Dennis, W. (1954b). Productivity among American psychologists. *American Psychologist, 9,* 191–194.

Dennett, D. C. (1995). *Darwin's dangerous idea: Evolution and the meanings of life.* New York: Simon & Schuster.

Ericsson, K. A. (1996). The acquisition of expert performance: An introduction to some of the issues. In: K. A. Ericsson (Ed.), *The road to expert performance: Empirical evidence from the arts and sciences, sports, and games* (pp. 1–50). Mahwah, NJ: Erlbaum.

Ericsson, K. A., Krampe, R. T., & Tesch-Römer, C. (1993). The role of deliberate practice in the acquisition of expert performance. *Psychological Review, 100,* 363–406.

Eysenck, H. J. (1993). Creativity and personality: Suggestions for a theory. *Psychological Inquiry, 4,* 147–178.

Eysenck, H. J. (1995). *Genius: The natural history of creativity.* Cambridge, England: Cambridge University Press.

Finke, R. A., Ward, T. B., & Smith, S. M. (1992). *Creative cognition: Theory, research, applications.* Cambridge, MA: MIT Press.

Galton, F. (1892). *Hereditary genius: An inquiry into its laws and consequences.* London: Macmillan.

Galton, F. (1972). *Hereditary genius: An inquiry into its laws and consequences* (2nd ed.). Gloucester, MA: Smith. (Original work published 1892).

Galton, F. (1874). *English men of science: Their nature and nurture.* London: Macmillan.

Gardner, H. (1983). *Frames of mind: A theory of multiple intelligences.* New York: Basic Books.

Gardner, H. (1993). *Creating minds: An anatomy of creativity seen through the lives of Freud, Einstein, Picasso, Stravinsky, Eliot, Graham, and Gandhi.* New York: Basic Books.

Gardner, H. (1998). Are there additional intelligences? The case for naturalist, spiritual, and existential intelligences. In: J. Kane (Ed.), *Education, information, and transformation* (pp. 111–131). Upper Saddle River, NJ: Merrill.

Goldberg, D. E. (1989). *Genetic algorithms in search, optimization, and machine learning.* Reading, MA: Addison-Wesley.

Guilford, J. P. (1967). *The nature of human intelligence.* New York: McGraw-Hill.

Hadamard, J. (1945). *The psychology of invention in the mathematical field*. Princeton, NJ: Princeton University Press.

Hayes, J. R. (1989). *The complete problem solver* (2nd ed.). Hillsdale, NJ: Erlbaum.

Holland, J. H. (1992). Genetic algorithms. *Scientific American, 267* (1), 66–72.

Howe, M. J. A. (1999). *The psychology of high abilities*. Washington Square, NY: New York University Press.

Huber, J. C. (1998a). Invention and inventivity as a special kind of creativity, with implications for general creativity. *Journal of Creative Behavior, 32*, 58–72.

Huber, J. C. (2000). A statistical analysis of special cases of creativity. *Journal of Creative Behavior, 34*, 203–225.

Jensen, A. R. (1992). Understanding *g* in terms of information processing. *Educational Psychology Review, 4*, 271–308.

Jensen, A. R. (1996). Giftedness and genius: Crucial differences. In: C. P. Benbow & D. J. Lubinski (Eds), *Intellectual talent: Psychometric and social issues* (pp. 393–411). Baltimore: Johns Hopkins University Press.

Jensen, A. R. (1998). *The g factor: The science of mental ability*. Westport, CT: Praeger.

Johnson, S. (1781). *The lives of the most eminent English poets* (Vol. 1). London: Bathurst et al.

Koza, J. R. (1992). *Genetic programming: On the programming of computers by means of natural selection*. Cambridge, MA: MIT Press.

Koza, J. R. (1994). *Genetic programming II: Automatic discovery of reusable programs*. Cambridge: MIT Press.

Langley, P., Simon, H. A., Bradshaw, G. L., & Zythow, J. M. (1987). *Scientific discovery*. Cambridge, MA: MIT Press.

Lombroso, C. (1891). *The man of genius*. London: Scott.

Ludwig, A. M. (1995). *The price of greatness: Resolving the creativity and madness controversy*. New York: Guilford Press.

Lykken, D. T. (1982). Research with twins: The concept of emergenesis. *Psychophysiology, 19*, 361–373.

Lykken, D. T. (1998). The genetics of genius. In: A. Steptoe (Ed.), *Genius and the mind: Studies of creativity and temperament in the historical record* (pp. 15–37). New York: Oxford University Press.

Lykken, D. T., McGue, M., Tellegen, A., & Bouchard, T. J. Jr. (1992). Emergenesis: Genetic traits that may not run in families. *American Psychologist, 47*, 1565–1577.

Martindale, C. (1990). *The clockwork muse: The predictability of artistic styles*. New York: Basic Books.

Martindale, C. (1995). Fame more fickle than fortune: On the distribution of literary eminence. *Poetics, 23*, 219–234.

Maslow, A. H. (1959). Creativity in self-actualizing people. In: H. H. Anderson (Ed.), *Creativity and its cultivation* (pp. 83–95). New York: Harper & Row.

May, R. (1975). *The courage to create*. New York: Norton.

Mednick, S. A. (1962). The associative basis of the creative process. *Psychological Review, 69*, 220–232.

Miller, G. F. (1997). Protean primates: The evolution of adaptive unpredictability in competition and courtship. In: A. Whiten, & R. Byrne (Eds), *Machiavellian intelligence II* (pp. 312–340). Cambridge, U.K.: Cambridge University Press.

Murray, P. (Ed.) (1989). *Genius: The history of an idea*. Oxford: Blackwell.

Over, R. (1988). Does scholarly impact decline with age? *Scientometrics, 13*, 215–223.

Over, R. (1989). Age and scholarly impact. *Psychology and Aging, 4*, 222–225.

Platz, A., & Blakelock, E. (1960). Productivity of American psychologists: Quantity versus quality. *American Psychologist, 15*, 310–312.

Poincaré, H. (1921). *The foundations of science: Science and hypothesis, the value of science, science and method* (G. B. Halstead, Trans.). New York: Science Press.

Price, D. (1963). *Little science, big science.* New York: Columbia University Press.

Quételet, A. (1968). *A treatise on man and the development of his faculties.* New York: Franklin. (Reprint of 1842 Edinburgh translation of 1835 French original).

Raskin, E. A. (1936). Comparison of scientific and literary ability: A biographical study of eminent scientists and men of letters of the nineteenth century. *Journal of Abnormal and Social Psychology, 31*, 20–35.

Roe, A. (1953). *The making of a scientist.* New York: Dodd, Mead.

Rogers, C. R. (1954). Toward a theory of creativity. *ETC: A Review of General Semantics, 11*, 249–260.

Rothenberg, A. (1986). Artistic creation as stimulated by superimposed versus combined-composite visual images. *Journal of Personality and Social Psychology, 50*, 370–381.

Rushton, J. P. (1990). Creativity, intelligence, and psychoticism. *Personality and Individual Differences, 11*, 1291–1298.

Serebriakoff, V. (1985). *Mensa: The society for the highly intelligent.* London: Constable.

Shockley, W. (1957). On the statistics of individual variations of productivity in research laboratories. *Proceedings of the Institute of Radio Engineers, 45*, 279–290.

Simonton, D. K. (1976). Biographical determinants of achieved eminence: A multivariate approach to the Cox data. *Journal of Personality and Social Psychology, 33*, 218–226.

Simonton, D. K. (1977a). Creative productivity, age, and stress: A biographical time-series analysis of 10 classical composers. *Journal of Personality and Social Psychology, 35*, 791–804.

Simonton, D. K. (1977b). Eminence, creativity, and geographic marginality: A recursive structural equation model. *Journal of Personality and Social Psychology, 35*, 805–816.

Simonton, D. K. (1978). Independent discovery in science and technology: A closer look at the Poisson distribution. *Social Studies of Science, 8*, 521–532.

Simonton, D. K. (1979). Multiple discovery and invention: Zeitgeist, genius, or chance? *Journal of Personality and Social Psychology, 37*, 1603–1616.

Simonton, D. K. (1984a). *Genius, creativity, and leadership: Historiometric inquiries.* Cambridge, MA: Harvard University Press.

Simonton, D. K. (1984b). Scientific eminence historical and contemporary: A measurement assessment. *Scientometrics, 6*, 169–182.

Simonton, D. K. (1985a). Intelligence and personal influence in groups: Four nonlinear models. *Psychological Review, 92*, 532–547.

Simonton, D. K. (1985b). Quality, quantity, and age: The careers of 10 distinguished psychologists. *International Journal of Aging and Human Development, 21*, 241–254.

Simonton, D. K. (1986). Stochastic models of multiple discovery. *Czechoslovak Journal of Physics, B, 36*, 138–141.

Simonton, D. K. (1988a). Age and outstanding achievement: What do we know after a century of research? *Psychological Bulletin, 104*, 251–267.

Simonton, D. K. (1988b). *Scientific genius: A psychology of science.* Cambridge, MA: Cambridge University Press.

Simonton, D. K. (1991a). Career landmarks in science: Individual differences and inter-disciplinary contrasts. *Developmental Psychology, 27*, 119–130.

Simonton, D. K. (1991b). Emergence and realization of genius: The lives and works of 120 classical composers. *Journal of Personality and Social Psychology, 61*, 829–840.

Simonton, D. K. (1991c). Latent-variable models of posthumous reputation: A quest for Galton's G. *Journal of Personality and Social Psychology, 60,* 607–619.

Simonton, D. K. (1992). Leaders of American psychology, 1879–1967: Career development, creative output, and professional achievement. *Journal of Personality and Social Psychology, 62,* 5–17.

Simonton, D. K. (1993). Blind variations, chance configurations, and creative genius. *Psychological Inquiry, 4,* 225–228.

Simonton, D. K. (1995). Personality and intellectual predictors of leadership. In: D. H. Saklofske, & M. Zeidner (Eds), *International handbook of personality and intelligence* (pp. 739–757). New York: Plenum.

Simonton, D. K. (1997). Creative productivity: A predictive and explanatory model of career trajectories and landmarks. *Psychological Review, 104,* 66–89.

Simonton, D. K. (1998a). Achieved eminence in minority and majority cultures: Convergence versus divergence in the assessments of 294 African Americans. *Journal of Personality and Social Psychology, 74,* 804–817.

Simonton, D. K. (1998b). Fickle fashion versus immortal fame: Transhistorical assessments of creative products in the opera house. *Journal of Personality and Social Psychology, 75,* 198–210.

Simonton, D. K. (1999a). Creativity and genius. In: L. A. Pervin, & O. John (Eds), *Handbook of personality theory and research* (2nd ed.). New York: Guilford Press.

Simonton, D. K. (1999b). Creativity as blind variation and selective retention: Is the creative process Darwinian? *Psychological Inquiry, 10,* 309–328.

Simonton, D. K. (1999c). *Origins of genius: Darwinian perspectives on creativity.* New York: Oxford University Press.

Simonton, D. K. (1999d). Talent and its development: An emergenic and epigenetic model. *Psychological Review, 106,* 435–457.

Simonton, D. K. (2000). Creativity: Cognitive, developmental, personal, and social aspects. *American Psychologist, 55,* 151–158.

Simonton, D. K. (2001). Talent development as a multidimensional, multiplicative, and dynamic process. *Current Directions in Psychological Science, 10,* 39–43.

Spearman, C. (1927). *The abilities of man: Their nature and measurement.* New York: Macmillan.

Sulloway, F. J. (1996). *Born to rebel: Birth order, family dynamics, and creative lives.* New York: Pantheon.

Terman, L. M. (1917). The intelligence quotient of Francis Galton in childhood. *American Journal of Psychology, 28,* 209–215.

Terman, L. M. (1925). *Mental and physical traits of a thousand gifted children.* Stanford, CA: Stanford University Press.

Walberg, H. J., Rasher, S. P., & Hase, K. (1978). IQ correlates with high eminence. *Gifted Child Quarterly, 22,* 196–200.

Walberg, H. J., Strykowski, B. F., Rovai, E., & Hung, S. S. (1984). Exceptional performance. *Review of Educational Research, 54,* 87–112.

Waller, N. G., Bouchard, T. J. Jr., Lykken, D. T., Tellegen, A., & Blacker, D. M. (1993). Creativity, heritability, familiality: Which word does not belong? *Psychological Inquiry, 4,* 235–237.

Winner, E. (1996). *Gifted children: Myths and realities.* New York: Basic Books.

Zusne, L. (1985). Contributions to the history of psychology: XXXVIII. The hyperbolic structure of eminence. *Psychological Reports, 57,* 1213–1214.

Chapter 12

Mental Retardation and *g*

Herman H. Spitz

1. Introduction

Arthur Jensen, so deserving of the tribute we give him in this volume, is, in the view of many, one of the giants in psychology. But beyond that he is very responsive and empathetic. In my experience he responds to correspondence with thorough consideration and detailed replies. Despite his stature in the field (and the abuse he has sometimes been subjected to) he has time to respond thoughtfully and fully. Concerning the group at the low end of the intelligence curve, he writes that he has "never been particularly interested in mental retardation in its own right, but . . . looked at it with a view to elucidating or testing hypotheses about mental abilities in general" (A. R. Jensen, personal communication, Jan. 24, 2001). I agree with this strategy (Spitz 1982). As Detterman (1987) expressed it, "any theory of mental retardation must also be a general theory of intellectual functioning" (p. 11). Any theory of intellectual functioning, I might add, is also a theory of mental retardation. It is incumbent upon scientists exploring the nature of intelligence to examine performance across the entire intellectual spectrum.

Jensen also wrote that persons with mental retardation "probably illustrate the nature of *g* more clearly than [do] persons at the top end of the curve" (A. R. Jensen, personal communication, Jan. 24, 2001). Repeatedly, basic research such as Jensen has carried out produces greater understanding of apparently unrelated problems; in this instance, the greater our understanding of *g* the greater our understanding of the nature of low intelligence.

For example, some time ago — before he fully realized the importance and ubiquity of Spearman's *g* — Jensen applied his theory of Level I and Level II forms of intelligence to, among others, the performance of groups with mental retardation. Level I was said to require basic, concrete performance, such as reproductive memory, in which no mental manipulation of the material is required before it is reproduced. Level II, on the other hand, requires mental manipulation. Jensen gave the Digits Forward short-term memory task as an example of a test that taps Level I ability, whereas Digits Backward draws upon Level II ability. In general, groups with mental retardation

The Scientific Study of General Intelligence: Tribute to Arthur R. Jensen
Copyright © 2003 by Elsevier Science Ltd.
All rights of reproduction in any form reserved.
ISBN: 0-08-043793-1

performed relatively well on Level I tasks (although there was an interaction with socioeconomic status and race) when compared with non-retarded groups, but poorly on the Level II tasks. Later he discovered that Level II "was indistinguishable from Spearman's *g*" (Jensen 1993: 186). Furthermore, Level I was not a unitary factor. Additionally, in using Level II there was a problem with construct validity. He abandoned the theory (which really was, as he said, more of a hypothesis) not only because Level I lacked scientific validity but because "Level I-Level II theory was essentially a special case of what I have termed *Spearman's hypothesis*" (Jensen 1993: 192). Using *g* as a hypothetical general principle explains at once a variety of diverse, sometimes apparently unrelated data, a far more desirable attribute than theories that attempt to explain each data set separately.

Mental retardation is not a single biological entity, although we sometimes treat it as if it were. It describes instances where intelligent and adaptive behavior is so ineffective that individuals have marked difficulty in school, at home, in certain occupations and in society generally. How low the intelligence must be for a person to be called mentally retarded is defined, and occasionally redefined, by mental health organizations. Consequently I will frequently use the term low intelligence in place of mental retardation.

The source of low intelligence is also elusive. All low intelligence is not, cannot be, derived from a single cause. In general, we define two general sources: (1) one or more of the innumerable physical, biological, chromosomal and environmental insults that can affect the expression of intelligence, and can affect it in different ways; and (2) the normal distribution and consequent hereditary expression that, in theory, produces a bell-shaped curve of intelligence. The greatest number of people called mentally retarded are from this latter group. They are represented primarily in the upper part of the mental retardation continuum and are likely to have one or more relatives who are mentally retarded. Those suffering from organic insult, on the other hand, tend to be represented primarily in the very lowest IQ range. There is, however, much overlap. Of course when individuals with a biological insult are added to the lower section of the normal curve it appends to the "normal" curve a small hillock or rise in the lower end. A pristine bell curve of IQ does not exist.

Now we ask how *g* is expressed in the lower portion of the curve, say less than IQ 70 or even a bit higher, when compared with its expression in the rest of the curve. This approach frequently assumes that low intelligence, whatever its source, will — in its most general form — manifest itself in a fairly uniform manner no matter what the cause of the low intelligence. Although it is risky to do so, for purposes of this paper I too will ignore diagnosis and review some of the relevant literature that examines the status of *g* in low IQ individuals, particularly as compared with the population that occupies the remaining portion of the intelligence curve.

2. Diminishing Returns and the Differentiation Hypothesis

Charles Spearman, the discoverer of *g*, was made aware that the *g*-saturation of an ability is dependant on "the class of persons at issue" (Spearman 1927: 217). He cited findings of Abelson indicating differences in the amount of *g* saturation of various mental abilities in 78 "normal" children when compared with 22 children who were, as they were called at the time, mentally defective. On a series of mentally challenging tasks the inter-test correlations (corrected for attenuation) were 0.466 for the normal children and 0.782 for the group that was defective. Until then, one might have wagered that a high inter-test correlation would indicate a greater *g*, but the test scores simply turned out to be more homogeneous for the lower IQ group. It appears that even though the power or efficiency of *g* is lower in low IQ groups, it diffuses more widely; that is, there is less scatter of the specific factors. This finding must indicate something about *g* in different ability groups, and what that something is has become the object of a colorful search that has recently heated up after a long quietus.

To explain, in part, the differential intercorrelations of low IQ and average IQ groups, Spearman made use of a general law drawn from economics: the law of diminishing returns. This law, he wrote, can be applied to the differing performances at different intelligence levels. He gave examples of how this law operated in other domains. In economics, adding more capital to a modest amount already spent on a piece of land does not increase the return proportionately. Similarly, adding twice as much coal to a ship engine going, say, 15 knots an hour, does not double the speed. In the study of intelligence, "the correlations always become smaller — showing the influence of g on any ability to grow less — in just the classes of persons which, on the whole, possess *g* more abundantly" (Spearman 1927: 219). Spearman did not elaborate, at least not in this book. He said nothing about investment of *g* in specific tests. He said only that the influence of *g* on certain abilities grows smaller in persons of high ability when compared with persons of low ability. Consequently, in persons of even higher ability the influence of *g* would be even smaller, but not a great deal smaller. Nevertheless his law has been interpreted (no doubt correctly) to mean that persons with an already high *g* (in the form of mental power or efficiency) do not need to invest it as much in tests of specific and group factors. Therefore, they would not gain much more of an advantage if they had been born with an even higher level of *g*: it would simply account for less of the variance in the battery of the tests, but not that much less.

As far as I know, Spearman had never predicted the finding that a mentally handicapped group would have a higher inter-test correlation than a normal group. His explanation, if it can be called that, for this apparent paradox was apparently post hoc. Changes or additions to theory based on new data is good science, but the debate about this explanation has never stopped (see Deary *et al.* 1996, for a short review, and also Jensen, in press). As with many such areas of research, much depends on the ability of groups being compared, the criterion used to select them and the material in the tests. Even after proposing the diminishing returns hypothesis, Spearman went on to consider various other variables that might have accounted for the results, saying only that because these other variables cannot by themselves account entirely for the phenomenon, "possibly there exists further a genuine law of diminishing returns for mental as for material processes" (p. 220). The law of diminishing returns, then, was not presented as a very strong hypothesis, at least not at that time, yet it has been pursued vigorously by a number of subsequent investigators. Spearman's somewhat vague application of the law of diminishing returns to mental tests left itself open to different interpretations.

Despite the small samples, Deary and Pagliari (1991) subjected the data given in Spearman (1927) to a principal component analysis and concluded that the g factor, derived as the first principle component, accounted for 52.6% of the variance in test scores for the non-retarded children, whereas it accounted for a whopping 80.8% of the variance for the low IQ group. They drew attention to Spearman's law of diminishing returns to explain these results, and also to the results given in the Detterman & Daniel (1989) study.

Detterman & Daniel (1989) obtained the average intercorrelations on the Wechsler (WAIS-R) subtests, as well as on a set of a computer-administered basic cognitive tasks, from college students (mean IQ = 115.5) and young adults with mental retardation (mean IQ = 67.5). The intercorrelation of measures from the basic cognitive tasks and the intelligence test scores, as well as with each other, was significantly higher for the group with mental retardation than for the higher IQ group. Detterman and Daniel then obtained the correlations on these tests using two groups of high school students, one with a mean IQ of 108 and another with a mean IQ of 93, a full standard deviation lower but not in the mentally retarded range. Nevertheless, the results were the same: the lower intelligence group had higher correlations.

In a second study they partitioned the standardization sample of the WAIS-R and WISC-R into five ability groups, based on only one of the subtests: Vocabulary, checked later by using Information, which proved to produce similar results. They used this method because, when delineating the groups, choosing on the basis of Full Scale scores introduced spurious negative correlations. The lowest ability group had IQ equivalents (Vocabulary or Information scores) of less than 78, the next group was within the 78 to 92 range, and so on, each covering 15-point intervals, with the highest group having an IQ equivalent of more than 122. Results showed that the average intercorrelation for all subtests was highest for the lowest ability group. The average intercorrelation of Wechsler subtests dropped (not entirely smoothly but generally systematically) as the groups went from the lower to the progressively higher ability level. In no instance was the subtest intercorrelation of the lowest ability group less than twice as high as that of the highest ability group. In fact in no instance was the subtest intercorrelation of the lowest group not significantly higher than that of the middle ability (93–107) group.

Lynn (1992) later reported similar results with a Scottish standardization sample of 1,369 children on the WISC-R, although he did not supply the IQ means. However, in Lynn's study the subtest correlation was significantly higher for the highest ability group than for the next to highest, whereas in the Detterman and Daniel study the two highest groups had about the same correlation. Nevertheless, in Lynn's study also the lowest ability group's subtest correlation of 0.44 was more than twice that of the highest ability group's correlation of 0.20, and three times as high as the penultimate group's correlation of 0.14. A good deal of evidence leaves little doubt that there is an inverse relationship between the size of the Wechsler subtest correlations and ability level, particularly prominent when groups in the mentally retarded and borderline range are compared with groups from much higher ability ranges.

Jensen (1998) interpreted Spearman's law of diminishing returns to mean that average and above average groups do not expend *g* on many of the specific tests. They have more diversified abilities. As Jensen (1998) put it, "The higher a person's level of *g*, the less important it becomes in the variety of abilities the person possesses. High-*g* persons have more diversified abilities, with more of the total variance in their abilities existing in non-*g* factors (i.e. the various group factors and specificity)" (p. 585). It follows then, that low IQ groups have less diversified abilities and therefore must expend more of what *g* they have on *all* the subtests. For low IQ groups, *g* accounts for more of the variance in these tests.

However, as Jensen (1998) remarked, "Others have interpreted this phenomenon in terms of what has become known as the *differentiation* theory" (p. 585). Detterman, for example, was uncomfortable with the finding of higher intercorrelations in the lower IQ group. Based on Spearman's theories, he argued, the intercorrelations of the lower IQ groups should be lower, not higher than the higher IQ groups. To explain what he thought was really a paradox, he referred to his previous proposal (Detterman 1987) that "intelligence can be viewed as a complex system of independent but interrelated parts" (Detterman 1991: 254), some of which were more important than others. Because not all abilities are of equal importance in performing a task, a person may have a high or low score on a task requiring a central ability, and this is crucial to whether the person is impaired or not. In Detterman's view, "*g* arises from this set of weights in combination with a person's independent ability" (p. 254).

Deary *et al.* (1996) equated the law of diminishing returns with the "differentiation hypothesis", originally used by Garrett to describe changes with age from childhood to adolescence and young adulthood. "Abstract or symbol intelligence changes in its organization as age increases from a fairly unified and general ability to a loosely organized group of abilities or factors" (Garrett 1946: 373). The hypothesis was recruited by Deary and others to describe changes when going from lower to higher ability levels, in which there is a transition from more indeterminate or formless application of one's ability to a more distinctive or differentiated application. Using the Differential Aptitude Test (DAT), Deary *et al.* (1996) separated 10,500 Irish school children into two groups whose mean IQs were roughly 90 and 110. The low group here was well above the mental retardation range, but it is of interest that a small but detectable effect was found even in this higher range of abilities. However, the effect was found only when one of three specific subtests of the DAT battery (either verbal reasoning, numerical ability, or space relations) was used to separate the participants into the two ability groups. Detterman & Daniel (1989), remember, had used the Wechsler Vocabulary subtest, so it appears that verbal ability is effective for separating ability groups in order to demonstrate the inverse correlation between IQ and subtest correlation.

In his detailed theory of intellectual development, of which this is an over-simplification, Anderson (1992) too equated Spearman's law of diminishing returns with the differentiation hypothesis. For Anderson, *g* is not higher in groups of higher intelligence; rather, the higher ability is related to the greater differentiation of basic abilities. Therefore, *g* decreases in importance as intelligence increases.

Jensen (in press) has recently dealt further with this issue. The comparison he made did not include a group with mental retardation but, again, it is of interest to anyone who uses intelligence tests as research instruments for studying groups of different ability levels, and the results are suggestive for our inquiry. He tested the widespread assumption that the magnitude of the low inter-test correlations in higher ability groups was uniform no matter what mentally challenging tests were used in the correlation matrix. No doubt floor effects play a role in reducing the intercorrelations of low IQ groups, but he reminded readers of Spearman's law of diminishing returns. In his study, Jensen used the standardization samples of the WISC-R and WAIS-R. All individuals from ages 5 to 74 who had IQs of 100 and below formed the low IQ group (mean IQ about 88), and the rest formed the high IQ group (mean IQ about 112).

After determining that the standard deviations of the high and low groups were so similar they could not account for the results to be reported, Jensen performed a number of analyses. Using Kaiser's method he substantiated previous findings that the mean subtest correlation was lower for higher IQ than for lower IQ groups in every age range. He then obtained the congruence coefficient between the first principal components (which, typically, he thereafter referred to as *g*) of the two ability groups, and found that the correlation matrixes of the high and low groups represented a very similar general factor.

From there on, *he ignored test and subtest scores* and looked only at the *g* loadings of the high and low groups on each subtest. In other words, he calculated the *g* loadings of each group separately, and then compared them with each other. First, using the total sample, he determined that the three subtests on the WISC-R that are most *g*-loaded are Vocabulary, Information and Similarities and the three that are least *g*-loaded are Coding, Mazes and Digit Span. Similarly, for the WAIS-R the three most *g*-loaded are Similarities, Vocabulary and Information and the three least *g*-loaded are Digit Symbol, Digit Span and Object Assembly.

Then, separately for the above average and below average groups, he calculated the differences in mean *g* loadings (*not* subtest scores) between the previously determined (on the general population) three most *g*-loaded subtest and three least *g*-loaded subtests. He made the same calculation for the below average group. As it turned out: *differences* were smaller at every age for the below average group than for the above average group. This resulted because on subtests that are *most highly g*-loaded based on the general population, both groups show high subtest *g* loadings of their own, but on those subtests that the general population had determined are *least highly g*-loaded, the subtest *g* loadings remained fairly high for the lower IQ group and dropped for the higher IQ group. As Jensen put it, those subtests in the battery "that are less *g*-loaded (where *g* loadings are based on the general population) consistently show greater decrements in their *g* loadings between low and high IQ groups than do the more highly *g*-loaded tests" (Jensen, in press). Consequently, he concluded that the Spearman effect (inverse relationship between subtest intercorrelations and IQ) is produced by the least *g*-loaded subtests in a battery and not, as might be expected, by the subtests that have the highest *g*-loadings.

This new finding indicated to Jensen that the "total scores of individuals in the upper range of ability distribution are considerably less *g*-loaded, and consequently are more adulterated by non-*g* factors and test specificity, than are the scores in the lower range" (Jensen, in press). Lower IQ subjects invest their *g* in more of the tests of specific and group factors than do high IQ subjects. Consequently, the psychometric *g* loadings are more evenly distributed across the subtests for the lower than for the higher IQ group. Based on these findings, the total score on the Wechsler Scales is not a good measure of *g* in individuals of above average mental ability, whereas the total score of lower IQ individuals is considerably more *g*-loaded.

Of course this tells us nothing about the differences between groups in amount of *g* available if it is properly tapped (we know the high IQ groups have more); it tells us, separately for each of these groups, only how their *g* is distributed on the subtests of these intelligence scales. Above average groups do not expend *g* on many of the specific tests because they have more diversified abilities that are independent from *g*.

These findings are very impressive. We knew that for the lower IQ groups *g* accounts for more of the variance in the total tests, but we did not know that the differences occur because the lower ability group invests relatively more *g* in less *g*-loaded subtests, not because of group differences on the highly *g*-loaded subtests. There is in fact very little difference in the *g* invested on the highly *g*-loaded subtests. These data will have to be substantiated in a very much lower IQ group before we can apply the general conclusions to groups with mental retardation. Based on past research there is no reason to doubt that it will apply to them as well, although groups with mental retardation can always provide us with surprises.

Psychometrically, to measure *g* by a total score Jensen (in press) suggested devising a battery of tests, each of which — using a general population sample — has high and approximately equal *g* loadings as the others. Other batteries must be devised to assess "various group factors or aptitudes and skills of practical significance, whatever their *g*". As for theory, we must deal with these new results (if confirmed using other tests), "that it is the highly *g*-loaded tests that differ the least in their loadings across different levels of ability, whereas the less *g*-loaded tests differ the most" (Jensen, in press).

The above analyses and conclusions pertain to subtest correlations and differences in subtest *g* loadings of two groups of different intelligence levels. It does not affect conclusions concerning comparisons of the rank order of performance on subtests that are, in turn, rank-ordered for *g* loadings (again based on the general population), which is another matter entirely and which will now be discussed.

3. Equal Mental Age (MA) and the Method of Correlated Vectors

One strategy for measuring the strength of *g* is to compare relative performance of bright and dull groups who are of equal MA on those subtests that have been shown by factor analysis of the entire standardization sample to require a high *g* (or high neural efficiency, or whatever *g* proves to represent). Spearman's (1927: 276) citation of a study in which groups who were mentally defective had particular difficulty with tests requiring the eduction of relations, and less difficulty in tests of repetition, points the way. Eduction of relations was, for Spearman, one of the prime probes for *g*.

In the late 1980s I gathered 4,304 protocols of people with low intelligence who took at least two of the four popular Wechsler Intelligence Scales (Spitz 1988): the Wechsler Adult Intelligence Scale (WAIS), the Wechsler Intelligence Scale for Children (WISC), and their revisions (the WAIS-R and the WISC-R) (Wechsler 1949, 1955, 1974, 1981). The groups were of far lower intelligence level than the groups used by many of the workers cited above. Finding large numbers of mentally retarded and borderline individuals who took at least two of the tests made it possible to compare how well the subtest rankings of each Scale, whose subtests are similar, correlate with every other. It turns out that except for the WAIS-WAIS-R comparison, each of the Scales intercorrelate significantly with each other; with rank order correlations ranging from 0.547 to 0.848.

The results distinguish those subtests on which the groups rather consistently scored well and those on which they score poorly relative to the other subtests. For three of the four Scales the highest two subtest scores for the groups with mental retardation and borderline intelligence were on Picture Completion and Object Assembly, in that order. Only on the WAIS-R is Object Assembly the highest, and Picture Completion third highest. At the other extreme, their poorest three subtest scores were generally, but not invariably, Vocabulary, Arithmetic and Information. (Of course this is only valid for group study not individual diagnosis, where there are large individual differences. For individuals, it is a probability measure.)

Now that we have some general idea of the performance ranking of mentally retarded groups on the subtests, we can determine how their performance is related to the subtests' g-saturation. Fortunately, a common hierarchical factor analytic technique has been performed on each of the Wechsler Scales using their standardization samples (Blaha & Wallbaum 1982; Blaha *et al.* 1974; Wallbrown *et al.* 1975; Wallbrown *et al.* 1974). The groups were approximately matched for particular age ranges of the standardization sample. This reduced the number of subjects to 200 each on the WISC and WISC-R and 300 each on the adult Scales. The rank order of the g-loadings of each subtest for each Scale, corrected for attenuation, were compared with the rank order of the subtest scores of the low intelligence groups. The Kendall coefficient of concordance was –0.63, for the WISC, –0.60 for the WISC-R, and –0.67 for the WAIS-R. However, it was 0.0 for the WAIS. There is no explaining the lack of correlation on the WAIS. For the others, the substantial negative correlations indicate that, in general, the higher the subtest's g-saturation, based on the standardization sample, the more difficult the test is for the low intelligence groups. This general method of analysis — in which the ranking of the subtests' g-loadings (or the ranking of some other variable, such as measures of heritability, and so on) are determined, and then the rank order performance of particular subgroups on those subtests is assessed — has been called by Jensen (1998) the "method of correlated vectors" (p. 143).

It is impossible in this limited space to list all the studies in which the rank order of subtest scores of groups with mental retardation are compared with groups of average, and sometimes much above average, intelligence. Consequently I will just give a flavor of this work. There were some minor differences in the findings, but the results have been quite similar, even using different tests. The purpose of this kind of research is obvious: to measure whether the *rank order* performance of low IQ groups on the subtests of an intelligence test differs from the *rank order* performance of groups with higher IQs. When subtest *g*-loadings are based on the general population, is subtest rank order performance of the two intelligence groups affected by the rank order of the subtest *g* loadings? Comparisons that have been made between low IQ and high IQ groups who are of equal mental age (MA) seem to me to be particularly interesting.

This kind of experiment is ready-made for the researcher, who can draw from the huge body of data generated by the clinical testing of groups with mental retardation, and from the standardization sample for the comparison group.

Some time ago, Thompson & Magaret (1947) extended the study of Laycock & Clark (1942) who had compared a mentally retarded group with a non-retarded group of equal MA on the 1937 Stanford-Binet Scale. Whereas Laycock and Clark used a small number of subjects and a limited number of items, Thompson and Magaret used the entire scale with a larger number of participants. The 441 participants who were mentally retarded had IQs ranging from 20 through 79, chronological ages ranging from 8 to 14 years, and MAs ranging from 2.6 to 10.5 years. They were matched on MA with 1.326 non-retarded individuals drawn from the standardization sample. For example, a mentally retarded individual with a MA of 5 years was matched with a non-retarded individual with a chronological age (CA) of 5 years, and so on.

Results indicated that 30 of the 79 items differentiated the groups. When these items were compared it was found that, in general, the items that were relatively more difficult for the low-IQ groups were the items that were more saturated with the general first factor reported by McNemar (1942) in his factor analysis of the standardization group of the Stanford-Binet. This first principle factor derived from the standardization group is, of course, considered an expression of Spearman's *g*. This is an early example of the use of correlated vectors and an early indication of the statistical finding that groups with mental retardation perform relatively more poorly on tests that are more highly *g*-saturated. *Even though the two groups were at the same MA level, they were not of equal brightness.* MA is a useful measure for matching groups, but IQ is a more valid measure of intelligence.

Three years later, Magaret & Thompson (1950) took from the standardization group a superior group of 197 individuals who tested above IQ 120, and matched them on MA with the average and retarded groups. This group of individuals with superior scores was necessarily much younger than the other two groups. Magaret and Thompson reported that those 11 items that were easier for the average than for the superior group were also lower in *g* saturation. There were 10 items that were easier and 7 items that were more difficult for the retarded group when they were compared with the superior group. The *g*-loadings of the seven items that were more difficult for the lowest IQ group had a significantly higher *g*-loading than did the items they found easiest. Interestingly, rote memory was among the difficult items, just as it had been when comparing the groups with low and average mean IQ. Rote memory is not always an easier item for groups who are mentally retarded, as it is sometimes thought to be, although it can be relatively good when they are compared with an intellectually gifted, much younger group.

Unfortunately, most of the experimenters who compared non-retarded and retarded groups on the Wechsler Scales did not, as did Thompson and Magaret, directly compare score rankings to the ranking of each subtest's *g* saturation. However, when the studies include large enough sample sizes and groups that are clearly separated on IQ level — with the mental level of the lower IQ group within the retarded and borderline limits — the pattern of differences is very distinct. Taken in total the data indicate that the low IQ groups have particular trouble with material that is highly *g*-saturated. They also indicate that matching these groups on MA does not match them on intelligence.

A most interesting study, for its content as well as its historical value, was Maude Merrill's doctoral dissertation, supervised by Lewis M. Terman and later published (Merrill 1924). In fact, in his own doctoral dissertation Terman had compared a small group of high IQ and low IQ children, so the concept of comparing the performance of extreme groups who are of equal MA was in the air. Indeed, such comparisons invite a discussion of the nature of intelligence. Merrill used the 1916 Stanford-Binet plus additional tests to compare a group of children in special classes, who had a mean IQ of 66, with a group of very high IQ children who were part of Terman's gifted children study. The two groups were of approximately equal MA and so the low IQ group was very much older. The reading, spelling and arithmetic levels of the two groups were also at roughly the same level.

Merrill's (1924) Stanford-Binet results sum up findings that, with a few exceptions, have been consistently reported, using either the Stanford-Binet or the Wechsler Scales (see Spitz 1982, for an early review). When matched on MA, the very high IQ group is superior on tests requiring verbal facility and reasoning, whereas the low IQ group is superior on tests requiring rote performance and maturation. The evidence indicates that, in general, the younger, very high IQ children are performing better than the older, low IQ children on items that load more heavily on the general factor.

It has long been known that the lower the intelligence the higher the constancy of mental tests (e.g. Goodman & Cameron 1978), which is further evidence of how *g* affects intelligence test performance in low IQ individuals over the life span. That is, for them an unchanging *g* pervades many more tests, whereas the performance of higher ability individuals is more affected by the more changeable non-*g* factors. Furthermore, experiments have indicated robustly that people with mental retardation have more difficulty with laboratory tasks requiring logic and problem solving than do non-retarded groups who are of equal MA (e.g. Spitz 1987). Logic and problem solving are very strong gauges of general intelligence. Understanding the fundamental principle that many more tests of mental ability express low but pervasive *g* in the performance of individuals who are of very low intelligence widens our understanding of the nature of mental retardation.

There is an interesting sidelight to results of repeated testing on the different intelligence scales. The low intelligence groups do not perform better on the later tests, contrary to expectations based on the "Flynn effect". Flynn had found that with individuals of average intelligence, the standardization group scored higher on the second, later test, thereby making it more difficult to get a high score on the second test than on the first and also indicating a rising intelligence. But, surprisingly, just the opposite happens when low IQ groups take both the WAIS and, many years later, the WAIS-R (Spitz 1989), which was normed 27 years after the WAIS. The newer test (the WAIS-R) produced higher scores. Similar results are found when low IQ groups takes both the WISC-R and, at a later date, the WAIS-R, which was normed seven years after the WISC-R.

Other findings supported this finding of a negative Flynn effect at the lower end of the intelligence curve. (The typical Flynn effect disappears but apparently does not reverse at the higher end of the curve.) The WAIS-R minus WAIS curve across the intelligence spectrum is so orderly (bow shaped) that a regression equation nicely describes the data (Spitz 1989). Are most people getting smarter while people with low intelligence are getting less intelligent? Not likely. Flynn (1985) attributed the contradictory findings in part to inadequate sample sizes in the standardization group at the lower intelligence levels. He had wisely recognized that allowances for massive gains in IQ might apply only for scores ranging from 90 to 110 (Flynn 1984: 39), but he did not predict that a lawful, gradually increasing reverse effect might be found below that range. This is another example of how, for whatever reason, the use of groups with low intelligence can occasionally produce surprises for unwary investigators.

4. Summary

There have been a number of different approaches to the study of *g* when groups with mental retardation are compared with non-retarded groups. The evidence from these psychometric studies indicates that groups with mental retardation have higher intercorrelations on the subtests of intelligence tests as well as on any battery of mentally challenging tasks than do groups of higher intelligence. New data obtained by Jensen suggest that the higher intercorrelation of low IQ groups is a result of greater investment of what *g* they have in all the subtests of an intelligence test, regardless of each subtest's *g* loadings when derived from large, representative samples. Low IQ groups have many fewer diverse abilities than do higher IQ groups and thus are more dependent on what *g* they have to execute a variety of tasks. As always, there are a few exceptions: *savants* who are mentally retarded have one (or, rarely, two) very well developed diverse ability, but that is dealt with in another chapter.

Although the intertest correlation does not tell us the strength of *g* in different groups, there are other strategies for making this measurement. Performance of groups of mentally retarded individuals, when compared with groups of higher ability (who are sometimes equated on MA), produces evidence that the mentally retarded groups perform most poorly on those tests that are the most highly *g*-loaded.

Results thus far require further substantiation, but at the same time the search for the nature of intelligence should turn also to an exploration of the biological nature of *g*. The discovery of the biological substrata of *g* would not only be a major scientific advance, it would be of immense interest and obvious utility to all those doing research with people who are mentally handicapped.

References

Anderson, M. (1992). *Intelligence and development: A cognitive theory.* Oxford, U.K.: Blackwell.

Blaha, J., & Wallbrown, F. H. (1982). Hierarchical factor structure of the Wechsler Adult Intelligence Scale-Revised. *Journal of Consulting and Clinical Psychology, 50*, 652–660.

Blaha, J., Wallbrown, F. H., & Wherry, R. J. (1974). Hierarchical factor structure of the Wechsler Intelligence Scale for Children. *Psychological Reports, 35*, 771–778.

Deary, I. A., & Pagliari, C. (1991). The strength of *g* at different levels of ability: Have Detterman and Daniel rediscovered Spearman's "Law of Diminishing Returns"? *Intelligence, 15*, 247–250.

Deary, I. J., Egan, V., Gibson, G. J., Austin, E. J., Brand, C. R., & Kellaghan, T. (1996). Intelligence and the differentiation hypothesis. *Intelligence, 23*, 105–132.

Detterman, D. K. (1987). Theoretical notions of intelligence and mental retardation. *American Journal of Mental Deficiency, 92*, 2–11.

Detterman, D. K. (1991). Reply to Deary and Pagliari: Is *g* intelligence or stupidity? *Intelligence, 15*, 251–255.

Detterman, D. K., & Daniel, M. H. (1989). Correlations of mental tests with each other and with cognitive variables are highest for low IQ groups. *Intelligence, 13*, 349–359.

Flynn, J. R. (1984). The mean IQ of Americans: Massive gains 1932 to 1978. *Psychological Bulletin, 95*, 29–51.

Flynn, J. R. (1985). Wechsler intelligence tests: Do we really have a criterion of mental retardation? *American Journal of Mental Deficiency, 90*, 236–244.

Garrett, H. E. (1946). A developmental theory of intelligence. *American Psychologist, 1*, 372–378,

Goodman, J. F., & Cameron, J. (1978). The meaning of IQ constancy in young retarded children. *Journal of Genetic Psychology, 132*, 109–119.

Jensen, A. R. (1993). Psychometric G and achievement. In: B. R. Gifford (Ed.), *Policy perspectives on educational testing* (pp. 117–27). Boston: Kluwer Academic publishers.

Jensen, A. R. (1998). *The g factor.* Westport, CT: Praeger.

Jensen, A. R. (in press). Regularities in Spearman's Law of diminishing returns. *Intelligence.*

Laycock, S. R., & Clark, S. (1942). The comparative performance of a group of old-dull and young-bright children on some items of the revised Stanford-Binet Scale of Intelligence Form. *Journal of Educational Psychology, 33*, 1–12.

Lynn, R. (1992). Does Spearman's *g* decline at high IQ levels? Some evidence from Scotland. *Journal of Genetic Psychology, 153*, 229–230.

Magaret, A., & Thompson, C. W. (1950). Differential test responses of normal, superior, and mentally defective subjects. *Journal of Abnormal and Social Psychogy, 45*, 163–167.

McNemar, Q. (1942). *The revision of the Stanford-Binet Scale.* Boston: Houghton Mifflin.

Merrill, M. A. (1924). On the relation of intelligence to achievement in the case of mentally retarded children. *Comparative Psychology Monographs, 2*, 1–100.

Spearman, C. (1927). *The abilities of man: Their nature and measurement.* New York: Macmillan.

Spitz, H. H. (1982). Intellectual extremes, mental age, and the nature of human intelligence. *Merrill-Palmer Quarterly, 28*, 167–192.

Spitz, H. H. (1987). Problem-solving in special populations. In: J. G. Borkowski, & J. D. Day (Eds), *Cognition in special children: Comparative approaches to retardation, learning disabilities, and giftedness* (pp. 153–193). Norwood, NJ :Ablex.

Spitz, H. H. (1988). Wechsler subtest patterns of mentally retarded groups: Relationship to *g* and to estimates of heritability. *Intelligence, 12*, 279–297.

Spitz, H. H. (1989). Variations in Wechsler interscale IQ disparities at different levels of IQ. *Intelligence, 13*, 157–167.

Thompson, C. W., & Magaret A. (1947). Differential test responses of normals and mental defectives. *Journal of Abnormal and Social Psychogy, 42,* 285–293.

Wallbrown, F. H., Blaha, J., Wallbrown, J. D., & Engin, A. W. (1975). The hierarchical factor structure of the Wechsler Intelligence Scale for Children-Revised. *Journal of Psychology, 89,* 223–235.

Wallbrown, F. H., Blaha, J., & Wherry, R. J. (1974). The hierarchical factor structure of the Wechsler Adult Intelligence Scale. *British Journal of Educational Psychology, 44,* 47–56.

Wechsler, D. (1949). *Manual for the Wechsler Intelligence Scale for Children.* New York: Psychological Corp.

Wechsler, D. (1955). *Manual for the Wechsler Adult Intelligence Scale.* New York: Psychological Corp.

Wechsler, D. (1974). *Manual for the Wechsler Intelligence Scale for Children-Revised.* New York: Psychological Corp.

Wechsler, D. (1981). *Manual for the Wechsler Adult Intelligence Scale-Revised.* New York: Psychological Corp.

Chapter 13

The Ubiquitous Role of *g* in Training*

Malcolm James Ree, Thomas R. Carretta and Mark T. Green

"Facts are very stubborn things, overruling all theories."

Jules Verne *Journey to the Center of the Earth*

1. Introduction

The relationship between general cognitive ability (*g*), and occupational performance has been the subject of theoretical speculation and applied research for a century. Many areas of study have contributed to understanding these relationships. These include investigations of the structure of ability, the predictive validity of *g* and other individual attributes (e.g. specific ability, personality, job knowledge) for training, and causal models of the relations among these variables.

Training is frequently the first or second broad component of occupational performance. Training inculcates the knowledge, skills and techniques required to perform the job or for promotions or new jobs, or just staying current with the changing demands of the "same" job.

In writing this chapter, we were struck by the persistence of a common mistake — the misidentification of a construct as the method used to measure it. In some of the studies reviewed later in this chapter, the study authors have called the construct by the name of the measuring device or by the appearance of the medium used for measurement. This increases the probability of misinterpreting the contributions of the sources of the variability to the measures.

* The views expressed are those of the authors and not necessarily those of the United States Government, the Department of Defense, or the United States Air Force.

Previously, we have noted that tests associated with the verbal factor contain large amounts of variance due to *g* and should be represented with a small v (for unique verbal contribution) and a large *g* proportional to the variance contribution of each component:

$$Verbal = v + g$$

Some tests (or other measures) are called verbal or mechanical because of the appearance of the questions. Walters *et al.* (1993) have termed this the "Topological Fallacy". Still others have used the new names assigned to cognitive components without noting that they are indistinguishable from *g* (see, e.g. Kyllonen 1993). This too is a form of the Topological Fallacy and has the potential to distort our understanding of the relationships among sources of variance in a measure. Early in his studies of *g*, Spearman posited the concept of the "indifference of the indicator". He meant that there are a myriad of ways and methods to measure *g* because of the ubiquity of *g* in cognitive tasks and measurements. It is important to separate the sources of variance in a measure to determine which are effective (Carretta & Ree, in press; Ree 1995). This can best be done by decomposing the measure into uncorrelated components or residualized factors.

2. Configuration of Abilities

2.1. History

Aristotle conjectured about the configuration or structure of human abilities distinguishing *dianoia* (ability), from *orexis* (emotional and moral faculty). "The thing that thinks, "*res cogitans*, is how the French secular philosopher Descartes conceived of ability. Peiró & Munduate (1994) report a treatise by the Spaniard Juan Huarte in 1575 on cognitive and other abilities in *Examen de ingenios para las ciencies* (more recently available as Huarte de San Juan 1991), later published in English as *The examination of men's wits: Discovering the great differences of wits among men and what sort of learning suits best with each genius*. These very early efforts are little known today and the scientific study of human abilities is often traced back to Galton, Binet, Spearman and the U.S. Army Alpha and Beta tests of World War I.

Spearman (1927) analyzed test batteries and proposed that every test measures a general factor (*g*) common to all tests, and one or more specific factors (s1 to sn) that are unique to each test. These constructs were often depicted with overlapping circles and ovals. General ability corresponded to a large circle and specific abilities to smaller ovals, arrayed racially (for illustrations, see Jensen 1980: 214 or Ree & Carretta 1998: 162). The amount of overlap between the large *g* circle and small specific abilities' ovals varies, depending on the extent to which a test measured *g* and one or more specific abilities. Eventually, Spearman acknowledged what has become known as group factors or "specifics" that appear in more than one category of test content such as verbal or spatial.

2.2. Flat and Hierarchical Configurations of Cognitive Abilities

The configuration of ability has been represented in many different ways. For example, Thurstone's (1938) flat model of Primary Mental Abilities did not include a general factor. Thurstone proposed there was no general factor and that ability consisted of seven independent "primary" factors, a position that later analyses forced him to recant (Thurstone & Thurstone 1941). Regardless of Thurstone and Thurstone's recantation, multiple aptitude theories strongly influenced psychology for decades (Fleishman & Quaintance 1984; Gardner 1983; Guilford 1956, 1959; Sternberg 1985). In psychometrics, the influence of multiple aptitude theories was especially powerful, where they led to the development of several multiple ability test batteries including the Armed Services Vocational Aptitude Battery (ASVAB), Differential Aptitude Test (DAT), Flanagan Aptitude Tests (FIT-FACT), General Aptitude Test Battery (GATB), and others (see Chapter 19 in this volume).

Notwithstanding the popularity of multiple aptitude theories, there has been an emergent consensus over the past 50 years that abilities have a pyramidal or hierarchical structure (e.g. Burt 1949; Vernon 1950, 1969). Burt (1949) proffered a five-level hierarchy with g at the apex, and successively expanding levels below. These levels, from higher to lower, are "General Intelligence", "Relations", "Association", "Perception" and "Sensation". Burt noted that the second level is made up of extensive group factors based on form and content. The successive levels are numerous and composed of narrower more specialized group factors.

Vernon's (1950, 1969) well-known hierarchical model also has g at its apex. On the next level are the two broad (i.e. major group) factors of verbal-educational (v: ed) and spatial-mechanical or spatial-perceptual-practical (k: m). These main group factors subdivide into minor group factors that further devolve to factors that are more specific.

Cattell (1971) and Horn (1978) generated a hierarchical model that does not include g. Instead, their model had two apexes, G_c (i.e. crystallized ability) and G_f (i.e. fluid ability). Four other apex factors have tentatively been added (Hakstian & Cattell 1978) representing memory (G_m), perceptual speed (G_{ps}), retrieval (G_r) and visualization (G_v). The need for further confirmation of these factors remains. The model offered by Jager (1967), which has several higher-order factors has not been influential.

Gustafsson (1988) suggested a combination of the Spearman-type g model and the Cattell-Horn fusion. He set G_f corresponding to g, G_c to v: ed, and G_v to k: m. Gustafsson (1980) noted the loading of G_f on g at 0.94, a near identity.

Hierarchical models of ability require higher-order sources as well as several specific lower-order sources. In cognitive ability, the highest-order factor (g) regularly accounts for more of the variance than do the specific factors combined. To understand the lower-order factors, it is important to "residualize" (Schmid & Leiman 1957), therefore removing the effects of g on the lower-order factors. The largest fraction of variance accounted for by a residualized specific factor in representative multiple-ability tests is about 8% (Carretta & Ree 1996; Ree & Carretta 1994: Stauffer *et al.* 1996). Frequently, this fraction is due to specific knowledge not specific ability. To understand this in relative terms, *g* typically accounts for from 30% to 65% of variance depending on the test battery composition. See Jensen (1980, Chapter 6) for a helpful review.

2.3. Fairness: The Same Factors Are Measured in All Groups

Several principles must be addressed when proposing the measurement of cognitive abilities in several groups. First is that the same factors should be measured for all groups. McArdle (1996), among others, has acknowledged that equality of factor loadings (i.e. factorial invariance) should be established before other group comparisons (e.g. mean differences) are considered. McArdle argues that failing factorial invariance, the psychological constructs being measured may be *qualitatively* different for the groups, thus creating ambiguity in the interpretability of the other comparisons.

Many studies have been conducted exploring the similarity of cognitive factors for race/ethnic, sex and socio-economic groups. Michael (1949) found virtually no differences in the cognitive factor structure for Whites and Blacks on U.S. Army pilot selection tests used in World War II. Likewise, Humphreys & Taber (1973) also found no differences in a comparison of factor structures for high and low socio-economic status boys from Project Talent.

Using 15 cognitive tests, DeFries *et al.* (1974) compared the structure of ability for Hawaiians of either European or Japanese ancestry. They found the same four factors and nearly identical factor loadings for the two groups.

The studies by Michael (1949), Humphreys & Taber (1973), and DeFries *et al.* (1974) examined common factors while others (Carretta & Ree 1995; Ree & Carretta 1995) have used hierarchical models to investigate the comparative structure of cognitive abilities for sex and ethnic groups. In a multiple race/ethnic and sex group cognitive ability factors comparison, Ree & Carretta (1995) examined a hierarchical model that included *g* and three lower-order factors of verbal/math, speed and technical knowledge. Ree and Carretta noted only small group differences on the verbal/math and speed factors. No significant differences were found for *g*! (however, see Chapter 10 in this volume).

Carretta & Ree (1995) compared cognitive-ability factor structures in large samples of young American adults. Their hierarchical model included *g* and five lower-order cognitive ability factors representing verbal, math, spatial, aircrew knowledge and perceptual speed. The model showed good fit and little difference for men and women and for five ethnic groups. Correlations between factor loadings for the sex groups and for all pairs of ethnic groups all approached $r = 1.0$. Regressions between pairs of groups showed no mean differences in loadings between males and females or among the race/ethnic groups. Similar results using two cognitive ability and psychomotor ability test batteries were observed for sex groups (Carretta 1997a; Carretta & Ree 1997). Cai *et al.* (1998) compared Chinese living in urban and rural communities and found similarity of cognitive ability factor structure. Adding these results to previous results (see, e.g.

Jensen 1980) presents a consistent picture of the near identity of cognitive ability structure for sex and ethnic groups.

3. Specific Abilities, Noncognitive Characteristics and Knowledge

Repeatedly it has been proposed that the measurement of specific cognitive abilities, noncognitive characteristics and knowledge is prerequisite for understanding human characteristics and occupational performance. For example, McClelland (1993) conjectured that in some circumstances motivation or other noncognitive characteristics would be better predictors of job performance than *g*. Sternberg & Wagner (1993) proposed substituting measures of practical intelligence and tacit knowledge rather than measures of what they term "academic intelligence". Sternberg and Wagner defined tacit knowledge as "the practical know how one needs for success on the job" (p. 2). They characterized "practical intelligence" as a more general form of tacit knowledge. Schmidt & Hunter (1993), in a commentary on Sternberg and Wagner, noted that the concepts of tacit knowledge and practical intelligence are redundant with the well-rooted construct of job knowledge.

4. Training and Academic Performance

Training and academic performance is generally measured using class grades or cumulative grade point average. These measures generally reflect the students' demonstrated acquisition of knowledge or skills gained in the classroom or laboratory.

4.1. Academic and Training Measures

The first step in a job is training in which new entrants must acquire the necessary knowledge and master the required skills. Training begins early with elementary education in reading, writing and arithmetic. Secondary school, vocational school, college, formal job training and on-the-job-training provide the opportunity to acquire additional specialized job knowledge and skills. In each of these training situations, *g* has been shown to be predictive of performance (Jensen 1998).

4.2. Predictive Utility of g

Jensen (1980: 319) provided these estimates of the validity of *g* for predicting academic training: elementary school — 0.6 to 0.7, high school — 0.5 to 0.6, college — 0.4 to 0.5, and graduate school — 0.3 to 0.4. Pragmatically, Jensen observed that the *apparent* decrease in the predictiveness of *g* was likely the result of artifacts such as range restriction and selective assortment into educational track. Thorndike (1986) provided an estimate of the predictive utility of *g* consistent with those of Jensen (1980). He examined the predictive utility of *g* for six high school course grades and found an average correlation of 0.532.

Jones (1988) used the unrotated first principal component loadings of a 10-test multiple-aptitude battery to estimate the tests' *g*-saturation. She then correlated the average validity of the 10 tests for predicting training performance for 37 jobs with these loadings and observed a correlation of 0.76. Jones also computed the correlation within each of four job families (administrative, electronics, general and mechanical) that covered the 37 jobs. No differences were found among the job families. Ree & Earles (1992) corrected Jones' *g* loadings for unreliability and observed a correlation of 0.98. They also obtained the same value in a replication in a different sample encompassing 150 jobs. Investigating the source of validity of aptitude tests, Jensen (1998) concluded "*g* is the ubiquitous agent of predictive validity over an extremely wide variety of jobs" (p. 286).

More than three decades ago McNemar (1964), in his presidential address to the American Psychological Association, reported that *g* was the best predictor of school performance in 4,096 studies that used the Differential Aptitude Tests. Moreover, Brodnick & Ree (1995) showed that *g* was a better predictor of college performance than was social class.

Roth & Campion (1992) illustrated the validity of a *g* composite for predicting training success for petroleum process technicians. The validity of the *g*-based composite was $r = 0.50$ after correction for range restriction.

Salgado (1995) reported biserial correlations of $r_b = 0.38$ (not corrected for range restriction) between a general cognitive ability composite and pilot training outcome in the Spanish Air Force. Using cumulative analyses, Salgado demonstrated that there was no variability in the correlations across five classes of pilot trainees.

Te Nijenhuis & van der Flier (2000) report that *g* was predictive of truck driver training in the Netherlands on a sample of foreign born and native participants. Uncorrected results for job knowledge criteria were $r = 0.222$ and $r = 0.245$ for immigrants and native born truck drivers, respectively. Their sample is of interest as it includes Turks, North Africans, Surinamese and (formerly) Yugoslavs. These findings buttress the ubiquity of *g* as a predictor.

Roznowski *et al.* (2000) demonstrated the predictive efficacy of *g* for learning electronics information from a computerized tutor. Their second study showed similar results for a flight-engineering tutor. They proposed a hierarchical model in which *g* was superior to paper-and-pencil cognitive factors and to factors derived from measures of information processing. This is consistent with Stauffer *et al.* (1996) who found measures of information processing (called cognitive components by their developers) to be mostly measures of *g*.

Although misunderstanding our previous use of "not much more than *g*" (see Visweswaran & Ones, 2002), Colquitt *et al.* (2000) have produced a comprehensive meta-analytically-based path analysis of the role of *g* in producing training outcomes. They showed *g* directly influencing declarative knowledge, skill acquisition, retraining self-efficacy and post training self-efficacy. They also found *g* to indirectly influence a host of other training effects such as motivation to learn, transfer and job performance.

Using a unit-weighted composite of the three tests from the Graduate Record Examinations — verbal, quantitative and analytic, a surrogate of *g*, Kuncel *et al.* (2001) demonstrated a meta-analytic correlation with graduate school grade point average as

$r = 0.45$. Using the same unit-weighted composite sans analytical, nearly identical results were found. Further analyses of their data showed that the combination of verbal and quantitative, a reasonable surrogate of g (see their Table 8) was predictive of comprehensive examination scores and faculty ratings of graduate performance.

Hunter & Hunter (1984) demonstrated through cumulative techniques that g was a ubiquitous predictor of training success and varied by job complexity. Ability data were from the General Aptitude Test Battery and training data were from a myriad of jobs. The more complex the job, the more valid g was for predicting training. Considering high to low job complexity, the validity ranged from $r = 0.59$ to $r = 0.54$.

4.3. Incrementing the Predictive Utility of g

Thorndike (1986) estimated the comparative validity of g versus specific ability composites for predicting results for about 1,900 enlisted U.S. Army trainees enrolled in 35 technical training schools. Specific abilities showed little incremental validity (0.03) beyond g and on cross-validation the multiple correlations for specific abilities usually shrunk below the bivariate correlation for g.

Using a large U.S. Air Force sample, Ree & Earles (1991) demonstrated that training performance was almost exclusively a function of g rather than specific factors. Participants were 78,041 enlisted men and women enrolled in 82 job-training courses. Ree and Earles examined whether g predicted training performance in about the same way regardless of the kind of job or its difficulty. Based on Hull's (1928) theory, it might be argued that although g was useful for some jobs, specific abilities were more important or compensatory and therefore, more valid for other jobs. Ree and Earles tested Hull's hypothesis with regression analyses. They sought to resolve whether the relationship between g and training performance was identical for the 82 jobs. This was accomplished by initially imposing the constraint that the regression coefficients for g be the same for each of the 82 equations, and then freeing the constraint and allowing the 82 regression coefficients to be estimated individually. Even though there was statistical evidence that the relationship between g and the training outcomes differed by job, these differences were so small as to be of no practical predictive consequence. The relationship between g and training performance was nearly identical across jobs. Using a single regression equation for all 82 jobs resulted in a reduction in the correlation of less than one-half of 1%.

In selection for technical training, specific ability tests may be given to qualify applicants on the assumption that specific abilities are predictive or incrementally predictive. For example, the U.S. Air Force uses specific ability tests for qualifying applicants for training as computer programmers and intelligence operatives. Besetsny, Earles & Ree (1993) and Besetsny, Ree & Earles (1993) examined these two specific ability tests to determine if they measured a construct other than g and if their validity was incremental to g. The samples were 3,547 computer-programmer and 776 intelligence-operative trainees and the criterion was training performance. Two multiple regression equations were computed for computer-programmer and intelligence-operative trainees. The first equation for each group had only g and the second g and specific cognitive abilities. The difference in R2 between these two equations was tested for each group of trainees to determine whether specific abilities incremented g. Incremental validity gains for specific abilities beyond g for the two training courses were 0.00 and 0.02, respectively. Although the specialized tests were designed to measure specific cognitive abilities thought to be incrementally predictive, they added nothing (0.00) or little (0.02) beyond g.

Similarly, interviews are sometimes used in the belief that they measure abilities and characteristics that are incremental to g. Walters *et al.* (1993) investigated the validity and incremental validity of an experimental structured interview for selecting U.S. Air Force pilot trainees. A series of tests were administered to 223 pilot trainees including the Air Force Officer Qualifying Test (AFOQT; Carretta & Ree 1996), computer-based cognitive and personality tests, as well as the structured interview. Experienced pilots who had completed a brief training course in interview techniques served as interviewers. The interview questions were designed to measure trainees' self-confidence and leadership, educational background, motivation to fly and flying job knowledge. Interviewers rated the trainees in these areas and provided ratings on probable success in pilot training, bomber-fighter flying and tanker-transport flying. The training criterion in the study was a dichotomous passing/failing pilot training outcome score. The validity of the predictors averaged: 16 AFOQT tests, 0.28; computer-based tests, 0.18; and the seven interview scores, 0.21. No incremental validity was found for the seven interview scores when added to the regression equation with the AFOQT and computer-based test scores. Ree & Carretta (1997) subsequently performed regression analyses using these data to compare full and restricted regression equations for predicting pilot training outcome. They found that adding the interview scores to a measure of g extracted from the AFOQT did not improve prediction and that the interview's predictive utility came from the measurement of g. Despite the intent of the interview designers to measure unique abilities beyond g, the interview failed to do so.

Using World War II data, Thorndike (1986) reported the incremental validity of specific composites versus g for the prediction of passing/failing pilot training for a sample of 1,000 trainees. An increment of 0.05 (0.64 vs. 0.59) was found for specifics beyond g. However, investigation revealed that specific job knowledge (i.e. aviation information) was tested and may have accounted for part of the increment.

Following Thorndike (1986), Olea & Ree (1994) tested the validity of g, specific ability, and specific knowledge for predicting several U.S. Air Force pilot and navigator training criteria. Measures of g, specific ability and specific knowledge were estimated from the principal components of the AFOQT (Skinner & Ree 1987). The AFOQT is a multiple aptitude battery containing measures of g and the five lower-order factors of verbal, math, spatial, perceptual speed and aircrew knowledge (Carretta & Ree 1996). The samples were approximately 4,000 pilot and 1,400 navigator trainees who were college graduates before entering training. Similar academic and work sample training criteria were obtained for the pilots and navigators. The criteria for the pilot trainees included academic grades, flying work samples (i.e. flight maneuvers), passing/failing training and an overall performance composite made by summing the other criteria. The criteria for the navigator trainees were academic grades, work samples of day and night celestial navigation, passing/failing training and an overall performance composite made by summing the other criteria. Results observed for the pilot and navigator trainees were similar. Analyses revealed that *g* was the best predictor for all pilot and navigator training criteria. For the composite criterion, which is the most inclusive and consequential measure of training performance, the validity after correction for range restriction was 0.40 for pilots and 0.49 for navigators. The non-*g* measures demonstrated an average incremental validity to *g* of 0.08 for pilot and 0.02 for navigator training. An examination revealed that the incremental validity for pilots was a consequence of specific aviation knowledge (i.e. aviation controls, instruments and principles), not specific cognitive abilities (i.e. math, perceptual speed, spatial verbal). It was not surprising that the non-*g* measures showed little incremental validity for navigator trainees, as the AFOQT does not contain measures of navigator-specific job knowledge.

Steindl & Ree (2000) investigated the same constructs in a sample of 230 randomly selected pilot candidates who entered the Norwegian Air Force Basic Flight School between 1988 and 1992. Martinussen & Torjussen (1998) initially used these data in the validation of their pilot selection battery. A wide-ranging battery of measures was administered including measures of *g*, personality and flying job knowledge. An interesting aspect of the study was that all the participants had to be fluent in a foreign language, English, prior to beginning training. Regression models confirmed the findings of Olea & Ree (1994) and path models showed the singular importance of *g* as a direct causative agent for learning English and an indirect causative agent for training success. The indirect effect on training performance was through English and job knowledge.

Hunter & Hunter (1984) provided an inclusive meta-analysis of the predictiveness of *g* for training criteria. They analyzed several hundred jobs across many job families and re-analyzed data from previous studies. The true validity of *g* was estimated to be 0.54 for job training criteria. In a similar manner, Levine *et al.* (1996) meta-analyzed 52 validation studies totaling 5,872 participants. Their estimate of the true validity of *g*-saturated cognitive tests (see their Appendix 2) was 0.668 for training criteria. In a meta-analysis encompassing 85 years of empirical research, Schmidt & Hunter (1998) examined the utility of measures of *g* and 18 other commonly used personnel selection methods (e.g. biographical data, conscientiousness tests, integrity tests, employment interviews, interests, job experience, peer ratings, reference checks). Their estimate of the predictive validity of *g* for training was 0.56. Combinations of predictors with the highest multiple correlations for job training were *g* plus an integrity test (mean validity of 0.67) and *g* plus a conscientiousness test (mean validity of 0.65). These meta-analyses and other research reviewed demonstrate that *g* predicts both academic and training criteria well.

4.4. Prior Job Knowledge and Training

Ree and colleagues (Ree *et al.* 1998/1999; Ree *et al.* 1995) added the construct of prior job knowledge to causal models of training. Prior job knowledge was defined as job-relevant knowledge that applicants bring to training. Ree *et al.* (1995) examined the causal effect of g and prior job knowledge on the acquisition of additional job knowledge and work sample performance during military aircraft pilot training. They reported that g had a strong causal influence on prior job knowledge, just as g had a strong effect on job knowledge in other studies. In training, no direct path was found from g to either of two pilot work sample performance factors derived from flying measures. However, g exerted an indirect influence on the pilot work samples, moderated through job knowledge acquisition. Included in this study was a set of three sequential training factors derived from academic courses. The direct relationship between g and the first sequential training factor was large, but was almost zero for the second sequential training factor, which builds on the knowledge of the first, and was low positive for the third sequential training factor that introduces substantially new material. Most of the causal influence of g was indirect through the acquisition of job knowledge in the sequential training courses.

Using cumulative data from 83 independent studies with a total sample of 42,399 participants, Ree *et al.* (1998/1999) constructed and tested path models to examine the causal roles of g and prior job knowledge in the acquisition of subsequent job knowledge. Their results supported a model in which g had a causal influence on both prior and subsequent job knowledge. There was a direct influence for g on both prior job knowledge and subsequent job knowledge. The g construct also had an indirect effect on subsequent job knowledge through prior job knowledge. An R2 of 0.80 was found for the model including all 83 jobs.

5. Differential Validity and Bias

Mean differences on tests between sex and race/ethnic groups have received much attention, especially when the tests are used for selection into educational and training programs (Hartigan & Wigdor 1989; Jensen 1980). Despite group mean differences in test performance (Carretta 1997b; Hyde 1981; Jensen 1980; Maccoby & Jacklin 1974; Roberts & Skinner 1996), there is no convincing evidence that well constructed tests are more predictive of educational or training performance for members of the majority group than for members of minority groups.

6. The Organizational Value of *g* as a Predictor

Individual differences in training that lead to individual differences in job performance are important to organizational effectiveness. Campbell *et al.* (1996) appraised the findings on the value of high and low job performance. Based on a conservative approach, they estimated that the top 1% of workers produces a return about 3.3 times as great as the lowest 1% of workers. Moreover, they estimated that the value might be from 3 to 10 times the return of the lowest 1%, depending on the variability of job performance.

Gottfredson (1997: 83) argued that ". . . no other measured trait, except perhaps conscientiousness . . . has such general utility across the sweep of jobs in the American economy". Hattrup & Jackson (1996) summarized the finding that specific abilities can be identified and measured, but concluded that they "have little value for building theories about ability-performance relationships" (p. 532).

The foundation for occupational performance is dependent on learning the knowledge and skills required for the job, and continues into on-the-job performance and beyond. These are dependent first on training. Training is dependent on *g*. Schmidt notes that this is one aspect of *g* theory and practice that has been demonstrated beyond even a debate. Our research findings and review of the literature clearly shows the ubiquitous role of *g* as a predictor of training.

References

Besetsny, L. K., Earles, J. A., & Ree, M. J. (1993). Little incremental validity for a special test for Air Force intelligence operatives. *Educational and Psychological Measurement, 53,* 993–997.

Besetsny, L. K., Ree, M. J., & Earles, J. A. (1993). Special tests for computer programmers? Not needed. *Educational and Psychological Measurement, 53,* 507–511.

Brodnick, R. J., & Ree, M. J. (1995). A structural model of academic performance, socio-economic status, and Spearman's *g*. *Educational and Psychological Measurement, 55,* 583–594.

Burt, C. (1949). The structure of the mind: A review of the results of factor analysis. *British Journal of Educational Psychology, 19,* 100–111, 176–199.

Cai, T., Gong, Y., Dai, X., & Tang, Q. (1998). Chinese intelligence scale for young children (CISYC). III: The study of factor structure. *Chinese Journal of Clinical Psychology, 6,* 203–206.

Campbell, J. P., Gasser, M. B., & Oswald, F. L. (1996). The substantive nature of job performance variability. In: K. R. Murphy (Ed.), *Individual differences and behavior in organizations* (pp. 258–299). San Francisco: Jossey-Bass.

Carretta, T. R. (1997a). Male-female performance on U.S. Air Force pilot selection tests. *Aviation, Space, and Environmental Medicine, 68,* 818–823.

Carretta, T. R. (1997b). Group differences on U.S. Air Force pilot selection tests. *International Journal of Selection and Assessment, 5,* 115–127.

Carretta, T. R., & Ree, M. J. (1995). Near identity of cognitive structure in sex and ethnic groups. *Personality and Individual Differences, 19,* 149–155.

Carretta, T. R., & Ree, M. J. (1996). Factor structure of the Air Force Officer Qualifying Test: Analysis and comparison. *Military Psychology, 8,* 29–42.

Carretta, T. R., & Ree, M. J. (1997). Negligible sex differences in the relation of cognitive and psychomotor abilities. *Personality and Individual Differences, 22,* 165–172.

Carretta, T. R., & Ree, M. J. (in press). Pitfalls of ability research. *International Journal of Selection and Assessment.*

Cattell, R. B. (1971). *Abilities: Their structure, growth, and action.* Boston, MA: Houghton Mifflin.

Colquitt, J. A., LePine, J., & Noe, R. A. (2000). Toward an integrative theory of training motivation: A meta-analytic path analysis of 20 years of research. *Journal of Applied Psychology, 85,* 678–707.

DeFries, J. C., Vandenberg, S. G., McClearn, G. E., Kuse, A. R., Wilson, J. R., Ashton, G. C., & Johnson, R. C. (1974). Near identity of cognitive structure in two ethnic groups. *Science, 183,* 338–339.

Fleishman, E. A., & Quaintance, M. K. (1984). *Taxonomies of human performance: The description of human tasks.* Orlando, FL: Academic Press.

Gardner, H. (1983). *Frames of mind: The theory of multiple intelligence.* New York: Basic Books.

Gottfredson, L. S. (1997) Why *g* matters: The complexity of everyday life. *Intelligence, 24,* 79–132.

Guilford, J. P. (1956). The structure of intellect. *Psychological Bulletin, 53,* 267–293.

Guilford, J. P. (1959). Three faces of intellect. *American Psychologist, 14,* 469–479.

Gustafsson, J. E. (1980, April). *Testing hierarchical models of ability organization through covariance models.* Paper presented at the Annual Meeting of the American Educational Research Association, Boston.

Gustafsson, J. E. (1988). Hierarchical models of individual differences in cognitive abilities. In: R. J. Sternberg (Ed.), *Advances in the psychology of human intelligence* (Vol. 4, pp. 35–71). Hillsdale, NJ: Lawrence Erlbaum.

Hakstian, A. R., & Cattell, R. B. (1978). Higher-stratum ability structures on a basis of twenty primary abilities. *Journal of Educational Psychology, 70,* 657–669.

Hartigan, J. A., & Wigdor, A. K. (Eds) (1989). *Fairness in employment testing: Validity generalization, minority issues, and the General Aptitude Test Battery.* Washington, D.C.: National Academy Press.

Hattrup, K., & Jackson, S. E. (1996). Learning about individual differences by taking situations seriously. In: K. R. Murphy (Ed.), *Individual differences and behavior in organizations* (pp. 507–547). San Francisco: Josey-Bass.

Horn, J. L. (1978). Human ability systems. In: P. B. Baltes (Ed.), *Life-span development and behavior* (Vol. 1, pp. 211–256). New York: Academic Press.

Huarte de San Juan, J. (1991). *Examen de ingenios para las ciencies* [Examination of wits for the sciences]. Madrid: Espasa Calpe.

Hull, C. L. (1928). *Aptitude testing.* Yonkers, New York: World Book.

Humphreys, L. G., & Taber, T. (1973). Ability factors as a function of advantaged and disadvantaged groups. *Journal of Educational Measurement, 10,* 107–115.

Hunter, J. E., & Hunter, R. F. (1984). Validity and utility of alternative predictors of job performance. *Psychological Bulletin, 96,* 72–98.

Hyde, J. S. (1981). How large are cognitive gender differences? A meta-analysis using ω^2 and d. *American Psychologist, 36,* 892–901.

Jager, A. O. (1967). *Dimensionen der intelligenz* [Dimensions of intelligence]. G Göttingen: Hogrefe, Germany.

Jensen, A. R. (1980). *Bias in mental testing.* New York: The Free Press.

Jensen, A. R. (1998). *The g factor: The science of mental ability.* Westport, CT: Praeger.

Jones, G. E. (1988). *Investigation of the efficacy of general ability versus specific abilities as predictors of occupational success.* Unpublished Master's thesis, Saint Mary's University of Texas, San Antonio, TX.

Kuncel, N. R., Hezlett, S. A., & Ones, D. S. (2001). A comprehensive meta-analysis of the predictive validity of the Graduate Record Examinations: Implications for graduate student selection and performance. *Psychological Bulletin, 127,* 162–181.

Kyllonen, P. C. (1993). Aptitude testing inspired by information processing: A test of the four-sources model. *The Journal of General Psychology, 120,* 375–405.

Levine, E. L., Spector, P. E., Menon, S., Narayanan, L., & Cannon-Bowers, J. (1996). Validity generalization for cognitive, psychomotor, and perceptual tests for craft jobs in the utility industry. *Human Performance, 9,* 1–22.

Maccoby, E. E., & Jacklin, C. N. (1974). *The psychology of sex differences*. Stanford, CA: Stanford University Press.

Martinusen, M., & Torjusen, T. (1998). Pilot selection in the Norwegian Air Force: A validation and meta-analysis of the test battery. *International Journal of Aviation Psychology, 8*, 33–45.

McArdle, J. J. (1996). Current directions in structural factor analysis. *Current Directions in Psychological Science, 5*, 11–18.

McClelland, D. C. (1993). Intelligence is not the best predictor of job performance. *Current Directions in Psychological Science, 2*, 5–6.

McNemar, Q. (1964). Lost our intelligence? Why? *American Psychologist, 19*, 871–882.

Michael, W. B. (1949). Factor analyses of tests and criteria: A comparative study of two AAF pilot populations. *Psychological Monographs, 63*, 55–84.

Olea, M. M., & Ree, M. J. (1994). Predicting pilot and navigator criteria: Not much more than *g*. *Journal of Applied Psychology, 79*, 845–851.

Peiró, J. M., & Munduate, L. (1994). Work and organizational psychology in Spain. *Applied Psychology: An International Review, 43*, 231–274.

Ree, M. J. (1995). Nine rules for doing ability research wrong. *The Industrial Psychologist, 32*, 64–68.

Ree, M. J., & Carretta, T. R. (1994). Factor analysis of the ASVAB: Confirming a Vernon-like structure. *Educational and Psychological Measurement, 54*, 459–463.

Ree, M. J., & Carretta (1995). Group differences in aptitude factor structure on the ASVAB. *Educational and Psychological Measurement, 55*, 268–277.

Ree, M. J., & Carretta, T. R. (1997). What makes an aptitude test valid? In: R. F. Dillon (Ed.). *Handbook on testing* (pp. 65–81). Westport, CT: Greenwood Press.

Ree, M. J., & Carretta, T. R. (1998). General cognitive ability and occupational performance. In: C. L. Cooper, & I. T. Robertson (Eds), *International review of industrial and organizational psychology* (Vol. 13, pp. 159–184). Chichester, U.K.: John Wiley.

Ree, M. J., Carretta, T. R., & Doub, T. W. (1998/1999). A test of three models of the role of *g* and prior job knowledge in the acquisition of subsequent job knowledge in training. *Training Research Journal, 4*, 135–150.

Ree, M. J., Carretta, T. R., & Teachout, M. S. (1995). Role of ability and prior job knowledge in complex training performance. *Journal of Applied Psychology, 80*, 721–780.

Ree, M. J., & Earles, J. A. (1991). Predicting training success: Not much more than *g*. *Personnel Psychology, 44*, 321–332.

Ree, M. J., & Earles, J. A. (1992). Intelligence is the best predictor of job performance. *Current Directions in Psychological Science, 1*, 86–89.

Roberts, H. E., & Skinner, J. (1996). Gender and racial equity of the Air Force Officer Qualifying Test in officer training school selection decisions. *Military Psychology, 8*, 95–113.

Roth, P. L., & Campion, J. E. (1992). An analysis of the predictive power of the panel interview and pre-employment tests. *Journal of Occupational and Organizational Psychology, 65*, 51–60.

Roznowski, M., Dickter, D. N., Hong, S., Sawin, L. L., & Shute, V. J. (2000). Validity of measures of cognitive process and general ability for learning, and performance on highly complex computerized tutors: Is the *g* factor of intelligence even more general? *Journal of Applied Psychology, 85*, 940–955.

Salgado, J. F. (1995). Situational specificity and within-setting validity variability. *Journal of Occupational and Organizational Psychology, 68*, 123–132.

Schmid, J., & Leiman, J. (1957). The development of hierarchical factor solutions. *Psychometrika, 22*, 53–61.

Schmidt, F. M. (2002). The role of general cognitive ability and job performance: Why there cannot be a debate. *Human Performance, 15*(1–2), 187–211.

Schmidt, F. L., & Hunter, J. E. (1993). Tacit knowledge, practical intelligence, general mental ability, and job knowledge. *Current Directions in Psychological Science, 2*, 8–9.

Schmidt, F. L., & Hunter, J. E. (1998). The validity and utility of selection methods in personnel psychology: Practical and theoretical implications of 85 years of research findings. *Psychological Bulletin, 124*, 262–274.

Skinner, J., & Ree, M. J. (1987). *Air Force Officer Qualifying Test (AFOQT): Item and factor analysis of Form O (Tech. Rep. No. AFHRL-TR-86–68)*. Brooks Air Force Base, TX: Air Force Human Resources Laboratory, Manpower and Personnel Division.

Spearman, C. (1927). *The abilities of man: Their nature and measurement*. New York: MacMillan.

Stauffer, J. M., Ree, M. J., & Carretta, T. R. (1996). Cognitive components tests are not much more than *g*: An extension of Kyllonen's analyses. *The Journal of General Psychology, 123*, 193–205.

Steindl, J. R., & Ree, M. J. (2000, November). *The role of cognitive ability and personality in the training success of Norwegian pilots*. A paper presented at the annual meeting of the International Military Testing Association. Edinburgh, Scotland, U.K.

Sternberg, R. J. (1985). *Beyond IQ: A triarchic theory of human intelligence*. New York: Cambridge University Press.

Sternberg, R. J., & Wagner, R. K. (1993). The *g*-ocentric view of intelligence and job performance is wrong. *Current Directions in Psychological Science, 2*, 1–5.

te Nijenhuis, J., & van der Flier, H. (2000). Differential prediction of immigrant versus majority group training performance using cognitive ability and personality measures. *International Journal of Selection and Assessment, 8*, 54–60.

Thorndike, R. L. (1986). The role of general ability in prediction. *Journal of Vocational Behavior, 29*, 322–339.

Thurstone, L. L. (1938). *Primary mental abilities. Psychometric Monographs No. 1*. Chicago: University of Chicago Press.

Thurstone, L. L., & Thurstone, T. G. (1941). *Factorial studies of intelligence. Psychometric Monographs No. 2*. Chicago: University of Chicago Press.

Vernon, P. E. (1950). *The structure of human abilities*. New York: Wiley.

Vernon, P. E. (1969). *Intelligence and cultural environment*. London: Methuen.

Viswesvaran, C., & Ones, D. S. (2002). Agreements and disagreements on the role of general mental ability (GMA) in industrial, work, and organizational psychology. *Human Performance, 15*(1–2), 212–231.

Walters, L. C., Miller, M., & Ree, M. J. (1993). Structured interviews for pilot selection: No incremental validity. *The International Journal of Aviation Psychology, 3*, 25–38.

Chapter 14

Education and *g*

Phillip L. Ackerman and David F. Lohman

1. Overview

A complete review on the relations between education and intelligence (or *g*) lies well beyond the scope of this chapter. An excellent review of the history of the field was provided by Snow & Yalow (1982; see also Snow 1982, 1996, and Chapter 13 in this volume). This chapter will attempt to highlight some of the central conceptual issues associated with evaluating the relationship between education and intelligence, will report on broad areas of research findings in the field, and attempt to integrate the literature to identify what is known and what fundamental questions remain for future study.

2. Jensen's Contributions

Although Jensen made substantive contributions to the study of intelligence and education/learning prior to 1969 (e.g. see Jensen & Rohwer 1968), the most critically important paper was the defining 1969 article in the *Harvard Educational Review* (Jensen 1969). In this article, Jensen set out a challenge to educators and psychologists, when he reported that prior attempts at raising IQ had shown relatively modest results. As such, he provided an important balance to the field, which in many ways had become entrenched in thinking that increases in IQ could be easily implemented by educational interventions. While this work is controversial even to the present day, it provided a perspective against which evaluations of the respective influences of IQ on education and education on IQ may be evaluated.

3. Concepts and Definitions

If we start with the question: "What is the relationship between education and *g*?" — it becomes apparent immediately that the answer to the question is dependent on how each of the terms is defined. The first step, then, must be a definition of terms. There are essentially three central terms that will be defined here: education, *g*, and IQ.

3.1. Education

The dictionary provides a "lexical" definition (i.e. a definition that describes how the word is used, see Robinson 1950). According to the *Oxford English Dictionary* (1971), education is defined first as "The process of nourishing or rearing a child or young person, an animal" (p. 833). The third definition is more specific: "The systematic instruction, schooling or training given to the young in preparation for the work of life; by extension similar instruction or training obtained in adult age. Also, the whole course of scholastic instruction which a person has received. Often with limiting words denoting the nature or the predominant subject of the instruction or kind of life for which it prepares, as *classical, legal, medical, technical, commercial, art education*" (italics in original). With these definitions in mind, then, we can broadly consider education as any aspect of child rearing, or more narrowly limit the discussion to instruction, schooling or training (whether to children or adults). For present purposes, we will concentrate on the narrow definition of education.

3.2. g

On the one hand, the dictionary is not helpful in defining *g* — because there is no entry for the term. On the other hand, the corpus of psychological literature is not very helpful, for the opposite reason — there are too many definitions of *g*. Most authors start with Spearman's notions of the "eduction of relations" and "eduction of correlates" (Spearman 1927). However, Spearman's own writing demonstrated either a confusion or evolution of thinking about *g* (depending on one's perspective). In his initial exposition of *g* (Spearman 1904), Spearman indicated that "[o]n the whole, then, we reach the profoundly important conclusion that *there really exists a something that we may provisionally term "General Sensory Discrimination" and similarly a "General Intelligence", and further that the functional correspondence between these two is not appreciably less than absolute.*" Spearman (1904: 272). However, elsewhere in the article, Spearman pointed out that the measures of intelligence with the highest *g* saturation were grades in "Classics" and peer ratings of "Common Sense".

Later, Krueger & Spearman (1907) determined that the Ebbinghaus Completion Test had a *g* saturation of 0.97. In 1914, Spearman described *g* as a "*general fund of mental energy*" (p. 103, italics in original). In a re-analysis of data from Simpson and Thurstone, Spearman reported that tests of verbal memory had even higher correlations with *g* than the Completion Test (e.g. Memory of passages and recognizing forms had a corrected correlation of $r = 1.08$ with *g*).

Spearman (1931) again refined his conceptualization of *g* as follows:

> "In particular, the *g* has been found to measure "noegenesis". This term denotes the following three actually and precisely observable mental

functions. The first is knowing of our own experience; we not only feel, but know that we feel; we not only strive, but know that we strive; we not only know, but know that we know. The second of the mental functions consists in that, when any two or more items are perceived or thought of, we may cognize relation between them . . . . An outstanding instance of this among tests is that of "synonyms and antonyms", where two words are given and the testee has to decide whether they are very alike or very unlike. Thirdly and lastly, when we perceive or think of any item and also of any appropriate relation, we may evoke the idea of the item which stands to the given one in the given relation. A well know[n] instance among tests is that of "opposites", where the testee is given some word and is told to say what is the opposite to it. These second and third functions are usually characterized as 'eductive' " (pp. 408–409).

By the late 1930s, Spearman settled on an operationalization for the measurement of *g*. In particular, Spearman was prepared to state:

"Far and away the greatest success in this direction [has] been achieved with respect to this all-important factor < *G* >. This can now be determined for a normal individual with an accuracy by which at any rate all the usual scholastic examinations are put to shame. Indeed, comparison may well be borne even with many approved physical measurements. And as to its possible further perfection, there seems no limit" (Spearman 1938: 79).

"Among the tests already available, I would specially commend to notice two of recent date and presenting notable advantages. One is that of Penrose and Raven, wherein some arrangement of figures in a rectangular design indicates to the subject the relationship which has to be discovered . . . . A fundamental but well known feature of these tests is their minimal dependence on language . . . . Another and rarer basic merit in them is their minimal dependence on previous experience and maximal dependence on pure eduction" (Spearman 1938: 80).

As will be discussed in more detail below, it is useful to separate *conceptualizations* of "*g*" from *measures* that are claimed to represent *g*. The conceptual definitions included a range of general to specific terms, such as General Mental Energy and Eduction of Relations and Correlates. From a measurement perspective, *g* was defined by Spearman to be represented by: Grades in Classics, peer ratings of common sense, scores on the Completion Test, Memory of passages and recognizing forms, synonyms and antonyms, and finally, by the test that ultimately became known as Raven's Progressive Matrices test.

Later authors (e.g. Jensen 1998) have suggested that what Spearman ultimately meant was that it doesn't matter what tests are used to assess *g*, that by virtue of the concept of "the indifference of the indicator" conjecture, *g* is rather best conceptualized as the factor that gives rise to the ubiquitous positive correlations among mental ability tests. This inductive approach lacks specificity, but provides a rubric for estimating *g* in a generally robust fashion — that is, if a wide-enough sample of ability tests is administered to a sample that is sufficiently heterogeneous in talent (e.g. see Thorndike 1994). Historically, empirical studies that employ such methods for assessing *g* tend to provide sufficient information to obtain omnibus intelligence, or IQ scores. Another approach is that advocated by Gustafsson (e.g. Gustafsson 1984; Gustafsson & Undheim 1996; Undheim & Gustafsson 1987). From Gustafsson's analysis of extant literature, *g* is essentially equivalent to Cattell's conceptualization of fluid intelligence (*Gf*) — which in turn is best identified by measures of reasoning and working memory (e.g. see Kyllonen & Christal 1990).

3.3. IQ

There is substantial overlap to some procedures that have been used for estimating *g* (i.e. determining a general factor underlying a battery of tests) and the procedure for estimating IQ (e.g. summing scores across a battery of ability tests, see Thurstone's Centroid method of factor analysis (Thurstone 1931)). When the number and breadth of tests making up a test battery is large, an individual's composite IQ test score is not usually substantially different from that individual's derived factor score on a general factor resulting from the common variance among the test correlations. As such, for the purposes of this chapter, omnibus IQ measures can be taken as useful surrogates for estimates of *g* (at least in terms of the modern approach toward *g*). Nonetheless, there is one important asymmetry regarding IQ and *g*. Most standardized IQ tests provide a reasonable estimate of *g* — whether derived from a factor analysis of test correlations or by an aggregation of scores across all the tests in the battery (e.g. see Thorndike 1987). However, not every test that purports to measure *g* is an IQ test. Some of the tests described by Spearman as highly saturated *g* measures (e.g. Completion Test, Memory of passages, synonyms and antonyms, etc) are highly correlated with IQ tests (in part, because the IQ tests, such as the Stanford-Binet or Wechsler scales include such measures as part of their respective battery). Other *g* tests, such as the predominantly non-verbal Raven's Progressive Matrices have decidedly lower correlations with IQ; while many tests that purport to represent "physiological *g*" (such as those predicated on choice reaction time, nerve conduction velocity, inspection time, and so on) have small to modest levels of overlap with IQ measures (for a review, see Jensen 1993).

4. Age, Development and Intelligence

One of the most intractable problems in evaluating the relationship between education and *g* is the problem of development and age. As near as we can tell, *g* theories have failed to provide any account of development across the lifespan. Spearman appears to have conceptualized *g* as either fixed or at least not monotonically increasing throughout the lifespan, as noted in the following criticism of the Binet approach to intelligence assessment.

> "Quite different again is the scale introduced by Binet, since this depends
> essentially on age. The unit consists of the difference between the

performance that some standard percentage of persons can do at any number of years of age and the performance that the same percentage of persons can manage when they are a year older. Such a scale — the "mental age" — has proved extraordinarily captivating with those who have been more educationalists than psychologists. And undeniably, it has achieved a wonderful success in actual practice. Yet at bottom, nothing could theoretically be more unsound. *For instance, it implies the absurd corollary that persons go on steadily improving in intelligence all their lives!*" (Spearman 1930: 567–568, italics added)

Moreover, Spearman rejected the role of experience on *g*, as he noted as follows:

"For, as we have seen, the very essence of what is measured by *G* consists in its originativeness: that is to say, it is *not* being experiential" (Spearman 1939: 250, italics in original).

There are numerous discussions of the genetics of *g* and the biology of *g* (e.g. see Jensen's 1998, very thorough review). In these formulations, an individual is endowed with a certain amount of *g* at conception (or at least a substantial percentage of the variance of *g* is accounted for by genes). The individual presumably carries this level of *g* through infancy, childhood and adulthood. Such a proposition is absurd, in the absence of cultural and educational influences. It seems to imply, as Plato did in *Meno* (Plato 1974) that an individual's reasoning skills, memory for digits and words, and knowledge are present at birth. The implication is that a feral child of above-average intelligent parents (e.g. a child raised by wolves, or in similarly complete human social isolation) would be expected to be able to educe relations and correlates nearly as well as his or her parents, who might have completed post-secondary education. Few (if any) investigators would probably make such an assertion regarding the lack of relationship between *g* and the environment. (Indeed, Jensen [1998, p. 113] argued that in the "case of Isabel" that it was only after the child was removed from social isolation and was "exposed to educational experiences" did her performance on intelligence tests improve.) Nonetheless, we are left without a theoretical basis for understanding the relationship between *g* and development. While some *g*-theorists are comfortable with asserting that *g* is "constant" throughout much of the lifespan, this assertion must be qualified by limiting the environmental variance to only allow for a specific range of cultures, even though these might range from Western European cultures on the one hand to nomadic Aboriginal tribes on the other hand. Moreover, at the level of measurement, such assertions *must* only refer to *g* as "relative standing, in comparison to an age-norm group" because all operationalizations of *g* show changes in average performance from young infancy to adulthood.

In contrast to the conceptual *g* approaches, IQ measures are *bounded* to an age-based framework. When Binet & Simon (1905) developed the precursor tests to modern IQ scales, they defined the construct of intelligence in a developmental and normative fashion. That is, intelligence test scores (originally Mental Age scores) make sense only in terms of an individual's relative standing, in comparison to same-age peers, and other students of older and younger ages. Stern's (1914) proposal, and Terman's (1916) implementation of the IQ (as [Mental Age/Chronological Age] × 100) was an attempt to present intelligence scores in a fashion that is independent of age. That is, the IQ score was developed to express an individual's intelligence by describing that individual's performance in comparison to average scores obtained by same-age, older and younger samples. This formulation depends on the finding that subjects of older ages were more likely to answer test questions correctly than younger subjects, ceteris paribus (all else being equal). As turned out to be rather obvious in hindsight, the concept of growth of mental abilities with age breaks down as individuals reach adulthood (e.g. see Lippmann 1922). Thus, when the average raw score performance of an older sample fails to exceed the performance of younger samples, the assumption of growth in mental abilities with age is violated. A subsequent development, the Deviation IQ (see, Pinneau 1961) expresses an individual's intelligence as *relative* to only samples of the same age (expressed in terms of the individual's standing on a standard normal distribution). The Deviation IQ avoids the "mental growth" issue — but it doesn't resolve the question of the nature of growth, maintenance and decline of intelligence during the lifespan.

In the abstract, raw scores on individual g measures or the component scales on IQ tests can be used in isolation across different age groups, without being subjected to the same limitation as IQ scores. In practice, though, this scaling problem is not usually avoided, because subjects of different ages end up answering different test questions. For example, tests of g for adults (such as the Raven test) are too difficult for small children, and test items designed to discriminate among small children do not well-discriminate among adult samples. Similarly, the items answered by a normal 3-year-old or 4-year-old on the Stanford Binet or Wechsler scales are quite different from those answered by a normal 30-year-old adult (e.g. see Bayley 1949, Honzik *et al.* 1948). This particular issue has been difficult to solve within the range of Western European school entrance (5 or 6 years of age) to school exit (age 18 or older). Recent advances in scaling and sampling methods, though, have made substantial progress in this regard (e.g. Embretson & McCollam 2000; Peterson *et al.* 1989).

A review of the age and intelligence literature is beyond the scope of this chapter. However, most of the literature on individual tests of intelligence and measures of g tends to support two broad findings: (1) Scores tend to increase from early childhood until at least early adulthood, with a trend toward negative acceleration as adulthood is reached (e.g. the Raven test shows increasing scores until an age range of 18–32 years of age); and (2) At adulthood, tests dominated by verbal content (e.g. vocabulary, reading comprehension, fluency) tend to continue to increase with age up to the 50s or 60s, albeit with a diminished rate of improvement, while tests of nonverbal abilities (e.g. working memory, inductive and deductive reasoning, quantitative problem solving, etc.) tend to decrease after the mid-20s. (For example, see review by Schaie 1996.)

5. The Effects of g and IQ on Educational Success

It is important to note first, that in Western European cultures, education is typically confounded with participant age, in that formal schooling starts in young childhood (age

5 or 6, or younger) and is usually completed at late adolescence or early adulthood (from age 16 to the mid-20s). Moreover, intelligence tests are used almost universally in the classification and selection of students for educational assignments. Such tests are sometimes used at school entrance (to determine 'readiness' for instruction), are often used for placement into special education or gifted and talented programs, are sometimes used for placement in some cases for vocational vs. academic tracks in adolescence, and are widely used for academic selection by post-secondary institutions, though in nearly all cases these tests are used in conjunction with other indicators of intellectual abilities and related constructs. Even when an institution of higher learning decides not to use intelligence tests for selection of applicants, prior selection (e.g. by elementary and secondary levels of education) has already substantially reduced the range-of-talent that exists in the potential applicant population. Self-selection, most likely partly predicated on an individual's self-estimate of abilities, also occurs in the application process for higher education, and for decisions made on dropping-out of high school. Therefore, it is likely that (at best) only in initial testing (e.g. ages 4–5) prior to entrance into formal educational settings, is it possible to estimate the direct influence of g or IQ on educational success in a way that is not confounded by prior selection and placement. Of course, even in such situations, one cannot rule out the effects of informal education (such as in the home or in preschool environments).

5.1. Childhood and Adolescent Education

Individual IQ tests reasonably well-predict school success of young children (at school entrance). Originally, Binet & Simon (1905) designed their scales to discriminate at the low end of the intelligence continuum. Early IQ tests were especially effective in predicting the success of less-able children in contrast to differentiating among above-average children, though more recent tests have been revised to provide reasonably accurate discriminations across the continuum from low to high levels of intelligence. Unfortunately, IQ or g estimates for 4 and 5-year-olds tend to have much lower reliability and validity than such estimates on older children, adolescents or adults (e.g. see Anastasi 1982). Omnibus IQ estimates of intelligence at young ages tend to have higher validity for predicting school success than g estimates predicated on strictly non-verbal tests. Various commentators have suggested that one major reason for this difference in validity estimates is due to the fact that early schooling has a more dominant dependence on development of verbal knowledge and skills (e.g. vocabulary, reading, writing), and that standard IQ measures have a substantial proportion of verbal content. To the degree that g is operationalized as non-verbal measures, its role in determining initial school success is modest at best. If g is conceptualized as the highest-order factor in a wide-ranging battery of verbal and non-verbal tests, it is virtually the same as IQ, and thus is highly predictive of initial school success.

Notwithstanding the confounds of prior educational selection and placement predicated on prior IQ scores, measures of IQ and g tend to increase in concurrent validity for school success as age increases through childhood and early adolescence, although this is partly attributable to increasing reliability of both predictor measures and criterion measures. IQ measures reasonably well-predict age of school leaving (or drop-out). As with testing at early ages, there are ubiquitous findings that omnibus IQ tests are more highly correlated with scholastic success indicators than are predominantly non-verbal *g* measures. (Insufficient data are available to make strong conclusions regarding the correlations of basic information processing measures of *g* and scholastic performance — but the general sense is that these measures perform far more poorly than even non-verbal reasoning *g* measures.)

5.2. Adult Education

IQ and non-verbal *g* measures are moderately correlated with initial college success (e.g. first year of college/university grade point average). The content of the test (omnibus vs. non-verbal) tends to track reasonably well with the content of the curriculum. For example, non-verbal reasoning tests tend to be more highly correlated with course grades in mathematics, and less well-correlated with course grades in literature and social science. The Stanford-Binet, while overall showing higher validity coefficients than the Raven test, tends to have the opposite pattern of correlations — higher in courses that have substantial verbal content, and lower in courses that have minimal verbal content.

It is interesting to note that both IQ and *g* measures show attenuation in predictive validity for college grades after the first year of college (e.g. see Humphreys 1968). Interestingly, the validity of IQ measures actually increases from the final year of college to the first semester/year of graduate or professional study (e.g. see Humphreys & Taber 1973). It has been argued elsewhere (see Ackerman 1994) that such results are consistent with the idea that IQ/*g* are important when a task or environment is novel, but when the student has been familiarized with the task/environment, IQ/*g* become less important determinants of performance. Supportive evidence for this assertion has come from a variety of sources, such as the increasingly important role played by individual differences in domain-specific knowledge as a predictor of post-graduate academic success (e.g. see Willingham 1974).

6. The Effects of Education on *g* and IQ

Several decades ago, Burks (1928) concluded that "the maximal contribution of the best home environment to intelligence is about 20 IQ points, or less, and almost surely lies between 10 and 30 points. Conversely the least cultured, least stimulating kind of American home environment may depress the IQ as much as 20 points. But situations as extreme as either of these probably occur only once or twice in a thousand times in American communities". It is important to keep in mind that when we discuss the effects of education on intelligence, the typical finding of changes are much smaller than those associated with extreme environments. Nonetheless, there is a potential for malleability in IQ, a fact that is at odds with the notion of fixed or innate intelligence.

6.1. Early Education

As stated earlier, age and schooling are typically confounded. It is, however, reasonable to assert that early formal schooling undoubtedly has an effect on both IQ and on the scores on tests designed to measure *g*. Children deprived of education of one sort or another (e.g. formal schooling, home schooling) inevitably show a decline in IQ (see discussion by Ceci 1991). In terms of raw test scores, this may mean that performance either increases at a slower level than it does for children in formal educational settings, or that scores do not change, or in fact scores may decline with increasing age in the absence of schooling. How large an effect education has on intelligence at young ages is hard to assess. Studies that contrast school attenders and school non-attenders at early ages are relatively few, and suffer from a variety of threats to validity (e.g. non-random assignment, inadequate specification of environments, the presence or absence of other influences such as socioeconomic status (SES) differences, etc.).

Ceci (1991) in a very thoughtful article, described several "classes of evidence" that education influences IQ. Although many of these sources of evidence also can be interpreted as suggesting that IQ influences school success, Ceci argued that such evidence is also supportive of the effects that school has on IQ scores. Several of these classes of evidence are briefly described:

(1) "Correlation between IQ and Years of School." Ceci reported that there are high correlations between IQ and the number of total years of school completed (*rs* between 0.60 and 0.80, even when SES is partialled out of the equation).

(2) "The influence of summer vacation on IQ." The point raised here is that assessed IQ tends to decline, on average, during the period in which school is not in session.

(3) "The effects of intermittent school attendance on IQ." On the basis of relatively old studies (those conducted in the 1920s and 1930s), the general sense of these studies is that children who attended school intermittently (for a variety of reasons, such as living in remote areas with intermittent school availability) had lower IQ scores than those children who attended school continuously.

(4) "The effect of delayed onset of school on IQ." When school is delayed for some children, their IQ scores are lower, in comparison to those children who start schooling at similar ages.

(5) "The effect of early termination of schooling on IQ." While this class of evidence reaches beyond early childhood and into late adolescence, it is generally found that individuals who terminate school early (e.g. prior to age 18) have lower IQs than those who proceed at least through secondary schooling.

(6) "Cohort effects associated with schooling and IQ." Based on some school systems imposing an absolute date-of-birth cut-off for starting formal schooling, it is possible to compare groups of children who differ only nominally in age, but differ by one year in amount of education. When such students are compared on IQ, those students starting school earlier have markedly higher IQ scores, at least within the first few years of schooling.

(7) "Historical changes in the schooling — IQ link." Known as the "Flynn effect" (after Flynn 1987), increases in the average raw scores of successive generations of samples during the 20th Century in several countries, might be at least partly attributable to the increase in average number of years of schooling in these populations.

Ceci (1991) argued that even if one or more of these sources of evidence are not necessarily decisive in showing that schooling positively affects intelligence level, in the aggregate, these data are concordant with such a proposition. It is important to note, though, that Ceci (1991) also argued that it is the *amount* of formal schooling that influences the growth of intelligence, rather than the *quality* of formal schooling. That is, studies of the quality of the educational experience have been far more inconsistent in supporting a linkage with increasing levels of intelligence.

Jones (1946/1975) gave a quite reasonable hypothesis of the effects of schooling on intelligence. He stated that IQ theory "implies a curvilinear relationship between education and test scores" for children of a given age. Children of school age with no education will make low scores, regardless of their natural talents or "educability". But, it is assumed that beyond a certain level of educational advancement, and within a normal range of school opportunities, increments in training will not be accompanied by corresponding increments in mental test scores. Ceci's (1991) review of the literature does not directly support this notion, but it is not inconsistent with the proposition, either.

Differentiating IQ from "pure" *g* measures is difficult, given either the overlap in measures (e.g. the Completion Test or memory for digits), or the unavailability of data (e.g. almost no data relate physiological measures of *g* to schooling). There has, though, been an evolution in thinking regarding the role of education on Raven test performance. In the original formulation by Penrose & Raven (1936), the authors state "The relations to be educed can be made novel and problematic at every stage in the series: they need not depend on previous education" (p. 98). In a subsequent test manual Raven *et al.* (1977) state that: "Together they [the Coloured and Advanced Series] provide a means to assess a person's present ability to perceive and think clearly, irrespective of past experience or present ability for verbal communication" (p. G3). In the most current manual (Raven 1990), this position is somewhat attenuated, as follows: "The available evidence suggests that 'g' is influenced by such things as open education at school and involvement in democratic child-rearing practices . . . . The effect is not dramatic, and the bulk of the variance is still between people who have grown up, or been educated in, the same type of environment" (p. 6).

Although it remains to be seen if indeed *g* measures such as the Raven test is less susceptible to the effects of schooling than traditional IQ measures, it may very well be that the reason for this is because there is less overlap between measures (e.g. both traditional school instruction and IQ tests have substantial verbal content, while the Raven has far less verbal content). Examination of cross-cultural testing with the Raven suggests, though, that cultural groups without formal schooling perform less well on the test than cultural groups with traditional formal education programs (e.g. see Raven 1990).

6.2. Adult Education

There have been several longitudinal studies on the impact of college education on IQ measures. Bloom (1964) summarized the results of these studies, and determined that, after accounting for both test reliability and estimated variability of the samples, the average increase in intelligence ranged from 0.66 to 0.82 SD units. In IQ terms, this represents a gain of 10 to 12 points. While these results do not rule out practice or memory effects, such results appear to be generally robust, ranging across tests such as the Army Alpha, the GATB and the Thorndike Intelligence Test.

7. Other Central Issues

7.1. Plasticity and Developmental Limitations and the Implications for the Effects of Education on Intelligence

After a number of early studies on the constancy of the IQ indicated that change in IQ levels for infant and child subjects were not correlated with initial status, Anderson (1939) suggested the "overlap hypothesis" as an explanatory mechanism. In Anderson's formulation, 100% of intelligence is present in an individual at "terminal status" (presumed by Anderson to be around age 16). At earlier ages, progressively smaller portions of intelligence are present in the individual, such that for the child entering school, perhaps only 40–50% of the child's intelligence is actually developed. While Anderson's proposition was based on a relatively small set of longitudinal studies, the general sense of the overlap hypothesis suggests an important limitation on the role of schooling on intelligence (echoed by later investigators, such as Bloom 1964; Carroll 1985). That is, as a larger proportion of intelligence is obtained (e.g. as the individual grows in age close to "terminal status") the malleability of intelligence decreases. Identical educational interventions could thus be expected to have the greatest impact on younger children than older children. Today, there are differing views on this perspective — indeed some researchers suggest that failures in attempts to raise IQ (such as Head Start) falsify both the overlap hypothesis and any general notions that intelligence is malleable (e.g. see discussion by Jensen 1969). However, such arguments are consistent with Ceci's (1991) proposition that the quality of education is generally unrelated to improvements in intelligence, while the quantity of schooling is indeed related to intelligence change.

Another aspect of Anderson's (1939) overlap hypothesis is that changes in IQ from year to year were uncorrelated with initial standing. This conclusion has been questioned, in part because of the existence of empirical data that suggest those children with high initial standing on IQ tend to show greater gains over time (for a detailed discussion, see Cronbach & Snow 1977; see also Snow & Yalow 1982). This aspect of development is discussed further below, in the section concerned with the Matthew Effect.

7.2. Investment Theories and Differentiation of Intelligence

Investigators such as Cattell (1971/1987; see Ackerman 1996 for a review) have suggested an alternative view on the growth, maintenance and decline of intelligence during development. In Cattell's formulation of the "investment hypothesis", individual growth in intelligence (mostly centered on crystallized intelligence [Gc]) is the result of the investment of cognitive/intellectual resources over an extended period of time. In the context of the effects of education on intelligence, an investment approach suggests that, while average intelligence may not change from one year of schooling to the next, individuals may differ predictably in their patterns of stability and change in intelligence. Some individuals may choose not to invest their cognitive/intellectual resources toward new knowledge and skill learning (e.g. such as "sitting through" classes rather than engaging in the curriculum). As such, these individuals might have stable raw scores on intelligence measures, which might in turn, result in lower IQ scores. Other individuals may be positively engaged in education, and as a result experience both raw and relative increases in intelligence test performance. Aggregate measures of intelligence, though, may not be particularly diagnostic of such differences in intellectual investment. Instead, assessment of component abilities (e.g. verbal, numerical and spatial group factors), or more specific domain knowledge measures (e.g. science, arts, humanities, etc.) may be more illuminating. While this proposition has yet to be tested empirically, if true, it may be that the effects of schooling on intelligence are obscured by consistent patterns of growth and decline, depending on the nature of the students' involvement in the educational curriculum. It is reasonable to speculate that by the time students complete post-secondary education, the changes in intelligence associated with education are likely to be best illuminated by an idiographic approach, or at least an approach that is more curriculum specific and knowledge-domain specific.

7.3. Matthew Effects

Drawing on a large corpus of studies in the domain of individual differences in reading skills, Stanovich (1986) described the nature of development in reading and subsidiary component skills as a Matthew effect ("after the Gospel according to Matthew: "For unto every one that hath shall be given, and he shall have abundance: but from him that hath not shall be taken away even that which he hath" (XXV: 29). That is, at least in the verbal domain, the effect of schooling and development is that "the rich-get-richer" – those individuals with initially high levels of skill show subsequently greater gains in future achievements. For an early study of this concept in the context of intelligence, see Thorndike (1966). In considering omnibus intelligence, various commentators over the 20th Century have suggested that, at the lower levels of IQ, a complementary trend is often found (namely, that those with low IQs tend to fall further and further behind). In fact, this finding was one of the methodological arguments against the use of the traditional IQ (MA/CA X 100) computation formula. The notion is that the intellectual repertoire differs markedly between two sets of individuals with the same Mental Age, but different Chronological Ages. Findings of Matthew effects in the intelligence domain, though, must be predicated on raw test scores, and only then, when the content of the test is relatively consistent from one age group to another (or when the time of testing is relatively short). As of this writing, there are mixed results regarding the Matthew effect on intelligence measures – some empirical studies appear to suggest Matthew effects in some domains (such as in the verbal domain – e.g. see those reviewed by Stanovich), while other studies fail to find Matthew effects, especially those in the non-verbal content domains.

The possibility of Matthew effects, though, further complicates the evaluation of the influence of education on intelligence, since these effects require evaluation of the magnitude of interindividual variance in test performance over time. As with studies of changes in adult intellect, examination of only mean differences may not present a complete accounting of the effects of schooling.

8. Integration

Nearly 100 years after Spearman's and Binet's seminal contributions to the theory and measurement of intelligence, a full understanding of the relationship between education and *g* lies well beyond our grasp. This state of affairs can be attributed to several key factors, as follows:

(1) The inherent confounding of age and educational level;
(2) Failure of the *g*-theory approach to provide an account of the growth, maintenance, and decline of intelligence over the lifespan;
(3) Failure of the *g*-theory approach to provide a coherent operationalization of assessment methods for measurement;
(4) Dependence on "nature's experiments" (Cronbach 1957) for information on the role of education on the development of intelligence;
(5) Too few studies on the nature of changes in intelligence as a result of education, especially for adults.

Given that age and educational level both tend to increase in a linked fashion, it is impossible to completely separate the effects of development/maturation from the effects of schooling. Innovative designs, such as the contrast between same-age cohorts who begin school or are delayed one year, are particularly attractive for study.

g-Theorists are apparently caught in a conundrum. On the one hand, if they admit that *g* grows, peaks and then declines with age (as IQ theorists have), *g* ceases to be a construct that is unrelated to development and experience. If *g* is influenced by experience, then it cannot be an immutable aspect of the individual. On the other hand, if they fail to admit that *g* changes with age, development and education, there is an inherent dissociation between the construct of *g* and any measure that purports to assess *g*. For example, even simple reaction time studies show a clear improvement from childhood to early adult ages.

The coherent operationalization of *g* assessment represents another serious challenge. In Spearman's evolving sense of exemplary measures of *g*, he first suggested sensory and other psychophysical assessments, then tests dominated by verbal abilities (the Ebbinghaus completion test – see Ackerman *et al.* 2001), and finally non-verbal tests of reasoning (the Raven test). The more basic information processing and physiological measures suggested by later researchers generally fail to relate to education, but also can be expected to have non-trivial changes in growth and decline over the lifespan. To date, no comprehensive representation of these various measures has been provided, that relates the measures to one another. In contrast, intelligence investigators (see, e.g. Carroll 1993; Marshalek *et al.* 1983; Vernon 1961) have generally settled on consensual representations of the component abilities that make up omnibus intelligence (which they call *g*, but this *g* differs in many ways from Spearman's conceptualization – see Gustafsson & Undheim 1996).

Traditional differential psychologists have been relegated to study "nature's experiments" (Cronbach 1957), in that a study of random assignment of children to "school" vs. "no school" is neither practical nor ethical. At the adult level, there is presumably somewhat more flexibility for policy makers. For example, in the 1960s, the U.S. military accepted 100,000 individuals of generally lower intelligence into the armed forces – and subsequently contrasted the performance of these individuals with those who passed the normal intelligence test screening. Colleges and universities often select individuals of widely differing intelligence levels, for a variety of reasons, rather than a 'top-down' selection. Thus, study of the effects of education on intelligence for adults may be more likely to provide critical information that cannot be readily obtained with children. Such an approach may be especially illuminating with the study of older or other non-traditional students.

If Ceci's (1991) assertion is correct – that is, that the quality of schooling has a much diminished influence on intelligence than the quantity of schooling, then aptitude-treatment interaction studies with intelligence scores as the dependent variable will find only modest effects. This has been the general conclusion of at least some observers (though see Cronbach & Snow 1977; Snow & Yalow 1982 for somewhat divergent perspectives).

9. Conclusions

The notion that "intelligence influences educational success" has been taken as a 'given' among most theorists and researchers over the past century. As Ceci (1991) noted, the notion that "education influences intelligence" is a much less-well accepted claim. The corpus of data suggests that both propositions are likely to be true to one degree or another, especially in terms of IQ test scores. The verisimilitude of these propositions, though, is most clearly demonstrated *at the margins*. Thus, individuals with very low measured intelligence are most highly likely to fail in mainstream educational assignments. Similarly, the complete absence of schooling appears highly likely to lead to very low measured intelligence. In between, the effects of intelligence on educational success and the effects of schooling on intelligence become attenuated. It is clear, however, that measured intelligence is not fixed and constant (e.g. see Bayley 1949; Thorndike 1940). It appears that, generally speaking, the effects of education on intelligence tend to be more marked with younger children than with adults – but this point is still somewhat controversial. The factors that influence change in intelligence may be general (such as Matthew Effects), or they may be multifaceted, such as involving constellations of traits (called trait complexes, after Snow 1963) that are mutually supportive or impeding for intellectual development (see Ackerman 1996, 2000; Ackerman & Heggestad 1997; Ackerman & Rolfhus 1999; Cattell 1971/1987, for discussions).

9.1. What about Spearman's g?

In this chapter, we have tried to address issues of education and intelligence that transcend the particular methods used to assess the construct of intelligence, partly because of the paucity of data that explicitly relates g measures (of the kind recommended by Spearman) to education. If we attempt to work back to the various extant operationalizations of g, some conclusions can be offered, while others must be deferred until more empirical data are available. For those measures that exemplify Spearman's initial operationalization of g (e.g. Completion Test, synonyms and antonyms, verbal memory), the results described for IQ measures are likely to be highly congruent, given two factors: (1) the overlap between these measures and the test content of most major omnibus IQ tests; and (2) the high verbal content of standard school instruction. For Spearman's subsequent operationalization (e.g. the Raven test), the influence of g on school success appears to be substantially attenuated, across the range of education from early childhood to adult schooling. It appears likely (though not yet substantiated by sufficient empirical data) that the effects of standard schooling on the Raven test are diminished in comparison to IQ measures. It should be noted, though, that there have been quite successful educational interventions that have resulted in substantial gains in performance on tests of non-verbal problem solving (see Denny & Heidrich 1990 for an example). Given the narrowness of the content of the Raven test, performance on the test is likely to be much more affected by drill-and-practice than traditional omnibus IQ tests. Whether such results represent a generalizable gain in intelligence beyond constrained non-verbal reasoning test items, remains to be seen.

As noted earlier, there are few empirical studies that demonstrate an association between basic information processing measures of g (e.g. simple reaction time, inspection time) or physiological measures of g (e.g. nerve conduction velocity) and probability of school success. There are virtually no studies that evaluate the effects of schooling or the lack of schooling on these measures. Whether these measures can be tied to education, either as causal determinants of success or as concomitant indicators of educational treatments, remains to be seen.

References

Ackerman, P. L. (1994). Intelligence, attention, and learning: Maximal and typical performance. In: D. K. Detterman (Ed.), *Current topics in human intelligence* (Vol. 4) *Theories of Intelligence* (pp. 1–27). Norwood, NJ: Ablex.

Ackerman, P. L. (1996). A theory of adult intellectual development: process, personality, interests, and knowledge. *Intelligence, 22*, 229–259.

Ackerman, P. L. (2000). Domain-specific knowledge as the "dark matter" of adult intelligence: gf/gc, personality and interest correlates. *Journal of Gerontology: Psychological Sciences, 55B* (2), p69–p84.

Ackerman, P. L., Beier, M. E., & Bowen, K. R. (2001). Explorations of crystallized intelligence: Completion tests, cloze tests and knowledge. *Learning and Individual Differences: A Multidisciplinary Journal in Education, 12*, 107–123.

Ackerman, P. L., & Heggestad, E. D. (1997). Intelligence, personality, and interests: Evidence for overlapping traits. *Psychological Bulletin, 121*, 219–245.

Ackerman, P. L., & Rolfhus, E. L. (1999). The locus of adult intelligence: Knowledge, abilities, and non-ability traits. *Psychology and Aging, 14*, 314–330.

Anastasi, A. (1982). *Psychological testing* (5th ed.). New York: MacMillan.

Anderson, J. E. (1939). The limitations of infant and preschool tests in the measurement of intelligence. *The Journal of Psychology, 8*, 351–379.

Bayley, N. (1949). Consistency and variability in the growth of intelligence from birth to eighteen years. *Journal of Genetic Psychology, 75*, 165–196.

Binet, A., & Simon, T. (1905). New methods for the diagnosis of the intellectual level of subnormals. *L'Année Psychologique, 11*, 191–244. Translated by Elizabeth S. Kite and reprinted in J. J. Jenkins & D. G. Paterson (Eds), *Studies of individual differences: The search for intelligence* (pp. 90–96). New York: Appleton-Century-Crofts.

Bloom, B. S. (1964). *Stability and change in human characteristics.* New York: Wiley.

Burks, B. S. (1928). The relative influence of nature and nurture upon mental development; a comparative study of foster parent-foster child resemblance and true parent-true child resemblance. *Yearbook of the National Society for the Study of Education*, (Pt. I), 219–316.

Carroll, J. B. (1985) Statement of Dr John B. Carroll, Professor of Educational Psychology, Harvard University. In: L. W. Anderson (Ed.), *Perspectives on school learning: Selected writings of John B Carroll* (1985). Hillsdale, NJ: Lawrence Erlbaum Associates.

Carroll, J. B. (1993). *Human cognitive abilities: A survey of factor-analytic studies.* New York: Cambridge University Press.

Cattell, R. B. (1971/1987). *Abilities: Their structure, growth and action.* [Revised and reprinted as *Intelligence: Its structure, growth, and action*]. Amsterdam: North-Holland.

Ceci, S. J. (1991). How much does schooling influence general intelligence and its cognitive components? A reassessment of the evidence. *Developmental Psychology, 27*, 703–722.

Cronbach, L. J. (1957). The two disciplines of scientific psychology. *American Psychologist, 12*, 671–684.

Cronbach, L. J., & Snow, R. E. (1977). *Aptitudes and instructional methods: A handbook for research on interactions.* New York: Irvington Publishers.

Denny, N. W., & Heidrich, S. M. (1990). Training effects on Raven's Progressive Matrices in Young, Middle-Aged, and elderly adults. *Psychology and Aging, 5*, 144–145.

Embretson, S. E., & McCollam, K. M. S. (2000). Psychometric approaches to understanding and measuring intelligence. In: R. J. Sternberg (Ed.), *Handbook of intelligence* (pp. 423–444), New York: Cambridge University Press.

Flynn, J. R., (1987). Massive IQ gains in 14 nations: what IQ tests really measure. *Psychological Bulletin, 101* (2), 171–191.

Gustafsson, J-E. (1984). A unifying model for the structure of intellectual abilities. *Intelligence, 8*, 179–203.

Gustafsson, J-E., & Undheim, J. O. (1996). Individual differences in cognitive functions. In: D. C. Berliner, & R. C. Calfee (Eds), *Handbook of educational psychology* (pp. 186–242). New York: Simon & Schuster Macmillan.

Honzik, M. P., Macfarlane, J. W., & Allen, L. (1948). The stability of mental test performance between two and eighteen years. *Journal of Experimental Education, 17,* 309–324.

Humphreys, L. G. (1968). The fleeting nature of the prediction of college academic success. *Journal of Educational Psychology, 59,* 375–380.

Humphreys, L. G., & Taber, T. (1973). Postdiction study of the graduate record examination and eight semesters of college grades. *Journal of Educational Measurement, 10,* 179–184.

Jensen, A. R. (1969). How much can we boost IQ and scholastic achievement? *Harvard Educational Review, 39,* 1–123.

Jensen, A. R. (1993). Spearman's *g*: Links between psychometrics and biology. *Annals of the New York Academy of Sciences, 702,* 103–129.

Jensen, A. R. (1998). *The g factor: The science of mental ability.* Westport, CT: Praeger.

Jensen, A. R., & Rohwer, W. D. Jr. (1968). Mental retardation, mental age, and learning rate. *Journal of Educational Psychology, 59,* 402–403.

Jones, H. E. (1946/1975). Environmental influences on mental development. Originally published 1946. In: J. K. Gardner, & H. Gardner (Eds), *Factors determining intellectual attainment.* New York, Arno.

Krueger, F., & Spearman, C. (1907). Die Korrelation zwischen verschiedenen geistigen Leistungsfahigkeiten. *Zeitschrift fur Psychologie (Leipzig), 44,* 50–114. (Translated by Werner W. Wittmann).

Kyllonen, P. C., & Christal, R. E. (1990). Reasoning ability is (little more than) working-memory capacity?! *Intelligence, 14,* 389–433.

Lippmann, W. (1922). The mental age of Americans. *New Republic, 32,* 213–215.

Marshalek, B., Lohman, D. F., & Snow, R. E. (1983). The complexity continuum in the radex and hierarchical models of intelligence. *Intelligence, 7,* 107–127.

Oxford English Dictionary (The Compact Edition) (1971). New York: Oxford University Press.

Penrose, L. S., & Raven, J. C. (1936). A new series of perceptual tests: Preliminary communication. *British Journal of Medical Psychology, 16,* 97–105.

Peterson, N. S., Kolen, M. J., & Hoover, H. D. (1989). Scaling, norming, and equating. In: R. Linn (Ed.), *Educational measurement* (pp. 221–262). New York: American Council on Education/Macmillan.

Pinneau, S. R. (1961). *Changes in intelligence quotient, infancy to maturity: new insights from the Berkeley growth study, with implications for the Stanford-Binet scales, and application to professional practice.* Boston, MA: Houghton Mifflin.

Plato (1974). *The Republic* (D. Lee, Trans.). New York: Penguin Books.

Raven, J. (1990). *Manual for Raven's Progressive Matrices and Vocabulary Scales: Research Supplement No. 3* (2nd ed.). San Antonio, TX: The Psychological Corporation/Oxford Psychologists Press.

Raven, J. C., Court, J. H., & Raven, J. (1977). *Raven's progressive matrices and vocabulary scales.* New York: Psychological Corporation.

Robinson, R. (1950). *Definition.* Oxford: Oxford University Press.

Schaie, K. W. (1996). *Intellectual development in adulthood: The Seattle longitudinal study.* New York: Cambridge University Press.

Snow, R. E. (1963). *Effects of learner characteristics in learning from instructional films.* Unpublished doctoral dissertation, Purdue University, Lafayette, Indiana.

Snow, R. E. (1982). The training of intellectual aptitude. In: D. K. Detterman & R. J. Sternberg (Eds), *How and how much can intelligence be increased* (pp. 1–37). Norwood, NJ: Ablex Publishing Corp.

Snow, R. E. (1996). Aptitude development and education. *Psychology, Public Policy, and Law, 2*, 536–560.

Snow, R. E., & Yalow, E. (1982). Education and intelligence. In: R. J. Sternberg (Ed.), *Handbook of human intelligence* (pp. 493–585). Cambridge: Cambridge University Press.

Spearman, C. (1904). "General intelligence", objectively determined and measured. *American Journal of Psychology, 15*, 201–293.

Spearman, C. (1914). The theory of two factors. *Psychological Review, 21* (2), 101–115.

Spearman, C. (1927). *The nature of "intelligence" and the principles of cognition*. London: Macmillan and Co.

Spearman, C. (1930). Disturbers of tetrad differences. Scales. *Journal of Educational Psychology, 21*, 559–573.

Spearman, C. (1931). Our need of some science in place of the word "intelligence". *Journal of Educational Psychology, 22*, 401–411.

Spearman, C. E. (1938). Measurement of intelligence. *Scientia, Milano, 64*, 75–82.

Spearman, C. (1939). "Intelligence" tests. *Eugenics Review, 30*, 249–254.

Stanovich, K. E. (1986). Matthew effects in reading. Some consequences of individual differences in the acquisition of literacy. *Reading Research Quarterly, 21*, 360–406.

Stern, W. (1914). *The psychological methods of testing intelligence*. (Translated from the german by Guy Montrose Whipple). Baltimore: Warwick & York. (listed as Educational Psychology Monographs, No. 13).

Terman, L. M. (1916). *The measurement of intelligence*. Boston, MA: Houghton Mifflin Co.

Thorndike, R. L. (1940). "Constancy" of the IQ. *Psychological Bulletin, 37*, 167–186.

Thorndike, R. L. (1966). Intellectual status and intellectual growth. *Journal of Educational Psychology, 57*, 121–127.

Thorndike, R. L. (1987). Stability of factor loadings. *Personality and Individual Differences, 8*, 585–586.

Thorndike, R. L. (1994). g. *Intelligence, 19*, 145–155.

Thurstone, L. L. (1931). Multiple factor analysis. *Psychological Review, 38*, 406–427.

Undheim, J. O., & Gustafsson, J. (1987). The hierarchical organization of cognitive abilities: Restoring general intelligence through the use of linear structural relations (LISREL). *Multivariate Behavioral Research, 22*, 149–171.

Vernon, P. E. (1961). *The structure of human abilities*. New York: Wiley.

Willingham, W. W. (1974). Predicting success in graduate education. *Science, 183*, 273–278.

Chapter 15

g, Jobs and Life

Linda S. Gottfredson

1. Horizontal and Vertical Aspects of *g*

Arthur Jensen has reinvigorated and redirected the study of human intelligence in major ways. Perhaps the most important has been to turn the field's attention back to Spearman's *g*, the general intelligence factor. The discovery that the same *g* factor emerges from diverse batteries of mental tests in diverse populations, together with the consequent option to derive scores for individuals on this common factor, has allowed intelligence researchers to make some crucial advances.

- To clearly distinguish "intelligence" (*g*) from the vehicles of its measurement (e.g. test format or content);
- To employ a common working definition of intelligence — *g* — despite using different tests of mental ability;
- To narrow the range of theoretical possibilities for what intelligence is, and to focus specifically on conceptions that emphasize a highly general (i.e. content- and context-free) set of mental capabilities or properties of the brain; and thereby
- To transcend some long-standing debates over the "real" meaning of intelligence and IQ: Which of the many verbal definitions of "intelligence" is correct for guiding research? (With *g* as the common yardstick, the question becomes moot.) Don't IQ scores represent just the arbitrary cultural knowledge that IQ tests happen to require? (No, they tap something much more general.)

The construct of *g* has arguably become our most valuable conceptual tool for probing the nature and origins of differences in "intelligence", as many chapters in this volume attest.

Another advantage of the *g* construct is that, in providing a common scale for measuring the differences in intelligence among people, the *g* factor also provides a common yardstick for comparing the mental *demands* of different *tasks*. Just as individuals can be distinguished in their levels of *g* (their "mental horsepower"), so too can tasks be distinguished in their *g loadedness* (the degree to which they call forth *g*). The classification of tasks and tests by *g* loading (their correlation with the *g* factor) has

The Scientific Study of General Intelligence: Tribute to Arthur R. Jensen
Copyright © 2003 by Elsevier Science Ltd.
All rights of reproduction in any form reserved.
ISBN: 0–08–043793–1

been essential in explaining why test results can differ substantially across different mental tests. In particular, we now know that some IQ tests and subtests are more *g* loaded than others (call forth *g* more effectively) and therefore should yield different patterns of results (for example, to better distinguish retarded from normal or gifted individuals). This variation in results stems not from flaws in intelligence tests or in the concept of intelligence itself, as was once alleged, but from the variability among tasks being used to evoke *g*.

The notion that tasks differ in their demands for *g* has importance far beyond psychometric testing, however. The notion is key to unraveling the consequences of intelligence in social life, what Jensen (1998) calls the horizontal aspect of *g*. Jensen himself has focused mostly on the vertical aspect of *g* (its biological roots), but he has provided the conceptual tools for others to advance its horizontal study. For instance, Jensen's insights on the properties of mental tasks have prompted sociologist Robert Gordon (1997) to analyze the psychometric properties of daily life as an intelligence test. He shows how the degree to which daily life mimics rather than departs from the properties of a reliable, valid test of intelligence helps to explain the pattern of both *g*'s impact across life as well as people's likelihood of perceiving that impact. Jensen's insights on mental tasks have also led to research (Gottfredson 1997; in press) on how differences in task attributes systematically shift *g*'s gradients of effect in employment, health and other domains of life. This chapter develops these themes further in order to show that, by turning attention to the psychometric properties of the tasks people perform, Jensen has opened up new ways of understanding how individual and group differences in *g* shape our individual and collective fates.

2. Life as a Mental Test Battery

"What role does intelligence play in our personal and collective lives?" To date, the answer to this question has been sought primarily in correlating individuals' scores on mental tests (such as IQ tests) with various personal outcomes (such as educational and occupational achievement). Considerable such research has been amassed, and I will summarize major portions of it. What the research has confirmed, besides the pervasive utility of *g*, is that the practical advantages of possessing higher levels of *g* depend on the nature of the tasks performed. In this sense, life is like a mental test battery containing subtests with a wide range of *g* loadings. Viewing life as a mental test (Gordon 1997) raises the following sorts of questions, which in turn prompt new ways of interpreting old evidence and gathering new data on *g*'s gradients of effect.

2.1. What is the Distribution, by g Loading, of the Many "Subtests" we Take in Life's Extensive Mental Test Battery?

Life is like a mental test battery in that the advantages of higher *g* are not uniform; rather, they depend on the complexity (and hence *g* loading) of the tasks we confront. Therefore, what is the distribution of tasks, by *g* loading, within different realms of life (work, family, health, etc.)? Do the distributions differ much from one realm to another, and why?

2.2. To What Extent Do We Take Common Versus Different Sets of "Subtests" in Life?

Life differs from a mental test battery in that we tend to take somewhat different batteries, that is, we are subjected to somewhat different sets of demands for *g*. For instance, we can become experts in some arenas (occupations, avocations, etc.) that other people do not. This non-comparability in undertakings allows us to create niches more compatible with our talents and interests, but it also makes it more difficult to compare the actual impact of *g* in our lives (Gordon 1997). To what extent, then, do we all take the same "subtests" in life?

2.3. To What Extent Do Our Differences in g Determine Which Set of Subtests we Take in Life?

Unlike IQ testers, life offers us some choice in the tests we take (e.g. raising children or not; trying to succeed as a teacher or plumber rather than a bank teller or truck driver). We have some freedom to pursue tasks within our competence and to avoid those that are either too easy or too hard. Our social worlds also parcel out opportunities and obligations to some extent according to our ability to handle them. Indeed, people often choose or are assigned different tasks precisely to avoid invidious distinctions in competence (Gordon 1997). As just suggested, differences in intelligence and their impact on everyday competence become difficult to perceive when people undertake non-comparable activities. (Is person A smarter as an electrician than person B is as a doctor?) However, we often pursue different activities precisely because we do differ in general intelligence. Accordingly, the very act of pursuing different activities often signals intelligence (Person B is likely to be smarter because doctors are brighter than electricians, on average). When we take different "tests", then, to what extent is that owing to ourselves — or others — selecting or refashioning the "tests" we take *based on our g level*?

2.4. To What Extent Are Life's Tests Standardized?

Mental testers work hard to standardize the conditions under which we take tests, precisely to rule out other influences on our performance. Not so life. Most parents want to give their children "a leg up". Such external advantages can either soften or accentuate the impact of *g*, depending on whether the least bright or the brightest individuals receive the most help or make the best use of it. Therefore, even when we do take common tests (e.g. mastering the elementary school curriculum, earning a livelihood, and so on), to what extent do we take them under standard conditions? Do people differ greatly, for instance, in the help or advance preparation they get — or extract — from their social environments? And to what extent is that help correlated — positively or negatively — with g? Positive correlations can magnify the practical value of having higher g, whereas negative correlations between g and help can compensate somewhat for (though never neutralize) lower levels of g.

2.5. Do Many Weakly g-Loaded Activities Cumulate to Produce Highly g-Loaded Life Outcomes?

Like the individual items on an IQ test, no single life task is likely to be very highly g loaded. g's impact in life may therefore stem largely from the consistency of its influence in long streams of behavior — that is, from virtually all life activities being g loaded to at least some small degree. Other factors are often more important than g in correctly answering any one particular IQ test item, but none has such a consistent influence throughout the test as does g. That is the secret of why IQ tests measure g so well — the "specificities" in the items cancel each other out when enough items are administered, but the effects of g accumulate. Perhaps so in life too. Might the many weakly g-loaded actions in life cumulate in the same manner to account for g's often strong and always robust correlations with the various overall outcomes in life, good and bad (good education, jobs, and income vs. unemployment, out-of-wedlock births, and incarceration)?

2.6. To What Extent, and How, Do a Society's Members (its "Test Takers") Create and Reshape the Mental Test Battery that the Society "Administers" to Current and New Generations?

As noted, people are not passive beings to which some independent, larger social order administers a preordained set of life tests. Rather, individuals shape their own lives in substantial measure by the many big and small choices they make over a lifetime. If their behavior is shaped to a significant degree by their differences in mental ability, as seems to be the case, so too will be the enduring patterns of behavior they collectively create across an entire society and which become institutionalized as elements of social structure. Therefore, just as our different capabilities may head us toward different rungs on the social ladder, might not our disparate choices for ourselves and others create or modify the ladder itself over time — for example, by gradually clustering economic tasks into stable sets (occupations) that differ widely in their information processing demands? Specifically, might the occupational hierarchy itself have evolved in response to enduring human variability in mental competence? And in what other ways might a society's attempts to accommodate this mental diversity be mirrored in the ways it structures itself over time?

In short, understanding the impact of g in social life requires knowing more about the mental demands of everyday life and how people try to adjust to or modify them. It requires examining the interaction between, on the one hand, a population whose members differ widely in *g* levels with, on the other hand, a social world whose tasks differ widely over age, place and time in their *g* loadings.

3. Jobs as Life Tests

What evidence is there that life is like a mental test battery, in particular, a highly *g*-loaded one? Some have claimed, for instance, that the general mental ability factor, *g*, is only "a tiny and not very important part" of the mental spectrum (Sternberg 1997: 11) and that it "applies largely, although not exclusively, to academic kinds of tasks" (Sternberg *et al.* 2000: xii). If that were so, then pursuing the foregoing questions would yield useless answers. The considerable evidence about occupations, employment and career development shows, however, that differences in *g* play a powerful role in the world of work.

Next to educational achievement, job performance has probably been the most exhaustively studied correlate of general intelligence. Personnel selection psychologists and job analysts have performed many thousands of studies to determine which aptitudes and abilities different jobs require for good performance. The large status attainment literature in sociology has correlated academic ability (it eschews the term intelligence) with life outcomes such as occupational level and income at different ages. These psychological and sociological literatures are not only vast but also provide a valuable contrast: namely, whereas on-the-job performance is a proximal, short-term correlate of *g*, occupation and income level are more distal, cumulative outcomes because they represent the culmination of a long process of developing and exercising job-related skills as well as negotiating an elaborate social system. This distinction between proximal and distal, discrete and cumulative outcomes becomes very important, as we will see, in understanding *g*'s role in other domains of life, from daily health self-care to ending up with illegitimate children or a prison record.

In what follows, I apply the perspective of occupations as mental tests to the sociological and psychological evidence, reviewed below, on occupational differentiation, job performance and occupational status attainment. Such application reveals that *g* exerts its effects in ways that are not unique to the workplace.

3.1. Hierarchy of Occupations' Recruitment Ranges for IQ

Jobs are similar to psychometric tests in the sense that they are constellations of tasks (items) that individuals are asked to perform, and where performance is judged against some standard of correct or incorrect, better or worse. These task constellations, or "tests", also tend to be reasonably stable and reliably different, that is, they can generally be classified into different "occupations" (classes of test). Just as there are many types of verbal ability tests, intelligence tests and the like, there are different varieties of teacher, electrician and physician.

An early hint that occupations might constitute reliably different mental tests came from several converging lines of research. The most systematic such evidence was the sociological work on the occupational hierarchy, which showed not only that all social groups rank occupations in the same order of prestige (Hodge *et al.* 1966), but also that the average IQ of an occupation's incumbents is correlated 0.8 to 0.9 with that occupation's prestige level (e.g. Canter 1956). Psychological research in both the military and civilian sectors revealed the same high correlation between occupational level and incumbents' IQs (e.g. Stewart 1947; U.S. Department of Labor 1970).

Figure 15.1 illustrates this phenomenon with more recent data from the Wonderlic Personnel Test (Wonderlic 1992). The occupations are ordered hierarchically according to their IQ recruitment ranges, but it is apparent that this ordering mirrors the prestige hierarchy of work. They range from the simplest, lowest-level jobs, such as a packer in a factory, to the most complex and prestigious jobs, such as an attorney. As shown in the figure, the range of IQs from which jobs recruit even the middle 50% of their applicants is wide (typically 15–20 IQ points, or 1.0–1.3 SD), but the recruitment range shifts steadily upward on the IQ continuum for increasingly higher-level jobs. (IQ ranges for actual hires are narrower — Gottfredson 1997 — and so probably differ more from one job to another for incumbents than they do for applicants.) Median IQ for applicants rises from about IQ 87 for packer to IQ 120 for attorney, an increase of over 2.0 SD.

In short, more demanding and more socially desirable occupations recruit their workers from higher reaches of the IQ distribution. This suggests that occupations are, indeed, life tests that differ markedly not only in manifest content but also in their demands for *g* — just as do the tests in any broad battery of mental tests. Figure 15.1 also gives a concrete sense of the wide range of jobs — life's occupational tests — that populate any economy.

3.2. Analyses of Jobs' Task Demands

That smarter workers get better jobs does not mean that better jobs actually require more brains, however. As many sociologists have rightly pointed out, employers may simply prefer, but not really need, smarter workers and may select them, among other reasons, simply for the greater status an elite workforce confers on the employer. Do higher level jobs actually require more brain power to get the work done? One answer comes from job analysis research. I review it in some detail because of its special importance for understanding jobs as mental tests. By illuminating the detailed task content of jobs, the research illustrates that jobs, like mental tests, are purposeful collections of individual tasks that call for skilled performance. And just as people's scores on mental test batteries have been factor analyzed to reveal more basic ability factors (e.g. Carroll 1993), so too have jobs' task demands been factor analyzed to uncover their more fundamental dimensionality.

Personnel researchers have collected extensive data on the aptitude and task demands of different jobs in order to improve hiring and training procedures, rationalize pay scales, and the like. Sociologists have collected parallel data on the socioeconomic requirements and rewards of occupations in order to better understand the nature and origins of social inequality. When factor analyzed, both sets of data reveal a task complexity factor among job demands that coincides with the occupational prestige

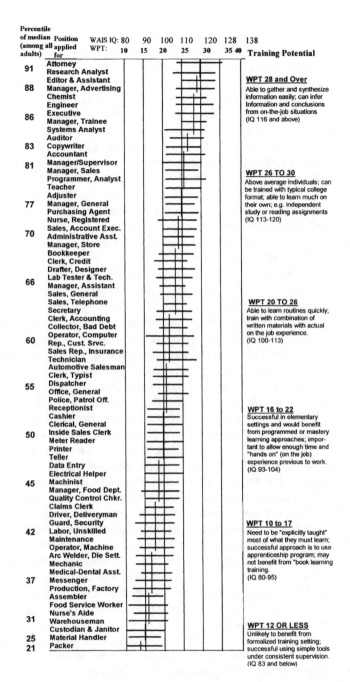

Figure 15.1: Wonderlic Personnel Test (WPT) scores by position applied for (1992). The bold horizontal line shows the range between the 25th and 75th percentiles. The bold crossmark shows the 50th percentile (median) of applicants to that job. Source: Wonderlic (1992: 20, 26, 27). Reprinted by permission of the publisher.

hierarchy. What Figure 15.1 only suggested, the job analysis data prove: there is a *g*-demands factor dominating the occupational structure that parallels the *g*-skills factor dominating the structure of human mental abilities.

Tables 15.1 and 15.2 summarize an analysis of several sets of job analysis data for most occupational titles in the United States economy around 1970. (See Gottfredson 1984, 1997, for a complete description of the data used to create the tables.) Table 15.1 shows the results of a principal components analysis that included the 32 broad "dimension" scores of the Position Analysis Questionnaire (PAQ), a well-known job analysis instrument, together with the rated demands for each of the aptitudes measured by the U.S. Employment Service's General Aptitude Test Battery (GATB).

The principal components analysis yielded 10 factors, the dominant one being the "overall complexity" of the job. The job attributes loading highly on this first factor include the PAQ dimensions of using many sources of information, processing information, making decisions and communicating those judgments, as well as the strictly cognitive GATB aptitudes (verbal, numerical, clerical and not physical strength). The complexity factor that dominates these job analysis data replicates earlier sociological work, which also described the primary distinction among occupations as a "complexity" dimension (Miller *et al.* 1980; Spaeth 1979). The other nine factors remind us that jobs differ along other dimensions as well — for instance, special aptitudes (e.g. spatial ability) and interests required (e.g. people vs. things). Nonetheless, occupations seem to be distinguished primarily by the complexity of their demands for information processing — that is, their demands for *g*.

Table 15.2 provides more evidence of this by correlating each of the 10 factors in Table 15.1 with more specific job attributes that were not included in the principal components analysis. Attributes are listed according to whether they correlate most highly with the complexity factor rather than with one of the nine other factors. The job characteristics are further subdivided according to whether they represent information-processing demands, different kinds of practical problem solving, level of responsibility and respect, degree of structure and supervision, interests required and so on.

With only two consistent exceptions, all information-processing demands (the top panel in Table 15.2) correlate most highly with the job complexity factor. The exceptions involve sight and vigilance with physical materials, and are associated, respectively, with the "work with complex things" and "vigilance with machines" factors. The information-processing demands that are correlated most highly with the task complexity factor involve compiling, combining and analyzing information and, hence, reasoning. They connote *g* itself. The information-processing demands differ in the degree to which they correlate with the job complexity factor, but this variation accords with the complexity of the processes that the demands represent: the more complex information processes (e.g. compiling, combining and analyzing information) correlate more strongly with overall job complexity than do the simpler ones (e.g. transcribing information and holding it in short-term memory).

Intelligence is often described in terms of problem solving, and many of the job requirements associated with the task complexity factor in the second panel of Table 15.2 are, in fact, general forms of problem solving. For example, requirements for advising, planning, decision-making, persuading and instructing correlate highly with

Table 15.1: Factor loadings from a principal components analysis (Varimax rotation) of 32 PAQ divisional factors and 9 DOT aptitude ratings.

PAQ and DOT ratings	Factors									
	1 Overall Complexity	2 Work With Complex Things	3 Vigilance With Machines	4 Operating Machines	5 Controlled Manual	6 Catering to People	7 Coordination Without Sight	8 Selling	9 Using Senses	10 Specified Apparel
2 — Using various info sources	0.92									
17 — Communicating judgments	0.91									
30 — Job-demanding circumstances	0.90									
DOT Verbal aptitude[a]	0.87			-0.26						
26 — Businesslike situations	0.82				-0.27					
23 — Personally-demanding situations	0.81					0.27				
7 — Making decisions	0.80				0.34		-0.26			
DOT Numerical aptitude[a]	0.80									
DOT Clerical perception[a]	0.76						0.29			
DOT Strength	-0.72				0.37					
8 — Processing Information	0.71						0.38			
12 — Skilled/technical activities	0.62	0.47								
10 — General body movement	-0.49					0.55				
24 — Hazardous job situations	-0.38		0.36		0.28				0.27	
DOT Form perception[a]		0.86					0.32			
DOT Finger dexterity[a]		0.81					-0.27			
DOT Spatial ability[a]		0.76	0.26							
DOT Motor coordination[a]	-0.30	0.72					0.40			
DOT Manual dexterity[a]	-0.52	0.70								
3 — Watching devices/materials		0.59	-0.38	-0.33	0.25		-0.34			
5 — Aware of environment			0.77							
11 — Controlling machines/processes			0.73							
32 — Alert to changing conditions			0.68	0.34	0.31	0.29				

Table 15.1: Continued.

PAQ and DOT ratings	Factors									
	1 Overall Complexity	2 Work With Complex Things	3 Vigilance With Machines	4 Operating Machines	5 Controlled Manual	6 Catering to People	7 Coordination Without Sight	8 Selling	9 Using Senses	10 Specified Apparel
14 — Misc. equipment/devices	-0.40		0.60							
9 — Using machines/tools	-0.28			0.70						
1 — Interpreting what sensed			0.30	0.63						
31 — Structured work	-0.48			0.59			0.29			
25 — Typical day schedule			-0.46	-0.46						
13 — Controlled manual activities	-0.27	0.38			0.63	-0.32				
20 — Exchanging job information			0.31	0.25	0.59		0.38			
22 — Unpleasant environment	-0.48		0.27		0.56					
19 — Supervisory/coordination			0.26			0.86	-0.32			
18 — General personal contacts						-0.49				
29 — Regular schedule							0.82			
16 — General physical coordination	0.25									
21 — Public/related contacts								0.80		
28 — Variable pay vs. salary								0.73		
6 — Using various senses									0.87	0.29
4 — Evaluating what is sensed									0.81	
27 — Optional vs. specified apparel										-0.82
15 — Handling/related manual			-0.34	0.37		0.35				-0.41
Eigenvalues	10.5	4.6	4.3	2.5	1.9	1.7	1.6	1.4	1.3	1.0
Variance (%)	25.7	11.3	10.6	6.2	4.6	4.2	3.8	3.4	3.1	2.5

[a] DOT aptitude scales are reversed for ease of interpretation.

Reprinted from Gottfredson, L. S. (1997). Why g matters: The complexity of everyday life. *Intelligence, 24* (1), 79–132. With permission from Elsevier Science.

Table 15.2: Job attributes that correlate most with the job complexity factor.

Correlate most with "complexity" factor	r	Correlate most with another factor	r	The other factor
I. Processing information (perceiving, retrieving, manipulating, transmitting it)				
compiling information, importance of	0.90	seeing (DOT)	0.66	work with complex things
combining information, importance of	0.88	information from events, extent of use	0.58	vigilance with machines
language, level of (DOT)	0.88	vigilance: changing events, importance of	0.57	vigilance with machines
reasoning, level of (DOT)	0.86	pictorial materials, extent of use	0.44	work with complex things
writing, importance of	0.86	apply measurable, verifiable criteria (DOT)	0.43	work with complex things
intelligence (DOT)	0.84	vigilance: infrequent events, importance of	0.41	vigilance with machines
written information, extent of use	0.84	patterns, extent of use	0.41	work with complex things
analyzing information, importance of	0.83	interpret others' feelings, ideas, facts (DOT)	0.22	catering to people
math, level of (DOT)	0.79			
math, level of	0.70			
quantitative information, extent of use	0.68			
coding/decoding, importance of	0.68			
oral information, extent of use	0.68			
talking (DOT)	0.68			
behavioral information, extent of use	0.59			
apply sensory/judgmental criteria (DOT)	0.55			
attention to detail, importance of	0.54			
transcribing, importance of	0.51			
short-term memory, importance of	0.40			
recognize/identify, importance of	0.36			

Table 15.2: Continued.

Correlate most with "complexity" factor	r	Correlate most with another factor	r	The other factor
II. Practical problem solving				
advising, importance of	0.86	supervising non-employees, importance of	0.64	catering to people
planning/scheduling, amount of	0.83	catering/serving, importance of	0.61	catering to people
decision making, level of	0.82	entertaining, importance of	0.59	catering to people
negotiating, importance of	0.79	non-job-required social contact, opportunity	0.25	catering to people
persuading, importance of	0.79			
staff functions, importance of	0.79			
coordinate without line authority, import of	0.74			
public speaking, importance of	0.68			
instructing, importance of	0.67			
direction/control/planning (DOT)	0.59			
dealing with people (DOT)	0.59			
dealing with people (DOT)	0.42			
III. Level of responsibility and respect				
prestige (Temme)	0.82	responsibility for materials, degree of	0.48	vigilance with machines
general responsibility, degree of	0.76	responsibility for safety, degree of	0.47	vigilance with machines
criticality of position, degree of	0.71			

Table 15.2: Continued.

Correlate most with "complexity" factor	r	Correlate most with another factor	r	The other factor
IV. Job structure				
self-direction (Temme)	0.88	complexity of dealing with things (DOT)	0.77	work with complex things
complexity of dealings with data (DOT)	0.83	follow set procedures, importance of	0.54	operating machines
work under distractions, importance of	0.78	meet set limits, tolerances, standards (DOT)	0.53	work with complex things
frustrating situations, importance of	0.77	specified work place, importance of	0.44	operating machines
interpersonal conflict, importance of	0.76	cycled activities, importance of	0.42	operating machines
strained contacts, importance of	0.69	perform under stress/risk (DOT)	0.27	vigilance with machines
complexity of dealing with people (DOT)	0.68			
personal contact required, extent of	0.66			
personal sacrifice, importance of	0.65			
civic obligations, importance of	0.64			
time pressure, importance of	0.55			
precision, importance of	0.53			
variety and change (DOT)	0.41			
repetitive activities, importance of	−0.49			
supervision, level of	−0.73			
repetitive or continuous (DOT)	−0.74			
structure, amount of	−0.79			

Table 15.2: Continued.

Correlate most with "complexity" factor	r	Correlate most with another factor	r	The other factor
V. Education and experience required				
education, level of curriculum	0.88			
general education development level (DOT)	0.86			
update job knowledge, importance of	0.85			
specific vocational preparation (DOT)	0.76			
experience, months/years	0.62			
training, months/years	0.51			
VI Focus of work/interests required				
interest in data vs. things (DOT)	0.73	"conventional" field of work (Holland)	0.51	coordination without sight
interest in creative vs. routine work (DOT)	0.63	"social" field of work (Holland)	0.45	catering to people
interest in social welfare vs. machines (DOT)	0.55	interest in science vs. business (DOT)	0.42	work with complex things
interest in producing vs. esteem (DOT)	−0.48	"investigative" field of work (Holland)	0.37	work with complex things
"realistic" field of work (Holland)	−0.74	"enterprising" field of work (Holland)	0.33	selling
		"artistic" field of work (Hollland)	0.20	work with complex things
VII. Physical requirements				
wet, humid (DOT)	−0.37	outside vs. inside location (DOT)	0.48	vigilance with machines
hazardous conditions (DOT)	−0.39	climbing (DOT)	0.42	controlled manual work
fumes, odors, dust, gases (DOT)	−0.45			
stooping (DOT)	−0.48			
noise, vibration (DOT)	−0.53			
physical exertion, level of	−0.56			
reaching (DOT)	−0.66			

Table 15.2: Continued.

Correlate most with "complexity" factor	r	Correlate most with another factor	r	The other factor
VIII. Other correlates				
salary, yes/no	0.70	commission, yes/no	0.53	selling
% government workers, males (census)	0.45	tips, yes/no	0.50	selling
% government workers, females (census)	0.45	licensing/certification	0.42	catering to people
% black, females (census)	−0.48	median age, males (census)	0.31	vigilance with machines
% black, males (census)	−0.53	mean hours, males (census)	0.31	controlled manual
wage, yes/no	−0.66	median age, females (census)	−0.28	coordination without sight
		mean hours, females (census)	−0.34	catering to people
		% female (census)	−0.37	controlled manual

Reprinted from Gottfredson, L. S. (1997). Why *g* matters: The complexity of everyday life. *Intelligence, 24* (1), 79–132. With permission from Elsevier Science.

the task complexity factor. Correlations are somewhat lower for more people-oriented than data-oriented problem solving (e.g. instructing vs. planning), but people-related problem solving is still much more typical at higher than lower levels of the job hierarchy (cf., Gottfredson 1986). Only the mostly non-intellectual people-related activities (e.g. catering to and entertaining people, supervising non-employees) correlate most highly with some other task factor ("catering to people").

Turning to the third and fourth panels in Table 15.2, jobs high on the work complexity factor are more prestigious, critical to the organization, and entail greater general responsibility. This finding is consistent with sociological research, cited earlier, on the common prestige hierarchy that characterizes occupations in all industrialized economies. As the structural attributes of jobs suggest, jobs that require considerable discretion and self-direction and which, accordingly, are not highly supervised and routinized, tend to be the most complex overall. The duties of such jobs also appear to entail psychological stress rather than physical stress.

Intelligence is also often described as the ability to learn quickly and efficiently. And, in fact, the fifth panel in Table 15.2 shows that more complex jobs tend to have more intense and more continuous training demands, whether that be formal education, specific vocational training, learning through extensive experience, or continually updating one's job knowledge. These training demands alone would make a job more *g* loaded overall.

Job analysis research by Arvey (1986) with different job attributes and different jobs reveals the same job complexity factor. In a set of 140 jobs from the petrochemical industry, his factor analyses revealed that a "judgment and reasoning factor" best distinguished among them. The chief elements of this factor, shown in Table 15.3, read like a description of intelligence as commonly understood by lay people and experts alike: for example, reason and make judgments, learn new procedures quickly and deal with unexpected situations.

Table 15.3: Job analysis items and factor loadings associated with judgment and reasoning factor developed from 140 petrochemical jobs.

Items	Factor Loading
Deal with unexpected situations	0.75
Able to learn and recall job-related information	0.71
Able to reason and make judgments	0.69
Able to identify problem situations quickly	0.69
React swiftly when unexpected problems occur	0.67
Able to apply common sense to solve problems	0.66
Able to learn new procedures quickly	0.66
Alert and quick to understand things	0.55
Able to compare information from two or more sources to reach a conclusion	0.49

Source: Arvey (1986: 148). Reprinted with permission from Academic Press, copyright 1986.

In summary, the job analysis data suggest not only that jobs differ greatly in their *g* loading, but also that this is the most fundamental distinction among them. That is, they differ primarily in the extent to which they call forth or "measure" *g*. If they were all to be populated by representative samples of the population, we might therefore expect the highest-level, more *g*-demanding occupations to function much like IQ tests (that is, workers' differences in job performance would simultaneously measure their differences in IQ), while lower-level, less *g*-loaded occupations would call forth or "measure" *g* less well. As we see next, this is just what yet another body of research reveals — jobs operate like differentially *g*-loaded mental tests.

3.3. Prediction of Job Performance

Personnel selection psychologists have only recently explicitly characterized their cognitive tests as measures of intelligence or *g*, but most now refer to them as measures of the general mental factor, *g* (see Visweswaran & Ones, in press). All mental tests measure mostly *g*, so I will refer to them all simply as measures of *g*, recognizing that they can vary in quality as measures of that construct. Very little research on the relation of mental abilities to job performance has actually extracted *g* scores, which means that the research typically understates the predictive value of *g* to some extent.

Table 15.4 summarizes the pattern of findings from the job performance literature. It is based on a review of several large military studies as well as the major meta-analyses for civilian jobs (Gottfredson, in press). Its first general point, on the "utility of *g*", is that *g* (i.e. possessing a higher level of *g*) has value across all kinds of work and levels of job-specific experience, but that its value rises with: (a) the complexity of work; (b) the more "core" the performance criterion being considered (good performance of technical duties rather than "citizenship"); and (c) the more objectively performance is measured (e.g. job samples rather than supervisor ratings). Predictive validities, when corrected for various statistical artifacts, range from about 0.2 to 0.8 in civilian jobs, with an average near 0.5 (Schmidt & Hunter 1998). In mid-level military jobs, uncorrected validities tend to range between 0.3 and 0.6 (Wigdor & Green 1991). These are substantial. To illustrate, tests with these levels of predictive validity would provide 30% to 60% of the gain in aggregate levels of worker performance that would be realized from using tests with perfect validity (there is no such thing) rather than hiring randomly.

The next point of Table 15.4, on *g*'s utility relative to other "can do" components of performance, is that *g* carries the freight of prediction in any mental test battery. Specific aptitudes, such as spatial or mechanical aptitude, seldom add much to the prediction of job performance, and they provide such increments only in narrow domains of jobs. General psychomotor ability can rival *g* in predictive validity, but its value rises as job complexity falls, which pattern is opposite that for *g*.

Turning to *g*'s utility relative to the "will do" components of performance (e.g. motivation), the latter add virtually nothing to the prediction of core technical performance beyond that provided by *g* alone. These "non-cognitive" (less cognitive) traits, however, substantially out-perform *g* in predicting the non-core, citizenship

Table 15.4: Major findings on g's impact on job performance[a].

Utility of g

(1) Higher levels of g lead to higher levels of performance in all jobs and along all dimensions of performance. The average correlation of mental tests with overall rated job performance is around 0.5 (corrected for statistical artifacts).

(2) There is no ability threshold above which more g does not enhance performance. The effects of g are linear: successive increments in g lead to successive increments in job performance.

(3) (a) The value of higher levels of g does not fade with longer experience on the job. Criterion validities remain high even among highly experienced workers. (b) That they sometimes even appear to rise with experience may be due to the confounding effect of the least experienced groups tending to be more variable in relative level of experience, which obscures the advantages of higher g.

(4) g predicts job performance better in more complex jobs. Its (corrected) criterion validities range from about 0.2 in the simplest jobs to 0.8 in the most complex.

(5) g predicts the core technical dimensions of performance better than it does the non-core "citizenship" dimension of performance.

(6) Perhaps as a consequence, g predicts objectively measured performance (either job knowledge or job sample performance) better than it does subjectively measured performance (such as supervisor ratings).

Utility of g relative to other "can do" components of performance

(7) Specific mental abilities (such as spatial, mechanical or verbal ability) add very little, beyond g, to the prediction of job performance. g generally accounts for at least 85–95% of a full mental test battery's (cross-validated) ability to predict performance in training or on the job.

(8) Specific mental abilities (such as clerical ability) sometimes add usefully to prediction, net of g, but only in certain classes of jobs. They do not have general utility.

(9) General psychomotor ability is often useful, but primarily in less complex work. Their predictive validities fall with complexity while those for g rise.

Utility of g relative to the "will do" component of job performance

(10) g predicts core performance much better than do "non-cognitive" (less g-loaded) traits, such as vocational interests and different personality traits. The latter add virtually nothing to the prediction of core performance, net of g.

(11) g predicts most dimensions of non-core performance (such as personal discipline and soldier bearing) much less well than do "non-cognitive" traits of personality and temperament. When a performance dimension reflects both core and non-core performance (effort and leadership), g predicts to about the same modest degree as do non-cognitive (less g-loaded) traits.

(12) Different non-cognitive traits appear to usefully supplement g in different jobs, just as specific abilities sometimes add to the prediction of performance in certain classes of jobs. Only one such non-cognitive trait appears to be as generalizable as g: the personality trait of conscientiousness/integrity. Its effect sizes for core performance are substantially smaller than g's, however.

Table 15.4: Continued.

Utility of g relative to the job knowledge

(13) *g* affects job performance primarily *indirectly* through its effect on job-specific knowledge.

(14) *g*'s direct effects on job performance increase when jobs are less routinized, training is less complete, and workers retain more discretion.

(15) Job-specific knowledge generally predicts job performance as well as does *g* among experienced workers. However, job knowledge is not generalizable (net of its *g* component), even among experienced workers. The value of job knowledge is highly job specific; *g*'s value is unrestricted.

Utility of g relative to the "have done" (experience) component of job performance

(16) Like job knowledge, the effect sizes of job-specific experience are sometimes high but they are not generalizable.

(17) In fact, experience predicts performance less well as all workers become more experienced. In contrast, higher levels of *g* remain an asset regardless of length of experience.

(18) Experience predicts job performance less well as job complexity rises, which is opposite the trend for *g*. Like general psychomotor ability, experience matters least where *g* matters most to individuals and their organizations.

ᵃ See Gottfredson (in press) for fuller discussion and citation. Table reprinted from Gottfredson (in press) with permission from Lawrence Erlbaum Associates.

dimensions of performance, although each typically in limited domains of work. Only the conscientiousness-integrity factor of personality inventories seems to have general utility across all kinds of work, but it is still notably less useful than *g* in predicting core performance. In short, no other single personal trait has as large and as pervasive an effect on performance across the full range of jobs as does *g*.

The last two general points of Table 15.4 are that job knowledge and job-related experience sometimes rival *g* in predictive validity, but that their value is always highly job-specific. The same *g* can be useful in all jobs, but knowledge and experience must be targeted to a particular kind of work (carpentry, accounting, etc.). The information-processing capability represented by *g* is highly generalizable; job knowledge and experience are not. Moreover, differences in knowledge among a job's incumbents result primarily from their differences in *g*, and complex jobs continue to require learning and problem solving (the exercise of *g*) for which previous knowledge and experience cannot substitute. That is, higher *g* remains useful, regardless of knowledge and experience, especially in higher level jobs. The advantages of higher *g* (say, another 10 IQ points) hold steady at increasingly higher levels of experience in a job, but the advantages of more experience (say, two years more than one's coworker) fade among workers with higher average levels of experience. Moreover, the predictive validity of experience falls at successively higher levels of job complexity — again, a pattern opposite that for *g*.

In short, possessing higher levels of *g* provides individuals a competitive edge for performing jobs well, especially a job's core technical duties. That edge tends to be small in low-level jobs, both in absolute terms and relative to other personal traits that might affect performance (such as reliability and physical strength). That edge is large in both regards, however, in higher-level, more complex jobs. Superior knowledge and experience may sometimes hide the functional disadvantages of lower *g*, but they never nullify them. Military research shows that less bright workers may out-perform brighter but relatively inexperienced workers, but that the brighter workers will out-distance their less able peers after getting a bit more experience (Wigdor & Green 1991: 163–164). Presumably, their superior information-processing skills allow brighter workers to apply past knowledge more effectively, deal faster with unexpected problems, extract more knowledge from their experience, and the like.

The job performance research also hints at another major difference between life tasks — the extent to which they are instrumental rather than socioemotional in character. As we saw, *g* is more important than personality traits in predicting performance of core technical duties (decontaminating equipment, repairing an engine, determining grid coordinates on a map, and so on), but it is less predictive in activities of a more interpersonal or characterological nature (being a reliable worker or helpful team-mate, showing leadership, impressing superiors and the like). For purposes of understanding the social consequences of *g*, we might therefore distinguish tasks not only along a complexity dimension, but also along a continuum from instrumental to socioemotional, as shown in Figure 15.2. We might expect the *g* loadings of tasks to be

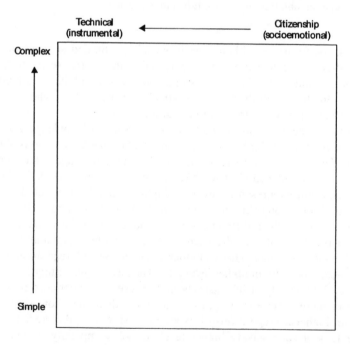

Figure 15.2: Matrix of life tasks.

highest in the upper left corner (complex instrumental tasks), and to drop steadily for tasks located nearer the lower right corner of Figure 15.2 (simple and socioemotional).

How do these results illustrate jobs as mental tests? First, they show that jobs, like mental tests, do indeed differ in their g loadings. And they differ just as the job analysis research had indicated they would: differences in g produce bigger, more consistent and more consequential differences in job performance (higher predictive validities) in more complex jobs (see Hunter & Schmidt 1996; Schmidt & Hunter 2000, for additional evidence). Conversely, some jobs are quite poor "tests" of g; that is, being bright does not boost performance on them very much. Thus, although the data show that higher levels of g are always useful to some extent, their value varies from great to slight depending on the activities involved. It is precisely such patterns of effect size that the study of task attributes such as complexity promises to illuminate.

Second, the foregoing results remind us that jobs also differ from psychometric tests in ways that may camouflage g's real effects unless those differences are taken into account. Because jobs are actually more like achievement tests than aptitude tests, their performance generally depends on specialized knowledge, which makes them sensitive to differences in exposure to relevant knowledge. That is why greater relative experience can temporarily level the playing field for lower IQ workers, camouflaging the longer-term disadvantages of lower g. Whereas IQ testers try to eliminate all such non-g advantages, real life is replete with them. These non-g influences do not neutralize the advantages of higher g, but they can make it more difficult to identify g's gradients of effect. As the fourth question earlier reminds us ("to what extent are life's tests standardized?"), we cannot trace g's impact in "real life" without understanding how life's "tests" depart from the ideal conditions for mental testing.

3.4. Prediction of Career Level

We turn now from job performance, which is a highly proximal effect of g in the workplace, to less proximal but more cumulative outcomes in employment such as income and occupation level. Being less proximal, we might expect them to be less dependent on g and more on institutional factors and social forces not under a worker's control. On the other hand, they represent a long series of behaviors and events of which the worker may be the only common component. This raises the possibility that less proximal outcomes may not necessarily be much less g loaded than more proximal ones, despite their being affected by a greater variety of external factors.

Correlations of IQ with socioeconomic success vary in size depending on the outcome in question, but they are consistent and substantial (see especially the re-analysis of 10 large samples by Jencks et al. 1979, ch. 4): years of education (generally 0.5–0.6), occupational status level (0.4–0.5), and earnings, where the correlations rise with age (0.2–0.4). The predictions are the same whether IQ is measured in Grades 3–6, high school, or adulthood (Jencks et al. 1979: 96–99). Moreover, they are underestimates, because they come from single tests of uncertain g loading (Jencks et al. 1979: 91). Various specific aptitude and achievement tests (both academic and non-academic) also predict education, occupation and earnings, but essentially only to the extent that they also measure g (Jencks *et al.* 1979: 87–96). This finding is consistent with that for the prediction of job performance: tests of specific abilities add little beyond g when predicting core performance. In short, g is what drives a test's predictions of socioeconomic success, and the predictions are substantial even from childhood when g is reasonably well measured.

Differences in g are clearly a major predictor of differences in career success, but why? The answer is not as obvious as it is for proximal outcomes such as on-the-job performance. Sociologists and economists have put much effort into modeling the interrelated processes of how people "get ahead" on the educational, occupational and income hierarchies (e.g. Behrman *et al.* 1980; Jencks *et al.* 1972, 1979; Sewell & Hauser 1975; Taubman 1977). Their statistical modeling suggests that "academic ability" (whether measured as IQ or standardized academic achievement) has both direct and indirect effects on each successive outcome in the education-occupation-income chain of development. Cognitive ability is by far the strongest predictor of education level relative to others studied (0.5–0.6 for IQ vs. 0.3–0.4 for parents' socioeconomic status (see Duncan *et al.* 1972, p. 38 for latter), and therefore seems to have large direct effects on how far people go in school. Educational level is, in turn, the major predictor of occupational levels attained. After controlling for educational attainment, mental ability's direct effect is much smaller on *occupational* than educational level, but still larger than the influence of family background. Jencks *et al.* (1979: 220) summarize mental ability as having a "modest influence" through age 25 in boosting young adults up the occupational ladder. Much the same pattern is found for *earnings*, after controlling for both education and occupation — the impact of IQ is mostly indirect. However, the direct effects of cognitive ability on earnings grow with age, leading Jencks *et al.* (1979: 119) to comment that IQ's direct effects are "substantively important" for raising earnings through at least middle age.

In summary, g is hardly the only predictor of career success, but it is a surprisingly strong one, both in absolute and relative terms. As complexly and externally influenced as it is, career development seems to be moderately tied to g level.

3.5. g's Causal Impact on Careers

IQ and SES background are not independent forces, of course. Sociologists tend to assume that IQ differences are largely created by differences in family resources, such as better educated parents, more books in the home, and the like. In other words, IQ scores really reflect mostly socioeconomic advantage. In contrast, many intelligence researchers assume that the accomplishments of parents and children have overlapping genetic roots. Namely, if parents have favorable genes for IQ, this genetic advantage will yield them greater socioeconomic success as well as brighter than average children who, consequently, will have their own favorable odds for socioeconomic success. If this assumption is true, then controlling for family background before assessing the causal impact of g actually controls away part of g itself and results in underestimating its impact.

Thus, although there is no argument among social scientists that IQ correlates moderately strongly with socioeconomic success, there is heated debate about whether higher intelligence might be a *result* rather than a *cause* of social advantage. The causal question has not been an issue in the job performance literature, partly because it strains credulity to attribute differences in job performance — for example, post-training success at assembling a rifle, reading maps, making good managerial decisions, and so on — to distal social forces rather than to proximal personal ones. The job performance research leaves no doubt, either, that earlier cognitive ability predicts *later* performance in training and on the job. It also shows that the most relevant distal characteristics, such as years of education, have scant value in predicting who performs best in a particular job (Hunter & Hunter 1984).

The causal question is still a major one, however, when the job outcomes at issue are broader, more personally consequential ones such as occupational prestige and income level attained. Although many social scientists still assume that intelligence is a result rather than a cause of social class differences, research continues to show the opposite. Sibling studies, for instance, provide evidence that *g* does, in fact, have a big causal influence and that social class has a comparatively weak one on children's adult socioeconomic outcomes. Biological siblings differ two-thirds as much in IQ, on the average, as do random strangers (12 vs. 17 IQ points). Despite growing up in the very same households, their differences in IQ portend differences in life outcomes that are almost as large as those observed in the general population (Jencks *et al.* 1979, ch. 4; Murray 1997a, 1997b; Olneck 1977: 137–138). Even in intact, non-poor families, siblings of below average intelligence are much less likely to have a college degree, work in a professional job, and have high earnings than are their average-IQ siblings, who in turn do much less well than their high-IQ siblings (Murray 1997b).

Behavioral genetic research also indicates that *g* is much more a cause than consequence of social advantage. First, research on the heritability of IQ indicates that differences in family advantage have a modest effect on IQ scores — about equal to that of genes — in early childhood, but that these family effects — called *shared environmental effects* — wash out by adolescence (Bouchard 1998; Plomin *et al.* 2000). Perhaps counterintuitively, the socioeconomic advantages and disadvantages that siblings share turn out to have no lasting effect on IQ. By late adulthood, the heritability of IQ is about 0.8, which means that phenotypic intelligence is correlating about 0.9 with genotypic intelligence (0.9 being the square root of 0.8). Environmental differences account for up to 20% of IQ differences in adulthood, but they represent *non-shared* effects that we experience one person at a time (such as illness), not family by family (such as parents' income and education). In short, differences in adult IQ are not due at all to differences in socioeconomic advantage.

Second, multivariate behavioral genetic analyses reveal not only that education, occupation and income level are themselves partly heritable (that is, our differences in education, occupation and income can be traced partly to our genetic differences), but that they also share some of the same genetic roots as does IQ. The heritabilities of educational level, occupational level and income are, respectively, about 0.6–0.7, 0.5, and 0.4–0.5 (e.g. Lichtenstein & Pedersen 1997; Rowe *et al.* 1998). More importantly, half to two-thirds of the heritability for each outcome overlaps the genetic roots of IQ.

Specifically, about 40%, 25% and 20% of the total (phenotypic) variation in education, occupation and income, respectively, can be traced to genetic influences that each *shares* with *g* (e.g. Lichtenstein & Pedersen 1997; Rowe *et al.* 1998). These overlapping heritabilities provide additional evidence that much variation in socioeconomic outcomes can be traced back to variation in *g*, in this case, to its strictly genetic component. In fact, behavioral genetic research has shown that most social environments and events are themselves somewhat genetic in origin (Plomin & Bergeman 1991).

To summarize, not only do differences in social environments and events not create differences in adult *g*, but career outcomes are themselves moderately genetic in origin, probably owing in part to genetic differences in *g*. "Getting ahead" is not only like taking a mental test battery, but one that taps genetically-conditioned mental abilities. Because getting ahead socioeconomically is a moderately rather than highly *g*-loaded life test, high *g* provides a big but not decisive advantage. As with other mental test batteries, the size of the advantage that higher levels of *g* confer differs from one subtest to another. It is largest in education, smallest in income, and intermediate for both occupational level attained and performance in the typical job.

3.6. Possible Mode of g's Cumulative Effects on Careers

The *g* factor has moderately large, causal effects on many long-term outcomes, as these and other data indicate, but its manner of effect is ill-understood. The sociological explanations are rudimentary and tend either to ignore or misconstrue the nature of intelligence, while psychological research on intelligence tends to ignore long-term career development. As noted before, the role of *g* in everyday life may largely mimic the role of *g* in IQ tests, where small effects can become big ones when other influences are less consistent — sort of a tortoise and hare effect. The following re-analysis of data from a longitudinal study of military careers illustrates this process. It also shows how the long-term impact of *g* can be underestimated by focusing too narrowly on the individual events that cumulate into a "career".

In 1966, during the era of President Johnson's Great Society programs, U.S. Secretary of Defense Robert McNamara inaugurated Project 100,000. Until its demise several years later, the project required each of the four military services to induct a certain percentage of men whose low level of mental ability would normally have disqualified them from service (percentiles 10–15 on the Armed Services Qualifying Test, AFQT, which corresponds to about IQ 80–85). The project was a social experiment intended to enhance the life opportunities of men who normally would have difficulty succeeding in civilian life. Part of the initiative therefore involved comparing the progress of the New Standards Men (NSM), as they were called, with a control group from each of the services. (See Laurence & Ramsberger 1991; Sticht *et al.* 1987, for details on Project 100,000, including the mixed nature of the four control groups.) Not all the New Standards Men actually were of low-normal ability (the threshold for mild mental retardation is IQ 70–75), because recruiters sometimes coached brighter applicants how to score poorly on the AFQT so that such men could enlist when the quota for bright men had already been met. Such instances, although probably proportionately small, would lead to underestimating somewhat the differences in career progress between New Standards and control men.

Table 15.5 provides the percentages of New Standards Men and control men who passed each of six basic hurdles in a military career: completing basic training, completing entry-level skill training and not being discharged for any reason during each of four successive periods during the first two years of service. The specialty (job) for which one is trained also affects the likelihood of performing well (e.g. low-ability men would be expected to perform better in lower-level jobs), so level of job specialty (technical vs. not) is listed too. Also listed are four criteria of success near the conclusion of the two years: pay grade, performance rating, non-judicial punishment and court martial conviction. The entries in Table 15.5 for each career stage refer to the percentage of men who, having entered that particular stage and became eligible to move to the next stage. Each successive stage therefore applies to successively fewer men — the dwindling pool of survivors, so to speak.

Analysts have often interpreted the data in Table 15.5 as showing that the New Standards Men did almost as well as the control men, and therefore that the military should welcome rather than avoid inducting low ability men (e.g. Sticht *et al.*'s 1987 book, *Cast-Off Youth*). Such positive interpretations might indeed seem warranted at first glance. The vast majority of New Standards Men succeeded at each level, and at a not much lower rate than did the control men. For instance, of men entering service in 1966–1969, 94.6% of the New Standards Men completed basic training compared to 97.5% of the control men. By 1969–1970 the need for military manpower had eased, and the services became more selective in who they would retain. Basic training retention rates for New Standards Men dropped considerably, especially in the three normally more selective services, from 94.6% overall in the earlier years to 87.6% in 1969–1970. The retention rate is nonetheless still high. Except in the Marine Corps, retention rates beyond basic training for New Standards Men seldom dropped much below 80% at any stage in the two-year careers. This would seem to paint a portrait of surprisingly consistent success for men of moderately low ability. Skeptics of Project 100,000 have pointed out that great pressure was put on the services to make the experiment succeed, and extra help and special leniency were no doubt offered the New Standards Men. Some were recycled through basic training several times. But however they were attained, the success rates do seem impressive.

This positive interpretation ignores two phenomena, however: rates of success relative to the control men, and *cumulative* rates of success over time. Table 15.6 shows the odds ratios calculated from each of the forms of success in Table 15.5. Odds ratios are one form of *risk ratio* used in epidemiology to quantify degree of risk *relative* to some comparison group, in this case the control men. To portray levels of risk, the ratios in Table 15.6 refer to the odds of *failure*, not success. They are calculated as (a) the odds of failure in the at-risk group (its members' odds of failure *rather than* success) divided by (b) the odds of failure in the comparison group. The odds ratio thus gives a sense of the *relative balance* of failure to success when moving from one group to another. To illustrate, the odds of *not* completing basic training were 5.4% to 94.6% (or 0.057) for New Standards Men and 2.5% to 97.5% (or 0.026) for control men, yielding an odds

Table 15.5: Success rates at different milestones in the first two years of military service: New Standards Men (NSM) and Control (C) Men (Percentages).

Stage in military career (for those who get that far)	Total		Army		Navy		Marine Corps		Air Force	
	NS	C	NS	C	NS	C	NS	C	NS	C
Completed basic training[a]										
entered 1966–1969	94.6	97.5	96.3	98.0	91.4	97.2	88.9	95.6	90.8	97.0
entered 1969–1970	87.6	95.6	94.5	97.5	83.0	94.1	62.2	85.9	85.6	96.2
Assigned to technical specialty[b] (e.g. *not* infantry, cook, driver, or clerk)	7.6	19.5	9.6	n.a.	4.7	n.a.	1.1	n.a.	4.2	n.a.
Completed entry-level skill training[c]	(91.9)[d]	(95.7)	92.8	96.3	86.8	91.3	92.8	96.8	89.1	96.0
Not discharged by:[e]										
13–15 months	81.1	92.8	88.4	91.9	86.8	96.1	56.4	91.5	80.8	94.4
16–18 months	82.9	92.0	88.6	90.9	88.4	95.4	64.8	89.0	78.3	95.8
19–21 months	82.7	91.0	88.4	89.7	86.3	94.7	67.2	89.3	76.0	94.6
22–24 months	86.1	90.7	88.9	90.0	89.8	94.0	69.0	88.2	76.9	92.5
Late-term performance										
promoted to paygrade E4 or E5 by 19–24 months[f]	66.7	81.6	85.7	94.1	13.0	70.1	75.1	87.4	16.5	30.1
rated "good" or "highly effective" worker at 22–24 months	(95.1)	(97.9)	97.5	98.9	89.6	96.9	85.7	96.1	91.2	92.9
no non-judicial punishment[h]	(83.4)	(90.6)	81.9	89.7	93.1	96.5	72.2	81.8	95.9	98.6
no court martial convictions[h]	96.8	98.4	96.8	98.4	99.0	99.7	94.7	95.3	99.8	~100.0

Table 15.5: Continued.

n.a. = not available.

[a] Laurence & Ramsberger (1991: 44).

[b] Laurence & Ramsberger (1991: 40). Electronic equipment repair, communications & intelligence, medical & dental, other technical.

[c] Sticht *et al.* (1987: 48)..

[d] Percentages in parentheses have been estimated by weighing the percentages in each of the services by the quotas for new standards men that each service was to meet in 1968 (respectively, 72%, 10%, 9% and 9% of all New Standards Men for the Army, Navy, Marine Corps, and Air Force, Laurence & Ramsberger, 1991: 29)..

[e] Laurence & Ramsberger (1991: 50).

[f] Laurence & Ramsberger (1991: 47). The disparities in rates can probably be traced to two key factors: (a) Navy and Air Force require tests for promotion; and (b) the jobs held by New Standards men in the Army and Marine were less technical (pp. 46, 49–50).

[g] Sticht *et al.* (1987: 54).

[h] Laurence & Ramsberger (1991: 49) "Total" figures for court martial convictions are from Sticht *et al.* (1987: 52).

Table 15.6: Odds ratios for *not* succeeding during the first two years of military service: New Standards Men (NSM) relative to Control (C) Men[a].

Stage in Military Career	Total	Army	Navy	Marine Corps	Air Force
Did not complete basic training					
entered 1966–1969	2.2	1.6	3.2	2.7	3.3
entered 1969–1970	3.1	2.3	2.5	3.7	4.3
Not assigned to technical specialty	2.9	2.3	5.0	20.0	5.6
Did not complete entry-level skill training	(2.0)	2.0	1.6	2.3	2.9
Discharged by:					
13–15 months	3.4	1.5	3.7	8.3	4.0
16–18 months	2.4	1.3	2.2	4.4	6.2
19–21 months	2.1	1.1	2.9	4.0	5.6
22–24 months	1.6	1.1	1.8	3.3	3.7
Late-term performance					
not promoted to paygrade E4 or E5 by 19–24 months	2.1	2.6	16.7	2.3	2.2
not rated "good or "highly effective" worker at 22–24 months	(2.4)	2.3	3.6	4.2	1.2
non-judicial punishment	(1.9)	1.9	2.0	1.4	3.0
court martial convictions	2.0	2.0	3.3	1.1	5.0

[a] Calculated from data in Table 15.5.

ratio of 2.2 (0.057/0.026). That is, the odds of failing rather than succeeding were more than twice as high for the New Standards Men as for the control men. Conversely, the New Standards Men's relative "risk" of success was less than half that of the control men (0.45, or the inverse of 2.2). In epidemiology, risk ratios of 2.0 to 4.0 represent a "moderate to strong" level of association, and above 4.0 a "very strong" association (Gerstman 1998: 128).

Risk ratios fall below 2.0 for New Standards Men only in the Army and in several of the more winnowed (e.g. longer-surviving) groups in the other services. The risk ratios thus paint a less positive picture of success: however high the success rates may be for New Standards Men in absolute terms, they tend to be markedly lower in relative terms in all the aspects of career development.

Figure 15.3 shows the cumulative consequences of one group having consistently lower rates of success at each stage in a cumulative or developmental process. It reflects the cumulative probability of men passing hurdles at each successive stage of a two-year career, from completing basic training to being recognized as a good worker after two years on the job. As shown in the figure, entering cohorts of New Standards Men experienced a higher probability of failure (discharge) than success (retention) by 18 months of military service. Of the New Standards Men entering basic training, fewer than half remained after 18 months, compared to almost three quarters (72.8%) of the control men. By that point, failure (discharge) had become the norm for New Standards Men whereas success was still the norm for control men. Their *rates* of failure had not increased at more advanced career stages (if anything, they fell), but because subsequent successes were contingent on earlier ones, their risks compounded faster with time than did those for the control men. As gamblers and investors know, even much smaller differences in odds or rates of return can compound over time to produce enormous differences in profit or loss.

In summary, careers are like mental tests in that what matters most is one's total score, not the odds of passing any particular item. The factor with the biggest impact on the total score is generally the one with the most pervasive influence, relative to all others, over the long haul. The advantage it provides may be small in any one task, but each new task adds its own sliver of advantage to the growing pile. Thus, the more long-term or multi-faceted an outcome, the more we ought to consider the consistency, not just the size, of any variable's impact.

3.7. g-Based Origins of the Occupational Hierarchy

This chapter, like most research on *g*, has focused on individual-level correlates of *g*. The most important impact of biologically-rooted variability in mental competence may occur at more aggregate levels, however, as Gordon (1997) described. At the level of the interpersonal context, for instance, our differences in *g* affect how and with whom we interact (cooperate, compete, marry, and so on) as well as the kinds of subcultures we produce. At the broader societal level, information, risk and disease can be seen to diffuse at different rates across different segments of the IQ distribution. Gordon also describes how social norms and political institutions evolve partly in response to the

	Completed Basic Training +	Completed Skills Training +	Not discharged within:				Success at two years
			13-15 + months	16-18 + months	19-21 + months	22-24 months	
NSM:	94.6	86.9	70.5	58.4	48.3	41.6	27.7 Good paygrade 39.6 Good performance rating 34.7 No non-judicial punishment 40.3 No non-judicial punishment
C:	97.5	93.3	86.6	80.0	72.8	68.8	56.1 Good paygrade 67.4 Good performance rating 62.3 No non-judicial punishment 67.7 No court martial conviction

Figure 15.3: Cumulative probability of remaining in the military for two years and then succeeding against four criteria: New Standards Men (NSM) and Control (C) Men[a].

social processes that are set in motion by noticeable and functionally important individual and group differences in mental competence. I therefore conclude the review of evidence on occupations by speculating about one such higher-order effect, specifically, how individual differences in mental competence may account for the emergence of the occupational prestige-complexity hierarchy.

People tend to take the occupational hierarchy for granted, but we can imagine other ways that a society's myriad worker activities might be chunked. Some sociologists have suggested that we either level these distinctions in occupational level or else rotate people through both good and bad jobs (e.g. Collins 1979), apparently on the assumption that virtually everyone can learn virtually any job. Their view is that the occupational hierarchy is merely an arbitrary social construction for maintaining the privileges of some groups over others (e.g. see the classic statement by Bowles & Gintis 1972/1973). Research on job performance and the heritability of *g* disproves their assumptions about human capability, however. Moreover, it hardly seems accidental that the key dimension along which occupations have crystallized over the ages (complexity of information processing) mirrors the key distinction in human competence in all societies (the ability to process information). Rather, the *g*-segregated nature of occupations is probably at least partly a social accommodation to a biological reality, namely, the wide dispersion of *g* in all human populations (Gottfredson 1985).

How might that accommodation occur? As described earlier, occupations are constellations of tasks that differ, not just in their socioeconomic rewards, but also in the human capabilities required to actually perform them and perform them well. It seems likely that both the systematic differences among task constellations (job differentiation) and the highly *g*-based process by which people are sorted and self-sorted to these constellations have evolved in tandem in recent human history. Both of these enduring regularities in human organization are examples of *social structure*. They would have evolved in tandem owing to the pressures and opportunities that a wide dispersion in human intelligence creates for segregating tasks somewhat by *g* loading.

Specifically, individuals who are better able to process information, anticipate and solve problems, and learn quickly are more likely to take on or be delegated the more complex tasks in a group, whatever the tasks' manifest content. For the same reason, persons with weak intellectual skills are likely to gravitate to or be assigned intellectually simpler tasks (see Wilk *et al.* 1995, on evidence for the gravitational hypothesis). Over time, this sorting and assignment process can promote a recurring *g*-based segregation of tasks because it provides a steady and substantial supply of workers whose levels of mental competence match those usually required by the work. Only when such *g*-differentiated supplies of *workers* are regularly maintained, can any *g*-related segregation of *tasks* emerge and become institutionalized over time as distinct occupations (e.g. into accountant vs. clerk, teacher vs. teacher aide, electrical engineer vs. electrician, nurse vs. hospital orderly).

If *g*-based distinctions among occupations can be sustained only when the workers populating those jobs differ reliably in their typical levels of *g*, then we might expect the *g*-based differences among jobs to grow or shrink depending on changes in the efficiency with which people are sorted to jobs by *g* level (Gottfredson 1985). More efficient sorting, if sustained, could lead eventually to greater distinctions among occupations, perhaps creating altogether new ones. Lower efficiency in sorting would narrow or collapse g-based distinctions among jobs, because the jobs in question would now have to accommodate workers with a wider dispersion in g levels. That is, a g-based occupational hierarchy could be expanded or contracted, like an accordion, depending on how much the means and variances in incumbents' g levels change along different stretches of the occupational hierarchy. Constellations of job duties (an *occupation*) therefore would be stable only to the extent that the occupation's usual stream of incumbents becomes neither so consistently able that it regularly takes on or is delegated more g-loaded tasks, thereby changing the usual mix of job duties, nor so wanting in necessary capacities that more complex tasks are shed from the occupation's usual mix of duties. Figure 15.1 suggests that the efficiency of g-based sorting of people to jobs is only modest, indicating that only modest levels of efficiency are needed to create a high degree of occupational differentiation.

We are less likely to notice work duties than workers being sorted to jobs, the former on the basis of their demands for g and the latter for their possession of it. However, both g-related sorting processes are always at work. The military provides a large-scale example of the task resorting process. Some decades ago, the Air Force outlined ways to redistribute job duties within job ladders so that it might better accommodate an unfavorable change in the flow of inductees, specifically, an anticipated drop in the proportion of cognitively able recruits when the draft (compulsory service) was ended in the 1970s. One proposal was to "shred" the easier tasks from various specialties and then pool those tasks to create easier jobs that less able men could perform satisfactorily (Christal 1974).

Purposeful reconfiguration of task sets to better fit the talents or deficits of particular workers can be seen on a small scale every day in workplaces everywhere, because many workers either exceed or fall short of their occupation's usual intellectual demands. Recall that all occupations recruit workers from a broad range of IQ, so some proportion of workers is always likely to be underutilized or overtaxed unless their duties are modified. However, it is only when the proportion of such misfit workers in a job rises over time that the modification of a job's g loading becomes the rule for all and not the exception for a few, and hence establishes a new norm for the now-reconfigured occupation.

The evolution of economies from agrarian, to industrial, to post industrial has provided much opportunity for occupational differentiation to proceed, because many new economic tasks have emerged over time. The internet information industry represents only the latest wave. With a greater variety of jobs and more freedom for individuals to pursue them, there is also increasing incentive for both individuals and employers to compete for the most favorable worker-job matches (respectively, individuals seeking better jobs and employers seeking more competent workers). Such competitive pressures will sustain occupational differentiation as long as individuals are free to buy and sell talent in the workplace.

These pressures can also be expected to *increase* occupational differentiation as economies become more complex and put ever-higher premium on information processing skills. Indeed, ours is often referred to as the Information Age. The prospect of greater occupational differentiation, and the greater social inequality it portends, have attracted much attention among social policy makers. Former U.S. Secretary of Labor Robert Reich, although rejecting the notion that people differ in intelligence, has nonetheless described the growing demand for what he calls "symbolic analysts" in clearly *g*-related terms: "The capacity for abstraction — for discovering patterns and meanings — is, of course, the very essence of symbolic analysis" (Reich 1992: 229). Like many others, Reich is concerned that increased occupational differentiation of this sort is leading to increased social bifurcation.

What we see here is the evolution of social structure in *g*-relevant ways, which is the issue raised by the sixth question earlier ("to what extent do a society's members create and reshape the mental test battery that it administers to new generations?"). That is, not only are jobs mental tests, but ones that societies actively construct and reconstruct over time. Reich's concern over the consequences of this ongoing process also illustrates how the relative risks for people along one segment of the IQ distribution can be greatly altered by the social and economic restructuring wrought by persons elsewhere on the IQ distribution. The evolution of work provides an example of high-IQ people changing social life in ways that harm low-IQ persons, but other domains of life provide examples where the effects flow in the opposite direction (Gordon 1997).

3.8. Jobs as a Template for Understanding the Role of g Elsewhere in Daily Life

Jobs collectively represent a vast array of tasks, both in content and complexity. While not reflecting the full range of tasks we face in daily life, many of them are substantially the same, from driving to financial planning. There is no reason to believe that *g* and other personal traits play a markedly different role in performing these same tasks in non-job settings, because *g* is a content- and context-free capability. To take just one example, the likelihood of dying in a motor vehicle accident doubles and then triples from IQ 115 to IQ 80 (O'Toole 1990).

To the extent that there is overlap between the task domains of work and daily life, the research on jobs and job performance forecasts what to expect from research on daily life. Namely, we will find that the many "subtests" of life range widely in their *g* loadings; that people "take" somewhat different sets of subtests in their lives; that their own *g* levels affect which sets they take, voluntarily or not; that life tests are even less standardized than jobs, which further camouflages *g*'s impact when taking any single life test; that life's full test battery is large and long, giving *g* more room to express itself in more cumulative life outcomes; and that social life (marriage, neighborhoods, etc.) will frequently be structured substantially along *g* lines.

More specifically, the research on job duties and job performance describes the topography of *g*'s impact that we can expect to find in social life: higher *g* has greater utility in more complex tasks and in instrumental rather than socioemotional ones; *g*'s utility can sometimes swamp the value of all other traits, but many other traits can also enhance performance and compensate somewhat for low *g*; and the practical advantages of higher *g* over a lifetime probably rest as much on the steady tail wind it provides in all life's venues as on its big gusts in a few.

4. Everyday Life as an IQ Test Battery

IQ scores predict a wider range of important social outcomes and they correlate with more personal attributes than perhaps any other psychological trait (Brand 1987; Herrnstein & Murray 1994). The ubiquity and often-considerable size of g's correlations across life's various domains suggest that g truly is important in negotiating the corridors of daily life. If this is so, then the common "tests" that we all take in life, outside of school and work, should provide clear evidence of g's role in our everyday lives. Two bodies of evidence are particularly informative in this regard — functional literacy and IQ-specific rates of social pathology. The former addresses the minutiae of daily competence; the latter addresses the cumulative consequences of daily competence or incompetence.

4.1. Functional Literacy: A Literate Society's Minimum Competency Test

If g has a pervasive and important influence in daily life, then we should be able to create an IQ test, *de novo*, from the "items" of everyday life. Indeed, it should be difficult to avoid measuring g with tests developed specifically to measure everyday competence. As we shall see, at least two sets of researchers, both of whom eschew the notion of intelligence, have nonetheless inadvertently created good tests of g from the daily demands of modern life.

The first test is the National Adult Literacy Survey (NALS), which was developed for the U.S. Department of Education by the Educational Testing Service (ETS; Kirsch *et al.* 1993). The second is the Test of Health Functional Literacy of Adults (TOHFLA), developed by health scientists working in large urban hospitals with many indigent patients (Williams *et al.* 1995). Functional literacy refers to competence at using written materials to carry out routine activities in modern life. Both the NALS and TOHFLA were developed in the wake of mounting concern that large segments of the American public are unable to cope with the basic demands of a literate society, for instance, filling out applications for jobs or social services, calculating the cost of a purchase, and understanding instructions for taking medication (see Gottfredson, in press, for additional information about the two tests).

The developers of both tests began with the same assumption, namely, that low literacy consists of deficits in highly specific and largely independent skills in decoding and using the written word. Guided by this hypothesis, the NALS researchers attempted to measure three distinct kinds of literacy by writing test items for three kinds of written material — prose (P), document (D) and quantitative (Q). Both sets of researchers, however, aimed for "high fidelity" tests, that is, they created items that measure real-world tasks in a realistic manner. So, for example, NALS respondents might extract information from news articles, locate information in a bus schedule, and use a calculator to calculate the cost of carpet to cover a room; TOHFLA respondents would read the label on a vial of prescription medicine to say how many times a day the medicine should be taken and how many times the prescription can be refilled. Sample items for the NALS are listed in Figure 15.4 and for the TOHFLA in Table 15.7. The

Proficiency Level	Sample Items[a]	Information-Processing Demands[b]
0	**69** Sign your name (D)	
	191 Total a bank deposit entry (Q)	*Level 1* (NALS ≤225) tasks require identifying or matching single pieces of information or performing a single, simple, specified arithmetic operation (like addition) in contexts where there is little or no distracting information. (Includes about 14% of white and 38% of black adults aged 16 and over.[c])
225	**224** Underline sentence explaining action stated in short article (P)	
	232 Locate intersection on a street map (D)	
	250 Locate two features of information in sports article (P)	*Level 2* (NALS 226-275) tasks introduce distractors, more varied information, and the need for low-level inferences or to integrate two or more pieces of information. Information tends to be easily identifiable, despite the presence of distractors, and numeric operations are easily determined from the format of the material provided (say, an order form). (Includes about 25% of white and 37% of black adults.)
275	**270** Calculate total costs of purchase from an order form (Q)	
	280 Write a brief letter explaining error made on a credit card bill (P)	
	308 Using calculator, determine the discount from an oil bill if paid within 10 days (Q)	*Level 3* (NALS 276-325) tasks require integrating multiple pieces of information from one or more documents, which themselves may be complex and contain much irrelevant information. However, the matches to be made between information and text tend to be literal or synonymous, and correct information is not located near incorrect information. (Includes about 36% of white and 21% of black adults.)
325	**323** Enter information given into an automobile maintenance record form (D)	
	328 State in writing an argument made in lengthy newspaper article (P)	
	348 Use bus schedule to determine appropriate bus for given set of conditions (D)	*Level 4* (NALS 326-375) tasks require more inferences, multiple-feature matches, integration and synthesis of information from complex passages or documents, and use of multiple sequential operations. (Includes about 21% of white and 4% of black adults.)
375	**368** Using eligibility pamphlet, calculate the yearly amount a couple would receive for basic supplemental security income (Q)	
	387 Using table comparing credit cards, identify the two categories used and write two differences between them (D)	
	410 Summarize from text two ways lawyers may challenge prospective jurors (P)	*Level 5* (NALS 376-500) tasks require the application of specialized background knowledge, disembedding the features of a problem from text, and drawing high-level inferences from highly complex text with multiple distractors. (Includes about 4% of white and less than 0.5% of black adults.)
500	**421** Using calculator, determine the total cost of carpet to cover a room (Q)	

Figure 15.4: Sample items and information-processing demands at five levels of NALS literacy.

Sources:
[a] Brown *et al.* (1996: 10). P = prose scale, D = documents scale, Q = quantitative scale.
[b] Brown *et al.* (1996: 11).
[c] Kirsch *et al.* (1993, Table 1.1A). Percentages are for Prose Scale.

Table 15.7: Percentage and relative risk (odds ratios) of patients incorrectly answering test items on the TOFHLA, by level of health literacy.

Test item		Literacy level		
		Inadequate	Marginal	Adequate
Numeracy items				
How to take medication on an empty stomach	%	65.3	52.1	23.9
	OR	**6.0**	3.2	1.0
How to take medication four times a day	%	23.6	9.4	4.5
	OR	**6.6**	2.2	1.0
How many times a prescription can be refilled	%	42.0	24.7	9.6
	OR	**6.8**	3.1	1.0
How to determine financial eligibility	%	74.3	49.0	31.5
	OR	**9.0**	3.0	1.0
When next appointment is scheduled	%	39.6	12.7	4.7
	OR	**13.5**	3.0	1.0
How many pills of a prescription should be taken	%	69.9	33.7	13.0
	OR	**15.6**	3.4	1.0
Prose Cloze passages				
Instructions for preparing for upper gastrointestinal tract radiographic procedure	%	57.2	11.9	3.6
	OR	**36.2**	3.7	1.0
Rights and Responsibilities section of Medicaid application	%	81.1	31.0	7.3
	OR	**54.3**	5.7	1.0
Standard informed consent document	%	95.1	72.1	21.8
	OR	**70.5**	9.4	1.0

Source of percentages: Williams *et al.* (1995, Table 3). Reprinted with permission from the American Medical Association.

tests are thus meant to sample common, practical tasks that are not tied to any particular knowledge base or special expertise.

Both tests have been individually administered to large samples in the United States, the NALS to a nationally representative sample of 26,091 adults aged 16 and older, and the 20-minute TOHFLA first being administered to 2,659 patients in two large urban hospitals. (Because the NALS was meant to provide a snapshot of the entire adult population, and not to calculate scores for individuals, no respondent took the entire, very long survey).

Although most NALS and TOHFLA tasks might seem relatively simple, large proportions of the American population have difficulty performing them correctly. As shown in Figure 15.4, fully 40% of whites and almost twice that proportion of blacks routinely function at only Levels 1 or 2, which NALS researchers have described as inadequate for "competing successfully in a global economy and exercising fully the rights and responsibilities of citizenship" (Baldwin *et al.* 1995: 16). The TOHFLA survey of urban hospital patients (Williams *et al.* 1995) classified 43% of patients as having either "inadequate" or "marginal" health literacy. Among the 26% of patients having inadequate literacy, Table 15.7 shows that two-thirds did not understand instructions on how to take prescription medication on an empty stomach or how many pills to take. Error rates for the two items were much lower for patients judged to have "adequate" literacy, respectively, 24% and 13%.

In a separate study of patients with chronic illnesses such as diabetes and hypertension, generally only about half of those with inadequate literacy knew even the most basic facts about their disease or how to cope with it, despite presumably having received instruction (Williams *et al.* 1998). Table 15.8 shows, for instance, that among diabetic patients with inadequate literacy, 62% did not know that they need to eat some form of sugar if they suddenly get sweaty, nervous or shaky (a signal that their blood sugar has dropped too low — also a fact that only about half knew).

Such low levels of functional competence were no surprise to the NALS and TOHFLA researchers. Rather, what greatly surprised both sets of researchers was to discover that low literacy actually represents a global poverty of higher order information-processing capabilities — the ability to learn, understand and solve problems. NALS analysts concluded that adult literacy reflects "problem solving", "complex information processing", and "verbal comprehension and reasoning, or the ability to understand, analyze, interpret, and evaluate written information and apply fundamental principles and concepts" (Venezky *et al.* 1987: 25, 28; Baldwin *et al.* 1995: xv). Health literacy researchers concluded that health literacy is the "ability to acquire new information and complete complex cognitive tasks", and that low literacy reflects "limited problem-solving abilities" (Baker *et al.* 1998: 795–797).

The health scientists also rediscovered what reading researchers had learned decades earlier in "work literacy" research for the Army (Sticht 1975): "literacy" reflects comprehension of both the spoken and written word. People with low literacy understand the spoken word no better than they do the written word. In other words, differences in functional literacy have nothing to do with reading and writing per se. Rather, "literacy" concerns information processing of any sort in either modality. The written word just provides a handy means of gauging this cross-modality competence.

The juxtaposition of the two sets of literacy studies is compelling because the research teams worked in different fields addressing different institutional needs, their tests differed greatly in manifest content and psychometric sophistication, and they were administered to quite different populations and in different contexts, and yet their results led the researchers to the same unexpected conclusion. As noted, they now describe

Table 15.8: Percentage and relative risk (odds ratios) of patients incorrectly answering selected questions about their chronic disease, by level of health literacy.

Patient does not know that		Literacy level		
		Inadequate	Marginal	Adequate
Diabetes				
If you feel thirsty, tired, and weak, it usually means your blood glucose level is high	%	40.0	30.8	25.5
	OR	**2.0**	**1.3**	**1.0**
When you exercise, your blood glucose level goes down	%	60.0	53.8	35.3
	OR	**2.7**	**2.1**	**1.0**
If you suddenly get sweaty, nervous, and shaky, you should eat some form of sugar	%	62.0	46.1	27.4
	OR	**4.3**	**2.3**	**1.0**
Normal blood glucose level is between 3.8–7.7 mmol/L (70–140 mg/dL)	%	42.0	23.1	11.8
	OR	**5.4**	**2.2**	**1.0**
If you feel shaky, sweaty, and hungry, it usually means your blood glucose level is low	%	50.0	15.4	5.9
	OR	**15.9**	**2.9**	**1.0**
Hypertension				
Canned vegetables are high in salt	%	36.7	24.0	19.2
	OR	**2.4**	**1.1**	**1.0**
Exercise lowers blood pressure	%	59.7	56.0	32.0
	OR	**3.1**	**2.7**	**1.0**
Blood pressure of 130/80 mm Hg is normal	%	58.2	32.0	28.8
	OR	**3.4**	**1.2**	**1.0**
Losing weight lowers blood pressure	%	33.2	16.0	8.3
	OR	**5.5**	**2.1**	**1.0**
Blood pressure of 160/100 mm Hg is high	%	44.9	30.0	8.3
	OR	**9.0**	**4.7**	**1.0**

Source of percentages: Williams *et al.* (1998, Tables 2 and 3).
Reprinted with permission from the American Medical Association.

literacy in the very language of critical thinking and information processing that researchers use to describe the manifestations of *g*.

We can therefore safely infer that both literacy tests are highly *g* loaded. But how *g* loaded are they? High enough to essentially constitute IQ tests, at least for non-immigrant populations? The answer is not clear for the TOHFLA, although different health literacy tests do behave like different IQ tests in certain ways: specifically, various health literacy scales correlate 0.7–0.9 with each other and with tests of known high *g* loading (Davis *et al.* 1998), such as the Wide Range Achievement Test (WRAT), even in samples that are highly restricted in range on ability.

I am not aware of any correlations of the NALS with IQ scores, but NALS technical reports provide other, more compelling evidence that the NALS is a reasonably good test of *g*: namely: (a) the NALS measures only a single factor; and (b) that factor is the ability to process complex information. The early NALS reports had scores on the three literacy scales correlating about 0.5 with each other, but then errors in calculation were discovered. When recalculated correctly, the three scales intercorrelated over 0.9, before correction for attenuation. Not surprisingly, the three separate scales produce virtually identical results — the same findings "in triplicate, as it were" (Reder 1998: 39, 44) — despite clear differences in item content. In short, the three different NALS scales measure the same general factor and virtually nothing else.

NALS researchers also carried out a lengthy analysis of test results that is rarely performed but which is invaluable for understanding the construct that a test is actually measuring — a detailed task analysis (separately for each of the three scales) to determine which of the items' attributes accounted for their differences in difficulty. The task analyses identified the same sources of item difficulty for all three scales, which the researchers labeled "processing complexity". Figure 15.4 summarizes the differences in processing complexity across the five NALS levels. They clearly represent differences in the complexity of information processing and problem solving, which, again, is the very language of *g*. In other words, NALS difficulty levels represent differences in demands for the information-processing skills that *g* embodies. They do not reflect readability per se (Kirsch *et al.* 1994), which supports the inference that functional literacy, as measured in large (non-immigrant) American samples, is mostly *g*.

We have just seen two examples where life yields a highly *g*-loaded mental test when researchers attempted to measure consequential differences in everyday competence, in this case, with written materials. But which domains of life activity might offer up such IQ tests, and why? Is literacy the exception? Probably not, but everyday literacy may be the prototype for where to find them. First, literacy tests sample highly instrumental tasks rather than socioemotional ones, that is, tasks primarily to the left side of Figure 15.2. The personnel selection research reviewed earlier suggests that instrumental activities depend more on *g* and less on personality traits than do interpersonal activities. Were we to build a life test from daily tasks of a more socioemotional nature, such as getting along with one's neighbors or influencing others, we would probably end up with a test that taps favorable personality traits more and *g* less than do either the NALS or the TOHFLA.

Second, literacy tasks constitute a life test that we are all obliged to take. They are among the common subtests in life, not only because we are all exposed to demands to use written materials, but also because they represent inescapable, ubiquitous self-maintenance tasks in any literate society. Adults who cannot perform the simpler tasks in the NALS scales in effect fail a minimum competency test for modern life. Ethnographic studies of mildly retarded adults poignantly describe how they often attempt to hide their inability to read, fill out job applications, and make change in order to avoid being stigmatized as incompetent and "retarded". But whether they succeed in hiding it or not, their low literacy renders them unable to live independent lives without considerable assistance (Koegel & Edgerton 1984).

Few functional literacy tasks may be discretionary if individuals want to protect their health and welfare over the long-run. It may matter little whether one occasionally fails to adequately describe the problems with an appliance needing repair, select the best values in a supermarket, capitalize on opportunities for cheaper goods and services, identify available social services, understand public issues affecting one's welfare, take medication properly, or recognize the symptoms of one's chronic illness that require immediate action, such as an imminent asthma attack or insulin reaction. Repeated such failure, however, especially across multiple arenas of life, can threaten one's health, disposable income and overall quality of life. Research on health literacy indicates, for example, that low-literacy individuals experience much higher health costs, poorer health and more frequent hospitalization (National Work Group on Literacy and Health 1998).

Moreover, the ability to master moderate- to high-complexity literacy tasks — for instance, to use bus and airline schedules, understand news articles and hospital consent forms, distinguish the merits of different employee benefits packages or credit cards, and recognize when and how to respond to the symptoms of one's chronic illness — enables one to participate more fully in civic and economic life, better exploit one's opportunities, waste less time and money, avoid accidents, better maintain one's health and simply live a less error-plagued daily existence. As functional literacy researchers have summed it up, "literacy is a currency not only in our schools, but in our society as well; and, as with money, it is better to have more literacy than less" (Kirsch & Jungeblut 1990: v–12). As health literacy researchers point out, it can also be a matter of life and death. Referring to the complicated new treatment regimens for heart attack victims, Baker *et al.* (1998: 791) warn that a "patient's ability to learn this regimen and follow it correctly will determine a trajectory toward recovery or a downward path to recurrent myocardial infarction, disability, and death".

Health self-care clearly constitutes a common test that none of us can afford to spurn. It is not entirely cognitive, of course (how many of us fail to act on our knowledge of proper diet and exercise?), but health researchers are concerned that the motivational component of patient "compliance" has been overestimated relative to its cognitive demands. Other realms of life also impose equally common tests on us — for instance, being a friend, neighbor, co-worker and law-abiding citizen — but, as suggested earlier, many of these are more socioemotional or characterological than is functional literacy. They can thus be expected to be less *g* loaded. On the other hand, equally instrumental tasks in some arenas of life are more discretionary and therefore do not constitute common life tests — many avocations, for instance. Because they are discretionary, fewer people will choose to undertake them. This means, in turn, that differences in quality of performance will depend more heavily on degree of exposure and length of practice, and thus that the utility of *g* will be somewhat camouflaged by differences in exposure and practice. That is, discretionary activities may or may not be fundamentally less *g* loaded than is functional literacy, but their dependence on *g* will be harder to ascertain because the "test takers" will be unrepresentative and highly self-selected.

4.1. "Making It": A Free Society's Decathlon

The earlier discussion of *g* and jobs suggested that there is a nexus of good life outcomes — socioeconomic outcomes, at least — that is associated with higher *g*. The behavioral genetic studies cited earlier reveal the association to be not only phenotypic, but also genetic to some degree. Figure 15.5 encapsulates that nexus of positive outcomes by arraying the levels of training and job potential that are typical for individuals at each of five broad segments of the IQ distribution, from the "high-risk" zone (IQ 75 and below) to the "yours to lose" zone (above IQ 125). Estimated IQ equivalents for the five NALS levels are indicated in the same figure. There are many factors besides *g* that affect success in education, training and employment, but the probability of success steadily improves at successively higher levels of IQ. These outcomes reflect the decathlon of socioeconomic life in a free society — citizens competing with one another in a long series of events to gain, and keep, a congenial place on the social ladder. The competitions are not entirely fair and open, of course, but they are free and open enough for competence — and hence *g* — to make a considerable difference in who succeeds. "Making it" socioeconomically does not represent a person's moral worth, but it does represent a common, valued pursuit in American life.

But what about the flip side of socioeconomic success — dropping out of high school, going to jail, bearing illegitimate children and other negative outcomes? This troubling nexus of social pathology, one that concerns social policy makers so, is part of the same decathlon of adult life in a free society as are the positive outcomes. One difference between the contests for obtaining good outcomes and avoiding bad ones, however, is that the latter often function as pass-fail tests: you either have or have not gone to prison, borne a child out of wedlock or gone on welfare. Failing these tests can be highly stigmatizing as well as debilitating, so they are tests that many people are loathe to fail or to have family members fail.

People of all IQ levels fail these tests, of course, and the role that *g* plays in the nexus of social pathology is still little understood. It is clear, however, that the probability of failure rises steeply toward lower levels of the IQ continuum. Moreover, IQ often predicts such outcomes at least as well as do the social class variables that social scientists had long assumed to account for why some people succumb and others do not (Herrnstein & Murray 1994; Gordon 1997).

Tables 15.9 and 15.10 illustrate how the relative risk of various unfavorable social outcomes rises steadily and substantially at each of 5 successively lower ranges of IQ, from above IQ 125 (about the 95th percentile) to below IQ 75 (about the 5th percentile). The data in Table 15.9 are based on young white American adults whose IQ scores were estimated from the Armed Forces Qualifying Test (AFQT), which is a reasonably good measure of *g* (Ree *et al.* 1998/1999; Herrnstein & Murray 1994, app. 3); Table 15.10 is based on NALS results for American white adults aged 16 and older, which results have also been translated into the IQ metric. The five score ranges overlap but are not identical across the two tests, with the five NALS levels in Table 15.10 for older adults representing somewhat higher levels of IQ than do the five levels in Table 15.9 for young white adults.

The two tables nonetheless reveal the same two trends. First, looking across the columns of odds ratios, relative risk at least doubles at each successively lower range of

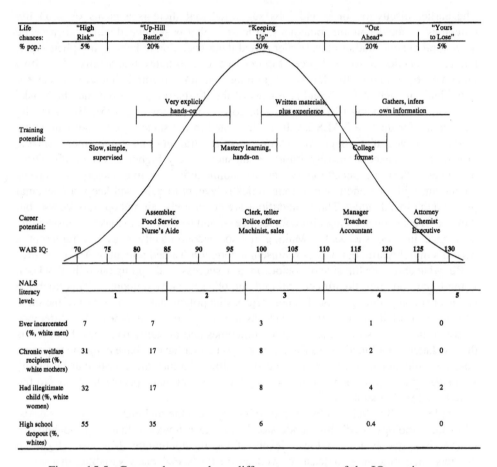

Figure 15.5: Career chances along different segments of the IQ continuum.

Source: Adapted from Figure 3 in Gottfredson, L. S. (1997). Why *g* matters: The complexity of everyday life. *Intelligence*, 24, 79–132, with permission from Elsevier Science.

[a] WPT = Wonderlic Personnel Test.

[b] NALS = National Adult Literacy Survey. See Gottfredson (1997) for translation of NALS scores into IQ equivalents.

[c] See Gottfredson (1997) for calculation of percentile.

Table 15.9: Relative risk of bad outcomes associated with lower IQ: Prevalence (%) and Odds Ratios (OR) for young white adults.

Outcome		IQ level				
		≥75	76–90	91–110	111–125	≥125
Bell Curve data: General population[a]						
Out of labor force	%	22	19	15	14	10
1 + mo/yr (men)	OR	1.6	1.3	1.0	0.9	0.6
Unemployed	%	12	10	7	7	2
1 + mo/yr (men)	OR	1.8	1.5	1.0	1.0	0.3
Ever in carcerated (men)	%	[7][b]	7	3	1	0
	OR	[2.4]	2.4	1.0	0.3	0.1[c]
Chronic welfare recipient	%	31	17	8	2	0
(women)	OR	5.2	2.4	1.0	0.2	0.05[d]
Had illegitimate children	%	32	17	8	4	2
(women)	OR	5.4	2.4	1.0	0.5	0.2
Lives in poverty as an	%	30	16	6	3	2
adult	OR	6.7	3.0	1.0	0.5	0.3
Went on welfare after 1st	%	55	21	12	4	1
child (women)	OR	9.0	2.0	1.0	0.3	0.1
High school drop out	%	55	35	6	0.4	0
	OR	19.0	8.4	1.0	0.1	0
Bell Curve data: Sibling pairs[e]						
Not working in professional	%	100	99	98	92	77
job	OR	hi[f]	2.0	1.0	0.2	0.1
Not a college graduate	%	100	97	81	50	18
	OR	hi[f]	7.6	1.0	0.2	0.1

[a] *Source of percentages:* Herrnstein & Murray (1994, pp. 158, 163, 247 194, 180, 132, 194 & 146 respectively).
[b] See text for explanation.
[c] Assuming that % rounded to zero from 0.4, which yields odds of 0.004 and an odds ratio of 0.13.
[d] Assuming that % rounded to zero from 0.4, which yields odds of 0.004 and an odds ratio of 0.046.
[e] Source of percentages: Murray (1997b).
[f] OR can not be calculated because the odds of 100:0 (its numerator) cannot be calculated.
Table from Gottfredson (in press) and reprinted with permission from Lawrence Erlbaum Associates.

Table 15.10: Economic outcomes at different levels of NALS literacy: Whites aged 16 and over (% and odds ratios).

Outcome		Prose Literacy Level				
		1 (≤225)	2 (226–275)	3 (276–325)	4 (326–375)	5 (376–500)
Employed only part-time	%	70	57	46	36	28
	OR	2.7	1.6	1.0	0.7	0.5
Out of labor force	%	52	35	25	17	11
	OR	3.2	1.6	1.0	0.6	0.4
Uses food stamps	%	17	13	6	3	1
	OR	3.2	2.3	1.0	0.5	0.2
Lives in poverty	%	43	23	12	8	4
	OR	5.5	2.2	1.0	0.6	0.3
Employed *not* as professional or manager	%	95	88	77	54	30
	OR	5.6	2.2	1.0	0.4	0.1

Source of percentages: Kirsch et al. (1993, Figures 2.5, 2.6, 2.7, 2.9 & 2.10).
Table reprinted from Gottfredson (in press) and reprinted with permission of Lawrence Erlbaum Associates.

IQ for the more cumulative outcomes, that is, for all but the two employment outcomes (not looking for work or being unemployed if looking, respectively). For example, compared to women of average IQ (IQ 91–110), women of somewhat below average IQ (IQ 76–90) are four times as likely to bear an illegitimate child (17% vs. 4%; ORs of 2.4 vs. 0.5, respectively) and eight times as likely to become chronic welfare recipients (17% vs. 2%; ORs of 2.4 vs. 0.2, respectively). The relative risk for women of low IQ (IQ 75 and below) is doubled yet again (ORs over 5.0). On the other hand, the relative risk of either social problem drops to near zero for high-IQ women.

Second, comparing these trends across different outcomes, we see that the risk gradients are steeper (shift more dramatically) for the more cumulative, pass-fail outcomes (chronic welfare use, living below the poverty line, dropping out of high school) than for the more episodic and more easily reversed outcomes (out of the labor force or unemployed for a month during the year). For instance, whereas odds ratios for the latter rise from under 0.6 to 1.6 when down up the IQ distribution, the ratios rise from under 0.3 to over 5.0 for poverty and welfare use. That the latter gradients are steeper is consistent with the hypothesis that *g* exerts its major effects on life outcomes largely by consistently tilting the odds of success and failure in the smaller events that eventuate in the more consequential outcomes. The results in Table 15.10 also support this thesis. Although they are based on a different test of ability (the NALS) in a much broader age segment of the population, they show the same pattern.

The heated debate over *The Bell Curve* (Herrnstein & Murray 1994) revealed, once again, that many if not most policy researchers assume that differences in intelligence do not play much role in who exhibits the behaviors that policy makers seek to reduce. They nonetheless seem willing to attribute causal importance to what are actually good surrogates for *g* — for instance, literacy and "basic skills" — if they attribute them to socioeconomic disadvantage rather than to *g*. To illustrate, a well-received 1988 report for the Ford Foundation (Berlin & Sum 1988) "explores the basic-skills crisis, presenting evidence that inadequate skills are an underlying cause of poverty and economic dependency" (p. 2). What was their measure of "basic skills?" The highly *g*-loaded AFQT. The report's authors concluded from their data that poverty is rooted substantially in skills deficits, but they minimize the implications of this by mistakenly conceiving "basic skills" as a collection of highly specific, discrete, remediable skills rather than a suite of relatively stable, highly general ones. In fact, as the bottom panel of Table 15.9 shows, risk gradients for *siblings growing up in the same household* parallel those in the general population for similar outcomes (Tables 15.9 and 15.10). This provides additional evidence that *g* plays a strong role *independent* of one's family circumstances.

How *g* plays a role in social pathology is unclear, as noted earlier. We might gain more insight, however, by treating each pathology as a long test battery or *career*. Indeed, we routinely talk about criminal careers in the same way we talk about educational careers — as a long stream of behavior that can push one over certain social thresholds, whether good ones (performing sufficiently well over the years to graduate from high school, college or graduate school) or bad ones (committing more numerous and more serious crimes that eventually lead to a first arrest, then a longer arrest record, a conviction and imprisonment one or more times). Disabling sexual careers can be conceptualized in the same manner — as a cumulating series of small mistakes and misjudgments that can precipitate life-altering events (illegitimate births, HIV infection).

This is essentially the same process we saw in Figure 15.3, which compared the careers of New Standards Men to those of a control group. At IQ 80–85, the New Standards Men are below average but still above the threshold for mild retardation. They can thus be compared to the second-to-lowest IQ range in Figure 15.5 (IQ 76–90), labeled "up-hill battle" (also column 2 in Table 15.9). The control men in the military study are probably somewhat above average in IQ (and therefore higher in IQ than the comparison group in Table 15.9), because federal law forbids the military to induct men from the lowest 10% of the ability distribution (below about IQ 80). The risk ratios that led to the majority of New Standards Men to "fail" (be discharged from the military) within 18 months on the job, like those for failing at each prior step along that road, generally hovered between 2.0 and 4.0 (Table 15.6).

These are similar to the risk ratios seen in Table 15.9 for social pathology among young white adults in the "up-hill battle" IQ range: their ratios generally range between approximately 2.0 and 3.0. (That the NSM odds ratios are somewhat larger than for the "up-hill battle" group may be due to the former's control group probably being somewhat brighter than the latter's.) No one would say that these levels of relative risk for social pathology are small in human terms but, as we saw, differences of this magnitude are often hastily dismissed as inconsequential when social scientists examine the role of low *g* in the individual events culminating in employment outcomes. Such haste is unwarranted for any sphere of life.

It is also useful to note that the predominance of failure over success among Project 100,000 men occurred despite the considerable help that they apparently received. Help tends to flow down the IQ continuum in any society, whether from family members or social service agencies, because that is one way that societies soften the consequences of low *g* for their least able members. The levels of help that the New Standards Men received, however, may not be routinely available in many domains in life. Help is prohibited, of course, on tests of aptitude and achievement, and it is probably discouraged whenever individuals and institutions seek "honest" signals of competence before entering long-term commitments (e.g. hiring, marriage). The point here is simply that "help" constitutes one of the common non-standard conditions under which we take life's tests, and that understanding such "non-standard" conditions is key to charting *g*'s gradients of effect in particular times and places. The more help that is routinely given to the least able, the less steep the IQ risk gradients will be, all else equal.

Turning from understanding the impact of low *g* to concerns over ameliorating it, we could predict that help would have to be as ubiquitous as are the risks created by low *g* — an impossible and intrusive enterprise — in order to maintain equally favorable life trajectories for low-IQ individuals. Flattening all risk gradients is not an option, but moderating them might be.

5. Conclusion

Understanding the role of *g* in the lives of individuals and societies requires that we psychometrically analyze the components of everyday life. Just as psychologists have task analyzed paid employment, so might researchers open up the psychometric black box of life's other daily demands. This strategy promises to speed our understanding of *g*'s gradients of effect in many arenas of social life, as well as help identify the personal and external factors that can steepen or flatten those risk gradients.

There are many other areas of life yet to be plumbed with the psychometric tools to which Jensen has pointed us. At the individual level, they include interpersonal relations, parenting and family life, health and safety, good citizenship, civic engagement and aging. As *g*-based gradients of risk play out at the individual level, they yield higher-order effects that are also ripe for study: *g*-based residential and social segregation; patterns of cooperation and competition, envy and respect, compassion and contempt; political tensions between populations that differ noticeably in *g*; evolution of social policy, law and mores in response to *g*-based social inequalities; the special difficulties of stemming preventable epidemics in some populations; and much more.

Most broadly, we might ask "what kind of mental test battery has modern life become?" Are developed societies ordering their activities and their members increasingly according to distinctions in *g*? If so, can — or should — the trend be reversed, accelerated, or ignored? If so, how might citizens in the "high-risk" and "up-hill battle" ranges of IQ (below IQ 90) be helped to weather the new challenges?

References

Arvey, R. D. (1986). General ability in employment: A discussion. *Journal of Vocational Behavior, 29* (3), 415–420.

Baker, D. W., Parker, R. M., Williams, M. V., & Clark, W. S. (1998). Health literacy and the risk of hospital admission. *Journal of General Internal Medicine, 13*, 791–798.

Baldwin, J., Kirsch, I. S., Rock, D., & Yamamoto, K. (1995). *The literacy proficiencies of GED examinees: Results from the GED-NALS comparison study.* Washington, D.C.: American Council on Education and Educational Testing.

Behrman, J. R., Hrubec, Z., Taubman, P., & Wales, T. (1980). *Socioeconomic success: A study of the effects of genetic endowments, family environment, and schooling.* New York: North-Holland Publishing Co.

Berlin, G., & Sum, A. (1988). *Toward a more perfect union: Basic skills, poor families, and our economic future.* (Occasional paper 3, Project on Social Welfare and the American Future). New York: Ford Foundation.

Bouchard, T. J. Jr. (1998). Genetic and environmental influences on adult intelligence and special mental abilities. *Human Biology, 70* (2), 257–279.

Bowles, S., & Gintis, H. (1972/1973). IQ in the U.S. class structure. *Social Policy, 3* (4 & 5), 65–96.

Brand, C. (1987). The importance of general intelligence. In: S. Modgil, & C. Modgil (Eds), *Arthur Jensen: Consensus and controversy* (pp. 251–265). New York: Falmer Press.

Brown, H., Prisuta, R., Jacobs, B., & Campbell, A. (1996). *Literacy of older adults in America: Results from the National Adult Literacy Survey.* Washington, D.C.: U.S. Department of Education, National Center for Education Statistics.

Canter, R. R. (1956). Intelligence and the social status of occupations. *Personnel Guidance Journal, 34*, 258–260.

Carroll, J. B. (1993). *Human cognitive abilities: A survey of factor-analysis studies.* New York: Cambridge University Press.

Christal, R. E. (1974). *The United States Air Force Occupational Research Project.* Lackland AFB, TX, Air Force Human Resources laboratory (AFSC). (NTIS No. AD774 574).

Collins, R. (1979). *The credential society: An historical sociology of education and stratification.* New York: Academic Press.

Davis, T. C., Michielutte, R., Askov, E. N., Williams, M. V., & Weiss, B. D. (1998). Practical assessment of adult literacy in health care. *Health Education & Behavior, 25* (5), 613–624.

Duncan, O. D., Featherman, D. L., & Duncan, B. (1972). *Socioeconomic background and achievement.* New York: Seminar Press.

Gerstman, B. B. (1998). *Epidemiology kept simple: An introduction to classic and modern epidemiology.* New York: Wiley.

Gordon, R. A. (1997). Everyday life as an intelligence test: Effects of intelligence and intelligence context. *Intelligence, 24* (1) 203–320.

Gottfredson, L. S. (1984). *The role of intelligence and education in the division of labor.* (Report No. 355). Baltimore: Johns Hopkins University, Center for Social Organization of Schools.

Gottfredson, L. S. (1985). Education as a valid but fallible signal of worker quality: Reorienting an old debate about the functional basis of the occupational hierarchy. In: A. C. Kerckhoff

(Ed.), *Research in sociology of education and socialization* (Vol. 5, pp. 119–165). Greenwich, CT: JAI Press.

Gottfredson, L. S. (1986). Occupational Aptitude Patterns (OAP) Map: Development and implications for a theory of job aptitude requirements (Monograph). *Journal of Vocational Behavior, 29*, 254–291.

Gottfredson, L. S. (1997). Why *g* matters: The complexity of everyday life. *Intelligence, 24* (1), 79–132.

Gottfredson, L. S. (in press). *g*: Highly general and highly practical. In: R. J. Sternberg, & E. L. Grigorenko (Eds), *The general intelligence factor: How general is it?* Mahwah, NJ: Erlbaum.

Herrnstein, R. J., & Murray, C. (1994). *The bell curve: Intelligence and class structure in American life*. New York: Free Press.

Hodge, R. W., Treiman, D. J., & Rossi, P. H. (1966). A comparative study of occupational prestige (pp. 309–334). In: R. Bendix, & S. M. Lipset (Eds), *Class, status, and power: Social stratification in comparative perspective* (2nd ed.). New York: Free Press.

Hunter, J. E., & Hunter, R. F. (1984). Validity and utility of alternative predictors of job performance. *Psychological Bulletin, 96* (1), 72–98.

Hunter, J. E., & Schmidt, F. L. (1996). Intelligence and job performance: Economic and social implications. *Psychology, Public Policy, and Law, 2* (3/4) 447–472.

Jencks, C., Bartlett, S., Corcoran, M., Crouse, J., Eaglesfield, D., Jackson, G., McClelland, K., Mueser, P., Olneck, M., Schwartz, J., Ward, S., & Williams, J. (1979). *Who gets ahead? The determinants of economic success in America*. New York: Basic Books.

Jencks, C., Smith, M., Acland, H., Bane, M. J., Cohen, D., Gintis, H., Heyns, B., & Michelson, S. (1972). *Inequality: A reassessment of the effect of family and schooling in America*. New York: Basic Books.

Jensen, A. R. (1998). *The g factor: The science of mental ability*. Westport, CT: Praeger.

Kirsch, I. S., & Jungeblut, A. (Eds.) (1990). *Literacy: Profiles of America's young adults*. Princeton: Educational Testing Service.

Kirsch, I. S., Jungeblut, A., Jenkins, L., & Kolstad, A. (1993). *Adult literacy in America: A first look at the results of the National Adult Literacy Survey*. Princeton, NJ: Educational Testing Service.

Kirsch, I. S., Jungeblut, A., & Mosenthal, P. B. (1994). *Moving towards the measurement of adult literacy*. Paper presented at the March NCES meeting, Washington, D.C..

Koegel, P., & Edgerton, R. B. (1984). Black six hour retarded children as young adults. In: R. B. Edgerton (Ed.), *Lives in progress: Mildly retarded adults in a large city* (pp. 145–171). Washington, D.C.: American Association on Mental Deficiency.

Laurence, J. H., & Ramsberger, P. F. (1991). *Low-aptitude men in the military: Who profits, who pays?* New York: Praeger.

Lichtenstein, P., & Pedersen, N. L. (1997). Does genetic variance for cognitive abilities account for genetic variance in educational achievement and occupational status? A study of twins reared apart and twins reared together. *Social Biology, 44* (1–2), 77–90.

Miller, A. R., Treiman, D. J., Cain, P. S., & Roos, P. A. (Eds) (1980). *Work, jobs, and occupations: A critical review of the Dictionary of Occupational Titles*. Washington, D.C.: National Academy Press.

Murray, C. (1997a). Brains, rather than family background, determine how well our children will do in later life, says author of The Bell Curve Charles Murray. *Sunday London Times*. (May 25).

Murray, C. (1997b). IQ and economic success. *The Public Interest*, (128), 21–35.

National Work Group on Literacy and Health (1998). Communicating with patients who have limited literacy skills: Report of the National Work Group on Literacy and Health. *The Journal of Family Practice, 46* (2), 168–176.

Olneck, M. R. (1977). On the use of sibling data to estimate the effects of family background, cognitive skills, and schooling. In: P. Taubman (Ed.), *Kinometrics: Determinants of socioeconomic success within and between families* (pp. 125–162). New York: North-Holland.

O'Toole, B. J. (1990). Intelligence and behavior and motor vehicle accident mortality. *Accident analysis and prevention, 22,* 211–221.

Plomin, R., & Bergeman, C. S. (1991). The nature of nurture: Genetic influence on "environmental" measures. *Behavioral and Brain Sciences, 14,* 373–427.

Plomin, R., DeFries, J. C., McClearn, G. E., & McGuffin, P. (2000). *Behavioral genetics* (4th ed.). New York: Worth Publishers.

Reder, S. (1998). Dimensionality and construct validity of the NALS assessment. In: M. C. Smith (Ed.), *Literacy for the twenty-first century* (pp. 37–57). Westport, CT: Praeger.

Ree, M. J., Carretta, T. R., & Doub, T. (1998/1999). A test of three models of the role of *g* and prior job knowledge in the acquisition of subsequent job knowledge. *Training Research Journal, 4,* 1–16.

Reich, R. (1992). *The work of nations.* New York: Vintage Books.

Rowe, D. C., Vesterdal, W. J., & Rodgers, J. L. (1998). Herrnstein's syllogism: Genetic and shared environmental influences on IQ, education, and income. *Intelligence, 26* (4), 405–423.

Schmidt, F. L., & Hunter, J. E. (1998). The validity and utility of selection methods in personnel psychology: Practical and theoretical implications of 85 years of research findings. *Psychological Bulletin, 124* (2), 262–274.

Schmidt, F. L., & Hunter, J. E. (2000). Select on intelligence. In: E. A. Locke (Ed.), *The Blackwell handbook of principles of organizational behavior* (pp. 3–14). Malden, MA: Blackwell Publishers.

Sewell, W. H., & Hauser, R. M. (1975). *Education, occupation, and earnings: Achievement in the early career.* New York: Academic Press.

Spaeth, J. L. (1979). Vertical differentiation among occupations. *American Sociological Review, 44,* 746–762.

Sternberg, R. J. (1997). *Successful intelligence: How practical and creative intelligence determine success in life.* New York: Penguin Putnam.

Sternberg, R. J., Forsythe, G. B., Hedlund, J., Horvath, J. A., Wagner, R. K., Williams, W. M., Snook, S. A., & Grigorenko, E. L. (2000). *Practical intelligence in everyday life.* New York: Cambridge University Press.

Stewart, N. (1947). Relationship between military occupational specialty and Army General Classification Test standard score. *Educational and Psychological Measurement, 7,* 677–693.

Sticht, T. (Ed.) (1975). *Reading for working: A functional literacy anthology.* Alexandria, VA: Human Resources Research Organization.

Sticht, T. G., Armstrong, W. B., Hickey, D. T., & Caylor, J. S. (1987). *Cast-off youth: Policy and training methods from the military experience.* New York: Praeger.

Taubman, P. (Ed.) (1977). *Kinometrics: Determinants of socioeconomic success within and between families.* New York: North-Holland Publishing Co.

U.S. Department of Labor (1970). *Manual for the USTES general aptitude test battery.* Washington, D.C.: U. S. Government Printing Office.

Venezky, R. L., Kaestle, C. F., & Sum, A. M. (1987). *The subtle danger: Reflections on the literacy abilities of America's young adults.* Princeton, NJ: Educational Testing Service.

Viswesvaran, D., & Ones, D. S. (Eds.) (in press). Role of general mental ability in industrial, work and organizational (IWO) psychology. *Human Performance,* (Special issue).

Wigdor, A. K., & Green, B. F., Jr. (Eds) (1991). *Performance for the workplace* (Vol. 1). Washington, D.C.: National Academy Press.

Wilk, S. L., Desmarais, L. B., & Sackett, P. R. (1995). Gravitation to jobs commensurate with ability: Longitudinal and cross-sectional tests. *Journal of Applied Psychology, 80* (1), 79–85.

Williams, M. V., Baker, D. W., Parker, R. M., & Nurss, J. R. (1998). Relationship of functional health literacy to patients' knowledge of their chronic disease. *Archives of Internal Medicine, 158*, 166–172.

Williams, M. V., Parker, R. M., Baker, D. W., Parikh, N. S., Pitkin, K., Coates, W. C., & Nurss, J. R. (1995). Inadequate functional health literacy among patients at two public hospitals. *Journal of the American Medical Association, 274* (21), 1677–1682.

Wonderlic Personnel Test, Inc. (1992). *Wonderlic Personnel Test and Scholastic Level Exam: User's manual*. Libertyville, I: Author.

Chapter 16

Crime, Delinquency and Intelligence:
A Review of the Worldwide Literature

Lee Ellis and Anthony Walsh

1. Introduction

The possibility that intelligence is correlated with criminal behavior has had a long and checkered history in the social sciences. Intelligence is such a quintessential human characteristic that we should not be surprised to find it underlying all sorts of behavior. Could this include behavior that violates the law? It is understandable that people would avoid adding insult to injury by attributing low intelligence to those who have been snared by the criminal justice system, often for doing things that many of the rest of us did without getting caught.

For over a century, some have speculated that low intelligence may lead to criminal behavior by hampering the ability to weigh the pleasure and pain involved in committing criminal acts, or more generally by diminishing humanity's moral sense. One of the earliest works emphasizing that there may be a causal link between low intelligence and criminality was an case study written by Richard Dugdale, entitled *"The Jukes": A Study of Crime, Pauperism, Disease, and Heredity* (1877/1895). Dugdale studied the lineage of a rural upstate New York family well known for its criminal activity, to which he gave the fictitious name of "Jukes". The family lineage was traced to a colonial-era character named "Max" whose descendants remained in relative isolation and propagated themselves primarily through incestuous marriage. Dugdale eventually traced hundreds of Max's descendants, among whom he found numerous cases of crime, pauperism, disease, illegitimacy, feeblemindedness, sexual promiscuity and prostitution. Of course, without a control group, any deductions from Dugdale's efforts were suggestive at best. Another famous lineage study was Henry Goddard's *The Kallikak Family: A Study in the Heredity of Feeble-mindedness* (1912/1931). This study traced two separate family lineages of a Revolutionary War soldier named, "Martin Kallikak, Sr". While on active service, Martin dallied with a feebleminded tavern girl with whom he fathered an illegitimate and feebleminded

The Scientific Study of General Intelligence: Tribute to Arthur R. Jensen
ISBN: 0–08–043793–1

son. From this lineage issued a variety of individuals of unsavory character, weak morality and low intelligence.

Martin produced another line of descendants with a "respectable" woman from a good Quaker family. The descendants of this lineage were much more prominent and well-respected in their communities. From the genealogies of these two families sharing a common male ancestor, but two different female ancestors, one "defective" and the other "respectable", Goddard (1912: 69) concluded that "degeneracy" was the result of "bad blood". Goddard (1912: 108) expressed alarm that the feebleminded branch of the Kallikaks were reproducing at twice the rate of the "respectable" branch, and suggested that feebleminded persons should be prevented from procreating by either sterilization or institutionalization. Not long after the first standardized tests of intelligence were published in English, Goddard began compiling information on the intelligence of delinquents and criminals in the United States. Based on these efforts, Goddard published another book called *Feeblemindedness* in which he concluded that "at least 50% of all criminals are mentally defective" a figure that was much higher than the 2–3% that he estimated for the general population (Goddard 1914: 9). Low intelligence translated into criminality, he believed, because the feebleminded lacked the ability to distinguish right from wrong. However, low intelligence by itself was not a sufficient explanation for criminality; temperament and environment must mingle with low intelligence to make a criminal. Over the next few decades, several researchers provided additional evidence that populations of criminals and serious delinquents scored substantially below average on standardized intelligence tests (e.g. Healy & Bronner 1939), although none of these subsequent studies put the majority of offenders in the range of being feeble minded.

The purported role of low intelligence in criminality was delivered a blow with the advent of large-scale mental testing for the armed services. Administering these tests to draftees during World War I revealed that 37% of the whites and 89% of the blacks received a diagnosis of feeblemindedness (Vold & Bernard 1986: 73). For critics of mental testing, these findings reflected the cultural bias of mental tests. Goddard himself was said to have changed his mind about the genetic origin of feeblemindedness based on these results, and began to feel that intelligence could be remedied almost entirely by education (Vold & Bernard 1986: 73).

By the 1930s, a few researchers began to challenge assertions that the IQ scores of criminals were significantly lower than the average for the population as a whole (reviewed by Zeleny 1933; Weiss & Sampliner 1944; Ferentz 1954). Claims of test bias and the assumption of some critics that intelligence testing had eugenic implications curtailed research involving intelligence in the field of criminology from the 1940s through the early 1970s (Wilson & Herrnstein 1985: 153).

2. The Resurgence of Interest in IQ

Renewed interest in the link between IQ and criminality erupted a quarter of a century ago with the publication of a review article by Travis Hirschi and Michael Hindelang (1977) in the *American Sociological Review*. This review concluded that a substantial inverse correlation existed between intelligence and involvement in delinquent and criminal behavior.

The conclusion reached by Hirschi and Hindelang was sharply criticized by a number of social scientists (e.g. Simons 1978), while others defended the conclusion (e.g. Herrnstein 1980: 48; Raine 1993: 232). Since the Hirschi and Hindelang article appeared, at least three selective reviews of the IQ-crime relationship have been published, all of which have characterized the relationship as ubiquitous and robust (Quay 1987a; Lynam *et al.* 1993; Stattin & Klackenberg-Larsson 1993).

Despite a reawakening of interest in the intelligence-criminality in the 1970s, today's criminologists continue to play down the role of intelligence in explaining delinquent and criminal behavior (Wright & Miller 1998). Evidence in this regard comes from a recent survey of criminologists, which found *low intelligence* ranked 19th among factors that were considered important causes of serious and persistent offending (Ellis & Walsh 1999). Furthermore, it is ironical to note that even though Hirschi has played an important role in drawing attention to the substantial relationship between intelligence and offending, the theory of delinquency and crime to which he subscribes — control theory — itself offers no specific explanation for why such a relationship should exist (Gottfredson & Hirschi 1990).

Given that nearly a quarter of a century has passed since the last exhaustive review of the intelligence-criminality relationship was published, an updated review is in order. To make the review as condensed as possible, we have organized the relevant references into two tables. One table deals with intelligence in general, and the other has to do with a phenomenon known as intellectual imbalance. As will be explained more later, *intellectual imbalance* refers to significant inconsistencies in scores between the two main components of standardized tests: the linguistic and the non-linguistic component.

3. Organizing the Evidence

Across the top of both tables, six categories of officially recorded crime statistics are identified. Delinquency, general/undifferentiated offenses (nearly always by adults), and offender recidivism are the first three categories. The next two columns in the table pertain to self-reported offending, one column for self-reported offenses in general and the other pertaining strictly to drug offenses (primarily the possession and use of marijuana and other illegal drugs). The last two columns of the table have to do with the clinical diagnoses of childhood conduct disorder and psychopathy (antisocial personality disorder).

In each table, research findings are represented according to the countries in which the studies were conducted. The countries are subsumed under the following seven broad geographical regions: Africa, Asia, Europe, the Middle East, North America, South-Central America and Caribbean, and the Pacific. The names of countries are those used at the time the study was published. Data specific for Hawaii were listed under *Pacific*, rather than *North America*. Also, as a Spanish speaking country, Mexico was subsumed under *South-Central America & Caribbean*, rather than *North America*; and Japan and Taiwan were subsumed under *Asia* instead of *Pacific*.

In addition to being grouped according to how each study measured delinquent and criminal behavior, studies in both tables are categorized as having found: (a) a significant positive; (b) a significant negative; or (c) non-significant relationship. Statistical significance was assessed by the researcher(s) who conducted each study.

A final methodological point is that there are some duplications in terms of the studies cited more than once in the same table. The reason for this is that a few studies examined the IQ-offending relationship using more than one measure of criminality.

4. Analysis of the Findings

4.1. Overall Intelligence

Table 16.1 presents the main findings from all of the studies we located that have investigated the relationship between intelligence and offending (including antisocial personality disorders). Giving attention first to the findings based on official definitions of offending, the majority of studies indicate that a significant negative correlation exists. Specifically, 68 studies of delinquency were found, and of these 60 (88.2%) found a significant negative correlation, and the remaining 8 studies found no significant relationship. For adult offending, 15 of the 19 (78.9%) studies found a significant negative correlation.

One finds a different picture when attention is turned to recidivism. Nineteen studies were located, only 7 (36.8%) of which reported a significant negative correlation, and 4 studies actually found a significant positive correlation. It appears that intelligence has little to do with whether former prisoners persist at offending beyond their first incarceration. This is surprising except when one notes that imprisoned offenders represent a very select proportion of the general population, and of offenders for that matter. Consequently, they are likely to be of lower intelligence than even the typical offender. Amongst this subgroup, intelligence appears to have little to do with one's chances of being arrested, reconvicted or re-imprisoned.

Regarding self reported offending, most of the evidence on offenses in general support the hypothesis that a significant inverse correlation exists between intelligence and delinquency/criminality. Specifically, 14 of the 17 studies (82.4%) support the hypothesis. Regarding self reports pertaining exclusively to illegal drug use, on the other hand, a very uncertain pattern has been found, with only half of the 6 relevant studies reporting an inverse relationship.

Turning to clinically diagnosed antisocial behavior, the evidence is entirely consistent with the hypothesized inverse intelligence-offending relationship. Nineteen studies were found — 5 pertained to adult antisocial personality disorder and 14 concerned childhood conduct disorders — and all revealed a significant inverse correlation.

Table 16.1: Relationship between intelligence and criminal/delinquent/antisocial behavior.

Nature of the Relationship	Criminal and Delinquent Behavior			Self-Reported Offenses		Antisocial Clinical Conditions	
	Delinquency	General & Unspecified Offenses	Recidivism	Victimful & Overall Offending	Illegal Drug Use	Childhood Conduct Disorders	Antisocial Personality
Negative	ASIA *India:* Shanmugam 1980 **EUROPE** *Denmark:* Moffitt et al. 1981; *England:* Eilenberg 1961; Gibson & West 1970; Rutter et al. 1975; Moffitt et al. 1981; Sturge 1982; Farrington 1987: 32; Nagin & Land 1993: 352; Farrington 1997a: 100; *Finland:* Jarvelin et al. 1995; Rantakallio et al. 1995; *Spain:* Diaz et al. 1984: 313; *Sweden:* Hartelius 1965; Jonsson 1967: 200; Jonsson 1975: 184; Stattin et al. 1997: 204 **NORTH AMERICA** *Canada:* Rogers & Austin 1934; *United States:* Fernald 1920: 527; Caldwell 1929; Elliott 1929: 574; Mendenhall 1932: Ruggles 1932; Glueck & Glueck 1934a, b: 292; Glueck 1935; Lane & Witty 1935; Charles 1936; Moore 1937: Owen 1937; Jameson 1938; Mann & Mann 1939; Lichtenstein & Brown 1938; Kvaraceus 1944; Franklin 1945; Altus & Clark 1949; Glueck & Glueck 1950; Shulman 1951; Diller 1952; Prentice & Kelly 1973; Murphy & d'Angelo 1963: 345; Naar 1965; Ahmad 1966; Conger & Miller 1966: 191; Robins & Hill 1966: 331; Wolfgang et al. 1972: 58; Miller et al. 1974; Yeudall et al. 1982: 261; Menard & Morse 1984; Lawrence 1985; Kandel et al. 1988; Denno 1990; Ward & Tittle 1994; Coughlin & Vuchinich 1996: 497; Rowe 1997: 150; Kasen et al. 1998: 58 **PACIFIC** *Australia:* Tennison-Wood 1932; McRae 1934; *Hawaii:* Werner 1987: 25; Werner & Smith 1992: 104; *New Zealand:* White et al. 1989; Lynam et al. 1993 **(62)**	**EUROPE** *Denmark:* Høgh & Wolf 1981; *England:* Goring 1913; West & Farrington 1973: 123; Farrington 1993a: 15; *Sweden:* Farrington 1997b: 97; *Finland:* Tiihonen et al. 1993; *Germany:* Goppinger 1983; *Sweden:* Stattin & Klackenburg-Larsson 1993 **NORTH AMERICA** *United States:* Zeleny 1933; Brown & Hartman 1938; McGarvey et al. 1981; Hains & Ryan 1983: 1540; Eisenman 1990 1991; Davis et al. 1991; Schweinhart et al. 1993 **(15)**	**EUROPE** *England:* Frank 1931; Shulman 1951; *Germany:* Schwind 1975; Richter et al. 1996: 339; *Sweden:* Stattin et al. 1997: 204 **NORTH AMERICA** *United States:* Tibbitts 1931; Shakow & Millard 1935 **(7)**	**EUROPE** *England:* Gibson & West 1970; West & Farrington 1973: 131; Farrington 1997b: 97 **NORTH AMERICA** *United States:* Hirschi 1969; Jessor 1976; Hirschi & Gottfredson 1977; Moffitt et al. 1981; Wiatrowski et al. 1981; Menard & Morse 1984; Lynam et al. 1993; Blackson & Tarter 1994: 818; Williams & McGee 1994 **PACIFIC** *New Zealand:* Moffitt & Silva 1988a; White et al. 1989; Hermnstein & Murry 1994: 246; Moffitt et al. 1995 **(16)**	**EUROPE** *Ireland:* Timms et al. 1973 **NORTH AMERICA** *United States:* Bear & Richards 1981; Codina et al. 1998 (females) **(3)**	**EUROPE** *England:* Rutter et al. 1970: 227; West & Farrington 1973; Rutter et al. 1975; McMichael 1979; Richman et al. 1982; Maughan et al. 1985; Farrington et al. 1990; Farrington 1993b: 15 *Netherlands:* Wiegman et al. 1992; *Scotland:* May 1975 **NORTH AMERICA** *Canada:* Andre et al. 1994; *United States:* Schonfeld et al. 1988; Robins et al. 1991: 278; Wentzel 1993: 360 **(14)**	**EUROPE** *Finland:* Virkkunen & Luukkonen 1977: 222 **NORTH AMERICA** *United States:* Wiens et al. 1959; Robins 1966: 156; O'Kane et al. 1996; Arnett et al. 1997: 1424 **(5)**

Table 16.1: Continued.

Nature of the Relationship	Criminal and Delinquent Behavior			Self-Reported Offenses		Antisocial Clinical Conditions	
	Delinquency	General & Unspecified Offenses	Recidivism	Victimful & Overall Offending	Illegal Drug Use	Childhood Conduct Disorders	Antisocial Personality
No Signif. Diff.	**EUROPE** *England:* Rutter *et al.* 1970: 227 **NORTH AMERICA** *Canada:* Valliant & Bergeron 1997; *United States:* Baker *et al.* 1929; Maller 1937; Lichtenstein & Brown 1938 **PACIFIC** *New Zealand:* Black & Hornblow 1973: 88 **(6)**	**EUROPE** *Germany:* Richter *et al.* 1996 **NORTH AMERICA** *United States:* Murchison 1926; Doll 1930; Townes *et al.* 1981 **(4)**	**EUROPE** *England:* Lane & Witty 1935; B Marcus 1955 **NORTH AMERICA** *United States:* Tolman 1938; Kirkpatrick 1937; Merrill 1947; Hartman 1940; Roberts *et al.* 1974: 835; Bendas 2000: 94 **PACIFIC** *New Zealand:* Black & Hornblow 1973 **(9)**	**NORTH AMERICA** *Canada:* Bogaert & Rushton 1989: 1075; *United States:* Broidy 1995: 550; Rowe 1997: 150 **(3)**	**NORTH AMERICA** *United States:* Wexler 1975; Codina *et al.* 1998 (males) **(2)**		
Positive			**EUROPE** *England:* Calhoun 1928; Hill 1936 **NORTH AMERICA** *United States:* Murchison 1926; Hartmann 1940 **(4)**		**NORTH AMERICA** *United States:* Kellam *et al.* 1980 **(1)**		

4.2. Intellectual Imbalance

Besides investigating the relationship between overall intelligence and offending behavior, numerous researchers have decomposed intelligence tests into their two main factorial components and compare each component to offending behavior. The result of this research has led to the identification of what is termed *intellectual imbalance*. Basically, if an individual scores significantly higher on one component of an IQ test than on another, he or she is said to be intellectually imbalanced. One can be intellectually imbalanced in either of two directions: the VIQ score can significantly exceed the PIQ, or vice versa.

Studies undertaken to determine if offenders are more likely to be imbalanced than persons in general are cited in Table 16.2. As one can see, the research indicates that offenders are more often imbalanced, and that the direction of the imbalance is in a specific direction: PIQ scores tend to exceed VIQ scores. This suggests that it is primarily the linguistic portion of standardized IQ tests that are unusually low among delinquents, criminals and persons with antisocial personalities. In other words, on average, offenders are nearer to the mean (or even above it) with regard to PIQ than regarding VIQ (Walsh 1991a; Lynam *et al.* 1993; Angenent & De Man 1996: 52). Most of the studies that have documented this imbalance have found the deficit to be in the range of 3 to 5 IQ points (e.g. Stattin & Klockenberg-Larsson 1993; Law & Faison 1996: 699).

By way of qualifications, two points are worth making. First, Table 16.2 shows that about 20% of the studies have not found a significant VIQ-PIQ difference. This is to be expected given the relatively small sample size in several of these studies. Second, one study actually found a significant difference in the opposite direction. Interestingly, this study is the only one pertaining to self-reported drug use. Given that Table 16.1 also revealed an excess of incongruous findings in regarding to self-reported drug use, we suspect that people whose offenses are confined to drug use are cognitively distinct from offenders who primarily engage in what we have termed victimful offending (Ellis & Walsh 2000: 9).

5. Artifactual Explanations for the IQ-Criminality Relationship

Some have interpreted the inverse relationship between IQ and crime as simply reflecting the tendency for low IQ offenders to be arrested and convicted at higher rates than high IQ offenders (Doleschal & Klapmuts 1973; also see Rutter & Giller 1984: 165; Quay 1987b: 107). There are three problems with this the "dumb-ones-get-caught" argument.

First, it is not just in official data that an inverse correlation has been found, but as shown in Table 16.1, most self-report data show the same pattern, except in the case of illegal drug use (West & Farrington 1973: 131). Second, the dumb-ones-get-caught argument does not explain why below average IQ scores are also found among children with conduct disorders, a diagnosis that nearly always *precedes* the onset of official delinquency (Rutter & Giller 1984: 165). Third, as was noted above, intelligence does

Table 16.2: The relationship between intellectual imbalance and criminal/antisocial behavior.

Nature of the Relationship	Criminal and Delinquent Behavior					Clinical Conditions	
				Self-Reported Offenses			
	Delinquency	Unspecified Offences	Recidivism	Victimful & Overall Offending	Illegal Drug Use	Childhood Conduct Disorders	Antisocial Personality Syndrome
PIQ significantly higher than VIQ	EUROPE *Denmark*: Buikhuisen et al. 1988; *England*: Payne 1960; Rutter et al. 1975; Rutter et al. 1979; Sturge 1982 NORTH AMERICA *United States*: Werder et al. 1943; Wechsler 1944; Franklin 1945; Sloan & Cutts 1945: 96; Altus & Clark 1949; Glueck & Glueck 1950; Diller 1952; Doppelt & Seashore 1959; Prentice & Kelly 1963; Camp 1966; Matarazzo 1972: 433; Ganzer & Sarason 1973; Andrew 1977; Ollendick & Hensen 1979; Haynes & Bensch 1983; Tarter et al. 1984; Tarter et al. 1985; Grace & Sweeney 1986; Walsh et al. 1987; Jensen & Faulstich 1988; Walsh 1990; Walsh 1991b; Culbertson et al. 1989; Cornell & Wilson 1992 PACIFIC *New Zealand*: Lynam et al. 1993: 193 **(30)**	EUROPE *Denmark*: Moffitt et al. 1981; *England*: Farrington 1993: 15; *Germany*: Richter et al. 1996: 338; *Sweden*: Stattin & Klockenberg-Larsson 1993 NORTH AMERICA *United States*: Barnett et al. 1989 **(5)**	EUROPE *Denmark*: Moffitt et al. 1981: 155 *England*: Farrington 1995: 941 NORTH AMERICA *United States*: Solway et al. 1975; Haynes & Bensch 1981; Blecker 1983 **(5)**	NORTH AMERICA *United States*: Moffitt et al. 1981; Maguin et al. 1993 PACIFIC *New Zealand*: Moffitt & Silva 1988b **(3)**		NORTH AMERICA *United States*: Wechsler 1958: 160; Camp 1977; Richman et al. 1982; Kender et al. 1985 PACIFIC *New Zealand*: McGee et al. 1986a; b; Henry et al. 1992a; b **(6)**	NORTH AMERICA *United States*: Wechsler 1944: 155; Fisher 1961 **(2)**
VIQ and PIQ not sign. different	NORTH AMERICA *United States*: Henning & Levy 1967; Foster 1959; Davis et al. 1991; Law & Faison 1996 **(4)**	EUROPE *England*: Farrington 1993: 15 PACIFIC *New Zealand*: Walters 1953 **(2)**		NORTH AMERICA *United States*: Meltzer et al. 1984; Tarter et al. 1985 **(2)**		EUROPE *England*: Farrington 1993: 15 **(1)**	EUROPE *Finland*: Virkkunen & Luukkonen 1977: 222 NORTH AMERICA *United States*: Strother 1944: 398; Naar 1965 **(3)**
VIQ significantly higher than PIQ					NORTH AMERICA *United States*: Fleming et al. 1982 **(1)**		

not appear to predict recidivism among incarcerated offenders. If the dumb-ones-get-caught argument had merit for explaining major variations in the offending-IQ relationship, one would expect the relationship to be true for recidivism as well. Nevertheless, it should be conceded that the IQ range in prison populations is substantially restricted to a below normal range, which places mathematical constraints on uncovering any small residual relationship that may exist (Jensen 1998: 295) For additional coverage of the "differential detection" hypothesis see Moffitt & Silva (1998) and Herrnstein & Murray (1994, ch. 11).

Others have suggested that the relationship between intelligence and offending may just reflect the link that both of these variables have with parental social status. In other words, because persons with high IQs tend to be reared by parents of high social status, and because offenders tend to be of low social strata (see below), the link between intelligence and criminality may be spurious. This possibility has been directly investigated, and found to be wanting based on three lines of evidence. First, studies have found that even after controlling for parental SES, a significant relationship continued to exist between low IQ scores and criminality (Metfessel & Lovell 1942: 143; West & Farrington 1977: 123; Hirschi & Hindelang 1977; McGarvey *et al.* 1981). Second, a review of the SES-offending relationship concluded that this relationship was much better established in the case of individual (achieved) social status than in the case of parental (background) social status (Ellis & MacDonald 2001). The opposite would be expected if it is parental status per se that is responsible for the IQ-criminality relationship. Third, even among siblings, one finds a negative correlation between IQ and criminality/delinquency. In other words, the IQ scores of criminal and delinquent siblings is 8 to 10 points lower than the scores for same-sex siblings with no offending history (Jensen 1998: 297). All three of these lines of evidence argue against the view that the IQ-criminality link can be dismissed as an artifact of parental social status.

6. Theoretical Explanations of the IQ-Offending Relationship

In light of the evidence that the relationship between intelligence and offending is real, it is somewhat surprising to find how few theoretical attempts have been made to explain the relationship, either singularly or in conjunction with the PIQ > VIQ relationship. None of the leading theories in criminology today offer an explicit explanation, particularly for the PIQ > VIQ relationship.

For those of us who teach criminology, it is disappointing to note how many texts in the field leave students with the impression that the jury is still out with respect to there being an IQ-offending relationship (see Wright & Miller 1998). Our suspicion is that there are two main reasons for lingering ambiguity in the face of strong evidence: First, criminologists may not be aware of the vast number of studies that have been conducted, and the consistency of their findings. Hopefully, the present review will help to inform them in this regard.

Second, most criminologists (and other social scientists) still seem to be uncomfortable with the IQ-offending relationship, since most of them still strongly favor the nurture side of the nature-nurture controversy when it comes to explaining criminal behavior (Sanderson & Ellis 1992; Ellis & Walsh 1999). Hopefully, social scientists will continue to work through these thorny issues with objectivity and come to a much more balanced view on the influence of genetic and social environmental factors.

In the meantime, we would like to offer some thoughts on how one might begin to theoretically explain the existence of an IQ-offending relationship, and why offenders are especially likely to do poorly on the linguistic portions of IQ tests. We believe that three theories can be of help in this regard, even though they are all still "minor players" in the field of criminology.

One of the three theories is moral maturation theory, as championed by Lawrence Kohlberg (1984a; b; c). Building on a foundation laid by Piaget (1968), Kohlberg contended that humans develop through stages in their moral reasoning, and that this maturation is at least modestly tied to intellectual maturation (Israely 1985: 34; Lickona 1976: 230). Several studies have provided support for the conclusion that intelligence is a good predictor of the speed with which children develop through Kohlberg's stages of moral reasoning (e.g. Sharma & Kaur 1992; Chovan & Freeman 1993; Narvaez 1993). If so, moral maturation may be at least partly a reflection of intellectual maturation, and a rapid rate of moral maturation appears to inhibit at least victimful forms of offending (Jensen 1998: 298). Other traits often linked to offending such as impulsiveness and orientation to the present also appear to be mediated in part by low intelligence (Jensen 1998: 298).

A second criminological theory that we think provides insight into the link between intelligence and offending behavior is hemispheric functioning theory (Ellis & Walsh 2000: 423). According to this theory, the two hemispheres of the neocortex make important contributions to people's abilities to obey linguistic instructions. In particular, studies have shown that the left hemisphere not only exercises a greater control over language (reviewed by Mountcastle 1962), but that it expresses a more social and "friendly" emotional tone than does the right hemisphere (Davidson & Fox 1989; Dawson *et al.* 1992; Schaffer *et al.* 1983; Silverman & Weingartner 1986). Theoretically, any deficiencies in development of the left hemisphere, or any difficulties it may have over-riding the functioning of the right hemisphere, could increase the probability of antisocial behavior.

As to why the two hemispheres seem to function differently from one individual to another, Ellis (1990) has proposed that testosterone, acting both perinatally and post-pubertally, is involved. In particular, to the degree that the right hemisphere is allowed to function independently, it will be functioning without the benefit of linguistic reasoning. It is worth noting that several studies have suggested that such a functional arrangement is more characteristic of male brains than of female brains (e.g. Wada *et al.* 1975; McGlone 1978; Yucel *et al.* 2001).

The third theory actually consists of varying proposals regarding the role of evolutionary forces in setting the stage for criminal behavior (for reviews see Ellis & Walsh 1997; Ellis 1998; Ellis & Walsh 2000: 432–466; Fishbein 2001: 19–25). These proposals converge on the following idea: that some individuals approach reproduction by emphasizing mating effort (i.e. having sex often, especially with numerous partners), while others emphasize a parenting approach (i.e. investing heavily in caring for a few offspring) (e.g. Low 1990; Rowe 1996: 270; Burgess & Drais 1999: 375). Other theorists refer to essentially the same idea by distinguishing an r-approach to reproduction and a K-approach. According to these theoretical proposals, individuals who focus on mating effort (an r-strategy) should exhibit a variety of behavior patterns that facilitate having numerous children in a brief amount of time. These interconnected behavior patterns often entail obtaining resources rapidly by whatever means, using the resources to attract sex partners, and employing other relatively inconsiderate methods of securing and controlling sex partners. In short, they are highly antisocial.

Because the methods used to succeed at a mating effort approach to reproduction tend to be crude and short term, those who use these methods have not been enfavored for developing high intelligence or long term planning abilities. For individuals who emphasize parenting effort, on the other hand, intelligence and long term planning become premium commodities (Rowe 1996). To reproductively succeed using parental effort usually requires establishing a lasting relationship with a sex partner, and then cooperating to rear and nurture a few children to do likewise in the next generation.

If evolutionary thinking along these lines is correct, genes should be making a substantial contribution to criminal behavior as well as to traits such as intelligence and the ability to plan ahead. We have recently shown that the evidence now strongly supports the "genetic influence hypothesis" regarding criminal/antisocial behavior (Ellis & Walsh 2000: 436–445). Others in the present volume will build the case for genetic influences on intelligence. This leads us to predict that several of the same genes that increase intelligence will serve to inhibit involvement in criminal/antisocial behavior.

7. Conclusion

In conclusion, intelligence can be considered an established correlate of delinquent and criminal behavior, especially when self-reported drug use and recidivism measures of offending are set aside. Given the difficulties researchers face when measuring the variables involved, along with the small sample size for several of the studies, the weight of the evidence is impressively consistent. The relationship does not appear to be attributable to the possibility that low-IQ offenders are more likely to be apprehended, or entirely due to the fact that parental social status is associated with low IQ and high offending rates.

The IQ-offending relationship is especially strong in the case of linguistic intelligence, and all but absent when it comes to spatial reasoning. Given the robustness of these conclusions, we submit that it is time for social scientists to focus their research efforts on theoretically explaining why these relationships exist.

Herein, we propose that at least three existing theories of criminal behavior may provide insight into these relationships. First, moral development theory asserts that there is an intimate link between how rapidly individuals develop intellectually and their development in moral reasoning. This implies that how the brain confronts intellectual tasks of several types may overlap with its ability to make moral decisions.

Second, hemispheric functioning theory focuses on evidence that the two hemi-spheres of the neocortex reason differently, with the left hemisphere being more adept than the right hemisphere at linguistic reasoning. Together with moral development theory, hemispheric functioning theory suggests that a failure in the normal development of brain centers that manage linguistic thought is important for understanding criminal/antisocial behavior.

Regarding the third theory, several researchers in the past decade have couched scientific explanations of criminal/antisocial behavior in an evolutionary framework. Central to most of these proposals has been the idea that individuals can successfully reproduce either by emphasizing mating effort or by focusing on parenting effort, and that criminality could be a manifestation of mating effort. Theoretically, individuals who focus their reproductive time and energy on short-term mating efforts need to obtain resources quickly, and they should avail themselves of as many mating opportunities as possible by whatever means. If so, criminality should be most characteristic of males. In many males, an early emphasis on mating effort may gradually give way to parenting effort later in life, although some of the least intelligent males may not make the transition until old age.

In conclusion, we believe that progress was made during the 20th Century in clarifying the nature of the relationships between intellectual functioning and criminal/antisocial behavior. The main task ahead of us in the 21st Century is to understand exactly how and why these relationships are as the evidence suggests.

Acknowledgment

We thank Travis Hirschi and Myrna Nelson for their helpful comments.

References

Ahmad, A. Z. (1966). A study of the relationship between test intelligence and delinquency. *Psychologia, 9*, 24–26.

Altus, W. D., & Clark, H. J. (1949). Subtest variation on the Wechsler-Bellevue for two institutionalized behavior problem groups. *Journal of Consulting Psychology, 13*, 444–447.

Andre, G., Kendall, K., Pease, K., & Boulton, A. (1994). Health and offence histories of young offenders in Saskatoon, Canada. *Mental Health, 4*, 163–180.

Andrew, J. (1977). Delinquency: Intellectual imbalance? *Criminal Justice and Behavior, 4*, 99–104.

Angenent, H., & De Man, A. (1996). *Background factors of juvenile delinquency*. New York: Peter Lang.

Arnett, P. A., Smith, S. S., & Newman, J. P. (1997). Approach and avoidance motivation in psychopathic criminal offenders during passive avoidance. *Journal of Personality and Social Psychology, 72*, 1413–1428.

Baker, H. J., Decker, F. J., & Hill, A. S. (1929). A study of juvenile theft. *Journal of Educational Research, 20*, 81–87.

Barnett, R., Zimmer, L., & McCormack, J. (1989). P > V sign and personality profiles. *Journal of Correctional and Social Psychiatry and Offender Treatment and Therapy, 35*, 18–20.

Bear, G. G., & Richards, H. C. (1981). Moral reasoning and conduct problems in the classroom. *Journal of Educational Psychology, 73*, 664–670.

Bendas, T. V. (2000). Gender investigations of leadership. *Voprosy Psikhologii*, (1), 87–95.

Black, W. A. M., & Hornblow, A. R. (1973). Intelligence and criminality. *Australian and New Zealand Journal of Criminology, 6*, 83–92.

Blackson, T. C., & Tarter, R. E. (1994). Individual, family, and peer affiliation factors predisposing to early-age onset of alcohol and drug use. *Clinical and Experimental Research, 18*, 813–821.

Blecker, E. G. (1983). Cognitive defense style and WISC-R P sign in juvenile recidivists. *Journal of Clinical Psychology, 39*, 1030–1032.

Bogaert, A. F., & Rushton, J. P. (1989). Sexuality, delinquency and r/K reproductive strategies: Data from a Canadian sample. *Personality and Individual Differences, 10*, 1071–1077.

Broidy, L. M. (1995). Direct supervision and delinquency: Assessing the adequacy of structural proxies. *Journal of Criminal Justice, 23*, 541–545.

Brown, A. W., & Hartman, A. (1938). A survey of the intelligence of Illinois prisoners. *Journal of Criminal Law Criminology, 28*, 707–719.

Buikhuisen, W., Bontekoe, E. H. M., Plas-Korenhoff, C., & Meijs, B. W. G. P. (1988). Biological, psychological, and social factors related to juvenile delinquency. In: W. Buikhuisen, & S. A. Mednick (Eds), *Explaining criminal behavior. Interdisciplinary approaches*. Leiden: E. J. Brill.

Burgess, R. L., & Drais, A. A. (1999). Beyond the "Cinderella effect": Life history theory and child maltreatment. *Human Nature, 10*, 373–398.

Caldwell, M. G. (1929). The intelligence of delinquent boys committed to Wisconsin industrial school. *Journal of Criminal Law, 20*, 421–428.

Calhoun, C. H. (1928). A follow-up study of 100 normal and 100 sub-normal delinquent boys. *Journal of Juvenile Justice, 12*, 236–240.

Camp, B. W. (1966). Performance in acting-out and delinquent children with and without EEG abnormality. *Journal of Consulting Psychology, 30*, 350–353.

Camp, B. W. (1977). Verbal mediation in young aggressive boys. *Journal of Abnormal Psychology, 86*, 145–153.

Charles, C. M. (1936). A comparison of the intelligence quotients of incarcerated delinquent white and American Negro boys and of groups of St. Louis public school boys. *Journal of Applied Psychology, 20*, 499–510.

Chovan, W., & Freeman, N. L. (1993). Moral reasoning and personality components in gifted and average students. *Perceptual and Motor Skills, 77*, 1297–1298.

Codina, G. E., Yin, Z., Katims, D. S., & Zapata, J. T. (1998). Marijuana use and academic achievement among Mexican American school-age students: Underlying psychosocial and behavioral characteristics. *Journal of Child & Adolescent Substance Abuse, 7*, 79–96.

Conger, J. J., & Miller, W. C. (1966). *Personality, social class and delinquency*. New York: Wiley.

Cornell, D., & Wilson, L. (1992). The PIQ > VIQ discrepancy in violent and nonviolent delinquents. *Journal of Clinical Psychology, 48*, 256–261.

Coughlin, C., & Vuchinich, S. (1996). Family experience in pre-adolescence and the development of male delinquency. *Marriage and the Family, 58*, 491–501.

Culbertson, F. M., Ferel, C. H., & Gabby, S. (1989). Pattern analysis of Wechler intelligence scale for children: Revised profiles of delinquent boys. *Journal of Clinical Psychology, 45*, 651–660.

Davidson, R. J., & Fox, N. A. (1989). Frontal brain asymmetry predicts infant's response to maternal separation. *Journal of Abnormal Psychology, 98*, 127–131.

Davis, A. D., Sanger, D. D., & Morris-Friehe, M. (1991). Language skills of delinquent and nondelinquent adolescent males. *Journal of Communication Disorders, 24*, 251–266.

Dawson, G., Klinger, L. G., Panagiotides, H., Hill, D., & Spieker, S. (1992). Frontal lobe activity and affective behavior of infants of mothers with depressive symptoms. *Child Development, 63*, 725–737.

Denno, D. W. (1990). *Biology and violence from birth to adulthood.* Cambridge, England: Cambridge University Press.

Diaz, A., Belena, A., & Baguena, M. J. (1984). The role of gender in juvenile delinquency: Personality and intelligence. *Personality and Individual Differences, 16* (2), 309–314.

Diller, L. (1952). A comparison of the test performances of delinquent and non-delinquent girls. *Journal of Genetic Psychology, 81*, 167–183.

Doleschal, E., & Klapmuts, N. (1973). Towards a new criminology. Crime and Delinquency *Literature, 5*, 607–626.

Doll, E. A. (1930). The relation of intelligence to criminality. *Journal of Social Psychology, 1*, 547–531.

Doppelt, J. E., & Seashor, H. G. (1959). Psychological testing in correctional institutions. *Journal of Counseling Psychology, 6*, 81–92.

Dugdale, R. (1877/1895). *The jukes: A study in crime, pauperism, disease, and heredity.* New York: Putnam.

Eilenberg, H. D. (1961). Remand home boys 1930–1955. *British Journal of Criminology, 2*, 111–131.

Eisenman, R. (1990). Six problems of a prison psychologist: A personal account. *Psychological Reports, 67*, 755–761.

Eisenman, R. (1991). I worked in prison: An insider's story. *Psychology: A Journal of Human Behavior, 28* (3–4), 22–26.

Elliott, M. (1929). *Correctional education and the delinquent girl.* Harrisburg, PA: Commonwealth of Pennsylvania.

Ellis, L. (1990). Left- and mixed-handedness and criminality: Explanations for a probable relationship. In: S. Coren (Ed.), *Left-handedness: Behavioral implications and anomalies* (pp. 485–507). North-Holland: Elsevier Science Publishers.

Ellis, L. (1998). NeoDarwinian theories of violent criminality and antisocial behavior: Photographic evidence from nonhuman animals and a review of the literature. *Aggression and Violent Behavior, 3*, 61–110.

Ellis, L., & McDonald, J. N. (2001). Crime, delinquency, and social status: A reconsideration. *Journal of Offender Rehabilitation, 32*, 23–52.

Ellis, L., & Walsh, A. (1997). Gene-Based Evolutionary Theories in Criminology. *Criminology, 35* (2), 229–276.

Ellis, L., & Walsh, A. (1999). Criminologists' opinions about causes and theories of crime and delinquency. *The Criminologist, 24* (July–August), 1–6.

Ellis, L., & Walsh, A. (2000). Criminology: A global perspective. Boston: Allyn and Bacon.

Farrington, D. P. (1973). Self-reports of deviant behavior: Productive and stable? *Journal of Criminal Law and Criminology, 64*, 99–110.

Farrington, D. P. (1987). Early precursors of frequent offending. In: J. Q. Wilson, & G. C. Loury (Eds), *From child to citizens* (Vol. III): *Families, schools, and delinquency prevention* (pp. 27–50). London: Springer-Verlag.

Farrington, D. P. (1993a). Understanding and preventing bullying. In: M. Tonry & N. Morris (Eds), *Crime and justice* (Vol. 17). Chicago: University of Chicago Press.

Farrington, D. P. (1993b). Childhood origins of teenage antisocial behaviour and adult social dysfunction. *Journal of the Royal Society of Medicine, 86*, 13–17.

Farrington, D. P. (1993). *Interactions between individual and contextual factors in the development of offending.* New York: Springer-Verlag.

Farrington, D. P. (1995a). The twelfth Jack Tizard memorial lecture. The development of offending and antisocial behavior from children: Key findings from the Cambridge study in delinquent development. *Journal of Child Psychology and Psychiatry, 360*, 929–964.

Farrington, D. P. (1995b). The development of offending and antisocial behaviour from childhood: Key findings from the Cambridge study in delinquent development. *Journal of Child Psychology and Psychiatry, 36*, 929–964.

Farrington, D. P. (1997a). The relationship between low resting heart rate and violence. In: A. Raine & P. A. Brennan, & D. P. Farrington & S. A. Mednick (Eds), *Biosocial bases of violence* (pp. 89–105). New York: Plenum.

Farrington, D. P. (1997b). Predictors, causes, and correlates of male youth violence. In: M. Tonry, & M. H. Moore (Eds), *Youth violence (crime and justice)* (Vol. 24). Chicago: University of Chicago.

Farrington, D. P., Loeber, R., & Van Kammen, W. (1990). Long-term criminal outcomes of hyperactivity-impulsivity-attention deficit and conduct problems in childhood. In: L. N. Robins, & M. Rutter (Eds), *Straight and devious pathways from childhood to adulthood* (pp. 62–81). New York: Cambridge University Press.

Ferentz, E. J. (1954). Mental deficiency related to crime. *Journal of Criminal Law, Criminology, and Police Science, 45*, 299–307.

Fernald, M. R. (1920). *A Study of Women Delinquents in New York State*. New York: Century.

Fishbein, D. (2001). *Biobehavioral perspectives in criminology*. Belmont, California: Wadsworth/Thomson Learning.

Fisher, G. M. (1961). Discrepancy in verbal and performance IQ in adolescent sociopaths. *Journal of Clinical Psychology, 17*, 60.

Fleming, J. P., Kellam, S. G., & Brown, C. H. (1982). Early predictors of age at first use of alcohol, marijuana, and cigarettes. *Drug and Alcohol Dependence, 9*, 285–303.

Foster, A. L. (1959). A note concerning the intelligence of delinquents. *Journal of Clinical Psychology, 15*, 78–79.

Frank, R. (1931). The hormonal causes of premenstrual tension. *Archives of Neurology and Psychiatry, 26*, 1053–1057.

Franklin, J. C. (1945). Discriminative value and patterns of the Wechsler-Bellvue Scales in the examination of delinquent Negro boys. *Educational and Psychological Measurement, 5*, 71–85.

Ganzer, F. J., & Sarason, I. G. (1973). Variables associated with recidivism among juvenile delinquents. *Journal of Consulting and Clinical Psychology, 40*, 1–5.

Gibson, H. B., & West, D. J. (1970). Social and intellectual handicaps as precursors of early delinquency. *British Journal of Criminology, 10*, 21–32.

Glueck, E. T. (1935). Mental retardation and juvenile delinquency. *Mental Hygiene, 19*, 549–572.

Glueck, S., & Glueck, E. (1934a). *Five hundred delinquent women*. New York: Alfred A. Knopf.

Glueck, S., & Glueck, E. T. (1934b). *One thousand juvenile delinquents*. Cambridge, MA: Harvard University Press.

Glueck, S., & Glueck, E. (1950). *Unraveling juvenile delinquency*. Cambridge, MA: Harvard University Press.

Goddard, H. H. (1912/1931). *The Kallikak family: A study in the heredity of feeble-mindedness*. New York: Macmillan.

Goddard, H. H. (1914). *Feeblemindedness: It's causes and consequences*. New York: Macmillan.

Goppinger, H. (1983). *Der tater in seinen sozialen Bezugen*. Berlin: Springer.

Goring, C. (1913). *The English convict: A statistical study.* London: His Majesty's Stationary Office (republished in 1972 by Patterson Smith, Monclair, NJ).

Gottfredson, M. R., & Hirschi, T. (1990). *A general theory of crime.* Stanford, CA: Stanford University Press.

Grace, W. C., & Sweeney, M. E. (1986). Comparisons of the P > V sign on the WISC-R and WAIS-R in delinquent males. *Journal of Clinical Psychology, 42,* 173–176.

Hains, A. A., & Ryan, E. B. (1983). The development of social cognitive processes among juvenile delinquents and nondelinquent peers. *Child Development, 54,* 1536–1544.

Hartelius, H. (1965). A study of male juvenile delinquents. *Acta Psychiatrica Scandinavica, 182 Suppl. Ad 40,* 1–154.

Hartman, A. A. (1940). Recidivism and intelligence. *Journal of Criminal Law and Criminology, 31,* 417–426.

Haynes, J. P., & Bensch, M. (1981). The P > V sign on the WISC-R and recidivism in delinquents. *Journal of Consulting and Clinical Psychology, 49,* 480–481.

Haynes, J. P., & Bensch, M. (1983). Female delinquent recidivism and the P > V sign of the WISC-R. *Journal of Clinical Psychology, 39,* 141–144.

Healy, W., & Bronner, A. (1939). *Treatment and what happened afterward.* Boston: Judge Baker Guidance Center.

Henning, J. J., & Levy, R. H. (1967). Verbal-performance IQ differences on white and Negro delinquents on the WISC and WAIS. *Journal of Clinical Psychology, 23,* 164–168.

Henry, P., Michel, P., Brochet, B., Dartigues, J. F., Tison, S., Salamon, R., & GRIM (1992). A nationwide survey of migraine in France: Prevalence and clinical features in adults. *Cephalalgia, 12,* 229–237.

Henry, B., Moffitt, T. E., & Silva, P. A. (1992). Disentangling delinquency and learning disability: Neuropsychological function and social support. *The International Journal of Clinical Neuropsychology, 13,* 1–6.

Herrnstein, R. (1980). In defense of intelligence tests. *Commentary, 69,* 40–51.

Herrnstein, R., & Murray, C. (1994). *The bell curve: Intelligence and class structure in American life.* New York: Free Press.

Hill, G. E. (1936). The intelligence of young male offenders. *Journal of Juvenile Research, 20* 20–27.

Hirschi, T. (1969). *The causes of delinquency.* Berkeley: University of California Press.

Hirschi, T., & Hindelang, M. (1977). Intelligence and delinquency: A revisionist view. *American Sociological Review, 42,* 571–587.

Hirschi, T., & Stark, R. (1969). Hellfire and delinquency. *Social Problems, 17,* 202–213.

Høgh, E., & Wolf, P. (1981). *Violent crime in birth cohort: Copenhagen 1953–1977: Project metropolitan.* Paper presented at the Symposium on Life History Research in Aggression and Antisocial Behavior, Monterey, California.

Israely, Y. (1985). The moral development of mentally retarded children: Review of the literature. *Journal of Moral Education, 14,* 33–42.

Jameson, A. (1938). Psychological factors contributing to the delinquency of girls. *Journal of Juvenile Research, 22,* 25–32.

Jarvelin, M-R., Laara, E., Rantakallio, P., Moilanen, I., & Isohanni, M. (1995). Juvenile delinquency, education and mental disability. *Exceptional Children, 61,* 230–241.

Jensen, A. R. (1998). *The g factor.* Westport: CT: Praeger.

Jensen, A. R., & Faulstich, E. (1988). Differences between prisoners and the general population in psychometric "g". *Personality and Individual Differences, 9,* 925–928.

Jessor, R. (1976). Predicting time of onset of marijuana use: A developmental study of high school youth. *Journal of Consulting and Clinical Psychology, 44,* 125–134.

Jonsson, G. (1967). Delinquent boys: Their parents and grandparents. *Acta Psychiatrica Scandinavia*, (Suppl. 43), 1–264.

Jonsson, G. (1975). Negative social inheritance. In: L. Levi (Ed.), *Society, stress and disease* (Vol. 2, pp. 181–186). London: Oxford University Press.

Kandel, E., Mednick, S. A., Kirkegaard-Sørensen, L., Hutchings, B., Knop, J., Rosenberg, R., & Schulsinger, F. (1988). IQ as a protective factor for subjects at high risk for antisocial behavior. *Journal of Consulting and Clinical Psychology*, *56*, 224–226.

Kasen, S., Cohen, P., & Brook, J. (1998). Adolescent school experiences and dropout, adolescent pregnancy, and young adult deviant behavior. *Journal of Adolescent Research*, *13*, 49–72.

Kellam, S. G., Ensminger, M. E., & Simon, M. B. (1980). Mental health in first grade and teenage drug, alcohol and cigarette use. *Drug and Alcohol Dependence*, *5*, 273–304.

Kender, J. P., Greenwood, S., & Conard, E. (1985). WAIS-R performance patterns of 565 incarcerated adults characterized as underachieving readers and adequate readers. *Journal of Learning Disabilities*, *18*, 379–383.

Kirkpatrick, M. E. (1937). Some significant factors in juvenile recidivism. *American Journal of Orthopsychiatry*, *7*, 349–358.

Kohlberg, L. A., & Candee, D. (1984). The relationship of moral judgement to moral action. In: L. Kohlberg (Ed.), *The psychology of moral development*. San Francisco: Harper and Row.

Kohlberg, L. (1984a). *Essays on moral development*. San Francisco, California: Harper and Row.

Kohlberg, L. (1984b). *Essays on moral development* (Vol. 2): *The psychology of moral development*. New York: Harper & Row.

Kohlberg, L. (1984c). *The psychology of moral development: The nature and validity of moral stages*. New York: Harper & Row.

Kvaraceus, W. C. (1944). Delinquent behavior and church attendance. *Sociology and Social Research*, *28*, 284–289.

Kvaraceus, W. C. (1944b). Juvenile delinquency and social class. *Journal of Educational Sociology*, *18*, 51–54.

Kvaraceus, W. C. (1944c). Delinquency: A by-product of the school. *School and Society*, *59*, 350–351.

Lane, H. A., & Witty, P. A. (1935). The mental ability of delinquent boys. *Journal of Juvenile Research*, *19*, 1–12.

Law, J. G. J., & Faison, L. (1996). WISC-III and *kait results in adolescent delinquent males. *Journal of Clinical Psychology*, *52*, 699–703.

Lawrence, R. (1985). School performance, containment theory, and delinquent behavior. *Youth and Society*, *17*, 69–95.

Lichtenstein, M., & Brown, A. W. (1938). Intelligence and achievement of children in a delinquency area. *Journal of Juvenile Research*, *22*, 1–25.

Lickona, T. (1976). Research on Piaget's theory of moral development. In: T. Lickona (Ed.), *Moral development and behavior* (pp. 219–265). New York: Holt, Rinehart and Winston.

Low, B. S. (1990). Sex, power, and resources: Ecological and social correlates of sex differences. *International Journal of Contemporary Sociology*, *27*, 49–73.

Lynam, D., Moffitt, T. E., & Stouthamer-Loeber, M. (1993). Explaining the relation between IQ and delinquency: Class, race, test motivation, school failure, or self control? *Journal of Abnormal Psychology*, *102*, 187–196.

Maguin, E., Loeber, R., & LeMahieu, P. G. (1993). Does the relationship between poor reading and delinquency hold for males of different ages and ethnic groups? *Journal of Emotional and Behavioral Disorders*, *1*, 88–100.

Mann, C. W., & Mann, H. P. (1939). An analysis of the results obtained by retesting juvenile delinquents. *Journal of Psychology, 8*, 133–141.

Marcus, B. (1955). Intelligence, criminality and the expectation of recidivism. *British Journal of Delinquency, 6*, 147–151.

Matarazzo, J. D. (1972). *Wechsler's measurement and appraisal of adult intelligence* (5th ed.). New York: Oxford University Press.

Maughan, B., Gray, G., Rutter, M., & Maugh, T. H. (1985). Reading retardation and antisocial behavior: A follow-up into employment. *Journal of Child Psychology and Psychiatry, 26*, 741–758.

May, D. (1975). Juvenile offenders and the organization of juvenile justice: An examination of juvenile delinquency in Aberdeen. *Ph.D. dissertation*, University of Aberdeen, Scotland.

McGarvey, B., Gabrielli, W. F., Bentler, P. M., & Mednick, S. A. (1981). Rearing social class, education, and criminality: A multiple indicator model. *Journal of Abnormal Psychology, 90*, 354–364.

McGee, R., Anderson, J., Williams, S., & Silva, P. A. (1986a). Cognitive correlates of depression in children and adolescents. *Journal of Consulting and Clinical Psychology, 56*, 903–908.

McGee, R., Williams, S., Share, D. L., Anderson, J., & Silva, P. A. (1986b). The relationship between specific reading retardation, general reading backwardness and behavioural problems in a large sample of Dunedin boys: A longitudinal study from five to eleven years. *Journal of Child Psychology and Psychiatry, 27*, 597–610.

McGlone, J. (1978). Sex differences in functional brain asymmetry. *Cortex, 14*, 122–128.

McMichael, P. (1979). The hen or the egg? Which comes first — antisocial emotional disorders or reading disability? *British Journal of Educational Psychology, 49*, 226–238.

McRae, C. (1934). *Psychology and education.* Sydney: Whitcombe & Tombs.

Meltzer, L. J., Levine, M. D., Karniski, W., Palfrey, J. S., & Clarke, S. (1984). An analysis of the learning style of adolescent delinquents. *Journal of Learning Disabilities, 17*, 600–608.

Menard, S., & Morse, B. J. (1984). A structuralist critique of the IQ-delinquency hypothesis: Theory and evidence. *American Journal of Sociology, 89*, 1347–1378.

Mendenhall, G. S. (1932). A study of behavior problems. *Psychological Clinic, 21*, 77–113.

Merrill, M. A. (1947). *Problems of child delinquency.* Boston: Houghton-Mifflin.

Metfessel, M., & Lovell, C. (1942). Recent literature on individual correlates of crime. *Psychological Bulletin, 39*, 133–164.

Miller, C. K., Zumoff, L., & Stephens, B. A. (1974). A comparison of reasoning skills and moral judgments in delinquent, retarded, and normal adolescent girls. *Journal of Psychology, 86*, 261–268.

Moffitt, T. E., Gabrielli, W. F., Mednick, S. A., & Schulsinger, F. (1981). Socioeconomic status, IQ and delinquency. *Journal of Abnormal Psychology, 90*, 152–157.

Moffitt, T. E., & Silva, P. A. (1988a). Self-reported delinquency, neuropsychological deficit, and history of attention deficit disorder. *Journal of Abnormal Child Psychology, 16*, 553–569.

Moffitt, T., & Silva, P. (1988b). IQ and delinquency: A test of the differential detection hypothesis. *Journal of Abnormal Psychology, 97*, 330–333.

Moffitt, T. E., Caspi, A., Silva, P. A., & Stouthamer-Loeber, M. (1995). Individual differences in personality and intelligence are linked to crime: Cross-context evidence from nations, neighborhoods, genders, races, and age-cohorts. In: J. Hagean (Ed.), *Current perspectives on aging and the life cycle* (Vol. 4). *Delinquency and disrepute in the life-course: Contextual and dynamic analyses* (pp. 1–34). Greenwich, CT: JAI Press.

Moore, J. E. (1937). A comparative study of the intelligence of delinquent and dependent boys. *Journal of Educational Psychology, 28*, 355–366.

Mountcastle, V. (1962). *Interhemispheric relations and cerebral dominance.* Baltimore: Johns Hopkins University Press.

Murchison, C. (1926). *Criminal intelligence.* Worcester, MA: Clark University.

Murphy, K. M., & d'Angelo, R. Y. (1963). The intelligence factor in the criminality of women. *American Catholic Sociological Review, 24,* 340–347.

Naar, R. (1965). A note on the intelligence of delinquents in Richmond, Virginia. *British Journal of Criminology, 5,* 82–85.

Nagin, D. S., & Land, K. C. (1993). Age, criminal careers, and population heterogeneity: Specification and estimation of a nonparametric, mixed Poisson model. *Criminology, 31,* 327–362.

Narvaez, D. (1993). High achieving students and moral judgment. *Journal for the Education of the Gifted, 16,* 268–279.

O'Kane, A., Fawcett, D., & Blackburn, R. (1996). Psychopathy and moral reasoning: Comparison of two classifications. *Personality and Individual Differences, 20,* 505–514.

Ollendick, R., & Hensen, M. (1979). Social skills training for juvenile delinquents. *Behavior Research and Therapy, 17,* 547–554.

Owen, M. B. (1937). The intelligence of the institutionalized juvenile delinquent. *Journal of Juvenile Research, 21,* 199–206.

Payne, R. W. (1960). Cognitive abnormalities. In: H. J. Eysenck (Ed.), *Handbook of Abnormal Psychology* (pp. 193–261). London: Pitman.

Piaget, J. (1968). *On the development of memory and identity.* Worcester, MA: Clark University Press.

Prentice, N. M., & Kelly, F. J. (1973). Intelligence and delinquency: A reconsideration. *Journal of Social Psychology, 60,* 327–337.

Quay, H. C. (1987a). Intelligence. In: H. C. Quay (Ed.), *Handbook of juvenile delinquency* (pp. 106–117). New York: Wiley.

Quay, H. C. (1987b). Patterns of delinquent behavior. In: H. C. Quay (Ed.), *Handbook of juvenile delinquency* (pp. 118–138). New York: Wiley.

Raine, A. (1993). *The psychopathology of crime: Criminal behavior as a clinical disorder.* San Diego, CA: Academic Press.

Rantakallio, P., Myhrman, A., & Koiranen, M. (1995). Juvenile offenders, with special reference to sex differences. *Social Psychiatry and Psychiatric Epidemiology, 30,* 113–120.

Richman, N., Stevenson, J., & Graham, P. J. (1982). *Pre-school to school: A behavioural study.* London: Academic Press.

Richter, P., Scheurer, H., Barnett, W., & Krober, H. L. (1996). Forecasting recidivism in delinquency by intelligence and related constructs. *Medicine, Science, and the Law, 36,* 337–342.

Roberts, A. H., Erickson, R. V., Riddle, M., & Bacon, J. G. (1974). Demographic variables, base rates, and personality characteristics associated with recidivism in male delinquents. *Journal of Consulting and Clinical Psychology, 42,* 833–841.

Robins, L. N. (1966). *Deviant children grown up: A sociological and psychiatric study of sociopathic personality.* Baltimore, MD: Williams and Wilkes.

Robins, L. N., & Hill, S. Y. (1966). Assessing the contributions of family structure, class and peer groups to juvenile delinquency. *Journal of Criminal Law, Criminology and Police Science, 57,* 325–333.

Robins, L. N., Tipp, J., & Przybeck, T. (1991). Antisocial personality. In: L. N. Robins, & D. Regier (Eds), *Psychiatric disorders in America* (pp. 258–290). New York: Free Press.

Rogers, K. H., & Austin, O. L. (1934). Intelligence quotients of juvenile delinquents. *Journal of Juvenile Research, 18*, 103–106.

Rowe, D. C. (1996). An adaptive strategy theory of crime and delinquency. In: J. D. Hawkins (Ed.), *Delinquency and crime: Current theories* (pp. 268–314). Cambridge: Cambridge University Press.

Rowe, D. C. (1997). A place at the policy table? Behavior genetics and estimates of family environmental effects on IQ. *Intelligence, 24*, 133–158.

Ruggles, E. W. (1932). An analytical study of various factors relating to juvenile crime. *Journal of Juvenile Research, 16*, 125–132.

Rutter, M., Tizard, J., & Whitmore, K. (1970). *Education, health, and behavior: Psychological and medical study of child development.* New York: Wiley.

Rutter, M., Cox, A., Tupling, C., Berger, M., & Yule, W. (1975). Attainment and adjustment in two geographical areas: I: The prevalence of psychiatric disorder. *British Journal of Psychiatry, 126*, 493–509.

Rutter, M., Maugham, G., Mortimer, P., & Ouston, J. (1979). *15,000 hours: Secondary schools and their effects on children.* Cambridge, MA: Harvard University Press.

Rutter, M., & Giller, H. (1984). *Juvenile delinquency: Trends and perspectives.* New York: Guilford Press.

Sanderson, S. K., & Ellis, L. (1992). Theoretical and political perspectives of American sociologists in the 1900s. *American Sociologist, 23*, 26–42.

Schaffer, C. E., Davidson, R. J., & Saron, C. (1983). Frontal and parietal electroencephalogram asymmetries in depressed and non-depressed subjects. *Biological Psychiatry, 18*, 753–762.

Schonfeld, I. S., Shaffer, D., O'Connor, P., & Portnoy, S. (1988). Conduct disorder and cognitive functioning: Testing three causal hypotheses. *Child Development, 59*, 993–1007.

Schweinhart, L. J., Baarnes, H. V., & Weikart, D. P. (1993). *Significant benefits: The High/Scope Perry preschool study through age 27.* Ypsilanti, MI: High/Scope.

Schwind, H. D. (1975). Verbrechen und schwachsinn. In: R. Sievers, & H. J. Schneider (Eds), Handworterbuch der Kriminologie (Vol. 3). Berlin: Gruyter.

Shakow, D., & Millard, M. S. (1935). A psychometric study of 150 adult delinquents. *Journal of Social Psychology, 6*, 437–457.

Shanmugam, T. E. (1980). *Psychological factors underlying juvenile delinquency.* Madras, India: University of Madras.

Sharma, V., & Kaur, K. (1992). Moral judgment as a function of intelligence, birth-order, and age of children. *Psychologia, 35*, 121–124.

Sharpe, K. J. (1992). Biology intersects religion and morality. *Biology and Philosophy, 7*, 77–88.

Shulman, H. M. (1951). Intelligence and delinquency. *Journal of Criminal Law and Criminology*, (March–April), 763–781.

Silverman, E. K., & Weingartner, H. (1986). Hemispheric lateralization of functions related to emotion. *Brain and Cognition, 5*, 322–353.

Simons, R. (1978). The meaning of the IQ-delinquincy relationship. *American Sociological Review, 43*, 268–270.

Sloan, W., & Cutts, R. A. (1945). Test patterns for defective delinquents on the Wechsler-Bellevue test. *American Journal of Mental Deficiency, 50*, 95–97.

Solway, J. S., Hays, J. R., Roberts, T. K., & Cody, J. A. (1975). Comparison of WISC Profiles of alleged juvenile delinquents living at home verses those incarcerated. *Psychological Reports, 37*, 403–407.

Stattin, H., & Klackenberg-Larsson, I. (1993). Early language and intelligence development and their relationship to future criminal behavior. *Journal of Abnormal Psychology, 102*, 239–378.

Stattin, H., Romelsjo, A., & Stenbacka, M. (1997). Personal resources as modifiers of the risk for future criminality. *British Journal of Criminology, 37*, 198–223.

Strother, C. R. (1944). The performance of psychopaths on the Wechsler-Bellvue test. *Proceedings of the Iowa Academy of Science, 51*, 397–400.

Sturge, C. (1982). Reading retardation and antisocial behaviour. *Journal of Child Psychology and Psychiatry, 23*, 21–31.

Tarter, R. E., Hegedus, A., Winsten, N., & Alterman, A. (1984). Neuropsychological, personality and familial characteristics of physically abused juvenile delinquents. *Journal of the American Academy of Child Psychiatry, 23*, 668–374.

Tarter, R., Hegedus, A., Winsten, N., & Alterman, A. (1985). Intellectual profiles and violent behavior in juvenile delinquents. *Journal of Psychology, 119*, 125–128.

Tennison-Wood, M. (1932). The causes of delinquency. *Australian Medical Journal, 32*, 12–19.

Tibbitts, C. (1931). Success or failure on parole can be predicted: a study of the records of 3,000 youths paroled from the Illinois State Reformatory. *Criminal Law, Criminology, and Police Science, 22*, 11–50.

Tiihonen, J., Eronen, M., & Hakola, P. (1993). Criminality associated with mental disorders and intellectual deficiency. *Archives of General Psychiatry, 50*, 917–918.

Timms, M. W., Carney, P. A., & Stevenson, R. D. (1973). A factor analytic study of drug abuse in adolescents. *Irish Journal of Psychology, 2*, 86–95.

Tolman, R. S. (1938). Differences between two groups of adult criminals. *Genetic and Psychological Monograph 20*, 353–458.

Townes, B. D., James, J., & Martin, D. C. (1981). Criminal involvement of female offenders: Psychological characteristics among four groups. *Criminology, 18*, 471–480.

Valliant, P. M., & Bergeron, T. (1997). Personality and criminal profile of adolescent sexual offenders, general offenders in comparison to nonoffenders. *Psychological Reports, 81*, 483–489.

Virkkunen, M., & Luukkonen, P. (1977). WAIS performances in antisocial personality disorder. *Acta Psychiatrica Scandinavica, 55*, 220–224.

Vold, G. B., & Bernard, T. J. (1986). *Theoretical criminology* (3rd ed.). New York: Oxford University Press.

Wada, J., Clarke, R., & Hamm, A. (1975). Cerebral hemispheric asymmetry in humans. *Archives of Neurology, 32*, 239–246.

Walsh, A. (1990). Standing trial versus copping a plea: Is there a penalty? *Journal of Contemporary Criminal Justice, 6*, 226–236.

Walsh, A. (1990). Illegitimacy, abuse and neglect, and cognitive development. *Journal of Genetic Psychology, 151*, 279–285.

Walsh, A. (1991). Race and discretionary sentencing: An analysis of obvious and nonobvious cases. *International Journal of Offender Therapy and Comparative Criminology, 35*, 7–19.

Walsh, A. (1991a). *Intellectual imbalance, love deprivation and violent delinquency: A biosocial perspective*. Springfield, IL: Charles C. Thomas.

Walsh, A. (1991b). Genetic and environmental explanations of juvenile violence in advantaged and disadvantaged environments. *Aggressive Behavior, 18*, 187–199.

Walsh, A., Petee, T., & Beyer, J. (1987). Intellectual imbalance and delinquency: Comparing high verbal and high performance IQ delinquents. *Criminal Justice and Behavior, 14*, 370–379.

Walters, R. H. (1953). Wechsler-Bellevue test results of prison inmates. *Australian Journal of Psychology, 5*, 46–54.

Ward, D. A., & Tittle, C. R. (1994). IQ and delinquency: A test of two competing explanations. *Journal of Quantitative Criminology, 10*, 189–212.

Wechsler, D. (1944). *The assessment of adult intelligence* (3rd ed.). Baltimore, MD: Williams and Wilkins.

Wechsler, D. (1958). *The measurement and appraisal of adult intelligence.* Baltimore, MD: Williams and Wilkins.

Weiss, H. R., & Sampliner, R. (1944). A study of adolescent felony violators. *Journal of Criminal Law, 34*, 377–391.

Wentzel, K. R. (1993). Does being good make the grade? Social behavior and academic competence in middle school. *Journal of Educational Psychology, 85*, 357–364.

Werder, A., Levi, J., & Risch, F. (1943). Performance of problem children on the Wechsler-Bellevue intelligence scale and the revised Stanford-Binet. *Psychiatric Quarterly, 17*, 695–701.

Werner, E. E. (1987). Vulnerability and resiliency in children at risk for delinquency: A longitudinal study from birth to adulthood. In: J. D. Burchard, & S. N. Burchard (Eds), *Primary prevention of psychopathology: Prevention of delinquent behavior.* Newbury Park, CA: Sage.

Werner, E. E., & Smith, R. S. (1992). *Overcoming the odds.* Ithica, NY: Cornell University Press.

West, D. J., & Farrington, D. P. (1973). *Who becomes delinquent? Second report of the Cambridge study in delinquent development.* London: Heinemann Educational Books.

West, D. J., & Farrington, D. P. (1977). *The delinquent way of life.* New York: Crane Russak.

Wexler, M. (1975). Personality characteristics of marijuana users and nonusers in a suburban high school. *Cornell Journal of Social Relations, 10*, 267–282.

White, J. L., Moffitt, T. E., & Silva, P. A. (1989). A prospective replication of the protective effects of IQ in subjects at high risk for juvenile delinquency. *Journal of Consulting and Clinical Psychology, 57*, 719–724.

Wiatrowski, M. D., Griswold, D. B., & Roberts, M. K. (1981). Social control theory and delinquency. *American Sociological Review, 46*, 525–541.

Wiegman, O., Kuttschreuter, M., & Baarda, B. (1992). A longitudinal study of the effects of television viewing on aggressive and prosocial behaviors. *British Journal of Social Psychology, 31*, 147–164.

Wiens, A. N., Matarazzo, J. D., & Gaver, K. D. (1959). Performance and verbal IQ in a group of sociopaths. *Journal of Clinical Psychology, 15* 191–193.

Williams, S., & McGee, R. (1994). Reading attainment and juvenile delinquency. *Journal of Child Psychology and Psychiatry, 35*, 441–459.

Wilson, J. Q., & Herrnstein, R. J. (1985). *Crime and human nature.* New York: Simon and Schuster.

Wolfgang, P., Figlio, R., & Sellin, T. (1972). *Delinquency in a birth cohort.* Chicago: University of Chicago Press.

Wright, R. A., & Miller, J. M. (1998). Taboo until today? The coverage of biological arguments in criminology textbooks 1961 to 1970 and 1987 to 1996. *Journal of Criminal Justice, 26*, 1–19.

Yeudall, L. T., Fromm-Auch, D., & Davies, P. D. (1982). Neuropsychological impairment of persistent delinquency. *Journal of Nervous and Mental Disease, 170*, 259–265.

Yucel, M., Sturart, G. W., Maruff, P., Verlakoulis, D., Crowe, S. F., Savage, G., & Pantelis, C. (2001). Hemispheric and gender-related differences in the gross morphology of the anterior cingulate/paracingulate cortex in normal volunteers: An MRI morphometric study. *Cerebral Cortex, 11*, 17–25.

Zeleny, L. D. (1933). Feeble-mindedness and criminal conduct. *American Journal of Sociology,* *38,* 564–576.

Part V

Reservations About *g*

Part V — Introduction

The purpose of Part V is to critically discuss reservations about *g* research, in order to obtain a balanced view of the pros and cons in the best tradition of science. Unfortunately, as mentioned in the general introduction, many critics chose to sit on the fence, if for a wide variety of reasons. This is rather damaging to the primary aim of allowing the reader to make a side-by-side evaluation of the relative strengths and weaknesses of the different approaches to intelligence in terms of validity and reliability.

However, Robert Sternberg agreed to write Chapter 17. Here he stresses that Arthur Jensen has amply validated the conjecture of Charles Spearman that there is a general factor of intelligence, but he also asks how general this general factor of intelligence is? Not much, according to Sternberg. In his view, the general factor is general and powerful only with respect to a relatively academic class of tasks. When broader tests of intelligence are used, the general factor dissipates. Moreover, other aspects of intelligence — including practical and creative ones — can predict various kinds of real-world performances and even academic performances as well as or better than do conventional tests of the general factor. This is an interesting and far-ranging statement, but Sternberg does not really make up for a proper and convincing comparison in Chapter 17. In order to better allow for an informed decision in this matter, the interested reader is advised to also consult Gottfredson (2001, 2002, in press, a, b) and, among others, Chapters 14, 15 and 19 in this volume, as well as Sternberg (2002); Sternberg *et al.* (2000); and Sternberg (in press).

Nathan Brody questions Jensen's genetic interpretation of racial differences in intelligence in Chapter 18, by critically reviewing studies of biological variables related to intelligence, studies of transracial adoptions, studies of racially mixed individuals, regression analyses, and statistical studies of between and within group heritability. In each of these cases Brody raises questions about the findings or presents other data. He concludes that there either are gaps in knowledge, inconsistent results, untested assumptions or flaws in reasoning, which makes him think that the evidence cited in favor of the genetic hypothesis is not persuasive.

Gerald Barrett, Alissa Kramen and Sarah Lueke take a number of new concepts of intelligence into the courtroom in Chapter 19. They observe that over the last 30 years there have been repeated attempts to improve upon our basic theories of intellectual abilities and the accompanying tests. These include such concepts as emotional intelligence (Goleman 1995), tacit knowledge (Wagner & Sternberg 1985), practical intelligence (Sternberg & Wagner 1986), competencies (McClelland 1973), and multiple intelligences (Gardner 1983).

The purpose of Chapter 19 is to critically examine these concepts for their practical and legal significance for employee selection systems in the public and private sectors. In a review of existing professional literature, they conclude that these "novel" concepts have neither practical nor legal significance. It is their belief that these theories and concepts have been poorly developed, poorly measured, and have yet to result in selection tests with any practical significance. There is no evidence that these variations of intelligence provide any incremental validity over cognitive ability tests in predicting job performance, nor is there evidence that adverse impact on minority applicants is reduced. Tests designed to measure these variations of intelligence fail to meet requirements of the professional standards (APA 1999), professional principles (SIOP 1987) and legal guidelines (EEOC 1978, 1979, 1980) for employee selection tests in the United States. They conclude that these so called novel concepts detract from legitimate theories of intelligence and from the development of constructs and operational tests, which will provide more effective employee selection tools and meet prevailing legal challenges.

Helmuth Nyborg presents in Chapter 20 a case study of collective fraud in 20th century academia and the public media in connection with a demonization of Arthur Jensen even since his famous "How much can we boost IQ and scholastic achievement" was published in *Harvard Educational Review* in 1969. He first lines up some historical examples of persecution, and then presents a simple model according to which Jensen's change of mind from largely neutral to a more biologically based thinking about restrictions on development collided head on with a strong Zeitgeist of unconditional equality and strongly prohibitive notions about inheritance. The account of the attacks on Jensen is divided into the immediate reactions around 1969–1971, and the later reactions, continuing until today. The late Steven Jay Gould and Richard Levontin figure prominently among the attackers. Section 5 then presents the defenders of Jensen. The question is raised in section 6, why so many were afraid to acknowledge even the slightest conservative effect of genes on human development and behavior, and why they preferred to regress to plausibility arguments rather than to reality. Section 7 provides an account of how destructive social reductionism, characterizing large parts of the 20th century, could infect many levels of academia and large parts of the public sphere with a collective fraud that, on the surface of it, looked very much like a superior moral stance in questions of equality and defence of the deprived. The chapter concludes with a simple prescription to cure the academic leftist disease of collective fraud in academia: break down the egalitarian fictions and begin again to act like scientists and demand the right to free inquiry. This is what Jensen has been doing all the time despite being viciously attacked.

Chris Brand, Denis Constales and Harison Kane expose in Chapter 21 deep concern over today's neglect of general intelligence *g*, and over the West's version of Lysenkoism where, by 2000, the denial of *g* has become virtually the official science policy. Some deplore *g* and its links to heredity, achievement and race, whereas others deploy both ancient and modern arguments that nothing can be 'measured' in psychology. These two contradictory positions of IQ's more scholarly detractors are especially considered in the chapter, as is the less-often-remarked problem for the London School that so few Christian-era philosophers and psychologists — prior to Herbert Spencer and Sir Francis Galton — made much room in their systems for *g*.

Despite considerable tacit acceptance of Plato's stress on the centrality of reason in human psychology, Plato's elitism and eugenicism are feared for their supposedly authoritarian implications. Thus Plato's acknowledgment that people have different general mental potential is set aside.

Chapter 21 further advances a hypothesis, supported empirically, which attributes neglect of *g* by intellectuals partly to their limited experience of real life — across the full IQ range. Data from 6,539 representative American subjects are searched to form groups having mean IQs 115 and 85 respectively, and it is found that the *g* factor accounts for almost twice as much mental ability variance among subjects in the lower-IQ group. After a decade of argument about H. E. Garrett's suggestion that intelligence 'differentiates' at higher levels of *g*, the present data arguably provide a decisive result — especially taking account of Jensen's criticisms of previous 'differentiation' findings, and using well separated IQ ranges. Heritable *g* is hugely important across the lower-IQ half of the population even though it is correctly felt to be of less relevance to the everyday choices made by higher-IQ people. Finally, it is suggested that, far from needing to be feared, Platonic realism actually enjoys distinguished support in modern philosophy and provides a basis for a new liberalism.

References

Gardner, H. (1983). *Frames of mind: The theory of multiple intelligences*. New York: Basic Books, Inc.

Goleman, D. (1995). *Emotional intelligence*. New York: Bantam Books.

Gottfredson, L. (2001). Book review. Practical intelligence in everyday life. *Intelligence, 29*, 363–365.

Gottfredson, L. S. (2002). *g*: Highly general and highly practical. In: R. J. Sternberg, & E. L. Grigorenko (Eds), *The general factor of intelligence: How general is it?* (pp. 331–380). Mahwah, NJ: Erlbaum.

Gottfredson, L. (in press, a). Dissecting practical intelligence theory: Its claims and evidence. *Intelligence, 30*.

Gottfredson, L. S. (in press, b). On Sternberg's "Reply to Gottfredson". *Intelligence*.

McClelland, D. C. (1973). Testing for competence rather than for "intelligence". *American Psychologist, 28*(1), 1–14.

Sternberg, R. J., Forsythe, G. B., Hedlund. J., Horvath, J. A., Wagner, R. K., Williams, W. M., Snook, S. A., & Grigorenko, E. L. (2000). *Practical intelligence in everyday life*. New York: Cambridge University Press.

Sternberg, R. J., & Wagner, R. K. (1986). *Practical intelligence: Nature and origins of competence in the everyday world*. New York: Cambridge University Press.

Sternberg, R. (2002). Reply to the book review on practical intelligence in everyday life. *Intelligence, 30*, 117–118.

Sternberg, R. (in press). *A reply to Gottfredson's and Brody's critique of the triarchic theory of successful intelligence and some of the work validating it*.

Wagner, R. K., & Sternberg, R. (1985). Practical intelligence in real-world pursuits: the role of tacit knowledge. *Journal of Personality and Social Psychology, 49*(2), 436–458.

Chapter 17

"My House is a Very Very Very Fine House" — But it is Not the Only House

Robert J. Sternberg

1. Introduction

There is a reason why *g* theorists of intelligence find *g* everywhere. *g* theorists find *g* everywhere because they never leave their house.

When children are young, they often feel that their house is somehow special. They know, of course, that there are other houses, and that these other houses serve as residences for other people. But these other houses are not special houses. They may be perfectly fine houses, but none of them is, in the words of the erstwhile soft-rock group, Crosby, Stills and Nash, "a very very very fine house". Certainly none of these other houses would constitute a home.

As the children grow up, and especially when and if they move, they discover that the special character of their house inhered not in the house itself, but in their feelings for that house. They learn that other houses are special to other people, and that, for them, their house is their home. In the words of Piaget (1972), the children lose much of their egocentrism, although they do not necessarily ever lose it all.

The thesis of this chapter is that *g* theorists, including my good friend and esteemed colleague Arthur Jensen, are like children who never quite grew up. They never have been willing to face that their house is, perhaps, a very very very fine house, but that it is not the only house. No matter what the evidence against their point of view — and it is substantial — they, like young children, will continue to explore their house and discover that no matter how many rooms there are, and no matter how many pieces of furniture, they all are similar in one way. Everything in the house belongs to that house. As for other houses, well, somehow they just do not count.

The Scientific Study of General Intelligence: Tribute to Arthur R. Jensen
Copyright © 2003 by Elsevier Science Ltd.
All rights of reproduction in any form reserved.
ISBN: 0–08–043793–1

2. The House of the *g* Theory of Intelligence

2.1. The Psychometric Approach

The evidence in favor of a general factor of intelligence is, in one sense, overwhelming. This evidence is so well documented by Jensen (1998) that there is no need to repeat it here. One would have to be blind or intransigent not to give this evidence its due. Not only is there evidence for the internal validity of the g factor, there also is evidence for its external validity as well. Again, Jensen's (1998) documentation, as well as that of others (see essays in Sternberg 1982, 1994, 2000), is scientifically impressive. The impact of Jensen's work on *g* to the field of psychology — in terms of both the support and the criticism it has generated — is a tribute both to Jensen and to his many ideas, including that of a general factor.

Of course, the idea of a general factor is not new, dating back at least to Spearman (1904, 1927). What makes Jensen's contribution particularly impressive, however, and perhaps unique, is Jensen's development of general-factor theory and the array of converging empirical operations Jensen has brought to bear upon demonstrating the internal and external validity of *g*. Jensen's 1998 book is exhaustive in documenting both his own work and that of others attempting to demonstrate the viability of *g*. Many other scientists, of course, also have attempted to document the viability of this theory (e.g. Carroll 1993; Herrnstein & Murray 1994; Schmidt & Hunter 1998; see essays in Sternberg & Grigorenko, in press).

2.2. Information-processing Approaches

Residents of the House of *g* are not limited to psychometric accounts. Information-processing accounts of the general factor are to be found as well (e.g. Brand 1996; Carroll 1976; Eysenck 1979, 1982; Jensen 1979). Indeed, I was once a rather uncomfortable resident of this House myself. In early work, I suggested that an important mission of intelligence research might be to identify the information-processing components underlying the general factor (Sternberg 1977; Sternberg & Gardner 1982, 1983). At this point, I believed that the major problem confronting intelligence research was the focus on individual differences — both conceptually and methodologically. The alternative I proposed — componential analysis — would analyze performance on test items of the kinds found on intelligence tests through information-processing components rather than psychometric factors. Each component would correspond to one of the constituents underlying *g*. The ultimate goal was to identify all such components underlying the general factor, as well as group and possibly even specific factors.

The father of this approach was not myself, of course, but rather Spearman (1923), who suggested that underlying the solution of analogies and related problems are three qualitative principles of cognition. In the 1970s and 1980s, a number of investigators suggested experimental and statistical methods for continuing Spearman's (1923) program of identifying the mental processes contributing to individual differences in the general factor (e.g. Embretson 1987; Hunt 1978, 1980; Pellegrino & Glaser 1980; Snow 1979, 1980; Sternberg 1977, 1980).

The data from my own research suggested that information-processing techniques essentially could be used to "rediscover" *g*. In this research, performance on cognitive tasks was decomposed into its underlying components. For example, reasoning on an analogy, classification or series problem — all of which have been found to be good measures of *g* (Cattell & Cattell 1963) — could be understood in terms of components such as encoding of stimuli, inference of relations between terms, mapping of higher order relations between relations, application of relations, comparison of proposed responses, justification of the preferred response and actual response. The time actually to respond was estimated as the regression residual of the other components, which were estimated as raw regression weights in equations predicting reaction time to varied types of test items. Although all of the components typically showed at least some correlations with scores on psychometric tests, distressingly, the residual response component (which was supposed to measure only preparation and response time) typically was by far the highest correlate of psychometric test performance (Sternberg 1983; Sternberg & Gardner 1983). In other words, the research suggested the discovery of a "general" information-processing component! Perhaps *g* truly was ubiquitous!

Underlying this research was a componential sub-theory seeking to specify the mental processes that underlie intelligent behavior by identifying and understanding three basic kinds of information-processing components, referred to as metacomponents, performance components, and knowledge-acquisition components.

Metacomponents are higher-order, executive processes used to plan what one is going to do, to monitor it while one is doing it, and evaluate it after it is done. These metacomponents include: (1) recognizing the existence of a problem; (2) deciding on the nature of the problem confronting one; (3) selecting a set of lower-order processes to solve the problem; (4) selecting a strategy into which to combine these components; (5) selecting mental representation on which the components and strategy can act; (6) allocating one's mental resources; (7) monitoring one's problem solving as it is happening; and (8) evaluating one's problem solving after it is done.

Performance components are lower-order processes that execute the instructions of the metacomponents. These components solve the problems according to the plans laid out by the metacomponents. Whereas the number of metacomponents used in the performance of various tasks is relatively limited, the number of performance components is probably quite large, and many are relatively specific to a narrow range of tasks (Sternberg 1985). Inductive reasoning tasks such as matrices, analogies, series completion and classifications involve a set of performance components that provide potential insight into the nature of the general factor of intelligence. That is, induction problems of these kinds show the highest loading on the general intelligence factor, or *g* (Jensen 1980; Snow & Lohman 1984; Sternberg & Gardner 1982). The main performance components of inductive reasoning are encoding, inference, mapping, application, comparison, justification and response.

Knowledge-acquisition components are used to learn how to do what the metacomponents and performance components eventually do. Three knowledge-acquisition components seem to be central in intellectual functioning: (1) selective encoding; (2) selective combination; and (3) selective comparison. Selective encoding involves sifting out relevant information from irrelevant information. Selective combination involves combining selective encoded information in such a way as to form an integrated, plausible whole. Selective comparison involves relating new information to old information already stored in memory.

The various components of intelligence work together. Metacomponents activate performance and knowledge-acquisition components. These latter kinds of components in turn provide feedback to the metacomponents. Although one can isolate various kinds of information-processing components from task performance using experimental means, in practice, the components function together in highly interactive, and not easily isolatable ways. Thus, diagnosis as well as instructional interventions need to consider all three types of components in interaction rather than any one kind of component in isolation. If one measures these components in relatively abstract, academic kinds of tasks, one will get the appearance of a general factor. Many investigators have been satisfied to stop there.

But understanding the nature of the components of intelligence is not, in itself, sufficient to understand the nature of intelligence because there is more to intelligence than a set of information-processing components. One could scarcely understand all of what it is that makes one person more intelligent than another by understanding the components of processing on, say, an intelligence test. The other aspects of the triarchic theory address some of the other aspects of intelligence that contribute to individual differences in observed performance, outside testing situations as well as within them.

3. The House of the Triarchic Theory of Human Intelligence

The basic idea of the triarchic theory of intelligence (Sternberg 1985, 1988, 1997, 1999a, 1999b) is that the components of intelligence, when applied to adaptation to, shaping of, and selection of real-world environments, create a profile of individual differences different from that of academic or analytical intelligence. This profile is one of practical intelligence. An additional profile of creative intelligence is created when individuals apply the components of information processing to relatively novel kinds of tasks and situations.

3.1. Practical Intelligence

3.1.1. In U.S. civilian settings   By the early 1980s, I was increasingly troubled by a phenomenon that every professor confronts multiple times in his career — students with higher intelligence-related test scores who perform poorly in undergraduate and graduate school and students with lower intelligence-related test scores who do not perform well at all. Coincidentally, the issue of a major news magazine in the week I am writing this chapter has a little column noting that Bill Bradley, who was a Rhodes Scholar and who graduated from Princeton University Magna Cum Laude, had a verbal SAT score of 485, whereas George W. Bush, who was a C student at Yale, had a verbal

SAT score of 566 (Time, February 7, 2000: 27). Perhaps more ironic than their college grades is the fact that neither score was particularly high, but this fact did not prevent Bradley from becoming a Senator, Bush from becoming a Governor, and both from becoming presidential candidates. Perhaps there is some practical facet of intelligence that is distinct from the more academic one measured by the SAT.

Richard Wagner and I proposed that there is a practical facet of intelligence that conventional tests of intelligence do not measure (Sternberg & Wagner 1986; Wagner & Sternberg 1985). Of course, we were not the first to make such a proposition (e.g. Neisser 1976). But we were committed to providing empirical demonstrations of the separation of academic and practical intelligence.

We believed that practical intelligence is based largely although not exclusively on *tacit knowledge*, or what a person needs to know to succeed in an environment that the person is not explicitly taught and that usually is not even verbalized. One of the inventories we developed was designed to measure tacit knowledge of business managers.

3.1.2. Relative domain generality of tacit knowledge   The *Tacit Knowledge Inventory for Managers (TKIM)* was administered to a sample of 64 business managers (Wagner 1987), as well as to business graduate students and Yale undergraduates. We found that scores on the test improved with experience — practical intelligence is not fixed. We further conducted two kinds of factor analysis on the tacit-knowledge scores of these business managers to examine the generality of the tacit-knowledge construct. A principal components analysis yielded a first principal component that accounted for 44% of the total variance, and 76% of total variance after the correlations among scores were disattenuated for unreliability. The residual matrix was not significant after extracting the first principal component. A first principal component accounting for about 40% of total variance is typical of analyses carried out on traditional cognitive-ability subtests. A confirmatory factor analysis was carried out to test alternative models of the factor structure of the tacit-knowledge inventory more formally. The results supported the generality of tacit knowledge. A model consisting of a single general factor provided the best fit to the data, and yielded small and non-significant differences between predicted and observed covariances.

The domain generality of tacit knowledge was given additional support when the identical tacit-knowledge framework was used to construct a new measure of tacit knowledge for the domain of academic psychology. A parallel study using samples of psychology professors, graduate students and undergraduates yielded a pattern of results nearly identical to that found in business samples. More importantly, a group of 60 undergraduates was given tacit-knowledge measures for both domains — business management and academic psychology — in counterbalanced order. After determining that order of administration did not affect the latent structure of the two tacit-knowledge measures, we calculated correlations between scores across measures. The magnitude of these cross-domain correlations was 0.58 for total score, 0.52 for managing oneself, 0.47 for managing tasks, and 0.52 for managing others (components of our tacit-knowledge construct), all significant at the 0.001 level. These results support the domain generality of individual differences in tacit knowledge.

3.1.3. The relationship of tacit knowledge to general intelligence

If individual differences in tacit knowledge appear to have some domain generality, have we accidentally reinvented the concept of "g", or general ability, which can be measured by an intelligence test? Results from several studies of tacit knowledge, in which participants have been given a traditional measure of cognitive ability in addition to a tacit knowledge-inventory, suggest that this is not the case.

Wagner & Sternberg (1985) gave the Verbal Reasoning subtest of the *Differential Aptitude Tests* (Form T) to a sample of undergraduates. The correlation between tacit knowledge and verbal reasoning was non-significant. In subsequent studies, a deviation-scoring system was used to quantify tacit knowledge, which made lower scores indicate better performance than higher scores. The correlation between tacit-knowledge scores and verbal-reasoning ability was again non-significant.

One important limitation of these results is that the subjects were Yale undergraduates and thus represented a restricted range of verbal ability. In addition, undergraduates have relatively little tacit knowledge compared to experienced managers. Rather different correlations between tacit knowledge and IQ might therefore be expected for other groups, such as business managers. We administered the *Tacit Knowledge Inventory for Managers* to a sample of managers who were participants in a leadership-development program at the Center for Creative Leadership (Wagner & Sternberg 1990). Participants in the program routinely completed a battery of tests including an intelligence test. For this sample, the correlation between tacit knowledge and IQ was once again not significant.

But even business managers represent a restricted range in IQ and perhaps in tacit knowledge as well. What would be the relation between tacit knowledge and IQ in a more general sample? In a study carried out at the Human Resources Laboratory at Brooks Air Force Base under the supervision of Malcolm Ree & Eddy (1988) examined relations between the *Tacit Knowledge Inventory for Managers and the Armed Services Vocational Aptitude Battery (ASVAB)* for a large sample of Air Force Recruits, 29% of whom were females, and 19% of whom were members of a minority group.

Eddy's (1988) study showed small correlations between tacit knowledge and *ASVAB* subtests. The median correlation was -0.07, with a range from 0.06 to -0.15. Of the 10 correlations, only two were significantly different from 0, despite the large sample size of 631 recruits. A factor analysis of all the test data, followed by oblique rotations, yielded the usual four *ASVAB* factors (vocational-technical information, clerical/speed, verbal ability and mathematics) and a distinct tacit-knowledge factor. The factor loading for the *Tacit Knowledge Inventory for Managers* score on the tacit-knowledge factor was 0.99, with a maximum loading for the score on the four ASVAB factors of only 0.06.

One final point about these results concerns the possibility that measures of tacit knowledge might identify potential managers from non-traditional and minority backgrounds whose practical knowledge suggests that they would be effective managers, even though their performance on traditional selection measures such as intelligence tests does not. Eddy (1988) did not report scores separately by race and sex, but did report correlations between scores and dummy variables indicating race and sex. Significant correlations in the 0.2 to 0.4 range between *ASVAB* subtest scores and both race and sex indicate that on the *ASVAB*, minority-group members scored more poorly than majority group members, and women scored more poorly than men. Non-significant correlations between tacit knowledge and both race (0.03) and sex (0.02), however, indicate comparable levels of performance on the tacit-knowledge measures between minority and majority-group members and between females and males.

3.1.4. The relationship of tacit knowledge to performance

In several early studies, we gave our tacit-knowledge measure to samples of business managers and examined correlations between tacit-knowledge scores and criterion-reference measures of performance in business. For example, in samples of business managers (Wagner 1987; Wagner & Sternberg 1985), we found correlations ranging from 0.2 to 0.4 between tacit-knowledge score and criteria such as salary, years of management experience, and whether or not the manager worked for a company at the top of the Fortune 500 list.

In the studies just described, the managers were sampled from a wide range of companies and only global criterion measures such as salary and years of management experience were available to be studied. When more precise criterion measures have been available, higher correlations between tacit knowledge and performance have been found. For example, in a study of bank-branch managers (Wagner & Sternberg 1985), the correlation between tacit knowledge and average percentage of merit-based salary increase was 0.48 ($p < 0.05$). The correlation between tacit knowledge and average performance rating for the category of generating new business for the bank was 0.56 ($p < 0.05$).

Further support for the predictive validity of tacit-knowledge measures is provided by the previously mentioned study of business managers participating in the Leadership Development Program at the Center for Creative Leadership (Wagner & Sternberg 1990). In this study we were able to examine correlations among a variety of measures, including the *Tacit Knowledge Inventory for Managers*. The appropriate statistic to determine what will be gained by adding a test to existing selection procedures, or conversely, what will be lost by deleting a test, is the squared semipartial correlation coefficient or change in R^2 from hierarchical regression analyses. We were able to provide an empirical demonstration of this type of validity assessment in the Center for Creative Leadership study.

Every manager who participates in the Leadership Development Program at the Center for Creative Leadership, Greensboro, North Carolina, completes a battery of tests. By adding the *Tacit Knowledge Inventory for Managers* to the battery, we were able to determine the unique predictive power of the inventory in the context of other measures commonly used in managerial selection. These measures included an intelligence test, a personality test, an interpersonal-orientation test, a test of field independence, two further tests of cognitive styles and a job-satisfaction questionnaire.

The criterion measure of managerial performance was behavioral-assessment-data ratings in two small-group managerial simulations. Beginning with zero-order correlations, the best predictors of the criterion score of managerial performance were tacit knowledge ($r = -0.61$, $p < 0.001$) and IQ ($r = 0.38$, $p < 0.001$). (The negative correlation for tacit knowledge is expected because of the deviation scoring system used, in which better performance corresponds to less deviation from the expert prototype and thus to lower scores.) The correlation between tacit knowledge and IQ was not significantly different from 0 ($r=-0.14$, $p>0.05$). We carried out a series of hierarchical regressions to examine the unique predictive value of tacit knowledge when used in conjunction with existing measures. For each hierarchical regression analysis, the unique prediction of the *Tacit Knowledge Inventory for Managers* was represented by the change in R^2 from a restricted model to a full model. In each case, the restricted model contained various measures, and the full model was created by adding the *Tacit Knowledge Inventory for Managers* as another predictor. If adding the tacit knowledge score resulted in a significant and substantial change in R^2, we could conclude that the predictive relation between tacit knowledge and the criterion measure was not subsumed by the set of predictors in the restricted model.

In every case, tacit knowledge accounted for substantial and significant increases in variance. In addition, when tacit knowledge, IQ and selected subtests from the personality inventories were combined as predictors, nearly all of the reliable variance in the criterion was accounted for. These results support the strategy of enhancing validity and utility by supplementing existing selection procedures with additional ones. They also suggest that the construct of tacit knowledge cannot readily be subsumed by the existing constructs of cognitive ability and personality represented by the other measures used in the study.

Williams & Sternberg (in press) also studied the interrelationship of tacit knowledge for management with demographic and experiential variables. (In this research tacit knowledge was defined as the sum of squared deviation of subjects' ratings from nominated-experts' score arrays on a tacit-knowledge measure). We found that tacit knowledge was related to the following measures of managerial success: compensation ($r=0.39$, $p<0.001$), age-controlled compensation ($r=0.38$, $p<0.001$), and level of position ($r=0.36$, $p<0.001$). Note that these correlations were computed after controlling for background and educational experience. Tacit knowledge was also weakly associated with enhanced job satisfaction ($r=0.23$, $p<0.05$). Demographic and education variables unrelated to tacit knowledge included age, years of management experience, years in current position, degrees received, mother's and father's occupations, mother's and father's educational level attained, and mother's and father's degrees received. (The lack of a correlation of tacit knowledge with years of management experience suggests that it is not simply experience that matters, but perhaps what a manager learns from experience.) A manager's years with current company was negatively related to tacit knowledge ($r=-0.29$, $p<0.01$), perhaps suggesting the possibility that deadwood managers often stayed around a long time. The number of companies that a manager had worked for was positively correlated with tacit-knowledge scores ($r=0.35$, $p<0.001$). Years of higher education was highly related to tacit knowledge ($r=0.37$, $p<0.001$), as was self-reported school performance ($r=0.26$, $p<0.01$). Similarly, college quality was related to tacit knowledge ($r=0.34$, $p<0.01$). These results in conjunction with the independence of tacit knowledge and IQ suggest that tacit knowledge overlaps with the portion of these measures that are not predicted by IQ.

This pattern of interrelationships between tacit knowledge scores and demographic and background variables prompted us to examine the prediction of our success measures using hierarchical regression. These analyses showed whether tacit knowledge contained independent information related to success — information distinct from that provided by background and experience. The pattern of results was similar across analyses. In the regression analysis predicting maximum compensation, the first variable entered in the regression equation was years of education, accounting for 19% of the variance ($p < 0.001$). The second variable entered was years of management experience, accounting for an additional 13% of the variance ($p < 0.001$). The third and final variable entered was tacit knowledge, accounting for an additional 4% of the variance ($p = 0.04$), and raising the total explained variance to 36%. In the regression predicting maximum compensation controlling for age, years of education was entered into the equation first, accounting for 27% of the variance ($p < 0.001$). And second, tacit knowledge was entered, explaining an additional 5% of the variance ($p = 0.03$). This final regression demonstrates the value of tacit knowledge to managers who are relatively successful for their age.

Several general conclusions can be drawn from the above regression analyses. First, it is difficult to predict success measures such as salary and maximum compensation, presumably due to the myriad effects upon such variables that were outside of the focus of this study. Nonetheless, approximately 40% of the variance in the success measures used in this study was explicable. For all four measures of success, the educational variable was the most important, followed in the case of salary and maximum compensation by an experiential variable (years of management experience). After education and experience were included in the equations, tacit knowledge still explained a significant proportion of the variance in success. Thus, tacit knowledge contains information relevant to the prediction of success that is independent of that represented by the background and demographic variables.

Although our greatest focus has been on the tacit knowledge of business managers, there is evidence that the construct also explains performance in other domains. In two studies of the tacit knowledge of academic psychology professors, correlations in the 0.4 to 0.5 range were found between tacit knowledge and criterion measures such as number of citations reported in the *Social Science Citation Index* and the rated scholarly quality of an individual's departmental faculty (Wagner 1987; Wagner & Sternberg 1985). More recently, we investigated the role of tacit knowledge in the domain of sales (Wagner *et al.* 1992). We found correlations in the 0.3 to 0.4 range between measures of tacit knowledge about sales and criterion measures such as sales volume and sales awards received for a sample of life insurance salespersons. In this work, we also have been able to express the tacit knowledge of salesperson in terms of sets of rules of thumb that serve as rough guides to action in sales situations. Expressing tacit knowledge in terms of rules of thumb may permit explicit training of at least some aspect of tacit knowledge. A preliminary training study in which undergraduates were trained in tacit knowledge relevant to the profession of sales found greater pre-test–post-test differences in tacit knowledge for groups whose training identified relevant rules of thumb than for those whose training did not make any such identifications (Sternberg *et al.* 1993).

3.1.5. Practical intelligence in U.S. military settings Once we had developed a tacit-knowledge inventory for each organizational level of management, we sought to obtain preliminary evidence of the validity of these measures in a new sample.

Specifically, we sought to establish that tacit knowledge, as measured by a *Tacit Knowledge Inventory for Military Leadership* (*TKML*), relates to an external criterion, that of leadership effectiveness. In addition, we sought evidence that tacit knowledge for military leadership predicts leadership effectiveness above and beyond measures that have been traditionally used to understand leadership like general cognitive ability and experience. We also aimed to show that tacit knowledge for military leadership is distinct from tacit knowledge for management. In other words, we sought further evidence that tacit knowledge is domain specific. We discuss the methods used to conduct our validation study and the results we obtained for leaders at the platoon, company and battalion levels (see Hedlund *et al.* 1998 for more details).

We administered the *TKML* along with our other measures (described below) to officers from 44 battalions stationed at six posts around the United States. The number of battalions sampled at each post ranged from four to ten. By sampling intact battalions, we were able to administer the tacit-knowledge inventory at all three levels of interest (battalion, company and platoon) and simultaneously to obtain judgments of leadership effectiveness from multiple perspectives. We obtained complete data from 368 platoon leaders, 163 company commanders, and 31 battalion commanders. In addition, we obtained ratings of leadership effectiveness from the superior officers of battalion commanders (i.e. brigade commanders), who themselves did not serve as participants.

In addition to the *TKML*, we administered measures of verbal ability (the *Concept Mastery Test — CMT*), experience, tacit knowledge for managers, and we obtained ratings of leadership effectiveness for all participants. In establishing the construct validity of our measure, we looked for evidence of convergent and discriminant validity. In other words, we expected the *TKML* to relate more highly to leadership performance than to verbal ability, experience or tacit knowledge for managers.

The *Tacit Knowledge Inventory for Managers* was also administered to further explore the discriminant validity of the *TKML*. We included the *TKIM* with the expectation that there may be some relationship of tacit knowledge across domains, but that leadership tacit knowledge should be more predictive of performance than tacit knowledge for managers.

We also asked participants to report the number of months they have been in their current position so that we could assess the relationship between job experience and tacit knowledge. We expected to find that tacit knowledge would relate moderately to experience, but that tacit knowledge would be a better predictor of performance than simply the amount of time one has spent in his or her job.

Finally, we administered a *Leadership Effectiveness Survey* (*LES*) to obtain a criterion against which to validate the *TKML*. The *LES* consists of single-item measures that ask respondents to rate the effectiveness of other officers on a seven-point scale. In the construct validation study, the survey called for separate judgments of effectiveness in the interpersonal and task-oriented domains of leadership as well as an overall assessment of leadership effectiveness.

We obtained 360-degree ratings from multiple sources including peers, superiors and subordinates. For battalion commanders we were unable to obtain peer ratings due to the limited interaction among battalion commanders, and for platoon leaders we did not obtain subordinate ratings due to the unavailability of non-commissioned officers to participate in the study. Because of space limitations, we cannot list all the results here (but see Hedlund *et al.* 1998; Sternberg *et al.* 2000). The main results were the following:

For platoon commanders, the validation of the *TKML* showed that tacit knowledge for military leadership at the platoon level is associated with greater tacit knowledge for managers ($r = 0.36$, $p < 0.01$) and greater verbal ability ($r = -0.18$, $p < 0.01$). (Note: A negative correlation reflects the scoring of the *TKML*; a smaller score indicates greater tacit knowledge.) The finding that tacit knowledge for military leadership correlated with verbal ability differs from findings in previous tacit-knowledge research. Finally, experience, as measured by months in current job, did not correlate significantly with tacit knowledge for military leadership. This finding is consistent with our earlier argument that the amount of experience one has does not guarantee that he or she has effectively learned from that experience.

More important than their relationships with one another, we were interested in the relationship of these predictors to leadership effectiveness. We found that platoon leaders with higher tacit-knowledge scores were rated higher on task effectiveness by their superior officers. Verbal ability only correlated significantly with ratings of task-oriented leadership by superiors. Tacit knowledge for managers and experience did not correlate significantly with any of the effectiveness ratings.

We examined the relationship between the *TKML* and *LES* further using hierarchical regression analysis. Specifically, we were interested in the incremental validity of the *TKML* above the combined *CMT* and *TKIM* scores in predicting leadership effectiveness. We entered scores on the two *CMT* scales and the *TKIM* in the first step of the regression, followed by scores on the *TKML* in the second step. For all three effectiveness ratings made by superiors, tacit knowledge for military leadership provided a significant increment in prediction above scores on the *CMT* and the *TKIM*, with the overall model R ranging from 0.19 to 0.21.

At the company level, we found that company commanders with more tacit knowledge for military leadership also had more tacit knowledge for management ($r = 0.32$, $p < 0.01$) and higher verbal ability ($r = -0.25$, $p < 0.01$). Experience did not relate significantly to tacit knowledge for military leadership. In terms of explaining leadership effectiveness, we found that their peers rated company commanders who scored higher on the TKML as more effective on overall and task leadership. Scores on the CMT also correlated significantly with subordinate ratings on all three dimensions of leadership effectiveness and with peer ratings of overall and interpersonal effectiveness. However, the direction of these correlations suggested that higher verbal ability was associated with lower effectiveness as a leader.

When we followed up these results with hierarchical regression analyses, we found that for peer ratings of effectiveness, tacit knowledge for military leadership provided a significant increment in prediction over verbal ability and tacit knowledge for managers. This increment was significant even when the *CMT* and *TKIM* together contributed a significant prediction in the first step of the regression analysis. The overall model R for predicting peer ratings ranged from 0.25 to 0.32.

At the battalion level, we found no significant relationships among the *TKML*, the *TKIM*, the *CMT* subscale scores, and job experience. However, we did find significant relationships with the criterion. Battalion commanders with greater tacit knowledge for military leadership were rated as more effective overall by their superiors ($r = -0.42$, $p < 0.05$). In addition, battalion commanders who scored higher on tacit knowledge for managers were rated as more effective on task-related leadership by their subordinates ($r = -0.36$, $p < 0.05$).

We were unable to follow up these results with hierarchical regression analyses because our sample sizes for relationships involving the criteria were less than 31. However, the pattern of correlations suggests that the *TKML* may be a better predictor of leadership effectiveness than the *CMT*. Our measure of verbal ability did not correlate significantly with any of the effectiveness ratings. Although the battalion level results are based on a relatively smaller sample, they are consistent with our findings at the company and platoon levels, and suggest that tacit knowledge for military leadership has some relevance to leadership effectiveness. We also found that from the subordinate's perspective, battalion commanders' tacit knowledge for management is related to their perceived effectiveness. This finding is consistent with Army doctrine and our earlier findings, which both indicate that part of the battalion commander's role involves managing a complex system.

The construct validation results also provided insight about the nature of tacit knowledge for military leaders. At all three levels, leaders who possessed greater tacit knowledge were rated as more effective by their superiors. For platoon leaders and battalion commanders, we found that the overall score on the TKML was predictive of effectiveness ratings, while for company commanders it was the subscale score on questions dealing with managing the boss that was predictive of superiors' ratings. The finding that officers who possessed tacit knowledge were viewed by their bosses as more effective leaders makes sense, given the way we scored the *TKML*. The expert profiles used to score the *TKML* were based on responses from officers who were designated as highly successful leaders. Their designation as successful was based on performance evaluations made by their superiors. Therefore, we would expect there to be some relationship between those who have greater tacit knowledge, as determined by their resemblance to the experts, and those who are rated as more effective by their superiors.

Our studies of practical intelligence do not question the importance of traditional analytical cognitive abilities. There is evidence that conventional tests of intelligence predict both school performance and job performance (Barrett & Depinet 1991; Schmidt & Hunter 1998; Wigdor & Garner 1982). What these studies do suggest is that there are other aspects of intelligence that may be independent of IQ and that are important to performance, but that largely have been neglected in the measurement of intelligence.

3.1.6. Practical intelligence around the world We have also tested our ideas about practical intelligence in a variety of settings around the world. Sometimes, we find that tacit knowledge is very similar from one place to the other. For example, in a study of tacit knowledge for basic office workplace skills, we found a correlation of

0.91 between patterns of preferred responses in the United States versus Spain (Grigorenko *et al.* 2000). But sometimes, very different results obtain from one country to another.

In a study near Kisumu, Kenya, we tested the practical intelligence of rural Kenyan children (Sternberg *et al.*, in press). We constructed a test of practical intelligence for children of roughly 11 to 15 years of age measuring indigenous tacit knowledge about natural herbal medicines that could be used to combat various illnesses. The test assessed knowledge of the names of the medicines as well as the conditions for which they are each used. This knowledge, never taught in school, is believed to be important for adaptation to the harsh environment of life in rural Kenya and is valued by the indigenous communities.

We found a significantly *negative* correlation of over –0.3 in magnitude between the scores on the indigenous test and the scores on crystallized intellectual abilities (comprising the *Mill Hill Vocabulary Scale* [in English] and a comparable test administered in the Dholuo language, which is spoken in the homes of the children, respectively), and no correlation with scores on tests of fluid (*Raven Coloured Progressive Matrices*). Such correlations are consistent with the triarchic theory of human intelligence rather than traditional psychometric theories positing a general ability at the top of a hierarchy of abilities (e.g. Carroll 1993; Cattell 1971; Gustafsson 1984, 1988; Horn 1994).

We cannot say for sure why we obtained negative or insignificant correlations. But based on the ethnographic observations of co-authors Geissler and Prince, both of whom are cultural anthropologists, we believe that the negative correlations for the more school-subject sensitive crystallized ability tests may have resulted from parents choosing to emphasize either an indigenous or a Westernized education, but not both, for their children. Some rural Luo parents see Western schooling as largely a waste of time, in that their children will spend their lives in a village where Western education buys them little or nothing. Other parents see Western education as the only ticket their children can obtain to leave the village and possibly obtain a university education and work in urban Kenyan society. But whatever the reason, the so-called "positive manifold" that has come to be taken for granted in the administration of tests of mental abilities disappeared when we went abroad to a developing-country non-Westernized environmental context and administered a test that measured knowledge viewed as adaptive in that environmental context.

When conventional psychometric tests are administered, they are typically administered in a static fashion, meaning that items are given with no feedback and no instruction to improve performance. Our own tests that we have described are administered in the same way. However, Vygotsky (1978), Feuerstein (1979) and others (e.g. Brown *et al.* 1983; Budoff 1967, 1987a, 1987b; Day *et al.* 1997; Guthke 1992; Lidz 1987) have suggested that it may be more useful to administer tests dynamically, with feedback and guided instruction (see review in Grigorenko & Sternberg 1998). The idea of such administration is that dynamic testing may measure a child's zone of proximal development (Vygotsky 1978), or the distance between the child's latent capacity and his or her developed ability. Such a zone may be a particularly important individual-differences construct among children in developing countries who have not had the kinds of Western educational experiences that can lead to high scores on Western types of cognitive-abilities tests.

In terms of the triarchic theory (Sternberg 1985), children from the developing world may have a far lower level of experience with Western types of tests than do children from the developed world. The tests thus may be measuring for these children a set of constructs that effectively is different from the constructs being measured for Western children. The children in the developing world also may not have developed as fully as have Western children the cognitive skills required for such tests.

In an international collaborative study, we gave 9- to 13-year-old children three dynamic tests of cognitive abilities of a Western character — verbal syllogisms, "20 questions", and card sorting (Sternberg *et al.* 2000). Children took a pre-test of a given kind, then received instruction and practice with feedback for about 10 to 15 minutes, and then received a post-test. The correlation between pre-tests and post-tests was only about 0.3. In other words, even a minor instructional period resulted in a fairly substantial change in the rank orders of the children's scores, rendering any conclusions drawn from the original and apparently unstable static "IQ-type" test scores suspect. But of course, the important question is not only whether the pre-test correlates with the post-test, but also, which test predicts better to future performance.

We also therefore looked at which measures better predicted later cognitive performance, the pre-tests or the post-tests. Later cognitive performance was operationally defined as performance on parallel forms of the cognitive tests given six months later. On average, the post-test was the better predictor. Thus, any general-ability factor elicited on the basis of the pre-test scores would measure an individual-differences construct that would be, at best, suspect, given the change in rank orders with minimal levels of feedback and instruction.

Some researchers have suggested not only the psychological importance of *g*, but its societal importance as well. For example, Herrnstein & Murray (1994) argued that in the United States, at least, an "invisible hand of nature" is forming a cognitive elite that is sorting people on the basis of general ability. Sternberg (1995, 1997), however, has argued that this sorting is not the result of any invisible hand of nature, but rather of a societal invention, namely, the extensive use of ability testing for college and graduate as well as professional school admissions. People who do not do well on conventional ability and related achievement tests (which measure largely the same constructs — Sternberg 1998) are denied the educational access routes that would enable them to enter more prestigious and high-paying jobs. Other criteria — such as race, ethnic group, religion, caste, socioeconomic class or physical appearance — can be and have been used to accomplish sortings, and also have been believed to be nature's call in social Darwinist interpretations of why the people who rise to the top of a society get there. For example, in the early history of the U.S., race was considered an entirely valid criterion for socially stratifying people, and a Black person born with a high IQ would retain a low position in society — usually that of a slave — regardless of his or her IQ. In almost any society, those who profit from the norms of that society will tend to value those norms and to want to impose them on others.

Contemporary Russian society belies any simple interpretation of the correlation of IQ with socioeconomic class. In contemporary Russia, many of those who are now at the socioeconomic top of society only a few years ago were on the margins of society and many of those who were at the socioeconomic top of the society are now at the margins. Scientists (including psychologists) in research institutes, for example, who are among the most educated in the society and presumably are among those with the highest IQs in Russian society, are now often not getting paid or are being paid only minimally. They live poorly and their work is no longer viewed as having the same prestige it once did because of the reordering of priorities that the society has experienced.

According to the triarchic theory of human intelligence (Sternberg 1985, 1997, 1999a, 1999b), practical intelligence is likely to have at least as great and probably a greater impact on societal success than is the kind of academic or analytical intelligence measured by conventional intelligence tests. Russia supplies a particularly interesting setting for studying such an idea, especially because of the rapid social change it is experiencing.

In a collaborative study in Voronezh, Russia, we were interested in the ability of mothers to adapt to the demands of a rapidly changing society (Grigorenko & Sternberg, in press). The Russian mothers took tests of fluid (the *Cattell Culture Fair Test of g*) and crystallized (tests of synonyms — antonyms and analogies) abilities as well as a self-report behavioral inventory assessing aspects of practical intelligence. We found that mothers higher in practical intelligence but not fluid and crystallized abilities were less depressed, more satisfied with their current life situation, and more confident of the future than were the mothers who were lower in practical intelligence. In other words, practical but not the more academic forms of intelligence seems to have been serving as a buffer against ill effects of rapid social change.

4. Educational Studies

Some of our studies have looked at creative as well as practical abilities, especially in educational settings. Consider some of our main studies (see also Sternberg & Lubart 1995).

4.1. The Triarchic Aptitude-treatment Interaction Study

A measure was developed to assess the components of the triarchic theory. The *Sternberg Triarchic Abilities Test* (*STAT*; Sternberg 1993) consists of three content domains (verbal, quantitative and figural) crossed with three domains of mental processing (analytical, creative and practical). The three domain of processing reflect the sub-theories outlined above. Analytical questions address the ability to learn from context and reason inductively (i.e. the relation of intelligence to the internal world). Creative questions address the ability to cope with novelty (i.e. the relation of intelligence to experience). And practical questions address the ability to solve real-world, everyday problems (i.e. the relation of intelligence to the external world).

There are three analytical subtests of the *STAT*, one for each content area (verbal, quantitative and figural). Analytical-verbal abilities are measured in the *STAT* by assessing the ability to learn from context. Vocabulary is viewed as a proxy for the ability to pick up information from relevant context (see Sternberg 1987). The analytical-quantitative consists of items that measure inductive reasoning ability in the numerical domain. The analytical-figural items similarly measure inductive reasoning ability with either figure classification or figure analogy problems. In the figure classification, the examinee must indicate which figure does not belong with the others.

The creative portion of the *STAT* also consists of three subtests (verbal, quantitative and figural). The creative-verbal questions require counterfactual reasoning and attempt to assess the ability to think in relatively novel ways. In the creative-quantitative questions, symbols are used in place of certain numbers requiring the examinee to make a substitution. The creative-figural items require the examinee to complete a series in a domain separate from the one in which they inferred the completion rule.

The practical portion of the *STAT* is designed to assess the ability to apply knowledge to problems with practical relevance. Practical-verbal items require the examinee to answer everyday inferential reasoning problems. Practical-quantitative items require the examinee to reason quantitatively with practical everyday problems of the kind he or she might face in everyday life. Items in the practical-figural portion require the ability to plan a route efficiently, given the information in a map or diagram.

In addition, there is a performance component to the *STAT*, consisting of three essay items, one each stressing analytical, creative and practical thinking. In the current version, the analytical problem requires students to analyze the advantages and disadvantages of having police or security guards in a school building. The creative problem requires students to describe how they would reform their school system to produce an ideal one. The practical problem requires students to specify a problem in their life, and to state three practical solutions for solving it. Essays are scored for analytical, creative and practical qualities, respectively, by trained raters.

In a pilot use of the *STAT* (Sternberg & Clinkenbeard 1995), a variety of ability tests were administered to 64 participants. The other tests used were the *Terman Concept Mastery Test* (primarily a test of crystallized abilities), the *Watson-Glaser Critical Thinking Appraisal* (a verbal test of critical thinking), the *Cattell Culture Fair Test of g* (primarily a test of fluid abilities), a homemade test of insight problems (adapted from Sternberg 1986). Respective correlations of the *STAT* with these tests were, for the analytical 0.49, 0.50, 0.50 and 0.47 (all significant); for the creative, 0.43, 0.53, 0.55 and 0.59 (all significant); and for the practical 0.21, 0.32, 0.36 and 0.21 (the second and third significant). Of the three processing domains measured by the *STAT*, the one that correlates the least with more traditional measures of general intelligence is practical ability.

In a first major study (Sternberg *et al.* 1996; Sternberg *et al.* 1999), we examined whether the triarchic theory would give rise to an aptitude-treatment interaction in the context of a college-level psychology course taught to high school students who were selected for their triarchic ability pattern, and then taught in a way that either better or more poorly matched their ability pattern, and whose achievement was assessed triarchically as well. Thus, a crucial aspect of this study was that identification of participants, instruction of participants, and assessment of participants' achievement were all based on the same, triarchic theory of intelligence. The motivation for this study was to show that conventional means of teaching and assessment may systematically undervalue creatively and practically oriented students: these students may have the ability to perform quite well, but may perform at lower levels than those of which they are capable because neither the form of instruction nor the form of assessment well matches their pattern of strength.

Participants were 199 high school students (146 females and 53 males), from among 326 who were tested, who were selected for participation in a summer program on the basis of their patterns of abilities. Program participants were socioeconomically and ethnically diverse.

Participants were identified via the *STAT* as high in analytical ability (20%), high in creative ability (19%), high in practical ability (18%), balanced high (i.e. high in all three abilities — 20%), and balanced low (i.e. low in all three abilities — 24%).

The 4-week-long instruction for the course involved common and unique elements for each instructional groups. Two parts were common: the college-level psychology text (a prepublication version of Sternberg 1995), which contained analytical, creative and practical content; and the morning lectures, taught by an award-winning teacher (a Yale professor of psychology), and which involved analytical, creative and practical elements. The experimental manipulation occurred in the afternoon, when participants were assigned to a discussion section that emphasized either memory, analytical, creative or practical processing, and that either was a better or a poorer match to the participants' tested pattern of abilities.

As an example, memory-oriented instruction might ask students to recall the main elements of the cognitive theory of depression; analytically-oriented instruction might ask students to compare and contrast the cognitive to the psychoanalytic theory of depression; creatively oriented instruction might ask students to invent their own theory of depression, drawing on but going beyond past theories; practically-oriented instruction might ask students to show how they could use existing theories of depression to help a depressed friend.

All participants were tested via homework assignments, a midterm examination, a final examination and an independent project. All assessments were evaluated for analytical, creative and practical achievement. The examinations included as well multiple-choice items that measured memory achievement.

All correlations of ability tests scores (analytical, creative, practical) with all measures of achievement were statistically significant (all $p < 0.01$), reflecting perhaps the fact that the instruction and assessment were guided by the same theory as was the identification instrument (i.e. the *STAT*). More important was the aptitude-treatment interaction, which also was statistically significant for all ability groups. In other words, students who were better matched triarchically in terms of their pattern of abilities outperformed students who were more poorly matched.

4.2. The Triarchic Instructional Studies

In a follow-up set of studies, we sought to show that in terms of simple main effects, triarchic instruction is potentially superior to other forms of instruction, regardless of students' ability pattern (Sternberg *et al*. 1998a, 1998b). The triarchic theory holds that students should be instructed in a way that helps them both to capitalize on their strengths and to remediate and compensate for weaknesses. Thus, ideally, students will be taught in all three ways (analytically, creatively, practically), as well as for memory, so that they both can capitalize on their strengths and learn to deal with their weaknesses. These studies were conducted in the students' own schools rather than in a special summer-school setting; their teachers were their actual classroom teachers; and the material they studied was the actual material they were studying as part of their regular instruction, suitably modified as necessary for the study.

Participants in a primary-school study included 213 third-grade students (106 boys and 107 girls) in two elementary schools in Raleigh, NC. Both schools serve a diverse population of almost exclusively lower socioeconomic status students, including large groups of African American, Hispanic and Asian students. A total of nine classes of 20–25 students each participated in the research.

During the intervention, students received an instructional unit on the topic of communities — a social-studies unit required for third-grade students in North Carolina. No formal text was used for the unit, but rather, materials were developed by teachers. The intervention took place for 10 weeks, 4 days per week, for 45 minutes per day, for a total of 30 hours of instruction.

Participants in a secondary-school study were 141 rising eighth-graders (68 boys and 73 girls) drawn from around the nation from predominantly white middle-class backgrounds. Students took a summer psychology course either in Baltimore, MD, or Fresno, CA, in connection with the Center for Academic Advancement at John Hopkins University.

The 10-section course took place in two intensive 3-week sessions. Classes met 5 days per week with 7 hours of class time per day.

In both studies, students were divided into three instructional groups: traditional (memory-oriented), critical-thinking (analytically-oriented), and triarchic (analytically, creatively, and practically oriented). Instructional time was the same in each condition, and all teachers were appropriately in-serviced.

To illustrate the three different instructional treatments, consider three ways in which a third-grade unit on public services (e.g. fire, police) can be taught. The approach taken in the traditional instruction was to have children memorize the names and functions of the various public services. In critical-thinking instruction, an additional analytical effort was undertaken, whereby students would compare and contrast the different services and evaluate which ones to keep — and why — in case of a budget crisis. In triarchic instruction, students might additionally be asked to invent their own public service, to describe its means and ends, and to compare this new public service with conventional ones.

Students in both studies were evaluated for memory-based achievement (via multiple-choice tests), as well as for analytical, creative and practical achievement (via essay tests). For example, a memory-oriented assessment might ask which of several officials is an elected official. An analytical assessment might ask students to write a page explaining what a person in a given governmental position (e.g. Mayor of Raleigh) does, why the position is needed, and why the position is one of authority. A creative assessment might ask the student to imagine a place where no one tried to be a good citizen, and to write about a third grader's visit to this place. A practical assessment might ask the student how to handle a situation in which he or she is in charge of teaching 8-year-old students visiting from England different kinds of government services available in Raleigh, NC.

The results from the two studies were roughly comparable. In general, triarchic instruction was superior to the other modes of instruction, even on multiple-choice memory-based items. (Exact statistics are contained in Sternberg *et al.* 1998b.) In the elementary-school study, students also were administered a self-assessment questionnaire, for which the students were asked how much they liked the course, how much they thought they learned in the course, and how well they thought they did in the course. The students in the triarchic group generally gave significantly higher ratings than did the students in the other two groups. For the first and third questions, the triarchic group ratings were significantly higher than the ratings in the other two groups. For the second question, the triarchic group rating was nonsignificantly higher than the rating for the analytical group and significantly higher than the rating for the traditional group.

5. Conclusion

Arthur Jensen is correct. There is a *g* factor within the range of tests commonly used to measure intelligence. No one has made a more compelling case for this fact than has Arthur Jensen. There also is a *g* factor within the range of teaching and assessment techniques commonly used in schools. As long as the educational system limits itself primarily to memory and analytical abilities in its identification, instruction and assessments procedures, psychologists will continue to be impressed with the robustness of the *g* factor. Once psychologists leave the house to which they have confined themselves for one century, they will find that there is much more to the world than *g*. It is time for psychologists to lead the way and leave the house, rather than serving as guards trying to keep other people in the house the psychologists seem to fear to leave.

Acknowledgments

Research for this article was supported by contract MDA903-92-K from the U.S. Army Research Institute and by a grant under the Javits Act Program as administered by the Office of Educational Research and Improvement, U.S. Department of Education. Grantees undertaking such projects are encouraged to express freely their professional judgment. This article, therefore, does not represent the position or policies of the Government, and no official endorsement should be inferred.

References

Barrett, G. V., & Depinet, R. L. (1991). A reconsideration of testing for competence rather than for intelligence. *American Psychologist, 46*, 1012–1024.

Brand, C. (1996). *The g factor: General intelligence and its implications*. Chichester, England: Wiley.

Brown, A. L., Bransford, J. D., Ferrara, R. A., & Campione, J. C. (1983). Learning, remembering, and understanding. In: J. H. Flavell, & E. M. Markman (Eds), *Handbook of Child Psychology* (Vol. III). New York: Wiley.

Budoff, M. (1967). Learning potential among institutionalized young adult retardates. *American Journal of Mental Deficiency, 72*, 404–411.

Budoff, M. (1987a). The validity of learning potential. In: C. S. Lidz (Ed.), *Dynamic assessment* (pp. 52–81). New York: The Guilford Press.

Budoff, M. (1987b). Measures for assessing learning potential. In: C. S. Lidz (Ed.), *Dynamic assessment* (pp. 173–195). New York: The Guilford Press.

Carroll, J. B. (1976). Psychometric tests as cognitive tasks: A new "structure" of intellect. In: L. B. Resnick (Ed.), *The nature of intelligence* (pp. 27–56). Hillsdale, NJ: Erlbaum.

Carroll, J. B. (1993). *Human cognitive abilities: A survey of factor-analytic studies*. New York: Cambridge University Press.

Cattell, R. B. (1971). *Abilities: Their structure, growth and action*. Boston: Houghton Mifflin.

Cattell, R. B., & Cattell, A. K. (1963). *Test of g: Culture fair, scale 3*. Champaign, IL: Institute for Personality and Ability Testing.

Day, J. D., Engelhardt, J. L., Maxwell, S. E., & Bolig, E. E. (1997). Comparison of static and dynamic assessment procedures and their relation to independent performance. *Journal of Educational Psychology, 89*, 358–368.

Eddy, A. S. (1988). *The relationship between the Tacit Knowledge Inventory for Managers and the Armed Services Vocational Aptitude Battery*. Unpublished masters thesis, St. Mary's University, San Antonio, TX.

Embretson, S. E. (1987). Improving the measurement of spatial aptitude by dynamic testing. *Intelligence, 11*, 333–358.

Eysenck, H. J. (1979). *The structure and measurement of intelligence*. New York: Springer-Verlag.

Eysenck, H. J. (Ed.) (1982). *A model for intelligence*. Berlin: Springer-Verlag.

Feuerstein, R. (1979). *The dynamic assessment of retarded performers: The learning potential assessment device theory, instruments, and techniques*. Baltimore, MD: University Park Press.

Grigorenko, E. L., Gil, G., Jarvin, L., & Sternberg, R. J. (2000). *Toward a validation of aspects of the theory of successful intelligence*. Manuscript submitted for publication.

Grigorenko, E. L., & Sternberg, R. J. (1998). Dynamic testing. *Psychological Bulletin, 124*, 75–111.

Grigorenko, E. L., & Sternberg, R. J. (in press). Analytical, creative, and practical intelligence as predictors of self-reported adaptive functioning: A case study in Russia. *Intelligence*.

Gustafsson, J. E. (1984). A unifying model for the structure of intellectual abilities. *Intelligence, 8*, 179–203.

Gustafsson, J. E. (1988). Hierarchical models of the structure of cognitive abilities. In: R. J. Sternberg (Ed.), *Advances in the psychology of human intelligence* (Vol. 4, pp. 35–71). Hillsdale, NJ: Erlbaum.

Guthke, J. (1992). Learning tests: The concept, main research findings, problems and trends. *Learning and Individual Differences, 4*, 137–151.

Hedlund, J., Horvath, J. A., Forsythe, G. B., Snook, S., Williams, W. M., Bullis, R. C., Dennis, M., & Sternberg, R. J. (1998). *Tacit Knowledge in Military Leadership: Evidence of Construct Validity. (Technical Report 1080)*. Alexandria, VA: U.S. Army Research Institute for the Behavioral and Social Sciences.

Herrnstein, R. J., & Murray, C. (1994). *The bell curve*. New York: Free Press.

Horn, J. L. (1994). Theory of fluid and crystallized intelligence. In: R. J. Sternberg (Ed.), *The encyclopedia of human intelligence* (Vol. 1, pp. 443–451). New York: Macmillan.

Hunt, E. B. (1978). Mechanics of verbal ability. *Psychological Review, 85*, 109–130.

Hunt, E. B. (1980). Intelligence as an information-processing concept. *British Journal of Psychology, 71*, 449–474

Jensen, A. R. (1969). How much can we boost IQ and scholastic achievement? *Harvard Educational Review, 39*, 1–123.

Jensen, A. R. (1979). g: Outmoded theory or unconquered frontier? *Creative Science and Technology, 2*, 16–29.

Jensen, A. R. (1980). *Bias in mental testing.* New York: Free Press.

Jensen, A. R. (1998). *The g factor: The science of mental ability.* Westport, CT: Praeger/ Greenwoood.

Lidz, C. S. (Ed.) (1987). *Dynamic assessment.* New York: The Guilford Press.

Neisser, U. (1976). General, academic, and artificial intelligences. In: L. B. Resnick (Ed.), *The nature of intelligence.* Hillsdale, NJ: Erlbaum.

Pellegrino J. W., & Glaser, R. (1980). Components of inductive reasoning. In: R. E. Snow, P. A. Federico, & W. E. Montague (Eds), *Aptitude, learning, and instruction: Cognitive process analyses of aptitude* (Vol. 1, pp. 177–217). Hillsdale, NJ: Erlbaum.

Piaget, J. (1972). *The psychology of intelligence.* Totowa, NJ: Littlefield Adams.

Schmidt, F. L., & Hunter, J. E. (1998). The validity and utility of selection methods in personnel psychology: practical and theoretical implications of 85 years of research findings. *Psychological Bulletin, 124*, 262–274.

Snow, R. E. (1979). Theory and method for research on aptitude processes. In: R. J. Sternberg, & D. K. Detterman (Eds), *Human intelligence: Perspectives on its theory and measurement* (pp. 105–137). Norwood, NJ: Ablex.

Snow, R. E. (1980). Aptitude processes. In: R. E. Snow, P-A. Federico, & W. E. Montague (Eds), *Aptitude, learning, and instruction: Cognitive process analyses of aptitude* (Vol. 1, pp. 27–63). Hillsdale, NJ: Erlbaum.

Snow, R. E., & Lohman, D. F. (1984). Toward a theory of cognitive aptitude for learning from instruction. *Journal of Educational Psychology, 76*, 347–376.

Spearman, C. (1904). 'General intelligence,' objectively determined and measured. *American Journal of Psychology, 15*, 201–293.

Spearman, C. (1923). *The nature of intelligence and the principles of cognition.* London: Macmillan.

Spearman, C. (1927). *The abilities of man.* London: Macmillan.

Sternberg, R. J. (1977). *Intelligence, information processing, and analogical reasoning: The componential analysis of human abilities.* Hillsdale, NJ: Lawrence Erlbaum.

Sternberg, R. J. (1980). The development of linear syllogistic reasoning. *Journal of Experimental Child Psychology, 29*, 340–356.

Sternberg, R. J. (Ed.) (1982). *Handbook of human intelligence.* New York: Cambridge University Press.

Sternberg, R. J. (1983). Components of human intelligence. *Cognition, 15*, 1–48.

Sternberg, R. J. (1985). *Beyond IQ: A triarchic theory of human intelligence.* New York: Cambridge University Press.

Sternberg, R. J. (1987). Most vocabulary is learned from context. In: M. G. McKeown, & M. E. Curtis (Eds), *The nature of vocabulary acquisition* (pp. 89–105). Hillsdale, NJ: Lawrence Erlbaum Associates.

Sternberg, R. J. (1988). *The triarchic mind: A theory of human intelligence.* New York: Viking.

Sternberg, R. J. (1993). *Sternberg Triarchic Abilities Test.* Unpublished test.

Sternberg, R. J. (Ed.) (1994). *Encyclopedia of human intelligence.* New York: Macmillan.

Sternberg, R. J. (1995). For whom the bell curve tolls: A review of The bell curve. *Psychological Science, 6,* 257–261.

Sternberg, R. J. (1997). *Successful intelligence.* New York: Plume.

Sternberg, R. J. (1998). Abilities are forms of developing expertise. *Educational Researcher, 27,* 11–20.

Sternberg, R. J. (1999a). Successful intelligence: Finding a balance. *Trends in Cognitive Sciences, 3,* 436–442.

Sternberg, R. J. (1999b) The theory of successful intelligence. *Review of General Psychology, 3,* 292–316.

Sternberg, R. J. (Ed.) (2000). *Handbook of intelligence.* New York: Cambridge University Press.

Sternberg, R. J., & Clinkenbeard, P. R. (1995). A triarchic model of identifying, teaching, and assessing gifted children. *Roeper Review, 17,* 255–260.

Sternberg, R. J., Ferrari, M., Clinkenbeard, P. R., & Grigorenko, E. L. (1996). Identification, instruction, and assessment of gifted children: A construct validation of a triarchic model. *Gifted Child Quarterly, 40* (3), 129–137.

Sternberg, R. J., Forsythe, G. B., Hedlund, J., Horvath, J., Snook, S., Williams, W. M., Wagner, R. K., & Grigorenko, E. L. (2000). *Practical intelligence.* New York: Cambridge University Press.

Sternberg, R. J., & Gardner, M. K. (1982). A componential interpretation of the general factor in human intelligence. In: H. J. Eysenck (Ed.), *A model for intelligence* (pp.T231–254). Berlin: Springer-Verlag.

Sternberg, R. J., & Gardner, M. K. (1983). Unities in inductive reasoning. *Journal of Experimental Psychology: General, 112,* 80–116.

Sternberg, R. J., Grigorenko, E. L., Ferrari, M., & Clinkenbeard, P. (1999). A triarchic analysis of an aptitude-treatment interaction. *European Journal of Psychological Assessment, 15,* 1–11.

Sternberg, R. J., & Grigorenko, E. L. (Eds) (in press). *The general factor of intelligence: Fact or fiction.* Mahwah, NJ: Lawrence Erlbaum.

Sternberg, R. J., & Lubart, T. I. (1995). *Defying the crowd: Cultivating creativity in a culture of conformity.* New York: Free Press.

Sternberg, R. J., Nokes, K., Geissler, P. W., Prince, R., Okatcha, F., Bundy, D. A., & Grigorenko, E. L. (in press). The relationship between academic and practical intelligence: A case study in Kenya. *Intelligence.*

Sternberg, R. J., Torff, B., & Grigorenko, E. L. (1998a). Teaching for successful intelligence raises school achievement. *Phi Delta Kappan, 79,* 667–669.

Sternberg, R. J., Torff, B., & Grigorenko, E. L. (1998b). Teaching triarchically improves school achievement. *Journal of Educational Psychology, 90,* 1–11.

Sternberg, R. J., & Wagner, R. K. (Eds) (1986). *Practical intelligence: Nature and origins of competence in the everyday world.* New York: Cambridge University Press.

Sternberg, R. J., Wagner, R. K., & Okagaki, L. (1993). Practical intelligence: The nature and role of tacit knowledge in work and at school. In: H. Reese, & J. Puckett (Eds), *Advances in lifespan development* (pp. 205–227). Hillsdale, NJ: Lawrence Erlbaum Associates.

Vygotsky, L. S. (1978). *Mind in society: The development of higher psychological processes.* Cambridge, MA: Harvard University Press.

Wagner, R. K. (1987). Tacit knowledge in everyday intelligent behavior. *Journal of Personality and Social Psychology, 52,* 1236–47.

Wagner, R. K., Rashotte, C. A., & Sternberg, R. J. (1992). *Tacit Knowledge in sales: Rules of thumb for selling anything to anyone*. Unpublished manuscript.

Wagner, R. K., & Sternberg, R. J. (1985). Practical intelligence in real-world pursuits: the role of tacit knowledge. *Journal of Personality and Social Psychology, 49,* 436–458.

Wagner, R. K., & Sternberg, R. J. (1990). Street smarts. In: K. E. Clark, & M. B. Clark (Eds), *Measures of leadership* (pp. 493–504). West Orange, NJ: Leadership Library of America.

Williams, W. M., & Sternberg, R. J. (in press). *Success acts for managers*. Mahwah, NJ: Lawrence Erlbaum Associates

Wigdor, A. K., & Garner, W. R. (Eds) (1982). *Ability testing: Uses, consequences, and controversies*. Washington, D.C.: National Academy Press.

Chapter 18

Jensen's Genetic Interpretation of Racial Differences in Intelligence: Critical Evaluation

Nathan Brody

1. Introduction

Jensen believes that Black-White differences in intelligence test scores are, in part, attributable to genetic differences.

In this paper I review the evidence he cites in support of this hypothesis and I explain why I do not find it persuasive. I know of no better way of demonstrating my appreciation of his skill as a scholar than to critically evaluate his arguments.

Jensen (1998) cites five kinds of studies in support of his hypothesis. These are: (1) studies of biological variables related to intelligence; (2) studies of transracial adoptions; (3) studies of racially mixed individuals; (4) regression analyses; and (5) statistical studies of between and within group heritability.

2. Biological Correlates of IQ

IQ is correlated with head size and with brain size as assessed by nuclear magnetic resonance tests. Rushton & Ankney (1996) reviewed the available literature on differences in head size among African-American and White samples based on data from autopsies and measurement of external head size. They concluded that African-Americans have head sizes that are approximately half of a standard deviation smaller than White Americans.

Kamin & Omari (1998) challenged Rushton and Ankney's conclusions. Rushton & Ankney (2000) wrote a critical response to the Kamin and Omari critique. The issues raised in these analyses are complex involving an analysis of various data sources of differing degrees of validity. I will rely in my comments on what I take to be the two most informative studies.

The Scientific Study of General Intelligence: Tribute to Arthur R. Jensen
Copyright © 2003 by Elsevier Science Ltd.
All rights of reproduction in any form reserved.
ISBN: 0–08–043793–1

Jensen & Johnson (1994) analyzed head circumference data from 14,000 pairs of four and seven-year-old siblings based on data collected for the National Collaborative Perinatal Project (Broman *et al*. 1987). They found a race X sex interaction. They obtained estimated brain sizes of 1,201 for White males, 1,163 for Black males, 1,131 for White females and 1,137 for Black females. Note that their data indicate that Black females have larger brain capacity than White females. Rushton & Ankney (2000) attribute these results to racial differences in the rate of female maturation. If this is correct, data on racial differences in adult brain size should be informative. Rushton and Ankney reported an analysis of head shape and size in 6,000 military recruits. Rushton and Ankey obtained a race X gender interaction that is analogous to that obtained by Jensen and Johnson. White males have marginally larger head sizes than Black males — Black females have marginally larger head sizes than White females.

The data indicating racial differences in brain size inferred from external measurements of head size is problematic. There are other sources of data based on autopsies that suggest that there may be racial differences in brain size. But these data are not based on large and systematically obtained samples. In my judgement the presence of a racial difference in brain size is not a firmly established finding.

There are several additional hypotheses that must be supported before it can be assumed that data on head and brain size differences provide support for a genetic explanation of racial differences in intelligence. It is necessary to demonstrate that head and brain size are heritable in both White and Black populations and that the covariance between head and brain size indices and IQ is genetically mediated in both White and Black populations. If either of these hypotheses is unsupported, then differences in head and brain size do not provide evidence for the genetic hypothesis. Actually there are data that suggest that both of these hypotheses are false. Jensen (1994) analyzed head size data on Black and White twins collected by Osborne (1980) to study relationships between head size and IQ. Jensen reported a correlation between the within family (within pair) difference scores for a combined index of three parameters of head size and IQ of 0.31 for MZ and 0.32 for DZ twin pairs. These data indicate that the covariance between these two measures is not attributable to genetic influences. Jensen's discussion of these results is as follows: "The within-pairs correlation between head size and *g* for MZ twins can be only a purely non-genetic correlation. The within-pairs correlation of DZ twins theoretically could be a pleiotropic genetic correlation, but this is unsupported by the fact that the obtained correlation in the DZ twins is no larger than the purely nongenetic correlation in the MZ twins" (Jensen 1994: 604). Jensen indicated that the relationship between head circumference might be mediated genetically but the data in this study based on 82 pairs of MZ twins and 61 pairs of DZ twins might have insufficient power to detect an actual relationship. Nevertheless, the data as reported contradict the hypothesis that the relationship between IQ and head circumference is pleiotropic. The fact that IQ and head circumference may both be heritable does not imply that the covariance between these variables is mediated genetically.

Rushton & Ankney (1996) analyzed twin data on the heritability of head circumference for Black and White twin pairs. Head circumference was clearly heritable for the sample of White twins. The MZ and DZ twin correlations adjusted for height and weight were 0.58 and 0.20, respectively. For Black twins the comparable correlations for MZ and DZ twin pairs were 0.41 and 0.31, implying that head circumferences was less heritable for Black twins than for White twins — although a formal test of the significance of difference in heritabilities for Black and White twin pairs was not statistically significant. The heritability of head circumference for the White sample was estimated to be between 0.47 and 0.56 — for the Black sample heritability was estimated to vary between 0.12 and 0.31. These data suggest that the determinants of head circumference may be different in Black and White twin pairs. Therefore the racial differences in head circumferences obtained in this study do not provide clear support for the hypothesis that the racial differences in IQ are influenced by genes that influence both head circumference and IQ.

Even if one accepts the problematic evidence indicating that Black individuals have slightly lower head size than White individuals, a closer examination of the available data suggests that these results do not provide support for the genetic hypothesis. The available evidence suggests that the relationship between head size and IQ is not mediated genetically and there is evidence that suggests that head size may not be substantially heritable among African-Americans.

Myopia (near-sightedness) is a biological variable that is positively correlated with scores on tests of intelligence. There is also evidence that African-Americans are less likely to be myopic than White Americans. Jensen reports data from military induction examinations that find the incidence of myopia among white recruits was 34% and among black recruits 8% — a difference of approximately one standard deviation. Racial differences in myopia are compatible with the genetic hypothesis. There are, however, many gaps in the evidence that would be necessary to argue that these data provide strong evidence for the genetic hypothesis. There is no information about the relationship between myopia and IQ within Black samples. There is no specific data on the heritability of covariances between myopia and intelligence in either White or Black samples. Thus critical evidence necessary to infer that differences in myopia support the genetic hypothesis is simply lacking.

3. Trans-racial Adoption

Analyses of adoption data indicate that IQs are influenced by the characteristics of the adopting families when children are young but these influences fade over time as children approach adolescence. Transracial adoption data for young children are less persuasive with respect to the influence of the adoptive family on IQ than data on older adoptees. In order to provide decisive evidence against the genetic hypothesis it would be necessary to demonstrate that children reared from birth by white adopted families have IQs that are determined by the characteristics of their adopted rather than their biological families. Ideally, the sample of children should be old enough for the usual influence of adopted families to be vanishingly small — (perhaps age 14 or above). If the data indicate that Black children adopted by White families develop IQs that are characteristic of their biological parents, the results would be supportive of the genetic hypothesis but not necessarily decisively supportive since the observable physical characteristics of Black adoptees maintain a cultural as well as a biological tie to their biological parents.

The Minnesota Transracial Adoption Study is the only transracial adoption study that includes longitudinal data. The study compares the IQ and academic achievement of White, Asian and Indian, Black and mixed race Black adoptees. The study is longitudinal including information about the performance of these adoptees when they had a mean age of 17. The adopted children were reared in relatively privileged White families in Minnesota by adoptive parents whose mean IQ was over one standard deviation higher than the population mean. The initial report of the study by Scarr & Weinberg (1976) interpreted the results of the study as being strongly supportive of an environmental interpretation of racial differences in intelligence. Scarr and Weinberg noted that the mean IQ of Black children in this study who were reared in White families was 107. The original report of the study dealt only with the results of the initial IQ tests when the children were age 7. Scarr and Weinberg noted that the Black children in this study had mean IQs that were above the U.S. white mean IQ. They argued that the relatively high IQ of Black children adopted in white homes provided strong evidence in favor of an environmental interpretation of mean differences in Black and White IQs.

There was one other feature of the data obtained in the initial report of the Minnesota study that provided evidence that was compatible with a genetic interpretation of the differences in IQ between Black and White Americans. The group of Black children who were adopted included 29 children who had two Black biological parents and 68 children who had one Black and one White biological parent. The former group had a mean IQ of 96.8 and the latter group had a mean IQ of 109. Despite their shared social identity these two groups of children differed in IQ. This difference might be attributable to genetic differences between the racial identities of their biological parents. Scarr and Weinberg noted that there is an alternative explanation for this differences in IQ of these two groups of Black adoptees. The interracial children had better pre-adoption histories than the children with two black parents, The former children were adopted earlier, had fewer pre-adopted placements, and lived in their adopted families for longer periods of time. They attributed the differences in performance on IQ tests between these two groups to differences in pre-adoptive histories.

Weinberg *et al.* (1992) reported the results of a ten-year follow-up of the subjects in the Scarr and Weinberg study. The follow-up data present a somewhat different pattern of results and do not lend themselves as readily to an environmental explanation of racial differences in IQ. The appropriate interpretation of these data has been the subject of disagreement between psychologists involved in the collection of these data and critics of their interpretation who favor a genetic interpretation of racial differences in IQ (Levin 1994; Lynn 1994; Waldman *et al.* 1994).

The Black adopted children in this study no longer have an IQ that is above the mean IQ of the White population of the U.S. Children with two Black parents have an IQ of 89.4 — a value that is approximately equal to the IQ of Black children reared in their own homes in this region of the United States. These data suggest that the IQ of these children was either not higher than or only slightly higher than the IQ they might have had if they had been reared by their biological parents. These data do not provide evidence indicating that children whose biological parents are Black would have higher

IQs if they were reared by privileged white parents in what has sometimes been called "the culture of the tests". The children who had two Black parents also had IQs that were nine points lower than the mean IQ of adopted inter-racial children with whom they presumably shared social identities and IQs that were slightly more than one standard deviation lower than that of White adopted children reared in comparable social circumstances.

Waldman *et al.* (1994; Weinberg *et al.* 1992) argued that their data are compatible with an environmental interpretation of racial group differences in IQ. They noted that the various adopted groups in this study differed in their pre-adoption experiences. Black adoptees had poorer pre-adoption experiences than other adoptees. It is also the case that the pre-adoptive experience of these children is related to their IQs at both the initial and follow-up testing. Measures of the pre-adoptive experiences account for 13% of the variance in adolescent IQ and 32% of the variance in childhood IQ. These data indicate that the late adolescent IQs of adopted children in the Minnesota study are influenced by two different kinds of variables — the racial identity of the biological parents of these children and the pre-adoptive experiences of these children. Both sets of variables are related to each other. The racial identity of the parents of the biological parents of these children and the pre-adopted family experiences of these children are confounded variables. It is impossible to ascertain whether the differences in performance in IQ for children with different racial backgrounds in this study are attributable to differences in their pre-adoptive experiences or to differences in the genetic characteristics of their biological parents, or to both of these variables in some unknown mixture of influence. The confounding of these variables is further illustrated by the results of regression analyses reported by Weinberg *et al.* (1992). They noted that an analysis in which racial group identity is entered as the initial set of variables followed by a consideration of pre-adoptive experiences indicates that the pre-adoptive experiences are no longer significantly predictive of the IQs of post adolescent adoptees. Similarly, a regression analysis in which measures of pre-adoptive experiences are considered prior to a consideration of the racial identity of the biological parents indicated that racial identity of the adoptees is not significantly related to post adolescent IQ. Therefore, these analyses cannot unconfound the respective influences of pre-adolescent placements and the biological racial identity of the adoptees.

Jensen (1998) noted that studies of the influence of early vs. late adoption on IQ indicate that children who are adopted early do in fact have higher preschool IQs than children who are adopted late but that by age 7 these differences are no longer present. He cited the results of a study by Fisch *et al.* (1976) as providing evidence for this conclusion. Fisch *et al.* compared the IQs of 77 white adoptees adopted prior to age 1 to the IQs of 17 adoptees adopted after age 1. They noted that children adopted prior to age 1 obtained significantly higher Stanford-Binet age 4 IQs than children adopted after age 1 (the mean 4-year-old IQs for these two groups of children are not given in their article). Fisch *et al.* noted that age 7 WISC scores were not significantly different for these two groups of children. The children adopted prior to age 1 had a mean full scale IQ at age 7 of 102.3 and the children adopted after age 1 had a mean full scale IQ of 97.9. Fisch *et al.* note that these means were not significantly different. Jensen indicates that the Fisch *et al.* study provides evidence for the view that age of adoption does not influence the IQ of older children. This appears to be a somewhat tendentious interpretation of these results. The mean differences obtained by Fisch *et al.* for age 7 IQ are certainly compatible with the assumption that age of adoption does influence IQ. Although the differences were not statistically significant, the small sample of adoptees older than 1 renders the power of the statistical test of the difference weak.

Jensen (1998) also cited the results of studies of late adopted Asian children as providing evidence for the assumption that age of adoption does not adversely influence IQ. While these studies do provide evidence that small samples of late adopted Asian children who have experienced poor pre-adoption experiences may obtain high IQs, the studies do not compare early and late adoptees. There is relatively little convincing evidence that permits an assessment of the influence of pre-adoption experiences and age of adoption on IQ. This suggests to me that an interpretation of the results of the Minnesota transracial adoption study that attributes group differences in IQ obtained in this study to the influence of pre-adoptive experiences is not contradicted by what is known about the influences of pre-adoption experiences.

There is an additional transracial adoption study that is not discussed by Jensen that provides evidence for an environmental interpretation of racial differences in intelligence. Moore (1986) administered IQ tests to a group of adopted children whose biological parents were both Black or who had one Black and one White parent. The children were adopted by either Black or White families who had comparable educational levels. The mean IQ of the children with two Black biological parents adopted by White parents was 109 and the mean IQ of the children whose biological parents were Black and White who were adopted by White parents was 107. These data do not exhibit the differences obtained in the Minnesota study. The Moore study differs from the Minnesota study in two possibly relevant ways. First, Moore's sample was smaller — there were 9 children whose biological parents were Black who were adopted by White families and there were 14 similarly adopted children who were biologically biracial. Second, the children were administered IQ tests at an earlier age than the follow-up tests administered in the Minnesota study.

Moore also found that Black and biracial children adopted by white families had IQs that were almost one standard deviation higher than the IQs of children with similar backgrounds who were adopted by Black families with comparable socioeconomic and educational backgrounds. The Moore study suggests that differences in the conditions of rearing associated with exposure to a White or a Black family account for Black-White differences in IQ. Although these results are clearly supportive of an environmental interpretation of racial differences they are not definitive. The data would be more dispositive if the sample were larger and if the children were older.

4. Racially Mixed Individuals

There are two studies of racially mixed individuals that contradict the genetic hypothesis. Jensen argues that these studies are not decisive. Eyferth (1961; Eyferth *et al.* 1960) obtained IQ data for children reared in Germany by their white German mothers whose fathers had been either Black or White soldiers who were stationed in

Germany at the end of World War II. The mothers whose children were either White or racially mixed were well matched for socioeconomic indices. The children were tested with a German version of the Wechsler tests when they were between 5 and 13 years old — the majority were tested between ages 10 and 13. The mean IQ of the White children was 97.2 and the mean IQ of the racially mixed children was 96.5. These results suggest that the IQ differences between White and Black individuals are attributable to environmental influences. Reared under comparable conditions in Germany, there are no IQ differences between racially mixed and white samples. This study has three desirable characteristics. First, the sample is not exceedingly small (there were 98 interracial children and 83 white children tested). Second, the children were old enough at the time of testing to have been influenced by the genetic characteristics of their biological parents. Third, the children were reared in relatively similar conditions — although it is possible that being non-white in Germany may have exposed the interracial children to negative social experiences.

While conceding that these data provide support for an environmental interpretation of Black-White differences in IQ, Jensen argued that these data are not critical for three reasons. First, he noted that black males were rejected for military service more often that White males and therefore Black soldiers were not as representative of the Black population as White soldiers. While this is correct, it is also true that Black soldiers did not perform as well as White soldiers on tests of intelligence used by the military.

Second, Jensen noted that IQ tests were not available for the biological parents of the children. This argument is not critical for the mothers of the children since the two groups of children were matched on relevant socioeconomic characteristics — it is unlikely that there would have been significant differences in the IQs of mothers of White and interracial children. No information was available about the biological fathers of these children other than their putative racial status. Jensen argued that it is possible that the biological fathers of these children were not representative of Black and White soldiers. It is possible that the White soldiers who fathered these children had lower IQs than other White soldiers and the Black fathers had higher IQ than other Black soldiers. While this is possible, it is also implausible. There is no reason to think that sexual relationships between Black and White soldiers with German women after World War II were differentially influenced by the IQ scores of the soldiers. Flynn (1980) discussed this issue in some detail. He suggested that there is no reason to think that the biological fathers of these children were not representative of the population of White and Black soldiers who were in Germany. Information about the IQs of the fathers would have been informative. Its absence does not lead to a plausible refutation of these findings.

Third, Jensen argued that IQ differences between White and interracial children might have been influenced by heterosis. Heterosis is the obverse of genetic inbreeding effects. Matings among individuals who are genetically unrelated increase the probability that genetically dominant genes that are associated with high IQ will be present among offsprings leading to an increase in the level of the IQ phenotype. Genetically diverse matings can increase scores on a heritable phenotype. There is relatively little data supporting the existence of heterotic effects for the IQ phenotype. Jensen cited the findings of a study conducted in Hawaii that reported that children whose parents were European and Asian had IQs that were approximately 4 points higher than children whose parents were both European (Nagoshi & Johnson 1986). Nagoshi and Johnson matched the parents for socioeconomic status and educational level. The biological parents in this study were not tested for IQ. It is possible that individuals of the same educational level who have interracial marriages might have higher IQs than individuals of who marry someone from the same race. Individuals who have high IQ may be less traditional in their marriage choices than individuals of low IQ. In addition, the extensive literature on the heritability of IQ indicates that virtually all of the genetic influence on IQ is additive rather than non-additive. If this is correct, then there should be little or no heterotic influence on IQ. In the absence of clear evidence for heterotic influences on IQ, Jensen's interpretation of the Eyferth results is not based on convincing evidence. While the Eyferth study is, in common with virtually all studies in this area, not definitive, it does provide evidence suggesting that the Black-White difference in performance on tests of intelligence is attributable to environmental influences.

Scarr *et al.* (1977) studied the relationship between degree of African ancestry for a sample of 181 Black individuals and performance on tests of intelligence. Scarr *et al.* constructed an odds index based on 12 genetic markers that were assumed to indicate the degree to which a person's genes were representative of individuals with African background and another index of the degree to which the genetic markers present were characteristic of European ancestry. The correlations between these indices and a measure of mental ability were –0.05 and –0.03. These data indicate that the degree to which a person's genes are characteristic of individuals with African backgrounds as opposed to European backgrounds is not predictive of performance on tests of intelligences. Jensen (1981; see also, Reed 1997) argued that the methods used to ascertain degree of racial admixture in this sample of African-Americans were not highly reliable and that the study had very weak power to detect differences that might have been present. The arguments involved are complex and it may well be that over time various genes that were once characteristic of African heritage have become dissociated. Thus it may be difficult to define the degree of racial mixture present in any contemporary African-American. Moreover, the phenomenon of African-American individuals who passed for white as well as an increase in inter-racial marriages in the United States renders the determination of a biologically meaningful distinction between Black and White individuals as well as an index of degree of African heritage increasingly problematic. To assert this is to indicate that the genetic hypothesis itself rests on somewhat shaky foundations.

5. Regression Phenomena

Regression to the mean occurs whenever *r* is less than 1.00. Jensen noted that regression effects for IQ are compatible with genetic influences on intelligence. This is hardly a remarkable assertion. We know that correlations between various individuals who are reared together vary in terms of the genetic relatedness of siblings. MZ twin correlations are higher than DZ twin correlations and biologically related siblings have higher correlations than non-biologically related siblings reared together. Since regression to the mean is derivable from correlation values, variations in correlation values that are compatible with the assumption that IQ is heritable will of necessity produce different degrees of regression towards the mean.

Regression effects may be observed in family studies of IQ. What, if anything, does this have to do with the genetic hypothesis? Jensen argued that racial differences in regression support a genetic explanation of the reasons for Black-White differences for IQ (Jensen 1973, 1998). Jensen noted that there are racial differences in regression. He obtained the IQs of all full siblings in grades 1–6 attending 14 elementary schools in a district in California. And he contrasted the IQ test scores of Black and White children whose siblings had identical IQs. Black children whose siblings had high IQs had lower IQs than White children whose siblings had the same IQ as the Black children. Why do Black children whose siblings have high IQ exhibit greater regression towards the mean than White children whose siblings have the same value? Jensen argued that the difference in regression supports the genetic hypothesis.

These data are compatible with the genetic hypothesis if one assumes that the racial differences in IQ occur for genetic reasons. But this provides independent evidence for the genetic hypothesis only if one assumes that what is at issue is correct. Assume that the reasons for between group differences in IQ are different from the reasons for within group differences in IQ and that genetic differences between the races are not implicated in between group differences. A Black person with an estimated true score IQ of 120 has an IQ that is 2.33 standard deviations above the putative black phenotypic mean of 85. A White person with an estimated IQ of 120 would have an IQ that is 1.33 standard deviations above the white mean of 100. Therefore, the predicted score of the sibling of the Black person will exhibit regression to the Black mean and the regression for the White sibling will exhibit regression toward the White mean. This observation does not inform us at all of the reasons why a Black individual with an IQ of 120 has a z score IQ value that is greater in the population of Black IQ values than a White person whose IQ is also 120 will be in the population of White values. In other words, differential regression occurs because Black people are Black and White people are White. The phenomenon is compatible with any hypothesis about the reasons for Black-White differences in IQ. It supports the genetic hypothesis only if one assumes that the genetic hypothesis is true in the first place.

Jensen (1998) cited a second analysis of these data that he believes supports the genetic hypothesis. Jensen obtained data on 16 additional tests including tests of scholastic achievement, short term memory and a test of psychomotor skills. He obtained sibling correlations for both Black and White samples for each of these tests. The average correlations for siblings were 0.28 and 0.30 for Black and White siblings, respectively. The White sample had higher mean performance on these tests than the Black sample — the mean difference was 1.03 standard deviations.

Jensen obtained White-Black mean differences expressed in standard deviation units for each of the tests in the battery. Jensen correlated the vector defining mean racial differences in performance on these 16 tests with the vector defining sibling correlations for these tests. When the sibling correlations were obtained from the Black sample, the correlation between the vector values for these tests was 0.61. The comparable correlation based on White sibling correlations was 0.80. These data imply that the magnitude of the Black-White differences in performance varies as a function of the degree to which siblings perform in a similar manner on these tests. Jensen argued that these results support the genetic hypothesis. Although Jensen does not explain his reasoning in detail, I believe that his argument is based on several assumptions. These are: (1) sibling correlations are dependent primarily on genetic similarities; (2) variations in sibling correlations across tests are dependent upon variations in the degree to which the tests are heritable; and (3) if the genetic hypothesis is correct, variations between racial groups are determined by the same variables that determine variations within racial groups. Since genetic variables are involved within groups they should be involved in determining performance differences between groups. Therefore, the vector defining sibling correlations construed as a measure of variations in genetic determinants of test performance ought to positively correlate with the vector defining Black-White differences in performance also construed as a measure of genetic differences in determinants of performance on tests.

Jensen argued that a purely environmental hypothesis would predict a negative correlation between the magnitudes of the sibling correlations and the magnitudes of the mean White-Black differences. Is Jensen's analysis of these data persuasive? The empirical results are unambiguous. Black-White variations in performance on a battery of tests are predictable by variations in sibling similarity in performance on these tests. Jensen assumed that variations in sibling similarity are determined by genetic influences rather than by environmental influences. He assumed that an environmental hypothesis would predict an inverse relationship between vectors of sibling similarity and mean racial difference in performance. The assumption is correct if it is assumed that the only environmental influences on tests of intelligence are non-shared influences that tend to make siblings reared in the same family dissimilar. While this assumption is supported by data for older siblings, it should be noted that it does not necessarily hold for younger siblings reared in the same family. The children tested in this study were young (recall that they were in grades 1–6). At these ages analyses of performance on tests of intelligence usually find some evidence of between family environmental influences on performance — although genetic influences are usually larger than environmental influences. The tests included measures of achievement that usually have lower heritability and often have between family environmental influences. This implies that variations in sibling correlations may reflect between family influences as well as genetic influences. The sibling similarity vector is probably determined by both genetic and environmental influences. If this is correct, the relationship between the vectors obtained in this study could have been mediated by environmental events.

Jensen's analysis of the results in this sibling study is compatible with the genetic hypothesis but the results provide at best weak support for the hypothesis because it is not formally tested with a genetically informed research design. It is possible, in principle, to obtain data that would provide a more specific test of the assumptions involved in Jensen's analysis. If Jensen's sibling study had included a substantial number of half as well as full siblings who were reared in the same family, it would have been possible to obtain measures of genetic and environmental influences on performance on each of the tests included in the battery. Vectors defining variations in genetic and environmental determinants of test performance could then be obtained for

Black and White samples and these vectors could be compared. Such analyses would lend themselves to a formal determination of independent genetic and environmental components of variance on the vector defining sibling correlations. The relationships between these independent components of variance on the vector could be compared across racial groups and a model could be tested indicating the respective contributions of genetic and environmental components of variance to the vector defining racial differences in performance on these tests. Such a formal model might provide support for Jensen's analysis of the meaning of variations in sibling correlations for a battery of tests. Such an analysis was not performed — a design using sibling correlations is not genetically informative since siblings may correlate for many reasons. This analysis leads to the conclusion that Jensen's analysis of sibling correlations in this study provides, at best, weak support for the genetic hypothesis.

6. Structural Equation Modeling

The method of using full and half siblings and formal structural equation models was used by Rowe & Cleveland (1996) to test the genetic hypothesis. Jensen cites the Rowe and Cleveland study as well as a study that he conducted using twin data as providing empirical support for the genetic hypothesis. Jensen noted that his study had a relatively small N and in some respects the data failed to conform to all of the necessary assumptions of the model he tested. Therefore, he relied on the results of the Rowe and Cleveland study. Rowe and Cleveland used data from the National Longitudinal Survey of Youth to test the genetic hypothesis. They obtained test scores for all of the Black and White full and half siblings in this study. There were 161 pairs of full Black siblings in the study, 314 full White siblings, 106 Black half siblings and 53 pairs of White half siblings. The academic achievement of the siblings was assessed on two reading tests and a test of mathematics. Rowe and Cleveland used structural equation models to test the genetic hypothesis. In order to test the hypothesis they began by testing different models of genetic and environmental influences on performance on these three tests of achievement. They were able to reject a model that assumed all of the variations in performance on these tests were attributable to genetic influences. An acceptable fit for a two factor model was obtained that assumed that variations in performance on these tasks were attributable to genes and to shared environmental influences. Separate analyses of the Black and White samples indicated that the same models fit both groups of subjects. Genetic factors were more important determinants of reading performance than they were of math performance. Shared environmental factors had a larger influence on performance in math than in reading. The two factor model of achievement was used to predict mean differences in achievement for Black and White subjects. The analyses were based on the assumption that the influences that caused within group variation were the same as those that caused between group variation. The model fitting procedure suggested that the Black sample had lower loadings on both the latent genetic and shared environmental factors that determined performance on these tests. Genetic differences between groups were assumed to account for 74% of the obtained difference in mean Black and White performance on the Reading Recognition test. Shared environmental influences accounted for 64% of the mean difference in performance on the Math test. The model predicted the obtained mean Black and White differences.

Rowe and Cleveland's study demonstrates that it is possible to test the genetic hypothesis using structural equation modeling procedures. Although their study provides evidence for the genetic hypothesis, the models they used were not highly sensitive to group differences in the determination of performance on these tasks. Rowe and Cleveland noted that the White sibling correlations obtained in this study conformed to the expectations derived from the assumption that performance on these tests was heritable. The average full sibling correlation on the three tests of achievement was 0.40 and the comparable half sibling correlation was 0.17. The correlations for Black siblings were not clearly in conformity with the assumption that the performance on these tests was heritable. For mathematics, Black half siblings had correlations of 0.42 versus full sibling correlations of 0.32 — a result opposite of that expected on the assumption that performance on the test was heritable. The Black full siblings had correlations of 0.38 on reading comprehension versus 0.33 for the black half siblings — a relatively small difference. Reading recognition was the only test on which Black full siblings had clearly larger correlations than Black half siblings (0.42 vs. 0.22). The mean Black full sibling correlation of these three tests was 0.37 and the mean Black half sibling correlation was 0.32. These data indicate that evidence for the heritability of these tests for the Black siblings is weaker than the evidence for the heritability of these tests for White siblings. Rowe and Cleveland reported that a test of a model assuming zero heritability for the Black sample was rejected. And, they reported that similar models fit both the White and Black sub-samples when analyzed separately. But the tests of these models could not have been very sensitive to violations of assumptions. Clearly a model that assumes that performance on these tests is heritable for the Black sample cannot be completely valid when the results that are obtained are opposite of those predicted by the assumption for one of the three tests (mathematics), and exhibit very small differences on a second test (reading comprehension). Moreover, Jensen (1998) argued that reading comprehension is a highly *g* loaded ability. Reading recognition is assumed to be less *g* loaded. The results of the formal modeling procedures fail to detect differences in the pattern of results for Black and White siblings that appear to be relatively large. If the differences in full and half sibling correlations for the Black siblings in this study were of the same order of magnitude as those obtained for White siblings on each of the tests, Rowe and Cleveland's analyses would provide clear evidence in support of the genetic hypothesis. Their analyses indicate that their model fitting procedures were not sensitive to the possibility that the determinants of performance on these tests were different for White and Black samples.

7. Conclusion

None of the five types of studies Jensen cites in support of his hypothesis are convincing. When examined critically, there are either gaps in knowledge, inconsistent results, untested assumptions and flaws in reasoning that tend to weaken Jensen's analyses. I do not find the evidence he cites in favor of the genetic hypothesis persuasive.

References

Broman, S. H., Nichols, P. L., Shaughnessy, P., & Kennedy, W. (1987). *Retardation in young children*. Hillsdale, NJ: Erlbaum.

Eyferth, K. (1961). Leistungen verschiedener Gruppen von Besatzungskindern in Hamburg-Wechsler Intelligenztest fur Kinder (HAWIK). *Archiv fur die gesamte Psychologie, 113*, 102–114.

Eyferth, K., Brandt, U., & Hawel, W. (1960). *Farbige Kinder in Deutschland*. Munchen: Juventa Verlag.

Fisch, R. O., Bilek, M., Deinard, A. S., & Chang, P-N. (1976). Growth, behavioral, and psychological measurements of adopted children: The influences of genetic and socioeconomic factors in a prospective study. *Behavioral Pediatrics, 89*, 494–500.

Flynn, J. R. (1980). *Race, IQ and Jensen*. London: Routledge & Kegan Paul.

Jensen, A. R. (1973). *Educability and group differences*. London: Methuen.

Jensen, A. R. (1981). Obstacles, problems, and pitfalls in differential psychology. In: S. Scarr (Ed.), *Race, social class, and individual differences in I.Q.* Hillsdale, NJ: Erlbaum.

Jensen, A. R. (1994). Psychometric *g* related to differences in head size. *Personality and Individual Differences, 17*, 597–606.

Jensen, A. R. (1998). *The g factor: The science of mental ability*. Westport, CT: Praeger.

Jensen, A. R., & Johnson, F. W. (1994). Race and sex differences in head size and IQ. *Intelligence, 18*, 309–333.

Kamin, L., & Omari, S. (1998). Race, head size, and intelligence. *South African Journal of Psychology, 28*, 119–128.

Levin, M. (1994). Comment on the Minnesota Transracial Adoption Study. *Intelligence, 19*, 13–20.

Lynn, R. (1994). Some reinterpretations of the Minnesota Transracial Adoption Study. *Intelligence, 19*, 21–28.

Moore, E. G. J. (1986). Family socialization and the IQ test performance of traditionally and transracially adopted black chidren. *Developmental Psychology, 22*, 317–326.

Nagoshi, C. T., & Johnson, R. C. (1986). The ubiquity of *g. Personality and Individual Differences, 7*, 201–208.

Osborne, R. T. (1980). *Twins: black and white*. Athens, GA: Foundation for Human Understanding.

Reed, T. E. (1997). "The genetic hypothesis": It could have been better tested. *American Psychologist, 52*, 77–78.

Rowe, D. C., & Cleveland, H. H. (1996). Academic achievement in Blacks and Whites: Are the developmental processes similar? *Intelligence, 23*, 205–228.

Rushton, J. P., & Ankney, C. D. (1996). Brain size and cognitive ability: Correlations with age, sex, social class and race. *Psychonomic Bulletin and Review, 3*, 21–36.

Rushton, J. P., & Ankney, C. D. (2000). Size matters: a review and new analyses of racial differences in cranial capacity and intelligence that refute Kamin and Omari. *Personality and Individual Differences, 29*, 591–620.

Scarr, S., Pakstis, A. J., Katz, S. H., & Barker, W. B. (1977). Absence of a relationship between degree of white ancestry and intellectual skills within a black population. *Human Genetics, 39*, 69–86.

Scarr, S., & Weinberg, R. A. (1976). IQ test performance of black children adopted by white families. *American Psychologist, 31*, 726–739.

Waldman, I. D., Weinberg, R. A., & Scarr, S. (1994). Racial-group differences in IQ in the Minnesota Transracial adoption Study: A reply to Levin and Lynn. *Intelligence, 19*, 29–44.

Weinberg, R. A., Scarr, S., & Waldman, I. D. (1992). The Minnesota Transracial Adoption Study: A follow-up of IQ test performance in adolescence. *Intelligence, 16*, 117–135.

Chapter 19

New Concepts of Intelligence: Their Practical and Legal Implications for Employee Selection

Gerald V. Barrett, Alissa J. Kramen and Sarah B. Lueke

1. Introduction

In the 1920s and 1930s basic theories of intellectual ability were developed along with operational tests which proved effective in predicting job performance (Spearman 1927; Thorndike 1936). In a series of studies and meta-analyses throughout the 1970s and 1980s, Schmidt and Hunter showed that cognitive ability was the best overall predictor of job performance (Hunter & Hunter 1984; Hunter 1986; Schmidt & Hunter 1981). Partially in reaction to the meta-analytic findings, research to expand on the definitions of competencies continued. The development of competencies by McClelland (1973) was followed by a discussion of tacit knowledge (Wagner & Sternberg 1985), practical intelligence (Sternberg & Wagner 1986), and multiple intelligence (Gardner 1999). In the 1990s, emotional intelligence became the intelligence of interest (Feist & Barron 1996; Goleman 1995, 1998a, 1998b; Graves 1999; Mayer *et al.* 1990).

All these new theories and proposed measurement instruments pose a challenge to traditional cognitive ability tests since it is claimed that these tests are more valid and have lower adverse impact. It is our contention that many of these tests are nothing more than pop psychology. It is distressing to see such books (i.e. Goleman 1998b) quoted as if they had some merit. We will review the themes present throughout all of these "creative" concepts and examine whether they have practical implications and can withhold legal scrutiny in the public and private sector.

2. Legal Challenges and the Daubert Standards

It is our opinion that despite all these theorists' claims of validity, if challenged in court, they would fail. The Daubert Standards for scientific tests are a set of guidelines for admissibility of scientific evidence into court (see Table 19.1).

The Scientific Study of General Intelligence: Tribute to Arthur R. Jensen
© 2003 Published by Elsevier Science Ltd.
ISBN: 0–08–043793–1

Table 19.1: Daubert criteria.

1   The theory must have been tested, or is at least able to be tested.
2   The theory (& expert) must have (been) published in peer reviewed publications.
3   There must be a known or potential error rate.
4   The theory must be generally accepted in the relevant scientific community.
5   The methods for testing the theory must meet scientific standards.

The criteria were set forth in Daubert v. Merrell Dow Pharmaceuticals (1993) and clarified through subsequent supreme court cases (General Electric Company v. Joiner 1997; Kumho Tire Company Ltd. v. Carmichael 1999) and federal district and appeals court cases (e.g. Black v. Rhone-Poulenc 1998; Butler v. Home Depot, Inc. 1997; Camp v. Lockheed Martin Corporation 1998; Clark v. Takata Corp. 1999; Gerlib v. R. R. Donnelley & Sons Co. 2001; Smith v. Ford Motor Co. 2000). (See American College of Trial Lawyers 1994, and Barrett 2000, for a discussion). In the U.S., the Daubert standards pertain to any selection instrument used or advocated by a plaintiff. This is part of American case law, but the basic principles of scientific standards are relevant to everyone considering a particular measure or construct's use for personnel selection.

In a typical disparate impact discrimination lawsuit, a series of steps occur. First, the plaintiff demonstrates adverse impact. Next, the defendant demonstrates that despite the adverse impact, the test is still valid. Third, the plaintiff's expert shows that there are alternative selection procedures with equal validity that result in less adverse impact. Fourth, the defendant's expert attempts to demonstrate that the alternative selection procedure is not as valid and doesn't decrease disparate impact. This is where the problem with new theories of intelligence comes in. They either implicitly or explicitly imply that they have a better approach. This has been the situation in court cases in which we've been involved (e.g. Adams v. City of Chicago 1996; Brown v. City of Chicago 1996, 1998; Firefighters Institute for Racial Equality v. City of St. Louis 2000; U.S. v. Garland 2000). At the start of the process, the defendants attempt to have the plaintiff's expert's evidence stricken using the Daubert standards, which act as a gatekeeping function. For purposes of illustration, we will show why we believe these new concepts of intelligence would not be accepted under the Daubert Standards.

3. Key Studies Cited by Advocates of New Concepts of Intelligence

It is clear that the key studies cited repeatedly by advocates of these new concepts do not meet the Daubert criteria for scientific evidence. In this section, we will review these studies and challenge each one as they would be challenged in a court as a basis for use of a particular measure as a personnel selection instrument.

Table 19.2.: Prediction of Foreign Service Officers (FSO) job performance using competency measures.

Test	Reliability	Validity
U.S. Knowledge	0.70	0.32**
Empathy (PONS)	0.20	0.11
Relevant Experience	—	0.16

(Participation in student government in high school plus college academic record minus sum of participation in musical activities in high school & college).
Data from an unpublished report by McClelland, D. C., & Dailey, C. (1973), and from Table 1, p. 70 of Barrett (1994).

3.1. PONS

The PONS test is designed to measure ability to read emotions. An unpublished report by McClelland & Dailey (1973) examining the PONS as a predictor of Foreign Service Officers' (FSO) job performance is often cited by advocates of emotional intelligence as supporting the validity of the PONS. However, as described in Barrett (1994), the U.S. Knowledge Test had higher reliability and validity compared to the PONS (see Table 19.2).

In fact, the validity coefficient for the Job Knowledge Test was significant, whereas the validity coefficient for the PONS did not reach statistical significance. By looking at Table 19.2, it is clear that the PONS, a measure of empathy, did not demonstrate a significant correlation with job performance. Despite this fact, Spencer & Spencer (1993) asserted that superior FSOs scored significantly higher on the PONS because they were better able to 'tune into' others' feelings. In addition, Goleman (1998a) asserted that the exam that measured academic subject correlated negatively with job performance for Foreign Service Officer; conversely, ability to read emotions (PONS Test) did predict Foreign Service Officer job performance. "Their (academic) scores were a poor indicator of how adept these new diplomats were on their feet — in fact, their on-the-job performance ratings actually correlated negatively with how well they did on the very test used to select them" (Goleman 1998a: 18, 332, note 4). Again, this statement regarding the PONS did not receive support by the data. In our review of the literature, we found no peer-reviewed articles which demonstrated that the PONS predicted job performance.

3.2. Tacit Knowledge

Dr Sternberg often relies on a study by Scribner (1984) to support his concept of tacit knowledge (Wagner & Sternberg 1985) as a predictor of job performance. However, Scribner used a very specific sample in a milk processing plant (preloaders, inventory workers, wholesale drivers, clerks) as well as 9th grade students. None of these would likely be considered representative samples by experts in the field. Four population groups (preloaders, inventory & drivers, clerks and students) were given 16 simulation problems and their strategies for solving the problem were examined (see Table 19.3).

From these results, Wagner and Sternberg concluded that tacit knowledge is a valid predictor of job performance. However, there was no measure of job performance in any of these studies, and none of the production workers were administered either an IQ test or a Tacit Knowledge inventory. The only relationship reported was that a standardized math test related to more optimum solutions for students. If a practitioner were to attempt to defend this study as evidence of the validity of tacit knowledge for predicting job performance, the study would certainly not meet the Daubert criteria. The theory was not tested and the methods used to test the theory would not meet scientific standards for test validation (APA 1999; EEOC 1978, 1980; SIOP 1987).

There have been studies that have attempted to empirically demonstrate a relationship between tacit knowledge and job performance. Wagner & Sternberg (1990) conducted a study at the Center for Creative Leadership using tacit knowledge to predict performance on two managerial simulations: Earth II and Energy International. *Tacit*

Table 19.3: Participants in Scribner (1984) descriptive case study of a dairy (from Table 1.1, p. 17).

Group	Number
Preloaders	5
Inventory	4
Wholesale Drivers	10
Clerks	11
Ninth Grade Students	30

Percent selected non-literal strategy when it is optimal (from Table 1.2, p. 23, Scriber 1984)

	(LPE & LME)
Preloaders	72%
Inventory & Drivers	65%
Clerks	47%
Students Scores on national math achievement test at or above grade level ($N = 12$)	42%[1]
Student scores on national math achievement test below grade level ($N = 18$)	15%[1]

Note: LPE = least physical effort; LME = least mental effort.
[1] From Note C.

Table 19.4: Center for Creative Leadership Studies/tacit knowledge (Wagner & Sternberg 1990).

Behavioral Assessment Data Rating (BAD)[1]	
TK	–0.61
IQ	0.38

[1] Sum of 8 dimensions for both simulations.
Separate correlations with the 8 dimensions were not reported.

Knowledge (or street smarts) was defined as the "work-related practical know-how that is learned informally on the job" and was measured by the *Tacit Knowledge Inventory for Managers* (TKIM; Wagner & Sternberg 1991), which consists of a series of work related situations. Wagner and Sternberg concluded that "scores on research measures of street smarts are quite predictive of ability to learn to solve practical problems in the office" (pp. 494–495) (see Table 19.4).

However, these conclusions would not be accepted under the Daubert standards. Several characteristics of the methodology used to demonstrate the predictability of tacit knowledge are problematic. First, tacit knowledge scores were calculated based on deviations of responses from an expert prototype of 15 additional participants in the Center for Creative Leadership's Leadership Development Program (LDP). They obtain scores for this "expert" group, obtain means on various dimensions, and subtract the individual score in the validation sample from the "prototype" score. You, in effect, have a difference score, which are known to have low reliability (Edwards 1994). This is not a typical scoring method used in personnel selection, and the authors do not provide evidence that this was acceptable. The criterion measures consisted of behavioral assessment data ratings on eight dimensions based on performance in the managerial simulations (activity level, led the discussion, influenced others, problem analysis, task orientation, motivated others, verbal effectiveness and interpersonal skills). In addition to the unusual method of using a deviation score, there are other problems with the scoring used in this study. When there were problems with finding correlations with the difference scores, they standardize scores on the test so that everyone has the same standard deviation (Wagner 1994). This adjustment of individuals' test scores would receive scrutiny under Civil Service rules and regulations. It is difficult to tell individuals that he/she has a lower test score than his/her observed score because it was changed to reflect the group standard deviation.

There are several issues with the dependent variables when this study is presented as a validation study. These are often used as predictors in assessment centers. There were no data presented relating managerial job performance and performance on the managerial simulations, neither correlational evidence nor evidence of content validity. Even if the simulations were related to job performance, this does not mean that tacit knowledge would also be related to job performance simply based on the evidence of a correlation between tacit knowledge and performance in the simulation (McCornack

1956). No data were presented relating predictors to each dimension. Participants were 45 participants in the Leadership Development Program from various jobs and organizational levels. This sample size is particularly small when one considers how many predictors were used in the regression equations. It is not evident exactly how the subtest scores were used, but even if one considers that subtests were combined to be one predictor score, there were eight predictors. This sample, both in terms of size and nature, will have problems with generalizability to managerial jobs. Wagner and Sternberg do not describe the nature of participants' jobs. Finally, there is a problem with the definition of tacit knowledge itself, which is defined as something learned on the job. The Uniform Guidelines (EEOC 1978) explicitly prohibit employers from selecting applicants based on knowledge learned on the job.

In another study on tacit knowledge, Colonia-Willner (1998) examined the relationship between the TKIM and job performance ratings of non-expert Brazilian bank managers.

Based on the results presented in Table 19.5, it is clear that although this study meets the Daubert standard of a tested theory, the test of this theory resulted in no relationship between tacit knowledge and job performance ratings. The questionable scoring method of the TKIM discussed with regard to the Wagner & Sternberg (1990) study (i.e. difference scores based on comparison to an expert prototype) was also used in this

Table 19.5: Expert versus non-expert bank managers in Brazil. In Raven's, DAT and TKIM Time Data from Table 5 of Colonia-Willner (1998).

Brazilian Bank Managers

Test	Expert ($N = 43$) M	Non-Expert ($N = 157$) M	P
Raven's score	17.67	14.83	<0.01
DAT score	27.60	22.41	<0.01
TKIM Time (min)	29.67	33.01	<0.01

(Time in minutes taken by the participants to grade the 91 strategies presented by TKIM)

TKIM Prediction of job performance for 157 Non-Expert Bank Managers (data from Table 4 of Colonia-Willner 1998).

TKIM	Job Performance
Overall	0.00
Self	0.01
Others	−0.06
Task	0.03

study. Finally, the results alluded to in the abstract of this article are somewhat misleading. Colonia-Willner stated in the abstract that the "TKIM predicted managerial skill, while the DAT and Raven's did not" (p. 45). However, when the results are examined more closely, it is evident that the TKIM did not predict job performance ratings. The statement made in the abstract refers to a relationship of $r = -0.12$ between overall TKIM score and an index of managerial success, which was a composite of management span (number of personnel supervised directly and indirectly), salary and job performance ratings. This is not a typical measure of job performance for a validation study. Based on the studies reviewed above, tacit knowledge would not survive legal scrutiny under the Daubert standards.

3.3. Competencies

Daniel (1992) proposed to identify critical leadership competencies for manufacturing supervisors and to test whether they can differentiate between top supervisors and a control group of supervisors in an electronics company. This study has never been cited by any of the major proponents of new concepts of intelligence. Two studies were conducted. The first study involved critical behavior interviews with 9 high-performing and 8 control supervisors and identified 13 competencies. In the second study, these 13 competencies were rated by the managers of 15 top supervisors and a control group of 23 supervisors ($N = 38$). Only the competency "image and reputation" differentiated the top supervisors from the control group ($t(32) = 3.11$, $p < 0.02$). However, "image and reputation" measures work behavior on the job. This study is an example of confusion between predictors and criteria in this study, and it does not meet the Daubert standards.

3.4. Interpersonal Accuracy

Davis & Kraus (1997) conducted a meta-analysis of relationships between individual differences and interpersonal accuracy (see Table 19.6).

Interpersonal accuracy has been defined in many ways, including accuracy in assessing another person's personality, affective or non-affective state, the role, identity or status of a target individual, or accuracy in predicting the actual behavior of a target person. Based on the results of this meta-analysis, Davis and Kraus concluded that a good judge (i.e. someone with a high level of interpersonal accuracy) is intelligent, more likely to view the world in a cognitively complex manner, and has good psychological adjustment. However, social intelligence was not significantly related to interpersonal accuracy, as would be expected. The findings of this meta-analysis have been cited by leading proponents of emotional intelligence. Goleman (1998b) asserted that "Those who are trusting — tend to be more highly attuned to feelings" (pp. 142, 350, note 20). However, it is evident from Table 19.6 that this relationship is rather small. No evidence regarding job performance was presented in this meta-analysis.

Table 19.6: (From Davis & Kraus (1997), Table 5.2, p. 157).

Individual Differences	Mean Effect	Fail Safe
Intellectual Functioning	0.23	465
Cognitive Complexity	0.27	30
Positive Adjustment	0.24	34
Social Intelligence	0.08	1
Interpersonal Trust	0.20	21

Note: Fail Safe = ". . . whenever the combined significance level was reliable, a 'fail-safe' number was calculated using the formula recommended by Cooper (1979), which provides an estimate of how many findings of zero association, not included in these analyses, would be necessary in order to make the combined significance level unreliable" (pg. 156).

3.5. Emotional Intelligence

Graves (1999) tested Mayer *et al.*'s (1999) Emotional Knowledge Test (EKT) as a predictor of performance on four assessment center exercises (see Table 19.7).

Graves found that emotional intelligence as scored by experts was significantly related to performance on the assessment center exercises. However, the magnitude of correlations was similar to the magnitude of the correlations between IQ and performance. The problems with using this study as validation evidence are similar to those discussed with regard to the Wagner & Sternberg (1990) study. The criterion measures were simulated jobs, which are assessment center exercises.

Table 19.8 reviews the available validation evidence.

Despite many claims that measures of emotional intelligence have been demonstrated as valid predictors of job performance (e.g. Bachman *et al.* 2000; Bar-On 1997, 2000; Goleman 1998a, 1998b), there is very little empirical evidence to support this statement.

Table 19.7: Correlation between EKT, IQ & performance
Composites ($N = 149$). (Data from Graves 1999, Table 24, p. 171).

Composite	Emotional Intelligence		IQ
	Expert Scored	Consensus Scored	
Peer	0.24**	0.12	0.25**
Assessor	0.27**	0.10	0.24**
Combined	0.31**	0.13	0.29**

Note: Criterion was peer and assessor ratings of performance on four job simulation exercises.

Table 19.8: Evidence of the relation between emotional intelligence and job performance.

Measure	Study	Sample	Results
Bar-On EQ-I 133 self-report items	Bachman *et al.* (2000)	Study 1 $N = 36$ debt collection officers Study 2 $N = 34$	No validity coefficients were reported. Study 1 No mean difference between Bar-on scores for most and least successful employees Study 2 Significant difference for empathy in the opposite direction
	Handley (1997)	Air force recruiters	No validity coefficients were reported. Handley reported that there were significant differences between successful and unsuccessful recruiters on 11 of 16 scales.
Emotional Competence Inventory (ECI) 110 self-report items asking participants to describe how representative each item is of their typical work behavior	Murensky (2000)	$N = 90$ executives in key leadership roles in an international oil corporation (13 female).	The criteria for "leader performance" was obtained using the Balanced Scorecard. • The correlation between the ECI Clusters and the Balanced scorecard was not significant.
EI 34 word pair items (e.g. insecure/secure) rated by interviewers.	Carrothers *et al.* (2000)	$N = 147$ medical school applicants	No validity coefficients were reported. No significant difference in EI scores between accepted and rejected applicants.

Table 19.8: Continued.

Measure	Study	Sample	Results
Short Version of the Multifactor Emotional Intelligence Scale (MEIS) Scenario based questions for 3 "branches" of emotional intelligence	Rice (1999)	$N = 26$ teams 9 of 26 teams were composed of 2 people, one of whom was the team leader.	Correlations of Total EIQ Scores with Overall Team Performance or Team Leader (pp. 65–73) *Predictor* *r* *Criterion* Team Mean EIQ Scores 0.25/0.30/0.08 Manager ranking/rating/Average team member ratings of team performance. Team leader EIQ scores –0.01/0.03/0.05 Manager team ranking/rating/Average team member team performance ratings. Team Average EIQ scores 0.34/0.03 Manager team leader ranking./performance ratings. Team EIQ 0.11 Average team member ratings of team leader. Team Leader EIQ 0.51/0.25/–0.18 Manager team leader ranking/ ratings/ Team member average performance ratings of team leaders. • Using a two-tailed test, none of the correlations shown in the table above were found to be significant (Rice shows two of the correlations to be significant).
Emotional Intelligence Scale by Schutte et al. (1998) 33 self-report items on a Likert-type scale.	Malouff & Schutte (1998)	$N = 26$ college seniors	$r = 0.38$, $p < 0.05$, one-tailed. After four months, supervisors rated the students' para-professional performance.

Table 19.8: Continued.

Measure	Study	Sample	Results
Emotional Knowledge Test (EKT) 5 dimensions scored by expert and consensus ratings, 1 dimension was also scored by the target.	Graves (1999)	$N = 149$ participants who were recruited through a newspaper advertisement and paid $130-$150	Criterion measures were assessor and peer performance ratings on assessment center exercises, not job performance.

Expert vs. consensus scores give very different results.

Coefficient alpha ranged from 0.15 to 0.82.

Emotional Intelligence composite with performance composite:

Table 24 (Graves 1999, p. 171).
Correlations between EIQ, IQ, and Performance Composites. ($N = 149$).

Composite
Emotional Intelligence
IQ

Expert Scored
Consensus Scored

Peer

    0.24**
    0.12
    0.25**

Assessor

    0.27**
    0.10
    0.24**

Combined

    0.31**
    0.13
    0.29**

Adapted from Graves (1999)
** $p < .01$, two-tailed.
Note: Peer = Peer composite based on average factor scores; Assessor = Assessor composite based on the average of the adjusted observed ratings.
Combined = Combined peer and assessor composites.

Table 19.8: Continued.

Measure	Study	Sample	Results
PONS (Measure of empathy)	McClelland & Dailey (1972)	$N = 115$ Foreign Service Officers	Test
			U.S. Knowledge Test
			Empathy (PONS)

	Reliability	Validity
U.S. Knowledge Test	0.70	0.32**
Empathy (PONS)	0.20	0.11

Note: Table adapted from Table 1 of Barrett (1994).
** $p < 0.01$, two-tailed.

It is important to note that none of the tests in this table are objective tests with correct answers. They are either self-report or rated by others. As can be seen in the table, none of the studies would pass all of the Daubert standards.

3.6. Group Intelligence

Williams & Sternberg (1988) defined group intelligence as "the full potential of a group of people working as a unit" (p. 356). They conducted a study to demonstrate the relationship between IQ and group performance (group product quality). Williams and Sternberg concluded that IQ was an essential component of group intelligence and as a predictor of group performance (see Table 19.9).

They also concluded that talkativeness and dominance were part of group intelligence. However, Goleman came to very different conclusions when he described this study in his 1998 book. Goleman (1998b) asserted that "In a classic study of group IQ by Wendy Williams and Robert Sternberg . . . the interpersonal skills and compatibility of the group members emerged as key to their performance (a result found time and time again). Williams and Sternberg found out that those who were socially inept . . . were a drag on the whole effort . . . All in all, the social effectiveness of the group predicted how well it would do, more than did the individual IQ of its members" (pp. 205, 358, notes 15, 16).

This is quite a different interpretation than that offered by the authors of the study: Williams & Sternberg (1988) stated that ". . . IQ was an essential component of intelligence; not only is a lot of IQ on average desirable, but also, one group member particularly high in IQ" (p. 375) and that ". . . having a fellow group member with a high desire to participate in such situations (demanding and uncomfortable social situations)

Table 19.9: Williams & Sternberg (1988).
Cognitive correlations of IQ with group product quality (from Table 7, p. 369).

IQ	Group Product Quality
Maximum (group member who scored highest)	0.65***
Mean (average score of 3 group members)	0.65***
Minimum (group member who scored lowest)	0.43*

Personality characteristics (from Table 7, p. 369)

	Group Product Quality
Empathy	NS
Extraversion	NS
Maximum Desire to Participate	−0.64***
Mean Private Self-Consciousness	0.41*

Multiple regressions of all written predictors on group product quality (from Table 8, p. 373)

$R^2 = 0.64$	Beta
Maximum IQ	0.50**
Maximum Desire to Participate	−0.48**

has a negative impact on the group's performance" (p. 370). Neither empathy nor extraversion predicted group product quality.

4. Conclusions Regarding the Daubert Standards

The first of the Daubert criteria states that the theory must have been tested, or is at least able to be tested. Gardner (1999) admits that he is not going to develop tests and attempt to empirically prove his theory. This admission would automatically rule out his expert testimony and preclude his concept of multiple intelligences from having any value for personnel selection in a real context. The concept of Emotional Intelligence also would fail to meet the Daubert standards, since there are no instruments which have demonstrated validity in predicting job performance. Goleman's (1995, 1998a, 1998b) theory is so diffuse it can never be tested, while Mayer *et al.* (1990) have a theory but negative results. Competencies as developed by McClelland (1973), Boyatzis (1994), and Spencer & Spencer (1993) is not actually a theory that can be tested, but a process of obtaining scores based on expert responses. Many competencies rely on past performance, but there is no definition of the construct of past performance. This has not been done with the measures of specific intelligence described here. Tacit knowledge (Wagner & Sternberg 1985), has been criticized due to its lack of a coherent definition (Gottfredson, in press). Without a definable construct/latent trait, there is no way a coherent measure can be developed. Constructs need to be defined, measures need to be developed, tested and then cross-validated.

The second of the Daubert criteria, that the theory (& expert) must have (been) published in peer reviewed publications, has also not been met by these new concepts. One of the outstanding features of all new concepts of intelligence is that they are primarily published in trade books and book chapters without adequate peer review. The number of actual publications in peer reviewed journals by these mentioned authors is very few, despite the fact that they have been around for 30 years.

The third is that there must be a known or potential error rate. Within selection contexts, either insufficient data exists or the data show that the instruments are not valid. It is impossible to determine the number of true positives, true negatives, false positives and false negatives to be expected in using the technique.

The fourth of the criteria says that the theory must be generally accepted in the relevant scientific community. All of the conceptualizations have been critiqued by practitioners and professionals in the area of Industrial/Organizational Psychology. It is doubtful that there is any acceptance of the concepts in the relevant field.

The fifth of the Daubert criteria asserts that the methods for testing the theory must meet scientific standards. All of the attempts to validate the instruments discussed here use non-standard procedures. They confuse predictors and criteria, make unwarranted statistical adjustments to the data, try schemes of using experts to develop prototypes, and manipulate data to get desired results when all else fails. Finally, none of the studies have ever used a predictive validation design.

5. Common Characteristics of Advocates of "New" Intelligences

All of the new concepts, including emotional intelligence, tacit knowledge, practical intelligence, competencies and multiple intelligence have common themes throughout their theories and research.

5.1. All of the "New and Innovative" Theorists Use a Strawman Approach

These theorists start by claiming that cognitive ability is given too much weight and that other attributes are important in predicting job performance or life outcomes. They say that the correlation between cognitive ability and job performance is 0.20, which accounts for 4% of the variance, so 96% of the variance is unaccounted for (Ghiselli 1966; Goleman 1998b). Of course, not even the early theorists of intellectual ability (e.g. Spearman 1904) ever said that it was the sole determinant of success in life. Certainly, it is possible that personality traits, attitudes and values might add incremental validity to cognitive ability in predicting job performance. The problem still is one of obtaining relevant non-cognitive measures that do add incremental validity in predicting job performance (Barrett *et al.* 2001). Research concerning these new concepts has continually failed to show incremental validity of any of their measures over cognitive ability in predicting job performance.

Goleman (1998b) implies that emotional intelligence should have incremental validity over cognitive ability with statements such as "Paradoxically, IQ has the least power in predicting success among that pool of people smart enough to handle the most cognitively demanding fields, and the value of emotional intelligence for success grows more powerful the higher the intelligence barriers for entry into a field. In MBA programs or in careers like engineering, law, or medicine, where professional selection focuses almost exclusively on intellectual abilities, emotional intelligence carries much more weight than IQ in determining who emerges as a leader". Goleman also relies on anecdotes (e.g. p. 22) in which two people have high ability, but what determines success is their emotional intelligence. Despite Goleman's claims and anecdotes, he provides absolutely no data to show the incremental validity of EQ tests.

Even personality measures, which Goleman cites as a scientific basis for emotional intelligence have failed to demonstrate incremental validity. It is doubtful that newly developed personality-based measures (i.e. emotional intelligence) will be able to find incremental validity where decades of research have failed. Goleman stated that emotional intelligence is based on 5 elements: self-awareness, motivation, self-regulation, empathy and adeptness in relationships. Each of these are non-cognitive constructs that have been researched elsewhere, and he relies on personality based research to support his propositions. For example, he cites research on early career self-confidence in predicting promotions and success in later career (Howard & Bray 1988), and longitudinal research on high-IQ individuals that found those most self-confident in their early career were most successful in their later career. This is consistent with Goleman's description of the essence of emotional intelligence, that "the new measure takes for granted having enough intellectual ability and technical know-how to do our jobs; it focuses instead on personal qualities, such as initiative and empathy, adaptability and persuasiveness" (p. 3). Goleman also describes Spencer and Spencer's (1993) research by saying that the need to achieve was found to be the strongest competence that distinguished star from average executives. Again, he is using this to say that among top level executives, achievement drive is what distinguishes among level of performance. No evidence is presented to support the incremental validity of emotional intelligence over cognitive ability in predicting performance. The majority of Goleman's evidence for the importance of empathy for superior job performance comes in anecdotal form (pp. 133–162). He also relies on Spencer & Spencer's (1993) work to say that developing others (sensing others' development needs and bolstering their abilities) was paramount to sales' manager performance because it was the competence most frequently found by top performers in the field. Again, this evidence is in no way a validation study following professional and legal guidelines, and none of the 286 studies reviewed by Spencer and Spencer were published in peer review journals. The ability to regulate oneself and effectively interact with others is part of Goleman's definition of emotional intelligence. A study conducted by Stewart & Carson (1995) was used by Goleman as an example of the importance of this trait. This study found that extraversion was negatively related to job performance. Extraversion is one of the Big Five factors of personality, which have been studied extensively as predictors of job performance.

Table 19.10 illustrates the lack of evidence that personality provides incremental validity over cognitive ability.

Many people cite Schmidt & Hunter (1998) in order to demonstrate an alternative selection procedure exists that is both valid and results in incremental validity over cognitive ability: personality (specifically conscientiousness and integrity). However, Schmidt & Hunter (1998) rely on simulations, not actual validity studies, so this cannot be used as evidence of incremental validity. This article is also often misinterpreted as a meta-analysis, which is untrue.

One of the few studies to empirically demonstrate incremental validity was Day & Silverman (1989). Day and Silverman found that interpersonal orientation had incremental validity over cognitive ability in predicting cooperation and a global job performance measure, and that ascendancy had incremental validity over cognitive ability in predicting potential for success. However, the manner of computing these personality variables was unusual. An individual's score on interpersonal orientation was calculated by subtracting the sum of two subscale scores from the sum of four other subscale scores. No definitions of the constructs themselves were given, nor have Day and Silverman's results ever been cross-validated. Finally, most of the studies presented in Table 19.10 tend "stack the deck" when looking for a personality trait that will result in incremental validity. These studies, as is often the case in practice, correlate all personality traits in a measure with job performance and then use only those that correlate in the regression equation. This is contrary to a rational model of test development where constructs are defined, specific hypotheses are made, and those hypotheses are tested. Despite claims and anecdotal evidence that new measures will have incremental validity, there is simply no empirical evidence.

5.2. Research of Dubious Relevance is Cited to Add Legitimacy to Their "New" Concepts

Often these researchers interpret research results directly opposite to actual findings (Barrett 1994), leave out of their discussion any positive results for cognitive ability, cite unpublished research they claim supports their viewpoint, which is often unattainable, and ignore early research on the topic.

Cherniss (2000) used a longitudinal study completed by Snarey & Valliant (1985) to assert that IQ has little relationship with how well people do at work. However, the authors of the study said that ". . . whenever intelligence is included among the variables, it emerges as a more significant factor than social or personality measures". Cherniss (2000) was simply wrong in his interpretation of the Snarey & Valliant (1985) article.

The most egregious case of citing inaccurate evidence is Goleman, who cites hundreds of articles in professional literature to support his propositions. In examining these studies, we found that he was often factually incorrect in his reporting. For

Table 19.10: Incremental validity of personality measures over cognitive ability tests for predicting performance in published studies.

Study	Sample	Predictor(s)	Criterion	R^2	ΔR^2
Allworth & Hesketh (2000)	245 Hotel employees	**Cognitive ability** • Raven's Progressive Matrices • Ball Clerical Speed and Accuracy Test • Numerical Reasoning Test	Supervisor ratings of job performance	0.0729	—
		Goldberg Agreeableness, Conscientiousness and Extroversion		0.1225	0.0496
Arneson *et al.* (1993)	50 insurance claims examiners	Claims Examiner Inventory and Basic Skills Test	Overall performance	0.35	—
		Hogan Personality Inventory and PROFILE		0.41	0.06
Black (2000)	284 New Zealand police recruits	**Cognitive ability**	Overall performance on practical and academic tests	0.11	—
		NEO-PI-R Conscientiousness		0.17	0.06
Cortina *et al.* (1992)[a]	314 State police recruits	Civil service exam	Supervisor final training ratings of recruits	0.16	—
		Inwald Personality Inventory		0.20	0.04
Crant (1995)	146 real estate agents	**General mental ability**	Job performance (houses sold, listings generated and commission income)	0.129	—
		NEO-FFI Conscientiousness		0.130	0.001
Day & Silverman (1989)	43 accountants	Wesman	Global composite of Potential for Success, Technical Ability, Timeliness of Work, Client Relations and Cooperation	0.019	—
		GPA		0.082	0.063
		Interpersonal Orientation (Positive weight in regression equation) Interpersonal Orientation was composed of: (affiliation + nurturance + degree of exhibition + social recognition) — (aggression + defendence)			
		Ascendancy (Negative weight in regression equation) Ascendancy was composed of: (dominance — abasement)		0.231	0.034
		Work Orientation (Positive Weight in regression equation) Work Orientation was composed of: (achievement + endurance) — play		0.259	0.028

Table 19.10: Continued.

Study	Sample	Predictor(s)	Criterion	R^2	ΔR^2
Fetzer *et al.* (2001)	152 customer service managers	**Reasoning Ability**	Performance Appraisal composite	0.027	—
		Personal Characteristics Inventory — Agreeableness		0.051	0.024
		Reasoning Ability	Interpersonal performance	0.030	—
		Personal Characteristics Inventory — Agreeableness		0.049	0.019
		Numeric Ability	Interpersonal performance	0.020	—
		Personal Characteristics Inventory — Agreeableness		0.039	0.019
		Numeric Ability	Integrity-type performance	0.046	
		Personal Characteristics Inventory — Agreeableness		0.062	0.016
Gellatly *et al.* (1991)	114 food-service organization unit managers	Personnel Assessment Form (PAF)	Overall supervisor ratings	0.004	—
		Personality Research Form-E (PRF-E) Self Reliant		0.107	0.103
Hattrup *et al.* (1998)	103 entry-level customer service and sales representatives	**Cognitive ability**	Sales performance	0.0961	—
		Conscientiousness (O'Connell 1994)		0.0970	0.0009
Jackson *et al.* (2000)	187 security officers	**Cognitive ability tests**	Standardized incident report score	0.57	—
		Jackson Personality Inventory-Revised Dependability		0.58	0.01
McHenry *et al.* (1990)	4,039 soldiers in nine army jobs	**General Cognitive Ability (ASVAB)**	Core Technical Proficiency	0.63	—
		Temperament/Personality composite computed from ABLE (Achievement Orientation, Dependability, Adjustment & Physical Condition)		0.63	0.00

Table 19.10: Continued.

Study	Sample	Predictor(s)	Criterion	R^2	ΔR^2
Mount *et al.* (1999)	146 civilian U.S. Army Managers	Wonderlic Personality Test	Supervisor ratings	0.029	—
		Personal Characteristics Inventory Conscientiousness		0.084	0.055
	103 sales representatives	Wonderlic Personality Test		0.04	—
		Personal Characteristics Inventory Conscientiousness		0.105	0.065
	121 district managers	Wonderlic Personality Test		0.058	—
		Personal Characteristics Inventory Conscientiousness		0.122	0.064
Mount *et al.* (2000)	376 clerical employees	**Wonderlic Personnel Test**	Quantity/Quality	0.02	—
		Personal Characteristics Inventory (Conscientiousness, Extraversion, Agreeableness, Openness, Emotional Stability)		0.136	0.116
		Wonderlic Personnel Test	Problem Solving	0.047	—
		Personal Characteristics Inventory (Conscientiousness, Extraversion, Agreeableness, Openness, Emotional Stability)		0.168	0.121
		Wonderlic Personnel Test	Interpersonal Relationships	0.001	—
		Personal Characteristics Inventory (Conscientiousness, Extraversion, Agreeableness, Openness, Emotional Stability)		0.051	0.049
		Wonderlic Personnel Test	Retention	0.002	—
		Personal Characteristics Inventory (Conscientiousness, Extraversion, Agreeableness, Openness, Emotional Stability)		0.080	0.078
Neuman & Wright (1999) (individual level data)	316 HR representatives	**Skills (Checking & Forms Completion) and Cognitive ability**	Peer ratings of task performance	0.12	—
		NEO-PI-R Conscientiousness and Agreeableness		0.20	0.08
Neuman & Wright (1999) (group level data)	79 four-person work teams	**Skills (Checking & Forms Completion) and Cognitive ability**	Supervisor ratings of task performance	0.28	—
		NEO-PI-R Conscientiousness and Agreeableness		0.36	0.08

Table 19.10: Continued.

Study	Sample	Predictor(s)	Criterion	R^2	ΔR^2
Oakes *et al.* (2001)	9,793 Air Traffic Controller trainees	**Cognitive ability**	Skill acquisition	0.039	—
		16PF (Q2, N, M, Q1, A, E, F, B, I, G, O, Q3 Factors)		0.041	0.002
Siem (1992)	325 Air Force Pilot Trainees	Battery without Automated Aircrew Personality Profiler (AAPP) (Air Force Officer Qualifying Test and Basic Attributes Tests only)	Training success	0.29	—
		Full model (AAPP included)		0.33	0.04

[a] Cortina *et al.* (1992) stated that "the incremental validity of one inventory over the other is not assessed . . . Analyses with the IPI entered before and after the MMPI were conducted. Because these analyses took up valuable space and added little information to those that are now presented, they were removed".

example, he cites McClelland's research to show that EIQ is more important than cognitive ability tests (Goleman 1998a). However, the results of that study showed that cognitive ability correlated 0.32 for Foreign Service Officers and empathy correlated 0.11. In addition, Goleman (1998b) referred to a study completed by Boyatzis *et al.* (1990) when he said that team leaders who were trained in team leadership competencies later had higher morale and had cut product development time by 30%. However, Boyatzis *et al.* stated that while the training in team leadership competencies clarified leadership it did not necessarily help with lack of management skills.

Goleman (1998a) also exhibited some selective reporting by not citing relevant articles that don't support his claims, including results that show cognitive ability as the best predictor (Crant 1995; Daniel 1992; Davis & Kraus 1997; Holahan *et al.* 1995). These articles consistently showed that intellectual functioning is a better predictor than concepts such as interpersonal trust, machiavellianism, personality and self-confidence. Sternberg has also ignored evidence contradicting his theories. Colonia-Willner (1998) found that the TKIM did not predict job performance. However, this study has been completely ignored by Sternberg (2001, 2002), as it does not support his theory that tacit knowledge should predict job performance.

5.3. Reinventing the Wheel and Ignoring Contradictory Evidence

Much of the literature on these creative concepts of intelligence uses old concepts without acknowledging their historical basis. As early as 1904, Spearman had measurement tools for academic intelligence and common sense. Certainly, Sternberg and Wagner's practical intelligence is not a new concept. While Spearman believed that common sense was highly related to general cognitive ability, this did not preclude

Sternberg and Wagner from asserting, with little or no evidence, that this is a separate concept.

In a similar fashion, competencies were used in industrial psychology tests as early as the 1930s (Bingham 1937). The term competencies has no agreed upon definition yet they seem to be no more than what has been called Knowledge, Skills, Abilities and Other characteristics (KSAOs) (Barrett 2000). There is no way to distinguish what have been referred to as abilities and what are now referred to as competencies. In 1995, abilities were defined as "an underlying characteristic of the person that leads to or causes superior or effective performance" (Boyatzis *et al.* 1995). Competencies were then defined in exactly the same way in a 1996 article (Boyatzis 1996). Such researchers did not acknowledge Daniel's (1992) published study examining leadership competencies of supervisors at an electronics company. In fact, the term competencies has been around for 60 years, first used by Walter Van Dyke Bingham in 1937. The new theorists have just recycled an old term without acknowledging the original researchers.

Social intelligence or emotional intelligence has been a subject of research since the 1920s. This line has continually faced the challenge of developing an operational definition and establishing validity of its use in predicting job performance. In fact, the George Washington Social Intelligence Test had validity levels higher than emotional intelligence tests that have been developed in recent times (Hunt 1928).

There continues to be confusion in the definition of emotional intelligence. There are two ways to measure emotional intelligence: objective and self-report tests. Both forms of EIQ tests should be considered to be extensions of objective and self-report empathy tests. There is no reason to believe that the new tests of EIQ are measuring a new concept and they share the same problems with past personality tests. These problems include low reliability, low or no criterion-related validity, limited construct validity, easily faked and differential validity for broad versus narrow trait assessment (Barrett *et al.* 2001). While the use of ability based EIQ measures helps with the problem of faking, the reliability and validity are too low (Barrett *et al.* 2001). There may not even be a single emotional intelligence construct. Barrett *et al.* (2001) found that the concept of emotional intelligence may not be one single construct. Two of the subscales of EQ, Emotion Perception (Music) and Emotion Perception (Sound) were negatively correlated (–0.38) (Davies *et al.* 1998). Even the label originated earlier than is typically noted. Mayer *et al.* (1990) are often credited for coining the term emotional intelligence, when in fact Payne (1985, 1986) used the term in his dissertation five years earlier.

Gardner's (1983) Multiple Intelligences theory presented human intelligence as a set of intellectual potentials including linguistic, musical, logical-mathematical, spatial, bodily-kinesthetic, intrapersonal and interpersonal. These are proposed by Gardner to be distinct components of human intelligence. However, he does not cite Spearman (1904), who also included a musical component, pitch discrimination, in his studies on intelligence. Contrary to Gardner, Spearman found that pitch discrimination was not distinct from general mental ability and found evidence for one general factor of intelligence. We do not wish to take a stand on the matter of whether musical ability is distinct from general mental ability, but simply wish to point out that Gardner completely ignored evidence contrary to his theory that had been available for almost 80 years.

5.4. Research Has Used Unorthodox Validation Methods

Many of the studies cited by these innovative researchers involve measures which confuse the independent variable (i.e. the predictor) and the dependent variable of job performance. The most graphic example of this was the Wagner & Sternberg (1990) study performed at the Center for Creative Leadership. They used as a measure of job performance two simulations involving groups of subjects interacting on a business problem. The performance of managers in the simulation were rated on nine dimensions. These simulations are routinely used in assessment centers to predict present or subsequent job performance. By a slight of hand, Wagner and Sternberg have turned performance on a predictor into job performance.

5.5. They Use Complex, Unorthodox, Usually Changing Methods to Score Tests

The evidence for competency testing, practical intelligence, and tacit knowledge all use unusual scoring procedures for their predictors. There are obvious problems with their expert prototype scoring and simulation approaches. One is that the "Psychological Corporation recommends that each organization conduct local validation studies to determine the job relatedness of TKIM" (Wagner & Sternberg 1991). Few organizations have the resources to complete a criterion related, concurrent validation study every time they want to use a valid selection test. The point is that there are no universal right answers with the Tacit Knowledge Inventory and the correct answers depend upon expert groups used in any one organization, in contrast to cognitive ability tests. In *Fink v. Finegan* (1936), the basic principles of a competitive examination procedure were outlined. These principles included having an objective standard or measure that is capable of being challenged and reviewed by other experts in the area, and there must be definite standards. It is clear from our review that the TKIM cannot be used in civil service testing because it does not meet the requirements of a competitive examination. This is true in every jurisdiction. Competitive examinations require that there be an effective competition among candidates. It also means that the test must be as objective as possible. This is impossible with the TKIM. Wagner & Sternberg (1991) pointed out that "there are no right or wrong answers for the response alternatives; the scoring is based on the amount of agreement between experts and applicants" (p. 23). Therefore, the measure will not satisfy the requirements of a competitive examination.

In addition, the distinction between concurrent and predictive validation designs is not well understood. Barrett *et al.* (1981) are often cited as evidence that validity coefficients obtained under concurrent and predictive designs tend to be similar. With non-cognitive tests, however, validity coefficients obtained using a predictive design are generally lower compared to validities obtained using a concurrent design (Hough 1998; Ones *et al.* 1993). The studies cited to support the use of specific intelligences are not based on predictive designs.

An additional problem with the TKIM is that there has been no cross-validation of the items. In the manual, Wagner & Sternberg (1991) state that there are 12 scenarios, each with 9 to 20 items. This means that there were over 120 items in the original TKIM, however, only 39 are reported to be significant. The alpha of these items is only 0.68, which is too low for use in individual selection. The process used to validate this test is similar to that used for BIBs (Biographical Information Blanks), which capitalizes on chance.

5.6. Ignore Professional and Legal Standards for Initial Selection and Promotion

The literature on these "creative" concepts of intelligence never refer to the U.S. professional and legal guidelines because they violate them. In our review of validation studies of actual incumbents or candidates, we did not find one study which met professional standards from any of these novel researchers. For example, Bar-On (1997) inappropriately used two studies (Handley 1997; Wagner & Morse 1975) to attempt to show the validity of his Emotional Quotient Inventory (EQ-I). One of the studies (Handley 1997) was an unpublished study in an Air Force Newsletter that only reported mean differences and did not report validity coefficients. In addition, the U.S. GAO stated that it is too early to evaluate its effectiveness (U.S. GAO 1998). Wagner & Sternberg's (1991) concept of tacit knowledge has little evidence to support its validity. In fact, the Users Manual reports no evidence of validity and no studies that use job performance (Barrett *et al.* 2001). There isn't one study where there was a direct comparison of these theories with cognitive ability to determine relative or incremental validity.

The Uniform Guidelines (Equal Employment Opportunity Commission. (1979, p. 2253-24; question #74) state that "content validity is not appropriate where the selection procedure involves knowledges, skills, or abilities which the employee will be expected to learn 'on the job' . . . . However, if such an ability . . . takes a substantial amount of time to learn, is required for successful job performance, and is not taught to those initial hires who possess it in advance, a test for that ability may be supported on a content validity basis". That is, selection tests cannot test for information that could be learned on the job in a short amount of time. The TKIM manual states "TKIM is also an excellent tool for training and development . . . Training directors can lead group discussions that will elaborate on the practical know-how and "rule of thumb" that underlie the expert managers' ratings" (Wagner & Sternberg 1991). This is an admission that whatever the TKIM measures can be trained in a short time and is therefore inappropriate to be used as a selection device. The test contains various work-related situations and items relevant to handling those situations. For example, one of the situations is a role play in which the vice-president of an electronics company needs to decide what to do about the company losing market share. These items do not display adequate coverage of performance on the job. The TKIM contains no content valid items.

A problem with competencies is that there are no empirical studies that show competencies are valid. Spencer & Spencer (1993) stated that criterion validity was the most important aspect of assessing a selection instrument. They also state that predictive validation studies are superior to other forms of validation. However, they provide no predictive validity evidence to support the use of competencies. While Spencer and

Spencer do claim that they have shown that competencies have predictive validity, they have confused validation studies with pilot studies. The use of very small sample sized precludes the use of any type of meaningful analyses (Schmidt *et al.* 1976).

5.7. *Claim Their Approach Will Have Superior Validity to CATs With No Adverse Impact*

All of the "novel" researchers claim that their new measures of competencies, emotional intelligence, practical intelligence and tacit knowledge have lower adverse impact when predicting job performance. There are three problems with this contention. First, there are very few examples, if any, demonstrating that any of these constructs actually predict job performance in real organizations. Second, we could find no evidence based on studies in any organization that these measures reduce adverse impact. Third, even when one considers personality tests, the alternative selection tests most researched as a means to reduce adverse impact, there is no conclusive evidence that a consistent reduction in adverse impact occurs. In fact, there is evidence that the use of a personality test in addition to a cognitive ability test may produce larger mean group differences than the use of a cognitive ability test alone (Kriska 2001). This result is a function of the correlation between predictors in the composite and the mean differences between races on the alternative test (Schmitt *et al.* 1997). In other words, a general statement that the introduction of a personality test to a cognitive ability test will result in a decrease in adverse impact cannot be made. A more accurate statement would be to say that in *some* cases, the use of personality tests in conjunction with ability tests *may* reduce adverse impact, but that in other cases it may in fact increase adverse impact. Therefore, even if there were empirical examples of these newer intelligence constructs' ability to predict job performance or produce less adverse impact than a traditional ability test, this would still not provide evidence of their ability to do so in a composite selection battery with a cognitive ability test.

References

Adams v. City of Chicago 1996 U.S. Dist. LEXIS 3567 (N.D. Ill. 1996)

Allworth, E., & Hesketh, B. (2000). Job requirements biodata as a predictor of performance in customer service roles. *International Journal of Selection and Assessment, 8*, 137–147.

American College of Trial Lawyers (1994, April 15). *Standards and procedures for determining the admissibility of expert evidence after Daubert.*

American Educational Research Association, American Psychological Association, National Council on Measurement in Education (1999). *Standards for educational and psychological testing.* Washington, D.C.: American Educational Research Association.

Arneson, S., Millikin-Davies, M., & Hogan, J. (1993). Validation of personality and cognitive measures for insurance claims examiners. *Journal of Business and Psychology, 7*, 459–473.

Bachman, J., Stein, S., Campbell, K., & Sitarenios, G. (2000). Emotional intelligence in the collection of debt. *International Journal of Selection and Assessment, 8*, 176–182.

Bar-On, N. (1997). *Bar-On emotional quotient inventory: Technical manual.* Toronto, ON: Multi-Health Systems, Inc.

Bar-On, R. (2000). Emotional and social intelligence: Insights from the Emotional Quotient Inventory. In: R. Bar-On, & J. D. A. Parker (Eds), *The handbook of emotional intelligence: Theory, development, assessment, and application at home, school, and in the workplace* (pp. 363–388). San Francisco, CA: Jossey-Bass.

Barrett, G. V. (1994). Empirical data say it all. *American Psychologist, 49* (1), 69–71.

Barrett, G. V. (2000, April). Recommended educational experience to prepare an I/O psychologist to be an expert witness. In: D. Zink (Chair), *Implications of legal developments.* Symposium conducted at the 15th annual meeting of the Society for Industrial and Organizational Psychologists, New Orleans, LA.

Barrett, G. V., Miguel, R. F., Tan, J. A., & Hurd, J. M. (2001, April). *Emotional Intelligence: The Madison Avenue approach to science and professional practice.* Presented at the 16th annual meeting of the Society for Industrial and Organizational Psychology, San Diego, CA.

Barrett, G. V., Phillips, J. S., & Alexander, R. A. (1981). Concurrent and predictive validity designs: A critical reanalysis. *Journal of Applied Psychology, 66,* 1–6.

Bingham, W. V. D. (1937). *Aptitudes and aptitudes testing.* New York: Harper & Brothers.

Black, J. (2000). Personality testing and police selection: Utility of the "big five". *New Zealand Journal of Psychology, 29,* 2–9.

Black v. Rhone-Poulenc, Inc. 19 F. Supp. 2d 592 (S.D.W. Va. 1998).

Boyatzis, R. E. (1994). Rendering unto competence the things that are competent. *American Psychologist, 49* (1), 64–66.

Boyatzis, R. E. (1996). Consequences and rejuvenation of competency-based human resource and organization development. *Research in Organizational Change and Development, 9,* 101–122.

Boyatzis, R. E., Cowen, S. S., & Kolb, D. A. (Eds) (1995). *Innovation in professional education.* San Francisco: Jossey-Bass.

Boyatzis, R. E., Esteves, M. R., & Spencer, L. M. (1990). Entrepreneurial innovation in pharmaceutical research and development. *Human Resource Planning, 15* (4), 15–29.

Brown v. City of Chicago, 917 F. Supp. 577 (N.D. Ill. 1996).

Brown v. City of Chicago, 8 F. Supp. 2d 1095 (N.D. Ill. 1998).

Butler v. Home Depot, Inc., 984 F.Supp. 1257 (N.D. Cal. 1997).

Camp v. Lockheed Martin Corporation, U.S. Dist. LEXIS 20750 (S.D. Tex. 1998).

Carrothers, R. M., Gregory, S. W., & Gallagher, T. J. (2000). Measuring emotional intelligence of medical school applicants. *Academic Medicine, 751,* 456–463.

Cherniss, C. (2000, April). Emotional intelligence: What it is and why it matters. In: R. C. Page (Chair), *Competency models and emotional intelligence: Are they useful constructs?* Symposium conducted at the annual meeting of the Society for Industrial and Organizational Psychology, New Orleans, LA.

Clark v. Takata Corp. 192 F. 3d 750 (7th Cir. 1999).

Colonia-Willner, R. (1998). Practical Intelligence at work: Relationship between aging and cognitive efficiency among managers in a bank environment. *Psychology and Aging, 13* (1), 45–57.

Cooper, H. (1979). Statistically combining independent studies. A meta-analysis of sex differences in conformity research. *Journal of Personality and Social Psychology, 37*(1), 131–176.

Cortina, J. M., Doherty, M. L., Schmitt, N., Kaufman, G., & Smith, R. G. (1992). The "big five" personality factors in the IPI and MMPI: Predictors of police performance. *Personnel Psychology, 45,* 119–140.

Crant, J. M. (1995). The proactive personality scale and objective job performance among real estate agents. *Journal of Applied Psychology, 80,* 532–537.

Holahan, C. K., Sears, R. R., & Cronbach, L. J. (1995). *The gifted group in later maturity.* Stanford, CA: Stanford University Press.

Daniel, T. L. (1992). Identifying critical leadership competencies of manufacturing supervisors in a major electronics corporation. *Group and Organization Management, 17* (1), 57–71.

Daubert v. Merrell Dow Pharmeceuticals, 509 U.S. 579 (1993).

Davies, M., Stankov, L., & Roberts, R. D. (1998). Emotional intelligence: In search of an elusive construct. *Journal of Personality and Social Psychology, 75* (4), 989–1015.

Davis, M. H., & Kraus, L. A. (1997). Personality and emphathic accuracy. In: W. Ickes (Ed.). *Emphathic Accuracy* (pp. 144–168). New York: Guilford Press.

Day, D. V., & Silverman, S. B. (1989). Personality and job performances: Evidence of incremental validity. *Personnel Psychology, 42* (1), 25–36.

Edwards, J. R. (1994). The study of congruence in organizational behavior research: Critique and a proposed alternative. *Organizational Behavior & Human Decision Processes, 58* (1), 51–100.

Equal Employment Opportunity Commission. (1978). Uniform guidelines on employee selection procedures. *Federal Register, 43* (166), 38290–38315.

Equal Employment Opportunity Commission. (1979). Adoption of questions and answers to clarify and provide a common interpretation of the uniform guidelines on employee selection procedure. *Federal Register, 44* (43), 11996–12009.

Equal Employment Opportunity Commission. (1980). Adoption of additional questions and answers to clarify and provide a common interpretation of the uniform guidelines on employee selection procedure. *Federal Register, 45* (87), 29530–29531.

Feist, G. J., & Barron, F. (1996, June). *Emotional intelligence and academic intelligence in career and life success.* Paper presented at the annual convention of the American Psychological Society, San Francisco, CA.

Fetzer, M. S., Fortunato, V. J., Kudisch, J. D., & Eidson, C. E. Jr. (2001). *Predictive and incremental validity in a customer service setting.* Poster presented at the 16th annual conference of the Society for Industrial and Organizational Psychology, San Diego, CA.

Fink v. Finegan (1936) 270 N. Y. 356.

Firefighters Institute for Racial Equality v. City of St. Louis 2000 U.S. App. LEXIS 19191 (8th Cir. 2000).

Gardner, H. (1983). *Frames of mind: The theory of multiple intelligences.* New York: Basic Books, Inc.

Gardner, H. (1999). *Intelligence Framed: Multiple intelligences for the 21st Century.* New York: Basic Books.

Gellatly, I. R., Paunonen, S. V., Meyer, J. P., Jackson, D. N., & Goffin, R. D. (1991). Personality, vocational interest, and cognitive predictors of managerial job performance and satisfaction. *Personality and Individual Differences, 12,* 221–231.

General Electric Company v. Joiner, 522 U.S. 136 (1997).

Gerlib v. R. R. Donnelley & Sons Co. 2001 U.S. Dist. LEXIS 17879 (N.D. Ill. 2001).

Ghiselli, E. E. (1966). *The validity of occupational aptitude tests.* New York: John Wiley & Sons, Inc.

Goleman, D. (1995). *Emotional Intelligence.* New York: Bantam Books.

Goleman, D. (1998a). What makes a leader? *Harvard Business Review, 76* (6), 92–102.

Goleman, D. (1998b). *Working with emotional intelligence.* New York: Bantam Books.

Gottfredson, L. S. (in press). Dissecting practical intelligence theory: Its claims and evidence. *Intelligence.*

Graves, J. G. (1999). Emotional intelligence and cognitive ability: Predicting performance in job-simulated activities. (Doctoral dissertation, California School of Professional Psychology, San Diego 1999). *Dissertation Abstracts International, 60* (5-B), 2398.

Handley, R. (1997). *Leveraging corporate performance through human capital profiling.* Unpublished manuscript.

Hattrup, K., O'Connell, M. J., & Wingate, P. H. (1998). Prediction of multidimensional criteria distinguishing task & contextual performance. *Human Performance, 11,* 305–319.

Holahan, C. K., & Sears, R. R., & Cronbach, L. J. (1995). *Self-confidence in high-IQ people and career success. The gifted group in later maturity.* Stanford: Stanford University Press.

Hough, L. M. (1998). Personality at work. In: M. Hakel (Ed.), *Beyond multiple choice: Evaluating alternatives and traditional testing for selection* (pp. 131–159). Hillsdale, NJ: Erlbaum.

Howard, A., & Bray, D. W. (1988). Self-confidence early in career predicts success later at AT&T. *Managerial lives in transition.* New York: Guilford Press.

Hunt, T. (1928). The measurement of social intelligence. *Journal of Applied Psychology, 12,* 317–334.

Hunter, J. E. (1986). Cognitive ability, cognitive aptitudes, job knowledge, and job performance. *Journal of Vocational Behavior, 29,* 340–362.

Hunter, J. E., & Hunter, R. F. (1984). Validity and utility of alternative predictors of job performance. *Psychological Bulletin, 96* (1), 72–98.

Jackson, D. N., Harris, W. G., Ashton, M. C., McCarthy, J. M., & Tremblay, P. F. (2000). How useful are work samples in validation studies? *International Journal of Selection and Assessment, 8,* 29–33.

Kriska, S. D. (2001, April). The validity-adverse impact trade-off: Real data and mathematical model estimates. In: J. P. Wiesen (Chair), *Reducing adverse impact while maintaining validity: The public sector experience.* Symposium conducted at the 16th annual conference of the Society for Industrial and Organizational Psychology, San Diego, CA.

Kumho Tire Company, Ltd. v. Carmichael, 526 U.S. 137 (1999).

Malouff, J., & Schutte, N. (1998). *Emotional intelligence scale scores predict counselor performance.* Paper presented at the Annual Convention of the American Psychological Society, Washington, D.C.

Mayer, J. D., DiPaolo, M., & Salovey, P. (1990). Perceiving affective content in ambiguous visual stimuli: A component of emotional intelligence. *Journal of Personality Assessment, 54* (3&4), 772–781.

Mayer, J. D., Salovey, P., & Caruso, D. (1999). *MSCEIT V. 2: The Mayer, Salovey, & Caruso Emotional Intelligence Test technical manual, Version 2: Mockup draft of 1st edition, July 28 2000.* Toronto, ON: Multi-Health Systems.

McClelland, D. C. (1973). Testing for competence rather than for "intelligence". *American Psychologist, 28* (1), 1–14.

McClelland, D. C., & Dailey, C. (1972). *Improving officer selection for the Foreign Service.* Boston, MA: Hay/McBer.

McClelland, D. C., & Dailey, C. (1973). *Evaluating new methods of measuring the qualities needed in superior Foreign Service Officers.* Boston: McBer.

McCornack, R. L. (1956). A criticism of studies comparing item-weighting methods. *Journal of Applied Psychology, 40* (5), 343–344.

McHenry, J. J., Hough, L. M., Toquam, J. L., Hanson, M. A., & Ashworth, S. (1990). Project A validity results: The relationship between predictor and criterion domains. *Personnel Psychology, 43,* 335–354.

Mount, M. K., Barrick, M. R., & Strauss, J. P. (1999). The joint relationship of conscientiousness and ability with performance: Test of the interaction hypothesis. *Journal of Management, 25,* 707–721.

Mount, M. K., Witt, L. A., & Barrick, M. R. (2000). Incremental validity of empirically keyed biodata scales over GMA and the Five Factor personality constructs. *Personnel Psychology, 53,* 299–323.

Murensky, C. L. (2000). *The relationships between emotional intelligence, personality, critical thinking ability, and organizational leadership performance at upper levels of management.* Unpublished doctoral dissertation, George Mason University, Fairfax, VA.

Neuman, G. A., & Wright, J. (1999). Team effectiveness: Beyond skills and cognitive ability. *Journal of Applied Psychology, 84,* 376–389.

Oakes, D. W., Ferris, G. R., Martocchio, J. J., Buckley, M. R., & Broach, D. (2001). Cognitive ability and personality predictors of training program skill acquisition and job performance. *Journal of Business and Psychology, 15,* 523–548.

O'Connel, M. S. (1994). *Development and validation in Mexico of a conscientiousness scale.* Dallas, TX: Select International.

Ones, D. S., Viswesvaran, C., & Schmidt, F. (1993). Comprehensive meta-analysis of integrity test validities: Findings and implications for personnel selection and theories of job performance. *Journal of Applied Psychology, 78,* 679–703.

Payne, W. L. (1985/1986). A study of emotion: Developing emotional intelligence; self-integration; relating to fear, pain and desire (theory, structure of reality, problem-solving, contraction/expansion, tuning in/coming out/letting go). *Dissertation Abstracts International, 47* (1), 203A. (UMI No. 8605928).

Rice, C. L. (1999). *A quantitative study of emotional intelligence and its impact on team performance.* Unpublished master's thesis, Pepperdine University, Malibu, CA.

Rudder v. District of Columbia, 890 F. Supp. 23 (D.D.C. 1995).

Schmidt, F. L., & Hunter, J. E. (1981). Employment testing: Old theories and new research findings. *American Psychologist, 36,* 1128–1137.

Schmidt, F. L., & Hunter, J. E. (1998). The validity and utility of selection methods in personnel psychology: Practical and theoretical implications of 85 years of research findings. *Psychological Bulletin, 124,* 262–274.

Schmidt, F. L., Hunter, J. E., & Urry, V. W. (1976). Statistical power in criterion-related validation studies. *Journal of Applied Psychology, 61* (4), 473–485.

Schmitt, N., Rogers, W., Chan, D., Sheppard, L., & Jennings, D. (1997). Adverse impact and predictive efficiency of various predictor combinations. *Journal of Applied Psychology, 82* (5), 719–730.

Schutte, N. S., Malouff, J. M., Hall, L. E., Haggerty, D. J., Cooper, J. T., Golden, C. S., & Dornheim, L. (1998). Development and validation of a measure of emotional intelligence. *Personality and Individual Differences, 25*(2), 167–177.

Scribner, S. (1984). Studying working intelligence. In: B. Rogoff, & J. Lave (Eds), *Everyday cognition: Its development in social context* (pp. 9–40). Cambridge, MA: Harvard University Press.

Siem, F. M. (1992). Predictive validity of an automated personality inventory for Air Force pilot selection. *International Journal of Aviation Psychology, 2,* 261–270.

Smith v. Ford Motor Co., 215 F.3d 713 (7th Cir. 2000).

Snarey, J. R., & Vaillant, G. E. (1985). How lower- and working-class youth become middle-class adults: The association between ego defense mechanisms and upward social mobility. *Child Development, 56* (4), 899–910.

Society for Industrial and Organizational Psychology (1987). *Principles for the validation and use of personnel selection procedures* (3rd ed.). College Park, MD: Author.

Spearman, C. (1904). "General Intelligence" objectively determined and measured. *The American Journal of Psychology, 15*, 259–293.

Spearman, C. (1927). *The abilities of man: Their nature and measurement.* New York: Macmillan Co.

Spencer, L. M., & Spencer, S. M. (1993). *Competence at work: Models for superior performance.* New York: John Wiley & Sons.

Sternberg, R. J. (2001). Successful intelligence: Understanding what Spearman had rather than what he studied. In: J. M. Collis, & S. Messick (Eds), *Intelligence and Personality: Bridging the Gap in Theory and Measurement* (pp. 347–373). Mahwah, NJ: Lawrence Erlbaum.

Sternberg, R. J. (2002). Successful intelligence: A new approach to leadership. In: R. E. Riggio, S. E. Murphy, & F. J. Pirozzolo (Eds). *Multiple intelligences and leadership.* Mahway, NJ: Lawrence Erlbaum Associates.

Sternberg, R. J., & Wagner, R. K. (1986). *Practical intelligence: Nature and origins of competence in the everyday world.* New York: Cambridge University Press.

Stewart, G. L., & Carson, K. P. (1995). Personality dimensions and domains of service performance: A field investigation. *Journal of Business and Psychology, 9* (4), 365–378.

Thorndike, R. L. (1936). Factor analysis of social and abstract intelligence. *Journal of Educational Psychology, 27* (3), 231–233.

United States General Accounting Office. (1998, January). *Military recruiting: DOD could improve recruiter selection and incentive systems (GAO/NSIAD–98–58).* Washington, D.C.: U.S.GAO.

United States of America v. City of Garland, Texas, No. 3-98-CV-0307-L (N.D. Tex.). (2000).

Wagner, R. K. (1994). Context counts: the case of cognitive ability testing for job selection. In: R. J. Sternberg, & R. K. Wagner (Eds), *Mind in context: Interactionist perspectives on human intelligence* (pp. 133–151). New York: Cambridge University Press.

Wagner, F. R., & Morse, J. J. (1975). A measure of individual sense of competence. *Psychological Reports, 36*, 451–459.

Wagner, R. K., & Sternberg, R. J. (1985). Practical intelligence in real-world pursuits: the role of tacit knowledge. *Journal of Personality and Social Psychology, 49* (2), 436–458.

Wagner, R. K., & Sternberg, R. J. (1990). Street smarts. In: K. E. Clark, & M. B. Clark (Eds), *Measures of leadership* (pp. 493–504). West Orange, NJ: Leadership Library of America, Inc.

Wagner, R. K., & Sternberg, R. J. (1991). *TKIM. The common sense manager. Tacit Knowledge Inventory for Managers: User Manual.* The Psychological Corporation.

Williams, W. M., & Sternberg, R. J. (1988). Group intelligence: Why some groups are better than others. *Intelligence, 12*, 351–377.

Chapter 20

The Sociology of Psychometric and Bio-behavioral Sciences: A Case Study of Destructive Social Reductionism and Collective Fraud in 20th Century Academia

Helmuth Nyborg

1. Demonization

The history of science abounds with examples of scientists killed, exiled or demonized for presenting the right message at the wrong time or to the wrong people. A direct line thus connects the poisoning of Socrates with the public burning of Giordano Bruno, the Catholic Church's condemnation of Galileo's view, and the Spanish Inquisition's devilish torture chambers with The Soviet Union's classical geneticists having to fight for life against Central Party-dictated Lysenkoism. The present chapter updates this tragic history by telling a 20th century sociological story about the demonization of the psychometric and bio-behavioral sciences in general, and of Professor Emeritus Arthur R. Jensen from University of California at Berkeley in particular.

1.1. The Past

Religious, romantic, political, moral or idealistic reasons motivated most of the persecutions. The medieval Church demanded, for example, that early cartographers put the Garden of Eden at the head of their maps to cover "six-sevenths" of the Earth in land, in accordance with the Bible. The data-oriented Gerardus Mercator thought that this representation was not only inaccurate but also dangerously misleading to those who wanted to find their way. What is more — he had the courage to say so in 1544. He was accordingly imprisoned for heresy with the intent to burn him at the stake. Somewhat surprisingly, considering the Zeitgeist of the time, he was subsequently released for "lack of evidence" (Jenkins 2000).

The Scientific Study of General Intelligence: Tribute to Arthur R. Jensen
Copyright © 2003 by Elsevier Science Ltd.
All rights of reproduction in any form reserved.
ISBN: 0–08–043793–1

The leaders of the Amsterdam Jewish community forbade in 1656 any contact with the philosopher Baruch Spinoza with the following words: "Nobody shall have oral or written communication with him. Nobody shall help him. Nobody may come closer to him than four steps. And nobody may read anything published by him".

Voltaire publicly questioned the official wisdom of France, and subsequently faced personal persecution and exile. Not only was he found guilty in defending Descartes, Newton and Pascal in *Lettres Philosophiques*, but he also referred to France as frivolous, superstitious and reactionary, and contrasted it to England. He had to hide in Lorraine in 1734 as the Paris police set out to arrest him. Voltaire did not mince his words, and dryly concluded: "It is dangerous to be right in matters on which the established authorities are wrong". If he knew that much, then why did Voltaire touch the matters at all? He provided that answer himself: "If I had not stirred up the subject (e'gaye' la matie're), nobody would have been scandalized; but then nobody would have read me". There are some truths that are better known to everybody, but somebody has to tell them. Voltaire and Art Jensen are equals here.

The ruthless hounding of classical Soviet geneticists, who dared questioning the demonstrably false Lysenkoist view and thus challenging the wisdom of The Central Committee of the Communist Party, extended the deadly line of destructive social idealism well into the 20th century. It is not known exactly how many fell prey to communistic ideology, but some recent estimates count the numbers to about 100 million people. The Third Reich also persecuted artists and scientists, preferably Jewish, and killed, relatively speaking, roughly as many individuals as fell victim to communist ideology (about 10 million, but then allow for the shorter time frame for committing these horrible crimes against Humanity). Even if not immediately apparent, these two ideologies, the a-biological Communist and the mistaken race-biology based Nazi, had two very different but equally important roles to play in the demonization of psychometrics and the bio-behavioral sciences in the 20th century. The communist ideology impact was to make the blind leading the seeing, and the Nazi ideology impact was to make everybody blind, deaf and dumb to anything but Aryan supremacy. Both ideologies had a hostile attitude to counter-intuitive data.

While Eastern Europe has a long history of suppressing free speech and academic freedom, the West still sees itself as a prime example of individual and academic freedom, with the U.S. in the forefront. This chapter purports to document that this is a false and dangerous illusion, in need of revision.

The point will be illustrated in different ways, but the overall purpose is to expose the perpetrators, count the dreadful personal, academic and public consequences of this surprising and all-embracing example of a 20th century collective fraud, and to suggest a remedy. The chapter provides illustrations of what happened to western psychometricians, bio-behavioral scientists and behavior geneticists devoted to data that ran counter to preconceived theories or idealistic, moral or political ideas, but who were not afraid to "e'gaye' la matie're". The examples are mostly taken from what happened to Arthur R. Jensen, who had a formidable sharpness and the audacity to openly challenge the official and sacrosanct notions that social equality presupposes biological identity, and that social and racial malleability is without end. The price he paid was high indeed, but he never shook his hands, and that is his greatness.

1.2. Contemporary Demonization

Many members of the London School of Differential Psychology, to which Hans Eysenck and Arthur Jensen also belong, has been demonized in the 20th century. The British psychologist Cyril Burt was, for example, accused of fiddling with his data on the similarity of twins. Because Burt was a leading proponent of the idea that intelligence is largely heritable, this cause célèbre was quickly exploited by social reductionist critics to throw a deadly blow to the entire notion of inheritance of intelligence. Yet, both the previous and the later methodologically better studies of the heritability of intelligence have come up with figures that, on average, compare favorably with Burt's original numbers. What remains of substance of the much hailed defamatory attacks is that an ageing Burt probably was inexcusably careless with the presentation of his own data. The really interesting question has now changed to the question of why so many critics still find the Burt case a good reason to reject the entire notion of the major inheritance of intelligence in face of the fact that, once you remove all Burt's data and use only the updated and technically much better evidence, it does not change one iota of the conclusion that genes count for about 80% of the familial transmission of ~~genes for~~ intelligence in late adulthood (but seemingly much less in childhood!)

When the late Hans Eysenck succeeded Burt as a prominent member of the London School, he also got viciously attacked for a life-long promotion of the study of individual differences with a non-exclusive emphasis on the biological side of human nature (see Nyborg 1997). Ironically, his critics associated his biological interest with underlying Nazi sympathy. It apparently made no impression on critiques that Hans had to fly his native Germany after being beaten up by schoolmates for refusing to join the Hitlerjugend. He even dared to openly challenge his Nazi schoolteacher in class when they were told that Jews were inferior people. Young Hans loved data, so he simply went to the local library to collect evidence that Jewish soldiers were, on average, more highly decorated than other German soldiers fighting in the First World War. Eysenck was not a Jew himself — just an unusually intelligent and brave young man! This bravery found good use in his long-life defense of psychometrics and the biological basis of personality and intelligence. He had to endure physical attacks and personal harassment in countless ways, and to have his lectures blocked at home or abroad.

The late Raymond Cattell may be considered a special kind of member of the London School. He was shamefully denied reception at the last minute in 1997 of a medal for a lifetime achievement award in psychology, endorsed by The American Psychological Association. The initiative to withhold the medal came from Barry Mehler, who also proposed that the late Stanley Porteus should no longer give his name to Porteus Hall at the University of Hawaii (for a characterization of Mehler, see Weyher: xl–xliii, in Lynn 2001). Mehler seems to have devoted his entire career to attacks on psychometrics and bio-behavioral research, and he has repeatedly attacked the Pioneer Fund for racism (ibid.). This fund supported the research of some members of the London School, as well as scientists outside the circle. Chris Brand, a long-time tenured lecturer at Edinburgh University, was sacked, and had to endure that his 1996 book: *The g factor: General Intelligence and its Implications*, was "de-published" by Wiley. The publisher simply took the book off the shelf where it had been on for sale for 6 weeks. Philippe Rushton of University of Western Ontario, Canada, was very close to being sacked and persecuted for "hate speech", and was actually subjected to a criminal investigation, that ended with nothing. A publisher withdrew and destroyed 45,000 copies of an abridged 2000 edition of his *Race, evolution, and behavior*, originally published by Transaction Publishers. With characteristic stamina Rushton successfully countered all the wild accusations and kept on with his important work (see Chapter 9 in this volume). Thomas Bouchard from Minnesota University in the U.S., an internationally recognized specialist using twins to study the inheritance of intelligence and personality, has routinely been ferociously attacked over many years. So have sociologists Bob Gordon from Johns Hopkins University and Linda Gottfredson from the University of Delaware, and many others. Readers interested in the unworthy details of these rueful stories may like to consult Lynn (2001).

1.3. The Demonization of Arthur R. Jensen

The above examples were meant to illustrate the fact that anybody critical of the prevailing social reductionism was demonized during the past two thirds of the 20th century. The attacks came not only from individuals, but also from academic institutions, professional organizations and the public media.

However, the attacks took on a particularly nasty form in the case of Arthur Jensen — perhaps because he has this tremendous capacity to accumulate solid data and to derive clear implications. The rule of the attackers seems to be that the better the data, the more vicious will be the punishment. The 16th century treatment prescribed for Spinoza looks surprisingly alike the 20th century treatment given Arthur R. Jensen: Stay away from him! Don't believe him! Disrespect him! Don't read him! Stop him!

Luckily, all this made no impression on Art. He followed Voltaire's advice to "e'gaye' la matie're", and refined the measurement of general intelligence *g*, critically discussed individual and groups difference in *g*, and enquired into the inheritance of *g*. There is no doubt, had Art not "e'gaye'ed" "la matiere" we would probably today have missed the most reliable and broadest applicable general measure psychology has ever devised. That would have been a sad story for the individual, the group, society and for science.

2. Jensen — The Scientist

2.1. Introduction

Arthur Jensen is the perfect case for illustrating which, and how, particular sociological components go into a well-coordinated attack on academic freedom. First, he is an impeccable scientist — at least in the eyes of all experts in his field. Moreover, he was able to radically change his mind in accordance with new data about restrictions on human development, but he also continued to use the classical methodological tools of psychology. I will on this basis argue that it was not a change of methods, but rather a change of mind, that made him the prime target for countless vitriolic attacks for years to come. The change of mind transformed him, in the eyes of his critics, from being a brilliant educational scientist with a non-offensive mainstream view and a clear devotion to better the conditions for the disadvantaged, into being a bad researcher doing bad science, and that for evil motives.

I am fully aware that all this may sound a bit exaggerated or even somewhat paranoid. Below I will therefore be very specific about each of the above stated claims. I will first substantiate the claim that Arthur Jensen is widely acknowledged by colleagues in his specialist fields — educational psychology and psychometrics — as a *primus inter pares*, then, that he is a master of methodology, that he did not fiddle with the data, that his findings are mainstream, and that he has no racial inclinations whatsoever.

2.2. Jensen — The Impeccable Educational Psychologist

A recent special issue of *Intelligence* praises Jensen as a professional in the full meaning of that term and as a person with extraordinary qualities (Detterman, ed., 1998). In fact, a reference to a passage by Galton (1869: 24–25) — "Kings among Men" was used to characterize Jensen as "A King among Men". Moreover, no less than four of his books or journal articles have reached the status of citation classics — defined by the Institute for Scientific Information as works with an unusually high frequency of citations in the scientific and professional journals. He is the 47th most cited psychologist in the twentieth century, and 12th among the 19 still alive (Haggbloom *et al.* 2002). In other words, judged by his academic success and the accolades, Jensen is a prototype of a high-caliber professional.

2.3. Jensen — The Infamous

It is therefore puzzling to see that the same Detterman could state with great confidence in the same 1998 issue of *Intelligence*, that Arthur Jensen will never receive the honors he rightly deserves. To fully understand this we have to go back to one fatal day in 1969, when Jensen's professional and personal life suddenly changed almost overnight. The day before he was a young honorable scientist with a promising career. The next day he was an outcast, rightly deserving verbal and physical abuse. It even became acceptable to many scientists that Jensen and his family deserved to live with realistic life threats. Ongoing projects were compromised, teaching made difficult, his office had to be secured, and his presence at campus required the company of bodyguards for personal safety. While on campus, angry students would regularly shout in choir: "Professor Jensen is in sight — he is teaching genocide". Over the next 30 years he would experience again and again that invited lectures at other universities in several countries were blocked by angry demonstrators. On one occasion he actually had to run for his life under the protection of 50 police officers, only to escape after being locked up in a closet for hours, and then "rescued" from the "scene of crime". As late as in 1999 demonstrators made an attempt to disturb an invited lecture at Edinburgh University, and he had to return to the States after being obstructed in delivering the honorary "Galton Lecture" in London.

Threatened and ridiculed at a personal and professional level, he had to get used to seeing fearful politically correct professional organizations promote far less qualified colleagues to stardom in the academic and professional hierarchies. Not that I have ever heard Arthur Jensen express even the slightest personal interest in stardom, but even Jensen cannot get around the fact of academic life, that the ultimate measure of one's professional standing is reflected in the recognition by our colleagues. Jensen is indeed "a man that will never receive honors!" So, what is wrong with him?

2.4. Jensen's Methods, Data and Interpretation

Did Jensen really deserve the extreme punishment from colleagues, organizations and the public? Perhaps he began to use shaky methods way back in the late 1960s? This obviously is not the case. The methods he used before and also after 1969 are pretty much standard in psychology. In fact, Art is generally acknowledged as one of the methodologically most skilled professionals in his field. In addition to exploiting classical techniques he has developed new sophisticated tools (such as correlated vector analysis (Jensen 1998, Appendix B), and I am not aware of any serious critique of these.

Did he begin to fiddle with his data around 1969? Wrong again. In the hundreds of attacks on him one rarely finds any accusation of questionable data, and in the few actual cases I have yet to see an instance where the discrepancy could not be explained rationally.

It is, of course, quite common in the history of science to see individuals get ousted from the good company for producing far-off-mainstream findings. Did Jensen begin to get "unusual" or "unexpected" results after 1969? Not at all! All his main observations confirm what everybody else finds in the field using similar techniques. In fact, those who have had the good fortune of working closely with him know painfully well, that he is extremely careful (bordering on the pedantic, if I may say so, Art?) in accepting what counts as good methods, solid empirical data and sound interpretation. In that respect many of his critics do not match him by half. Even more interesting, there is now considerable consensus in professional circles with respect to most of Jensen's main conclusions — those he arrived at before, as well as those reached after 1969. Most of the basic problems he addressed can now be considered basically solved, and research can safely progress in new directions (Jensen 1998), which is precisely what Jensen, and many others with him, are busy doing right now.

2.5. Is Jensen a Racist?

In the *Harvard Educational Review* (*HER*) article Jensen (1969) began the section on Race Differences by stating: "The important distinction between the individual and the population must always be kept clearly in mind in any discussion of racial differences in mental abilities ... Whenever we select a person for some special educational purpose ... we are selecting an individual, and we are selecting him and dealing with him as an individual for reasons of his individuality ... The variables of social class, race, and national origin ... are irrelevant as a basis for dealing with individuals". Later Jensen writes: "Furthermore, since, as far as we know, the full range of human talents is represented in all the major races of man and in all socioeconomic levels, it is unjust to allow the mere fact of an individual's racial or social background to affect the treatment accorded to him. All persons rightfully must be regarded in the basis of their individual qualities and merits, and all social, educational, and economic institutions must have built into them the mechanisms for insuring and minimizing the treatment of persons according to their individual behavior".

This is hardly the view of a racist generalizing blindly and derogatorily across hundreds or thousands of individuals. Rather we see the fingerprints of a responsible and careful educational psychologist with an open eye for existing individual variation, irrespective of race. I will later go back to the puzzling question how on earth Jensen's critics could nevertheless accuse him of being driven by a contemptible, fundamentally racist attitude.

2.6. Is Jensen Opposing Racial Desegregation?

Could all the hate directed towards Jensen be partially a function of him opposing racial desegregation in schools? To the contrary, Jensen has always maintained the position of being opposed to segregated schools (e.g Jensen 1972: 51). He is concerned, however, that segregation takes place so that all children benefit from it, as racial balance in schools may not by itself solve existing educational problems. Educational diversity and desegregation need not be incompatible goals, he says, but ". . . ignoring individual differences in children's educational needs could be most destructive to those who are already the most disadvantaged educationally. The allocation of a school's resources for children with special educational problems cannot be influenced by race; it must be governed by individual needs. Making an association . . . between the "nature-nurture" question and the issue of racial desegregation of schools is, in my opinion, a most flagrant non sequitur". Again, this is hardly the view of a racist segregationist, but rather a balanced expression of concern for the disadvantaged, irrespective of color.

2.7. If Not Jensen — Then Who is to Blame?

If Jensen really is not to blame, then who is? Many of Jensen's opponents came from what can somewhat loosely be called the academic left (Gross & Levitt 1994/1998). My first tentative hypothesis was, accordingly, that the demonization of Jensen was a simple function of a predominantly academic left-wing dissatisfaction with the notion of a largely inherent human inequality in intelligence, threatening their honorable idea of basic solidarity with the poor. This quickly appeared to be much too narrow an analytic framework, even if the gusty impact of the academic left remained central in the auspices of an extended model (to be presented later).

3. A Simple Model for Demonization

3.1. Introduction

It gradually transpired that the full answer to the question of whom to blame for the demonization of Jensen, required nothing less than a full-scale analysis of all the sociological components that interacted to produce the war-like climate surrounding psychometric, differential psychology, behavioral genetics and the bio-behavioral sciences in general. The analysis required a focus going far beyond the left or right oriented ideologies of some of the combatants. It had to involve also the academic institutions and the public context in which it unfolded.

The analysis was accordingly divided into two parts, even if the overall purpose of the analysis was to expose the destructive play of social reductionism, amounting to a collective fraud, committed by surprisingly many academics and their organizations, by irresponsible universities, and by some professional and even cross-national organiza-tions, all seemingly guided by a debilitating political correctness ideology.

The deeper irony of all this is that the collective fraud seems originally planted by the academic left in order to promote human happiness and solidarity with the disadvantaged, but it ended up killing both of these honorable intentions, in addition to seriously threatening the academic freedom of individuals, and thereby the entire foundation of modern universities.

The first part of the analysis takes on a very specific form — that of a single case pseudo-experimental study, with a few independent variables and a mapping of the kind and level of demonization. The second part of the analysis, to be presented later, incorporates a number of semi-dependent variables that are useful for the full appreciation of the intricate pattern of collective fraud, spun in a worrisome unison by many parts of modern academia and the public. The variables will be defined as they are used, but a brief overview of all variables in the two-part study may help grasp the larger picture.

Jensen radically changed his mind in the late 1960s, and this change appears in the first analysis as an independent variable with two modes: one biologically neutral and uncontroversial, the second one biologically related and deeply offensive. The second independent variable in the first study pertains to major variations in the prevailing Zeitgeist in the 20th century, a parameter with 4 modes.

The remaining variables, introduced in the second stage of the analysis, include genes for a (in)flexible personality that make it difficult to change one's mind, religious beliefs, moral and ethic agendas, an idealized search for the "truth", a widespread fear of elitism, racism, sexism or inequality, a subjective craving for pedagogical optimism, an urgent need for scientific recognition among peers, the explicit or implicit moral objectives of funding by organizations, public media ideologies, the desire for being political correct and, finally, the implicitly or explicitly stated purposes of political, professional and academic programs.

It is a fact that there is no simple co-variation among these many inter-dependent variables. Sometimes they act mainly in isolation to restrain individual academic freedom, sometimes synergistically, or they may even interact non-linearly — possibilities that obviously do not facilitate an effect analysis.

3.2. Independent Variables in the First Part of the Analysis

3.2.1. The two Arthur Jensen decision modes The first decision mode is a pre-1969 mainstream science nurture mode with uncontroversial implications. The second is a post-1969 nature mode with controversial implications.

In the first mode Jensen concentrated on laboratory research and theoretical problems, involving university undergraduates and serial rote learning problems, a topic as far removed as one could get from the focus of his later 1969 HER article on IQ, achievement, race and genetics. Then, in the mid-1960s Jensen decided to radically change his mind. This section maps the purely empirical reasons for the change, and demonstrates that it had nothing to do with subconscious or preconceived attitudes.

Jensen entertains the personal philosophy that even if a scientist is mostly interested in theory he/she should try and bring this expertise to bear on practical problems whenever needed. Therefore, when a school psychologist asked him to point out a good culture-free or culture-fair test that would work for children diagnosed as educationally mentally retarded (EMR) Jensen — as the helpful person he always is — accepted the challenge. He first did some empirical work to empirically confirm the school psychologist's suspicion that available tests were quite valid for white middle-class children but did not work well for minority lower-class children. Despite an IQ of 75 or lower, EMR children did not seem nearly as retarded as the white middle-class children with comparable IQs. Thus, when compared to white middle-class children with similarly low IQ, they appeared much brighter socially as well as in playful interactions. Jensen began to wonder whether it was possible to devise a testing procedure to bring this phenomenon under closer scrutiny. The first step was to ponder whether most IQ tests actually assessed prior learning outside the test room, where minority children obviously might be culturally disadvantaged. Next step was to develop various "direct learning tests" that measured the rate of learning, something new in the test room. In this phase of clarification, Jensen realized that culturally disadvantaged EMR children from low socioeconomic status (SES) homes performed much better relative to middle-SES EMR children with the same low IQ. He took this to mean that the direct learning tests picked up important behavioral and cognitive differences between low-SES and middle-SES EMR children that the usual IQ tests simply missed.

A first reflection on the results suggested that the culture-fair test had been invented. But Jensen did not stop there. With the characteristic incisiveness that permeates all of Jensen's research, his ensuing research involved large-scale studies of school children. Moreover, Jensen also ". . . inevitably became deeply immersed in the rapidly growing

educational literature of the 1960s on the psychology of the culturally disadvantaged —
at that time a new term for the children of the poor, specially racial minorities such as
Negroes, Mexican-American, Puerto Ricans and American Indians, as well as poor
whites" (Jensen, 1972, p. 7). Unfortunately, many of the reports at the time were still in
the form of unpublished research reports, and they were accumulating rapidly, so
Jensen, with characteristic meticulousness, ". . . felt a need to scan all these reports,
winnow them to find the most substantial and methodologically sound studies, classify
them, and digest and organize the results into a reasonably coherent body of knowledge
which could be summarized in a book . . ." (ibid., p. 7).

The attempt to develop tests fair to culturally deprived low SES minority children
must strike everybody as laudable. So must the colossal work Jensen put into the
systematization and updating of the relevant educational literature. I have taken quite a
number of colleagues by surprise when informing them that Arthur Jensen truly worked
along such lines. They knew for sure from several critical sources that he was the prime
enemy of the deprived of this world — in particular of blacks.

However, a genuine surprise was also in store for Jensen. In his own words: "What
stuck me as most peculiar as I worked my way through the vast bulk of literature on the
disadvantaged was the almost complete lack of any mention of the possible role of
genetic factors in individual difference in intelligence and scholastic performance. In the
few instances where genetics was mentioned, it was usually to dismiss the issue as
outmoded, irrelevant, or unimportant, or to denigrate the genetic study of human
differences and proclaim the all-importance of the social and cultural environment as the
only source of individual and group difference in the mental abilities relevant to
scholastic performance. So strongly expressed was this bias in some cases, and so
inadequately buttressed by any evidence, that I began to surmise that the topic of
genetics was ignored more because of the particular author's social philosophy than
because the importance of genetic factors in human differences had been scientifically
disproved. . . . At that time I was largely but not utterly ignorant of the research on the
genetics of mental abilities" (Jensen, 1972, pp. 7–8). It became obvious to Jensen that,
in order to fully understand what caused individual difference in intelligence and
scholastic performance, he also had to review the total world literature on the genetics
of human abilities. That was the frugal time for a radical change of mind, informed
basically by data and in a spirit of a genuine surprise.

He wrote a number of articles on what he had learned. The articles elicited an
invitation to talk in 1967 at the annual convention of the American Educational Research
Association (AERA; Jensen 1968). At the meeting he pointed out that present education
had failed by not taking into account innate or acquired differences in abilities. He
further pointed out that the ideal of equality of educational opportunity can actually do
harm, quite like a physician treating all patients with the same medicine. He finally
noted that optimal instructional procedures may not be discovered if we do not take into
account the wide range and diversity of abilities, with the effect that we may unwittingly
alienate many children.

In the process of reviewing literature, Jensen became impressed with the Coleman *et
al.* report on Equality of Educational Opportunity, published in 1966. This study was
based on more than half a million children, and presented massive evidence that ". . .

discrepancies in educational achievement by different social class and racial groups are correlated to only a slight degree with inequalities in those variables over which schools traditionally have control. The data made it abundantly clear that biological and social environmental factors associated with social class, race, and family background accounted for most of the variance in intellectual ability and scholastic performance" (p. 10). At the next annual meeting of the AERA in 1968 Jensen presented his Level I-Level II theory on a triple interaction among social class, intelligence and rote learning ability.

The two AERA addresses led to an invitation to write the now (in)famous article "How much can we boost IQ and scholastic achievement" for the *HER* (Jensen 1969). The invitation was quite explicit, and the reader is strongly urged to carefully inspect the outlay *in toto*, presented on page 11 in Jensen (1972). Thus, contrary to what many still believe today, and in face of the fact that the HER editorial board later denied it, Jensen was *explicitly invited* to comment, among many other things, on his ". . . position on social class and *racial differences in intelligence*" (my emphasis). The article was published on 28 February 1969. This is the day the basis of *Jensenism* was established: "The theory that an individual's IQ is largely due to heredity, including racial heritage. [1965–1970]; after Arthur R. Jensen (born 1923), U.S. educational psychologist, who proposed such a theory; see -ism] — **Jen'sen-ist, Jen'sen-ite'**, n., adj." (e.g. *The Random House and Webster's Unabridged Dictionaries*).

The *HER* article proved that Jensen had felt forced by solid empirical evidence to switch from mode 1 of publicly laudable neutral research on serial learning effects and on the helping of the culturally disadvantaged, to mode 2 acknowledging: (1) the existence of individual and race difference in intelligence; (2) the failure of compensatory education; (3) that a purely environmental hypothesis may perhaps not any longer suffice; and (4) that help for the disadvantaged better acknowledges the differences.

Then all hell broke loose. To fully understand the violent dynamics of this we have to connect Jensen's change of mind to the prevailing Zeitgeist mode, in which the *HER* article surfaced.

3.2.2. Zeitgeist modes   The model operates with four Zeitgeist modes: (1) a pre-1940 form where biological explanations were generally accepted; (2) a 1940–1980 blank slate form where Lysenkoism, behaviorism and hostile anti-nature attitudes dominated, fuelled partly by communist ideology, partly by Nazi misuse of eugenics to promote nasty genocide programs; (3) a brief 1980–1990 relational-interpretative form of anti-science interlude; and, finally (4) a post-1990 period where new evidence from progressive neuro-biological sciences (molecular sciences, neurochemistry, neurophysiology, neuroimaging) and behavioral genetics slowly began to make biological explanations partly acceptable to at least some researchers outside orthodox academic left circles.

This simple model predicts that had Jensen presented his newly established conclusions in the *HER* article during the pre-1940 Zeitgeist mode 1 he would have received largely laudatory critique. This was the time when the eugenics movement flourished in many countries, and it was quite common to talk seriously about a genetic basis for individual and group differences in intelligence. Biological explanations were generally accepted and recommendations by the political right, as well as by the left, were used in support of "progressive" social policies in many countries.

Segerstråle (2000) mentions several factors that may explain the turning away from mode 1 biological or nature explanations toward the mode 2 "official environmentalism" or nurture explanations so domineering in the twenties and thirties in the U.S. Among them are the growing social influence of immigrants and northern urban blacks, the Great Depression, a growing skepticism against social Darwinist arguments and the dwindling support for the eugenics movements after reports of escalating Nazi sterilization practices. Add to this the 1968 American Anthropological Association unanimous resolution to denounce racism (Degler 1991), and it becomes understandable that ". . . there was a dramatic decrease in articles on race and sex differences (ibid., pp. 203–205). Segerstråle also cites Barkan (1992) and Degler (1991) for observing that anthropologists Franz Boas, Ruth Benedict and Margaret Mead were successfully promoting the notion of the importance of culture over biology in explaining behavior, and Provine (1973) for noting ". . . the strong political drive for an environmentalist attitude in academia this time". A UNESCO 1952 statement made it virtually illegitimate to use race as an explanatory factor; it emphasized that there were no differences among the races, and this was largely accepted on face value by large sections within academia and also outside it. Barkan (1992, pp. 342–343) found that ". . . biological explanations [were] replaced by cultural analysis. Rigid views of hierarchies among human groups largely yielded to relativism and indeterminism".

From 1980 onwards, a number of philosophical and text-reading movements were formed, where deconstructionism, post-modernism and debunking of science prevailed. Many of these movements included hostile reactions towards biological thinking but also science in general.

The tides slowly change again around 1990 or so, thanks to the exponentially increasing knowledge from functional genomics and the molecular sciences, combined with truly breathtaking developments in behavior genetics and brain imaging sciences. Surprisingly, even if it has once again become somewhat acceptable to mention the biological side of human nature — at least in some circles — in mode 3 and 4, this is, unfortunately, also is the time when political correctness prevails not only in academia at-large but also in the public press. Post-modernist theory and "standpoint" epistemologies make some progress in debunking science, and Jensen's lectures are still occasionally obstructed during this period.

Anyway, Jensen had no choice but to present his mode 2 thinking in the *HER* article in the middle of the 1940–1980 mode 2 Zeitgeist, simply because that was the time when he first discovered that he in the first part of his professional career had seriously underestimated the biological side of his work. Jensen has, as mentioned, an unusual high regard for data, he is honest, and he is willing to let science be guided by data, even if they speak against his previous view.

Finally, he had the personal flexibility needed to turn around 180 degrees and re-interpret the observations in the cold light of new and better evidence. This is more than can be said for many of his opponents. As will be demonstrated later, they openly distrusted unequivocally good data, and even admitted in public that they preferred to interpret them in reassuring light of already pre-formed notions (i.e. they subjected texts to moral reading, see below). The difference in the mental flexibility of Jensen and his critics will play a role in the second part of the analysis.

As soon as Jensen's decision mode 2 collided with Zeitgeist mode 2, the following predictable but unworthy series of events played out.

4. The Attacks

4.1. The Immediate Reactions

Jensen's HER article was immediately given unprecedented publicity, and many of the reactions could be likened more to an emotional hullabaloo than to presenting counter-factual evidence.

I will give a fairly detailed description of the reactions, because I know from personal experience that many people simply find it impossible to believe the many unworthy postures of "honorable" scientists. They either flatly reject that the unfair attacks on Jensen ever took place, or they may say that he most certainly deserved a "qualified response", or they may even call it a balanced discussion. To counter such an evasion from facts, I will in this section draw heavily on Jensen's own account of some of the details of the retaliations from the time of the publication in 1969 and up to 1971 (Jensen 1972).

After reading the section, I will ask the reader to judge the scientific honesty of those same scientists who questioned Jensen's honesty, as he went from decision mode 1 to 2 in Zeitgeist mode 2. To be fair, the later section on "Defenses" also outlines some basically positive reactions, but the present section serves the main purpose of illustrating the nature and causes for the inexcusably bad academic climate. It was so bad that Jensen exclaimed in despair, "Most of the main points of my [HER] article were never mentioned, being completely displaced by the racial issue, which was often a grotesque parody of what I had actually written".

4.1.1. Reactions in or by academic journals   It is instructive to first monitor the timid reactions of the editorial office of the *Harvard Educational Review* in the aftermath of Jensen's 1969 *HER* article (1972). The Board undoubtedly was under great pressure from many individuals and organizations as part and parcel of a collective fraud (see later), but the ensuing events ". . . are unprecedented in the history of scholarly publication in America . . ." because ". . . the Boards academic wisdom and adherence to traditional principles of scholarly publication were pathetically wanting" (p. 23).

Among other things, the Board sent out a false statement, denying that they actually had invited Jensen to comment on race differences. The board then denied Jensen a copy of the statement, but sent it out to everybody else asking for it. The Board then halted the Winter issue with Jensen's article and declined orders from University bookstores. The reason they gave for this was that "The Jensen article . . . presents a view of intelligence that we feel must be read in the context of expert discussion from other psychologists and geneticists". Apparently, what they really meant was that academics cannot be trusted to think for themselves, and so they needed the proper guidance by the critics of Jensen to reach a "correct view". The Board then decided not to sell reprints to Jensen of his own article, even if everybody else could order them. Next, it was hinted that Jensen's rejoinder to the critics could not be published in the ensuing Spring issue, but rather would appear in the much later Summer issue. They then reversed this decision, but only after massive intervention. Still, the Board refused to sell reprints of the original article to Jensen, even if other authors could still obtain copies of their articles in the usual way! However, after the Board was reminded by eight ". . . faculty members of the Department of Educational Psychology at a large Eastern university . . ." that the "interim distribution of the article appears to be at best anti-intellectual and at worst a form of censorship" (pp. 26–27). Jensen was finally "allowed" to buy copies of his own article!

It may be hard to believe, but the sad story of the cowardice of the *HER* editorial board does not end here. The Spring issue was planned to have four or five discussants of Jensen's original article, but was upped to seven. Being fair, as always, Jensen found that for the most part they were ". . . reasonably thoughtful, scholarly attempts to deal with the issues by my paper", and characterized by a ". . . generally moderate tone and lack of any essential disagreement with the main points of my article . . ." (p. 27). However, the Board had refused to publish previously invited papers from two high-caliber solicited contributors — Ellis Page from the University of Connecticut and Michael Scriven from the University of California at Berkeley — despite being delivered on time. The two papers apparently did not only fail to sufficiently "put down" Jensen's stance. They even dared take a critical stance on his critics. Being under such pressure the Board apparently could not allow itself to take any chances.

Worse was still to come! The Summer 1969 issue of *HER* contained some twenty articles and letters ". . . most of them only masquerading as serious critiques of my article. Likening me to Hitler (p. 592) . . . was apparently not beneath the Editorial Board's standards . . ." as was not the fact that some of these articles ". . . contained factual, methodological, and theoretical errors and unsubstantiated accusations against my article". The Board further accepted to publish Deutsch's strong claim that "perhaps so large a number of errors [in Jensen's article] would not be remarkable were it not for the fact that Jensen's previous work has contained so few, and more malignant, all the errors referred to are in the same direction: Maximizing differences between blacks and whites and maximizing the possibility that such differences are attributable to hereditary factors" (p. 254). It is telling to note that Deutsch was not able to back up his charges despite repeated requests to do so. When finally forced by demands of the Committee of Scientific and Professional Ethics and Conduct of the American Psychological Association, Deutsch came up with a ". . . by any standard . . . pathetic document" (Jensen 1972: 28–29).

The Board of *HER* demonstrated further anomalies. It now refused Jensen the right to rejoinder to the critique! The Nobel Laureate in physics, William Shockley, fared no better. He was able to demonstrate that there were fatal errors in one of the critical *HER* articles: "Social Allocation Models of Intelligence: A Methodological Inquiry" by Light and Smith (1971) from Harvard University. The model suggested that even if the heritability of intelligence was as high as 0.80, the mean White-Black IQ difference could be accounted for entirely in terms of environmental differences. What Shockley demonstrated was that the model generated a number of completely absurd results, highly discrepant with common observations. Despite the fact that the Shockley paper expressed no opinion at all in the matter of race differences, but simply pointed out essential logical infirmities and wide discrepancies from well-known facts in the Light and Smith article in *HER*, the Board nevertheless refused to publish Shockley's critique. This is another example of *HER*'s inexcusable censure, pure and simple. Shockley's paper was eventually published in another journal in 1971.

4.1.2. Reactions by academic institutions

4.1.2.1. The American Psychological Association   The powerful American Psychological Association sponsored a division called The Society for the Psychological Study of Social Issues (SPSSI). This division issued on May 2 1969, a statement, meant to discredit major points in Jensen's 1969 *HER* article. Parts of the statement were aggressively distributed to newspapers across the nation and to several professional journals, to be published *in toto* (e.g. American Psychologist, November 1969: 1039–1041). The statement contained remarkably sweeping counter-conclusions (but no data) about observations for which there already was substantial confirmation, or the arguments were twisted. For example, it said ". . . we believe that statements specifying the hereditary components of intelligence are unwarranted by the present state of scientific knowledge . . . such statements may be seriously misinterpreted". Not one word about the massive confluent evidence from twin and adoption studies. It stated that: "The evidence points overwhelmingly to the fact that when one compares Negroes and Whites of comparable cultural and educational background, difference in intelligence test scores diminish markedly". No mention of the fact that when one controls for education much of the IQ variance is taken away. The statement said that ". . . a more accurate understanding of the contribution of heredity to intelligence will be possible only when social conditions for all races are equal and when this situation has existed for several generations". It was not stated that this, obviously, would make all future studies on race difference virtually impossible, nor did it acknowledge that such a restrictive condition was not really called for, either.

With respect to compensatory education it said: "One of our most serious objections to Jensen's article is to his vigorous assertion that compensatory education has apparently failed". "We maintain that a variety of programs . . . have been effective and . . . carefully planned intervention . . . can have a substantially positive influence on the performance of disadvantaged children". One should have thought that APA sponsored honest scientists would have felt obliged at this point to back up their strong counterclaim with clear evidence, or that the APA would have asked for it.

The statement further pointed out ". . . a number of Jensen's key assumptions and conclusions are seriously questioned by many . . . It is thus an oversimplification to try and explain complex behavior in terms of "heredity *versus* environment" (original emphasis). Having examined Jensen's data ". . . we find that observed racial differences in intelligence can be attributed to environmental factors". Present-day intelligence tests are "Largely developed and standardized on white middle-class children . . ." and ". . . tend to be biased against black children . . .".

It may be hard to believe, but SPSSI people then reaffirmed their "... long-held position of support for open inquiry on all aspects of human behavior". They emphasized in particular that "... in the study of human behavior a "variety of social factors may have large and far-reaching effects ..." so "... the scientist must examine the competing explanations ... and ... exercise the greatest care in his interpretation". I feel confident that at least some APA ears must have turned red, at least in retrospect.

Jensen's response came promptly, and was published in the same November issue of American Psychologist. Had Jensen actually set heredity versus environment, or denied the possible impact of a variety of social factors in his *HER* article (or elsewhere, for that matter)? Not at all! What he said was: "The preponderance of the evidence is, in my opinion, less consistent with a strictly environmental hypothesis than with a genetic hypothesis, *which of course, does not exclude the influence of environment or its interaction with genetic factors*" (p. 82, my emphasis). Moreover, Jensen explicitly warned readers against the error of pitting heredity versus environment in a section sub-headed "Heredity versus Environment" (pp. 44–46).

It may very well be that the SPSSI people capitalized on the chance that even responsible scientists would not themselves take the trouble to read Jensen's original *HER* article, but the question still remains: Why on earth should the SPSSI people lie openly and want to blatantly misrepresent Jensen's position? How could honest APA scientists hold a "... position of support for open inquiry ..." when they at the same time call for the impossible scenario that the social and cultural condition for whites and blacks must be kept equal for generations, before anybody can even publish in the field? My guess, and that of others, is that such a claim is a camouflaged attempt to censure, and to cover a closed mind that would forever preclude proper analysis.

The SPSSI people claimed that IQ tests are inevitably biased against black children. This is patently wrong, but this claim had at least one good effect. It made Jensen undertake the formidable task of reviewing the entire world literature on test bias. This resulted in a book (Jensen 1980), which confirmed that well standardized tests contain no ethnic bias when properly used, and when applied in other cultures with proper caution.

With respect to the SPSSI claim that compensatory education programs are effective and notably lift the performance of disadvantaged children — where was their documentation for this? Where is the evidence today, a third of a century and millions of dollars later? True, when one compares blacks and whites, holding education and culture constant, the usual 15 point difference in IQ shrinks but, as mentioned previously, this takes a sizeable part of the variation out of the equation as IQ differences account for a significant proportion of the educational variation. Perhaps the SPSSI people ought to take seriously their own call to "... exercise the greatest care in ... interpretation".

4.1.2.2. Reactions by the American Anthropological Association   On March 5 1970, the American Anthropological Association (AAA) presented a list of 16 resolutions to all its members, in which they obfuscated Jensen's position, implied positions he never held, and called Jensen a "chauvinist, biased racist".

Resolution 15 thus concluded that Jensen's article ". . . is not consistent with the facts of psychology, biology or anthropology". It said that ". . . Jensen's article is wholly inadequate . . .", and that, "All races possess the abilities needed to participate fully in the democratic way of life and modern technological civilization".

Resolution 16 then requested that all members return to their homes from the meeting and ". . . use all available outlets in the national and local media to inform the general public concerning the correct facts about the nature of human variability".

Like with the previous APA statements, we again see a seriously flawed statement from a "responsible" professional organization, reflecting a chilling lack of obligation to present "facts" to substantiate their strong counterclaims. Instead of presenting all relevant data they ran a data-free cheap-shut vendetta against Jensen.

As usual, Jensen got it right when he commented: "In science the only thing that really counts is a preponderance of the facts and converging lines of evidence" (1972: 42). This honest view apparently does not resonate well within broad professional psychology and anthropology circles, and makes one wonder what science really meant to these corrupt moralizing and politicizing organizations.

4.1.3. Claims from other sides for breach of honesty and ethics   Jensen had further reason to wonder. He repeatedly wondered why his critics could get away easily with vicious *ad hominem* attacks, an approach so readily embraced by wide circles — while suspending most critical and scientific standards?

He wondered why there apparently were no costs associated with writing in a nationally syndicated newspaper: "Some of the more outraged souls, black and white, would like to settle the whole thing by proving that they have IQ enough to tie a noose that will fit Jensen's neck".

He wondered why six distinguished Berkeley social science professors could get away with writing in the Berkeley student newspaper that Jensen ". . . was extremely naïve about the nature of cultural differences in test performances" whereas nobody apparently bothered to ask the distinguished professors what precisely they had done to enlighten us? Could they muster more than pure and simple disrespect? We actually do not know till this day!

Jensen wondered why he could not hear the voices of the remaining hundreds of social science professors in this discussion? Obviously, even first year students with a rudimentary understanding of fair play and knowledge of the basic rules of science ought to have felt obliged to set the record straight? Few did. As I will argue later, we here begin to see the vague contours of a far-reaching collective fraud with the purpose of framing Jensen. They could neither frame him on his data nor on his methods, but they could exploit the frontal collision between Jensen's politically incorrect mode 2 nature decision, and their own beloved Zeitgeist mode 2 nurture conviction.

One discussant in the *HER* Spring 1969 issue claimed that Jensen was "girding" himself for a "holy war against environmentalists". Did any of the other critics go back to Jensen's 1969 *HER* article to check for themselves whether his position was war-like or not, and faithfully go back to correct this untrue statement? Not one, as far as I can see! Did any of the critics double-check Jensen's major conclusion, and report back that Jensen actually provided clear and frank support of the notion that environmental factors were also important? Not one. Possible faint attempts to correction drowned in the mud.

There are two competing interpretations of all this. Either, most of the environmentalists did not read Jensen's source text but relied on misrepresenting second-hand sources, as ammunition for their crusade. Or, they actually read the original but subjected it to "moral reading" (Segerstråle 2000), whereby the ". . . critics [of sociobiology] employed a particular style of textual exegesis . . . aimed at revealing the true meaning [of sociobiology]" so that ". . . the critics' interpretation of the true meaning [of sociobiology] came to overrule their targets' protests. The critics profited from the prevailing post-war taboo on biological explanation of behavior" (p. 2).

Considering the sometimes no more than superficial similarity between the sociobiology and IQ "wars", it seems a reasonable assumption that Jensen's critics also applied the "moral reading" approach when studying IQ and race texts. They could, of course, also have headed for something else, partly obscure to themselves, in a self-perceived "non-war" against Jensen, but I will concur with Segerstråle, that moral reading is the more likely interpretation.

A group called *"Psychologists for Social Action"* urged at the Annual Spring 1969 convention of the Eastern Psychological Association, that Jensen should be expelled or at least censured by the APA. There is no register of what other members at the meeting had to say to these tactics, which reminds me of other sinister epochs in history. Spinoza, Voltaire, and the witches of all times would surely have recognized the patterned silence surrounding controversial matters. Apparently, no scholars openly disagreed with the mob at the meeting. Perhaps some honest members bent their head in shame, but most kept their mouth shut for personal comfort.

In this way Jensen's critics could, at no apparent costs, question the existing and well-documented individual and group differences in intelligence. Considering their earlier call for open inquiry and honest assessment, it is almost empirically bizarre that the critics called upon the Rosenthal & Jacobson 1968 study — *Pygmalion in the Classroom* — which concluded that increased self-esteem improves performance. Perhaps they hoped, by some sort of analogy, that black IQ could be raised by improving black self-esteem? What critics did not say, perhaps did not know or, more likely, did not care about, is that all later major reviews of the Rosenthal effect have come out negative. There is, in fact, no support at all for Rosenthal's strong claim, and all replications of the original study have failed to confirm the idea that teacher expectancy raises IQ or promotes scholastic achievement. All this seems to boil down to a rather obvious strategy: rather than openness and honesty, the professional Eastern Psychological Association and, by association, the authoritative APA, were trying to frame Jensen according to the prescription: don't care about science, as long as the attacks visibly harm Jensen!

4.1.4. Campus activities   Various handbills were passed out on campus asking students to join demonstrations in Jensen's class. Placard-bearing students gathered at the University's Board of Regents with the message: "Fire Jensen", or held up such placards under his office windows while shouting "Fight racism! Fire Jensen", or pamphlets with his picture and the text: "HITLER IS ALIVE AND WELL AND

SPREADING RACIST PROPAGANDA AT BERKELEY". Come and help fight in the struggle against racism at Jensen's class!" To attain maximal effect, time and place of the lectures was kindly provided. At the same time a sound-truck circled campus with full volume on its loudspeaker for the simple message: "Fight racism! Fire Jensen!" Slogans scrawled on his office door or in the elevators: "Jensen Must Perish" or "Kill Jensen", kept appearing despite being removed as fast as they were scribbled.

"*Students for a Democratic Society*" (SDS) made up their own screwed definitions of true democracy and academic freedom. They thus succeeded in preventing a lecture at the University of California's Salk Institute at La Jolla campus, Jensen reports, by continuously clapping hands in relay, so as not to tire out. After about an hour of this, the lecture was called off. The lecture the next day had to be delivered to privately announced invitees. This strategy angered the SDS students so much that the campus police at Berkeley got wind that the SDS Berkeley chapter had held a rally to plan reprisals with threats so virulent that it was deemed advisable that Jensen should be accompanied on the campus, to and from classes, and in the parking lot, by two plain-clothes bodyguards, for two weeks. I wonder precisely which kind of democracy they had in mind. Most appalling, it appears that neither their professors, nor anybody from campus administration, saw able to comment on the deep irony here. Almost everybody ducked for cover, but not Jensen.

4.1.5. Threats to the home Three years after the publication of the *HER* article threatening phone calls were still made at home late at night, despite an unlisted phone number. At one time the threats were deemed so realistic by the police that the Jensen family had to abandon their house and move elsewhere for a while.

4.1.6. The silencing of colleagues Jensen was far from alone in being harassed and in having his rights to free speech hurt. Luckily, some of these colleagues neither accepted to be silenced. Professors Richard Herrnstein, William Shockley, Philippe Rushton and others also had their lectures cancelled by demonstrators. In 1971 Herrnstein wrote an article in *The Atlantic Monthly* suggesting that a society based on equality of opportunity would turn out to be a society where social stratification is based on IQ classes. The idea was originally set forth by Young (1958) and further elaborated in 1994 by Herrnstein and Murray in *The Bell Curve*, and convincingly confirmed by others, including Gottfredson (Chapter 15 in the present volume). Herrnstein's lectures were interrupted, and posters were carried around campus with the text: "Wanted for racism".

4.2. The Later Reactions

4.2.1. Introduction Did all the fuss end there back in the early seventies? Jensen certainly hoped so. A little more than three years after the original publication of the *HER* article he wrote in the preface to his *Genetics and Education* (1972): "The storm of ideologically, often politically, motivated protests, misinterpretations, and vilification prompted by this article has by now fortunately subsided, with most encouraging signs of being displaced in professional journals and conferences (and now to a large extent even in the popular press) by rational and sober consideration of the educational and societal implications of the important issues raised in this article. The heat and smoke have largely abated, which is all to the good; yet the concerned interest of the kind I had originally hoped my article would stimulate has continued to grow".

Jensen surely was up for a great surprise here. His positive evaluation of the situation in academia reflected the wishful thinking of an honest and hard working scientist, who wanted to go back to work again. Little did he anticipate the heat still in store for him for another 30 years in the 20th century. The unmeasured amount of outright hatred, personal persecution, defamation and vilification even spilled over into the 21st century! In 1999 demonstrators tried to block a lecture by Jensen at Edinburgh University. Jensen was asked to give an invited Lecture at the Galton Institute in London, but demonstrators successfully took over the arrangement. The police were called in, but they apparently were not asked to make any difference to troublemakers and scientists: they simply cleared the building for everybody! Jensen had to return to the U.S. without being able to address the audience.

I fear that the damage done by the dismissive organizers of the meeting not only allowed for an obvious breach of free speech, but it also provided a clear message to the demonstrators about how to succeed in future actions with no personal risk!

4.2.2. Salvador Luria   The molecular biologist at MIT and self-declared socialist, Salvador Luria (1974a, 1974b), was interviewed by Segerstråle about his view on Jensen, IQ and race research in the early seventies. A Nobel Laureate, Luria saw himself perfectly justified in straightforwardly dismissing IQ research as scientifically and socially useless, and accusing Jensen and IQ research of just politicizing.

Luria said: "Jensen started an article in the *Harvard Educational Review* by saying that compensatory education had been tested and it had failed. That was not so, and I fought . . . because that was a political, a straight political issue, white vs. black . . . Jensen's was a definitive political action . . . IQ data are a reasonable predictor for . . . certain people['s] . . . function in a certain type of school . . . beyond that, that IQ has any relation to anything . . . from the point of view of success in other ways, I would say it cannot be denied, but there is zero evidence here. I read a little bit more: there is zero evidence to me . . . *there is no evidence for intelligence* . . . having expert teachers interview children we would get much more information than in IQ tests . . . *those tests . . . are not based on any scientific background.* You see, it has something in common with Creation science. You say something, and then you insist it may be so because somebody said it in a book . . . claims about a high heritability of IQ [are] 'nonsense' . . . the question of how to get the most out of each person according to his or her ability was not a biological problem. These were all 'socio-political traps' beyond the scope of science" (interviewed in February 1982, and reported in Segerstråle (2000: 245 ff., italics added by Segerstråle).

I have previously dubbed such an approach *The Lord Nelson strategy* (Nyborg 1972). You put the sextant in front of your blind eye, and report that you see nothing. This was precisely what Lord Nelson did, and he commanded the British fleet to continue bombarding Copenhagen, even after the Danish King had presented the white flag for surrender within sight. The total destruction of the city bastions and abduct of the Danish fleet were the goals, and fair play or correct observation had nothing to do with it.

In other words, either Luria is a simple ignorant opening his mouth too much in matters he obviously knew not enough about, or he deliberately looked away from solid data and perhaps thought he could get away with a gross misrepresentation of Jensen's position and data. It is certainly to be hoped that young 21st century scientists will inevitably be very uneasy whenever they see how cavalierly scientists of the highest ranks thought they could gallop to sweeping conclusions, riding on fast horses but with surprisingly little empirical baggage. Luria's statement: "I read a little bit more: there is zero evidence to me . . ." comes true in a way that perhaps does not serve his image as a responsible scientist well!

4.2.3. The Sociobiology Study Group of Science for the People   (1976) also rode on fast horses. They simply declared to the world, that: "The claims that there is a high heritability of IQ . . . have now been thoroughly debunked".

4.2.4. The American Anthropological Association   A major critical attack on Jensen and IQ research was further launched in the form of eight articles, collected under the title *Race and intelligence by The American Anthropological Association* in the early seventies (Brace *et al.* 1971). The titles alone tell a story, if neither about strict scientific objectivity nor about neutrality: *"The Promotion of Prejudice"*, *"Cultural Myopia"*, *"Illogical IQ Theory"*, *"Flaw in Jensen's use of heritability data"*, *"Pseudo-issues"*, *"Racialist Comeback"*, *"Inadequate Evidence and illogical Conclusions"*, *"How Racist use 'Science' to degrade black people"* or *"Jensen's dangerous half truth"*.

In addition, the authors accused Jensen of one-sidedness, and *The American Anthropological Association* endorsed the accusation! It may be no coincidence that Franz Boas was one of the founding fathers of this organization, and that Margaret Mead and other luminaries of his school were loyal members (see later).

4.2.5. Richard Lewontin and Stephen Jay Gould   Segerstråle (2000) provides an interesting analysis of the last quarter of the 20th century research on sociobiology. I will in several instances in this chapter draw on Segerstråle's excellent analyses, partly because she points to parallel events in the equally heated sociobiology and IQ debates, and partly because she enjoyed a unique insider position in the critics' camp. However, I part company with her interpretation of Jensen's role in the controversy (see later).

Segerstråle notes that Richard Lewontin, professor of biology at Harvard University, a member of the *Sociobiology Study Group*, was considered by many the chief opponent of sociobiology and ". . . the upholder of good and moral science against bad and dangerous pseudo-science" (p. 18). Here bad science means science that can be socially abused, whereas good science produces pure knowledge. Another vocal member of the group was professor at the Museum of Comparative Zoology, Stephen J. Gould. The study group later connected to the Boston chapter of *Science for the People*, a national forum for left-wing academic activism (Walsh 1976), under the name *The Sociobiology Study Group for Science for the People*.

Segerstråle was granted observer status at some of their meetings and reports on critical discussions of "biological determinism" and on psychometric studies showing a sex difference in math ability in an atmosphere ". . . of righteous moral indignation at dangerous 'biological determinist' theories and their creators" (p. 21). The group was very active and successful in promoting their view, and was even granted a two-day symposium at the meeting for the prestigious *American Association for the Advancement of Science* (AAAS) in Washington, D.C., in February 1978, to carry through well-attended critical discussions of sociobiology.

Segerstråle's account of the personal attacks on sociobiologist Edward O. Wilson at the meeting looks like a *déjà vu* of what had already happened to Arthur Jensen: "Just as Wilson is about to begin, about ten people rush up on the speaker podium shouting various epithets and chanting: 'Racist Wilson you can't hide, we charge you with genocide!' While some take over the microphone and denounce sociobiology, a couple of them rush up behind Wilson (who is sitting in his place) and pour a jug of ice-water over his head, shouting 'Wilson, you are all wet! (p. 23).

Again we see the previously mentioned disturbing aspect of the obvious attempts to censure free speech: nobody from the AAAS intervened. No officials showed the demonstrators and mockers of academic freedom to the door, or called the police to have them doing it. This particular type of irresponsibility on the part of officials is an unhappy feature that we will see repeating itself in many later situations where Arthur Jensen and others came under attack. It may be no coincidence that Stephen Jay Gould was later called to preside over this organization (see later).

4.2.6. Edward Wilson's reservations   Segerstråle raises an interesting question: Why was sociobiologist Wilson not more cautious about suggesting links between genes and human behavior, when he saw how badly Jensen and Herrnstein were treated earlier? But he was, she observed. On page 554 in his major opus *Sociobiology* Wilson (1975) actively played down the social significance of IQ — despite clear evidence to the contrary! In fact, Wilson went out of his way to downscale the importance of IQ in the last chapter of *Sociobiology* and instead emphasized other bases for social success. Frankly, I find it hard to believe that a man of Wilson's stature and insight did not know the facts, such as those presented in Chapter 15 in this volume, or much earlier in the 20th century. Wilson even tried another common strategy to avoid being framed like Jensen — he succumbed to the idea that race is not a meaningful biological concept.

However, these concessions did not help Wilson a bit, because the academic leftists nevertheless applied their "moral reading" strategy and became able to reveal the "hidden message" in his writings as reflecting a justification of existing social and racial inequalities. His was a no-win position, even if he downplayed the race and intelligence cards, and neither were Herrnstein's and Jensen's, whom certainly did not downplay any of them.

4.2.7. Lewontin   It is an interesting twist that Lewontin accused American academics of falling back to old attitudes and using ". . . untrue statements, facts which are not facts, logic which is not logic, and prove that there are important genetic differences between races" (1975a, 1975b, 1975c) while, at the same time, the Civil Rights Act in

1964 prohibited discrimination in hiring, and thus promoted equal opportunity ideas and affirmative action, and countered notions of inequality, racism, sexism, biologism, conservatism and elitism.

4.2.8. The New York Times Segerstråle takes it as a good illustration of how firmly the academic intelligentsia was holding on to ". . . the 'total' environmentalist position . . ." when in 1973 *The New York Times* published a *Resolution against Racism*, signed by over 1,000 academics from different institutions across the U.S. Not only did it declare: ". . . all humans have been endowed with the same intelligence". It also condemned the research by Jensen and others as both unscientific and socially pernicious. It went as far as to threaten, that "racist" researchers "deserve no protection under the name of academic freedom" and it urged liberal academics to resist "racist" research and teaching.

This culpable resolution indicates that more than 1,000 scientists in the U.S. thought that scientific results are to be construed or annulled by simply signing a pamphlet. The resolution reminds me of the prescriptions the Jewish community in Amsterdam gave on the perpetrator Spinoza in 1656, of the Nazis prescriptions on how to treat Jews, artists and homosexuals in the 1930s and 1940s, and of the pamphlet signed by hundreds of German scientists to testify on the bad quality of Albert Einstein's "Jewish" science. Not without good humor, Einstein later remarked that just one good argument would have sufficed.

Alas, there is little reason for humor in the fact that so many American 20th century scientists had learned so little from the horror stories of fascist or communist suppression of scientists or artists with "entartede" or "false consciousness" views. The prominent member of *Science for the People*, Joe Alper (1982) bundled Edward O. Wilson and Arthur R. Jensen under one hat, and declared to the world that they together were "the scientific racists of the past" rather than "the Ku Klux Klan or the Birchers". Do we see guilt by association and blood from the past spilled over honest scientists on a low-cost basis? Did any of the thousand plus scientists have any quarrel with that?

4.2.9. Who is lying: Plato and Jensen — or Gould himself? Gould (1981, 1996) devoted a whole book to expose Plato's and Jensen's lies, and called it *The Mismeasure of Man*. Gould said: "This book is about the scientific version of Plato's tale. The general argument may be called biological determinism" and is about ". . . the claim that worth can be assigned to individuals and groups by measuring *intelligence as a single quantity*" (p. ii, original emphasis).

Gould was even more specific, when in 1996 he let the 1981 version of *The Mismeasure of Man* reprint. He now ". . . treats *one particular form of quantified* claim about the ranking of human groups: the argument that intelligence can be meaningfully abstracted as a single number capable of ranking all people on a linear scale of intrinsic and unalterable mental worth . . . this limited subject embodies the deepest (and most common) philosophical error, with the most fundamental and far-ranging social impact, for the entire troubling subject of nature and nurture, or the genetic contribution to human social organization" (p. 20, original emphasis).

The result of ranking people according to intelligence in a single series of worthiness is, according to Gould, ". . . invariably to find that oppressed and disadvantaged groups — races, classes, or sexes — are innately inferior and deserve their status. In short, this book is about the Mismeasure of Man" (p. 21).

But who is lying here? The simplest and most direct way to find out is to transcend the borders of academia, and check for oneself whether people out there in the real world can in fact be ranked usefully by Jensen's general intelligence *g* measure, in a way that makes sense in terms of test reliability and predictive validity. Gottfredson and many others have already taken the trouble to collect the relevant evidence, and the reader is urged to inspect the results in Chapter 15 of this volume.

Gould, of course, knows of these data, but he does not accept their usefulness. Why not? Because Gould sees Howard Gardner's (1983) concept of multiple intelligence as ". . . the major challenge to Jensen in the last generation, to Herrnstein and Murray [1994] today, and to the entire tradition of rankable, unitary intelligence marking the mismeasure of man" (p. 22). Gardner's exceedingly broad definition of intelligence allows for an easy and attractive escape from one-dimensional intelligence ranking. Thus, most people are good at something; it may not be intelligence as traditionally defined, but if we just call it intelligence we can justifiably say that most people are intelligent. If we just incorporate talents for dancing or football, for understanding other people, or oneself, or nature, we can establish a multidimensional realm of intelligence that supplants the single series of unworthiness measure, and prove that oppressed and disadvantaged groups — races, classes or sexes — are not innately inferior and deserve their status. Apparently, we don't even have to establish scales for measuring these intelligences (Gardner has not), we don't have to check whether four of these intelligences inter-correlate significantly and reflect *g* (they do), and we don't have to take into account whether the remaining intelligences inter-correlate significantly (they don't), or whether they have predictive validity (they don't; see Jensen 1998, or consult Chapter 19 in this volume).

4.2.10. Gouldian self-promotion   Having demonstrated in *The Mismeasure of Man* that Plato and Jensen are lying, Gould (1981/1996) goes on to assure the reader that he feels quite competent in doing what he must do: "I feel I have a decent and proper grasp of the logic and empirics of arguments about biological determinism. . . . I am fully up to snuff (I would even be arrogant and say "better than most") . . . in fallacies of supporting data . . . my special skill lies in a combination . . . rarely combined in one person's interest . . . special expertise in handling large matrices of data . . . I therefore felt particularly competent to analyze the data, and spot the fallacies, in arguments about measured differences among human groups. . . . I therefore found my special niche [and] . . . combine the scientist's skill with the historian's concern" and focus upon ". . . deep and instructive fallacies (not silly and superficial errors) in the origin and defense of the theory of unitary, linearly ranked, innate, and minimally alterable intelligence" (pp. 24–26).

Gould is, in his own words, not at all bothered by such a narrow-minded complaint as: "Gould is a paleontologist, not a psychologist; he can't know the subject and his book must be bullshit". That is simply nonsense, Gould says: "The subject that I did chose . . . represents a central area of my professional expertise — in fact, I would go further and say . . . that I have understood this area better than most professional psychologists who have written on the history of mental testing, because they do not have expertise in this vital subject, and I do" (p. 40). Given this formidable insight, what then has Gould to say about the measurement of intelligence he so detests?

4.2.11. Gould on factor analysis　Gould assures us that he feels at home in judging factor analysis, the purpose of which is to derive common axes in a positively correlated data matrix. He was therefore terrified to learn that this technique ". . . might have arisen in a social context to a particular theory of mental functioning with definite political meaning . . . that Spearman had invented the technique of factor analysis specifically to study the underlying basis of positive correlation among test".

What was so terrifying about that? Well, ". . . principal components of factor analyses are mathematical abstractions, not empirical realities — and . . . every matrix subject to factor analysis can be represented just as well by other components with different meanings, depending on the style of factor analysis applied in a particular case. Since the chosen style is largely a matter of researcher's preference, one cannot claim that principal components have empirical reality (unless the argument can be backed up with hard data of another sort . . ." "Spearman had invented factor analysis to push a certain interpretation of mental tests — one that had plagued our century with its biodeterminist implications". . . . "Factor analysis had been invented for a social use contrary to my beliefs and values". I felt personally offended . . . and this book . . . ultimately arose from this insight and feeling of violation. I felt compelled to write *The Mismeasure of Man*". "Furthermore . . . the harmful hereditarian version of IQ had not developed in Europe . . . but in my own country of America, honored for egalitarian traditions" (pp. 43–44). The mathematics of IQ testing, ". . . the key error of factor analysis lies in reification, or the conversion of abstractions into putative real entities" (1996: 48).

Perhaps Gould's fear would have been even larger had he fully understood the nature and power of factor analysis, a topic treated with exceptional expertise by world authorities like John Carroll (1993; or Chapter 1 in this volume) or by Jensen (1998: *The g Factor* book).

4.2.12. Gould on biological determinism　Why is biological determinism so dangerous, asks Gould? ". . . because the errors of biological determinism are so deep and insidious, and . . . appeal to the worst manifestations of our common nature . . . reductionism . . . reification . . . dichotomization . . . hierarchy . . . When we rejoin our tendencies to commit these general errors with the sociopolitical reality of a xenophobia, that so often (and so sadly) regulates our attitude to "others" judged inferior, we grasp the potency of biological determinism as a social weapon — for "others" will be thereby demeaned, and their lower socioeconomic status validated as a scientific consequence of their innate ineptitude rather than society's unfair choices" (p. 27).

If we do not counter it we will see: ". . . resurgences of biological determinism correlate with episodes of political retrenchment . . . or . . . fear among ruling elites, when disadvantaged groups sow serious social unrest". "What argument against social change could be more chillingly effective than the claim that established orders, with some groups on top and other at the bottom, exist as an accurate reflection of the innate and unchangeable intellectual capacities of people so ranked?" "Resurgences of biological determinism correlate with periods of political retrenchment and destruction of social generosity". We must therefore raise awareness, that ". . . calls for solidarity among demeaned groups should not be dismissed as mere political rhetoric, but rather applauded as proper reactions to common reasons for mistreatment" (p. 28).

The reader is here invited to speculate on which direction Gould's fear would take if biological determinism were not an error of interpretation but a fact of life. Would Gould blame nature for the destruction of social generosity, and to what effect? Moreover, if we knew more about the causes or mechanisms of biological determinism, would we not be better able to intervene and much more effective in easing the conditions for the disadvantaged? Gould's hostile and square position leaves no room for alternatives to blaming Jensen and others for things they are not responsible for and actually tries to counter.

4.2.13. Gould on individual and group differences   Arthur Jensen is responsible, in Gould's opinion, for one such recurrence ". . . with a notoriously fallacious article on the supposed innateness of group differences in IQ . . ." which coincided with ". . . the onset of a conservative reaction that always engenders renewed attention for the false and old, but now again useful, arguments of biological determinism" (p. 30). Gould does not even consider that Jensen actually published his *HER* article precisely at the time when he realized that he had seriously underestimated the biological impact on development, and had to switch to decision mode 2. Gould just could not resist the temptation to politicize the change and claim it coincided with a conservative swing. Ironically, Zeitgeist mode 2 points to the golden heydays where academic leftists like Gould had their greatest hit rate in fighting what they saw as biological determinist attitudes. Apparently, to Gould the matter is just a question of interpretation — yours or mine? And whatever you say or write, it has to reflect your moral or political stand!

However, Gould did not consider updating his 1981 *The Mismeasure of Man* book until the *The Bell Curve* by Herrnstein and Murray, surfaced in 1994. *The Bell Curve* signified, in Gould's opinion ". . . a swing of the political pendulum to a sad position that requires a rationale of affirming social inequalities as dictates of biology" where ". . . the theory of unitary, rankable, innate, unalterable intelligence acts like a fungal spore, a dinoflaggellate cyst, or a tardigrade tun — always present in abundance, but in an inactive, dormant, or resting stage, waiting to sprout, engorge, or awake when fluctuating eternal conditions terminate slumber". Should anybody be particularly surprised that the ". . . publication of *The Bell Curve* coincided with . . . a new age of social meanness unprecedented in my lifetime . . . " and that this new ". . . meanspiritedness [is consonant] with an argument that social spending can't work because, contra Darwin, the misery of the poor does result from the laws of nature and from the innate ineptitude of the disadvantaged?" (p. 32).

Again Gould manages, in a florid and hostile manner, to tie an empirically loaded work, drawing upon solid data collected by hundreds of scientists over several decennia, to subjective motives reflecting the most evil and asocial tendencies of his time.

4.2.14. The critics as rational firefighters This tactics makes it understandable why Gould and other critics so often emphasize the meanspiritedness, the notorious fallacy, the falseness, and the social meanness of Jensen and others. We just have to combine the moral reading style of the critics with their left oriented position and pessimistic view on the lack of solidarity with the poor, and we see immediately why the critics simply must define themselves as defenders of human freedom, equality and dignity, and why they felt they had to assume a very active outgoing role here. Lewontin *et al.* (1984) provide at good example of this in the following passage, characterizing their almost "Einsatz kommando"-like urge:

> "Critics of biological determinism are like members of a fire brigade, constantly being called out in the middle of the night to put out the latest conflagration, always responding to immediate emergencies, but never with the leisure to draw up plans for a truly fireproof building. Now it is IQ and race, now criminal genes, now the biological inferiority of women, now the genetic fixity of human. All these deterministic fires need to be doused with the cold water of reason before the entire neighborhood is in flames" (p. 266).

Gould stresses again and again the urgent need for policing academia, because, in the brutal but necessary fight against biological determinism we must:

> ". . . never flag in our resolve to expose the fallacies of science misused for alien social purpose . . ." for a simple reason: "We pass through this world but once. Few tragedies can be more extensive than the stunting of life, few injustices deeper than the denial of an opportunity to strive or even to hope, by a limit imposed from without, but falsely identified as lying within" (Gould 1996: 50).

It pays off to ponder again whether it is nature, and not Jensen, who stunts life and denies opportunities? Just think for a moment, if the new insight from the molecular and brain sciences is combined with behavioral genetics' brand new way of defining the impact of environmental factors (within versus between family, and shared versus non-shared), would hold the best promise for optimizing the conditions for the deprived? Gould never entertains such a possibility, because he sees evil plots everywhere, and surely knows whom to blame!

4.2.15. Postmodernism According to Segerstråle (2000) the "old" academic left eventually partly transformed itself, so that: "The new 'cultural left' in academia, . . . instead focused their energy on postmodernist theory and 'standpoint' epistemologies, where sociobiologists were . . . now being dismissed as old-fashioned defenders of the truth" (p. 308).

Seen in this perspective, it is perhaps little surprise to note that some postmodernists express a rather hostile attitude to IQ testing. In the recent symposium — *Psychological Assessment from a Social Constructivist Point of View* — at the *XXVII Meeting of the International Psychology Congress* in 2000 in Stockholm, Sweden, Yvonna Lincoln and

Kenneth and Mary Gergen questioned the basic validity and legitimacy of psychometric test.

Some of their critique was directed at the idea that test administrators actually believe in an objective reality. Testers further assume that they can measure and predict the characteristics of the objects. Testers believe that their methods of measurement are independent of what they measure, and that the choice of measures will not influence the studied subject. Test administrators believe that observer status is objective, but this is suspect because, irrespective of the unit of measurement and method, objectivity is compromised by the theoretical orientation and purpose of the study.

A further problem with IQ testing is, according to Kenneth Gergen, that psychometrics disregard our relational and situated connectedness. Mary Gergen went on to question the value of psychometric studies of individuals, because what really is measured is the construction of the meeting between the tester and the tested, and the chosen method sets the agenda for what actually can be seen. It is, in fact, the semantic content that defines the understanding of the individual under scrutiny.

Yvonna Lincoln finally questioned the entire legitimacy of psychology as a discipline, because it is based on the test ideology taken from psychometrics — "we" can and "the others" cannot. To solve this crisis we have to open up to a constructive dialogue about ideologies, according to Lincoln.

This is a good example of a straw-man approach. The post-modernists first set up a completely unrealistic description of the blatant idiocy of IQ testers, and then shoot them down in one cheap stunt. Frankly, I have never met any serious psychometrics subscribing to such outdated positivist positions, neither have I found any example of it in the modern psychometric literature.

Let us turn the post-modern critique on its head for a moment: how long and how cheaply can the critics get away with notoriously side-stepping the massive evidence for the high psychometric test reliability and predictive validity, amassed over close to a century. Post-modernist critics repeatedly violate the "Total evidence rule" by reporting a fraction of the empirical evidence as if it was all. Their meetings nevertheless attract a large and often enthusiastic crowd. When they return to their home institutions they eagerly share their important new insight with students and colleagues. As this happens again and again, I am forced to conclude that something amounting to a collective blindness to certain data has infected much of modern academia.

5. The Defenders

5.1. Introduction

Even if the resistance to Jensen's work was overwhelming, there were also some notable examples of scientists who dared to defend Jensen, even if this brought them right into the frying pan as well.

5.1.1. Edson and Stevens One of them was Lee Edson (1969) from the *New York Times Magazine*. Jensen found that he stood out as producing a "... thorough, thoughtful, and well-balance story . . ." on the incident. Edson's article stimulated more letters-to-the-editor than any other article *New York Times Magazine* had ever received.

In one such letter Harvard psychology professor S. S. Stevens expressed the opinion that: "The environmentalists have had the microphone in recent years and they have talked up an American brand of Lysenkoism, which holds that brain power can be taught. That notion draws much of its powerful appeal from the hope we all feel that somehow we can shake the world and make it better, right now. Practically everybody is trying to improve somebody".

Stevens further wrote: "That concept of the IQ has, I believe, proved itself the most important quantitative concept contributed thus far by psychology", and that " we gain nothing by turning our backs on the process of biological inheritance which sets the design for our size and appearance, and for much of our behavior".

5.1.2. Bereiter Another defender was Bereiter (1970), who inspected all the early fuss and came to the interesting conclusion that apparently "the educator need not concern himself with genetics because, in the first place, he is constrained to working with environmental variables and must therefore do the best he can with them . . . and because, in the second place, education deals with individual children of unknown genetic potential, so that normative data on genetic differences have no application" (p. 298).

However, even if valid points for the teacher in the classroom, they are potentially relevant at the level of educational policy dealing with populations rather than with individuals. Here, individual differences in intelligence should encourage us, according to Bereiter, to look for alternative teaching methods that do not rely so heavily upon IQ abilities, and also influence our expectations of what can be accomplished.

5.1.3. Zigler Also Zigler (1968) revealed little patience with the environment reductionists: ". . . our nation has more to fear from unbridled environmentalists than . . . from those who take the biological integrity of the organism seriously. It is the environmentalists who have been writing review after review in which genetics are ignored and the concept of capacity is treated as a dirty word. It is the environmentalists who have placed on the defensive any thinker who . . . has had the temerity to suggest that certain behaviors may be in part the product of read-out mechanisms residing within the programmed organism. It is the unbridled environmentalist who emphasizes the plasticity of the intellect, who tells us one can change both the general rate of development and the configuration of intellectual process, which can be referred to as the intellect, if we could only subject human beings to the proper technologies. In the educational realm, this has spelled itself out in the use of panaceas, gadgets, and gimmicks of the most questionable sort. It is the environmentalists who suggest to parents how easy it is to raise the child's IQ . . . It is the environmentalist who have argued for pressure-cooker schools, at what psychological costs, we do not yet know".

5.1.4. Shockley A much less forgiving critic of social reductionism and equality-makings, than Jensen, was that of the late physics professor and Nobel Laureate William Shockley, mentioned earlier. He urged without success the U.S. National Academy of

Sciences to sponsor research on the genetics of intelligence. Shockley diagnosed the major problem here as a thought-blockage caused by a theologico-scientific delusion, called the "apple of God's eye obsession" — God meaning, for some, the proper socio-biological order of the universe. True believers hold that God has designed nature's laws so that good intentions suffice to ensure humanity's well-being; the belief satisfies a human need for self-esteem. Any evidence counter to man's claim to be the "apple of God's eye" . . . provokes retaliation . . . or else the . . . obsession had to be painfully revised". An important antithesis to a feature of the contemporary form of the "apple of God's eye obsession" is, according to Shockley: ". . . the theory that intelligence is largely determined by the genes and that races may differ in the distribution of mental capacity" (Shockley 1971: 307).

5.1.5. Davis Davis (1978) also went to the rescue. He found that the critics were confusing the normative with the empirical while falling prey to "The moralistic fallacy", because they suffered from a "fear of facts". Perhaps this fear emanated on the basis of a fear of potential social misuse of data! Davis (1976) certainly thought so when commenting on research in the effects of having an XYY karyotype and on behavior genetics in general: ". . . I suggest . . . It is the conviction that an attention to genetic factors in behavior will have reactionary social consequences . . ." and that ". . . attention to genetic factors in behavior 'only serves to propagate the damaging mythology of the genetic origins of "antisocial behavior", and so it interferes with the job of eliminating the social and economic factors involved in such behavior".

However, we should never, in the words of Davis, try to 'legislate the facts of nature'. Davis (1986) also commented on the raging IQ debate, and on Gould's frontal attack on IQ research in general and on Jensen in particular. He stressed that Gould's critique of research on race and sex differences in cognitive abilities rested mainly upon outdated craniology and other mistakes of the past, whereas Gould largely omitted the much more sophisticated contemporary approaches, thus misleading the public about current research. Instead of truthfully reporting on reliable methods and high predictive validities, Gould questioned whether general intelligence, *g*, really existed at all. Logically, as he concluded that it does not, he accordingly also had to dismiss its heritability. This would be the *coup de grâce* to the idea of IQ being inherited.

5.1.6. Page and 50 American scientists Ellis Page (1972) united with 50 other scientists, including Jensen, Eysenck, Herrnstein and four Nobel price winners, to send out a resolution. The resolution was a reaction to the fact that reporting on the importance of heredity for human behavior had ". . . brought psychologists and other scientists under extreme personal and professional abuse at Harvard, Berkeley, Stanford, Connecticut, Illinois, and elsewhere".

After referring to anti-scientific moves in the past, the statement reported on today's ". . . similar suppression, censure, punishment, and defamation . . ." where ". . . positions are often misquoted and misrepresented; emotional appeals replace scientific reasoning; arguments are directed against the man rather than against the evidence. Among the attackers are non-scientists, political militants on campus, academics committed to environmentalism, knowable scientists that are silent out of fear".

The result is that "... it is virtually heresy to express a hereditarian view, or to recommend further study of the biological bases of behavior. A kind of orthodox environmentalism dominates the liberal academy, and strongly inhibits teachers, researchers, and scholars from turning to biological explanations or efforts".

This statement of support elicited much criticism. Vetta (1973) thus noted in an amendment to the resolution in *American Psychologist* that the signers could not have seen much of Jensen's work because, had they investigated it, they could not have "... failed to notice the deficiencies, the contradictions, and the outright misrepresentations". Vetta may have done a good old moral reading of Jensen's text and spotted the errors but, like Deutsch, could not tell the world about them in any precise manner.

5.1.7. Segerstråle I have drawn extensively on Segerstråle's 2000 book, because she was in a rather unique situation to comment on the sociobiology and IQ debates. Originally educated in organic chemistry and biochemistry at the University of Helsinki, Segerstråle moved from hard science to the sociology of science, doing her doctoral research at Harvard University. This unique background allowed her to, for example, consider the nature-nurture debate from a biological as well as from the sociological-philosophical perspective. Moreover, Segerstråle actively participated in some of the meetings on the academic left, allowing her to peek into the hinterland of the critics and thus provide us with a better understanding of the context for their moves. Finally, Segerstråle personally interviewed many of the prominent combatants on both sides of the fence.

Segerstråle notes that there is little doubt that Lewontin's sociopolitical position was based on his devotion to Marxism in practice, which served as "... a 'coupled' moral-cum-scientific agenda ..." that made him think that "good science" is unproblematic, and "bad science" is in need of explanation. His two specific tasks were accordingly to "... demonstrate the 'scientific error' of scientists with 'incorrect' political beliefs, and.. to unmask these beliefs in their scientific text and show how the latter 'errors' led to the former one" (ibid.: 41).

In an early critique of Jensen, Lewontin (1970) strived to "... display Professor Jensen's argument, to show how the structure of his argument is designed to make his point and to reveal what appear to be deeply embedded assumptions derived from a particular world view, leading him to erroneous conclusions".

Like Gould and other leftists, Lewontin often practiced an aggressive and hostile *ad hominem* character assassination approach, and did not even shy away from talking about the common "carelessness, shabbiness and intellectual dishonesty ..." in the study of intelligence (1975a). He claimed that such students "... sometimes tell deliberate lies because they believe that small lies can serve big truths (1981).

In the public TV broadcast Lewontin (1975b) further said: "We know now that brain size has nothing to do with intelligence ...", and that earlier and contemporary scientists were "... lying about genetic differences while posing as experts".

Were that the case, we have several "liars" writing chapters to the present volume, including the editor (see Chapters 6, 9 and 10, respectively). Is it really a lie that brain size correlates about 0.3–0.40 with IQ? Is it a small or a big lie that the inheritance for IQ rises from a lowly 0.20 in early childhood to a hovering 0.75 in late adulthood? If no lie, then we see examples of the remarkable disrespect Lewontin and other academic leftists show for, what experts consider solid data. We see an almost unrestrained urge to communicate false messages to the public, in the service of self-assumed moral considerations and self-proclaimed openness in scientific matters. However, an old word says: never throw stones if you live in a glass-house. If data were stones, the critics were soon homeless.

Halfway through her book, Segerstråle (2000) mentions a striking feature of the whole debate: "The burden of proof was on sociobiologists and IQ researchers to prove their innocence, not on the accusers to prove the formers' guilt . . . 'politically correct' academics felt that they could require sociobiologists and others to be careful in their actions and choice of words, while they did not see the need to censor their own language when they accused the former of political intent. Sociobiologists were held to high standards, while the critics of sociobiology felt they could get by with easy dismissals of sociobiological theorizing . . . Anti-sociobiologists were allowed to see all sorts of links between sociobiology and unsavory politics, but the sociobiologists were not allowed to respond that sociobiology's alleged political intent was a 'lie' (or, 'simple lie')" (p. 192).

Segerstråle's analysis of the logic behind the critics' reasoning suggests that it was not traditionally scientific but rather of a moral-legalistic kind, applied to science, and here we are back once again to the moral reading strategy. When critics apply moral reading to texts, they: ". . . imagine the worst possible political consequences of a scientific claim. In this way, maximum moral guilt might be attributed to the perpetrator of this claim" (2000: 206). Plato was thus a big liar, not because he assumed human diversity exists and is largely innate, but rather because people can be defined on a scale according to their worth — some are inherently gold, others silver and then there are those of bronze (Chorover 1979: 25).

Segerstråle (2000) also asks how we can explain the critics' astounding disregard for the original context of their citations, and concludes that: "In fact, one might describe the critics' data selection process as a rather blatant case of what Charles Babbage in his The Decline of Science in England (written in 1830!) famously called 'cooking', that is, selecting only those pieces which (in his words) 'will do for serving up'". Perhaps the critics saw only the pertinent parts of the text to be criticized and disregarded the rest as noise? A moral reading could also be used as pedagogical material ". . . showing the 'innocent reader' just how sociobiological explanations were cleverly constructed to support a particular political point" (p. 212).

This view harmonizes well with my impression of Gould. He leans more on tremendous rhetoric skills, the Lord Nelson strategy, and broad public acceptance of no limits to human development, than on adherence to honest empirical evidence, logic, and obedience to the "Total Evidence Rule", which says that nothing but the whole truth will suffice.

5.1.8. Gross and Levitt   Gross & Levitt (1994) provided a scorching analysis of the academic situation in their book — *Higher Superstition: The Academic Left and its Quarrels with Science*. They launched a heavy attack on the Academic Left (AL), and it surely is no coincidence that they begin the book with a citation from Bertrand Russell's (1968) autobiography: "I find that much unclear thought exists as an excuse for cruelty, and that much cruelty is prompted by superstitious beliefs".

A major point is that muddleheadedness has throughout history been a much more potent force than malevolence or nobility as it ". . . blunts our wisdom, misdirects our compassion, clouds whatever insights into the human condition we manage to acquire". Gross and Levitt have few illusions about the likely impact of their writings: "Even if it be the most futile of all things to crusade against the muddleheadedness of the AL people, this quixotry is at least to be preferred to just passively registering the damage done to science by the AL" (p. 1). This critique rang a bell: many of Jensen's most vocal critics confessed to a leftist political inclination.

Gross and Levitt wanted, first of all to avoid muddleheadedness in their own quarter, so they set out to ". . . first define what unites the AL individuals". They found that ALs do not ". . . have a well-defined theoretical position with respect to science . . . but a noteworthy uniformity of tone, and that tone is unambiguously hostile . . . [toward] some of the uses to which science is put . . . toward the system of education . . . toward the *actual content* of scientific knowledge and toward the assumption . . . [that] scientific knowledge is reasonably reliable and rests on a sound methodology . . ." to an extent that ". . . irrationality is courted and proclaimed with pride" (pp. 2–3; authors' emphasis). The group of ALs, furthermore, typically comprises humanists and social scientists, rarely working physical scientists. ALs can often be identified under the umbrella of post-modernism in fields like literary criticism, social history, cultural studies, cultural constructivism, postmodern philosophy, feminist theory, deep ecology, deconstruction, and so forth.

"The assumption that makes specific knowledge of science dispensable is ". . . above all, the moral authority with which the academic left emphatically credits itself . . . sufficient to guarantee the validity of the critique" (p. 6).

Higher Superstition then goes on to analyze the impact of AL on a multitude of areas that, while highly interesting by themselves, would bring us too far away from the present context. Moreover, my selective quotes from their informative and broad-spectered analysis do little justice to Gross and Levitt's painstaking attempt to define what they mean by the academic left. However, they suffice to bring better into focus the fact that it was people from the AL camp that provided the most explosive ammunition for the ferocious attacks on Jensen. This is not to deny that Jensen has also been attacked by irrational right wing fundamentalists, some with a clear theologico-creationist leaning, but the ALs were definitely not only more vocal but also more vicious.

Let me repeat the important source for the concern Gross and Levitt expressed for the sanity of modern academia — ". . . an open hostility toward the actual content of scientific knowledge and toward the assumption . . . that scientific knowledge is reasonably reliable and rests on a sound methodology. (Gross & Levitt 1994: 2). This is one of the major concerns that forces Gross and Levitt to ". . . attack [the] . . . academic or cultural left . . . constructivists and relativist sociologists of science . . . for challenging science's ability to produce knowledge which was in any sense 'truer' than other types of knowledge. There is a sense of solidarity within the academic left, a solidarity of a political rather than an intellectual nature . . . a preoccupation with science as power ... [a] distrust of experts ... [an] obsession with textual analysis ..."

I entirely concur with Gross and Levitt in this analysis, and will in the last part of this chapter corroborate on the grave consequences they see of the serious politically and morally inspired attacks on science. The irony of the story is that Jensen — one of the most apolitical persons I know — highly unwillingly got caught in the middle of this battle.

5.1.9. Carroll. Carroll (1997) found several good reasons to respond to the unfair and surprisingly uninformed critique of intelligence research. He first noted that the publication of Herrnstein and Murray's *The Bell Curve: Intelligence and Class Structure in American Life* from 1994 had spawned a veritable cottage industry in which numerous reviews, critiques, editorials were written — rarely by the informed specialist — to express mainly negative views of their data, analyses and conclusions. Thus, works by Fraser (1995) and Jacoby & Glauberman (1995) doubt the emphasis on individual difference in intelligence as a factor in social success, and question the concept of intelligence, the instruments, and the methodology of psychometrics. With never-failing energy Gould (1994) repeated the claim that Herrnstein and Murrey were mistaken in "... assuming that intelligence 'is depictable as a single number, capable of ranking people in linear order, genetically based, and effectively immutable" (p. 139).

One unfortunate result of all this commotion has been, according to Carroll, that many 'public intellectuals' see psychometric research and intelligence as discredited pseudoscience alien to the ideals of a democracy (Giroux & Searls 1996). As Carroll finds that psychometrics is a sound and fair-minded scientific discipline, he undertook the task to re-examine the six propositions that Herrnstein and Murray stated as being beyond significant technical dispute in psychometric research, to see whether they in fact live up to the current consensus among most experts. This re-examination is all the more important, because Carroll is considered by most experts in psychometrics one of the most central scientists for empirically supporting the modern hierarchical model of intelligence. It really is a shameful sign of contemporary thinking that most critics prefer Gould's self-confident but not well-informed treatment of factor analysis to Carroll's eminent and empirically cautious 1993 book, or to Jensen's 1998 book on *The g factor*.

The six propositions had been widely criticized as being false and pseudoscientific, but Carroll found them on the re-examination:

> "... to be reasonably well supported. Most experts agree that there is a general factor *g* on which human beings differ. It is measured to some degree by most tests of cognitive aptitude and achievement, but more accurately by tests designed to measure it. It corresponds to most people's concept of intelligence. It is quite stable over the lifespan, and properly constructed and administered IQ tests are not demonstrably biased against different social groups. It is substantially influenced by genetic factors, but also by environmental factors".

Carroll also found that some psychometric findings about *g* have been poorly presented to the public or widely misunderstood, so he urges the public to recognize that:

(1) psychometrics (literally, mental measurement) is a rigorous scientific discipline that has resolved many questions concerning cognitive abilities; (2) general ability scores should be taken not as direct measures of hereditary intelligence, but rather as measures of rate of progress over the life span in achieving full mental development; (3) there are many other cognitive abilities besides *g*; (4) important sources of variation in *g* or IQ are environmental; (5) the IQ is possibly more an indicator of how fast the individual can learn than it is of the individual's capability of learning; and (6) much more research is needed to resolve questions about the role of individual differences in cognitive abilities in a democratic society. These conclusions can be reached whatever one's views may be about the validity of Herrnstein and Murray's claims about the significance of variation in intelligence for social problems".

Carroll accomplished two things with his analysis. First, he showed — once again — that the psychometric analyses of intelligence are well founded in the empirical world, something the critics either flatly deny or try hard to circumvent. Second, the conclusion is entirely independent of Herrnstein's and Murray's treatment in *The Bell Curve*, but neither does it contradict their book.

The critics are now, once again, pushed to the wall by empirical and methodological arguments, and their accusations for underlying "bad motives" or "unconscious race aversions" lose power. Carroll is careful, nevertheless, to point out that we still have much to learn, that there still are lacuna in our knowledge, and so forth. But the overall conclusion is clear: psychometrics is not the pseudo-science the public is made to believe by the critics.

5.2. Truth and Asymmetry

When dealing with the controversy between, on the one side, sociobiologists, psychometrics and behavioral geneticists and, on the other side, the critics, Segerstråle (2000) in many ways defended Jensen against the unfair attacks. However, we now arrive at a point where I disagree with Segerstråle's otherwise insightful analyses. The main reason for the divergence is, that Segerstråle sees both parties as defenders of the truth: ". . . it is just that they have different conceptions of where the truth lies" (2000: 1). In contrast, the IQ controversy has nothing to do with symmetrical defenses of some truth.

In fact, there are several ways to demonstrate that the IQ controversy was deeply asymmetrical. One of the parties is fairly well characterized by a series of brutal and merciless *ad hominem* attacks by a group of aggressive and ruthless ideologues, moved more by self-assumed moral authority than truth or, as Gross & Levitt (1994/1998) prefer to express it, by a shameless moral one-upmanship, going far beyond truth and data. The other party is better characterized as a group of hard-working scientists moved more by empirical arguments than by anything else; their endeavor involves correlations and experimentally controlled data and not at all some self-assumed moral authority.

I agree completely with Segerstråle when she invites the reader to inspect ". . . the relentlessness with which the critics kept attacking their targets, who were accused not only of "incorrect" political and moral stances, but also of "bad science"." However, the character of the plot changes radically, when we inspect the sincere and honest presentations, and the tempered and fact-oriented rejoinders by Arthur Jensen. There is nothing in Jensen's work or in his personality that compares to the hostile and vicious attacks launched routinely by the academic leftist firefighters. It takes little effort to see that it is complete nonsense to talk about Jensen's hostility, because there is none. Neither is there, to the best of my knowledge, any serious critique of the empirical side of Jensen's works, which cannot be explained rationally.

Segerstråle further sees the controversy as a clash of different traditions coming from two different academic camps; they live in two different worlds of factual knowledge and taken-for-granted assumptions. She then uses social psychological theory to predict that any incoming information will be aligned with existing convictions, well-known cognitive defense mechanisms will protect members of each camp from being challenged on their existing knowledge, and members within each camp will reinforce each other's beliefs.

This diagnosis has obvious shortcomings in terms of asymmetry. The critics disregarded factual knowledge on the basis of their standpoint, whereas Jensen took nothing for granted. The critics singled out Jensen and the behavioral geneticists for ridicule and punishment, but not vice versa. The critics kept repeating the vicious attacks as good "firefighters" must do, whereas Jensen and the behavioral geneticists spent much time in developing new methods and steadily amassing a mountain of increasingly more precise data — that substantiated their own position and increasingly lamed the critic's claim.

Perhaps Segerstråle may have missed the vital asymmetry in the scientific and personal approaches of the two parties because of a common inclination of many philosophers to emphasize reasoning and logic over data. According to her, everybody had a battle to win, and everybody deserved a prize for this. However, in terms of precious data, only one party deserves a prize in the controversy — a prize for amassing a surplus of confluent evidence. The critics basically continued to flatly deny, misrepresent or ridicule that very same evidence and endlessly repeated their moral condemnation of the collectors.

I may agree with Segerstråle when she in Chapter 15 — *Capitalizing on Controversy* — states: ". . . it was in each side's interest to define the 'issue' under debate in a way that benefited their own side, so that they themselves would be seen as being correct and the opponents wrong" (p. 299). However, I do not see the evidence to back up the claim that ". . . both parties . . . may have been interested in keeping the controversy going because of the chances for short-term and long-term profit . . .". Even if Segerstråle reports mainly on the sociobiology debate that occupies most of her fine book, Jensen and the behavioral geneticists are by association hit as well by the accusation.

In fact, nothing could be more wrong. Jensen is a self-declared strongly non-political person to the extent of being embarrassed over this himself. He responds to critique with data, analyses and interpretation, not for harvesting profit — politically or morally. His real intent is to hasten back and check the real world for its reality. This claim is easy to check: just inspect his many works or the responses he offers the many critics. Similarly, the behavior geneticists I know are preoccupied with amassing family, twin and adoption data, or with the analysis of quantitative trait loci, or study the molecular basis of intelligence, rather than fueling any kind of controversy. It is, in fact, quite difficult to see whatever interests Jensen or behavior geneticists could possibly have in keeping any kind of controversy going. They already had paid so dearly for hostile publicity fueled by the critics, in terms of loosing funding or attracting negative attention from colleagues and professional organizations. Therefore, to "... depict the participants as involved in competition for peer recognition, pursuing recognition-capital in both the scientific and moral realms", frankly makes little sense in Jensen's case. He would happily skip the publicity for personal and professional survival — and for gaining new data apt to guide the treatment of deprived children.

In other words, Segerstråle's analysis goes wrong precisely where she makes too close an analogy between the ongoing sociobiology, IQ and behavioral genetics debates. It may be true that in the sociobiology debate, "... those who stood to gain the most were scientists who could promote their own scientific theories as both scientifically and morally/politically superior by probing another scientist both scientifically and morally wrong ... by ascribing scientifically and morally untenable views to suitable opponents ..." (p. 303). However, Jensen and the behavior geneticists obviously had been much better off, if their critics had left them alone to do their research and present their results without having to fight the time-consuming demonization, politization and accusations of morally wrongdoing. They generally believe that good data ought to speak for themselves. Where Segerstråle correctly emphasizes the socio-political, philosophical and opportunistic sides of the critique she pays, in my opinion, too little attention to the hard science aspects of Jensen's and the behavior geneticists' work.

On the final page of her *Defenders of the Truth*, Segerstråle condenses her major point: "I am arguing that moral/political concerns, far from being an obstacle to be eliminated, were in fact a *driving force* both in generating and criticizing scientific claims in this field, and that the field was better off because of this. We see, then, the importance of moral and metaphysical commitments in science. They motivate scientific work, they sustain it in the face of adversity, and they drive scientists to closely scrutinize the claims of opponents. It seems to me that moral/political criticism is an important and healthy phenomenon in science, particularly in fields which depend largely on plausibility arguments" (p. 408, original emphasis).

This may be the way many philosophers of science or sociology see it. We are theoretical, moral and political beings, and this is what drives us as scientists. It is good for us to be challenged on moral/political grounds, because only then we will do our utmost to optimize the task in hand. Segerstråle misses here, as said before, the importance of experimental design and solid data, that Jensen and the behavior geneticists see as the essence of their endeavors. She also misses the importance of pure multidirectional and genuine curiosity that might drive a scientist in any direction, in accordance with the serendipity principle that partly informs Jensen: he originally set out in one direction, but the findings persuaded him in the 1960s to radically change his mind. Despite being harassed, threatened, loosing funding, ridiculed and wasting oceans of time on trying to respond to ridiculous accusations and wild misrepresentations of his position, he continued to pour out solid data, to satisfy his curiosity, and to test entirely new hypotheses.

Far from being the case that "The characters in my story are all defenders of the truth — it is just that they have different conceptions of where the truth lies", it seems to me that nobody in the IQ wars in fact defended truth in any proper sense of that term. True statements about the world is heavily linked to positivism (or mathematics) — but the last real positivist probably died shortly after the turn of the 19th century. What seemed to have taken place is that the academic left distorted the evidence and substituted truth with moral one-upmanship in the IQ controversy, whereas others, in particular Jensen, carefully collected and defended data along the lines of confluence and increasing precision, and talked a lot about probabilities, but never called upon truth.

The fundamentally different nature of the two enterprises, and of the combatants, is worth keeping in mind. It was Jensen who refined 20th century psychology's most reliable, stable and broadest applicable measure — general intelligence g — extended it, and brought it safely into the 21st century, despite the twists, shouts and obvious malevolence of the academic left. A man of lesser ability, personal courage and scientific integrity would long ago have succumbed to the virulent antiscientific assaults, and psychometrics would have had much less to offer science today. Rather than one truth against another, it was a battle of data against misconceived moral ideology.

A further asymmetry was safely identified by Segerstråle: "Instead of checking for themselves . . . it seems that many academics rather took the critics' interpretation at face value . . . why read the original when the critics' conclusion was eminently plausible?" (2000: 14–15). So many of the critics did not care to read the original works and check essential facts before they jumped to unsound conclusions.

Another thing is whether they all exercise "coupled reasoning", i.e. held a belief that a scientific position different from one's own must be politically motivated? Davis' 1983 critique of Gould may seem like just another example of the coupled reasoning that the critics were originally accused of using. Gould was blinded by Marxist ideology and such a bad scientist will inevitably make error upon error when discussing IQ research, according to Davis. Segerstråle concluded that from each side's perspective, the other side's position clearly looked ideologically biased. The critics ". . . wanted to unveil and debunk IQ research as 'bad' science . . ." with "its potential social misuse . . .". However, for Davis ". . . the promise of good science was connected to its potential social usefulness", and so he had to debunk the politically inspired attacks on good science (p. 233).

Perhaps Segerstråle's claim that many participants in the sociobiology debate applied extensive coupled reasoning is correct, but Jensen certainly did not, even if he was the most viciously attacked. My professional and personal acquaintance with Jensen tells me that he is resolutely apolitical, and I have seen him react with visible impatience whenever someone asks for his most likely political stance in IQ matters. I feel pretty sure his reaction will be: Look at the data; what does it tell you? Anybody who cares to read his many and detailed responses to critiques will immediately spot this strategy. To give an example, my own position on the likelihood of a sex difference in g differs from Jensen's (see Chapter 10 in this volume), but I have never heard Art link this scientific disagreement to political motives on my part; he rather challenges me on my methods and data, and this is precisely as it should be.

In other words, Segerstråle may have a point that many apply moral reading of opponent texts in the search for "hidden or unconscious" moral or political truth, but I must insist that moral reading is wasted on Jensen's texts. On the other side, Jensen obviously hopes that his research can be put to good use for individuals in school and elsewhere, but this is no license to include Jensen in the camp of researchers who apply coupled reasoning, not even if Gould and others say so three times. There is no scientific use in linking people devoted to coupled reasoning together with scientists aiming to demonstrate empirically that IQ research can be used to smooth the progress of individual learning. Davis actually referred to Jensen's warning that great harm would come to individuals in the educational system if we do not maximize the opportunity for development in each individual, entirely regardless of race or income. If this is coupled reason, it is at least of a completely different nature than the one characterizing Gould and other critics, who detests evaluation and ranking of individuals according to IQ scales, and sets out to destroy those who do.

5.3. Lewontin, IQ and Natural Science

There is an interesting twist to Lewontin's (1975a) critique of research on intelligence, a foible that demonstrates one of his particular kinds of selective blindness to existing data. His basic position is that "... the only truly scientifically interesting questions about cognitive traits can be asked at the molecular level". Psychometricians were motivated, yes, and what motivates them "... 'must' be their underlying sociopolitical bias that was driving these researchers to bad science" (Segerstråle 2000: 201). In other words, bad psychometric ideology or motives lead to bad methods and bad science. It is indeed remarkable that Lewontin either did not realize, or perhaps did not want to acknowledge, that Spearman as far back as the beginning of the 19th century defended a molecular analysis — yes, explicitly urged his colleagues to identify the secrets behind his general intelligence factor g — undoubtedly pure physics and chemistry of the brain, he ventured. With that feat, physiology would have achieved one of its greatest triumphs, he said. It was just that Spearman did not command proper methods for doing molecular analyses, and it is not fair to criticize a scientist for not having access to then non-existing methods he would have loved to use.

Lewontin also appears to have missed the fact that Jensen had over many years steadily accumulated data to suggest that g is related to a multitude of brain physiological parameters, and that he explicitly used this evidence to argue that g is not just the "wisp of archane mathematical machinations", that he was accused of blindly believing in. Jensen even pursued the question whether g - physiology connections go through ontogenetic, phylogenetic, or perhaps environmental mechanisms. The late Hans Eysenck, also viciously attacked by the leftists for unsound abstractions, repeatedly stressed the essentially biological nature of personality and g. Hans actually discussed at some length which (brain) chemicals would be relevant for such a proposition. Lewontin and other critics seem to miss that many neuroscientists successfully use brain imaging techniques to illustrate that important neurochemical parameters correlate with cognitive problem solving. The present editor (Nyborg 1994) wrote an entire book on the molecular basis of human nature and intelligence.

How could Lewontin fail to acknowledge all these attempts to reveal the "molecular" basis of *g*, and instead postulate all kinds of malevolent political motives or bad science? If this type of highly selective reporting is not bad science, then what is? But then again, it becomes fully understandable how Lewontin could reach the conclusion that our present ignorance is enormous and ". . . the need for the socially powerful to exonerate their institutions of responsibility for the problems they have created is extremely strong . . ." and that ". . . any investigations into the genetic control of human behaviors is bound to produce a pseudo-science that will inevitably be misused" (Lewontin 1975a).

Segerstråle (2000: 202) concluded that, apparently: ". . . it was *morally wrong for a scientist to produce anything else than absolutely certain knowledge*" (original emphasis). She further noted that this represents ". . . in a nutshell the general moral-cum-scientific spirit characteristic of the Sociobiology Study Group . . ." (p. 203). May I add: this is not just bad science, it is a distortion and antithesis to science.

6. Genes, Culture and Human Development

6.1. Introduction

Why were so many people desperately afraid to acknowledge even the slightest conservative effects of genes on human development and behavior? Given a choice, why would most people rather subscribe to an extreme version of the environmental paradigm, such as the one nourished by the founder of modern anthropology, Franz Boas, and his followers in the first third of the 20th century, than admit to even a moderate form of genetic determinism? Jensen certainly wondered.

Sociobiologist Edward O. Wilson also took up this dilemma in his latest opus, *Consilience: The Unity of Knowledge* from 1998. Point of departure for the discussion was the "Standard Social Science Model (SSSM), as defined by Cosmides & Tooby (1992). The SSSM sees culture as a system of symbols and meanings that mould individual minds and social institutions. This idea sounded reasonable enough to Wilson, but the SSSM also sees culture as the product of environment and historical antecedents, not reducible to elements of biology and psychology, and here Wilson strongly dissents, because the model implies that the human mind cannot create culture but is the product of that culture. Obviously, the SSSM cannot be defended just on the basis of fear that genetic determinism is morally wrong as it easily lends support to sexism, racism, war and class division as inevitable phenomena.

6.2. Plausibility, Reality and Explanations

Likewise, why are so many social scientists readily prepared to see another scientist as a moral pariah if he dared question the unfounded notion that developmental differences are 100% determined by environmental factors? Sheer ignorance is not the case for all ". . . otherwise objective and dispassionate intellectuals [who] display such vehement moral indignation and even zealous combativeness toward any explanation of human behavior differences, especially social class and racial differences, that propounds genetic factors as playing a part" (Jensen 1972: 55).

Obviously, Jensen had good reasons to mull over this question. His preliminary answer reflects an incredible fair and decent man's reasoning, considering the hateful context for the discussion. He even goes as far as to believe that those who have most strongly opposed him have ". . . done so out of noble but mistaken sentiments . . ." and that ". . . their motives are not entirely discreditable". As he says: "We all feel some uneasiness and discomfort at the notion of differences among persons in traits that we especially value, such as mental abilities, which have obviously important educational, occupational, and social correlates . . . our first tendency is to minimize them or explain them away. This is even more true when we are confronted with group differences; it seems to us so intrinsically unjust that some socially defined groups, through no fault of their own, should be disadvantaged with respect to traits which all persons value that we are easily inclined to deny such differences or at least attribute them to relatively superficial and external causes and appearances, such as prejudice, biased tests and observations, discriminatory schooling, racism, and other similar explanations which tend to place blame and guilt on other persons and forces in society. And there is considerable plausibility to such thinking . . ." (ibid.: 55–56).

Where then does all this "plausibility" come from? Two places, according to Jensen: a human proclivity to place blame for disadvantage or misfortune, and simple Skinnerian shaping. To see the blame placing mechanism we just have to look back to ancient times, where ". . . natural disasters such as volcanos, earthquakes, and floods were blamed on the ill-will of personified gods". Whereas the physical sciences now provide "natural" explanations for this ". . . the social sciences still have not moved beyond personified blame, leveled at "society", "the establishment", "Capitalism", or whatever — personified entities at which we can vent our anger much as one can feel angry at an individual who intentionally commits a personal offense" (p. 56).

Jensen then goes on to offer illustrative examples of Skinnerian shaping from his own rich experiences in teaching psychology and education. Any statement that minimizes, explains away, glosses over, or places blame on personified institutions for mental and educational differences between individuals or groups ". . . is met by an unmistakable rush of warm approval from the audience" (p. 56). This approval ". . . shapes more than anything else the speaker's utterances further toward eliciting more waves of warm approval from the audience . . . lessens the audience's anxiety . . . almost palpable, with bits of laughter and the rustle of relaxing tensions among the listeners", with the effect of reinforcing the speaker in that direction, often unconsciously and even against his will".

From my own experiences from lecturing on the development of individual and groups differences in intelligence and behavior genetics, these reactions certainly make you think twice next time you present the data. Try a little exercise for yourself. Give a brief lecture on sex differences in intelligence, and begin with the massive documentation for a male superiority in 3-D spatial abilities. You immediately see a surprisingly coordinated and self-reinforcing tension. The audience suddenly moves, some straighten up, turn toward the neighbor and whisper a brief comment. The others nod approvingly, send an overbearing smile, or even laugh demonstratively loud. Some begin to eagerly scribble hasty notes on paper, preparing for an angry rebuttal, that will surface a few minutes later. At that time it simply is not possible to cure the open hostility of the audience, even if you now document, that females are superior to males in some verbal abilities. Minds are set for blaming somebody — the messenger of the bad message. Now present the same data to new students, but this time first report on the female verbal superiority. You will see approving smiles, and then you can get away unhurt reporting on the male superiority in spatial ability.

These students are not dumb. What is failing here is that many (most?) modern psychology students are not trained properly in independent and critical scientific thinking. They rather think in plausibility terms, and are well accustomed to argue in politically correct ways. They prefer moral to empirical reasoning and reading, and many are impressed by post-modern relativism, to such an extent that they automatically launch an antiscientific critical program as if that was the last word on the matter. To many of them science and data are texts waiting to be contextualized — not carefully controlled attempts towards increased precision. Most are not aware that they are betraying scientific stringency, and feel good by attacking any messengers of "bad" information. They got their coupled-reasoning lessons from Gould, Lewontin, and modern French philosophers, and they want to feel good, socially safe and justified.

Jensen (1972: 57) asked several colleagues what intellectual reasons they could see for denying a genetic basis for behavioral differences. The most common reason was that ". . . such knowledge, if it is established and generally accepted by the scientific and intellectual community, might be used by some persons for evil purposes, to promote racial prejudice, discrimination, and segregations and to justify or rationalize the political suppression, and economic exploitation of racial minorities and the Nations' working class in general".

Jensen is not moved by such arguments: ". . . these consequences do not logically follow from the recognition of genetic behavioral differences. Nearly all scientifically important knowledge can be used for good or ill. Intellectuals should be concerned with men's purposes and the uses to which knowledge will be put; they should never think in terms of suppressing knowledge or the quest for it".

Another expressed worry is the fear that differences in gene frequencies for some traits will automatically compromise the moral ideal of equality expressed in "all men are created equal", and would hinder equality before the law, education, civil rights etc. But this is not so, Jensen says: "Realization of the moral ideal of equality proclaimed in the Declaration of Independence, of course, does not depend upon either phenotypic or genotypic equality of individuals' psychological qualities".

Still another misconception that pops up repeatedly in the attacks on Jensen is that genetic differences between populations are ". . . somehow, *sui generis*, intrinsic, unchangeable, protoplasmic differences" (author's emphasis, p. 57). This is a completely wrong and ignorant notion, promulgated in racist tracts, Jensen says: "There is nothing at all "intrinsic" or "immutable" about human gene pools", as specific gene frequencies reflect mainly "... varying degrees of geographic and social isolation of breeding groups and natural selection", through differing environmental pressures.

6.3. Summing Up the Critique

When carefully analyzed the critique boils down to a number of sociopolitical and moral attitudes that for the most part can be condensed to the following statements (of unknown source), that defenders have to take into account:

(1) All individuals and human groups are the same with respect to intelligence, personality and behavior.

(2) Academics must speak with one voice thereabout.

(3) It is the duty of scholarly and other organizations to enforce politically correct ways of talking about the origin of individual and group differences.

(4) However, should any difference be found, it must be ascribed to environmental factors.

(5) The prime task of the social scientists is then to change these environmental factors in such a way that the difference disappears.

(6) Should any difference resist environmental intervention, it should be ascribed to the need for further research, lack of funding, or too little time to correct.

(7) Never should the differences be explained by genetic factors or gene-environment correlation or interaction.

(8) Should the differences nevertheless suggest a genetic component, environmental factors must immediately be invoked to annul them.

(9) Should the differences nevertheless remain, stricter than normal scientific criteria must be established before any genetic influence is accepted by, say, requesting identical environment for all individual or groups.

(10) Any behavioral scientists claiming even a moderately genetic effect must immediately be sanctioned against.

(11) Non-environmentalist outcomes should be misrepresented, strawmen invented and torn apart, or possible but implausible alternative solutions should be put into effect.

(12) It should be emphasized that there are certain subjects that should not be investigated at this time in history.

(13) Should any scholar be unable to understand or accept the much stricter criteria for differential psychological research, he should be punished.

(14) Should any journalists be unable to understand the rules for politically correct presentation, higher editorial levels must intervene and correct.

7. Destructive Social Reductionism and Collective Fraud

7.1. Introduction

The critique of Jensen is a perfect example of how 20th century academic freedom has come under siege in the West, as it was previously in the East. It suggests that the hostility of the academic left towards individualism and biological explanations plays a major role in ruining the research climate in modern academia, despite superficial declarations of adherence to open-minded research and obligatory cocktail-party proclamations of freedom for all.

The more we look into the literature on this depressing scenario, the more destructive the social reductionist point of view appears, and the more serious becomes the threat to academic freedom, even to a former left-oriented person like myself.

Segerstråle raised a pertinent question, also pondered by Gross and Levitt: How on earth could the environmentalist/culturalist position become so forceful in academia, and why was it automatically linked to progressive politics. Segerstråle traces the answer to ". . . the post-Second World War situation and particularly . . . the famous UNESCO agreement in 1952, which effectively put a ban on biological research in human behavior. It was precisely this taboo that sociobiologist Wilson, and before him, IQ researcher Arthur Jensen and the behavioral geneticists, were breaking" (2000: 30).

There is more to the story than that, however. As we saw, the demonization of Jensen could be dealt with analytically at a surface level in terms of the previous simple model, according to which Jensen switched from neutral decision mode 1 to biological mode 2 in Zeitgeist mode 2, a change towards biological thinking at a time where all such manifestations were banned, punished on a personal basis, and where confirmatory data were seen as politically motivated. Clearly, the broad sweep, the generality, and the noticeable hostility towards Jensen across many layers of academic and public life cannot be fully appreciated within such a narrow analytic frame.

We need to eyeball the full social-academic-organizational-political-public horizon in order to understand in details why so many scientists, professional and international organizations, and the press at large, could so easily unite in such a surprisingly effective self-reinforcing synchrony, and act almost like a well-disciplined team to muster the brutal and direct force against apostates. We have to combine all the destructive elements of social reductionism — such as the role of religion, the egalitarian fiction, the self-perceived moral superiority of the critics, the open suppression of empirical alternatives, the corruption of professional organizations, the urge toward political correctness, the threats to biological projects and funding — in order to fully understand the explosive sequence of events and how they finally amount to nothing less than a large scale collective academic fraud, and even "inverse" fraud. The following section introduces some semi-dependent variables needed for the second part of the analysis.

7.2. Semi-dependent Variables

7.2.1. Equality   Garrett (1961) described a journalistic credo called "egalitarian orthodoxy" involving flat denial or a softening of the likelihood that genes may partly explain race, sex or individual differences in intelligence, personality or interests etc.

Linda Gottfredson is even more explicit here. In an article — Egalitarian fiction and collective fraud (1994) she said: "Social science today condones and perpetuates a great falsehood . . . or 'egalitarian fiction' . . . that racial-ethnic groups never differ in average . . . *g* . . . general . . . ability . . ." While individual scientists' intellectual dishonesty is well-known, little attention has been given to the ways in which collectives of scientists ". . . have perpetuated frauds on the scientific community and the public at large".

She further noted that no scientist in the collective can probably be accused of fraud in the usual sense, but ". . . their seemingly minor distortions, untruths, evasions, and biases collectively produce and maintain a witting falsehood" (ibid.: 53).

Which social processes could be responsible for this? asks Gottfredson. After having established the general agreement among experts about the existence of a real average difference, she points to the results of an important study by Snyderman & Rothman (1988) — *The IQ controversy: The media and public policy* — providing strong evidence that the general public receives a highly distorted view of opinion among 'IQ experts' (ibid.: 54). The public press has left the opinion that many experts agree that intelligence cannot be defined well, that IQ tests cannot be used outside the school, and that they are biased against minorities, even if most experts are of the opposite opinion. This is interesting because the study also showed that most experts privately agree with Arthur Jensen, who is constantly exposed in the media for holding just such views. Despite the change in expert view toward Jensen, obviously guided by the overwhelming weight of the evidence, the public impression has not moved correspondingly. Gottfredson takes Snyderman & Rothman's findings to suggest that many ". . . experts misrepresent their belief or are keeping silent in the face of a public falsehood. It is no wonder that the public remains misinformed on this issue" (p. 55).

Linda Gottfredson was close to being sacked from Delaware University in the U.S. for accepting a research grant from the previously mentioned Pioneer Fund for investigating IQ-occupation relationships. Her characterization of the rather bleak situation in 20th century academia is illustrative:

> "Perhaps the most aggressively perpetrated collective fraud in the social sciences today is that which sustains the egalitarian fiction. This is the frequent but false assertion that intelligence is clustered equally across all human populations, that is, that there are, on average, no racial-ethnic disparities in developed mental competence" (Gotfredson 2000).

Gottfredson's notion of collective fraud will be used in the present analysis, but the scope will not be restricted to race differences in intelligence, but will include the entire social reductionistic conspiracy against any researcher, who dares investigate individual or group differences in physique, intelligence, personality, achievement, or behavior in general, and the evolutionary, genetic, physiological or brain bases of these differences. I will term this the "Grand academic leftist collective fraud" hypothesis.

7.2.2. The role of religion and philosophy

Jensen notes that definitions always arise in a particular context of understanding, and that contexts differ from one period to another (termed Zeitgeists in this chapter), and from one scientist to another. The early context for intelligence was Platonic philosophy and Christian theology. Jensen (1998: 1) observed: "This vastly delayed the study of . . . intelligence . . . as manifesting individual differences . . . [intelligence] was identified with the soul and seen as a perfect, immaterial, universal attribute of humans, and both definitions were counterproductive. It took a Darwin (1859/1872) to counter blatant environmentalism (e.g. Locke 1690) and to realize that the evolution of intelligence is basically a biological phenomenon common to man and other animals, a Spencer (1820–1903) to defend Darwin, counter dualism, and hammer out that, intelligence is a physiological mean for individually adjusting internal to external conditions, a Galton (1822–1911, 1869) to establish differential psychology which sets the study of individual and group differences on a solid scientific track, and a Spearman (1904) to define and measure intelligence objectively".

7.2.3. The egalitarian fiction Gottfredson (1994) saw no need to mingle her words when she wrote that egalitarians often assert that the egalitarian promise is absolute truth beyond scientific scrutiny whereas the opposite view may be discredited through misrepresentation, by contradicting arguments never made while ignoring what was actually said, by attributing political preferences to an author that he never has had, or by simply alleging fraud or gross incompetence with no substantiation. "The study of race and intelligence is something they tell us, that no decent person — let alone a serious scientist — would ever do and that every decent person and serious researcher would oppose. Thus, in a kind of Orwellian inversion, marked by what Gordon (1993) calls 'high talk and low blows,' the suppression of science presents itself as science itself. Intellectual dishonesty becomes the handmaiden of social conscience, and ideology is declared knowledge while knowledge is dismissed as mere ideology". This is all the more tragic because enforcement of the egalitarian fiction ". . . tries to defy a reality and produces what it was meant to avoid, that is, producing pejorative racial stereotypes, fostering racial tensions, stripping members of lower-scoring groups of their dignity and incentives to achieve, and creating permanent social inequalities between the races".

7.2.4. The role of funding organizations Most scientists need funding in order to do research, and most funding agents make an attempt to define what they find worth funding. As demand is usually much larger than supply, the individual scientist has to conform to — or at least better pay close attention to — which projects the funding agents think are worth supporting. This is all well known, but what is perhaps less acknowledged is, that the basic motivation of most major philanthropic funds in the U.S., and probably also in Europe, changed markedly in recent times.

Heather MacDonald (2000) took the trouble to describe the change in a series of essays, now collected and published as a book — *The burden of bad ideas*. According to MacDonald, quite radical changes took place in, what in the present context corresponds to the middle of Zeitgeist mode 2, i.e. around 1960–1970, where large funding agents got increasingly inspired by left oriented ideas emanating from within the American academy, from political think tanks, and from organizations for the arts and sciences.

Before the change, such foundations as Carnegie, Ford, Mellon, Mott and Rockefeller gave most of their money to establish concert halls, hospitals, libraries, museums or universities, with the goal of extending the opportunities of the less fortunate. After the change, the foundations began to support projects that, instead of seeking mobility and success for the less privileged, rather promoted "advocacy" and "empowerment" by way of "community action" and "collaboratives" to overthrow the "racist, sexist, and classist edifice" upon which America had been founded. This change of mind, from traditional values, to prevailing left oriented political-economic-cultural themes had, according to MacDonald, a profound effect on research at The Ivy League Universities, the National Institutes of Health, the Centers for Disease Control, but also the New York State Regents, the New York Times, and the Smithsonian Institute were affected by the change of mind.

Obviously, the changes also affected the nature of educational policy, and research on "critical-thinking skills", "community-building", "brainstorming", "student-centered learning" substituted to some extent the older "content-based" curricula and ability guided teaching.

MacDonald is, according to Peter Savodnik (2000: 38), almost alone in describing this major change in funding in the U.S. in the 1960s, and he ends by concluding: "The hugely wasteful social-engineering experiments have . . . wrought . . . widespread havoc on the people least able to defend themselves against the well-funded programs of America's radical establishment".

Project Head Start comes to mind here. It was the conspicuous lack of documentation for a clear benefit for the culturally deprived children involved in this multi-million dollar program that alerted Arthur Jensen, and the negative outcome of his (and other's) analysis got him into trouble. While we are still waiting for a documentation of the lasting positive effects of such programs, we can speculate on how easily the academic left was able to redirect major funding their particular way.

Whatever the answer is to that question, the massive redirection of research funding no doubt socialized many researchers away from what they originally planned, and towards projects that conform to the new goals. This most certainly would drain the funding for psychometrics and behavioral genetics.

7.2.5. Individual suppression of academic freedom   Gottfredson (1994) wondered why the experts keep their mouth shut about the obvious, and provided the answer herself: Because IQ experts have learned to "live within a lie", quite like the people living under communist rule in Eastern Europe, as so aptly noted by Vaclav Havel. Here ordinary citizens were complicit in their own tyranny because they silently had to play the game of the rulers and thus unwillingly became supporters of the tyranny they detested.

Coleman, who is perhaps best known for his monumental report on *Equality of educational opportunity* (Coleman *et al.* 1966) knew precisely how it is to live within a lie. He, thus, later (1990–1991) reflected with regret on why he deliberately neglected certain unpopular aspects of his otherwise eminent social science analysis. The excuse he gave was, that academics establish norms for themselves for which kinds of questions to raise and which to avoid. One of the most influential norms is: never ever raise questions about possible biological roots to intellectual race- and sex-related differences. All academics "know" by heart that such questions rapidly and inevitably raise incredible tensions forcing their faculty to harsh repercussions, so they have to be avoided at all costs, even if truth is one of them. Unfortunately, not only truth suffers here. Coleman admitted that our possibilities of ever coming to grip with important aspects of the causal basis for the social phenomena studied may be permanently stultified.

7.2.6. Collective suppression of academic freedom While the reasons for individuals to keep their mouth shut in dangerous matters like IQ are fairly obvious, it is more complicated to answer the question why groups of experts keep their mouth shut about the obvious? Could it be that there is now a collectively structured silence, where groups of social scientists deliberately subordinate scientific norms to political preferences and create a kind of pseudo-reality?

Wolf (1972) noted that many contemporary social scientists keep ". . . presenting inconclusive data as if it were decisive; lacking candor about 'touchy' subjects . . .; blurring or shaping definitions (segregation, discrimination, racism) to suit 'propagandistic' purposes; making exaggerated claims about the success of favored policies (compensatory education and school integration) while minimizing or ignoring contrary evidence". They are under great professional and institutional pressure, because peer recognition is the currency of academic and scientific life and decisive for promotion, status, and funding. Even the smallest digression from politically correct ambitions could irreparably damage an otherwise successful professional career. Even just expressing respect for the "right" people counts on the positive side, whereas ". . . honoring, defending, or even failing to condemn the 'wrong' sort of individual or idea . . ." might stain one's reputation (p. 56).

According to Gottfredson (1994), such a system breeds intellectual corruption. This is precisely what appears to be happening today in the social sciences on matters of race and intelligence. While certainly being a personal annoyance, all these threatening activities had the unfortunate effect of silencing colleagues who otherwise might have joined in the defense of Jensen's cause. Jensen received a large number of supportive letters, but many of the writers explicitly stated that they preferred to remain anonymous, so as not to be subjected to a similar treatment. Jensen (1972) gave an example of a colleague who got his paper returned with proper payment and a letter from the editor explaining ". . . we have finally decided against entering the controversy altogether". When Jensen urged the author to try and publish his paper elsewhere, he said: ". . . because of the abuse which you have received, I have no intention of submitting my paper for publication elsewhere" (p. 47)

Gordon (1993) argues that many social scientists demonstrate their party loyalty to the egalitarian fiction by enforcing it in myriads of small ways in their academic routine by off-handedly dismissing race differences in intelligence as racist claims, blaming the victim, or discouraging students and colleagues from doing "sensitive" research. Overt censorship is common to those "not knowing where to step".

Gottfredson (1994) finds that ". . . the lie is gradually distorting and degrading all institutions and processes where intelligence is at least somewhat important . . . public schools, higher education, the professions, and high-level executive work" (p. 58). She concluded that ". . . society is being shaped to meet the dictates of a collective fraud. The fiction is aiding and abetting bigots to a far greater degree than any truth ever could, because its specific side-effects — racial preferences, official mendacity, free-wielding accusations of racism, and falling standards — are creating deep cynicism and broad resentment against minorities, blacks in particular, among the citizenry".

7.2.7. Collective bias in academia   All this had the chilling effect of silencing large parts of academia, and began more and more to look like a sweeping collective fraud, extending downwards to university administrators and funding agents, and upwards to huge professional organizations, and to public policy where individual politicians could harvest easy votes, and where the political left and right parties, creationists, and others with heavily vested interests in evading the role of biology and individual differences in intelligence for human behavior, and keep a kind of socially based pseudo-solidarity with the disadvantages.

There are many further ways to censor than the overt forms, according to Gordon (1993). One is to establish speech-codes on campus, another to subject National Institute of Health research application to an extra layer of review for politically "sensitive" grant proposals, still another to ban particular funding sources. The latter became the policy of the University of Delaware because, as the University said, funding of research on race ". . . conflicts with the university's mission to promote racial and cultural diversity" (Gottfredson 1994: 56).

7.2.8. Collective bias in professional organizations   It is not just individuals who can be harmed by opposing the current dogma of the social sciences that all differences in intelligence — individual, sex, or race differences — are caused by some form of discrimination or omission. So can scientific organizations, and they are noticeably sensitive to this potential danger. Gottfredson (1994) explains: "It raises the public and scientific respect for the organization whenever it honors an individual that lives well up to the dogma, and degrades it in the eyes of others should a non-dogmatic person be awarded. It provides respect to issue statements conforming to the dogma even, or perhaps in particular, if it pours scorn on non-conformers, like Jensen".

7.2.9. Bias in national and cross-national organizations   Even such high-profiled organizations like UNESCO and the UN take part in the collective fraud. I previously referred to factually incorrect statements by such organizations. Recently, United Nations Secretary General, Kofi Annan declared that intelligence: ". . . is one commodity equally distributed among the world's people" (Hoyos & Littlejohn 2000). It takes only a brief inspection of the massive cumulative long-term documentation for marked national differences in IQ by Lynn & Vanhanen (2002) to see, that such counter-factual statements neither serves the credibility of the organization as such nor its top representatives. It may very well be that the purpose of the statement was meant politically or strategically, but cross-national policy based on lies — great or small — might easily bounce back in non-productive ways.

7.2.10. Devastating political correctness (PC)   Webster's New World Dictionary of American English (1994) describes political correctness as ". . . orthodox liberal opinion on matters of sexuality, race ... usually used disparagingly to connote dogmatism, excessive sensitivity to minority causes ..." Weyher (1998) refers in a discussion of PC to a cover story in Newsweek (24 December 1990) where it is said that: "P.C. is Marxist in origin, in the broad sense of attempting to redistribute power from the privileged class (white males) to the oppressed masses. It represents the values of social equality and social justice over that of free speech".

"For the first time in our history, Americans have to be fearful of what they say, of what they write, and of what they think. They have to be afraid of using the wrong word, a word denounced as offensive or insensitive, or racist, sexist, or homophobic". These words are from a lecture by Bill Lind at a conference at George Washington University in 1998. We have seen PC in other countries, now we have it here, and primarily on campuses, but it is spreading throughout society. Historically, PC is Marxism translated from economic into cultural terms, and the parallels to classical Marxism are very obvious, according to Lind. It is the child of a totalitarian ideology and it is deadly serious: "... the student or faculty member who dares to cross any of the lines set up by the gender feminist or the homosexual-rights activists, or the local black or Hispanic group, or any of the other sainted "victims" groups that PC revolves around, quickly find themselves in judicial trouble. Within the small legal system of the college, they face formal charges ... and punishment".

The formally installed "speech codes" at some campuses reflect PC, and the strong statements from minority students organizations against Jensen, as well as the violent reaction towards anybody transgressing the not so fine line, all tell a story of repression of academic freedom, that surely will inform researchers of any stripes of what is best to do here and now, and it may explain in part why individuals as well as large professional groups bow to PC. Whatever the PC term precisely refers to, transgression of it can issue a deadly blow to one's scientific reputation.

7.3. Summing It All Up

Gross & Levitt (1998) took the trouble to sum it all up. They stressed that the critics rode on a too high moral horse. Perhaps they were too good to be true. They were willing to sacrifice Jensen at the price of their own scientific integrity and honesty. They practiced selective reading, omitted major points, denied well-established research, and were carried to fame on morally well-sounding statements that sat well with the public. Educators, eager to find some consolation for the slow progress in raising the learning curves for the disadvantaged, welcomed the promises of easy progress and participated all too willingly in the attacks on messengers of bad news. Colleagues noticed the unmerciful treatment of Jensen and bent their heads in silence. Young scientists soon realized that their future could not safely be built on pursuing a career in psychometrics or behavioral genetics. Granting committees, such as the Pioneer Fund soon realized that funding people like Jensen rapidly raised critical questions about their own sinister motives — didn't they have hidden racist leanings, didn't they have neo-nazi connections, etc. The smears would take no end, even if they showed the critics to the door by exposing their errors (Lynn 2001).

7.4. The "Inverse" Fraud of Gould and Lewontin

Fraud is defined in the present context as the critic's deliberate distortion of solid evidence on individual and group differences in physique, intelligence, personality and behavior, and as the misrepresentation of scientists that collect such data. However, the critics also use the term fraud but in an inverse form. To the critics, fraud could be spotted through moral reading and massaging of texts to reveal the truly evil motives behind apparently innocent data.

Gould was a tireless master of inverse fraud. He thus warned us ". . . how theory and unconscious presupposition always influence our analysis and organization of presumably objective data" (1996: 49). Previously, in his original (1981) version of *The Mismeasure of Man*, he had said: "If the cultural influences upon science can be detected in the humdrum minutiae of a supposedly objective, almost automatic quantification, then the status of biological determinism as a social prejudice reflected by scientists in their own particular medium seems secure" (p. 58). Moreover: "In reanalyzing . . . classical data sets, I have continually located *a priori* prejudice, leading scientists to invalid conclusions from adequate data, or distorting the gathering of data itself. In a few cases . . . we can specify conscious fraud as the cause of inserted social prejudice. But fraud is not historically interesting except as gossip because the perpetrators know what they are doing and the *unconscious* biases that record subtle and inescapable constraints of culture are not illustrated. In most cases discussed in this book, we can be fairly certain that biases — though often expressed as egregiously as in the cases of conscious fraud — were unknowingly influential and that scientists believed they were pursuing unsullied truth" (Gould 1996: 59, original emphasis).

Many other examples of inverse fraud can be found in the 1986 book by Schiff and Lewontin — *Education and class: The irrelevance of IQ genetic studies*. In the foreword, Halsey accurately reflects the particular direction and aggressive intent of the book by stating: ". . . the authors steadfastly and indeed belligerently declare their ideological bias to environmentalism . . ." (in Schiff & Lewontin 1986: v), and on the next page he characterizes Sir Cyril Burt ". . . as a dominating figure who slid from obsession through pseudo-science into outright fraud" (p. vi).

The Schiff and Lewontin book refers to Franz Boas (1912), who in 1909–1910 measured the heads of 13,000 immigrants born in Europe and of their children born in America. Boas found striking effects on the cranial form as a function of the length of exposure to an American upbringing. Boas, who often targeted "scientific racism" or false thinking about races, took this result as proof that racial head characteristics depend on environmental rather than genetic factors, and concluded that those who think otherwise are racists. In particular the disciples of Boas, such as anthropologists Ruth Benedict, Margaret Mead and Ashley Montagu were instrumental in promoting this kind of social reductionist view of human nature.

However, Sparks & Jantz (2002) have 90 years later re-examined Boas' published data and found, that the effects of the new environment on head form were "insignificant". They found "negligible" differences between parents' and childrens' head form, in comparison to the differentiation among ethnic groups. It is food for thought that Gould, Lewontin and many other critics have used this study to bolster a social-reductionistic view on race. They are the people who call for the uttermost caution in interpretation of data, while at the same time accuse Jensen of dishonesty.

Schiff informs us on page xi: ". . . that questions concerning genetic effects are essentially irrelevant to . . . access to education. Later (in Schiff & Lewontin 1986: xiii) he declares that ". . . theories of innate differences arise from political issues . . .", and in their introduction to the book Schiff & Lewontin state that ". . . we try to show that, as far as education is concerned, most genetic studies are not only unsound but are also irrelevant" (p. xiii).

Discussing phrenology Schiff & Lewontin (1986) state, "As it turns out, there is no correlation at all between the size of an adult's brain and his or her ability to perform intellectually" (p. 7). They therefore see their book as a direct attempt ". . . to oppose the errors of biological theory of *social* class, and to present competing evidence that class is a social phenomenon, *created* by the structure of social relations, and not dictated by our genes" (p. 14, original emphasis), and they further claim that ". . . the nature-nurture debate is actually a smokescreen for a debate over the interaction between individual differences and social structure" (p. 17).

Many IQ experts try to cover this by using double-talk, and "The most sophisticated type of double-talk concerning the word "intelligence" is that of Jensen (1980), whose technical analysis boils down to the definition attributed to Binet ("intelligence is what my test measures")".

Schiff & Lewontin (1986) conclude the first part of their book by stating that ". . . procedures used to validate "intelligence" tests are as socially determined as the tests themselves. The high degree of sophistication of some of their procedures only serves to mask an unwillingness to face the social, psychological, and ethical questions posed by the construction and use of IQ tests" (pp. 32–33), that ". . . discussions about IQ usually fail to distinguish clearly between questions of fact and questions of values. In addition, they are often obscured by technical confusion". There is a ". . . refusal to consider social class as a basic component of present reality. Finally, the circular nature of attempts to validate IQ scores stems from this same inability to question current social values".

The authors then react strongly against the idea that social inequality may be attributed ". . . to differences in innate ability between the children of the different social classes, as revealed by differences in the distributions of IQ scores" because ". . . white middle-class people decide who is intelligent and who is not", and as long as ". . . teachers, filled with goodwill and with ethnocentric naïvity, view human intelligence through their own school training, the academic failure of working-class children will be built into the school and social system" (p. 125).

In counting the many errors about genetics and their social consequences Schiff & Lewontin (1986) draw attention to a "striking feature": ". . . the degree to which a supposedly "Scientific" field is permeated with basic conceptual and experimental errors . . . much of the discussion of the biology of intelligence would simply evaporate if fundamental biological and statistical notions were applied to the genetics of human behaviour with the same degree of rigour and logic that is standard in, say, the study of milk yield in cattle or body weight in mice" (p. 169).

Discussing the why of intelligence testing, Schiff & Lewontin (1986) state that "The purpose of the IQ test is to identify the potential winners presumably so that society will not waste its precious resources on those whose abilities are insufficient" and behind lies "... the claim that this social organization is an inevitable manifestation of human biology, that the war of all against all is a natural law" (pp. 184–185).

In a section called Error 12: If it is new and complicated it must be true, Schiff & Lewontin (1986) say: "Partly through self-delusion, and partly through a deliberate attempt to mystify the innocent, some of those who have written about the genetics of IQ have tried to make the story more believable by making it more complicated" by "... introducing a complex mathematical model involving many variables and parameters and finding the set of parameters that best fits the data" and so "... for that reason alone seem deeper and more 'scientific'" (e.g. Eysenck 1979: 3) and "It is absurd to think that the numbers that come from such models have any meaning" (pp. 185–187).

This is an excellent example of an inverse fraud win-win strategy running along the line: If heads I win, if tails you loose. If Jensen used the same old simple outworn methods, the field has stagnated; if Jensen developed new and more complicated methods a false sense of depth is pretended. Never mind if the new methods provide more reliable results with broader applicability in other areas. Jensen has to be framed in a catch 22-situation.

But the story of inverse fraud does not end here. The social implications of the many conceptual errors that have been propagated in the field of IQ studies come together, according to Schiff & Lewontin (1986), to press home a single major theme where the bottom line is: "Differences between social class and races are heritable and unchangeable ...". Therefore "... social policy that attempts to change either the structure or the assignment of groups to it is misdirected, as waste of time, and even harmful because it raises hopes that are bound to be dashed. It is essentially an argument for the inevitability and justice of the status quo. It is fairly obvious who the argument serves" (p. 187).

Bouchard & McGue are also treated unkindly by Schiff & Lewontin (1986). They reported in 1981 on resemblance correlations for 43 parent-offspring and 69 siblings. The comment from Schiff & Lewontin (ibid.) was: "Since these studies provide essentially no genetic information, one can wonder why society has paid scientists to repeat essentially the same observation for so long". Apparently, when scientists strive to reproduce potentially controversial observations they are at fault, and this principle can be used as a weapon against the enemy. Again, either way, you lose. Presumably, the many later confirmative studies raise even more serious questions about the sinister motives of those who did them and those who financed them.

Schiff & Lewontin (ibid.) motivate the writing of their book with the goal of providing the reader with a key to the literature on nature-nurture and IQ, so that by following their prescriptions the reader will be able to focus on the general principles rather than on any particular study, and "... concentrate on the questions rather than on the answers" (p. 192).

Key reading seems here to be just another word for moral reading or coupled reasoning: disregard the data and concentrate instead on why the researcher took the trouble to investigate the biological basis of race or intelligence. This kind of reading is, in fact, essential for understanding the true nature of social reductionist critique and its destructive nature. However, what is at stake here is more than a particular moral standing or reading of texts in the nature-nurture and IQ debates; rather it is an example of an immoral and destructive instruction how to dismiss data, however solid, in order to promote what Gottfredson defines as collective fraud.

It is therefore not surprising to see that Schiff & Lewontin (1986) concluded: "In our opinion, the most striking fact of the whole IQ story is the contrast between the use of IQ to account for social heredity and the deliberate or unaware avoidance of a direct analysis of that heredity", and that ". . . a significant fraction of the scientific establishment has handled this issue in what appeared to be an inappropriate way" (pp. 223–225). The psychometric approach to human intelligence misses ". . . the capacity to ask questions, to oneself and to others". "The biological deterministic approach . . . misses another specific feature of homo sapiens. It is homo sapiens who decide . . . how his society is organized . . .".

7.5. Inverse Illusions

Schiff and Lewontin have, quite like Gottfredson and others, a rather pessimistic view of the calamities in academia, but the signs differ radically.

To Schiff & Lewontin (1986), most workers in academia seem to suffer from two contradictory illusions: "The illusion of complete academic freedom . . . a denial or lack of awareness of social and economic pressures influencing scientific workers . . ." and the opposite illusion of ". . . complete helplessness . . . Most scientists fail to recognize that the type of question they ask and the type they choose to ignore derive both from social pressure and from a personal choice" (pp. 226–227).

To Gottfredson and others, Schiff, Lewontin and Gould tried their uttermost to limit the academic freedom; moreover Jensen *et al.* were painfully aware of the many pitfalls associated with the long haul of collecting solid data that could stand the test of critical control in a climate so hostile to their research.

While Jensen found himself mostly engaged in hard empirical work, Schiff & Lewontin (1986) felt free to speculate — without a self-perceived obligation to collect the relevant data — what the problem really was. They saw fit to conclude: ". . . the amount of knowledge about child behavior accumulated among schoolteachers is greater and of a different sort than that accumulated by academic psychologists. Even more instructive . . . is the fact of trying to change [educational processes] . . . scientists may not possess the most important part of the existing knowledge about human behavior, specifically about human intelligence . . . those who believe that they have a monopoly on something may not be the best judges of the legitimacy of that monopoly".

These hypotheses definitely deserve interest to the extent Schiff & Lewontin want to make comparisons among the predictive validity of teacher knowledge and the predictive validity of *g*. They did not do any of the hard work needed. However, the data are already out there. Why didn't they call upon it?

Lewontin & Schiff instead offer the following truly breathtaking scenario: ". . . the direct observation of human mental processes is potentially available to four billion observers. The scientific authority granted to a few concerning the functioning of the human mind may then be largely usurped". They seem to suggest: skip science, and thy will see the light! This is an inverse illusion.

7.6. Gould in Hell?

Gould's self-esteem seems not slighted towards the meek end. He never doubted that he was on the right path when he said: "May I end up next to Judas Iscariot, Brutus, and Cassius in the devil's mouth at the center of hell if I ever fail to present my most honest assessment and best judgment of evidence for empirical truth".

Speaking metaphorically, of course, I am afraid his wish will come true (provided that anybody any longer believes in such spooky things!) Neither did Gould present an honest assessment of those he countered nor did he pass the best judgment of their empirical findings. No doubt his social ambitions and care for the disadvantaged were deeply rooted in an honest responsibility, but he was a person who fought for a beautiful ideal of equality by attacking innocent scientists that as faithfully as possible presented data as they saw them, painfully aware of all the possibilities for making errors that are built into such an enterprise. Gould, and other academic leftists, never abstained from vicious *ad hominem* attack at the cost of their scientific integrity. This stands in sharp contrast to most of those they attacked and demeaned, with Jensen as the prominent counter-example.

Gould neither understood nor accepted the massive critique of his position, and he turned aggressively against anybody who questioned him. His description of his own reaction to colleagues taking him to task is telling. "The nadir certainly arrived (with a bit of humor in the absurdity) in the Fall 1983 issue of the archconservative journal, The Public Interest, when my dyspeptic colleague Bernard D. Davis published a ridiculous personal attack on me and the book under the title "Neo-Lysenkoism, IQ, and the Press". Gould also attacked *The Bell Curve* by Herrnstein & Murray (1994) in strong words by critiquing the illogic of the general argument, and the inadequacies of the book's empirical claims. Gould then became ". . . particularly pleased because Mr. Murray became so apoplectic about this article . . ." (Gould 1996: 48).

This is neither the language of science, nor is his exhilarations particularly productive, even if Gould may have scored points in certain quarters with this style ". . . because many people felt that I had provided a comprehensive and fair (if sharp) commentary . . ."

7.7. The Burden of the Academic Left

Gross & Levitt (1994/1998) went as far as to worry that the existence of the academic left ". . . has to be read as the manifestation of a certain intellectual debility afflicting the contemporary university: one that will ultimately threaten it". At the same time, Gross & Levitt are eager to assure us that obviously not all the left-oriented in academia or elsewhere are to be blamed, even if ". . . that's where most (but certainly not all) of the silliness is coming from . . ."

The damage done to universities by the leftists can hardly be underestimated, say Gross & Levitt: "Prestige-laden departments in the humanities and the social sciences are thickly populated — in some by now well-known cases we might say, without opprobrium, "dominated — by radical thinkers". Not only academic institutions, but also "Scholarly associations are often dominated by these same stars . . ." Here they refer to an analysis by Fromm (1993). It is no longer unusual to see that administrators at universities either themselves are ". . . prominent left-wing figures . . ." or ". . . more bland . . .". Either way, they have to take into account the fact that the local campus left is an important and stable segment of the academic community, whose views must be taken into account . . ." Therefore: "Often, when administrations take official positions on social issues — particularly those involving race, ethnicity, and gender questions — the tone, and the jargon as well, is indistinguishable from that of the militant left" Gross & Levitt (1994/1998: 34).

One might add here that this applies in particular, whenever individual, sex, or race differences in intelligence, are in question, or behavioral genetics results are presented. The remarkable passivity of many university officials whenever Jensen was obstructed or attacked springs to mind here.

Gross & Levitt noted that contemporary academic presses ". . . pour out dozens upon dozens of volumes, grounded in left-wing theory . . ." and that there are ". . . learned journals . . . whose purpose is avowedly political and unapologetically leftist. Universities by the score are delighted to host conferences and symposia . . ." that resound with left-wing rhetorics (p. 34).

7.8. Where Lefties Go In, Righties Go Out!

Gross & Levitt wonder how this regrettable deterioration and corruption had taken place in academia. Taking into account the isolation and neutering of significant left-wing sentiments in the world of "real" politics, Gross & Levitt speculate that, perhaps ". . . recruitment into academic careers, especially outside the exact sciences, has been altered in a way that lures people with left-wing sympathies and hopes for radical social change into scholarly careers, while simultaneously bright young students of conservative bent are less and less enchanted at the prospect of joining the professoriate . . . a diffuse phenomenon, largely inadvertent and unplanned . . . [but where] . . . the process has had the crucial goodwill of a kind of academic "silent majority", the great body of professors who, while they may distance themselves from doctrinaire ideological formulations and exotic new social theories, somehow continue to believe vaguely that the left, broad construed, remains (after all these decades) "the party of humanity", the locus of right thinking; and that it deserves to be nurtured and encourages even if it goes overboard from time to time in the vehemence of its views" (Gross & Levitt, 1994/1998: 35).

8. The Future

8.1. What Can Be Done to Counter the Collective Fraud?

Even if truly worried over the widespread corruption of academia by the left, Gross & Levitt (1994/1998) do not call for a "depoliticization" of the classroom. Honest and undogmatic intellectuals, left-oriented or not, is what Gross & Levitt call for (p. 35).

Another countermove is to continue to amass data. This is precisely what Jensen and many others have been doing, and these data have bolstered the claims Jensen made in his 1969 "*How much can we boost IQ and scholastic achievement*" HER article. Thus, despite many claims to the contrary, the 15 points black-white IQ difference has not diminished over time, even if it fluctuated. Rushton & Jensen (2003) continue to illustrate that an increasing amount of evidence is consistent with the notion that the race difference has genetic as well as environmental components (see also Chapter 9 in the present volume, and Chapter 18 for reservations). The support for a heritability estimate of IQ of about 0.80, as originally suggested by Burt, pours in from family studies (that do not allow for separation of genetic and environmental effect), and from twin and adoption studies (that do allow for the separation). We also now know that IQ heritability is low in early childhood (0.20), and that it increases steadily over the life-span to reach the above mentioned 0.80 in late adulthood. It has been demonstrated again and again that properly administered IQ tests are not culturally biased, that IQ measures have better reliability and predictive validity than any other measure provided by 20th century psychology. It is also generally acknowledged that the insane discussion of whether IQ or *g* is a reified thing in the head is a long since dead issue. What really counts is its operational definition and practical validity.

One of the most ironic aspects of the nature-nurture debate is that behavior genetics has succeeded in developing new and more precise measures of the effects of environmental factors on development, than the social reductionist could ever dream of. Where environmentalists still claim that early rearing or deprivation exert a massive impact on development, but never providing the much-needed tabulation of effects, behavior genetics separates the shared and non-shared factors, and studies them in within- and between-families designs. The results have been stunning. The longer an adopted child remains in a new family the more it differentiates away from it developmentally, psychologically, behaviorally and physically, and the more it grows towards increasing similarity with the biological parent it does not know. The heritability coefficients grow with age for all these traits, and the intelligence of the child becomes increasingly similar to that of the biological parents, whereas it looses all similarity with the intelligence of the foster parents after age 5 or 6. These observations contradict traditional social learning theory, and they keep pouring in.

Gottfredson's (1994) cure against the collective fraud is to break down the egalitarian fiction, and avoid all its harm. This does not require heroism, but rather "... for scientists to act like scientists — to demand, clearly and consistently, respect for truth and for free inquiry in their own settings, and to resist the temptation to win easy approval by endorsing a comfortable lie" (p. 59). It may sound easy, but it is not. It has been said that a theory dies only when its inventor dies or, phrased more elegantly by Max Planck: ". . . a new scientific truth does not triumph by convincing its opponents and making them see the light, but rather because its opponents eventually die, and a new generation grows up that is familiar with it".

This suggests that the readiness with which we accept, construct or defend certain types of theory may have a genetic basis. In fact, traditionalism, a core dimension of attitudes involving conservative versus liberal views on a wide range of issues, has been found to show a heritability of about 0.30 in adoption and several twin studies (for overview, see Plomin *et al.* (2001: 246–247). However, there is higher assortative mating for traditionalism than for any other psychological trait (about 0.50). When this is taken into account, the heritability for traditionalism rises to 0.50 and the shared environmental influence drops to about 15% (Eaves *et al.* 1989).

The surprisingly robust and unshakeable nature of a given individual's scientific persuasion or philosophical orientation may thus be understood in terms of an underlying genetic propensity to hold a liberal or conservative beliefs. To the extent this makes sense, stubborn traditionalism is a factor that has to be encompassed in any serious understanding of the sociology of science. It may be manifested in the dogmatic search for particular "truths" or a moral or ethical agenda at the academic left, or it may explain the dogmatic inflexibility of conservative scientists to change their mind. In any case, Jensen cannot have genes for traditionalism. As I have demonstrated, he has on several occasions radically changed his mind when the data told him to do so (e.g. his level I–level II theory, and the role of genetics in development). Others most likely have them, perhaps in a dominant allele form, and this would work against any easy remedy for the devastating consequences for the operations of the academic left, the steadfastness of the Zeitgeist, and the unbelievable solidity of personal certainty about where to find the truth. The genetic predisposition may also partly explain why the science wars became so vitriolic, and why it is so very very difficult to change the course of science through revolutionary shifts. The other parts of the explanation may be identified in the dynamic social interaction of the many semi-dependent factors outlined in this chapter and made responsible for the synergy of the collective fraud.

An important factor in countering this inertia is to change the education of young scientists. Instead of teaching them to win arguments through persuasion, misrepresentation, ridiculing, censoring, or sacking, we ought to instruct them to critically search for solid data, and let the data speak with the weight that confluent evidence gives it. In short, let them in the words of Gottfredson do what they are expected to do: to act like responsible scientists. This obviously will not remove all the stones in their way, but it will at least not let them be trapped so easily by the snares of social reductionisms and collective fraud.

A third factor is to ensure that the administrative layers of academia are instructed in countering prevailing PC, and that funding agents let go their tendency to support only facile PC areas.

Finally, let only those who patiently and competently search for durable data get a price. Jensen is such a person. He is a King! He deserves the throne.

References

Alper, J. (1982). Book review of The legacy of Malthus. *Science for the People*, (March–April), 30–31.

American Psychologist (November 1969). pp. 1039–1041.

Babbage, C. (1830). *Reflections on the decline of science in England*. The British Library.

Barkan, E. (1992). *The retreat of scientific racism*. Cambridge: Cambridge University Press.

Bereiter, C. (1970). Genetics and educability: Educational implications of the Jensen debate. In: J. Hellmuth (Ed.), *Disadvantaged Child* (Vol. 3), *Compensatory education: A national debate* (pp. 279–299). New York: Brunner-Mazel.

Boas, F. (1912). *Changes in bodily form of descendants of immigrants*. New York: Columbia University Press.

Bouchard, T. J. Jr., & McGue, M. (1981). Familial studies of intelligence; A review. *Science, 212*, 1055–1059.

Brace, C. L., Gamble, G. R., & Bond, J. T. (Eds) (1971). *Race and intelligence. Anthropological Studies, No. 8*. Washington, D.C.: American Anthropological Association.

Brand, C. R. (1996). *The g Factor: General intelligence and its implications*. Chichester, U.K.: Wiley & Sons (Withdrawn, but a revised (2001) version is available free online at http://www.douance.org/qi/brandtgf.htm

Carroll, J. B. (1993). *Human cognitive abilities: A survey of factor-analytic studies*. New York: Cambridge University Press.

Carroll, J. B. (1997). Psychometrics, intelligence, and public perception. Special issue: Intelligence and social policy. *Intelligence, 24* (1), 25–52.

Chorover, S. (1979). *From genesis to genocide*. Cambridge: MIT Press.

Coleman, J. S., Campbell, E., Mood, A., Weinfeld, E., Hobson, D., York, R., & McPartland, J. (1966). *Equality of educational opportunity*. U.S. Department of Health, Education, and Welfare.

Cosmides, L., & Tooby, J. (1992). The psychological foundation of culture. In: J. Barkow, L. Cosmides, & J. Tooby (Eds), *The adapted mind* (pp. 19–136). New York: Oxford University Press.

Darwin, C. (1859/1872). *On the origin of species by means of natural selection, or the preservation of favored races in the struggle for life*.

Davis, B. D. (1976). Speech at the Cambridge Forum (10 April). *The Davis controversy. The Present Illness*. Special Issue.

Davis, B. D. (1978). The moralistic fallacy. *Nature, 272*, 390.

Davis, B. D. (1983). Neo-Lysenkoism, IQ, and the press. *The Public Interest*, (Fall), 41–59.

Davis, B. D. (1986). *Storm over biology: Essays on science, sentiment, and public policy*. Vuffalo, NY: Prometheus Books.

Degler, C. (1991). *In search of human nature: The decline and revival of Darwinism in American social thought*. Oxford: Oxford University Press.

Detterman, D. K. (Ed.) (1998). Special issue, A King among men: Arthur Jensen. *Intelligence, 26*, 3, 175–318.

Eaves, L. J., Eysenck, H., & Martin, N. G. (1989). *Genes, culture, and personality: An empirical approach*. London: Academic Press.

Edson, L. (1969). *New York Times Magazine* (August 31).

Eysenck. H. J. (1979). *The structure and measurement of intelligence*. New York: Springer Verlag.

Fraser, S. (Ed.) (1995). *The Bell Curve Wars: Race, intelligence, and the future of America*. New York: Basic Books.

Fromm, H. (1993). Scholarship, Politics and the MLA. *Hudson Review, 46* (1), 157–168.

Galton, F. (1869). *Hereditary genius: An inquiry into its laws and consequences*. London: Macmillan. (Cleveland, OH: World 1962).

Gardner, H. (1983). *Frames of mind: The theory of multiple intelligences*. New York: Basic Books, Inc.

Garrett, H. E. (1961). The equalitarian dogma. *Perspectives in Biology and Medicine, 4*, 480–484

Giroux, H. A., & Searls, S. (1996). The bell curve debate and the crisis of public intellectuals. In: J. L. Kincheloe, S. R. Steinberg, & A. D. Gresson (Eds), *Measured lies: The Bell Curve examined*. New York: St. Martin's Press.

Gordon, R. A. (1993). *The battle to establish a sociology of intelligence: A case study in the sociology of politicized disciplines*. Baltimore, MD: The Johns Hopkins University, Department of Sociology.

Gottfredson, L. (1994). Egalitarian fiction and collective fraud. *Society, 31* (3), Whole No. 209.

Gottfredson, L. S. (2000). 'Equal potential: a collective fraud'. *Society, 37* (5), vii/viii.

Gould, S. J. (1981/1996). *The Mismeasure of Man*. New York: W. W. Norton/Harmondsworth, U.K.: Penguin Books.

Gould, S. J. (1994, November 28). Curveball: Review of R. J. Herrnstein, & C. Murray, *The Bell Curve: Intelligence and class structure in American life* (New York: Free Press, 1994). *The New Yorker*, 139–149 [reprinted in Jacoby & Glauberman (1995), pp. 3–13.]

Gross, P. R., & Levitt, N. (1994/1998). *Higher superstition: The academic left and its quarrels with science*. Baltimore: Johns Hopkins University Press.

Haggbloom, S. J., Warnick, R., Warnick, J. E., Jones, V. K., Yarbrough, G. L., Russell, T. M., Borecky, C. M., McGahhey, R., Powell, J. L. III, Beavers J., & Monte, E. (2002). The most eminent twentieth century psychologists. *Review of General Psychology, 6*, 139–152.

Halsey, G.: Foreword to Schiff, M., & Lewontin, R. (1986). *Education and class: The irrelevance of IQ genetic studies*. Oxford, U.K.: Clarendon Press.

Herrnstein, R. J. (1971). *I.Q. Atlantic Monthly* (September), pp. 43–64.

Herrnstein, R. J., & Murray, C. (1994). *The Bell Curve: Intelligence and class structure in American life*. New York: The Free Press.

Hoyos, C., & Littlejohn, M. (2000, April 4). "Annan draws up a road map to guide UN". *Financial Times*, p. 16.

Jacoby, R., & Glauberman, N. (Eds) (1995). *The Bell Curve debate. History, documents, opinions*. New York: Times Books.

Jenkins, S. (2000). *Times, 28*, vi.

Jensen, A. R. (1968). Social class, race, and genetics: Implications for education. *American Educational Research Journal, 5*, 1–42.

Jensen, A. R. (1969). How much can we boost IQ and Scholastic Achievement. *Harvard Educational Review*, (Reprint Series No. 2), 1–123.

Jensen, A. R. (1972). *Genetics and education*. London: Methuen & Co LTD.

Jensen, A. R. (1980). *Bias in mental testing*. New York: Free Press.

Jensen, A. R. (1998). *The g factor: The science of mental ability*. Westport, CT: Praeger.

Lewontin, R. C. (1970). Race and intelligence. *Bulletin of the Atomic Scientists*, (March 2–8).

Lewontin, R. C. (1975a). Genetic aspects of intelligence. *Annual Review of Genetics, 9*, 387–405.

Lewontin, R. C. (1975b). *Transcript of Nova program*. WGBH Boston, #211, Transmission by PBS, 2 February (after Segerstråle 2000).

Lewontin, R. C. (1975c). Interview. *The Harvard Crimson, 3* (December).

Lewontin, R. C. (1981). *The inferiority complex. Review, The mismeasure of man.* The New York Review of Books, 22 October.

Lewontin, R. C., Rose, S., & Kamin, L. (1984). *Not in our genes.* New York: Pantheon Books.

Lind, B. (1998). *The origins of political correctness: On accuracy in academia.* Paper presented at the 13th AIA Annual Summer Conference at the George Washington University, July 10.

Locke, J. (1690). *An essay concerning human understanding.*

Luria, S. E. (1974a). What can biologists solve? *The New York Review of Books, 7* (February, 22–28).

Luria, S. E. (1974b). Reply. *The New York Review of Books,* (2 May), 45.

Lynn, R. (2001). *The science of human diversity: A history of the Pioneer fund.* New York: University Press of America.

Lynn, R., & Vanhanen, T. (2002). *IQ and the wealth of nations.* Westport, CT: Praeger.

MacDonald, H. (2000). *The burden of bad ideas.* New York: Ivan R. Dee Publ.

Nyborg, H. (1972). *Psykologi og genetik: En introduktion til psykogenetik* (Psychology and genetics: An introduction to psychogenetics). København: Munksgaard.

Nyborg, H. (1994). *Hormones, sex, and society: The science of physiology.* Westport, CT: Praeger.

Nyborg, H. (1997). *The scientific study of human nature: Tribute to Hans J. Eysenck at Eighty.* Oxford, U.K.: Pergamon.

Page, E. B. (1972). Behavior and heredity. Resolution. *American Psychologist, 27* (July), 660–661.

Plomin, R., DeFries, J. C., McClearn, G. E., & McGuffin, P. (2001). *Behavioral Genetics* (4th ed.). New York: Worth Publishers.

Provine, W. P. (1973). Geneticists and the biology of race crossing. *Science, 182,* 790–796.

Rosenthal, R., & Jacobson, L. (1968). *Pygmalion in the classroom. Teacher expectation and pupils' intellectual development.* New York: Holt, Rinehart and Winston, Inc.

Rushton, J. P. (2000, 2nd abridg. ed.). *Race, Evolution, and behavior.* New Brunswick, NJ: Transaction Publishers.

Rushton, J. P., & Jensen, A. R. (2003). Thirty years of research on black-white differences in cognitive ability. *Psychology, Public Policy, and the Law,* (in press).

Russell, B. (1968). *The autobiography of Bertrand Russell.* Boston: Atlantic Monthly Press.

Savodnik, P. (2000). Bad ideas matter most. *The Weekly Standard,* (October 30), 38.

Schiff, M., & Lewontin, R. (1986). *Education and class: The irrelevance of IQ genetic studies.* Oxford, U.K.: Clarendon Press.

Segerstråle, U. (2000). *Defenders of the truth: The battle for science in the sociobiology debate and beyond.* Oxford, U.K.: Oxford University Press.

Shockley, W. (1971). Dysgenics, geneticity, raceology: A challenge to the intellectual responsibility of educators. *Phi Delta Kappan, 53,* 297–307.

Snyderman, M., & Rothman, S. (1988). *The IQ controversy: The media and public policy.* New Brunswick, NJ: Transaction Books.

Sociobiology Study Group of Science for the People (1976). Sociobiology — another biology determinism. *Bioscience, 26*(3), 182, 184–186.

Sparks, C. S., & Jantz, R. L. (2002). *Proceedings of the National Academy of Sciences.*

Spearman, C. (1904). General intelligence, objectively determined and measured. *American Journal of Psychology, 15,* 201–293.

Vetta, A. (1973). Amendment to the resolution on scientific freedom regarding human behavior and heredity. *American Psychologist,* (28 May), 444.

Walsh, J. (1976). Science for the people. Comes the revolution. *Science, 191,* 1033–1055.

Webster's New World Dictionary of American English (1994). *3rd College edn*. New York: MacMillan.

Weyher, F. H. (1998). The Pioneer fund, the behavioural sciences, and the media's false stories. *Intelligence (Editorial)*, 26 (4), 319–336.

Wilson, E. O. (1995). *Sociobiology: The new synthesis*. Cambridge, MA: Harvard University Press.

Wilson, E. O. (1998). *Consilience: The unity of knowledge*. New York: Alfred Knopf.

Wolf, E. P. (1972). Civil rights and social science data. *Race*, *XIV* (2), 155–182.

Young, M. (1958). *The rise of the meritocracy, 1970–2033*. (s. 15n).

Zigler, E. (1968). *The nature-nurture issue reconsidered: A discussion of Uzgiris' paper*. Paper read at Conference on Sociocultural Aspects of Mental Retardation, Peabody College, Nashville, Tennessee, June (cited in Jensen 1972, p. 355).

Chapter 21

Why Ignore the *g* Factor? — Historical Considerations

Christopher R. Brand, Denis Constales and Harrison Kane

1. Neglect of *g*

Readers of this book honouring Emeritus Professor Arthur Jensen (of the University of California at Berkeley) need little introduction to the preference among many of today's psychologists, educators, politicians and commentators for denying, or at least ignoring the *g* factor. Around 1960, Arthur Jensen narrowed his research focus as a differential psychologist to the role of heritable *g* in explaining educational outcomes — not least the attainments of Blacks and Whites in the U.S.A. Following his invited article in *Harvard Educational Review* (1969), Jensen became the best-known exponent of and martyr to the central thesis of psychology's London School. Subsequently, an intensifying inquisition against 'the Jensenist heresy' inspired by egalitarians such as Leon Kamin, Stephen Jay Gould, Richard Lewontin, Steven Rose and Barry Mehler has kept other Western academics cowed.

1.1. Opposition to g

Opposition to *g* has really come to dominate turn-of-the-century psychology. Experimental psychologists have slowly re-discovered *general intelligence* after years of behaviourism (e.g. Mackintosh 1997; Conway *et al.* 1999), yet they talk of it only as 'working memory' and decline to show interest in measuring it reliably in individuals or in examining its heritability. Social psychologists wishing to avoid *g* have felt it safer to avoid *all* talk of trait differences and to engage in a rhetoric that further denies the existence of human races. Differential psychologists should have been enjoying the credit for proving the general equality of the sexes in intelligence (however, see Chapter 10 in this volume for a different view), for allowing bright children from poor home backgrounds to be routed towards the highest educational achievement, and for exempting mentally subnormal people from the rigours of the criminal law. Instead, they

The Scientific Study of General Intelligence: Tribute to Arthur R. Jensen have paid a high price for pointing out that there are differences between the races and social classes in a *g* factor that is substantially heritable. For thirty years, only the Pioneer Foundation (Weyher 1999) has been willing to fund research by psychologists accepting heredity as a co-determining factor.

1.2. Consequences for Education

The consequences for education have been still more serious. To acknowledge deep-seated differences in general intelligence had always seemed pessimistic in a post-Nietzschean West which no longer held out to its citizens the hope of future equality in a Christian heaven; and, unlike the late Hans Eysenck, Arthur Jensen entertained no optimistic notion that behaviour therapy might quickly allow ameliora-tion of the psychological problems revealed by his work. From the first storm of controversy over *How much can we boost IQ and scholastic achievement?* through *Bias in Mental Testing* (Jensen's 'Old Testament', vindicating the fairness of IQ-type tests) to his magnum opus, *The g Factor: the Science of Mental Ability* (his 'New Testament', covering psychogenetic studies), Jensen defied the politics of neosocialism which attributes all the problems of 'minorities' to 'disadvantages', 'prejudices' or 'low expectations' that can be rectified by interventions of a social, as distinct from a biological type. Consistently, Jensen doubted there could be any great degree of intellectual equalization for children having serious educational problems in a computerized world where high levels of *g* are increasingly demanded.

Seizing on such 'pessimism', critics ignored the positive aspects of Jensen's thesis. Instead of IQ differences being addressed realistically by the use of school streaming or tracking as progressive educators had once maintained (see Ravitch 2000), modern educationists have refused to admit that society works by division of labour. A view has been adopted in the West to the effect that all children (except perhaps the mentally retarded) have equal intellectual potential — at least so long as they are kept within a rigid state school system that frowns on individuation of teaching and allows specialization only for children having gifts for music and ballet. By the 1990s, poor performance from any group of children came to be blamed not on genetic differences but on alleged failures by teachers and on wider 'low expectations' and 'racism' (whether 'institutionalized' or otherwise). Desperate to 'turn round' failing inner-city schools, Britain's 'New Labour' government in 1999 began appointing 'superheads' at salaries of £70,000 p.a. and with no ancillary expense spared. There was much talk of 'situations' and 'cultures of failure' that would soon be rectified. Yet, denied the possibility of expelling unruly pupils, three of the superheads soon resigned in despair and the eleven selected 'Fresh Start' schools had no better academic results after a year of their new regimes than they had at the beginning (*Independent* [London] (2000), 2 (ii), 8). Universities also had to ignore intelligence: they risked serious criticism in the 1990s if they failed to represent 'minorities' *pro rata* in their ranks; and they repeatedly sought fresh admissions criteria which might enable them to admit more non-White and state-school applicants, even if to do so they might lower academic standards. Doubts about programmes of 'affirmative action' were invariably denounced as 'racist' — thus inhibiting sensible discussion. Indeed, no proposal for real improvement, even to increase U.K. medical practitioners' fluency in English, went without criticism as 'racist'. Jensen's own record of support for the racial desegregation of U.S. schools was not enough to stop Steven Rose (1997) calling him 'the grandfather of modern scientific racism' and declaring 1969 'the beginning of the last big wave of scientific racism'.

1.3. Further Protests

Notoriously, opposition to *g* came to a head when Richard Herrnstein & Charles Murray (1994) published, in *The Bell Curve*, their estimates of the wider social importance of the *g* factor. Large-scale IQ testing and follow-up of U.S. youth had, by 1990, shown that *g* differences were more important than differences in parental socio-economic status (SES) in accounting for life outcomes at age 30 in qualifications, employability, law-abidingness and procreational self-control. That such *g* differences should be thought even 40% heritable by Herrnstein & Murray incensed America's academics, especially since *The Bell Curve* also set out reasons for thinking the intellectual differences between Blacks and Whites to be deep-seated. Herrnstein and Murray were swiftly and widely denounced as 'attempting to revive scientific racism' (e.g. by Washington State University's Obed Norman 1995).

1.4. New Evidence

The years 1994 to 2000 provided new support for the London School. There was a study from Africa of a 25-IQ point difference between Blacks and Whites (Rushton & Skuy 2000). Genetic engineering of 'Doogie' mice yielded a substantial improvement on learning tasks (Tang *et al.* 1999). A review showed the general unimportance of parental SES in accounting for children's differences in personality or intellect (Bruer 1999) — contradicting the belief of Richardson (1999) that "IQ tests are merely clever numerical surrogates for social class". There was a finding by Robert Plomin of some genes for IQ (http://news.bbc.co.uk/hi/english/sci/tech/newsid_850000/850358.stm). New evidence appeared favouring streaming in schools (see Brand 1998). The international journal *Intelligence* devoted a whole issue in 1998 to articles that were largely celebratory of Jensen's work; and the editor of *Intelligence*, Douglas Detterman (who had himself once hoped the *g* factor would "go away"), condemned as "absurd environmentalism" the theories of a British behaviourist then employed at the University of Exeter, M. J. A. Howe (e.g. 1997). Nevertheless, these advances for the London School counted for little in the media or in the universities of the West where politically correct 'sensitivity' to the problems of minorities almost had become the norm.

1.5. Neo-socialist Impact

It is easy to explain how public egalitarianism increased in parallel with Arthur Jensen's lifetime of scholarly effort to understand intelligence differences and their origins. The self-declared imperative of socialists was always to help the poor, or at least 'the working class'. Today, as the West has learned the folly of communism and seen the collapse of most of the regimes that ever adopted it, left-wing politicians in democratic countries have no longer been able to offer economic policies of state control, high taxation, welfare extravagance and serious redistribution of wealth. Instead, a busy new method of rectifying 'disadvantage' has been found: the neosocialists of modern America and Britain have offered to minorities — whom they encourage to immigrate — not hard cash but the perquisites of 'affirmative action'.

1.6. Wilful Ignorance

Nevertheless, to understand the motives of Jensen's opponents is still not to have a full appreciation of the extent of their opposition. Critics ignore John Carroll's (1993) establishment of *g* as accounting for far more mental ability variance than all other factors put together (see Chapter 1 in this volume). They set aside Tom Bouchard *et al.*'s (1990) evidence from separated monozygotic twins of a high heritability for *g* — saying *a priori* that "phenomena such as canalization, divergent epigenesis, exon-shuffling (which modifies gene-products to suit current developmental needs), and even developmental modification of gene-structures themselves, now make dubious the idea of a one-to-one relationship between incremental accumulations of 'good' or 'bad' genes, and increments in a phenotype" (Richardson 1999). Critics neglect Linda Gottfredson's (e.g. 1997) demonstration of the *g* levels required in different occupations (see Chapter 15 in this volume). Still more astonishing, environmentalists and egalitarians themselves lack any positive account of how intelligence differences arise.

1.7. Gene-environment Interaction

The chief current recourse of the critics of the London School is to say that genes always work 'in interaction with the environment'. According to the Provost of King's College, Cambridge (Bateson & Martin 2000): "The continuous process of exchange between individuals and their environments that underlies development makes a nonsense of the notion that an individual's characteristics can be predicted from their genes and experiences". Critics apparently think that this will dissuade people from manipulating genes to achieve the kind of eugenic effects that are already achievable in plants and animals.

1.8. Secular Rise in IQ

When an appeal to 'interactionism' is thought too risky or over-used, the second refuge is in the work of James Flynn (e.g. 1984) telling of the secular rise in IQ-test scoring that was first noticed in 1948. Unfortunately for this notion, these test-score gains are greatest on sub-tests of copying skill [Coding or Digit Symbol] that are relatively poor measures of *g* (Rushton 1999); and no-one has ever explained them or been able to speed them up. Flynn himself had hoped that Black test scores might be rising as fast as those of Whites once did; and Hunt (1999) still thought the Black-White gap was "clearly decreasing" and had already declined to 0.8 SD units (i.e. 12 IQ points). However, Murray (1999) reported *National Longitudinal Survey of Youth* data from the previous generation showing no closing of the racial gap in fluid *g*; Nyborg & Jensen (2000) found a highly significant ($p < 0.00001$) Black-White difference of 1.174 in psychometric *g* in a sample with an *N* of 4,037; and in 2000 the U.S. federal Department of Education said the Black-White gap in reading had actually been *increasing* through the 1990s — leaving the average Black 17-year-old of 2000 reading only about as well as the average White 13-year-old. Statewide achievement testing in *New York State* in 2002 found large race differences persisting that could not readily be attributed to the socio-economic backgrounds of pupils (Hartocollis 2002).

1.9. Componentialists, Constructivists and Philosophers

That appeals to complexity have to substitute for empirical demonstration of powerful social-environmental effects on intelligence is the basic flaw in the opposition to Jensen. Yet, beyond the complexity-venerating responses to London School achievements, there are two lines of arguments, which come from eminent and well-informed psychologists and which continue the critique of *g* more seriously into the present. They can be called *componentialist* and *constructivist* respectively. In addition, there is one line of attack on *g* which has not yet been tried by critics but which probably should have been tried: it is to ask, 'If Jensen is essentially right about *g*, why have so many great philosophers, thinkers and scientists of the past showed so little appreciation of the occurrence of *g* differences?' This can be titled the problem of *classic neglect*.

2. Suggested Alternatives to Acknowledging

2.1. Componentialism

Undoubtedly the simplest and strongest reply to the London School would be to point to *g*'s being only *one* of several measurable dimensions of mentality — and perhaps not even the dimension having the greatest power to account for human differences in behaviour, personality and achievement. Just as *g* can seem less important when it is considered that people also differ in looks, wealth, health and strength, so *g* can be played down by setting it alongside other personality features like the Big Five (extraversion, anxiety, independence, conscientiousness, tender-mindedness — see Brand 1997) which so appeal to today's psychometricians. Even within the realm of mental abilities, it may be argued that there are several independent factors, or at least factors that correlate so weakly as to make talk of *g* irrelevant.

Such multifactorial hopes continue the time-honoured ambitions of philosophers and psychologists to identify the main 'components of the mind.' Whether Plato with his three, Aristotle with his greater but undecided number, Aquinas with his eight (eventually ten), Gall with his 28, Spurzheim with his 35, Guilford with his 150 or Sternberg with his 666 components (including interaction effects), many have held out a vision from which some egalitarian satisfaction might be extracted. Certainly the failure of any definite number of components to emerge seems no deterrent to positive psychologists. In the past decade, Harvard's Howard Gardner has advocated some seven (gradually becoming eight-and-a-half — Traub 1998; but possibly dropping to three — Gardner 1999) 'intelligences' without ever citing the work of multifactorial theorists like Louis Thurstone who might have been his guide; and Daniel Goleman (1995) has proposed an entirely new type of intelligence, 'emotional intelligence' (EQ) that he deems to have eluded a century of correlational psychology — his confidence undimmed by the failure of himself or his supporters to come up with any way at all in which EQ can be objectively or reliably measured. The great merit of componentialism is that it can always be envisaged that new forms of observation or testing might allow the emergence of new dimensions — just as cognitive psychologists now have Chomskyan modules for aspects of language acquisition and evolutionary psychologists envisage that (some) people's minds may house previously unremarked 'landscape seekers' and 'cheater detectors.' As knowledge of the brain grows, there is more evidence of brain centres specialized for recognizing vegetables (but not fruit), proper names, and people of other races. Such discrete faculties might realize the wildest dreams of any nineteenth-century phrenologist.

To such ambitions there can be no entirely compelling answer — even though Nathan Brody (1992) and Arthur Jensen (1998) have explained that Gardner's scheme is 'arbitrary and without empirical foundation.' Plainly, it is the precise hope of any scientist of the mind to discover previously unnoticed aspects of mental functioning and of individual differences. Just as some successful form of conversational psychotherapy may eventually be discovered, and some further generations of 'positive discrimination' may at last boost Black IQ, it just *could* be that expensive new forms of in-depth child assessment being developed by non-psychometricians at Harvard and Oxford may achieve more than a re-invention of the wheel. Where once IQ testers tried to test children's IQs adequately in group sessions lasting 40 minutes, today's psychologists in America are granted leisurely hours of observation, with one observer per child, to try to find aspects of game-playing that might be used as a new criterion to counsel university entry for low-IQ applicants from 'underprivileged' backgrounds. London School theorists can only remark what must be the decreasing likelihood that any stone has been left unturned in the hunt for mental abilities which they themselves once led — studiously exploring from 1920 to 1960 numerous schemes allowing talk of non-g factors (usually called 'specific' or 'group' factor). Notably, factor analytic methods showed long ago how levels of intelligence may differ somewhat across verbal, numerical, spatial and musical symbol systems — for example, one person in eight has a statistically significant ($p < 0.05$) discrepancy between verbal and spatial intelligence (Wechsler 1939).

What must be specially remarked in 2001, however, is the latest failure to deliver a substantially improved componentialism. For twenty years, Britain's leading psychologist, Nicholas Mackintosh, has occupied the Chair of Experimental Psychology at

Cambridge University. Following service on a U.K. government commission into the poor educational performance of Black children, Mackintosh — best known as a learning theorist of animal behaviour — increasingly concentrated on the topic of intelligence; and his 1997 book *IQ and Human Intelligence* was the product.

Although this work opens with condescension towards IQ, a magisterial impartiality is largely preserved on matters of fact. Unusually for a psychology professor in the public eye, Mackintosh does not blame IQ psychologists for the restrictive 1924 U.S. Immigration Act; nor for Britain's mid-century selective system of grammar schools. He is emphatic that IQ allows prediction of a child's educational future that goes substantially beyond whatever can be predicted from parental SES; he allows that the nature of *g* as mental speed has been becoming clearer, whether because inspection time tests correlate at 0.40 with IQ or because tests of working memory and 'Tower of Hanoi' ability correlate as high as 0.77; and he rejects the wish of psychologists like Stephen Ceci and Anders Ericsson to distract attention to special learning abilities, and the wish of Leda Cosmides and Nicholas Humphrey to talk of specialized social intelligence.

Despite having come to hold views that would actually qualify him for membership of the London School, Mackintosh is concerned throughout his book to go beyond *g* and identify sub-factors of intelligence, and most notably to envisage some distinction between verbal and spatial intelligence (which abilities, he concludes, have their own special links to verbal and spatial memory). Yet all that Mackintosh has to show for his componentialist concern is summed up in his high regard for the work of Snow and Yalow (1982) whom once distinguished four sub-factors to *g* (verbal, spatial, crystallized, memory). Altogether, Mackintosh's modest multifactorialism best approximates the London School model proposed by Sir Cyril Burt and Philip Vernon in the nineteen-fifties (e.g. Mackintosh: 266). By the end of his book, Mackintosh admits that "some readers may feel disappointed, even cheated" by his answers to the main questions about human intelligence; and, while remarking the "risk of concluding . . . on a somewhat sceptical or sour note", he concedes the existence of the *g* factor as classically envisaged. Altogether, *IQ* and *Human Intelligence* is probably the worst news for componentialists since Eysenck and Burt noticed the many considerable correlations between Thurstone's theoretically independent 'primary abilities' (Eysenck 1939). Mackintosh dismisses the classic multifactorial effort of J. P. Guilford and likewise the recent notions of Howard Gardner — saying "if [Gardner] means there is no positive manifold, he is simply wrong".

2.2. Constructivism

If the quest to establish a compensatory componentialism has failed, an alternative for egalitarians is to downplay *g* itself. Since 1982, the most popular critique of IQ and all its works has been Stephen Jay Gould's *The Mismeasure of Man*. In that book, Gould disparaged the IQ testing movement by pretending it had some close connection with nineteenth-century claims that brain size was the main determinant of intelligence — claims for which Gould felt there was insufficient good evidence by the standards of a century later. In fact 1990s brain scan evidence actually did yield several correlations of around 0.40 between cerebral volume and IQ — correlations which to this day remain unremarked by Gould. He achieved the feat of persuading his many readers to forget about the twentieth-century history of IQ and see the *g* factor as a preposterous legacy of Victorian imperialism, responsible for untold damage to race relations and working class life chances.

More important than Gould's neglect of post-1969 IQ research (documented in Rushton 1996) was his claim that there is really no such thing as *g*, except by a statistical sleight of hand. In particular, Gould maintained it was wrong to 'reify' intelligence — to talk of it as something which had any existence or any possibility of being measured. In this, Gould struck a chord with many psychologists — not least with those personality theorists who had long doubted the possibility of 'measuring personality' or any similar aspects of human individuals. Had not the behaviourist philosopher Gilbert Ryle (1949) pointed out that, rather than talk of people 'being intelligent' or 'having intelligence', it would be less metaphysical and more precise to describe just which actions they performed and which problems they solved 'in an intelligent way' or 'intelligently'? Once, J. B. Watson and his latter-day followers had removed all mental concepts from the repertoire of much academic psychology. Now Gould would finish the job by eliminating the most dangerous survivor from the days of mentalism.

In fact, Gould's own campaign against reification was deeply flawed.

> First, Gould ignored the fact that both Jensen and Eysenck themselves had — in days when positivism was more popular than it is today — expressed reservations about the status of *g*. In 1969, Jensen had written: "We should not reify *g* as an entity, of course, since it is only a hypothetical construct intended to explain covariation among tests" (p. 9). And in 1981 Eysenck wrote: "[I]t is . . . meaningfulness, or proven usefulness in explanation and prediction, that is important in a theoretical concept; . . . the notion of "existence" is philosophically meaningless in relation to concepts" (p. 82). Even today, Jensen (1998) recommends dissociating *g* from intelligence — breaking *g*'s real-world connection and using it only as a scientific handle to avoid confusion and the overheated discussions of intelligence with which he has been painfully familiar. (Anderson (2000) has especially complained that Jensen's operationalization of intelligence as only the *g* factor serves to avoid serious theorizing about mental structures.)
>
> Secondly, Gould's point about *g* being *bound* to show up in factor analysis would always have been perfectly familiar to the humblest user of that statistical technique. What matters, however, is not the tautological emergence of a first factor, accounting for as much variance as possible in a matrix, but rather the *size* of that factor. Especially important is the ratio of the first factor to further independent factors — which *g* invariably dwarfs in mental ability matrices by ratios of five-to-one.
>
> Thirdly, despite the idea of *g* being some kind of trick, Gould was actually to prove perfectly sympathetic to mental measurement when it

came to the *oblique* factors and multiple components that have attracted so many American psychologists. By the end of his book, Gould is found cheerfully praising the componential vision of Thurstone and hoping for more of the same from modern researchers — thus showing himself quite content that there *is* a mental realm of ability factors in which notions of existence and quantification have some relevance. By 1999, Gould was even to be found in his sixteenth book, *Rocks of Ages: Science and Religion in the Fullness of Life*, trying to negotiate a stand-off between science and religion, so far was he from any thoroughgoing materialism.

2.3. Materialist Critique

Not so easily set aside, however, are some theorists who have written at length about the iniquity of attempting or pretending to measure mental abilities. The most accessible of these to English-speaking psychologists is the Australian educationist, Roy Nash (1990).

Nash's "materialist critique of IQ" argues essentially that IQ is no more than a descriptor of test performance and that there is no reason to posit some underlying reality, 'intelligence', as an *explanation* of performance. Nash is not hostile to IQ as a descriptive exercise — so long as it remains purely descriptive. Indeed, he defends Jensen against those who think it invalid to make comparisons between the intelligence levels of different species.

> "Jensen is quite right — the great apes *are* more intelligent than the dogs, and, provided they have had some experience with sticks, ropes and boxes, are remarkably good at this sort of problem solving. It is pure obfuscation to try to argue that chimpanzees are not 'really' more intelligent than dogs, that 'intelligence' is a human concept, that dogs can find their way home better than chimpanzees, and so on and so forth. Words may be difficult to define in terms that everyone will find acceptable, but there is a central meaning to words and if we cannot say meaningfully that chimpanzees are more intelligent than dogs we might as well give up the effort of communication in this area at all."

But Nash regards the phenomenon of intelligence differences as arising not from differences in traits or faculties but rather from children's rates of progress through the 'syllabus' that their culture provides. Following Jean Piaget, Nash is content that children "are likely to accrue knowledge, processes or whatever at different rates but in a similar order". Thus the phenomenon of a *g* hierarchy arises as a variety of different factors — including physiological differences — impact on children's rates of learning. To talk otherwise of some measurable mental possession of intelligence, says Nash, is just "pseudoscience".

> "The entire problematic of IQ theory seems to be based on an error of startling simplicity. People can hear, and their hearing can be tested, they are able to hear this or that well, and for that there must be all sorts of reasons, but no one would dream of offering in explanation of relatively poor hearing — 'not enough construct of hearing ability.' That would be a very poor way to refer to the actual physiological mechanism of hearing. Why are some people able to perform tasks held to demand cognitive thought better than others? According to IQ theory because they possess greater 'cognitive ability.' That they possess greater 'cognitive ability' may be demonstrated by their performance on tests of 'cognitive ability.' It is not difficult to understand why so many contemporary cognitive psychologists stand well back from an argument with a built-in self-destruct device which ticks as loudly as this one."

Unlike Gould, Nash does not hamstring himself by relaxing his criticism for other psychometric measures by which he is less politically exercised. Rather, he extends his hardcore-nominalist condemnation beyond London School theorists to psychometricians as a whole. Further, he wins a certain plausibility for his argument by pointing to the uncertainties entertained by Jensen and Eysenck themselves about g as they sometimes departed from the faculty conception held by the Aristotelian Charles Spearman. (Effectively, Eysenck and Jensen sometimes opted to accept the 'test theory pragmatism' which treats IQs as nothing but convenient numbers, while at other times they called g a "biological reality". Nor does Nash settle for condemning only what he takes to be the muddle and pretentiousness of psychometrician-psychologists: he is equally scathing about Nicholas Mackintosh, fearing (correctly — see above) that the latter's approach over the years "contributes to the legitimation of IQ".

Nash insists not just that IQ theorists have never managed to quantify any property beyond or beneath the performances that yield IQ estimates, but that there is no such property to be measured. This complaint, based on the fact that IQs are essentially rankings and have no true zero point, is one which also impressed the British psychometrician-psychologist Paul Kline (2000) before his death and which has led Kline's able student, Paul Barrett (e.g. 2001), to doubt whether present paradigms for g can be usefully continued. It is therefore worth examining in some detail Nash's claim that a Czech logician, Karel Berka, has succeeded in showing that IQ involves no true measurement of anything.

2.4. Berka's Wider Concept of Measurement

Berka's main work on the philosophical theory of measurement is his *Measurement: Its Concepts, Theories and Problems* (1983). There are two important points about the context in which Berka's book was written. In 1980, Czechoslovakia was under Communist rule, so the book adheres carefully to basic Marxist-Leninist tenets which are repeatedly invoked when alternatives are considered and choices have to be made. Secondly, Berka expressly intended to present critical objections to what he called the "wider" concept of measurement — the view that almost all human actions can be viewed to some extent as measurements (intentionally or not), so that, for example, responses to psychometrists' questions need no further philosophical justification to provide a basis for scientific measurement. (Some philosophers argue that a person who tosses a coin is 'measuring its fairness', and that a person who drinks tea is 'measuring temperature'.) Thus Berka's book tries to answer the question: "Can one formulate a theory of measurement which is in full accordance with Marxism-Leninism and which allows only of 'narrow' measurement?"

Philosophically, this is a valid and interesting question. The slump in the popularity of Marxism-Leninism today is accidental and irrelevant. Yet other, quite different, questions could be asked. For instance: "Can one formulate a wider doctrine of measurement that is in full accordance with Marxism-Leninism?" Or: "What could be the Marxist-Leninist objections to *disallowing* 'wider' measurement (Berka having already investigated the Marxist-Leninist objections to *allowing* 'wider' measurement.)?" Or: "Can one formulate a theory of wide or narrow measurement which is in full accordance with rationalism?" — or with positivism, empiricism or any other philosophical doctrine.

Thus it is largely pointless for critics of IQ to quote Berka's rejection of extraphysical measurements similar to IQ. One of Berka's essential underlying assumptions is that only certain very special actions can be termed "measurements", and the restrictions he makes on purposive actions easily disqualify as measurements not only IQ, but even such a tangible and widely used concept as *economic utility*. Berka's rejection of IQ as measurement is not a consequence of any of his arguments or investigations. Rather, it follows at once from his openly stated purpose to give the most restrictive interpretation possible to the term "measurement".

In Berka's view, counting cannot be accepted as a form of measurement, however non-intuitive this rejection may seem. Similarly, statistics are completely absent from Berka's view of science. IQ is admitted by Berka only as a form of "quasi-quantification". Berka thus accepts that IQ values can actually be meaningfully compared and ordered. He only objects to them being added to each other and arithmetically averaged. However, it can be argued that accepting IQ as quasi-quantification is actually quite sufficient to justify most talk of IQ measurement — as follows.

The IQ values of a population have a distribution which is a good approximation to the Gaussian bell curve. This curve is symmetrical around its arithmetical average, so the mean of the distribution coincides with the median value. According to Berka, the arithmetical average makes no sense, being based on 'meaningless' addition and division; but the median *does* make sense so long as the values considered can be ordered uniquely — so long as they are "quasi-quantified". *Even though the mean as such is not 'meaningful' in Berka's view, its actual value will coincide with that of the median; and the median is itself meaningful since it only requires ordering to be defined — not any adding or averaging.*

Similarly, the standard deviation of the distribution (which is used to calibrate the IQ scale) is obtained from an average of squared deviations, and is thus not meaningful in Berka's view. But the difference between, for example, the first and the third quartile values *is* meaningful, being based only on ordering. Again, the value of this difference will coincide in any normal distribution with a fixed multiple of the standard deviation (1.3489 times the standard deviation).

Thus the answer to Berka's critique and to those who invoke it is simple. All statements about the mean IQ and standard deviations of different populations can be rewritten in "quasi-quantified" terms which would be completely equivalent and entirely acceptable to Berka. Opponents of IQ cannot, therefore, truly claim to follow Berka in 'dismissing IQ as quasi-quantification.'

Opponents further like to claim they are following Berka when they liken IQ testing to ranking people by the numerical value of their telephone numbers (numbers that indeed *cannot* be meaningfully compared). But that analogy is entirely misleading. Phone-number ranking is not *quasi-*, but *pseudo-*quantification in Berka's terminology. IQ's critics like to feel they have a philosopher on their side in dismissing means and standard deviations for IQ as 'meaningless.' Yet, on Berka's own account, IQ values are a perfectly respectable form of quasi-quantification, for which statistical descriptions in terms of ordering (e.g. the median and quartile values) are well-defined. When the observed distributions for a population and for its sub-populations look like normal distributions, and pass suitable statistical tests for normality, this is true scientific evidence for the reality of IQ values (at least at the population level). Thus it is fully justifiable to represent them *via* the most widely used descriptors, the mean and the standard deviation.

2.5. Constructivism Again

Is such argumentation against Berka, Nash and Kline sufficient to carry the day against an outright 'constructivist' who holds more widely that there is no reality — not even material reality — because all we can know are words and a vast language game that allows no escape from culture and politics? For example, the Parisian philosopher, Jean François Lyotard, was a leading 'anti-racist' and Marxist — though he never went so far as to join the French Communist Party. A key saying of his was that he "could not accept that there was any reality that the philosopher could observe". Biography was a particular object of his scorn: "*La biographie, c'est l'imbécillité*", he would pronounce, since 'people' did not really exist. Together with Michel Foucault, Jacques Derrida and Gilles Deleuze, Lyotard was responsible for 'postmodernism' — the late-twentieth-century version of Western philosophical idealism (see Introduction to *The g Factor* (Brand 1996)). (Full considerations of the inanities and hypernegativity of Parisian poststructuralism and constructivism are provided by Mark Lilla (1998) and by Gerard Delanty (1998). For a summary, see 'Reconstructivism deconstructed' at http://www.crispian.demon.co.uk/McDNLArch4b)

Much constructivism consists merely in making impossible and pedantic demands for tight definitions of terms like intelligence and race and then denying there can be any reality when these definitions are not forthcoming. The constructivist may insist that heredity has not been demonstrated — except as a 'social fact' — unless every last genetic detail of DNA is known and a full account furnished of how genes do their work.

Needless to say, the meaninglessness of the concept of 'race' is an especially treasured item in the constructivist repertoire. It is as if the constructivist could never have a useful discussion of 'trees' because it is hard to say whether a *bonsai* is a tree or a bush. Like its practical arm of Political Correctness (PeeCee), constructivism aims to banish sensible scientific discussion and research at least to the distant future. However, there are four reasons why the demands of constructivists merit no serious reply at present.

(1) The constructivist rhetoric that has come to dominate much social psychology as well as the academic world of the arts is a continuation of the idealistic and relativistic traditions of philosophy. These reached their previous high point as Hegel and Nietzsche urged no truth was to be found beyond, respectively, the social collective and the individual will. Today, unconstrained idealism finds its practical expression in the PeeCee movement emanating from Harvard which insists on speech control so as to be polite about (in fact, to ignore) the real problems posed by minorities. As a corollary, PeeCee expects minorities to achieve social rewards (degrees, jobs, parliamentary representation etc.) *pro rata* and not according to any criterion of merit.

   Unfortunately, the constructivist's idea of the importance of words and 'labels' in stage-managing human nature has been largely confuted by the advance of psychiatric medicine in the twentieth century. While theorists like Foucault pontificated about the 'social creation of madness' and its convenience for capitalists and authoritarians, the mental hospitals of the West were actually having their human contents emptied on to the streets thanks to breakthroughs by drug companies. By contrast, despite Britain's 'comprehensive' schools becoming the fief of teachers of left-wing persuasions and great modern piety about 'disadvantage' and 'learning difficulties', levels of educational attainment fell (by international standards) thanks to the simple reality-feature of comprehensivisation — which largely precludes teaching in accordance with ability levels. Thus have genuine twentieth-century changes quite simply contradicted those who believed that madness would be cured by re-labelling, and educational levels raised by avoiding all talk of stupidity and failure.

(2) Sceptical doubts as to the existence of core realities are invariably self-undermining and of dubious use to the 'progressive' causes that idealists typically wish to advance. In their wish not to talk of IQ or race or sex — preferring the non-biological terms 'ethnicity' and 'gender' — constructivists invite the question of what they themselves will ever be able to say about anything. Anti-essentialism has been notably attacked by the left-wing anti-racist crusader, Kenan Malik (1996). Just as radical critics once used to ask the Scottish existentialist psychiatrist, Ronald Laing, what he could really do for schizophrenics if he did not believe in the diagnosis, so Malik doubts constructivists' ability to say or do anything about poverty, low intelligence, racism or sexism. "Relativism", he observes, "undermines the capacity to challenge racism". To claim that humans are equal requires an acknowledgment of *some* human essence in which some important equality can occur. By contrast, Malik points out, "Poststructuralism inevitably leads to the questioning of equality itself".

(3) The idea that some scientists "cling to the dogma [of an 'objective external world']
imposed by the long post-Enlightenment hegemony" was approvingly explored in
an article in the refereed social-science journal, *Social Texts*. Unfortunately for the
constructivists who usually read and write for *Social Texts*, the article was entirely
meaningless and had been written as a spoof by a physicist at New York University,
Alan Sokal (1996). What the journal had published from Sokal was a Trojan horse
bedecked with all the buzzwords, academic references and flattery for the journal's
own editors that these postmodernists could have wished. Here, after all, was a real-
life physicist saying right-on things such as: "The *pi* of Euclid and the *g* of Newton,
formerly thought to be constant and universal, are now perceived in their ineluctable
historicity". This was irresistible material for the journal's Special Issue entitled
'Science Wars' (May 1996). Here was a splendid chance to pray Gödel's theorem,
chaos theory and quantum mechanics in aid of modern neosocialist relativism and
outright nihilism. Today, however, Sokal can — like Doctor Johnson kicking his
table — simply laugh at all those associated with the journal. Says Sokal (1998),
"Anyone who believes that the laws of gravity are mere social conventions should
try transgressing those conventions from the windows of his flat on the 21st floor".
Apparently only two non-scientists had realized from reading a draft that his article
was a spoof.

(4) The days of the *philosophe engagé* are long since over in Paris. As the French saw
Hungary, Solidarity, Solzhenitsyn, Cambodia and Leipzig 1989, they gave up their
intellectuals. Derrida is now marginal, at best, to French thinking about cognitive
science and philosophy of mind — thinking which increasingly runs in English-
speaking grooves [as witness the top French psychology journal, *Cahiers de
Psychologie Cognitive*, which publishes in English]. (The only problem is that
Derrida has found a new stamping ground on American campuses — among *les
grands enfants* who do not understand their country's general success and wish
Whites to beat their breasts about America's failure to solve its Black problem. No
wonder Derrida has a new saying as he professes to admire the 'states' rights' of
America and advocates Black power: "*La deconstruction, c'est l'Amérique*".)

2.6. Classic Neglect

In view of the feebleness of even their best arguments against a real, measurable and
powerful *g* factor, it is perhaps unsurprising that the critics of the London School largely
settle for what Raymond Cattell called *ignoracism*. They try to ignore the writings of
Eysenck & Jensen — bestirring themselves only to advise the 'publishing' trade of the
trouble that they will make for any pro-IQ works appearing in bookshops. Nevertheless,
it is surprising that critics have not used a line of criticism that should have a big appeal
for idealistic anti-empiricists: to cite the authority of philosophers against the Jensenist
heresy.

PeeCee is a religion that is currently at the stage where Christianity was before Emperor Constantine took it by the scruff of the neck in 314 A.D. and put it to imperial work. Because of this immaturity, no modern authorities of much general stature in psychology itself can be found to challenge London School ideas. Reliance has had to be placed instead on a biologist (Gould), a neuroscientist (Rose) and behaviourists like Howe & Kamin who have spent their working lives committed to a mentality-denying exercise that has itself been officially rejected by modern cognitive science and the rest of psychology. However, a more promising scene opens up for the critic who looks to the past. Psychology's founding fathers — who were what would be called philosophers or (especially in the case of the rationalist philosophers) scientists — showed a clear propensity to do without the *g* factor.

It was famously observed by the mathematician-philosopher, Alfred Whitehead, that Western philosophy can be characterized as a series of footnotes to Plato. Certainly the quest for truth and goodness on which Plato embarked (drawing on Socrates, and followed pretty faithfully by Aristotle) has arrived after 2,400 years at a miserable state of affairs where no modern philosopher is known to the general public apart from the self-contradictory and depressive Ludwig Wittgenstein. Unlike his mentor, the realism-seeking Bertrand Russell, Wittgenstein had no interest in science and was happy to leave psychology to the arid evasions of behaviourism while he dismissed as 'language games' the West's classic concerns with metaphysics — with how to describe objectively the world that lies beyond the efforts of the physicist. Thus it is that, in today's public debates (e.g. Sturrock 1998) over the concerns of Parisian Professor Luce Irigay to modify or qualify Einstein's equation $E = MC^2$ because it is sexist (entirely concerned with things going very fast in straight lines), no big-name philosopher can be found to speak for science against PeeCee.

Needless to say, Lyotard's proposal that 'people do not exist' goes equally unchallenged by any philosopher feeling able to draw on 100 years of empirical psychology and its findings. Although differential psychologists find impressive personal continuities over time (not least in IQ which correlates 0.78 with itself across forty years of adulthood — Schwartzman *et al.* 1987), philosophy in the English-speaking world still shares David Hume's sceptical worry that a person cannot be proved to be anything more than a changeful "bundle of sensations".

Often it is Plato who is blamed for the West's follies, as befits his philosophical pre-eminence. Certainly it was Plato who provided the most enduring answer to the materialism of thinkers such as Democritus and the relativism of the Sophists. Building on the mathematical discoveries of Pythagoras, Plato argued that there was a world of truth beyond the senses and urged men to seek such truth, claiming that in it they would also find freedom, beauty, goodness and justice. Plato envisaged three types of being: the timeless, unchanging *Ideas* of a realm of intelligible and true Being; the objects of sense-perception in a realm of Becoming; and the human soul whose business was to mediate between the first two realms. Plato's improvement on materialism and relativism markedly resembles that of the greatest modern philosopher of science, the late Sir Karl Popper, who finally came to a 'three world' metaphysical theory (of *products of mind, mental experiences and dispositions* and *physical objects*). Plato's school, the Academy, lasted almost a thousand years and remained — thanks also to Aristotle — an abiding influence on the Christian world.

However, there were three enduring problems for three-worldism.

The first was that there were not enough truths to stock the 'higher' realm, for the truths of geometry and the laws of logic and the 'clear and distinct' intuition of Descartes that must exist can take one only so far.

The second problem was causal to the first. It proved hard to agree criteria by which to decide what was and what was not a higher truth. In particular, it proved hard to provide a resounding endorsement of empirical science — at least until Popper provided his rationale that scientific truth required not positive demonstration but the failure of attempts to falsify a theory's predictions.

Thirdly, it proved hard to establish any interesting number of *moral* truths. Though Kant worked hard to argue that one should behave as if one's behaviour might become a universal maxim, this was not very suitable to coping with individual differences and Kant's authority was eventually dented by Einstein's proving that space-time was not in fact neatly four-dimensional as Kant had stoutly maintained it must be. Nor was utilitarianism much help, again because of individual differences: partly, individual happiness is substantially under genetic control; partly happiness is caused idiosyncratically in different people, defying the grander utilitarian ideas of improving the human condition. Lastly, Plato's own insistence that the good life should essentially involve a quest for higher truth understandably came to be taken by others as a puritanical abjuration of the world of the senses and of sex. Plato's model of the human soul resembles the one that would be adopted by Freud, of a charioteer (the voice of reason, Freud's *ego*, allowing reality-contact and wisdom) battling to get the best from two very different horses, one passionate and impulsive (the appetitive *id*) and the other more organized and focussed (the purposeful *superego*). People who adopt such a model can understandably slip towards thinking that the charioteer might be better off working with just the one, relatively controlled horse and doing without the passionate horse altogether. The later formulations of mystical neoplatonism encouraged such slippage, as did the Church.

Of course, Christianity did not altogether forget the body. Indeed, it insisted on a bodily resurrection as a key part of the after-life of the believer. In particular, Aristotle's less mystical version of Platonic realism eventually became central to Christianity as articulated by Saint Thomas Aquinas. The mediaeval church was happy to accept that the existence of God could be proved by reason as well as by faith and it happily added to its repertoire Aristotle's never very forcefully expressed belief that the earth was the centre of the universe, as well as his more considered beliefs in the inferiority of women and in the naturalness of slavery. (Aristotle was a romantic who had loved his wife dearly till her early death — when he proceeded to have children by her slave; but he had departed from Plato's views that women were the equals of men and that Greek should not enslave Greek.) More importantly, Aristotle's two categories of cognitive and affective functions departed from Plato's three-world view that allowed a distinction between the realms of intellect (products) and intelligence (operations). Indeed, the Church would pay a high price for linking itself to Aristotle, for the latter's insistence on teleological causation would prove unacceptable to John Locke, Voltaire and the many other Enlightenment thinkers who took Galileo and Isaac Newton as their heroes. Having embarked on making truth claims about the natural world, the Church was unable to resist the temptation to have fights with Darwin and Freud, following which it lost most of its following in the West even though maintaining an active dysgenic influence in Africa. Psychology, too, paid a price: wrapped up in Aristotle's articulation of logic, concern with intelligence (as distinct from the intellectual work of reason) was lost until it was revived by Herbert Spencer (1855); and it was yet another eighty years before Raymond Cattell (e.g. 1936) began to make the vital distinction between *fluid* and *crystallized* intelligence g_f and g_c (however, see Chapter 1 in this volume.)

Even Aristotle — the Christian King Solomon, adept in science as much as philosophy — had not proved able to sustain his self-selected supporters. So Western philosophy collapsed into a set of unedifying arguments about whether there were any native faculties that gave secure access to bits and pieces of truth — or whether a sufficient basis for human knowledge could be found empirically in individually learned associations from the world of the senses. Even at their high points, neither rationalists nor empiricists came up with very much. Instead, their writing involves a constant struggle to keep the wolves of scepticism, relativism and nihilism from the door. Eventually, following Kant's 'transcendental idealism' — admitting it might be hard to have true knowledge of reality but claiming some of our ideas just *had* to be right — the high road to all-round idealism was wide open.

First, Hegel gloried in what had to be the work of the insuperable social collective; then Nietzsche held out the unreasoned hope of a Superman. Martin Heidegger, the philosopher most revered by constructivists today, played an active part in encouraging Nazism while at the same time inspiring Jean Paul Sartre who would pass on to the post-1945 world an 'existential' denial of essence and truth together with a sympathy for communism. Today, though science and mathematics remain the practical bulwark of everyday truth claims in the West, few would care to provide a defence of why this is so; and many in faculties of arts and social science now challenge even the best-established truths of psychology — about IQ and race — in their pursuit of an ideological egalitarianism no less fanatical than the Christian gene-denying belief in the 'brotherhood' of man.

Any simple return to Platonism has seemed ruled out at once by Plato's sympathy for eugenics and by his seeing no need for private property. Plato even felt able to propose a considerable scheme of censorship, especially of the poetry and pictures which he thought could so easily mislead people into untruth. Indeed, it is Plato's determinist and authoritarian tendencies that repelled his natural supporter, Popper, from endorsing Platonism. Long unhappy with evolution theory and with the genetic and biological realm that could usefully have made a Fourth World in his own metaphysics, Popper

(1945) was unhappy with Plato's question of 'Who should rule?' Sadly, Popper saw Plato's concern with human nature as no more worthy than the "gibberish" of Hegel's "renaissance of tribalism" which began "the tragi-comedy of German idealism"; and, when he finally arrived at his own three-world metaphysics late in life, Popper (e.g. 1994) had no inclination to examine its political implications or to revise his youthful condemnation of Plato.

In fact, it is far from obvious that Plato should be blamed for the collapse of his system. Plato's faith in the work of human reason extended far beyond discovering the truths of mathematics. The high-born and personally courageous Plato was able to derive from his principles a system of governance which he believed would improve both on aristocracy and on the democracy that had demanded the death of his hero, Socrates. It would also furnish a model of mind. Plato is the only philosopher to have made axiomatic to his thought the 'principle of specialization' — that each person is himself and not another thing, and that behaviour should be expected to reflect individual differences and thus achieve the highest co-operation and happiness. In Plato's utopian Republic, people would occupy positions according to their own individual natures (metaphorically: gold, silver, brass or iron). Yet open and reasoned discussion among the 'guardian' leaders would be essential to government and inter-generational social mobility was expected, rather than any static caste system. Plato saw the qualities of his selected philosopher-kings, following from their intelligence and knowledge, as likely to include at once courage, self-discipline, a broad vision, a good memory and quickness in learning. Plato's thought clearly allows the presentation of a rich morality and complete politics even if ardent democrats will be a little shocked.

By insisting on the importance of reason in public affairs, Plato was arguably just spelling out what actually tends to happen in all decent Western democracies where, by one route or another, intelligence, education and money all help secure more access to political power. And Plato gratifies any differential psychologist by his frank endorsement of inherited personality differences and the need for society to be adapted sensibly to them. Platonic authoritarianism is no greater than could be expected in a democratic Athens recently defeated by Sparta. The reasons for the West's rejection of Platonism must be found elsewhere.

Doubtless Plato's elitism proved less than ideal to the running of the Alexandrian empire that was soon to emerge. Empires need to sweet-talk their different tribes, nations and races into a passable co-operation, so the topic of innate human differences is best avoided. Certainly, Christianity sensed a tension with its own stress on the 'brotherhood of man' which required equal respect all round or even a positive veneration of the poor, meek and needy. By the time of Saint Augustine, official Christian philosophy became quite strictly egalitarian — abandoning through the Dark Ages any attempt to rely on human reason and instead adopting the criterion of blind faith.

Yet, to a psychologist, the most obvious problem with the Platonic scheme is just that Plato relied on reason rather than on general intelligence to provide the key method in the search for truth. As is appreciated today, there are many trivial reasoning tasks that are quite often failed by people of good general intelligence — though doubtless even more frequently failed by low-IQ people. Plato's biggest problem was to have adopted a criterion that is not easily defensible as a way of selecting his 'guardians'; and he was optimistic enough to believe that many would be able to master reasoning and pursue truth directly if they had a proper education. IQ testing could have solved Plato's problem. Recognizing *g* would have provided at once a guiding method for selecting officials, a social goal to be pursued, and the likelihood of persisting individual differences in achievement that would validate his Republic.

Unsurprisingly, subsequent enthusiasts for equality, democracy and utilitarianism did little to rectify Plato's omission. And rationalist philosophers persisted with the original Platonic task of detecting by reason what *had* to be true about the world — and what they thought would appear readily to any who accepted philosophical discipline. Yet there is a peculiarity that critics of IQ should have noted. How is it that, in the epistemological and metaphysical struggles of the West, no one till Spencer (1855) and Galton (1869) said plainly that the high road to truth (and also to a just and contented society) might be *via* not reasoning, let alone any 'pursuit of happiness', but *via* general intelligence?

The matter can be put more simply: How could a great philosopher like Thomas Hobbes have said "As to the faculties of the mind . . . . I find a greater equality amongst men than [in] physical strength"? Having once formulated questions about human equality and about whether human knowledge is innate or learned, how could philosophers have avoided the observation that some people are more generally intelligent than others? Doubtless, thinking men would have occasionally made, like Doctor Johnson, the observation that "[True genius] is a mind of large general powers accidentally determined to some particular directions". But what prevented them exploring and testing the idea? By the eighteenth century, the faculty philosophy of Scotland's Thomas Reid tried to preserve liberalism from Hume's scepticism by replacing the fruitless search for innate ideas with a recognition of the faculty of 'common sense.' Following England's Francis Bacon and running alongside Joseph Gall's phrenology, Reid's belief in constitutional determinants of thought was the antecedent of the views of Galton, William McDougall, Charles Spearman and Burt. Is such theorizing, though backed by twentieth century research, doomed to be but a flash in the philosophers' pan?

2.7. The Differentiation Hypothesis

Fortunately, it is possible to advance a hypothesis as to how so many intelligent people — including the chattering classes and media personages of modern times — remain in denial about *g* differences as they pursue their schemes for rectifying the human condition by social skills training. Indeed, critics of *g* can be pretty thoroughly obliged. One can simply accept that there is no strong *g* factor to be found *in the people among whom the educated, not to mention the hyper-educated, chiefly have their everyday being*. This 'differentiation hypothesis' dates back to an observation of Spearman's (1927) though it was chiefly advocated in the twentieth century by the distinguished American psychologist, Henry Garrett, who chaired Columbia University's psychology department and once served as president of the American Psychological Association (e.g. Garrett 1938, 1946, 1980). The idea is that the g 'differentiates' at higher levels of mental ability, perhaps as people reach serious options to specialize rewardingly in particular skills and topics. Thus the g factor is markedly stronger (i.e. accounts for more ability variance among testees) in samples having lower average intelligence — whether lower IQ or lower Mental Age. (For fuller presentations of theorizing and a history of empirical work, see Chapter 2 of *The g Factor* by Brand 1996; or Appendix A of *The g Factor* by Jensen 1998.)

Because differentiation of g is usually studied by comparing the cognitive performance of high- and low-IQ individuals, researchers invariably encounter nagging problems associated with restriction of the range of ability in their samples. For example, in the most widely cited modern study of the hypothesis, Detterman & Daniel (1989) divided the standardization samples of the WISC-R and WAIS into five ability groups based on scores in either the Vocabulary or Information subtests of the Wechsler. Within each ability group, average correlations between abilities were calculated, providing an indicant of the pervasiveness of Spearman's g. Differentiation was demonstrated dramatically in so far as average correlations among subtests decreased monotonically from about $+0.70$ for the lowest IQ group (<78) to about $+0.35$ for the highest IQ group (>122). However, as a means of equating the variances in the ability groups, Detterman and Daniel applied statistical corrections for restriction of range. As Jensen (1998) has explained, an underlying assumption of the correction for restriction of range is that the "true" correlation between the variables in question (i.e. subtests) is equal throughout the full range of the latent trait (here, Spearman's g). The basic idea of cognitive differentiation is that abilities are *not* uniformly interrelated across the entire spectrum of intelligence. Therefore, such statistical corrections run counter to the very hypothesis under study. Other studies (Lynn 1992; Lynn & Cooper 1993) that replicated Detterman and Daniel's methods similarly failed to consider restriction of range, and therefore provide only circumstantial evidence in support of differentiation.

In the largest study of differentiation to date, researchers from the Edinburgh Structural Psychometrics Group (ESPG) analyzed Irish standardization data for the Differential Aptitude Test (DAT; Deary *et al.* 1996). The DAT consists of eight subtests measuring verbal ability, abstract reasoning, numerical reasoning, clerical speed, mechanical reasoning, spatial ability, spelling, and language use. Deary *et al.* divided the normative sample ($N = 10,353$) into four smaller groups, based on age and ability. Average IQs of the low- and high-ability groups were 90 and 110 respectively. Test scores were equated for variance. The authors' primary finding was that the g factor (first principal component) accounted for about 49% of the variance among the less able children, and 47% among children of above average ability. This 2% difference in variance was thus vanishingly slight — possibly attributable to the relatively small mean IQ difference (20 points) between ability groups and to the higher ability children themselves being at no very high level of mental development. The handful of other studies (e.g. Fogerty & Stankov,1995) in this area are plagued by small sample sizes that drastically limit their generalizability. In order to evaluate the true nature of g in groups of varying ability, the researcher must compose high- and low-IQ groups of sufficient size so that they have equal standard deviations on the selection test, while also differing substantially in IQ.

The most recent study of cognitive differentiation comes from the University of Nevada (with help from the ESPG) (Kane & Brand 2001). This study was specifically designed to avoid the methodological imperfections of earlier investigations that may have clouded results. The research used normative data ($N = 6,359$) from the Woodcock-Johnson (1989; Woodcock, 1990) Psychoeducational Battery Revised (WJ-R) which is an individually administered test of academic achievement and cognitive abilities. The standardization sample is representative of the population of the United States and covers a wide age range, from childhood to adulthood. The WJ-R is an operational representation of the Horn-Cattell theory of crystallized (g_c) and fluid (g_f) abilities (e.g. Horn & Cattell 1966; Horn 1985). Twenty-one diverse subtests measure an array of eight primary abilities within the g_c/g_f framework. The WJ-R has excellent psychometric properties, and a number of empirical studies (e.g. Bickley *et al.* 1995) corroborate its clinical and theoretical validity. The WJ-R also provides an excellent representation of Carroll's (1997) Three Stratum Theory of cognitive abilities, with the eight cognitive clusters corresponding to Stratum II. Complemented by fourteen subtests of academic achievement, the WJ-R is the most comprehensive battery of cognitive processing tests available to researchers. The diverse nature of the WJ-R provides a "good" g (Jensen & Weng 1994); and the theoretical framework enables insight into possible mechanisms of differentiation.

In contrast to the sophisticated procedures used in previous studies (e.g. Deary *et al.* 1996), Kane & Brand used a relatively simple and straightforward approach to identify high- and low-IQ groups. First, scores on the Numbers Reversed, Listening Comprehension, and Verbal Analogies subtests were averaged to create a composite variable, 'SortIQ'. These subtests were not involved in calculating Broad Cognitive Ability (BCA) or in any subsequent analysis, and therefore provided an independent estimate of overall intelligence. The simple correlation between SortIQ and BCA was 0.94. Dividing the entire data set at the mean of SortIQ yielded two ability groups. Next, desired characteristics for the ability groups were assigned. Sample size for both groups was set at 500. Standard deviations were set at 7.5, or about half of the value typically observed in the general population. Means for the high- and low-IQ groups were set at 115 and 85, respectively. Once these characteristics were fixed, z-scores were calculated within each ability group, using BCA as the criterion variable. Finally, individuals were randomly sampled by z-score intervals, with the desired number of subjects sampled at each z-score interval corresponding to the proportion observed in the normal distribution. These simple procedures resulted in two ability groups being formed, each normally distributed and equated for variance, with respective means of 115 and 85. Sixteen subtests were chosen for analysis, with each subtest identified by previous research (McGrew 1997) as being a strong indicator of its respective primary g_c/g_f factor.

A series of analyses compared the primaries measured by the WJ-R across each ability level. Evidence for cognitive differentiation was unequivocal. In the low- and high-IQ groups, the g factor (the first unrotated principal component) accounted respectively for 52% and 29% of the variance in cognitive performance. Simply stated, for individuals of lesser intellect, general intelligence is the dominating influence, accounting for nearly twice the amount of variance in overall cognitive performance on

Table 21.1: Primary abilities' g loadings in high- and low-IQ groups.

Primary Ability	g Loading	
	Low IQ	High IQ
Fluid Intelligence (g_f)	0.89	0.80
Visual Processing (g_v)	0.88	0.77
Processing Speed (g_s)	0.95	0.75
Long-Term Retrieval (g_{lr})	0.69	0.65
Crystallized Intelligence (g_c)	0.84	0.39
Auditory Processing (g_a)	0.81	0.65
Short-Term Memory (g_{sm})	0.72	0.39
Quantitative Reasoning (g_q)	0.86	0.72

sixteen tests. Conversely, above-average individuals display markedly more specialization, or differentiation of their mental abilities.

The g loadings of the various cognitive clusters are presented in Table 21.1.

The patterns of loadings are consistent with the observations made by Spearman (1927) and with his 'law of diminishing returns.' (Spearman himself interpreted g-differentiation to mean that successive g-increments have diminishing effects across the full range of abilities.) Factor loadings also suggest possible mechanisms of differentiation. Quite the largest decline in g-factor loadings occurred on measures of crystallized intelligence (g_c). The loading of g_c on g declined from 0.84 for the low-IQ group to 0.39 for the high-IQ group. In the Horn-Cattell model, g_c is indicative of an individual's store of information. Thus, a possible conclusion is that low-IQ individuals, more than their above-average counterparts, depend on g for the acquisition of knowledge and information. To the annoyance of its detractors, this finding offers compelling evidence that g plays a causal role in the formation of an individual's fund of knowledge and information. This result is also in keeping with the ideas of Garrett (1946). He offered the first coherent theory of differentiation, in which through the course of mental development, g becomes increasingly invested in specialized activities that result in differentiation. Presumably, the gifted have more intellectual capital to invest than the less able; so in them cognitive differentiation is more pronounced.

The next largest difference in g factor loadings occurred on measures of g_{sm}, which is usually interpreted as indicating working memory (WM) capacity. Over the past decade or so, researchers have assigned an increasingly important role to WM as an explanatory agent in understanding individual differences in human cognitive performance. Mackintosh (above) finds this idea attractive and Kyllonen & Christal (1990) went so far as to equate WM capacity with Spearman's g, citing a simple correlation between them of 0.91. This finding supports the idea that g determines WM for low-ability groups but shows that g cannot be understood as WM in people of higher ability. Not surprisingly, the Nevada study also provides evidence that high-IQ individuals, more than low-IQ individuals, rely on "noncognitive" constructs (e.g. introversion, motivation) for successful performance. For the gifted, aspects of personality complement intellect to assure exceptional accomplishment.

Clearly, the diminishing influence of *g* on quite a few abilities at the higher levels of intelligence suggests that distinct, non-*g* abilities play important parts in the accomplishments (and personal eccentricities) of the gifted. Conversely, *g* serves as quite the most prominent source of mental limitations in the less able. Indeed, *g* is such a source of intellectual limitation among low-IQ individuals that educationists have achieved expenditures on the retarded that are a hundredfold greater than those on high-*g* children (Herrnstein & Murray 1994). The *g* factor is particularly strong among Black testees: studying thousands of South African secondary school pupils, Lynn & Owen (1994) found *g* correlated 0.62 with subtest variation in Blacks but only 0.23 among Whites (who were two standard deviations higher in IQ); and Rushton & Skuy (2000, their Table 3) similarly found that 83% of Standard Ravens Matrices were better correlated with total Ravens IQ scores in Blacks than in Whites.

The Nevada study is the most methodologically adequate attempt so far to assess the differentiation hypothesis — involving more subjects, more subtests, better sampling and a bigger (30-point) IQ range. Its striking results confirm the need to consider the range of ability when venturing theories of intelligence and attainment. After all, what lasting impressions do average or poor musicians, writers, or mathematicians make? Mediocre accomplishment is seldom documented, simply because its preservation would be of no lasting benefit to society. The thing to remember is that individuals who are noticed and remembered for their accomplishments come from an extremely restricted range of abilities to which their precise *g* levels may apparently be of little immediate importance. When this is ignored, it is easy to see why the importance of Spearman's *g* in the rest of the population can often be under-rated. Thomas Edison once remarked that genius was "1% inspiration and 99% perspiration". For Edison and others of his intellectual gentry, that ratio may summarize important truths. For duller people, however, inspiration (and thus *g*), will be both scarce and also a more important determinant of intellectual outcomes.

3. Conclusions

Despite the heroic efforts of Arthur Jensen, realism about the *g* factor has been in short supply in recent years. Critics of IQ ignore the strongly positive correlations that obtain between all mental abilities — especially across the lower reaches of intelligence; and they set impossibly high standards of 'measurement' that are never met elsewhere in social science. Claiming to fear that acceptance of *g* differences must lead to the type of regimented society that Plato once envisaged, critics deplore London School ideas as 'fascist'.

In fact, the already strong case for *g* has strengthened steadily in recent years as the ambitions of massively-funded multifactorialists have come to grief. Now it turns out that the failure of many intellectuals of the past to recognize the importance of *g* can be explained by their lack of contact with low-IQ people: 50% of Western philosophers could not even bring themselves to marry, let alone have the extensive contacts with normal youngsters that characterised the militaristic and paedophilic society of Plato's Athens. How Galton and Burt differed from other psychologists of their day was in their wide experience of life — Galton as an adolescent surgeon working with his medical family around Birmingham, and Burt undertaking live-in social work in the slums of Liverpool. Alfred Binet, too, thanks to government funding, saw the problems of low IQ at first hand.

Moreover, there is in fact no necessity for the facts of life about *g* to lead to authoritarian social arrangements. Plato himself envisaged that his utopia run by philosopher-kings would involve much discussion, choice, social mobility and indeed sexual opportunity; it was Aristotle, not Plato, who set about justifying slavery and female subordination — whereas Plato counselled individuation of treatment rather than the use of group labels; Plato recommended outright censorship only in the primary education of trainee guardians — a principle endorsed world-wide today, for all societies make many restrictions on what can be shown to pre-adolescent children; and any true liberalism is essentially *assisted* by Plato's recognition that people differ importantly from each other and thus should not be forced into identical schooling, employment or marital contracts.

Liberalism has been advocated in the past by Protestants, nationalists, hedonists and empiricists wanting to throw off the chains for which they blamed Aristotle and the Catholic Church. But negative liberalism has a bizarre feature: for what is the point of liberalism unless there are radically different individuals to be liberated? Liberalism is altogether more likely to flourish if the truth is acknowledged that each person is a debating society, as Plato and Freud both thought, and that society should mirror and articulate that arrangement in ways likely to lead to such moral progress as is possible. The bloody experiments of 1642 in Britain, of 1789 in France, of 1917 in Russia and of 1933 in Germany give no reason at all to think that utopias arise from ideologies of brotherly equality. Instead of seeking an equality that invariably turns out to deny freedom, it is time to put freedom *first*.

That the most important truths of human psychological nature steer us logically towards intelligent and informed choice would not have surprised Plato — who after all wanted such choice to apply even to the question of breeding the next generation. Presently the breakdown of marriage in the West is promising a much reduced White population which will come increasingly from the least responsible parents. It is time to admit the realities of human *g* differences — which have classically liberal consequences when properly considered. To his eternal credit, Arthur Jensen — though perhaps no Platonist himself — has helped mightily to keep that option open.

References

Anderson, M. (2000). An Unassailable Defense of g but a Siren-song for Theories of Intelligence. *Psycoloquy, 11* (013), *Intelligence g Factor*, (28).

Barrett, P. T. (2003). Quantitative science and intelligence. *International Journal of Psychophysiology*, (in press).

Bateson, P., & Martin, P. (2000). Recipes for humans. *Guardian* [London], 6 ix.

Berka, K. (1983). *Measurement: Its Concepts, Theories and Problems*. Written originally in Czech (Mereni: Pojmy, Teorie, Problemy), the book was translated into English in 1983 and published as one of the Boston Studies in the Philosophy of Science (Robert S. Cohen, & Marx W. Wartofsky, Eds).

Bickley, P. G., Keith, T. Z., & Wolfe, L. (1995). The three-stratum theory of intelligence: Test of the structure of intelligence across the life span. *Intelligence, 20*, 309–328.

Bouchard, T. J. Jr., Lykken, D. T., McGue, M., Segal, N. L., & Tellegen, A. (1990). Sources of human psychological differences: the Minnesota Study of twins reared apart. *Science, 250*, 223–228.

Brand, C. R. (1996). *The g Factor: General Intelligence and its implications*. Chichester, U.K.: Wiley & Sons (Withdrawn, but a revised (2001) version is available free online at http://www.douance.org/qi/brandtgf.htm

Brand, C. R. (1997). Hans Eysenck's personality dimensions: their number and nature. In: H. Nyborg, *The scientific study of human nature: Tribute to Hans Eysenck at eighty* (pp. 17–35). Oxford: Pergamon.

Brand, C. R. (1998). Fast track learning comes of age. In: Camilla P. Benbow, & David Lubinski (Eds), *Intellectual Talent*. Baltimore, John Hopkins University Press. *Personality & Individual Differences, 24* (6), 899–900.

Brody, N. (1992). *Intelligence* (2nd ed.). San Diego, CA: Academic Press.

Bruer, J. T. (1999). *The Myth of the first three years*. New York: Free Press.

Burt, C. (1954). The differentiation of intellectual ability. *British Journal of Educational Psychology, 24*, 76–90.

Carroll, J. B. (1993). *Human cognitive abilities: A survey of factor-analytic studies*. Cambridge, U.K.: Cambridge University Press.

Carroll, J. B. (1997). The three-stratum theory of cognitive abilities. In: D. P. Flanagan, J. L. Genshaft, & P. L. Harrison (Eds), *Contemporary intellectual assessment: Theories, tests, and issues* (pp. 122–130). New York: The Guilford Press.

Cattell, R. B. (1936). *A guide to mental testing*. London University Press.

Conway, A. R., Kane, M. J., & Engle, R. W. (1999). Is Spearman's *g* determined by speed or working memory capacity? *Psycoloquy, 10* (74): ftp://ftp.princeton.edu/pub/harnad/Psycoloquy/1999.volume.10/ Psyc.99.10.074.intelligence-g-factor.16.conway; http://www.cogsci.soton.ac.uk/cgi/psyc/newpsy?10.074

Deary, I. J., Gibson, G. J., Egan, V., Austin, E., Brand, C. R., & Kellaghan, T. (1996). Intelligence and the differentiation hypothesis. *Intelligence, 23*, 105–132..

Delanty, G. (1998). *Social science: Beyond constructivism and realism*. Oxford: Oxford University Press.

Detterman, D. K., & Daniel, M. H. (1989). Correlations of mental tests with each other and with cognitive variables are highest for low IQ groups. *Intelligence, 13*, 349–359.

Eysenck, H. J. (1939). In: L. L. Thurstone (Ed.), *Primary mental abilities. British Journal of Educational Psychology, 9*, 270–275.

Flynn, J. R. (1984). The mean IQ of Americans: massive gains 1932 to 1978. *Psychological Bulletin, 95*, 29–51.

Fogerty, G. J., & Stankov, L. (1995). Challenging the law of diminishing returns. *Intelligence, 21*, 157–174.

Galton, F. (1869). *Hereditary genius: An inquiry into its laws and consequences*. London: Collins.

Gardner, H. (1999). *Reframing intelligence*. New York: Basic Books.

Garrett, H. E. (1938). Differentiable mental traits. *Psychological Record, 2*, 259–298.

Garrett, H. E. (1946). A developmental theory of intelligence. *American Psychologist, 1,* 372–377.

Garrett, H. E. (1980). *IQ and racial differences*. Torrance, CA: Noontide Press and Brighton Historical Review Press.

Goleman, D. (1995). *Emotional intelligence*. New York: Bantam.

Gottfredson, L. (1997). Why *g* matters: the complexity of everyday life *Intelligence, 24,* 79–132.

Gould, S. J. (1984). *The Mismeasure of Man*. Harmondsworth, U.K.: Penguin.

Gould, S. J. (1989). *Rocks of ages: Science and religion in the fullness of life*. New York: The Ballantine Publishing Group.

Hartocollis, A. (2002). Racial gap in test scores found across New York. *New York Times,* 28 iii (Education). (http://www.nytimes.com/2002/03/28/education/28SCOR.html?ex = 1018293517 &ei = 1&en = da6f180f5274fedc)

Herrnstein, R., & Murray, C. (1994). *The Bell Curve*. New York: Free Press.

Horn, J. L. (1985). Remodeling old models of intelligence. In: B. B. Wolman (Ed.), *Handbook of intelligence: Theories, measurements and applications* (pp. 267–300). New York: Wiley.

Horn, J. L., & Cattell, R. B. (1966). Refinement and test of the theory of fluid and crystallized ability intelligence. *Journal of Education Psychology, 57,* 253–270.

Howe, M. J. A. (1997). *IQ in Question*. London: Sage.

Hunt, E. (1999). The modifiability of intelligence. *Psycoloquy, 10* (072); *Intelligence g Factor,* (14). http://www.cogsci.soton.ac.uk/psyc-bin/newpsy?article = 10.072&submit = View + Article.

Jensen, A. R. (1969). How much can we boost IQ and scholastic attainment? In: *Environment, heredity and intelligence*. Cambridge, MA: Harvard Educational Review.

Jensen, A. R. (1998). *The g factor: The science of mental ability*. Westport, CT: Praeger.

Jensen, A. R., & Weng, L. J. (1994). What is a good *g*? *Intelligence, 18,* 231–258.

Kane, H., & Brand, C. R. (2001). *The Structure of Intelligence in groups of varying cognitive ability: a test of Carroll's three-stratum theory*. [Submitted]

Kline, P. (2000). *A psychometrics primer*. London: Free Association.

Kyllonen, P. C., & Christal, R. E. (1990). Reasoning ability is little more than working memory capacity? *Intelligence, 14,* 389–433.

Lilla, M. (1998). The politics of Jacques Derrida. *New York Review of Books, 25,* vi.

Lynn, R. (1992). Does Spearmans *g* decline at high IQ levels? Some evidence from Scotland. *Journal of Genetic Psychology, 153,* 229–230.

Lynn, R., & Cooper, C. (1993). A secular decline in Spearmans *g* in France. *Learning and Individual Differences, 5,* 43–48.

Lynn, R., & Owen, K. (1994). Spearman's hypothesis and test score differences between Whites, Indians and Blacks in South Africa. *Journal of General Psychology, 121,* 27–36.

Mackintosh, N. J. (1997). *IQ and human intelligence*. Oxford and New York: Oxford University Press.

Malik, K. (1996). *The meaning of race: Race, history and culture in western society*. Basingstoke: Macmillan.

McGrew, K. S. (1997). Analysis of the major intelligence batteries according to a proposed comprehensive g_f-g_c framework. In: D. P. Flanagan, J. L. Genshaft, & P. L. Harrison, *Contemporary intellectual assessment: Theories, tests, and issues* (pp. 151–174). New York: The Guilford Press.

Murray, C. (1999). http://www.lrainc.com/swtaboo/taboos/cmurraybga0799.pdf

Nash, R. (1990). *Intelligence and realism: A materialist critique of IQ*. Basingstoke: Macmillan.

Norman, O. (1995). http://www.vancouver.wsu.edu/fac/norman/kuhn.html

Nyborg, H., & Jensen, A. R. (2000). Black-white differences on various psychometric tests: Spearman's hypothesis tested on American armed service veterans. *Personality and Individual Differences, 28*, 593–599.

Popper, K. (1945). *The open society and its enemies*. London: Routledge & Kegan Paul.

Popper, K. (1994). *Knowledge and the body-mind problem: In defence of interaction*. London: Routledge. [Based on lectures given at Emory University, USA, in 1969.]

Ravitch, D. (2000). *Left back: A century of failed school reforms*. New York: Simon & Schuster.

Richardson, K. (1999). Demystifying g. psycoloquy: 10(048). *Intelligence g Factor*, (5).

Rose, S. (1997). http://www.carf.demon.co.uk/feat01.html

Rushton, J. P. (1996). Race, intelligence and the brain: the errors and omissions of the "revised" edition of S. J. Gould's. *The Mismeasure of Man. Personality & Individual Differences, 21*.

Rushton, J. P. (1999). Secular gains in IQ not related to the g factor and inbreeding depression unlike Black-White differences: A reply to Flynn. *Personality & Individual Differences, 26*, 381–389.

Rushton, J. P., & Skuy, M. (2000). Performance on Raven's Matrices by African and White university students in South Africa. *Intelligence, 28* (4), 251–265.

Ryle, G. (1949). *The concept of mind*. London: Hutchinson.

Schwartzman, A. E., Gold, D., Andres, D., Arbuckle, T. Y., & Chaikelson, J. (1987). Stability of intelligence: a forty-year follow-up. *Canadian Journal of Psychology, 41*, 244–256.

Snow, R. E., & Yalow, E. (1982). Education and intelligence. In: R. J. Sternberg (Ed.), *A Handbook of Human Intelligence* (pp. 493–586). Cambridge, MA: Cambridge University Press.

Sokal, A. (1996). Transgressing the boundaries: towards a transformative hermeneutics of quantum gravity at http://www.nyu.edu/gsas/dept/physics/faculty/sokal/index.html. {For further demonstration of the ease with which plausible constructivist nonsense can be generated, see http://www.elsewhere.org/cgi-bin/postmodern}

Sokal, A. (1998). Interviewed in *Scientific American*, iii.

Sturrock, J. (1998). In: A. Sokal, & J. Bricmont (Eds), *Intellectual impostures. London review of books* (Vol. 16, p. vii).

Spearman, C. (1927). *Abilities of man*. London: Macmillan.

Spencer, H. (1855). *Principles of Psychology* (Vols I & II) (4th edition in 1889). London: Williams & Norgate.

Tang, Ya-ping, Shimizu, E., Dube, G. R., Rampon, C., Kerchner, G. A., Zhuo, M., Liu, G., & Tsieni, J. Z. (1999). Genetic enhancement of learning and memory in mice. *Nature, 401*, 63–68.

Traub, J. (1998). Multiple intelligence disorder. *New Republic, 26* (x), 20–23.

Wechsler, D. (1939). *The measurement and appraisal of adult intelligence*. Baltimore: Williams & Wilkins.

Weyher, H. F. (1999). The Pioneer Fund, the Behavioral Sciences, and the Media's False Stories. *Intelligence, 26* (4), 310–336.

Woodcock, R. W. (1990). Theoretical foundations of the WJ-R measures of cognitive ability. *Journal of Pyschoeducational Assessment, 8*, 231–258.

Woodcock, R. W., & Johnson, M. B. (1989). *Woodcock-Johnson Psycho-Educational Battery-Revised*. Chicago: Riverside.

Part VI

Epilogues

Chapter 22

An Arthurian Romance

Rosalind Arden

"Nurture counts more than nature, baby"

Robert Winston in the Sunday Times, July 1st 2001

"Nothing has an uglier look to us than reason, when it is not of our side"

Edward Frederick Halifax

1. Prejudice and Justice

Unlike the other contributors in this book, I'm not a scientist and my degree in Art History isn't an obvious entrée into the world of individual differences. I came to know Arthur Jensen and something of his science as an 'outsider'. I've taken the liberty of butting in on the discussion because of a passion to see justice done, both to the man and to his subject. The subject is acutely relevant to the modern world with its magnified cognitive complexity; the science is crucial if we are to escape from serial failure in social policy. As for the man, Arthur has chosen science over personal popularity; his resolute integrity is even heroic. But my first impression of Arthur was very different; I suspected him of sporting horns.

I did my degree when my two children were at primary school. The course was a Marxist-informed, Foucauldian, 'social construction of the self' kind of affair. It was taught with great verve; the experience was, for me, an entirely invigorating change from previous years of endless stain removal and mopping. However, as soon as I'd graduated, I fell in love with science — which I had rather forgotten since a childhood crammed with ponds, microscopes and nature clubs. I decided to work on science documentaries such as the 'Equinox' television series on Britain's Channel Four. A television documentary later provided the impetus for me to learn about intelligence

The Scientific Study of General Intelligence: Tribute to Arthur R. Jensen
© 2003 Published by Elsevier Science Ltd.
ISBN: 0–08–043793–1

research. I started with the full canteen of shining intellectual prejudices typical of a liberal, educated journalist. The learning process has taken me a long way from where I began. Since I remember what my thoughts and biases were then, I try to polish them now and again so as to remind myself why it is important to communicate effectively about intelligence and individual differences.

I first heard of Arthur Jensen in 1994 while working on a BBC series presented by the malacologist and geneticist Steve Jones (University College London). The six films were about genes and human origins. The brief of the assistant producers was to find stories that demonstrated "what happens when scientific information about genes is dropped into various cultural contexts". The sub-text, which we all agreed on, was that it makes no sense to say 'a gene for . . .'. All of us on the team perceived biology to be entirely subsumed by culture. I suppose it was a post-modern series; ideas wafted in and out of the programmes that were, on the whole, rather unintelligible. But we were sensitive to human diversity and very well-meaning.

2. Princess of Darkness

Herrnstein and Murray's book 'The Bell Curve' came out in the Summer I started at the BBC. Although I hadn't seen a copy, I knew that it was both bad and wrong. In fact it was rather delicious to revile it, one was so *right* in doing so. I'm not sure that anyone I know had seen a copy, but we talked about it a fair bit in the office and one of my friends tried to get Charles Murray to agree to give us an interview — to provide one programme with a frisson of wickedness. 'The Bell Curve' did not make as big a splash in the British media as it had done in the USA, so when Charles Murray did not agree to be interviewed by our series, we turned our attention elsewhere. I was not at that time particularly interested in intelligence. But even with that brief exposure, I developed one strong opinion. The prime spot, the throne of the prince of darkness, so far as this hereditarian nonsense about IQ was concerned, definitely belonged to Arthur Jensen. I remember that his name conjured for me a sense of almost beyond the pale madness. That he was utterly wrong-headed I felt with conviction. Not that I had read any of his papers.

3. Intelligence, Genes, and the Standard View

Two years after working on the BBC series, I was trying to think of a good idea for a one-hour science documentary. Days and dozens of calls later, I ended up one afternoon in the office of behavioural geneticist Robert Plomin to learn what I could about his work on individual differences in intelligence. He was leading an intriguing new genetic study. Plomin had designed a way to try to find specific genes implicated across the range of intelligence. He agreed to let us film the work his team were doing in London, Cardiff, Iowa and Pennsylvania. There are a number of approaches one can take in intelligence research. One route is to go from the top down — to try to quantify and analyse the behaviour and then move down through the layers eventually to genes and molecules. Another way is to start with various genes and move up through layers of possible mechanisms to arrive once more at the observable behaviours. These two methods are not mutually exclusive; they may easily be incorporated together in a single research programme. Plomin and his team seemed to be attacking the problem from both ends simultaneously with some success. I knew immediately that it would be a good story for television. That was my focus, to develop the story in such a way that I could get a television editor excited about paying for a film.

When I went to visit Plomin, I was ignorant of the scientific literature on intelligence and individual differences. Nonetheless I kept a suite of opinions that I wasn't even aware of explicitly. They emerged over time, often in discussions with others or in response to reading various papers. I think, from having talked to people about it subsequently, that my thoughts at that time characterise almost the 'standard view' of intelligence among liberal, pro-social and reasonably well-educated people.

I now recognise that we lay people outside the psychometric community have a combination of intuition and ideology instead of a theory of intelligence. But that is to be expected. We don't go around in our daily lives thinking 'gosh it's Tuesday, I really ought to develop a coherent theory of intelligence' any more than we think that we need to develop a theory of energy consumption in order to eat. Hunger does that perfectly well. We do not need a proper scientific theory of intelligence in order to think.

But if we want to answer questions like 'why are some people brighter than others?' we do need to turn to science. Instead, we more often confuse our theories of social justice with our assumptions about intelligence. I will come back to this point later because it is really at the heart of why I am writing this chapter.

Channel Four Television expressed an interest in commissioning a film about intelligence and the work of the Plomin team. So I plunged into reading what I could of 'the literature', without a compass to begin with. Gradually I hooked somewhat into the network — they seem to exist around the key practitioners in any subject — where I heard through the grapevine that Arthur Jensen was coming to give a talk in London. I told my partner that I intended to call Arthur and invite him to have tea with me. I am appalled to confess that my desire to meet Arthur that first time was exactly analogous to the gruesome desire that many journalists would have in getting an 'exclusive interview' with spectres such as Harold Shipman (the British serial poisoner) or some Hannibal Lecter type apparition. Arthur's acceptance of my invitation to tea was a thrill, like the prospect of going to a dance with a devil. I took him to Brown's in London because, in my imagination, the grave and sophisticated ambience of the fine hotel would provide an excellent backdrop for this éminence grise of badness, this well-mannered gentleman with a trident under his waistcoat.

4. Having Tea with Arthur

Worryingly, evidence is less of an antidote to illusion than one might hope. Over assam and cucumber sandwiches Arthur was gracious, thoughtful and engaging. Still I wanted to call out 'look everybody, I'm having tea with Arthur Jensen'. Not that any of the cosmopolitan beauties in buttery leather and peacock silk would have been any the wiser (nor would they have raised an eyebrow had I been entertaining Nabokov I suspect). Arthur is around five foot ten and of medium build. His large, smooth face reminded me of a goshawk with a wide forehead, gently curving nose, very clear blue eyes and slightly electrified eyebrows. A novelist would describe his mouth as that of an aesthete, rather severe, not the lips of a sensualist. His overall bearing combined the beginning of frailty that comes with age, plus the vigour that I guessed were the endowments of a disciplined and health-promoting life. His posture was upright, he wore, I believe some kind of greyish suit with a v-necked woolly under the unbuttoned jacket and those shoes that physicists usually wear — very sensible and quite the wrong colour. In conversation, Arthur's face is rather immobile, most of the expression comes from the eyes, which are lively and lambent. I was struck by the contrast between this man's reputation — bête noire, incendiary, proponent of racist science — and his presence in the flesh. He was mild, serious, gentle, unassuming.

Arthur's unworldliness reminded me of Chauncy Gardner the Peter Sellers character in the film 'Being There' whose simple utterances were mistaken for profundity. Like Gardner's fame, Arthur's fame (or notoriety) seemed utterly accidental, something of which he was almost oblivious. He was either unaware of, or unwilling to uphold certain social mores too. For example, when we talked about the work for which he has become well known, he would talk about 'Blacks' or 'Whites' without going sotto voce. This made me feel uncomfortable; I remember covertly checking other scone eaters to see whether they had heard, trying to pull my head into my body, like a tortoise; without success, of course. I should say that Arthur was not making racist comments; my unease stemmed from his lack of restraint, his willingness to talk about 'Blacks and Whites' the way we talk about trees and hedges. My own discomfort (which I mention because I am sure it is common) arose from a fear of being exposed to racism within me, near me, or other people thinking it of me. I was definitely curious about whether this man was emotionally racist or whether he was simply perversely blind to what were widely taken to be the human implications of his scientific research.

We talked a lot about music, one of Arthur's great passions. He plied me with stories that manifested his devotion to various maestros, such as how he managed to bluff his way into Toscanni's rehearsals. Arthur's memory for the details of an event and what such and such a conductor had said circa 1932 was alarming. I am having to work here, to avoid invention, about that afternoon a few years ago, and I'm much younger than he is. I was very much taken with his enthusiasm for knowledge, for new insights, fresh approaches to understanding the world. As a science producer, I've met dozens of 'top scientists' yet it's always a treat to meet someone with an unjaded palette, a ravenous appetite to learn. I've been surprised at how many successful scientists are mealy-mouthed in the face of new evidence, unmoved by data that disconfirm treasured theories or ideologies. Jensen exhibited an intense if choosy interest in life. He wasn't indiscriminately wide open to just any old thing, but his excitement did seem to be kindled by a healthy variety of topics. The 'healthy' is clearly a value judgement, I mean only to say that spending time with someone with only one interest is a little hard going.

The life of Gandhi has been a key influence and source of inspiration for Arthur who is quite a Gandhi scholar. Arthur told me some amusing stories about the life of this man whose insistence, on combining asceticism with a large entourage carrying the technology of the time, caused one of his patron-admirers to say 'you've no idea how much money it costs me to keep you in the poverty to which you are accustomed'. Arthur felt impelled to do something useful with his life and viewed Gandhi as an exemplar of time well spent. However, Arthur's respect for Gandhi did not persuade me (by association) that Arthur was a Good Person: Hitler, after all, was a vegetarian. Oh no, I wasn't about to be 'bought off' so easily.

We broached the subject of intelligence and the causes of differences between individuals. Arthur talked about his work and that of others including Hans Eysenck, whose post-graduate student he had been for some years. He told me about Eysenck's enviable approach to writing a book. No writer's block or displacement activities for Hans; he would come into the office in the morning and pace up and down while dictating a continuous flow to his secretary. He would stop after a couple of hours to resume other tasks for the afternoon, beginning dictation again the next morning. Within a number of weeks the completed book was transcribed by the dutiful secretary and delivered to the publisher. We talked about the relatively new discipline of evolutionary psychology and how it is essential for scientists to develop a proper understanding of intelligence, both from the species perspective (insights into function and phylogeny), and the point of view of individual differences.

After a few hours we parted. I left Arthur on Piccadilly expecting to help him into a taxi. He airily waved my offer away; he remembered London pretty well, he said, and preferred to walk. I would not have been the least surprised had he told me he had memorised a street map from his time as a graduate student, but he's probably made many interim trips to London since then. We left on pleasant terms. My afternoon had been a mixture of unfulfilled expectation (no whiff of burning flesh) and pleasure in hearing the vividly related stories about conductors and their foibles. For Arthur, I'm sure it was simply another sandwich, another journalist.

Arthur's reputation as a Caligula of the far right rests on a paragraph in his 1969 Harvard Educational Review article in which he discussed a putative relationship between genes and racial intelligence differences. Briefly, Arthur suggested that one might not need to invoke special reasons to distinguish intelligence differences between races from differences within races. He claimed that genes might play a part in intelligence differences between Blacks and Whites in the same way that genes were thought play a role in intelligence differences among Whites.

The link between intelligence and important factors such as income and status makes it socially important to understand the causes of differences between individuals (regardless of race). An alternative explanation to the genetic hypothesis that Arthur adumbrated seemed very likely to be true. The environment that many Black people inhabit (in both Britain and the USA) is often vastly different from the environment of Whites (I mean to include the psycho-social environment as well as the economic background). I thought that the effects of having a lower income, poorer resources and being subjected to racism would easily be potent enough to account for the well observed performance difference on IQ tests. I wondered how seriously Arthur took the effects of enduring racism. I wondered why he had chosen to work on race differences, a subject that seemed to be socially divisive. I should say that after this first meeting I remained agnostic about Arthur and the question of racism. I was undecided in my opinion of whether Arthur was racist over and above the ordinary way in which we all carry various prejudices around with us, however much we protest this ugly fact.

5. The Burden of Knowledge

Over the next few months I continued to read the scientific literature on research into individual differences. It's an extensive literature so I sought help from people with a range of viewpoints to guide me to important articles. I was also aided by a couple of academic books that came out around that time such as Sternberg and Grigorenko's edited collection 'Intelligence Heredity and Success' — in places quite a fizzing collection of papers that disagreed with one another rather fruitfully. I telephoned or met several scientists whose work seemed important within the discipline. I've found in most of my encounters with new areas of science, that there is usually a strong consensus about who's 'important' in any given subject, almost without regard to which 'side' they purport to be on. These 'people maps' help enormously in orienting beginners in a new territory.

It's a common experience that when you first go somewhere new — either a physical place or an intellectual territory — you have all sorts of insights and responses that become dulled through familiarity. This is true of people making television documentaries — one starts on a subject as an 'outsider', but after a few weeks or months marinating in the subject, one becomes saturated. After that it is a struggle to maintain that jargon-less position of not-knowing. Surprisingly quickly it seems, colleagues begin to say 'you've forgotten the audience, you're going too fast, remember what you used not to know' and so on. I had that experience when I began learning about intelligence research. I started with an inexplicit but nonetheless well developed conceptual framework, the standard tabula rasa environmentalist view. My ideas changed in the light of what I read. I began to understand about the heritability of intelligence and the powerful effect of genes. The evidence was abundant, good quality, overwhelmingly persuasive. Then I would go into editorial meetings at Channel Four and talk to people who held exactly the opinions I had begun with.

In one particular respect, making a film about intelligence research was signally different from my earlier experience of working on a film about superstring theory. Big Science — particle physics, string theory — rightly captures people imaginations, for it is wonderful stuff. It was a tremendous privilege to talk to giants in the subject and to be the recipient of so much generosity from experts who kindly gave up their time to tutor me. The big difference for me was that with physics, especially such an exciting but arcane branch (as it was then, now it's booming), I went in saying 'I don't know, teach me', whereas when I went to meet Robert Plomin to learn about his research, my attitude was much more, 'well I have a sackful of my own views already, but by all means, please try to cram in a little of what you know'. So there was much less openness, much less willingness to say 'I don't know'. I found when talking to friends about the film project that I wasn't the only one to come to the subject with lots of pre-conceptions. With superstrings, friends would say 'what the heck are they?' leading me to cobble together anything I could muster, whatever I'd heard or read that morning probably. When we talked about intelligence, though, it was another story; everybody had an opinion, everyone thought they knew all about it already. The reasons for the two kinds of responses to the two different subjects are obvious but perhaps worth articulating.

Unlike superstrings, which would need a particle accelerator as big as the solar system to persuade them to leave a legible signature, the behaviours that say 'intelligent life' are easily observable phenomena. Indeed studies reveal that spouses match each other more closely on intelligence than on any other trait. This suggests that we are intuitive experts in the art of intelligence measurement. There are counter examples, but it is nonetheless a general truth. There are many possible explanations for this assortative mating. Like other constructs such as 'beauty', we usually know it when we see it; and we know it doesn't reside merely in the tilt of the nose or the curve of the hip. Incidentally, we also know that our intuitions are imperfect. We can be thrown off the scent when people have the 'wrong' accent or the 'wrong' clothes. Intelligence like beauty can be under-appreciated for social reasons. Kate Moss was presumably beautiful before she was 'discovered' by someone in the beauty industry, yet her accent, her milieu and her clothes made her potential to be a world famous supermodel less obvious.

6. The Art of Balancing Contrasting Views

Working on the television project was more challenging than I had anticipated. This was partly because of certain industry practices and partly because I felt threatened in several ways, which made me feel uncomfortable. Commissioning editors often require that documentary television producers achieve 'balance' by offering contrasting points of view. This sounds innocuous, until you face a subject where the debate that the scientific community is having is not the debate that the public thinks they are having. The public thinks that the debate in intelligence is about whether genes are important or not. The scientists moved on from that discussion decades ago. They are trying to figure out not whether genes are important or not, but which genes are important. They are looking for correlates in neuroscience or trying to understand non-genetic pathways in biological development.

Television often distorts subjects by taking the view that audiences will only be interested if the film has some tension — usually generated by conflict. Tension is a natural and successful element of much television drama, but it is sometimes contrived and misleading in documentary. When I produced the film about Plomin's work, I sought diligently for opposing views. I came across the work of Stephen Ceci. Ceci is passionate about understanding intelligence using non-genetic approaches. Thinking I had found my legitimate opposition we went to film an interview with him. Although I was very happy to meet Professor Ceci (he has an interesting perspective and great personal integrity), I was heartily disappointed to hear him say 'I'd be extremely surprised if anything Plomin did failed to replicate'. So much for my oppositional viewpoint. In the end I was faced with the choice of recruiting a polemicist from outside the field, or dragging in to the film a scientist without a serious reputation in the subject.

7. Confusions Surrounding Intelligence

At roughly the time I first met Arthur, I was struggling with three aspects of the subject. Firstly, I was uneasy with the idea that one could measure something as complicated as human intelligence. Secondly, I had a common sense explanation for intelligence differences between people — privilege and the lack of it. I didn't understand why genes had to be included in the discussion. In addition, I felt that genetic influence would imply a fatalistic attitude towards achievement. The third facet, vague but potent, was the miasma of shame that seemed now and then to infuse the subject. This was the fog of eugenics, of Nazi racist ideology. There is a fourth issue that I will return to later — an amorphous but serious anxiety about race and genetics. Just thinking about that was like a 'final frontier' for me. But first the easier aspects of my confusions.

7.1. Definitions and Measures of Intelligence

The first point is about definition and measurement. Ian Deary from Edinburgh University set me straight on definitions. He pointed out that a clear definition is often the end point of science, not the starting point. It's quite legitimate to study something in order to find out what it is rather than the other way around. This might sound obvious to the point of facile, but I know I am not the only one to have wasted time debating the utterly spurious point that 'we need to know what intelligence is before we can find out about it'. As for measuring intelligence, I did not have to be repelled by the notion that the might of the astronomically well-connected human brain can be captured by a single number. That is simply not the claim. The claim is that a reasonable battery of IQ-type tests will yield, with stolid reliability and with remarkable accuracy, a ranking order that shows where each person stands relative to others in the population under study. This point about the relative nature of IQ scores is important. The power of IQ scores lies in the fact that they show, better than any other single variable, the level of one person's intellectual 'juice' relative to another's. In any case it is mistaken to imagine that any psychometrician thinks that IQ scores capture everything that is interesting, lovable or worthwhile about a person.

7.2. The Causes

My second confusion was about the causes of differences. Why look further than nurture in the form of class, social and economic factors which confer advantage with reckless caprice? It is an intuitively reasonable explanation. The problem with relying on common sense is that it serves us a little unevenly. What we call common sense is a bundle of implicit quasi-knowledge stemming from various sources. These include evolved intuitions (such as 'don't eat it if it smells putrid'), assumptions about the natural world that stem from our limited perceptions (such as 'the sun revolves around the earth') and bits and pieces of information that we pick up from the world, only some of which will be based on science. It became clear to me that I was mistaken in thinking that the contents of my mind had been selected purposefully, as a child collects pebbles on a beach. The contents of my head are partly chosen by me for good reasons, but lots of them have simply blown in, the mental equivalents of bits of old crisp bag, tarred, straggly feathers, ring pulls from discarded cans. My assumptions are by no means all well founded or even apparent to me. My common sense told me that the powerful impact of the environment on intelligence differences is obvious. It took me some time to understand that I needed sometimes to ask whether my hunches were grounded on good science or a more brownfield site.

7.3. "What About the Nazis?"

Distinguishing scientific questions from social issues was absolutely crucial in dealing with the last of the three areas that bothered me. I wanted to know why people always said 'well what about the Nazis?' when I told them I was doing a film about IQ. I also hoped that in finding out I would be better equipped to gauge the moral temperature of Arthur and other scientists in the field.

The Nazi Holocaust is iconic in its status as a landmark for everything vile, depraved and cruel that humans can do to one another. Because of this, it is actually very hard to think clearly about anything to do with the regime at all. I can illustrate this point nicely. The Nazis were quick to recognise the health hazards of smoking cigarettes. Alone, In Europe, they campaigned against tobacco with some success. In post-war Britain, everything associated with Nazis or even Germans was repudiated, including the anti-smoking movement. Britain gave up 'giving up' for decades because it smacked of Nazi Germany. I needed to find out whether intelligence research was contaminated by association in the same way. I found two points of contact between the Nazis and intelligence research.

The first point is that the Nazis did mental testing. They used tests to identify mental defectives (in contemporaneous language). Was this a baleful programme? The French psychologist Alfred Binet first developed a systematic approach to mental testing in 1904. Binet's explicit programme was to identify feeble-minded students so that he could offer them additional educational support. Testing is not in itself a nasty enterprise. The moral status of a testing programme depends on questions such as what the testers are doing it for, and whether those being tested are volunteers or not. Testing people for 'defectiveness' in order to exterminate, involuntarily sterilise or incarcerate is invidious beyond words. I don't know enough about the type and application of tests used by the Nazis to comment on the scientific status of their mental testing programmes. They could easily have been valid and effective. The important point is to distinguish the science from the social policy. They are not mutually inter-dependent. I will come back later to an important point about testing and the Holocaust.

7.4. Eugenics — The "Red-rag" Word

The second point of contact between intelligence research and the Nazis is that the Nazis embraced eugenics. Eugenics is, as Richard Dawkins once said, a 'red-rag' word. It is almost impossible for anything coherent or sensible to come out of a paragraph with the word in it. Let's try to separate the science from the social meaning of eugenics. There are two sorts of eugenics, positive and negative. 'Positive' eugenics is the amplification through selective breeding of heritable traits that are judged to be beneficial. A good example of this exists in modern day Singapore where the Prime Minister, Lee Kuan Yew, has talked about the benefit to the country's human capital of encouraging intelligent families to have more children. 'Negative' eugenics aims to curtail deleterious traits in a population through various programmes of weeding people out. Possible methods include infanticide, homicide, abortion, sterilisation, legislation, social policy and even social pressure.

Eugenics was founded by Charles Darwin's half cousin Francis Galton. Galton was the larger-than-life father of research into intelligence and individual differences. Galton recognised that personality as well as physical characteristics were heritable but, like Darwin, he lacked a good theory of genetics — the agency of inheritance. Galton thought that it would be both possible and good to boost desirable traits and to avoid many illnesses and disabilities through selective breeding. Galton's vision of an 'improved' society was shared by many of the intelligentsia; leading thinkers both left wing and right took up the spirit of eugenics with great enthusiasm.

The Nazis took up both positive and negative eugenics but the spirit of Nazi eugenics was very different from Galton's conception. Galton's 'improvements' to society were based on values that elevated health and virtues such as the enjoyment of hard work. The traits that Galton valued were an ad hoc collection. Some of them (such as vigour) overlap with traits that contribute to the modern concept of 'fitness', but they were not supported by a consistent biological theory. Nor was the Nazi eugenic programme based on a coherent biological theory. The Nazis had a different aim from Galton. Their intention was to use eugenic practices to create a state based on Nationalist ideology that promoted Aryanism. 'Racist' is rather an etiolated term to describe the agenda, since its success depended on genocide; it required the extermination of all non-Aryan people in the state's jurisdiction.

Galtonian eugenics differed from Nazi eugenics on another substantive point. Where Galton favoured educating people in the benefits of elective human husbandry, the Nazis empowered the state to make reproductive choices on people's behalf. This distinction remains important today. I might wish for a child who enjoys hard work, but I would resist the state's right to determine that my child showed an inappropriate level of moral turpitude and shiftlessness. It is one thing to make value judgements about various traits and judge them to be good or bad — we all do that. But that is not to say the state rather than the individual should have dominion over our 'breeding' choices. Galtonian eugenics was about encouraging individuals to make salutary choices (the original term which he abandoned was viriculture, which carries the meaning rather well).

Nazi eugenics was a programme of torment and slaughter founded on racism and ideology, not science. But, of course, we don't excoriate the Nazis simply for their failure to use science properly. It is their values that shock us to breathlessness. They used whatever means would allow them to achieve their goals — from surgical appliances to gas chambers. It is a mistake to dignify that yoking of ideology to brute mechanisms by calling it science.

7.5. Nazi Abuse of Eugenics

Backtracking for a moment, science does have something to say about mental testing and the Holocaust. The important point I alluded to earlier is this. If the Nazis had taken seriously the idea that testing reveals the mental component of biological fitness, then a systematic testing programme would have ensured the protection of the Jewish people. The Nazis failed to use biologically informed eugenic principles when they led the Jews to the gas chambers. There is a lot of literature on mental ability, genetics and Jews. The Jews are quite clearly, as a group, the cognitive élite of Europe. As with any population science, this statement is probabilistic and epidemiological in nature. It makes no predictions about particular individuals, but only speaks about averages. In the light of this, it is possible to interpret the Nazi Holocaust as another example of the proletariat revolting against the cognitive elite — as later happened in Pol Pot's killing fields of Cambodia. Incidentally, one of the great modern fears of testing is that if an élite is identified, they will subjugate the underclasses. H. G. Wells' story *The Time Machine* is a good literary example. In that story, the upper caste Eloi had dominion over the cave dwelling, lower caste Morlocks. In life rather than literature, it is nearly always the other way around. History usually reveals the élites being persecuted by the masses, or by a despot who fears the élite.

I admit to recognising certain confusions in my own and others' reactions to eugenics. As usual these muddles persist because we conflate science or technology with policy. It is the *aim* of the Nazis that we repudiate. No science or technology could have lessened the crime of the policy; though certainly the crime of the policy was harnessed to an indescribably evil strategy. But it is essential that we understand the distinction between science or technology and the uses to which they are put.

7.6. Eugenics, Sex, and the Individual

Many parents today actually welcome certain eugenic practices. We are grateful for tools such as amniocentesis. These investigative procedures inform us about the condition of the foetus. They are often used in decisions about whether or not to carry to term a foetus with disabilities. Amniocentesis is certainly eugenic, as are other screening tools that lower the rate of babies being born with painful, severe and sometimes terminal diseases. I think it is fair to say that we are all biased towards some of the percepts of eugenics — none of us would wish our children to be born with severe disabilities, though we feel uncomfortable owning up to it. Another confusion is that while we publicly derogate the prospect of intelligence screening, in practice the greatest use of screening is in mothers who are at risk for carrying a child with Down syndrome. Down syndrome is the largest single cause of mental retardation. This chromosomal defect causes several health problems, but let us not disguise the fact that the retardation aspect of the disorder is a great concern for prospective parents.

The last point I want to make about eugenics is that, at a basic level (sometimes with family involvement), mate choice (our choice of sexual partners) is almost entirely eugenic in its function. For other species, and ancestrally for humans, mate choice was a potentially dangerous exercise. It necessitates search costs, demands time and energy, exposed us to predators and jealous rivals. In the absence of variation in heritable fitness there would be very little point to it. One might just as well mate with the first creature of the appropriate sex that one encounters. Mate choice happens because of the genetic advantage to offspring, conferred by parents having sex with 'good quality' partners. Mate choice is a grindingly powerful engine of evolution. All species that have two sexes (including some hermaphroditic species such as slugs) engage in choosing partners for sex. We sophisticated modern humans don't choose our partners with a conscious view to having 'designer children'. Indeed many of us choose not to have children at all. But the long arm of evolution has shaped in our own minds, propensities to find attractive, features that are 'cues of biological 'fitness' such as good health and a degree of charitableness. This does not mean that we always choose 'high fitness' partners, but it unquestionably tilts us toward them. We are not conscious of the way evolution has shaped our proclivities any more than we are consciously aware of our kidney function, yet our preferences and our renal systems serve us well. Mate choice is none other than pre-copulatory eugenics.

8. Dining with Arthur (and Barbara)

I found the process of familiarising myself with the literature on intelligence daunting; not just because of my ill-suited background, but also because of the discipline it required. Nor had I ever worked on a subject that exercised my emotions so much. I received some help in this from Arthur who came to England in the summer of 99 to do some research. We didn't sit around talking about the agonies of reconciling various inconsistent intellectual positions. Arthur is not given to that style at all. I learned more by example, from listening and talking to him about various research projects he was interested in.

8.1. What "Is" and What "Ought"

I got to know him better during this period. We had a few meals together and I met his wife Barbara (he told me 'she is the best decision I ever made'). I came to admire him immensely for all kinds of reasons. One of them relates to the business of thinking about unsavoury issues such as eugenics. Arthur possesses a clarity of thought that borders on the pathological. I mean by this, that at times he reminds me of the Commander Data character in Star Trek. Data is a humanoid robot endowed with extraordinary processing power, but has been programmed without emotions. This can be used to great comic effect when he misunderstands, say, a woman's sexual approach. Yet occasionally Data's unique lack of sentiment enables him to rescue his colleagues from a catastrophic situation. Arthur isn't emotionless in quite this way, but he does maintain an impenetrable firewall between his understanding of 'things as they are' and 'things as one would like them to be'. He has immense intellectual courage; he never evades or side-slips facts because they reveal unsightliness. What I first read as lack of emotion, I now see as a remarkable humility. Arthur cares far more about the truth, about good data, than he does about his reputation, his standing, even his comfort and personal safety.

Like many people, I feel like a skewered halibut when pressed about certain unwelcome facts, flapping and writhing to get off the point. Arthur does not share my squeamishness; he's extremely bald, non-judgemental, factual. I used to misunderstand this as science without the humanising 'common touch'. I know better now, it's because he cares very deeply. Arthur has spent years trying to make a contribution in the field of education for the disadvantaged. He is data-driven because he feels passionately that social progress requires us to develop a clear grasp of the world as it actually exists. I share his view that policies for a make-believe world are doomed to failure.

I have thought a great deal about Arthur because he is, in some respects, indexical of an intellectual position. He has, like the hoover, become eponymous. Jensenism carries its own much-battered portmanteau. I've thought about the difficulty of standing up for him, which sounds schoolgirl-pathetic; but is nonetheless at times a reality. I want to explain why.

8.2. Good and Bad Guys

Arthur stands for the 'bad guy position' whereas people who think that IQ differences have no genetic basis find the 'good guy' position theirs for the taking. It is shamefully hard to resist the safety of running for what is perceived to be the moral high ground and turn instead towards the science. Science is after all, the most reliable source of answers to the empirical questions about what causes us to vary.

In developed industrial societies (as opposed to hunter-gatherer societies) the value of high intelligence is amplified. Whereas some benefits certainly accrue to the brightest men and women in pre-agrarian societies (there is some evidence of this), the advantages of intelligence in a socially mobile, modern society are huge. They include access to better education, housing, jobs, money, health care (in some regions) and holidays. When we think about social justice and fairness, most of us think that we have made progress. We have switched (or slowly and bloodily disengaged) from a system in which people were born into political power into one in which that power is vested in elected representatives of the people. Money and influence, however, did not immediately shake loose and become widely available to all after we gained democracy. Social inequality, income inequalities are still with us.

8.3. Meritocracy and Justice

In Britain, the hard to define but deadly easy to decipher, notion of 'class' provided some of the stickyness that prevented assets from flowing freely around the nation.

British society is not class-free in the new Millennium, but the virtues of merit, of social mobility, of allowing people to rise through the ranks according to the breadth of capacity rather than length of vowels, are widely praised. Yet what do we expect of a merit-based society? We expect a meritocracy to deliver fairness. In a proper meritocracy, opportunity will be open to all. Presumably some environmental equalisation will take place so that accident of birth no longer determines important outcomes such as education, health and wealth. The bright child in the sink estate will not waste her potential nor will the intellectually flaccid Duke find shelter in a sinecure afforded by nepotism. Many of us hope that such a meritocracy will substantially reduce income inequality. We might also feel that at last we have a society in which people get what they deserve to a great extent. These are serious errors.

A fully meritocratic society would exaggerate the inequalities. We must not confuse equality of opportunity with equality of outcome. If it were possible to iron out all gross environmental differences between us, the remaining differences would all be genetic. All remaining mental ability differences would then be heritable differences. In the 'equal environments' scenario, instead of being attenuated, the differences between us would be even larger. Where money adhered before to family and class, in a meritocracy, money would attach to genes. Now, rich but dim folk are sheltered by family money and bright but poor folk at least have some chance of success. In a full-fledged meritocracy, the divisions between smart alecs and dunderheads would cut very deep. This does not imply that we should avoid merit or meritocracy. But it's certainly crucial that we understand the science so that we can think ahead and see what a meritocracy would really imply and how we should respond to it.

8.4. Nature Versus Nurture

The concept of fairness inflects the way we view genetic explanations of individual differences. Most of us would like the good things in life to be fairly and evenly distributed among all people regardless of size, sex, race or belief. After all, part of the function of government is to provide a mechanism for sharing out various 'goods'. These goods include tangibles such as money and intangibles such as health and dignity, for example. In experimental economics, there is lots of evidence that our species behaves much more fairly than is 'rational' in the economic sense — we're not saints, but we're not totally grasping either. We know that physical attractiveness is uneven, genetic, unfair, hard to change and advantageous, but we're so accustomed to it, that though we try to 'beauty up', we know more or less what our range is. Intelligence is like beauty in this respect. It is a chance affair, it can be a benefit, but we don't judge our friends or loved ones by it. We know that it is just part of the package and that there is a lot more to a person than their ranking on the beauty pageant of life. Part of our resistance to genetic explanations of individual differences derives from antipathy towards making explicit the intrinsic unfairness of a genetic lottery.

The business about nature and nurture is variously described as a false dichotomy or a tired perspective. Yet it still rakes in the column inches and citations. We see a note of triumphalism in newspaper articles or even journal papers that 'find for' the environment. "Nurture counts more than nature, baby", crows one article written by a Labour Peer from this week's cuttings. What is so great about nurture? What is the basis of our gut reaction in favour of environmentally causal hypotheses? My guess is that we have at least a tripartite confusion. One, we think that we are choosing between malleability and determinism — the environment is amenable to change whereas genes aren't. Neither of these statements is true. The environment can be notoriously difficult to change and genetic predispositions can be compensated for (think of eyeglasses, hair dye, low-salt diets). Two, we are muddled about blame. When something bad happens we are eager to identify the locus of blame. This is well illustrated by countless heart-wrenching newspaper stories in which a series of events leads to a dreadful calamity. Suppose a Black child is failing at school; we want to know why. Our emotions and sense of fairness rightly tell us that the racism and poverty endured by this child are bad. But it is a mistake to assume that the racism and poverty which we repudiate are the cause of her poor performance. We don't want to blame the child herself for her performance, yet we feel we must assign blame somewhere, so we blame the environment. When we set it out honestly, it becomes clear that it is the will to blame that confuses us. We think we have two alternatives: blame the child (her genes) or blame the environment. Again, this is false. We don't have to assign blame. Our goal should be informed understanding. It is perfectly legitimate to improve the quality of this child's environment regardless of whether or not it improves scholastic performance.

The child's performance could be poor for a number of reasons. Are we even fighting her corner by claiming that her environment kept her from succeeding? We can easily see the error in this by imagining the reverse. As a thought experiment, imagine a world where racism and poverty increase academic performance. Would we then approve of racism and poverty? Most certainly not. Racism and poverty are environmental features that a civilised society must march against, quite regardless of their effects on performance. As an aside, racism and poverty have often been given as reasons for the success of various 'geniuses', as in stories that begin 'he fought so hard to get away from his background'. They do not make us approve of the background that our genius worked so hard to escape. Science will enable us to find out about causal directions and effects of environments. But we cannot afford to conflate social justice with the science of individual differences.

The third pillar supporting our veritable temple of confusion, is that we imagine that if it is widely known that parenting effort does not raise IQ, then parents won't bother with it. Yet running along a damp beach with sand squeezing between the toes might not change a child's IQ, but it might make the day one to remember. Plenty of experiences enrich life, without enhancing IQ. Raising IQ is surely not the goal of providing a child with a 'good environment'.

Lots of the issues that I had to confront when I first met Arthur had to do with my capacity to learn new facts that did not sit well with my own theories of social justice. I want to be very clear about this. The transition that I have experienced, my Arthurian romance, did not begin by my having one interpretation of the data only to be seduced by another. I scarcely knew anything of the data when I began. The change is that I have become more perceptive about the distinction between my comfort with certain facts, and the objective truth status of facts. The two are unconnected. The status of a fact depends on the totality of evidence that supports it. My comfort level is personal to me and reflects my concepts about how I would like the world to be.

We are curiously equivocal about genes and their effects. We say we dislike 'genetic determinism' yet every time a baby is born to a human mother, we thrill to the perfection of the tiny anemone hands and feet. We rarely stop to praise biological (mostly genetic) determinism for seeing to it that we get the right species. How terrifying pregnancy would be, if for nine months we had to ponder the possibility of being delivered of a fine baby bobcat or weasel. I've encountered two opposing views on the connection between genes and intelligence. One view is that it is absurd to suggest that genes contribute very much to intelligence. The other is that it's ludicrous to claim that genes are not largely responsible for intelligence. The third thing I've noticed is that these opinions are frequently found lurching from neuron to neuron in the same brain.

No one believes that just anyone could become Mozart or Einstein if they simply 'put their back into it'. Nor are we asinine enough to blame severe mental retardation on laziness or bad parenting. We seem happy assigning genetic influence to both the right and the left tail of the gaussian distribution. What about the rest of the range — where most of us sit? Do we imagine that genes kick in at the sharp ends but don't influence all the rest of us in the zone that is in and around the average? It is hardly parsimony. We should expect genes to influence our intelligence right along the range — as they do with height or with any other personality trait.

Differences in ability are striking to teachers and parents. But we are both inconsistent and tortured about these differences at the level of policy. This makes us not kinder, but ineffectual and dishonest. I recently visited eight state schools to interview principals and administrators with the purpose of finding an elementary school for my daughter. I picked up various leaflets that the schools distributed for the edification of parents. One of them stridently insisted that 'every child is gifted, you just have to identify the special talent belonging to your own child and nurture it'. This is patently false. Most children are average. That is what average means; this fact is harder to escape than the earth's gravity. Some children are extremely un-gifted and some are 'gifted' (such a horrid term, but frequently used in the USA where they go in for that sort of thing). Is it helpful to tell some poor woman that if she hasn't found the special gift of her intellectually deeply un-gifted child that she has not searched properly? Why not instead take the heat off, admit that there is the same gaussian diversity in intelligence that exists in every other complex variable in nature across all two-sex multi-celled species. The mother would probably be relieved to hear that she is perfectly entitled to love and nurture her child without needing the child's 'special gift' to legitimise her parental care.

Parents with several children usually notice that their children are not perfectly equal in intelligence. Do they love their children in rank order of their intelligence? I don't know whether this question has been studied systematically or not but, anecdotally, I don't see evidence of that. Indeed what little evidence there is, supports a prediction consistent with evolutionary theory — that parental resource allocation tracks reproductive value (number of likely future children) rather than intelligence. When we think about what counts in a person, intelligence is one of many qualities that we esteem. David Buss's, landmark study of traits preferred by mates, conducted in 37 different cultures, found a universal desire for kindness ahead of intelligence. Among friends, and employees, we value lots of characteristics such as loyalty, integrity and conscientiousness as well as intelligence. Intelligence is by no means a sine qua non. Murray & Herrnstein (1994) put it nicely; "intelligence is a trait not a virtue".

It is crucial for us to think clearly about intelligence and what it means for us, both privately and publicly. One reason that we should bother to set this out is because it is virtually certain that scientists will, in time, learn very much more about the genetic basis of the differences in intelligence between individuals. Anyone even peripherally involved with the subject has a moral duty to work towards generating clarity rather than fear. If scientists, policy makers and the press are clear-headed about the facts then future discoveries will be greeted with interest not dread. What will happen otherwise when the first laboratory creates a 'smart chip' that picks up all the known intelligence enhancing alleles in our DNA? It will be a quick and easy to read off the likely range of an individual's intelligence. The second step will follow, someone will want to compare allelic frequencies across various racial groups. Should this be stopped in case we find out directly from the DNA that groups vary in allelic frequencies? We have an opportunity to extricate ourselves from the confusion caused by muddling our values with science. It is incumbent upon us to avoid being caught on the hop.

8.5. The Race Question

Now to that fourth 'final frontier' point I mentioned much earlier. Genetics and race; one cannot write about Arthur and avoid it. I asked him once after dinner, on his way to the tube, if he was racist. I thought at the time that I was being a bit daring. When I look back on it I feel ashamed because I was not, as I thought, bearding the lion in his den, I was simply being callow and jejune. I came to understand that later from his answer. Anyway, what he said was this: 'I've thought about this a lot and I've come to the conclusion that it's irrelevant'. He did not mean that *racism* is morally irrelevant. He meant that against the importance of developing a proper scientific theory of individual differences in intelligence, the personal attributes of Arthur R. Jensen are trivially insignificant. It is typical of Arthur that he deflected attention away from himself toward the subject he cares about. Had someone asked me the same question, I would have fallen over myself in my haste to lunge for the moral high ground, to demonstrate what a good person I am. I find it almost intolerable to be thought racist. Readers will know that Arthur has spent decades being very widely abused and accused of racism. It is striking that he rarely defends himself. He is obdurate that the science is distinguished from the scientist and he cares a great deal more about the former.

Just before we begin the discussion about race I want to comment on the term itself. It hardly needs to be said that we are one species. I have never met a scientist who thinks a race is a discrete group of people. Race is better thought of as pools of concentration of various gene frequencies. Rather than thinking about rigid boxes, it is more accurate to think of pools that flow into one another. The mechanism that creates the pools is sex, and the mechanism that creates the flow is sex. Gene frequencies of one type or another ebb and flow according to the intensity of the inbreeding or outbreeding of any particular population. Most of the literature on race differences in intelligence is devoted to descendents of three major racial groups, African, Caucasian and East Asian. None of these are taken to be immutable 'types'. Nor are any of these three major groups thought by anyone I've ever met to be homogeneous. Africans have more diversity than the other groups, but they all show moderate diversity. It very much depends on which end of the binoculars you are looking through. We all look exquisitely similar down one end; from the opposite end, some differences are apparent.

Race differences and racism are two different things. They are often muddled together to nobody's benefit. The suggestion that studying race differences is intrinsically racist is a logical absurdity and harmful. Race is an emotive subject. That is not at all absurd; such ghastly things have happened because of racism. It is not surprising that we rather shrink from the task of thinking clearly about racial differences. But difficulty is not an excuse, just a challenge. There are already several well-known examples of biological differences, which it is immoral not to explore, such as different reactions to drugs, different propensities to disease and so on. It is vital to explore racial differences when we develop new drugs for exactly the same reasons that we must take sex, age and pregnancy into account. One quick point about studying race is that, racism needs neither facts nor science to support it. Racism is endemic within White, Black and East Asian populations. Racism exists where there is cognitive stratification and where there is none. Racism is not caused by intelligence differences.

Average intelligence differences between racial groups is a nettle with even more stingers than other topics of racial differences. Why? My guess is that we have confusions about how we value intelligence. What are the facts and how should we separate them from our values?

We know that on average, Blacks score around 15 points lower on IQ type tests than Whites. We know that on average, East Asians score around 7 points higher than Whites on IQ type tests. We do not have any direct evidence that the causes of these differences are genetic. However these differences are fairly stable. We know too that if we invoke socio-economic status and racism as the explanation for lower average test performance, then the same factors should lower the average scores of East Asians wherever they have suffered those privations. But East Asians' average scores do not look that way, even in the presence of those factors. I don't know of any evidence that contradicts the genetic hypothesis but I know of much that supports it. It seems that there are a number of questions we could ask ourselves in order to help us sort out the muddle. I'm not intending to try to answer these questions, I just thought it a good idea to set them out.

(1) What is the cause of the Black–White IQ difference?
(2) If the differences were found to be influenced by genes, what would follow?
(3) Could anything good come from a proper scientific understanding of racial differences in IQ?
(4) What bad would come from such knowledge?
(5) Should the scientific enquiry be stopped?
(6) Could anything bad come from a lack of knowledge about race differences?
(7) What would we like the differences to derive from? And why?

(8) If the Black–White difference on IQ scores was found to be in the opposite direction would we find it more acceptable?

The value of setting out various questions is that it can help us to unpick the tangled threads of the scientific issues versus the social issues. The two questions I want to return to are the third and the eighth.

The short answer to question 3 — 'Could anything good come from a proper scientific understanding of racial differences in IQ?' — must be that policies based on ignorance certainly haven't done anybody any good. The longer answer is that scientific understanding is essential if we have any hope of making sound policy.

One good example of this is education. In Britain our educational system is something of a procrustean bed. Many children will not and cannot succeed because they do not have the mental ability to accomplish the only available esteemed goals — A levels or university. Rather than worrying about whether the way to enable more children to have higher education is by lowering the entrance requirements or increasing student loans, we should learn from the science of intelligence research and be much more visionary. It is not a matter of re-defining entrance thresholds, we should be providing children with achievable goals all along the ability range. Providing challenges for children *wherever* along the range they fall, taking account of their needs, instead of pretending that whipping the teachers will create more students able to pass A level physics. The cognitive diversity of the population is seriously under-appreciated. That is true for both ends of the distribution, there is as little point in whipping Oxbridge for elitism as whipping the state school teachers for poor achievement. We must be able to stretch out the range at the top of the distribution as well as accommodate students along the rest of the range. If we take diversity seriously, we will appreciate very quickly that race, after all, is something of a distraction. In terms of policy, it's not race that's salient, it's range.

Range is more important than race in many issues of policy because of the distribution of IQ. If we plot the bell shaped curve for the distribution of intelligence among Whites and add to the same graph the gaussian distribution for Blacks we find the overlap is 80%. Knowing someone's colour tells us precious little about them. By chance alone we would expect to find a greater IQ gap between any two Whites drawn at random from the White population, than we would find by randomly selecting a person from each of those two populations. The bell-shaped curve that represents a Gaussian distribution is the most powerful tool in our armoury in enabling us to predict the range that we need in education and the world of work. As well as advising us about the range, the bell curve is informative about proportions. It tells us how many people diverge from the average, and in what proportion and direction. Surprisingly, 30% of the whole variance exists in only 3% of the population, so the ability range at both ends is rarely adequately met. The failure to understand population IQ distributions is pernicious. Both individuals (often teachers) and institutions become beating sticks when those assessing performance take little account of the range and distribution of the performers.

Now to answer question eight. 'If the Black–White difference on IQ scores was found to be in the opposite direction would we find it more acceptable?' Our answer depends, of course, on who is reading the question. My hunch is that it would be a cause for celebration among many people who aver racism. The kick we would get out of this reversal, merely illuminates the fact that we don't like racism. The argument (replete with delicious cliché) goes something like: 'if X is shown to have innately lower average intelligence than Y, then X will be consigned to the scrapheap'. Would it be better if Y was on the scrapheap? Who ordered the scrapheap? It is not a logical part of the proposition, but it keeps sneaking in like a tomcat at the back door. Surely we shouldn't build our fortress against racism on such flimsy ground as the population average in one particular complex trait? It's so obviously nonsensical. It can only be that case that we are running scared from genetic influences on average intelligence differences between individuals or populations because we can't face up to the fact that we have conflated intelligence with human worth, a truly egregious error.

We are slavish and pusillanimous when it comes to intelligence research. We should welcome any proper scientific insights that increase the effectiveness with which we can make good social policy. Instead, we grovel in scientific self-abasement, fearing that we will lose our claim to moral rectitude if we acknowledge the subtle and minor differences between us. Our proper revulsion of racism should not lead us to make the mistake of policing what we learn about the world and each other. Suppose it is true that the Black–White average difference in performance on IQ type tests owes exclusively to genetic differences. Would that make Whites superior? If it would, then we are definitely forced to admit that every parent of two children with non-identical IQ scores has one inferior child and one superior child. The logic is inescapable. It must follow too, that among our friends, and in every marriage (few spouses have identical IQ scores) there is a mixture of inferior loved ones and superior loved ones. We know this is quite false. We are hiding under the bed for nothing.

If what we want is for humans to respect and care for one another regardless of who they are, we don't need permission from science. If we are concerned about inequalities in goods such as health or wealth, we can create policies to ameliorate those differences. Moreover, without a proper understanding of the causes of those differences, continued failure is certain.

Arthur's suggestion that genes could contribute to Black/White differences in average intelligence is supported by massive amounts of data and by a strong consensus among the silent, scientific majority of psychometricians. But new evidence could alert us to the fact that this view is wrong. One fact I would stake my mortgage on is that, if data showing the error of Arthur's work came to light, he would be the first to publish them; his honesty and integrity run deep and wide.

9. Arthur — A Great Scientist

I am grateful to Arthur for his intellectual generosity for which he is well known among his colleagues. I have certainly experienced a volte-face, I have come to admire Arthur immensely. I am very proud of my friendship with someone who by reputation, I once vilified. Thinking about intelligence has been rewarding, often uncomfortable, always provoking. It has forced me to try to articulate what it is exactly that I care about in people, what matters. Intellectual honesty, the willingness to be open to facts that look at first glance to be frightening, does not come easily. Arthur is a renunciate. He has chosen the stony path of scientific truth over the smoother course of popularity and public acceptance. If Arthur had worked in any other field, I'm certain that honours would have fallen into his lap, for he is a great scientist. The battle between the forces of reason and ideology is frightening, even for a bystander. I have felt at times like a person at sea, clinging for all I'm worth to the mast while the winds are blowing hard. When the calm comes, I see that the winds of science could not blow me on to treacherous rocks that would scupper my values; they have instead blown me further on course towards being able to implement them.

Reference

Herrnstein, R. J., & Murray, C. (1994). *The bell curve: Intelligence and class structure in American life*. New York: The Free Press.

Chapter 23

Jensen as a Teacher and Mentor

Philip Anthony Vernon and Other Former Students

1. Introduction

When Helmuth Nyborg invited me to contribute a chapter titled "Jensen as a teacher and mentor" my first reaction was to wonder why, out of all of Arthur's former students, Helmuth had chosen me. I also decided, quite quickly, that this was a task that it would not be fair for only one person to undertake. Surely, many of Arthur's students would want to share their perspectives and memories of the times they had spent with him. Moreover, each would likely have some unique stories or anecdotes that, in combination, would provide a more complete picture of Arthur in his role as a teacher and mentor. I therefore resolved that I would contact as many of Arthur's former students as I could and would ask them to send me a short account of their favorite memories of him.

This sounded like a good plan but proved to be a lot harder than I had thought it would be.

I first contacted Paul Ammon, one of Arthur's colleagues in the School of Education at the University of California, Berkeley, and a professor from whom I had taken some courses during my doctoral program there. Paul helped me find a current graduate student, Becki Bell, who agreed to work as a short-term research assistant for me. Becki's task sounded easy: find me the names and dissertation titles of all of the graduate students that Arthur had advised during his long career at Berkeley. (Of course, I could have asked Arthur for this information directly, but I did not want him to wonder what I was up to. In addition, my University library was unable to help me find the information electronically).

Becki's first stop was the Dean's Office where she quickly learned that there was no master list of dissertations that had been completed in the School of Education, or at least not one that she could access. Her next stop was the Education library in Tolman Hall. Here she found bound copies of dissertations and, turning to their Certificates of Examination, she identified those on which Arthur had been chief advisor (or Chairman, as they are referred to at Berkeley). The one snag was that the library only kept dissertations for the previous 10 years, a period during which Arthur had only supervised a few students! Back to the drawing board.

It seemed most unlikely, even though the library didn't keep them, that the University would simply discard dissertations after 10 years. Asking around, Becki discovered that, in fact, old dissertations were stored in the Northern Regional Library Facility, a large building in Richmond, just 20 minutes away from the Berkeley campus. She told me by email that she would be visiting this facility in a few days: it sounded as though our search would soon be rewarded.

Three days later, I was eager to open the email that arrived from Becki. Instead of finding the students' names that I was hoping for, however, Becki's email read: "Bad news! I went to the NRLF in Richmond and the dissertations are there but NOT ARRANGED IN ANY ORDER!" In order to make the best use of available space, the dissertations at NRLF are stacked by size, not by subject; thus, any Education dissertation might end up next to an Engineering or a Foreign Language or any other dissertation. It would be a Herculean task to identify those that were even written by Education students, let alone those completed by Arthur's students: a task neither I nor Becki herself was prepared for her to undertake.

In the meantime, I had been in touch with Barbara Nakakihara, the former division secretary in Arthur's department and now a staff personnel analyst still in Berkeley's School of Education. Barbara was able to add a few more names to the list that Becki had compiled and she also suggested that, in fact, Arthur had not had as many graduate students as I had assumed he had. All in all, I ended up with the names of 9 people who had completed their dissertations with Arthur. I was able to track down and contact 7 of these and all of them agreed to share their recollections. What follows are the pieces they sent me, arranged alphabetically, plus my own account, plus a contribution from Bill Rohwer, who did not do his thesis with Arthur but who worked for several years as his research assistant and subsequently became one of his colleagues.

I have not edited any of these pieces, and their titles are those their authors gave them. As I had hoped, although there is some not-unexpected overlap, each one also contributes something unique; in total, they paint a picture of a man who, for a variety of reasons, was and is deeply admired by his students, all of whom are proud to refer to him as their mentor.

2. Jensen as a Teacher and Mentor

2.1. Sri Ananda, WestEd: My Recollections of Arthur Jensen

It was spring of 1978 when I first met Arthur Jensen. I was 21 years old and at the end of my first year as a doctoral student in educational research methodology and measurement. I wasn't really committed to my studies and was unsure whether I wanted to stay in graduate school. I was more interested in other things — community issues, relationships, and fun (not necessarily in that order). Still, I signed up for one of Dr

Jensen's seminars on test bias and was curious about the course. Having read and heard much about the controversy that surrounded Dr Jensen's work, I was unsure of what to expect.

Meeting him at that first class was a pleasant surprise. He was clearly in command of the subject area and current research on test bias. At the same time, he was soft-spoken, unassuming and completely approachable. Moreover, I found the course topic fascinating: this was my first graduate level class that dealt in-depth with a timely and complex testing issue.

It was also the first of several courses that I ultimately took from Arthur Jensen. We soon developed a strong student-teacher relationship — the first one that I developed with a professor. I could talk to him about any research interest, including my eventual dissertation topic: aging and intelligence. Largely through his courses and his interest in my work, I found much-needed grounding for my graduate studies. I decided to try and stick it out with my studies.

During my years as a graduate student, there are several fond memories that I have of Arthur Jensen. Of all these memories, two remain foremost in my mind. The first is of my oral exams. Like most students, I was extremely nervous about taking my "orals". What would the faculty ask me? What if I couldn't answer a question? What if they thought I was incompetent? What if I didn't pass?!

The first hour or so of my orals went well — at least in my mind. I felt OK about the questions posed and confident of the answers I provided. Then, just as I started to relax a little, my faculty advisor, Leonard Marascuilo, posed a very tough, real-life statistical/methodological problem from out of the blue and asked me how I would solve it. I was momentarily stunned and panicked because I didn't have a clue how to approach it. Luckily for me that moment was short-lived because as soon as the question was raised, Dr Jensen's hand shot up in the air. With an unbridled enthusiasm that is unexpected from an internationally known scholar, he pleaded: "Can I try to answer it? Can I try?" Of course, Dr Marascuilo had no choice but to let Dr Jensen take a stab at the solution of a problem intended to challenge *my* skills. What an immense relief for me! I felt saved from total humiliation.

Almost 20 years later, I cannot for the life of me remember that dreaded methodological problem. However, I will never forget the image of Arthur Jensen emphatically raising his hand and calling out for a chance to try and solve this challenging problem. Such is his intellectual curiosity and natural zest for challenging problems.

The second memory is not of a discrete event, but instead involves Dr Jensen's overall role as chair of my dissertation committee. Before I finally started work on my dissertation, I had already moved 400 miles away from Berkeley to Los Angeles and taken about two years off to work and start a family. Worried that I might end up ABD (all but dissertation) forever, I quit work and moved back temporarily to the San Francisco Bay Area with a baby in hand, hoping to focus on my dissertation. Somewhat self-conscious about my absence, I went to see Dr Jensen, told him that I was now ready to start my dissertation, and asked him to chair the dissertation committee. He agreed.

Dr Jensen was immensely helpful throughout this dissertation development process. He helped me refine my research design. His grant foundation helped support my research. He was always available to me for advice and support, giving me thoughtful feedback on dissertation chapters in a timely fashion. No other professor had ever given me this level of attention and support. When it came time to march on graduation day, I was proud to have him there to confer my degree. His support did not end that day. Throughout the years, he continued to send me articles about his research and other work he thought might be of interest to me.

Since receiving my doctorate, I have worked as an assessment specialist on a variety of national, state, and local testing and accountability efforts. For the last ten years, I have worked at WestEd, a regional education laboratory with headquarters in San Francisco. The program that I direct at WestEd consists of a staff of over 20 individuals that are helping a dozen different states to implement student and teacher assessment systems in support of accountability reform. In my work, I am constantly struck by the continued relevance of many of the issues Dr Jensen has studied over the last several decades. Sometimes I agree with his positions, other times I seek different answers. Nevertheless, the clarity and rigor of his work continue to challenge me not to shy away from complex and difficult solutions to ongoing problems of equity and excellence.

In summary, I remain inspired by Dr Jensen's commitment to his work and am indebted to him for his support. He was a wonderful mentor, in charge of his content areas, striving for methodological rigor in all his work, and deeply committed to helping his students succeed. I don't know how I would have completed my graduate studies without his support.

2.2. *Jeffery P. Braden, University of Wisconsin-Madison: Reflections on Arthur Jensen as a Mentor*

I came to the University of California-Berkeley to study school/neuropsychology. It was by sheer accident that Arthur Jensen became my mentor and advisor. At the time, I was working full time as a school psychologist at the California School for the Deaf in Fremont. Because I had difficulty leaving my job before 3 o'clock, and because Arthur taught courses beginning at 4:30, I selected many courses with Art. Thus, it was not by design, but by default, that I first studied with Arthur Jensen.

When I first came in contact with Arthur Jensen, I wanted to help him see the error of his ways. I had heard *about* Jensen as an undergraduate. There was inevitably a story told about how wrong he was, and how badly ideology influenced his research. Of course, I didn't realize until much later that none of my undergraduate professors had ever invited me to read anything written by Art. It was sufficient for them to present and for me to hear their conclusions, and to attack his credibility and scholarship. Therefore, I felt it was my duty as an enlightened undergraduate in the mid-eighties to help Art Jensen see the error of his ways.

It is safe to say that Art influenced my thinking more than I influenced his. Over the course of classes and readings, I came to realize that issues that were so conveniently resolved by undergraduates were in fact more complicated. Thus, it is safe to say that Art changed what I thought — but far more importantly, Art changed *how* I thought.

Among the influences Art had on me and my thinking were the following:

— *How to write*. Art taught me how to write in an appropriate academic style. He did so with high quality, high frequency feedback. I would say he accomplished this without excessive praise. I still have a copy of the first draft of a position paper that I submitted to Art (I show it to my own students every year to let them know how writing can improve with feedback). This first draft has an average of 16.07 marks or comments per page. It also has the following comment (back of page 8): "This paragraph is some of the worst writing I have ever seen. I can't even understand it well enough to attempt a revision . . .". This comment helped me to discriminate feedback from praise! However, the third draft of the paper is the only manuscript I have ever published that was accepted without revision. Thus, it provides a good example of how feedback can affect learning, and a good example of how far I came as a result of Art's guidance.

— *Intellectual persistence*. I remember during a class I took with Art on behavior genetics that I once asked him a question, which he could not answer. I was delighted at being able to "stump the professor". (I can't remember the question, but I do recall the satisfaction at having asked a question to which Art didn't know the answer). However, I got my comeuppance the following week, when Art took the first half hour of the class providing the answer and handing me four or five articles that explained his response. He clearly expected me to read these and to come back with a statement that indicated my understanding of his answer. I ended up spending a good five or six hours the week after that class grinding through weighty, formula-ridden articles on behavior genetics in an effort to divine an intelligent reply. Art was the consummate scholar, in that he never rested until he found the answer to a question.

— *In God We Trust — all others must have data*. Although this motto comes from the school psychology literature, I think Art modeled this principle better than any professor I have seen. That is, when confronted with a challenge, he inevitably would dig for data, either by collecting his own additional data, or by reanalyzing extant data, or otherwise using information to guide his response. Although Art's writing certainly does not lack style or wit, it is his inexorable use of data to grind down arguments that I most admire.

— *Operationalizing hypotheses*. A complementary tactic that Art frequently used in responding to critics and challenges, in addition to the use of data, was to operationalize hypotheses. Time and time again, critics posed alternative accounts or explanations of his data. Frequently, these accounts were possible, if not plausible, and they would be presented as "proof" that Art was wrong. However, Art had the uncanny knack of translating arguments from concept into testable hypotheses, and then usually managed to provide data showing that the criticism was unfounded. This is a talent that I have tried to emulate in my own work, although with less success than Art.

— *Willingness to ask the unaskable*. Art modeled an ability to tolerate the emotional reactions of others when framing research questions. He once described himself as high on psychoticism, and thus explained his lack of concern regarding others' social reactions to his work. I am not sure if I agree with the diagnosis, but the intervention that he modeled was powerful. As a result, I have had a higher degree of comfort addressing controversial and politically incorrect questions — much to the discomfort of some of my friends and colleagues.

— *The power of a few good ideas.* Art modeled pattern recognition in problem solving, and the power of some simple ideas that can recur in work. An example of these ideas is the fallacies he outlined in test bias. I invoke them frequently in a variety of contexts, including the use of special norms with deaf children, assessment accommodations for students with disabilities, and the generalizability of research findings. I cannot claim to have contributed to the literature similarly powerful ideas, but I am a student of their use, and frequently apply them in applied and research contexts.

Although I cannot claim to have internalized these habits of mind as effectively as Art, nor to execute them with his brilliance, I nonetheless value these characteristics of scholarship. I feel that Art profoundly influenced my role as a scholar, in part with the content that I have studied (I continue to have a strong interest in cognitive abilities, particularly their structure and nature/nurture issues), but also through the qualities of inquiry that he modeled. I have attempted to inculcate my students with similar habits of mind, although I cannot claim a high degree of effectiveness in this regard. In summary, I feel that Art influenced both what I think, and more importantly, the way I think about issues in psychology and society. For that, I will always be grateful.

2.3. Angela Gedye, Sunny Hill Health Centre for Children: Recollections of Dr A. R. Jensen by a Former Graduate Student

In the early and mid 1970s, I was a foreign student (Canadian) taking psychology classes from Dr Arthur Jensen. Later, I chose him as my graduate advisor and head of my doctoral committee. The place was the University of California, Berkeley. The period was fairly soon after the publication of his 1969 *Harvard Educational Review* article which generated widespread controversy. For most of those years, I was his *only* graduate student because students feared being ostracized as "racist" if associated with him. Those of us who experienced him as a person, and read his work carefully, knew otherwise. I was honored to be under the tutelage of such a rare kind of intellect.

Apart from his tremendous breadth of expertise, he also had an exceptional depth of knowledge. He expressed ideas orally as clearly as he wrote them in papers. In a letter I sent him soon after my Ph.D. was completed, I wrote: "Ever since my first course with you, I have always appreciated the breadth of the expertise you command and the ease with which you communicate it. I love your digressions". In any class, he could and would often expand on an issue or a piece of research, providing little-known or behind-the-scenes information about the research or the researcher. These "digressions" were as rich as the text material and always fascinating. If a student did not understand something, he was very facile at taking complicated concepts and stating them in easy-to-understand language. He was never arrogant about his tremendous intellect, nor did he make us feel inferior for knowing so little compared to him. I remember thinking what an exceptional teacher he was.

As an academic under attack for his research findings, he showed inordinate composure and understanding. In situations where protestors showed up at his classes, trying to malign, ridicule, or humiliate him, he remained composed, not defensive, and he sincerely tried to answer their questions. When he discussed other academics' critiques of his work, he addressed the issues raised and never made *ad hominem* arguments or disparaging comments. Similarly, when he travelled to other parts of the world to speak and protestors disrupted his speech or prevented him from speaking, he spoke with understanding about those hostile to him. He showed astonishing patience with his critics and extraordinary coping skills in response to relentless professional and personal criticism. I continue to admire his unflinching composure in the face of opposition.

During office hours with him as my advisor, I was always impressed by his ability to quote figures from tables in articles published even decades earlier. Each time I left feeling a boost of energy and excitement about research ideas. He encouraged independent thinking and independent research, not variations on the theme of his own research pursuits. (This was in contrast to research experience I had with other professors there.) I came to see a difference between research that addresses meaningful questions and research that produces minor iterations on a theme and adds another entry to one's list of publications. (I made a vow to myself in graduate school never to publish any work unless I thought it was a meaningful contribution. This was a factor in my decision after graduation not to seek an academic position, where "publish or perish" pressures prevailed. Indeed, my first publication came 8 years after my PhD was completed.) I am also grateful to both Dr Jensen and Dr Marjorie Honzik who emphasized the need to be very sure about what you publish because your name will always be associated with a paper if it turns out later to be inaccurate or invalid. They both described the extra lengths they would go to in order to check the accuracy of their findings.

In subsequent years, I have sought Dr Jensen's advice and perspective usually on dealing with professional attacks and resistance when one introduces new ideas. Throughout all these years, he remains a formative influence on my values as a researcher and a model of courage in pursuing truth regardless of the opposition encountered.

2.4. John H. Kranzler, University of Florida: Arthur R. Jensen — Scholar, Teacher and Mentor Nonpareil

Let me begin by saying that it is with great pleasure that I share some of my personal reflections on Professor Arthur R. Jensen, a truly extraordinary scholar, teacher and mentor. I first met Professor Jensen in 1985, shortly after beginning a doctoral program in the Department of Educational Psychology at the University of California, Berkeley. As a student of school psychology, I was very interested in issues relating to the use and interpretation of intelligence tests in the schools, particularly those pertaining to test bias. Moreover, while an undergraduate student at the University of Oregon, I had taken courses on information-processing theory from Michael Posner and Ray Hyman. I was fascinated by Professor Jensen's research that extended their work in experimental psychology to investigate the relationship between the speed and efficiency of elemental cognitive processing and general cognitive ability. Fortunately for me, the School Psychology Program at Berkeley allowed its students to study with any professor in the department. Professor Jensen seemed like the most logical choice for me as a faculty advisor and I was anxious to meet him.

By all rights, Professor Jensen shouldn't have played an important role in my life. After all, he was a world-famous researcher in education and psychology and I was a lowly first-year graduate student seeking a degree in school psychology. He was also rarely on campus that year, spending most of his time working at home, free from the distractions of pesky students like me. One day, however, I happened to catch Professor Jensen in his office. Gathering up my nerve, I knocked on his door, introduced myself, and boldly stated that I wanted to work with him. He replied that he didn't have a position available at the moment, but that if I was interested in his research, I should read some of his most recent work and come back and talk with him about it. He then handed me an imposing stack of pre-prints and articles that he had published within the last year.

The following week I returned for our discussion, albeit with an admittedly poor grasp of the literature I had just read and re-read. How does psychometric g relate to neo-Piagetian theories of Robbie Case, Pasqual-Leone, and others that I was reading so much about in my developmental classes? He replied, without hesitation, "g is M-space". I was dumbstruck. In one sentence, he had shown me that intelligence and cognitive development were not really as distinct as I had viewed them, and that there is some bigger picture out there into which all of what I was learning must somehow fit. Professor Jensen then proceeded to discuss in detail the history and current state of knowledge on intelligence for over an hour. An hour! By the end of our discussion he had outlined a study that he wanted to see conducted that would directly address questions raised by critics surrounding the effects of practice, administration order, and retinal displacement in his research with the Hick paradigm. I was more than willing to be involved. Under Professor Jensen's guidance, I conducted this study with Patti Whang, a fellow graduate student at the time and now a Professor at Auburn University (see Patti's reflections below). The results of this study — my first refereed journal publication — were published in *Intelligence* in 1987.

I had the good fortune to work for Professor Jensen as a research assistant on a number of different projects at the Institute for the Study of Educational Differences from 1986 to 1990. During that time, he was the perfect mentor. This is not a word I use lightly. I have long believed that many doctoral programs in my field do not do an adequate job of socializing students for jobs in academia. Although many do an adequate job of teaching the requisite declarative knowledge (i.e. ideas, concepts and theory), most do not do a good job teaching the procedural knowledge (i.e. how professors work) that is needed by an aspiring academic to succeed. For example, there is seldom instruction in writing grants or in subtle nuances of revising manuscripts for publication. Professor Jensen, however, was instrumental in my socialization for life as an assistant professor. Immediately after agreeing to take me on as an advisee, he established an apprentice-like relationship. For the next four years, he provided only as much guidance as needed at the right times for his advisees, much like the conductor of an orchestra, throughout all phases of the research process, from developing hypotheses to submitting articles for publication. Most importantly, he taught me how to ask good research questions (i.e. empirically refutable), to think critically and independently, and to keep an open mind. He modeled the behavior of the quintessential scientist every single day. Throughout that period, as busy as he was with his research, he was always available and accessible. Drafts of my dissertation were always returned — dripping in red ink, edited closely for content and style — the next day! Professor Jensen also took the time to sit down with me to go over his comments on numerous drafts and answered question after question from me on his feedback. To this day, I am amazed at how much time and energy he put into mentoring his students. I cannot imagine a better mentor.

While at Berkeley, I also had the privilege of experiencing Professor Jensen's considerable talents in the classroom. I am not exaggerating when I say that his seminar on behavior genetics was one of the finest examples of college teaching that I have ever experienced. His presentation of ideas, often very complex ideas, was always amazingly clear. Although the area of behavior genetics was new and often difficult for me, he engaged the class in an almost effortless fashion in such a way that the material was understandable to all. He was particularly adept at bringing even the driest material to life with stories of actual events and the people behind the research. Professor Jensen also demanded the best from his students. His exams were extremely thorough and challenging and famously difficult. At the end, however, I came away from that class not only informed and inspired, but entertained as well. Once, years later while talking to a colleague here at the University of Florida, I commented that I thought that the best researchers made the best teachers. She laughed. After thinking about it, I had to admit that I had indeed over-generalized. I should have been more specific. The best researcher I have ever known was also the best teacher — Professor Jensen.

Professor Jensen was key in my developing the abilities and confidence to become a professor. I look back on my days at the University of California, Berkeley with extreme fondness. This is due in large part to Professor Jensen: scholar, teacher, and mentor *nonpareil*.

2.5. Terry Michelsen, Antioch Unified School District: Arthur R. Jensen

When I entered the doctoral program at UC Berkeley, I was already 47 years old and had retired from an Air Force career only four years earlier. Initially, Professor Jensen was not my mentor, but as it became increasingly apparent that my interests lay in cognitive development, I asked him if he would consider chairing my committee, and he graciously consented. Since my Air Force retirement plus the GI Bill did not quite cover family expenses in the Bay Area, I began advertising my services as an editor and typist of theses and dissertations. Professor Jensen became one of my first clients, and he continued to bring me articles and book chapters to prepare for publication until shortly before I finally received my Ph.D. in December 1990. I cannot imagine a more prolific writer or one who is able to organize the material and make his points with greater clarity than Arthur Jensen. It became almost a weekly ritual. He would park his Mercedes on Euclid Avenue, in front of our house, and mount the stairs to the front door with heavy footsteps that could belong to no one else but the Professor. My wife did not even have to look out the window to know who was at the door. He always had a thick sheaf of yellow, lined paper filled with his characteristic scrawl and replete with arrows and numbers signaling me to go back two pages and type old paragraph 4 between new paragraphs 3 and 5. Actually, he had been doing this so long that his instructions were easy to follow. His handwriting, however, was something else. It at first reminded me more of Arabic than English cursive as I labored to decipher this word or that phrase. I soon, however, became adept at transforming those yellow sheets into typed manuscript, and eventually wondered why I had ever had a problem. During the late 1980s, Professor Jensen bought a computer and a word processing program and began typing some of his own material. His first attempts were tentative, since he continued to bring those yellow sheets to my door. With time, however, the rumbling on my front steps became more and more infrequent. Fortunately, I had been awarded the doctorate by that time and had taken a full-time job as a school psychologist, so I gave up editing and typing for a living with few regrets.

Despite his affable manner, I have always felt that, deep down, Arthur Jensen is a shy man who is slightly uncomfortable with people he doesn't know well. Uncomfortable, I say, until the subject of music comes up. He told me that in his youth he had aspired to become a musician but had come to the conclusion that he would never be good enough to reach the top of that profession, so he chose to study psychology at Columbia University. Nevertheless, he and Barbara always had season tickets to the San Francisco Opera, and if there was an opera by Wagner — or better yet, the Ring Cycle — anywhere within a reasonable distance (which included Bayreuth), he was there. He must have a vast music library, because he converses with authority about composers, conductors, and soloists, frequently interjecting into his musical critiques amusing anecdotes from their lives.

One day, instead of handing me the usual yellow sheets, Professor Jensen gave me a copy of a test he had devised to determine which upper-division undergraduates would be required to enrol in Psychology 201 (a survey course on the history of psychology) and which would escape this somewhat obnoxious requirement. He asked me to look it over and let him know what I thought of it. That evening, I began reading through it. While most of the material was familiar to me, correct responses required an intimate knowledge of the contributions of well known and lesser known researchers — knowledge that is normally acquired only after years in the field. The next day, Jensen came by and asked me what I thought of the test. I said, "It appears to me that all upper division students are going to be enrolling in Psych 201". He looked surprised and distressed and replied, "I don't understand. I showed the test to Leo Postman and HE didn't have any trouble with it!"

2.6. Steven M. Paul, University of California-San Francisco: Reflections on Dr Arthur Jensen

Honesty, integrity, and accuracy, these are the words that first come to mind when I reflect on my impressions of Dr Arthur Jensen. Dr Jensen was my faculty advisor at UC Berkeley, where I received my Ph.D. in educational psychology. I was lucky enough to serve as his research assistant for many years. I learned more from our private conversations and work together than from the many formal courses I have taken over the years.

From an academic perspective, Dr Jensen showed me, by his own actions, the value of accuracy and thoroughness in research. I learned to check and double-check my calculations or statistical analyses I may have done, well before I would consider presenting them to him. There was no question that the high standards that he would require of himself should be also met by those who worked with him. Having Dr Jensen as an advisor was an incredible advantage. Any paper that I wrote that passed his scrutiny would not require any further revisions. The first academic article that I submitted for publication was accepted without the need for any changes or additions. This is because that article had already been criticized and revamped to meet the expectations of the toughest reviewer around.

Although his academic standards and accomplishments are perhaps the first things that come to mind, I also remember how impressed I was with his humanity and nonacademic pursuits. Arthur Jensen is a true man of the world. His interests, skills and passions are astounding. For one, he is the consummate storyteller. He would often fascinate me for hours with his tales of international travel and adventure. Not only were his stories full of revelations about other cultures and customs new to me, his delight in relating his experiences was inspirational. I had not traveled anywhere outside of the United States when I first met Dr Jensen. Thanks in large part to his enthusiasm, I have since traveled all over the world myself. When I was working with him, Dr Jensen's favorite international destination was India. He immersed himself in all things Indian, especially the food. He is an excellent cook of Indian delicacies with an impressive knowledge of spices. I remember his pride in being able to withstand and actually enjoy the hottest of spicy dishes that he would prepare himself with ingredients he had brought home from his travels. His stories were always about the different people he met and revealed a true concern and compassion for people from all walks of life.

Another of Dr Jensen's passions is classical music. He would regale me with stories of the concerts that he had attended and in particular the conductors that he appreciated the most. I believe that in his youth he would manage to somehow gain admittance to symphony rehearsals in order to see his favorite conductors at work. He is very knowledgeable about music and didn't appreciate when liberties were taken with classical scores. He would tell me that many people in the world play the first four notes of Beethoven's Fifth Symphony inaccurately. They are all of the same duration. The last of the four is not to be held longer than the first three. That kind of desire for precision perhaps provides an insight into the workings of a brilliant mind.

My educational experiences with Arthur Jensen, academic and otherwise, have helped to shape the person that I am today. I strive to achieve the same high standards and integrity that he showed me as a kind and generous mentor.

2.7. Bill Rohwer, University of California-Berkeley: My Indebtedness to Arthur R. Jensen

My career owes much of its early direction and development to Art Jensen. Even so, when our association began, it would have taken extraordinary perspicacity to foresee how powerful his influence would be.

At the time, I was a graduate student at Berkeley, but not in Art's department. Art was on the faculty of the School of Education and I was in the middle of my doctoral work in the Department of Psychology. The birth of my first child had created an urgent need for more income. The half-time research assistantship I held in Psychology provided too little money, and no one in my department could offer me additional work. Instead, one of my professors told me that he had heard that Art had a grant and might need some help, so I went to see him.

During the interview, Art explained that he was conducting research at the intersection of verbal learning and individual differences. At that point, I knew next to nothing about either of these domains, and yet Art hired me. To this day, I don't know why, unless he was as desperate for help as I was for money. What I do know is that he enabled me to support my family and avoid dropping out of school, and that his mentorship over the next few years would prove pivotal for my career.

His mentoring came in the form of what he said and what he did. Both forms seemed to flow effortlessly from his own nature.

I had easy access to what he said because I often worked in his faculty office at a table no more than ten feet from his desk. He loved to talk and, when he was at that desk, talk he often did. He talked with admiration of the productivity of Thorndike and Eysenck, and with infectious enthusiasm of the genius of Beethoven and Toscanini. He also talked of his own renunciation of a budding career as a concert musician and I'll never forget his explanation of this decision. He came to the realization, he said, that as a musician he would never be of the first rank, so he turned to a career, in psychology, that did not require real native talent to achieve eminence. I found his explanation quite daunting as I was struggling mightily even to qualify for entry to this (undemanding) career.

Daunting, too, was what Art did. His abilities were amazing: he could put his finger unerringly on significant issues and frame them in entirely new ways; he could design research that decisively analyzed these issues; and he could write about his ideas and research with clarity, fluency and a degree of ease that made me (and still does) unspeakably envious.

What Art did also included an extraordinary generosity that, in my case alone, took countless forms. As I've already mentioned, soon after I met him he gave me work that I needed in the worst way. In that work, he provided both the guidance and the latitude necessary for me to find a line of productive research. He invited me along whenever he consulted other experts about his own research. He took me to my first convention and introduced me to his peers. From the beginning he freely included me as co-author of his publications and eventually promoted me to first author. Then, as I was finishing my dissertation and seeking a faculty position, he was instrumental in arranging the only offer I received, from the Berkeley School of Education. And, if that wasn't enough, shortly after I joined the faculty, he made a key contact and referral that enabled me to obtain my first research grant.

For all of this, I'm deeply grateful.

2.8. Tony Vernon, University of Western Ontario: Arthur Jensen — Teacher, Mentor, and Friend

I started my Ph.D. program at Berkeley in 1977, where I had applied to work with Arthur Jensen in the School of Education. Through my father, I had already met Arthur several times and, when he heard that I would be driving to California from my home in Canada, Arthur told me that he would be at his house on Clear Lake and invited me to stay there for a few days before completing the trip to Berkeley.

I arrived at Clear Lake on August 7 — I remember the date because it was my birthday. Somehow, Arthur knew this and had arranged for us to celebrate the occasion with dinner at a nearby restaurant. Thus began a relationship that would continue over the next several years and, indeed, continues to this day.

The following morning, Arthur was back to business: although he was "on vacation", he had work to do. The first thing he did was to offer me a position as his research assistant and to assign me the task of writing a review article on his Level I/Level II theory of mental abilities. He had introduced this theory some 10 years earlier and had collected reprints of every article, by himself and by anyone else, that pertained to it. He presented me with these reprints, stacked in a huge box, and said "happy reading!"

With a brief interlude during which I went down to Berkeley to find an apartment for the year, I ended up spending the rest of that August at Clear Lake, working my way through all the Level I/Level II articles and making notes for my review. During this time, my and Arthur's workdays would start early — he was usually in his office above the guesthouse by 8 in the morning — and would continue with a short break for lunch until 3 or 4 in the afternoon. At that time, Arthur would take a long swim in the lake — a mile or more — and would sometimes take his Sunfish out for a sail. Then came the serious (but enjoyable) business of preparing dinner: typically something Indian or

Mexican. Arthur loved India and its culture — not many people know that he wrote a biography of Gandhi when he was still a teenager! — and he was a superb cook. I grew to love the fiery hot dishes that he prepared.

Observing Arthur's work habits was inspirational. He would head up to his study where, at that time, he didn't even have a typewriter, let alone a computer. Instead, he did all his writing long-hand, with a fountain pen, on legal size pads of yellow paper, and later had it typed by a secretary or another research assistant. He could write for hours and seldom made many revisions. Those who have read his articles know that his writing is exceptionally clear but it's also the case that he appeared to write almost effortlessly. I know that I have attempted to emulate his style but I also know that it doesn't come as easily for me as it seemed to for him!

After putting in 7 or 8 hours at his desk, Arthur didn't slow down. Unless a concert or an interesting news story was being broadcast, Arthur's evenings seldom included television. Instead, he was more likely to read or, when he had company, to talk. Arthur is a great conversationalist who loves to talk and it was always fascinating to listen to him. He would talk about his work, about articles he had read recently, or about any of his other passions: especially music. Arthur was himself an accomplished musician: indeed as a young man he had played clarinet in a symphony orchestra and only gave up this career because he felt that he was not sufficiently talented. But he still loved music and had lots of tales about his favorite musicians and conductors: especially Wagner and Toscanini. He also loved animals — you could set your watch by the Clear Lake ducks that flew onto his lawn at 4pm for their daily afternoon feeding — and he told me that as a boy he used to collect snakes that he would give to the San Diego zoo.

As his student, I took several of Arthur's courses: on intelligence and mental abilities, on test bias, and on behavior genetics. Arthur was a gifted teacher who never relied on lecture notes. Moreover, in addition to presenting the material that he wanted to cover, his lectures would invariably include interesting asides or embellishments about the topics or the people he was lecturing on. Going to his office to ask him a question would frequently result in a lecture in itself — but I mean this in a good sense: Arthur is exceptionally knowledgeable and he loves to share his knowledge. I learned at least as much from these off-the-cuff "office lectures" as I did in his formal classes. His own thirst for knowledge was also infectious. Even after he was a professor at Berkeley, Arthur continued to sit in on courses over in the Psychology Department (in one of which, he met his wife-to-be, Barbara), and he was so enthusiastic about whatever he had heard or read that it was difficult not to want to learn from him.

As a research advisor, Arthur was the perfect model. His own research is methodologically rigorous and he is incredibly productive. He allowed me (and the other students working with him at that time) considerable freedom in choosing research topics, but he was also always available for consultation and advice when needed. Through his own example, I know that he brought out the best in me, and I have continued to value his comments and suggestions on work-in-progress ever since. I also valued Arthur's willingness to tackle topics that, due to their controversial nature, often led to his being criticized, and sometimes demonstrated against and even physically attacked. He was a staunch believer that knowledge is always preferable to ignorance —

no matter what the topic — and he never allowed the opinions of others to stop him from doing what he believed in: this was a lesson well worth learning.

I consider myself very fortunate to have had the opportunity to work with Arthur: first as his student and, after graduating, continuing to work on a number of projects and papers with him. I will always admire him as an advisor, a teacher, and a mentor and I am proud to be able also to call him a friend.

2.9. Patricia A. Whang, Auburn University: A broad education — Reflections on a Storied Past

With the passage of time, it is sometimes the little things that loom largest in one's mind. Thus, when I reflect on what having Arthur Jensen as a boss, a role model and a dissertation chair has meant to me, it is to those things which at the time seemed inconsequential, that I must pay homage to.

I vividly remember my first meeting with Dr Jensen as a graduate student. I remember walking into his fourth floor office in Tolman Hall with great trepidation and little direction, and walking out with a handful of articles on *g*. Those articles were my intellectual sustenance as a graduate student. Oh, how I worked hard to grapple with the ideas, re-reading, underlining, and marveling at the clarity with which the complex ideas were written. I also remember that fateful day not long after that first meeting when, quite unexpectedly, I received the phone call that elevated me from just another graduate student to Arthur Jensen's research assistant. What an honor, what excitement, what a challenge! Little could I have imagined how that office, which had seemed so intimidating and so foreign, would come to resonate in my memory as the space where I was afforded an education, in the broadest sense of the word. For this, I will always be eternally grateful.

This office was neither fancy nor ostentatious. In fact, it stands out in my memory as rather gray and functional, largely because of the gray color of the institutional desks, chairs and bookcases. Despite what one might imagine, the bookcases were not crammed with books. In fact, the shelves were virtually empty. This is because writing was done at the lake house, where, in addition to peace and solitude, Dr Jensen could also take advantage of the lake by having a swim in the afternoon.

Because Dr Jensen was not dependent on his office space in the ways most professors were, he shared it with his research assistants. Thus, when I think about my desk across from Dr Jensen's, what I remember most fondly are the stories. In my mind's eye, memories of these discussions are not fully rendered unless they capture the rather mischievous glimmer of Dr Jensen's blue eyes as he would lean back in his office chair, with glasses clasped in one hand. Hearing, for example, about his adventures in India and the beauty of the land and people had me longing to pay a visit. I also learned a considerable amount about such things as dahl, how bread is cooked on the walls of a tandoori oven, and how the recipes of Madhur Jaffrey are close to authentic. This topic of conversation should be of no surprise to those who know of Dr Jensen's passion for cooking Indian cuisine. As Mrs Jensen explained to me, their kitchen at the lake house has two stoves, two sinks, and two refrigerators, so as to accommodate this passion.

Another frequent topic of conversation was music. If my memory serves me well, I remember hearing stories of Dr Jensen playing the clarinet while growing up and I have vague memories of Dr Jensen talking about having strongly considered pursuing music as a major. Though he obviously pursued other interests, his passion for music never abated. For example, I can make out the skeletal remains of a story about his sneaking into a rehearsal of, I believe, Horowitz, while a graduate student in New York City. I remember more distinctly the happiness with which he recalled having been allowed to stay during the rehearsal. Furthermore, Dr Jensen not only held season tickets for the San Francisco opera, but he also endeavored to patronize the opera productions in the cities he was visiting. Thinking about Dr Jensen's love of music reminds me of his habit of humming softly as he walked, rather briskly, down the corridors of Tolman Hall. Obviously, there is much more to Dr Jensen than what can be deduced from his scholarly contributions.

I loved those stories and of course Dr Jensen had many that reflected a rather tumultuous period of our discipline's history. There were so many stories about the fallout from his *Harvard Educational Review* article. There were stories of police escorts to classes, classes disrupted by demonstrators and the subsequent need to hold them in ever-changing locations, and invited addresses to such overflowing audiences that they had to be piped into additional rooms. I also remember how Mrs Jensen had to hurriedly load up boxes of data and drive away with them in order to preserve them. When I watch *60 Minutes*, I have to chuckle when I think about Dr Jensen's description of being interviewed by Mike Wallace and the way that Wallace would lunge at this interviewee to get a startled look. The funny part is that only the looks and not the lunges became a part of the televised segment. Even with the passage of years, instructions for how to approach suspicious mail remained posted on one of the bookcases.

It is hard to capture the breadth and depth of what I learned from those stories, but they still stick with me and at some level must inform who I am because many have become my stories too. I love sharing a story about Hans Eysenck. I shared Dr Jensen's amazement at Eysenck's ability to write books and articles by tape recording them as he walked around his office. Later, a secretary would transcribe the tapes into a manuscript. When Dr Jensen asked Eysenck how he could write whole articles and books without notes, Eysenck was quick to assure him that he was working from notes. With that assurance, he reached into his desk drawer and pulled out a sheet of paper with the briefest of outlines as proof. I can still hear Dr Jensen's chuckle of astonishment at this as he emphasized "just one sheet of paper for the whole book!". I also remember a rather cautionary tale about a psychologist who was such a perfectionist about his writing that he only wrote one article and eventually committed suicide: definite lesson to be learned from that tale! Perhaps there are also lessons to be learned from the stories Dr Jensen told about the Nobel Prize winning physicist William Shockley. One in particular stands out in my mind. Dr Jensen was invited to the Shockley's for dinner but he ended up eating alone with Mrs Shockley. Apparently, Dr Shockley was in the middle of working on a problem and did not want to be distracted from this work by any dinner guest.

I find myself grasping for words with which to express how having Arthur Jensen as a boss, role model and dissertation chair has contributed to my life. The contributions are so deep and pervasive that I am finding them difficult to tease out and present in a nice, neat package. I share a small part of my education, stories told in casual conversation, in hopes that if you, the reader, understand how this one aspect of my education has touched my life, you can begin to have some inkling of what it has meant to me to learn from Dr Jensen. I will always be eternally grateful.

Bibliography of Arthur R. Jensen

1955

1. Symonds, P. M., & Jensen, A. R. (1955). A review of six textbooks in educational psychology. *Journal of Educational Psychology, 46*, 56–64.

1956

2. Jensen, A. R. (1956). *Aggression in fantasy and overt behavior.* Unpublished doctoral dissertation, Columbia University, New York.

1957

3. Jensen, A. R. (1957). Aggression in fantasy and overt behavior. *Psychological Monographs, 71*, (445), Whole No. 16.
4. Jensen, A. R. (1957). Authoritarian attitudes and personality maladjustment. *Journal of Abnormal and Social Psychology, 54*, 303–311.
5. Pope, B., & Jensen, A. R. (1957). The Rorschach as an index of pathological thinking. *Journal of Projective Techniques, 21*, 59–62.

1958

6. Jensen, A. R. (1958). Personality. *Annual Review of Psychology, 9*, 295–322.
7. Jensen, A. R. (1958). The Maudsley Personality Inventory. *Acta Psychologica, 14*, 312–325. (Reprinted in: Savage, R. D. (Ed.) (1958), *Readings in Clinical Psychology.* Pergamon Press).
8. Symonds, P. M., & Jensen, A. R. (1958). The predictive significance of fantasy. *American Journal of Orthopsychiatry, 28*, 73–84.

1959

9. Jensen, A. R. (1959). The reliability of projective techniques: Review of the literature. *Acta Psychologica, 16*, 3–31.

10. Jensen, A. R. (1959). *The reliability of projective techniques: Methodology* (pp. 32–67). Amsterdam: North-Holland Publishing Co.
11. Jensen, A. R. (1959). A statistical note on racial differences in the Progressive Matrices. *Journal of Consulting Psychology, 23,* 272.
12. Jensen, A. R. (1959). Review of the Thematic Apperception Test. In: O. K. Buros (Ed.), *Fifth mental measurements yearbook* (pp. 310–313). Highland Park, NJ: Gryphon Press.
13. Jensen, A. R. (1959). Review of the Family Relations Test. In: O. K. Buros (Ed.), *Fifth mental measurements yearbook* (pp. 227–228). Highland Park, NJ: Gryphon Press.
14. Jensen, A. R. (1959). [Review of *Perceptual processes and mental illness,* by H. J. Eysenck, G. W. Granger, & J. D. Brengelmann.]. *Journal of Nervous and Mental Diseases, 128,* 469–471.

1960

15. Jensen, A. R. (1960). Holistic personality. [Review of *Understanding personalities,* by R. Leeper, & R. Leeper, & P. Madison.] *Contemporary Psychology, 5,* 353–355.
16. Jensen, A. R. (1960). Some criticisms of automated teaching. *California Journal of Instructional Improvement, 3,* 32–35.
17. Jensen, A. R. (1960). Teaching machines and individual differences. *Automated Teaching Bulletin, 1,* 12–16. (Reprinted in: Smith, W. I., & Moore, J. W. (Eds), *Programmed learning* (pp. 218–226). New York: Van Nostrand, 1962).

1961

18. Jensen, A. R. (1961). On the reformulation of inhibition in Hull's system. *Psychological Bulletin, 58,* 274–298.
19. Jensen, A. R. (1961). Learning abilities in Mexican-American and Anglo-American children. *California Journal of Educational Research, 12,* 147–159.
20. Symonds, P. M., & Jensen, A. R. (1961). *From adolescent to adult* (pp. viii + 413). New York: Columbia University Press.

1962

21. Jensen, A. R. (1962). The von Restorff isolation effect with minimal response learning. *Journal of Experimental Psychology, 64,* 123–125.
22. Jensen, A. R. (1962). An empirical theory of the serial-position effect. *Journal of Psychology, 53,* 127–142.
23. Jensen, A. R. (1962). Temporal and spatial effects of serial position. *American Journal of Psychology, 75,* 390–400. (Reprinted in: Slamecka, N. J. (Ed.) (1967), *Human learning and memory: Selected readings* (pp. 117–124). New York: Oxford University Press).
24. Jensen, A. R. (1962). Is the serial position curve invariant? *British Journal of Psychology, 53,* 159–166.

25. Jensen, A. R. (1962). Transfer between paired-associate and serial learning. *Journal of Verbal Learning and Verbal Behavior, 1*, 269–280.

26. Jensen, A. R. (1962). Spelling errors and the serial position effect. *Journal of Educational Psychology, 53*, 105–109. (Reprinted in: Otto, W., & Koenke, K. (Eds) (1969), *Readings on corrective and remedial teaching* (pp. 346–352). Boston: Houghton-Mifflin; Johnson, P. E. (Ed.) (1972), *Learning: Theory and practice* (pp. 173–179). New York: Crowell).

27. Jensen, A. R. (1962). Extraversion, neuroticism and serial learning. *Acta Psychologica, 20*, 69–77.

28. Jensen, A. R. (1962). The improvement of educational research. *Teachers College Record, 64*, 20–27. (Reprinted in: 1963, *Education Digest, 28*, 18–22; Courtney, E. W. (Ed.) (1965), *Applied research in education* (pp. 304–316). Totowa, NJ: Littlefield, Adams & Co.).

29. Jensen, A. R. (1962). [Review of *Programmed learning: Evolving principles and industrial applications. Foundation for Research on Human Behavior*, edited by J. P. Lysaught] *Contemporary Psychology, 7*, 33.

30. Jensen, A. R. (1962). Reinforcement psychology and individual differences. *California Journal of Educational Research, 13*, 174–178.

31. Jensen, A. R., & Blank, S. S. (1962). *Association with ordinal position in serial rote-learning. Canadian Journal of Psychology, 16*, 60–63.

32. Jensen, A. R., Collins, C. C., & Vreeland, R. W. (1962). A multiple S-R apparatus for human learning. *American Journal of Psychology, 75*, 470–476.

1963

33. Jensen, A. R. (1963). Serial rote-learning: Incremental or all-or-none? *Quarterly Journal of Experimental Psychology, 15*, 27–35.

34. Jensen, A. R. (1963). Learning abilities in retarded, average, and gifted children. *Merrill-Palmer Quarterly, 9*, 123–140. (Reprinted in: DeCecco, J. P. (Ed.) (1964), *Educational technology: Reading in programmed instruction* (pp. 356–375). New York: Holt, Rinehart, and Winston, Inc.).

35. Jensen, A. R. (1963). Learning in the preschool years. *Journal of Nursery Education, 18*, 133–139. (Reprinted in: Hartup, W. W., & Smothergill, Nancy L. (Eds) (1967), *The young child: Reviews of research* (pp. 125–135). Washington, D.C.: National Association for the Education of Young Children).

36. Jensen, A. R., & Roden, A. (1963). Memory span and the skewness of the serial-position curve. *British Journal of Psychology, 54*, 337–349.

37. Jensen, A. R., & Rohwer, W. D. Jr. (1963). Verbal mediation in paired-associate and serial learning. *Journal of Verbal Learning and Verbal Behavior, 1*, 346–352.

38. Jensen, A. R., & Rohwer, W. D. Jr. (1963). The effect of verbal mediation on the learning and retention of paired-associates by retarded adults. *American Journal of Mental Deficiency, 68*, 80–84.

1964

39. Jensen, A. R. (1964). The Rorschach technique: Are-evaluation. *Acta Psychologica, 22*, 60–77.

40. Jensen, A. R. (1964). *Learning, briefly.* [Review of *Learning: A survey of psychological interpretations*, by W. F. Hill.] *Contemporary Psychology, 9*, 228–229.

1965

41. Jensen, A. R. (1965). An adjacency effect in free recall. *Quarterly Journal of Experimental Psychology, 17*, 315–322.
42. Jensen, A. R. (1965). Rote learning in retarded adults and normal children. *American Journal of Mental Deficiency, 69*, 828–834.
43. Jensen, A. R. (1965). *Individual differences in learning: Interference factor* (pp. 1–160). Cooperative Research Project No. 1867, U.S. Office of Education.
44. Jensen, A. R. (1965). Scoring the Stroop Test. *Acta Psychologica, 24*, 398–408.
45. Jensen, A. R. (1965). Review of the Maudsley Personality Inventory. In: O. K. Buros (Ed.), *Sixth mental measurements yearbook* (pp. 288–291). Highland Park, NJ: Gryphon Press.
46. Jensen, A. R. (1965). Review of the Rorschach Test. In: O. K. Buros (Ed.), *Sixth mental measurements yearbook* (pp. 501–509). Highland Park, NJ: Gryphon Press. (Reprinted in: Bracht, G. H., Hopkins, K., & Stanley, J. C. (Eds) (1972). *Perspectives in education and psychological measurement* (pp. 292–311). New York: Prentice-Hall).
47. Jensen, A. R. (1965). Review of the make a picture story test. In: O. K. Buros (Ed.), *Sixth mental measurements yearbook* (pp. 468–470). Highland Park, NJ: Gryphon Press.
48. Jensen, A. R., & Rohwer, W. D. Jr. (1965). Syntactical mediation of serial and paired-associate learning as a function of age. *Child Development, 36*, 601–608.
49. Jensen, A. R., & Rohwer, W. D. Jr. (1965). What is learned in serial learning? *Journal of Verbal Learning and Verbal Behavior, 4*, 62–72. (Reprinted in: Slamecka, N. J. (Ed.) (1967), *Human learning and memory* (pp. 98–110). New York: Oxford University Press).
50. Battig, W. F., Allen, M., & Jensen, A. R. (1965). Priority of free recall of newly learned items. *Journal of Verbal Learning and Verbal Behavior, 4*, 175–179.

1966

51. Jensen, A. R. (1966). The measurement of reactive inhibition in humans. *Journal of General Psychology, 75*, 85–93.
52. Jensen, A. R. (1966). Social class and perceptual learning. *Mental Hygiene, 50*, 226–239. (Reprinted in: Rogers, Dorothy (Ed.) (1969), *Readings in child psychology*. New York: Brooks-Cole Publishing Co.).
53. Jensen, A. R. (1966). Individual differences in concept learning. In: H. Klausmeier, & C. Harris (Eds), *Analyses of concept learning* (pp. 139–154). New York: Merrill, 1966. (Reprinted in: Butcher, H. J., & Lomax, L., (1971). *Readings in human intelligence* (pp. 100–114). London: Methuen).
54. Jensen, A. R. (1966). Cumulative deficit in compensatory education. *Journal of School Psychology, 4*, 37–47.
55. Jensen, A. R. (1966). Verbal mediation and educational potential. *Psychology in the Schools, 3*, 99–109. (Reprinted in: Torrance, E. P., & White, W. F. (Eds) (1975), *Issues and advances in educational psychology* (2nd ed., pp. 175–188). Ithaca, IL: F. E. Peacock).
56. Jensen, A. R. (1966). Conceptions and misconceptions about verbal mediation. In: M. P. Douglas (Ed.), *Claremont Reading Conference* (pp. 134–141). Thirtieth Yearbook, Claremont Graduate School.

57. Jensen, A. R. (1966). Intensive, detailed, exhaustive. [Review of *Paired-associates learning: The role of meaningfulness, similarity and familiarization*, by A. E. Goss & C. F. Nodine.] *Contemporary Psychology, 11*, 379–380.
58. Jensen, A. R., & Rohwer, W. D. Jr. (1966). The Stroop Color-Word Test: A review. *Acta Psychologica, 25*, 36–93.

1967

59. Jensen, A. R. (1967). Varieties of individual differences in learning. In: R. M. Gagné (Ed.), *Learning and individual differences* (pp. 117–135). Columbus, Ohio: Merrill. (Reprinted in: Roweton, W. E. (Ed.) (1972), *Humanistic trends in educational psychology*. New York: Xerox Co.).
60. Jensen, A. R. (1967). Estimation of the limits of heritability of traits by comparison of monozygotic and dizygotic twins. *Science, 156*, 539. Abstract.
61. Jensen, A. R. (1967). Estimation of the limits of heritability of traits by comparison of monozygotic and dizygotic twins. *Proceedings of the National Academy of Science, 58*, 149–156.
62. Jensen, A. R. (1967). The culturally disadvantaged: Psychological and educational aspects. *Educational Research, 10*, 4–20.
63. Jensen, A. R. (1967). How much can we boost IQ and scholastic achievement? *Proceedings of the California Advisory Council on Educational Research.*

1968

64. Jensen, A. R. (1968). Social class, race and genetics: Implications for education. *American Educational Research Journal, 5*, 1–42. (Reprinted in: Gordon, I. J. (Ed.) (1971). *Readings in research in developmental psychology* (pp. 54–67). Glenview, IL: Scott, Foresman, & Co.; Clarizio, H. F., Craig, R. C., & Mehrens, W. H. (Eds) (1970). *Contemporary issues in educational psychology*. New York: Allyn & Bacon).
65. Jensen, A. R. (1968). Patterns of mental ability and socioeconomic status. *Science, 160*, 439. Abstract.
66. Jensen, A. R. (1968). Patterns of mental ability and socioeconomic status. *Proceedings of the National Academy of Sciences, 60*, 1330–1337.
67. Jensen, A. R. (1968). Social class and verbal learning. In: M. Deutsch, I. Katz, & A. R. Jensen (Eds), *Social class, race, and psychological development* (pp. 115–174). New York: Holt, Rinehart, & Winston. (Reprinted in: DeCecco, J. P. (Ed.) (1967). *The psychology of language, thought, and instruction* (pp. 103–117). New York: Holt, Rinehart, & Winston).
68. Jensen, A. R. (1968). The culturally disadvantaged and the heredity-environment uncertainty. In: J. Hellmuth (Ed.), *Disadvantaged child* (Vol. 2, pp. 29–76). Seattle, Washington: Special Child Publications.
69. Jensen, A. R. (1968). Another look at culture-fair testing. In: *Western Regional Conference on Testing Problems, Proceedings for 1968, Measurement for Educational Planning* (pp. 50–104). Berkeley, California: Educational Testing Service, Western Office. (Reprinted in: Hellmuth, J. (Ed.), *Disadvantaged child* (Vol. 3), *Compensatory education: A national debate* (pp. 53–101). New York: Brunner/Mazel).

70. Jensen, A. R. (1968). Influences of biological, psychological, and social deprivations upon learning and performance. In: *Perspectives on human deprivation* (pp. 125–137). Washington, D.C.: U.S. Department of Health, Education, and Welfare.

71. Jensen, A. R. (1968). Discussion of Ernst Z. Rothkoph's Two scientific approaches to the management of instruction. In: R. M. Gagné, & W. J. Gephart (Eds), *Learning research and school subjects* (pp. 134–141). Itasca, IL: F. E. Peacock.

72. Jensen, A. R. (1968). The biology of maladjustment. [Review of *Studies of troublesome children*, by D. H. Stott.] *Contemporary Psychology, 13*, 204–206.

73. Jensen, A. R., & Rohwer, W. D. Jr. (1968). Mental retardation, mental age, and learning rate. *Journal of Educational Psychology, 59*, 402–403.

74. Deutsch, M., Katz, I., & Jensen, A. R. (Eds) (1968). *Social class, race, and psychological development* (pp. v + 423). New York: Holt, Rinehart, & Winston.

75. Lee, S. S., & Jensen, A. R. (1968). Effect of awareness on 3-stage mediated association. *Journal of Verbal Learning and Verbal Behavior, 7*, 1005–1009.

1969

76. Jensen, A. R. (1969). How much can we boost I. Q. and scholastic achievement? *Harvard Educational Review, 39*, 1–123. (Reprinted in: Environment, heredity, and intelligence. *Harvard Educational Review*, Reprint Series No. 2, 1969 (pp. 1–123); *Congressional Record* (May 28, 1969, Vol. 115, No. 88, pp. H-4270–4298); Bracht, G. H., Hopkins, K., & Stanley, J. C. (Eds) (1972). *Perspectives in educational and psychological measurement* (pp. 191–213). New York: Prentice-Hall; Barnette, W. L. Jr. (Ed.) (1976). *Readings in psychological tests and measurements* (3rd ed., pp. 370–380). Baltimore: Williams & Wilkins).

77. Jensen, A. R. (1969). Reducing the heredity-environment uncertainty. *Harvard Educational Review, 39*, 449–483. (Reprinted in: Environment, heredity, and intelligence. *Harvard Educational Review*, Reprint Series No. 2, 1969 (pp. 209–243)).

78. Jensen, A. R. (1969). Intelligence, learning ability, and socioeconomic status. *Journal of Special Education, 3*, 23–35. (Reprinted in: *Mental Health Digest*, 1969, 1, 9–12).

79. Jensen, A. R. (1969). *Understanding readiness: An occasional paper* (pp. 1–17). Urbana, IL: ERIC Clearinghouse on Early Childhood Education, National Laboratory on Early Childhood Education.

80. Jensen, A. R. (1969). Jensen's theory of intelligence: A reply. *Journal of Educational Psychology, 60*, 427–431.

81. Jensen, A. R. (1969). The promotion of dogmatism. *Journal of Social Issues, 25*, 212–217; 219–222.

82. Jensen, A. R. (1969). Criticism or propaganda? *American Psychologist, 24*, 1040–1041.

83. Jensen, A. R. (1969). An embattled hypothesis [interview]. *Center Magazine, 2*, 77–80.

84. Jensen, A. R. (1969). Education ills: Diagnosis and cure? [Review of *Who can be educated?* by M. Schwebel.] *Contemporary Psychology, 14*, 362–364.

85. Jensen, A. R. (1969). [Review of *Pygmalion in the classroom*, by R. Rosenthal & Lenore Jacobson.] *American Scientist, 57*, 44A-45A.

86. Jensen, A. R. (1969). Race and intelligence: The differences are real. *Psychology Today, 3*, 4–6. (Reprinted in: Sexton, Patricia C. (Ed.) (1970). *Problems and policy in education.* New York: Allyn & Bacon; Jacoby, R., & Glauberman, N. (Eds) (1995). *The Bell Curve debate: History, documents, opinions.* New York: Random House).

87. Rohwer, W. D. Jr., & Jensen, A. R. (1969). A reply to Glass. *Journal of Educational Psychology, 60*, 417–418.

1970

88. Jensen, A. R. (1970). A theory of primary and secondary familial mental retardation. In: N. R. Ellis (Ed.), *International review of research in mental retardation* (Vol. 4, pp. 33–105). New York: Academic Press.
89. Jensen, A. R. (1970). Hierarchical theories of mental ability. In: B. Dockrell (Ed.), *On intelligence* (pp. 119–190). Toronto: Ontario Institute for Studies in Education.
90. Jensen, A. R. (1970). IQ's of identical twins reared apart. *Behavior Genetics, 1*, 133–148. (Reprinted in: Eysenck, H. J. (Ed.) (1973). *The measurement of intelligence* (pp. 273–288). Lancaster, U.K.: Medical and Technical Publishing Co.).
91. Jensen, A. R. (1970). Race and the genetics of intelligence: A reply to Lewontin. *Bulletin of the Atomic Scientists, 26*, 17–23. (Reprinted in: Baer, D. (Ed.) (1973). *Heredity and society: Readings in social genetics* (pp. 300–311). New York: Macmillan; Block, N. J., & Dworkin, G. (Eds), *The IQ controversy* (pp. 93–106). New York: Pantheon).
92. Jensen, A. R. (1970). Can we and should we study race differences? In: J. Hellmuth (Ed.), *Disadvantaged child* (Vol. 3), *Compensatory education: A national debate* (pp. 124–157). New York: Brunner/Mazel. (Reprinted in: Grigham, J. C., & Weissbach, T. A. (Eds) (1971). *Racial attitudes in America: Analysis and findings of social psychology* (pp. 401–434). New York: Harper & Row; *Journal of the American Anthropological Association*, 1971, Anthropological Studies. No. 8.; Wrightsman, L. S., & Brigham, J. C. (Eds) (1973). *Contemporary issues in social psychology* (2nd ed., pp. 218–227). Monterey, CA: Brooks/ Cole).
93. Jensen, A. R. (1970). Learning ability, intelligence, and educability. In: V. Allen (Ed.), *Psychological factors in poverty* (pp. 106–132). Chicago: Markham.
94. Jensen, A. R. (1970). The heritability of intelligence. *Science & Engineering, 33*, 40–43. (Reprinted in: *Saturday Evening Post*, Summer, 1972; Rubinstein, J., & Slife, B. D. (Eds) (1980). *Taking Sides: Clashing views on controversial psychological issues* (pp. 232–238). Guilford, CN: Dushkin Publishing Group; Zimbardo, P., & Maslach, C. (Eds) (1973). *Psychology for our times: Readings* (pp. 129–134). Glenview, IL: Scott, Foresman).
95. Jensen, A. R. (1970). Statement of Dr. Arthur R. Jensen to the General Subcommittee on Education of the Committee on Education and Labor, House of Representatives, 92nd Congress, second session. *Hearings on Emergency School Aid Act of 1970* (pp. 333–342). (H.R. 17846) Washington, D.C.: U.S. Government Printing Office.
96. Jensen, A. R. (1970). [Review of *Behavioral genetics: Methods and research*, edited by M. Manosevitz, G. Lindzey, and D. D. Thiessen. New York: Appleton-Century-Crofts, 1969.] *Social Biology, 17*, 151–152.
97. Jensen, A. R. (1970). Parent and teacher attitudes toward integration and busing. *Research Resume*, No. 43, California Advisory Council on Educational Research, May, 1970.
98. Jensen, A. R. (1970). Selection of minority students in higher education. *Toledo Law Review*, Spring–Summer, Nos. 2 & 3, 304–457.
99. Jensen, A. R., & Rohwer, W. D. Jr. (1970). *An experimental analysis of learning abilities in culturally disadvantaged children* (pp. 1–181). Final Report. Office of Economic Opportunity, Contract No. OEO 2404.

1971

100. Jensen, A. R. (1971). Individual differences in visual and auditory memory. *Journal of Educational Psychology, 62*, 123–131.

101. Jensen, A. R. (1971). Controversies in intelligence: Heredity and environment. In: D. W. Allen, & E. Seifman (Eds), *The teacher's handbook* (pp. 642–654). Glenview, IL: Scott, Foresman & Co.

102. Jensen, A. R. (1971). The role of verbal mediation in mental development. *Journal of Genetic Psychology, 118*, 39–70.

103. Jensen, A. R. (1971). Heredity, environment, and intelligence. In: L. C. Deighton (Ed.), *Encyclopedia of education* (Vol. 4, pp. 368–380). New York: Macmillan.

104. Jensen, A. R. (1971). The race X sex X ability interaction. In: R. Cancro (Ed.) (1971). *Contributions to intelligence* (pp. 107–161). New York: Grune & Stratton.

105. Jensen, A. R. (1971). A note on why genetic correlations are not squared. *Psychological Bulletin, 75*, 223–224.

106. Jensen, A. R. (1971). Hebb's confusion about heritability. *American Psychologist, 26*, 394–395.

107. Jensen, A. R. (1971). Twin differences and race differences in IQ: A reply to Burgess and Jahoda. *Bulletin of the British Psychological Society, 24*, 195–198.

108. Jensen, A. R. (1971). Erblicher I. Q. oder Pädagogischer Optimismus vor einem an deren Gericht. *Neue Sammlung, 11*, 71–76.

109. Jensen, A. R. (1971). *Do schools cheat minority children? Educational Research, 14*, 3–28.

110. Jensen, A. R. (1971). The phylogeny and ontogeny of intelligence. *Perspectives in Biology and Medicine, 15*, 37–43.

111. Jensen, A. R. (1971). Heredity and environment: A controversy over IQ and scholastic achievement. In: H. C. Lindgren, & F. Lindgren (Eds), *Current readings in educational psychology* (2nd ed., pp. 323–327). New York: Wiley.

1972

112. Jensen, A. R. (1972). *Genetics and education* (pp. vii + 379). London: Methuen (New York: Harper & Row).

113. Jensen, A. R. (1972). A two-factor theory of familial mental retardation. In: J. deGrouchy, F. J. G. Ebling, & I. W. Henderson (Eds) (1972), *Human genetics* (pp. 263–271). Proceedings of the 4th International Congress of Human Genetics, Paris, September, 1971. Amsterdam: Excerpta Medica.

114. Jensen, A. R. (1972). Review of Analysis of Learning Potential. In: O. K. Buros (Ed.), *Seventh mental measurements yearbook* (Vol. I, pp. 622–625). Highland Park, NJ: Gryphon Press.

115. Jensen, A. R. (1972). The case for IQ tests: Reply to McClelland. *The Humanist, 32*, 14.

116. Jensen, A. R. (1972). The causes of twin differences in IQ: A reply to Gage. *Phi Delta Kappan, 53*, 420–421.

117. Jensen, A. R. (1972). Genetics and education: A second look. *New Scientist, 56*, 96–98.

118. Jensen, A. R. (1972). Scholastic achievement and intelligence (Statement to the U.S. Senate Select Committee on Equal Educational Opportunity). In: *Environment, Intelligence, and Scholastic Achievement* (pp. 55–68). (A compilation of testimony to the Select Committee on Equal Educational Opportunity, United States Senate, 92nd Congress, 2nd Session, June 1972.) Washington, D.C.: U.S. Government Printing Office, 1972. (Reprinted in: *Saturday Evening Post*, 1972, *244* (No. 2), 150–152).

119. Jensen, A. R. (1972). Interpretation of heritability. *American Psychologist, 27*, 973–975.

120. Jensen, A. R. (1972). I.Q. and Race: Ethical issues. *The Humanist, 32*, 5–6.

121. Jensen, A. R. (1972). Heritability and teachability. In: J. E. Bruno (Ed.), *Emerging issues in education* (pp. 57–88). Lexington, MA: D. C. Heath.
122. Jensen, A. R. (1972). *Comment on De Fries' paper.* In: L. Ehrman, G. S. Omenn, & E. Caspari (Eds) (1972), *Genetics, environment, and behavior* (pp. 23–25). New York: Academic Press.
123. Jensen, A. R. (1972). Discussion of Tobach's paper. In: Lee Ehrman, G. S. Omenn, & E. Caspari (Eds) (1972). *Genetics, environment, and behavior* (pp. 240–246). New York: Academic Press.
124. Jensen, A. R. (1972). Educabilité, transmission hereditaire et differences entre populations. (Educability, heritability, and population differences.) *Revue de Psychologie Appliquée, 22,* 21–34.
125. Jensen, A. R. (1972). [Review of *Race, culture and intelligence,* edited by K. Richardson, D. Spears, & M. Richards (Middlesex, England: Penguin, 1972).] *New Society, 491,* 408–410.
126. Jensen, A. R. (1972). Sir Cyril Burt [Obituary]. *Psychometrika, 37,* 115–117.
127. Jensen, A. R. (1972). Jensen on Hirsch on "jensenism". *Educational Researcher, 1,* 15–16.
128. Jensen, A. R. (1972). Assessment of racial desegregation in the Berkeley Schools. In: D. Adelson (Ed.), *Man as the measure: The crossroads* (pp. 116–133). (Community Psychology Series, No. 1. American Psychological Association, Div. 27). New York: Behavioral Publications, Inc.
129. Jensen, A. R. (1972). Educability, heritability, and population differences. *Proceedings of the 17th International Congress of Applied Psychology.* Brussels, Belgium: Editest.
130. Jensen, A. R. (1972). Letter-to-the-Editor [on genetic IQ differences among social classes]. *Perspectives in Biology and Medicine, 116,* 154–156.
131. Jensen, A. R. (1972). Review of WLW Culture Fair Inventory. In: O. K. Buros (Ed.), *Seventh mental measurements yearbook* (Vol. 1, pp. 720–721). Highland Park, NJ: Gryphon Press.
132. Jensen, A. R. (1972). The IQ controversy: A reply to Layzer. *Cognition, 4,* 427–452.
133. Jensen, A. R. (1972). Empirical basis of the periodic table of human cultures. In: E. Haskell (Ed.) (1972), *Full circle: The moral force of unified science* (pp. 156–164). New York: Gordon & Breach.

1973

134. Jensen, A. R. (1973). A case for dysgenics. *The Journal: Forum for Contemporary History, 2* (4), 1–6.
135. Jensen, A. R. (1973). Some facts about the IQ. *The Journal: Forum for Contemporary History, 2* (7), 6–8.
136. Jensen, A. R. (1973). Expanding the thesis: The IQ controversy. [Review of *IQ in the meritocracy,* by R. J. Herrnstein. Boston: Little-Brown, 1973.]. *Book World, Chicago Tribune,* June 24, 1973.
137. Jensen, A. R. (1973). On "Jensenism": A reply to critics. In: B. Johnston (Ed.), *Education yearbook, 1973–74* (pp. 276–298). New York: Macmillan Educational Corporation.
138. Jensen, A. R. (1973). Race, intelligence and genetics: The differences are real. *Psychology Today, 7,* 80–86. (Reprinted in: Durland, W. R., & Bruening, W. H. (Eds) (1975). *Ethical issues* (pp. 403–414). Palo Alto, CA: Mayfield; *Whitehead, Joan M. (Ed.) (1975). Personality and learning 1* (pp. 345–351). London: Hodder & Stroughton; Schell, R. E. (Ed.) (1977). *Readings in developmental psychology Today* (pp. 230–234), (2nd ed.). New

York: Random House; Brigham, J. C., & Wrightsman, L. S. (Eds) (1977). *Contemporary issues in social psychology* (3rd ed.). Monterey, CA: Brooks/Cole).

139. Jensen, A. R. (1973). Critics of the IQ. [Review of *The fallacy of IQ*, edited by C. Senna. New York: The Third Press, 1973]. *The Georgia Review, 27*, 439–445.

140. Jensen, A. R. (1973). Personality and scholastic achievement in three ethnic groups. *British Journal of Educational Psychology, 43*, 115–125.

141. Jensen, A. R. (1973). Let's understand Skodak and Skeels, finally. *Educational Psychologist, 10*, 30–35.

142. Jensen, A. R. (1973). Skinner and human differences. In: H. Wheeler (Ed.), *Beyond the punitive society* (pp. 117–198). San Francisco: W. H. Freeman.

143. Jensen, A. R. (1973). *Educability and group differences* (pp. xiii + 407). London: Methuen (New York: Harper & Row).

144. Jensen, A. R. (1973). *Educational differences* (pp. xiii + 462). London: Methuen. (New York: Barnes & Noble).

145. Jensen, A. R. (1973). Bildungsfähigkeit, Erblichkeit und Bevolkerungsunterschiede. *Neue Anthropologie, 1*, 37–43.

146. Jensen, A. R. (1973). Level I and Level II abilities in three ethnic groups. *American Educational Research Journal, 4*, 263–276.

147. Jensen, A. R. (1973). Wie sehr können wir Intelligenz *Quotient und scheinlische Leistung steigert? In: H. Skowronek (Ed.) (1973), *Umwelt und Begabung*. Stuttgart, W. Germany: KlettCotta. (Paperback edition published by Ullstein Taschenbuch Verlag, 1982).

148. Jensen, A. R., & Frederiksen, J. (1973). Free recall of categorized and uncategorized lists: A test of the Jensen hypothesis. *Journal of Educational Psychology, 65*, 304–312.

1974

149. Jensen, A. R. (1974). What is the question? What is the evidence? [Autobiography]. In: T. S. Krawiec (Ed.) (1974), *The psychologists* (Vol. 2, pp. 203–244). New York: Oxford University Press.

150. Jensen, A. R. (1974). Kinship correlations reported by Sir Cyril Burt. *Behavior Genetics, 4* (1), 1–28.

151. Jensen, A. R. (1974). [Review of Abilities: *Their structure, growth, and action*, by R. B. Cattell. Boston: Houghton-Mifflin, 1971.] *American Journal of Psychology, 87*, 290–296.

152. Jensen, A. R. (1974). [Review of *Genetic diversity and human equality*, by Th. Dobzhansky. New York: Basic Books, 1973.]. *Perspectives in Biology and Medicine, 17*, 430–434.

153. Jensen, A. R. (1974). How biased are culture-loaded tests? *Genetic Psychology Monographs, 90*, 185–244.

154. Jensen, A. R. (1974). Effects of race of examiner on the mental test scores of white and black pupils. *Journal of Educational Measurement, 11*, 1–14.

155. Jensen, A. R. (1974). Ethnicity and scholastic achievement. *Psychological Reports, 34*, 659–668.

156. Jensen, A. R. (1974). Cumulative deficit: A testable hypothesis? *Developmental Psychology, 10*, 996–1019.

157. Jensen, A. R. (1974). Interaction of Level I and Level II abilities with race and socioeconomic status. *Journal of Educational Psychology, 66*, 99–111. (Reprinted in: Wittrock, M. C. (Ed.) (1972). *Learning and instruction* (pp. 270–290). Berkeley, CA: McCutchan).

158. Jensen, A. R. (1974). Equality for minorities. In: H. J. Walberg (Ed.), *Evaluating educational performance* (pp. 175–222). Berkeley, CA: McCutchan.
159. Jensen, A. R. (1974). The strange case of Dr. Jensen and Mr. Hyde? *American Psychologist*, *29*, 467–468.
160. Jensen, A. R. (1974). Educability and group differences. *Nature*, *250*, 713–714.
161. Jensen, A. R. (1974). Race and intelligence: The case for genetics. *The Times Educational Supplement*, London, September 20, 1974, No. 3095, 20–21.

1975

162. Jensen, A. R. (1975). The price of inequality. *Oxford Review of Education*, *1* (1), 13–25.
163. Jensen, A. R. (1975). Les fondements scientifiques des inegalités ethniques. *Le Monde Diplomatique*, June 1975, No. 255, 19.
164. Jensen, A. R. (1975). A theoretical note on sex linkage and race differences in spatial ability. *Behavior Genetics*, *5*, 151–164.
165. Jensen, A. R. (1975). The meaning of heritability in the behavioral sciences. *Educational Psychologist*, *11*, 171–183.
166. Jensen, A. R. (1975). *Panorama of modern behavioral genetics*. [*Review of Introduction to behavioral genetics*, by G. E. McClearn & J. C. DeFries. San Francisco: Freeman, 1973]. *Contemporary Psychology*, *20*, 926–928.
167. Jensen, A. R. (1975). Race and mental ability. In: J. F. Ebling (Ed.), *Racial variation in man* (pp. 71–108). London: Institute of Biology/Blackwell.
168. Jensen, A. R. (1975). Gibt es Unterschiede zwischen Schwarzen und Weissen? *Psychologie Heute*, Jan. 1975, 63–75.
169. Jensen, A. R. (1975). Interview: Rasse und Begabung. *Nation Europa*, September 1975, 19–28.
170. Jensen, A. R., & Figueroa, R. A. (1975). Forward and backward digit span interaction with race and IQ: Predictions from Jensen's theory. *Journal of Educational Psychology*, *67*, 882–893.

1976

171. Jensen, A. R. (1976). Race differences, strategy training, and improper inference. *Journal of Educational Psychology*, *68*, 130–131.
172. Jensen, A. R. (1976). Equality and diversity in education. In: N. F. Ashline, T. R. Pezullo, & C. I. Norris (Eds) (1976), *Education, inequality, and national policy* (pp. 125–136). Lexington, MA: Lexington Books.
173. Jensen, A. R. (1976). Addendum to human diversity discussion. In: B. D. Davis, & P. Flaherty (Eds) (1976), *Human diversity: Its causes and social significance* (pp. 223–228). Cambridge, MA: Ballinger.
174. Jensen, A. R. (1976). Twins' IQ's: A reply to Schwartz and Schwartz. *Behavior Genetics*, *6*, 369–371.
175. Jensen, A. R. (1976). *Eine Zweifactorentheorie des familiären Schwachsinns*. *Neue Anthropologie*, *4*, 53–60.
176. Jensen, A. R. (1976). Test bias and construct validity. *Phi Delta Kappan*, *58*, 34–346.
177. Jensen, A. R. (1976). Heritability of IQ [Letter-to-the-Editor]. *Science*, *194*, 6–14.

178. Jensen, A. R. (1976). The problem of genotype-environment correlation in the estimation of heritability from monozygotic and dizygotic twins. *Acta Geneticae Medicae et Gemellologiae, 25*, 86–99.

1977

179. Jensen, A. R. (1977). An examination of culture bias in the Wonderlic Personnel Test. *Intelligence, 1*, 51–64.
180. Jensen, A. R. (1977). Cumulative deficit in IQ of blacks in the rural South. *Developmental Psychology, 13*, 1841 91. (Reprinted in: Willerman, L., & Turner, R. G. (Eds) (1979), *Readings about individual and group differences* (pp. 83–91). San Francisco: W. H. Freeman).
181. Jensen, A. R. (1977). Race and mental ability. In: A. H. Halsey (Ed.), *Heredity and environment* (pp. 215–262). London: Methuen.
182. Jensen, A. R. (1977). An unfounded conclusion in M. W. Smith's analysis of culture bias in the Stanford-Binet intelligence scale. *Genetic Psychology Monographs, 130*, 113–115.
183. Jensen, A. R. (1977). Did Sir Cyril Burt fake his research on heritability of intelligence? *Phi Delta Kappan, 58*, 471–492. (Reprinted in: *Education Digest*, March, 1977, 42, 43–45).
184. Jensen, A. R. (1977). Die falschen Anschultdigungen gegen Sir Cyril Burt. *Neue Anthropologie, 5*, 15–16.

1978

185. Jensen, A. R. (1978). Genetic and behavioral effects of nonrandom mating. In: R. T. Osborne, C. E. Noble, & N. Weyl (Eds), *Human variation* (pp. 51–105). New York: Academic Press.
186. Jensen, A. R. (1978). Sex linkage and race differences in spatial ability: A reply. *Behavioral Genetics, 8*, 213–217.
187. Jensen, A. R. (1978). Sir Cyril Burt in perspective. *American Psychologist, 33*, 499–503.
188. Jensen, A. R. (1978). The current status of the IQ controversy. *Australian Psychologist, 13*, 7–28.
189. Jensen, A. R. (1978). The nature of intelligence and its relation to learning. In: S. Murray-Smith (Ed.), *Melbourne studies in education* (pp. 107–133). Melbourne University Press. (Reprinted in: *Journal of Research and Development in Education, 12*, 79–95).
190. Jensen, A. R. (1978). Racism refuted [Correspondence]. *Nature, 274*, 738.
191. Jensen, A. R. (1978). Zum Stand des Streits um die Intelligenz. *Neue Anthropologie, 6*, 29–40.
192. Jensen, A. R. (1978). IQ controversy. *Baltimore Sun*, Nov. 24, 1978, p. A12.
193. Jensen, A. R. (1978). Citation Classics (How much can we boost IQ and scholastic achievement?). *Current Contents, No. 41*, (October 9), 16.

1979

194. Jensen, A. R. (1979). *g*: Outmoded theory or unconquered frontier? *Creative Science and Technology, 2*, 16–29.

195. Jensen, A. R. (1979). [Review of *Inheritance of creative intelligence*, by J. L. Karlsson. Chicago: Nelson-Hall, 1978.] *Journal of Nervous and Mental Diseases, 167*, 711–713.
196. Jensen, A. R., & Marisi, D. Q. (1979). A note on the heritability of memory span. *Behavior Genetics, 9*, 379–387.
197. Jensen, A. R., & Munro, E. (1979). Reaction time, movement time, and intelligence. *Intelligence, 3*, 121–126.
198. Jensen, A. R., & Osborne, R. T. (1979). Forward and backward digit span interaction with race and IQ: A longitudinal developmental comparison. *Indian Journal of Psychology, 54*, 75–87.

1980

199. Jensen, A. R. (1980). *Bias in mental testing* (pp. xiii + 786). New York: The Free Press (London: Methuen).
200. Jensen, A. R. (1980). Uses of sibling data in educational and psychological research. *American Educational Research Journal, 17*, 153–170.
201. Jensen, A. R. (1980). Chronometric analysis of intelligence. *Journal of Social and Biological Structures, 3*, 103–122.
202. Jensen, A. R. (1980). Précis of Bias in Mental Testing. *Behavioral and Brain Sciences, 3*, 325–333.
203. Jensen, A. R. (1980). Correcting the bias against mental testing: A preponderance of peer agreement. *Behavioral and Brain Sciences, 3*, 359–371.
204. Jensen, A. R. (1980). A critical look at test bias: Fallacies and manifestations. *New Horizons, 21*, 44–64.
205. Jensen, A. R., & Inouye, A. R. (1980). Level I and Level II abilities in Asian, White, and Black children. *Intelligence, 4*, 41–49.

1981

206. Jensen, A. R. (1981). *Straight talk about mental tests* (pp. xiv + 269). New York: The Free Press.
207. Jensen, A. R. (1981). Raising the IQ: The Ramey and Haskins Study. *Intelligence, 5*, 29–40.
208. Jensen, A. R. (1981). Obstacles, problems, and pitfalls in differential psychology. In: S. Scarr (Ed.), *Race, social class, and individual differences in IQ* (pp. 483–514). Hillsdale, NJ: Erlbaum.
209. Jensen, A. R. (1981). Reaction time and intelligence. In: M. Friedman, J. P. Das, & N. O'Connor (Eds), *Intelligence and learning* (pp. 39–50). New York: Plenum.
210. Jensen, A. R. (1981). Impressions of India. *Update* (Graduate School of Education, University of California, Berkeley), Winter.
211. Jensen, A. R. (1981). Citation Classic (The Stroop color-word test: A review). *Current Contents, 13*, 20.
212. Jensen, A. R. (1981). An interview with Arthur Jensen. *Communique* (National Association of School Psychologists), *10*, 3–5.
213. Jensen, A. R. (1981). Taboo, constraint, and responsibility in educational research. *New Horizons, 22*, 11–20.

214. Jensen, A. R. (1981). A nontechnical guide to the IQ controversy. *New Horizons, 22,* 21–26.
215. Jensen, A. R., Schafer, E. W. P., & Crinella, F. (1981). Reaction time, evoked brain potentials, and psychometric *g* in the severely retarded. *Intelligence, 5,* 179–197.

1982

216. Jensen, A. R. (1982). Intelligence. In: S. B. Parker (Ed.), *Encyclopedia of science and technology* (5th ed.). New York: McGraw-Hill.
217. Jensen, A. R. (1982). Bias in mental testing: A final word. *Behavioral and Brain Sciences, 5,* 339–340.
218. Jensen, A. R. (1982). The chronometry of intelligence. In: R. J. Sternberg (Ed.), *Advances in the psychology of human intelligence* (Vol. 1, pp. 255–310). Hillsdale, NJ: Erlbaum.
219. Jensen, A. R. (1982). Reaction time and psychometric *g*. In: H. J. Eysenck (Ed.), *A model for intelligence* (pp. 93–132). New York: Springer.
220. Jensen, A. R. (1982). Changing conceptions of intelligence. *Education and Training of the Mentally Retarded, 17,* 3–5.
221. Jensen, A. R. (1982). The debunking of scientific fossils and straw persons. [An essay-review of *The mismeasure of man*, by S. J. Gould.]. *Contemporary Education Review, 1,* 121–135.
222. Jensen, A. R. (1982). Level I/Level II: Factors or categories? *Journal of Educational Psychology, 74,* 868–873.
223. Jensen, A. R. (1982). The race concept: Physical variation and correlated socially significant behavioral variation. *Current Anthropology, 23,* 649–650.
224. Jensen, A. R., & Reynolds, C. R. (1982). Race, social class, and ability patterns on the WISC-R. *Personality and Individual Differences, 3,* 423–438.

1983

225. Jensen, A. R. (1983). Sir Cyril Burt: A personal recollection. *Association of Educational Psychologists Journal, 6,* 13–20.
226. Jensen, A. R. (1983). Effects of inbreeding on mental-ability factors. *Personality and Individual Differences, 4,* 71–87.
227. Jensen, A. R. (1983). The nonmanipulable and effectively manipulable variables in education. *Education and Society,* 51–62. (Reprinted in: *New Horizons,* 1983, *24,* 31–50).
228. Jensen, A. R. (1983). [Review of *The testing of Negro intelligence* (Vol. II), edited by R. T. Osborne, & F. C. J. McGurk.] *Personality and Individual Differences, 4,* 234–235.
229. Jensen, A. R. (1983). [Review of *The inheritance of personality and ability*, by R. B. Cattell.] *Personality and Individual Differences, 4,* 365–368.
230. Jensen, A. R. (1983). The definition of intelligence and factor score indeterminacy. *The Behavioral and Brain Sciences, 6,* 313–315.
231. Jensen, A. R. (1983). Again, how much can we boost IQ? [Review of *How and how much can intelligence be increased*, edited by D. K. Detterman & R. J. Sternberg.] *Contemporary Psychology, 28,* 756–758.
232. Jensen, A. R. (1983). Critical flicker frequency and intelligence. *Intelligence, 7,* 217–225.
233. Jensen, A. R. (1983). Taboo, constraint, and responsibility in educational research. *Journal of Social, Political and Economic Studies, 8,* 301–311.

234. Jensen, A. R. (1983). Beyond Groth's sociological criticism of psychometrics. *Wisconsin Sociologist, 20,* 102–105.
235. Jensen, A. R., & Reynolds, C. R. (1983). Sex differences on the WISC-R. *Personality and Individual Differences, 4,* 223–226.
236. Reynolds, C. R., & Jensen, A. R. (1983). WISC-R subscale patterns of abilities of blacks and whites matched on full scale IQ. *Journal of Educational Psychology, 75,* 207–214.
237. Sen, A., Jensen, A. R., Sen, A. K., & Arora, I. (1983). Correlation between reaction time and intelligence in psychometrically similar groups in America and India. *Applied Research in Mental Retardation, 4,* 139–152.

1984

238. Jensen, A. R. (1984). Francis Galton (1822–1911). In: R. J. Corsini (Ed.), *Encyclopedia of psychology* (Vol. 2, p. 43). New York: Wiley.
239. Jensen, A. R. (1984). Karl Pearson (1857–1936). In: R. J. Corsini (Ed.), *Encyclopedia of psychology* (Vol. 2, pp. 490–491). New York: Wiley.
240. Jensen, A. R. (1984). Charles Edward Spearman (1863–1945). In: R. J. Corsini (Ed.), *Encyclopedia of psychology* (Vol. 3, pp. 353–354). New York: Wiley.
241. Jensen, A. R. (1984). Louis Leon Thurstone (1887–1955). In: R. J. Corsini (Ed.), *Encyclopedia of psychology* (Vol. 3, pp. 426–427). New York: Wiley.
242. Jensen, A. R. (1984). Law of filial regression. In: R. J. Corsini (Ed.), *Encyclopedia of psychology* (Vol. 2, pp. 280–281). New York: Wiley.
243. Jensen, A. R. (1984). Cultural bias in tests. In: R. J. Corsini (Ed.), *Encyclopedia of psychology* (Vol. 1, pp. 331–332). New York: Wiley.
244. Jensen, A. R. (1984). Inbreeding in human factors. In: R. J. Corsini (Ed.), *Encyclopedia of psychology* (Vol. 2, pp. 191–192). New York: Wiley.
245. Jensen, A. R. (1984). General intelligence factor. In: R. J. Corsini (Ed.), *Encyclopedia of psychology* (Vol. 2, p. 48). New York: Wiley.
246. Jensen, A. R. (1984). Heritability. In: R. J. Corsini (Ed.), *Encyclopedia of psychology* (Vol. 2, p. 108). New York: Wiley.
247. Jensen, A. R. (1984). Test bias: Concepts and criticisms. In: C. R. Reynolds, & R. T. Brown (Eds) (1984), *Perspectives on bias in mental testing* (pp. 507–586). New York: Plenum.
248. Jensen, A. R. (1984). Political ideologies and educational research. *Phi Delta Kappan, 65,* 460–462.
249. Jensen, A. R. (1984). The limited plasticity of human intelligence. *New Horizons, 25,* 18–22.
250. Jensen, A. R. (1984). Mental speed and levels of analysis. *The Behavioral and Brain Sciences, 7,* 295–296.
251. Jensen, A. R. (1984). Test validity: *g* versus the specificity doctrine. *Journal of Social and Biological Structures, 7,* 93–118.
252. Jensen, A. R. (1984). Jensen oversimplified: A reply to Sternberg. *Journal of Social and Biological Structures, 7,* 127–130.
253. Jensen, A. R. (1984). [Review of *Intelligence and national achievement,* edited by R. B. Cattell.] *Personality and Individual Differences, 5,* 491–492.
254. Jensen, A. R. (1984). Sociobiology and differential psychology: The arduous climb from plausibility to proof. In: J. R. Royce, & L. P. Mos (Eds), *Annals of theoretical psychology* (Vol. 2, pp. 49–58). New York: Plenum.

255. Jensen, A. R. (1984). Constraint and responsibility in educational research. *Journal of Social, Political and Economic Studies.* * side mangler.
256. Jensen, A. R. (1984). *The black-white difference on the K-ABC: Implications for future tests.* Journal of Special Education, *18*, 377–408.
257. Jensen, A. R. (1984). Objectivity and the genetics of IQ: A reply to Steven Selden. *Phi Delta Kappan, 66*, 284–286.
258. Agrawal, N., Sinha, S. N., & Jensen, A. R. (1984). Effects of inbreeding on Raven Matrices. *Behavior Genetics, 14*, 579–585.
259. Vernon, P. A., & Jensen, A. R. (1984). Individual and group differences in intelligence and speed of information processing. *Personality and Individual Differences, 5*, 411–423.

1985

260. Jensen, A. R. (1985). Compensatory education and the theory of intelligence. *Phi Delta Kappan, 66*, 554–558. (Reprinted in: Slife, B. (Ed.), *Taking sides: Clashing views on controversial issues* (8th ed.). Guilford, CT: Dushkin).
261. Jensen, A. R. (1985). Armed Services Vocational Aptitude Battery. *Measurement and Evaluation in Counseling and Development, 18*, 32–37.
262. Jensen, A. R. (1985). Review of the Predictive Ability Test, Adult Edition. In: J. V. Mitchell, Jr. (Ed.), *The ninth mental measurements yearbook* (Vol. 2, pp. 1184–1185). Lincoln, NE: University of Nebraska Press.
263. Jensen, A. R. (1985). Review of Minnesota Spatial Relations Test, Revised Edition. In: J. V. Mitchell, Jr. (Ed.), *The ninth mental measurements yearbook* (Vol. 2, pp. 1014–1015). Lincoln, NE: University of Nebraska Press.
264. Jensen, A. R. (1985). Methodological and statistical techniques for the chronometric study of mental abilities. In: C. R. Reynolds, & V. L. Willson (Eds), *Methodological and statistical advances in the study of individual differences* (pp. 51–116). New York: Plenum.
265. Jensen, A. R. (1985). Race differences and Type II errors: A comment on Borkowski and Krause. *Intelligence, 9*, 33–39.
266. Jensen, A. R. (1985). The nature of the black-white difference on various psychometric tests: Spearman's hypothesis. *The Behavioral and Brain Sciences, 8*, 193–219.
267. Jensen, A. R. (1985). The black-white difference in *g*: A phenomenon in search of a theory. *The Behavioral and Brain Sciences, 8*, 246–263.
268. Jensen, A. R. (1985). Humphrey's attenuated test of Spearman's hypothesis. *Intelligence, 9*, 285–289.
269. Jensen, A. R. (1985). Immunoreactive theory and the genetics of mental ability. *The Behavioral and Brain Sciences, 8*, 453.
270. Cohn, S. J., Carlson, J. S., & Jensen, A. R. (1985). Speed of information processing in academically gifted youths. *Personality and Individual Differences, 6*, 621–629.

1986

271. Jensen, A. R. (1986). Intelligence: "Definition," measurement, and future research. In: R. J. Sternberg, & D. K. Detterman (Eds), *What is intelligence? Contemporary viewpoints on its nature and definition.* Norwood, NJ: Ablex.
272. Jensen, A. R. (1986). The theory of intelligence. In: S. Modgil, & C. Modgil (Eds), *Hans Eysenck: Searching for a scientific basis for human behavior.* London: Falmer Press.

273. Jensen, A. R. (1986). *g*: Artifact or reality? *Journal of Vocational Behavior, 29*, 301–331.
274. Jensen, A. R. (1986). [Review of *Academic work and educational excellence: Raising student productivity*, edited by T. M. Tomlinson & H. J. Walberg.] *Educational Evaluation and Policy Analysis, 8*, 447–451.
275. Jensen, A. R., & Vernon, P. A. (1986). Jensen's reaction time studies: A reply to Longstreth. *Intelligence, 10*, 153–179.

1987

276. Jensen, A. R. (1987). Citation Classic: (Educability and group differences). *Current Contents: Social & Behavioral Sciences, 19* (46).
277. Jensen, A. R. (1987). Citation Classic: (Bias in mental testing). *Current Contents: Social & Behavioral Sciences, 19* (46).
278. Jensen, A. R. (1987). Process differences and individual differences in some cognitive tasks. *Intelligence, 11*, 107–136.
279. Jensen, A. R. (1987). Unconfounding genetic and nonshared environmental effects. *The Behavioral and Brain Sciences, 10*, 26–27.
280. Jensen, A. R. (1987). The plasticity of "intelligence" at different levels of analysis. In: J. Lochhead, J. Bishop, & D. Perkins (Eds), *Thinking: Progress in research and teaching*. Philadelphia: Franklin Institute Press.
281. Jensen, A. R. (1987). Individual differences in mental ability. In: J. A. Glover, & R. R. Ronning (Eds), *A history of educational psychology*. New York, Plenum.
282. Jensen, A. R. (1987). The *g* beyond factor analysis. In: R. R. Ronning, J. A. Glover, J. C. Conoley, & J. C. Witt (Eds), *The influence of cognitive psychology on testing* (pp. 87–142). Hillsdale, NJ: Erlbaum.
283. Jensen, A. R. (1987). Differential psychology: Towards consensus. In: M. Modgil, & C. Modgil (Eds), *Arthur Jensen: Consensus and controversy*. London: Falmer Press, Ltd.
284. Jensen, A. R. (1987). *g* as a focus of concerted research effort [Editorial]. *Intelligence, 11*, 193–198.
285. Jensen, A. R. (1987). Intelligence as a fact of nature. *Zeitschrift für Pädagogische Psychologie, 1*, 157–169.
286. Jensen, A. R. (1987). Individual differences in the Hick paradigm. In: P. A. Vernon (Ed.), *Speed of information processing and intelligence*. Norwood, NJ: Ablex.
287. Jensen, A. R. (1987). Mental chronometry in the study of learning disabilities. *Mental Retardation and Learning Disability Bulletin, 15*, 67–88.
288. Jensen, A. R. (1987). Further evidence for Spearman's hypothesis concerning black-white differences on psychometric tests. *The Behavioral and Brain Sciences, 10*, 512–519.
289. Jensen, A. R., & McGurk, F. C. J. (1987). Black-white bias in "cultural" and "noncultural" test items. *Personality and Individual Differences, 8*, 295–301.
290. Naglieri, J. A., & Jensen, A. R. (1987). Comparison of black-white differences on the WISC-R and the K-ABC: Spearman's hypothesis. *Intelligence, 11*, 21–43.

1988

291. Jensen, A. R. (1988). Mongoloid mental ability: Evolution or culture? *Mensa Research Bulletin, 24*, 23–25.

292. Jensen, A. R. (1988). [Review of *Practical intelligence: Nature and origins of competence in the everyday world*, edited by R. J. Sternberg & R. K. Wagner.] *Personality and Individual Differences, 9*, 199–200.
293. Jensen, A. R. (1988). Speed of information processing and population differences. In: S. H. Irvine (Ed.), *The cultural context of human ability.* London: Cambridge University Press.
294. Jensen, A. R. (1988). Review of the Armed Services Vocational Aptitude Battery. In: J. T. Kopes & M. M. Mastie (Eds), *A counselor's guide to vocational guidance instruments.* The National Vocational Guidance Association.
295. Jensen, A. R. (1988). Sex differences in arithmetic computation and reasoning in prepubertal boys and girls. *Behavioral and Brain Sciences, 11*, 198–199.
296. Jensen, A. R., & Faulstich, M. E. (1988). Psychometric *g* in black and white prisoners. *Personality and Individual Differences, 9*, 925–928.
297. Jensen, A. R., Larson, J., & Paul, S. M. (1988). Psychometric *g* and mental processing speed on a semantic verification test. *Personality and Individual Differences, 9*, 243–255.
298. Jensen, A. R., Saccuzzo, D. P., & Larson, G. E. (1988). Equating the Standard and Advanced Forms of the Raven Progressive Matrices. *Educational and Psychological Measurement, 48*, 1091–1095.
299. Cohn, S. J., Cohn, C. M. G., & Jensen, A. R. (1988). Myopia and intelligence: A pleiotropic relationship? *Human Genetics, 80*, 53–58.
300. Kranzler, J. H., Whang, P. A., & Jensen, A. R. (1988). Jensen's use of the Hick paradigm: Visual attention and order effects. *Intelligence, 12*, 371–391.

1989

301. Jensen, A. R. (1989). The relationship between learning and intelligence. *Learning and Individual Differences, 1*, 37–62.
302. Jensen, A. R. (1989). Philip Ewart Vernon (1905–1987) [Obituary]. *Psychologist, 44*, 844.
303. Jensen, A. R. (1989). "Revised" Updated. [Review of *Intelligence: Its structure, growth and action*, by R. B. Cattell.] *Contemporary Psychology, 34*, 140–141.
304. Jensen, A. R. (1989). Raising IQ without increasing *g*? A review of "The Milwaukee Project: Preventing mental retardation in children at risk." *Developmental Review, 9*, 234–258.
305. Jensen, A. R. (1989). "Total perceived value" as the basis of assortative mating in humans. *The Behavioral and Brain Sciences, 12*, 531.
306. Jensen, A. R. (1989). New findings on the intellectually gifted. *New Horizons, 30*, 73–80.
307. Jensen, A. R., Cohn, S. J., & Cohn, C. M. G. (1989). Speed of information processing in academically gifted youths and their siblings. *Personality and Individual Differences, 10*, 29–34.
308. Buckhalt, J., & Jensen, A. R. (1989). The *British Ability Scales* Speed of Information Processing subtest: What does it measure? *British Journal of Educational Psychology, 59*, 100–107.
309. Kranzler, J. H., & Jensen, A. R. (1989). Inspection time and intelligence: A meta-analysis. *Intelligence, 13*, 329–347.
310. Reed, T. E., & Jensen, A. R. (1989). Short latency visual evoked potentials (VEPs), visual tract speed, and intelligence. Significant correlations. Abstract. *Behavior Genetics, 19*, 772–773.

1990

311. Jensen, A. R. (1990). Speed of information processing in a calculating prodigy. *Intelligence, 14*, 259–274.
312. Jensen, A. R. (1990). Straight history. [Review of *Schools as sorters: Lewis M. Terman, applied psychology, and the intelligence testing movement, 1890–1930*, by P. D. Chapman.] *Contemporary Psychology, 35*, 1147–1148.
313. Jensen, A. R., & Reed, T. E. (1990). Simple reaction time as a suppressor variable in the chronometric study of intelligence. *Intelligence, 14*, 375–388.

1991

314. Jensen, A. R. (1991). Spearman's *g* and the problem of educational equality. *Oxford Review of Education, 17* (2), 169–187.
315. Jensen, A. R. (1991). General mental ability: From psychometrics to biology. *Psychodiagnostique, 16*, 134–144.
316. Jensen, A. R. (1991). Speed of cognitive processes: A chronometric anchor for psychometric tests of *g*. *Psychological Test Bulletin, 4*, 59–70.
317. Jensen, A. R. (1991). IQ and Science: The mysterious Burt affair. *The Public Interest. No. 105*, 93–106.
318. Jensen, A. R. (1991). Review of G. E. Thomas (Ed.), "*U.S. race relations in the 1980s and 1990s: Challenges and alternatives*" (New York: Hemisphere Publishing Corporation.) *Personality and Individual Differences, 12*, 321–322.
319. Jensen, A. R. (1991). Spirmanov *g* factor: Veze izmedu psihometrije i biologije. *Psihologija, 24*, 167–193.
320. Kranzler, J. H., & Jensen, A. R. (1991). The nature of psychometric *g*: Unitary process or a number of independent processes? *Intelligence, 15*, 397–422.
321. Kranzler, J. H., & Jensen, A. R. (1991). Unitary *g*: Unquestioned postulate or empirical fact? *Intelligence, 15*, 437–448.
322. Reed, T. E., & Jensen, A. R. (1991). Arm nerve conduction velocity (NCV), brain NCV, reaction time, and intelligence. *Intelligence, 15*, 33–47.

1992

323. Jensen, A. R. (1992). Understanding *g* in terms of information processing. *Educational Psychology Review, 4*, 271–308.
324. Jensen, A. R. (1992). Spearman's hypothesis: Methodology and evidence. *Multivariate Behavioral Research, 27*, 225–233.
325. Jensen, A. R. (1992). More on Psychometric g and "Spearman's hypothesis." *Multivariate Behavioral Research, 27*, 257–260.
326. Jensen, A. R. (1992). Scientific fraud or false accusations? The case of Cyril Burt, In: D. J. Miller, & M. Hersen (Eds), *Research fraud in the behavioral and biomedical sciences*. New York: Wiley & Sons, Inc.
327. Jensen, A. R. (1992). The importance of intraindividual variability in reaction time. *Personality and Individual Differences, 13*, 869–882.

328. Jensen, A. R. (1992). Preface. In: R. Pearson (Ed.), *Shockley on race, eugenics, and dysgenics* (pp. 1–13). Washington, D.C.: Scott-Townsend.

329. Jensen, A. R. (1992). Mental ability: Critical thresholds and social policy. *Journal of Social, Political and Economic Studies, 17*, 1–11.

330. Jensen, A. R. (1992). The Cyril Burt scandal, research taboos, and the media. *The General Psychologist, 28*, 16–21.

331. Jensen, A. R. (1992). The relation between information processing time and right/wrong responses. *American Journal on Mental Retardation, 97*, 290–292.

332. Jensen, A. R. (1992). Vehicles of *g. Psychological Science, 3*, 275–278.

333. Jensen, A. R., & Reed, T. E. (1992). The correlation between reaction time and the ponderal index. *Perceptual and Motor Skills, 75*, 843–846.

334. Jensen, A. R., & Wilson, M. (1992). Henry Felix Kaiser (1927–1992). *In Memorium* (pp. 88–91). Berkeley: University of California.

335. Reed, T. E., & Jensen, A. R. (1992). Conduction velocity in a brain nerve pathway of normal adults correlates with intelligence level. *Intelligence, 16*, 259–278.

1993

336. Jensen, A. R. (1993). Psychometric g and achievement. In: B. R. Gifford (Ed.), *Policy perspectives on educational testing* (pp. 117–227). Norwell, MA: Kluwer Academic Publishers.

337. Jensen, A. R. (1993). Test validity: g versus "tacit knowledge". *Current Directions in Psychological Science, 2*, 9–10.

338. Jensen, A. R. (1993). Why is reaction time correlated with psychometric *g*? *Current Directions in Psychological Science, 2*, 53–56.

339. Jensen, A. R. (1993). Spearman's hypothesis tested with chronometric information processing tasks. *Intelligence, 17*, 47–77.

340. Jensen, A. R. (1993). Spearman's g: Links between psychometrics and biology. *Annals of the New York Academy of Sciences, 702*, 103–131.

341. Jensen, A. R., & Sinha, S. N. (1993). Physical correlates of human intelligence. In: P. A. Vernon (Ed.), *Biological approaches to the study of human intelligence* (pp. 139–242). Norwood, NJ: Ablex.

342. Jensen, A. R., & Whang, P. A. (1993). Reaction times and intelligence: A comparison of Chinese-American and Anglo-American children. *Journal of Biosocial Science, 25*, 397–410.

343. Kranzler, J. H., & Jensen, A. R. (1993). Psychometric *g* is still not unitary after eliminating supposed "impurities": Further comment on Carroll. *Intelligence, 17*, 11–14.

344. Reed, T. E., & Jensen, A. R. (1993). Choice reaction time and visual pathway nerve conduction velocity both correlate with intelligence but appear not to correlate with each other: Implications for information processing. *Intelligence, 17*, 191–203.

345. Reed, T. E., & Jensen, A. R. (1993). Cranial capacity: New Caucasian data and comments on Rushton's claimed Mongoloid-Caucasoid brain-size differences. *Intelligence, 17*, 423–431.

346. Reed, T. E., & Jensen, A. R. (1993). A somatosensory latency between the thalamus and cortex also correlates with level of intelligence. *Intelligence, 17*, 443–450.

1994

347. Jensen, A. R. (1994). Afterword: Deafness and the nature of mental abilities. In: J. P. Braden (Ed.), *Deafness, deprivation, and IQ* (pp. 203–208). New York: Plenum.
348. Jensen, A. R. (1994). Phlogiston, animal magnetism, and intelligence. In: D. K. Detterman (Ed.), *Current topics in human intelligence* (Vol. 4): *Theories of intelligence* (pp. 257–284). Norwood, NJ: Ablex.
349. Jensen, A. R. (1994). Review of "Intelligence" (2nd ed.) by N. Brody. *American Journal on Mental Retardation, 98*, 663–667.
350. Jensen, A. R. (1994). Reaction time. In: R. J. Corsini (Ed.), *Encyclopedia of Psychology* (2nd ed., Vol. 3, pp. 282–285). New York: Wiley.
351. Jensen, A. R. (1994). Humphreys's "behavioral repertoire" an epiphenomenon of g. *Psychological Inquiry, 5*, 208–210.
352. Jensen, A. R. (1994). Francis Galton. *In: R. J. Sternberg (Ed.), Encyclopedia of Intelligence* (Vol. 1, pp. 457–463). New York: Macmillan.
353. Jensen, A. R. (1994). Charles Edward Spearman. In: R. J. Sternberg (Ed.), *Encyclopedia of Intelligence* (Vol. 2, pp. 1007–1014). New York: Macmillan.
354. Jensen, A. R. (1994). Hans Jurgen Eysenck. In: R. J. Sternberg (Ed.), *Encyclopedia of Intelligence* (Vol. 1, pp. 416–418). New York: Macmillan.
355. Jensen, A. R. (1994). Race and IQ scores. In: R. J. Sternberg (Ed.), *Encyclopedia of Intelligence* (Vol. 2, pp. 899–907). New York: Macmillan.
356. Jensen, A. R. (1994). Psychometric g related to differences in head size. *Personality and Individual Differences, 17*, 597–606.
357. Jensen, A. R. (1994). Paroxysms of denial. *National Review, 46*, (Dec. 5), 48–50. (Reprinted in: Jacoby, R., & Glauberman, N. (Eds) (1995), *The Bell Curve debate: History, documents, opinion*. New York: Random House.
358. Jensen, A. R., & Johnson, F. W. (1994). Race and sex differences in head size and IQ. *Intelligence, 18*, 309–333.
359. Jensen, A. R., & Ruddell, R. B. (1994). Guy Thomas Buswell. *In Memorium* (pp. 46–49). Berkeley: University of California.
360. Jensen, A. R., & Weng, J-J. (1994). What is a good g? *Intelligence, 18*, 231–258.
361. Jensen, A. R., & Whang, P. A. (1994). Speed of accessing arithmetic facts in long-term memory: A comparison of Chinese-American and Anglo-American children. *Contemporary Educational Psychology, 19*, 1–12.
362. Jensen, A. R., & Wilson, M. (1994). Henry Felix Kaiser (1927–1992) (Obituary). *American Psychologist, 49*, 1085.
363. Kranzler, J. H., Whang, P. A., & Jensen, A. R. (1994). Task complexity and the speed and efficiency of elemental information processing: Another look at the nature of intellectual giftedness. *Contemporary Educational Psychology, 19*, 447–459.
364. Shaughnessy, M. F. (1994). An interview with Arthur R. Jensen. *The School Field, 4*, 129–154.

1995

365. Jensen, A. R. (1995). Psychological research on race differences (Comment). *American Psychologist, 50*, 41–42.
366. Jensen, A. R. (1995). Wanted: A unified theory of individual and group differences. (Abstract). *Behavior Genetics, 25*, 272.

367. Jensen, A. R. (1995). IQ and science: The mysterious Burt affair. In: N. J. Mackintosh (Ed.), *Cyril Burt: Fraud or framed?* Oxford: Oxford University Press.

1996

368. Jensen, A. R. (1996). Secular trends in IQ: Additional hypotheses. In: D. K. Detterman (Ed.), *Current topics in human intelligence* (Vol. 4): *The environment* (pp. 147–150). Norwood, NJ: Ablex.
369. Jensen, A. R. (1996). Inspection Time and *g*. (Letter), *Nature, 381*, 729.
370. Jensen, A. R. (1996). The locus of biological *g*. In: I. Mervielde (Ed.), *Abstracts of the 8th European Conference on Personality.* University of Ghent, Belgium, July 11, 1996, p. 54.
371. Jensen, A. R. (1996). Giftedness and genius: Crucial differences. In: C. P. Benbow, & D. Lubinski (Eds), *Intellectual talent: Psychometric and social issues* (pp. 393–411). Baltimore: John Hopkins University Press.
372. Jensen, A. R. (1996). [Review of R. Plomin, "Genetics and experience" (1997)]. *Journal of Social and Evolutionary Systems, 19*, 307–311. (Reprinted in: *European Sociobiological Newsletter*, May 1997, No. 44, 24–28).

1997

373. Jensen, A. R. (1997). The puzzle of nongenetic variance. In: R. J. Sternberg & E. L. Grigorenko (Eds), *Intelligence, heredity, and environment* (pp. 42–88). Cambridge: Cambridge University Press.
374. Jensen, A. R. (1997). The neurophysiology of *g*. In: C. Cooper, & V. Varma (Eds), *Processes in individual differences* (pp. 108–125). London: Routledge.
375. Jensen, A. R. (1997). Psychometric g and the race question. In: J. Kingma, & W. Tomic (Eds), *Reflections on the concept of intelligence* (pp. 1–23). Greenwich, CT: JAI Press.
376. Jensen, A. R. (1997). Introduction (to section on intelligence). In: H. Nyborg (Ed.), *The scientific study of human nature: Tribute to Hans J. Eysenck at eighty.* New York: Elsevier.
377. Jensen, A. R. (1997). The psychometrics of intelligence. In: H. Nyborg (Ed.), *The scientific study of human nature: Tribute to Hans J. Eysenck at eighty.* New York: Elsevier.
378. Jensen, A. R. (1997). Eysenck as teacher and mentor. In: H. Nyborg (Ed.), *The scientific study of human nature: Tribute to Hans J. Eysenck at eighty.* New York: Elsevier.

1998

379. Jensen, A. R. (1998). Adoption data and two *g*-related hypotheses. *Intelligence, 25*, 1–6.
380. Jensen, A. R. (1998). *The g factor.* Westport, CT: Praeger.
381. Jensen, A. R. (1998). Spearman's law of diminishing returns. In: A. Sen & A. K. Sen (Eds), *Challenges of contemporary realities: A psychological perspective* (pp. 107–123). New Delhi: New Age International, Ltd.
382. Jensen, A. R. (1998). The g factor in the design of education. In: R. J. Sternberg, & W. M. Williams (Eds), *Intelligence, instruction, and assessment* (pp. 111–131). Hillsdale, NJ: Erlbaum.

383. Jensen, A. R. (1998). The suppressed relationship between IQ and the reaction time slope parameter of the Hick function. *Intelligence, 26,* 43–52.
384. Jensen, A. R. (1998). Jensen on "Jensenism." *Intelligence, 26,* 181–208.

1999

385. Jensen, A. R. (1999). Review of "Psychological testing of American minorities" by R. J. Samuda. *Personality and Individual Differences, 26,* 1143–1145.
386. Jensen, A. R. (1999). Review of "Intelligence: A new look" by H. J. Eysenck. *The Galton Institute Newsletter, 32,* 6–8.
387. Caryl, P. G., Deary, I.. J., Jensen, A. R., Neubauer, A. C., & Vickers, D. (1999). Information processing approaches to intelligence: Progress and prospects. In: I. Mervielde, I. Deary, F. de Fruyt, & F. Ostendorf (Eds), *Personality Psychology in Europe* (Vol. 7, pp. 181–219). Tilburg Univ. Press.

2000

388. Jensen, A. R. (2000). Hans Eysenck's final thoughts on intelligence. Special review of "Intelligence: A new look" by H. J. Eysenck (1998), Transaction Books. *Personality and Individual Differences, 28,* 191–194.
389. Jensen, A. R. (2000). Review of "Eminent creativity, Everyday creativity, and health" by M. A. Runco & R. Richards (Eds), Ablex, 1998. *Personality and Individual Differences, 28,* 198–199.
390. Jensen, A. R. (2000). Elementary cognitive tasks and psychometric *g*. In: A. Harris (Ed.), *Encyclopedia of Psychology.* New York: APA/Oxford University Press.
391. Jensen, A. R. (2000). Twins. In: A. Harris (Ed.), *Encyclopedia of Psychology.* New York: APA/Oxford University Press.
392. Jensen, A. R. (2000). Charles Spearman: Founder of the London School. *The Galton Institute Newsletter,* No. 36, 2–4.
393. Jensen, A. R. (2000). Testing: The dilemma of group differences. *Psychology, Public Policy, and Law, 6,* 121–127.
394. Jensen, A. R. (2000). Hans Eysenck: Apostle of the London School. In: G. A. Kimble, & M. Wertheimer (Eds), *Portraits of pioneers in psychology* (Vol. IV, pp. 338–357). Washington, D.C.: American Psychological Association and Mahwah, NJ: Erlbaum.
395. Jensen, A. R. (2000). Charles Spearman: Discoverer of *g*. In: G. A. Kimble, & M. Wertheimer (Eds), *Portraits of pioneers in psychology* (Vol. IV, pp. 92–111). Washington, D.C.: American Psychological Association and Mahwah, NJ: Erlbaum.
396. Jensen, A. R. (2000). Was wir über den *g*-Faktor wissen (und nichtwissen). In: K. Schweizer (Ed.), *Intelligenz und Kognition: Die kognitiv-biologische Perspektive der Intelligenz* (pp. 13–36). Landau: Verlag für Empirische Pädagogik.
397. Jensen, A. R. (2000). *The g factor: Psychometrics and biology* (pp. 37–57). Novartis Foundation Symposium 233. *The nature of intelligence.* Chichester, England: Wiley.
398. Jensen, A. R. (2000). Some recent overlooked research on the scientific basis of "The Bell Curve." commentary on Reifman on Bell-Curve. *Psycoloquy, 11* (106).
399. Jensen, A. R. (2000). "The *g* factor" is about variance in human abilities, not a cognitive theory of mental structure. Reply to Anderson. *Psycoloquy, 11* (041).

400. Jensen, A. R. (2000). A nihilistic philosophy of science for a scientific psychology? Reply to Barrett. *Psycoloquy, 11* (088).

401. Jensen, A. R. (2000). Name-calling is a disappointing substitute for real criticism. Reply to Brace. *Psycoloquy, 11*, (009).

402. Jensen, A. R. (2000). Artificial intelligence and *g* theory concern different phenomena. Reply to Bringsjord. *Psycoloquy, 11* (086).

403. Jensen, A. R. (2000). The heritability of *g* proves both its biological relevance and its transcendence over specific cognitive abilities. Reply to Bub. *Psycoloquy, 11* (085).

404. Jensen, A. R. (2000). Processing speed, inspection time, and nerve conduction velocity. Reply to Burns. *Psycoloquy, 11* (019).

405. Jensen, A. R. (2000). The Ubiquity of mental speed and the centrality of working memory. Reply to Conway et al. *Psycoloquy, 11* (038).

406. Jensen, A. R. (2000). Is there a self-awareness of one's own *g* level? Reply to Demetriou. *Psycoloquy, 11* (04).

407. Jensen, A. R. (2000). Mixing up Eugenics and Galton's Legacy to research on intelligence. Reply to Fancher. *Psycoloquy, 11* (017).

408. Jensen, A. R. (2000). Psychometric scepticism. Reply to Harrington. *Psycoloquy, 11* (039).

409. Jensen, A. R. (2000). The locus of the modifiability of *g* is mostly biological. Reply to Hunt. *Psycoloquy, 11* (012).

410. Jensen, A. R. (2000). A "simplest cases" approach to exploring the neural basis of *g*. Reply to Ingber. *Psycoloquy, 11* (023).

411. Jensen, A. R. (2000). A fuzzy boundary of racial classification attenuates IQ difference. Reply to Jorion. *Psycoloquy, 11* (022).

412. Jensen, A. R. (2000). A potpourri of *g*-related topics. Reply to Kovacs & Pleh. *Psycoloquy, 11* (087).

413. Jensen, A. R. (2000). IQ tests, psychometric and chronometric *g*, and achievement. Reply to Kush. *Psycoloquy, 11* (014).

414. Jensen, A. R. (2000). Race differences, *g*, and the "default hypothesis." Reply to Locurio. *Psycoloquy, 11* (004).

415. Jensen, A. R. (2000). Cognitive components as chronometric probes to brain processes. Reply to Mackintosh. *Psycoloquy, 11* (011).

416. Jensen, A. R. (2000). Behavioral and biological phenomena equally "real" and related. Reply to Partridge. *Psycoloquy, 11* (018).

417. Jensen, A. R. (2000). "Biological determinism" as an ideological buzz-word. Reply to Raymond. *Psycoloquy, 11* (021).

418. Jensen, A. R. (2000). Nothing 'mystifying' about psychometric *g*. Reply to Richardson. *Psycoloquy, 11* (042).

419. Jensen, A. R. (2000). Correlated vectors, *g*, and the "Jensen effect". Reply to Rushton. *Psycoloquy, 10* (082).

420. Jensen, A. R. (2000). Evoked potentials, testosterone, and *g*. Reply to Tan. *Psycoloquy, 10* (085).

421. Jensen, A. R. (2000). Evoked brain potentials and *g*. Reply to Verleger. *Psycoloquy, 10* (084).

422. Nyborg, H., & Jensen, A. R. (2000). Testosterone levels as modifiers of psychometric *g*. *Personality and individual differences, 28*, 601–607.

423. Nyborg, H., & Jensen, A. R. (2000). Black-white differences on various psychometric tests: Spearman's hypothesis tested on American armed services veterans. *Personality and Individual Differences, 28*, 593–599.

2001

424. Jensen, A. R. (2001). Misleading caricatures of Jensen's statistics: A reply to Kaplan. *Chance, 14*, 22–26.
425. Jensen, A. R. (2001). Spearman's hypothesis. In: S. Messick, & J. Collis (Eds), *Intelligence and personality: Bridging the gap in theory and measurement* (pp. 3–25). Mahwah, NJ: Erlbaum.
426. Jensen, A. R. (2001). Vocabulary and general intelligence. Commentary on Bloom's "How children learn the meanings of words". *Behavioral and Brain Sciences, 24*, 1109–1110.
427. Nyborg, H., & Jensen, A. R. (2001). Occupation and income related to psychometric *g*. *Intelligence, 29*, 45–55.

2002

428. Jensen, A. R. (2002). Galton's legacy to research on intelligence (The 1999 Galton Lecture). *Journal of Biosocial Science, 34*, 145–172.
429. Jensen, A. R. (2002). Review of Intelligence testing and minority students: Foundations, performance factors, and assessment issues by R. R. Valencia & L. A. Suzuki (Sage, 2001). *Intelligence, 30*, 216–217.
430. Jensen, A. R. (2002). General cognitive ability (*g* factor) assessment. In: R. Fernandos-Ballesteros (Ed.), *Encyclopedia of Psychological Assessment*. London: Sage.
431. Jensen, A. R. (2002). Psychometric *g*: Definition and substantiation. In: R. J. Sternberg, & E. L. Grigorenko (Eds), *The g factor: How general is it?* Mahwah, NJ: Erlbaum.

In Press

432. Jensen, A. R. (in press). Regularities in Spearman's Law of Diminishing Returns. *Intelligence*.
433. Jensen, A. R. (in press). Do age-group differences imitate racial differences? *Intelligence*.
434. Jensen, A. R. (in press). The mental chronometry of giftedness. In: D. Boothe, & J. C. Stanley (Eds), *Giftedness and cultural diversity*.
435. Jensen, A. R. (in press). Psychometric *g* and mental chronometry. *Cortex*.
436. Jensen, A. R. (in press). Mental chronometry and the unification of differential psychology. In: R. J. Sternberg, & J. Pretz (Eds), *Cognition and intelligence*. Cambridge: Cambridge University Press.
437. Rushton, J. P., & Jensen, A. R. (in press). African-White IQ differences from Zimbabwe on the Wechsler Scale for Children-Revised. *Personality and Individual Differences*.
438. Rushton, J. P., & Jensen, A. R. (in press). Thirty Years of research on Black-White Differences in IQ. *Psychology, Public Policy, and Law*.

Author Index

Subject Index